P9-DTA-332

# LANGUAGE ASSESSMENT
# AND INTERVENTION
## for the Learning Disabled

**Elisabeth Hemmersam Wiig**

*Boston University*

**Eleanor Messing Semel**

*Boston University*

Charles E. Merrill Publishing Company
*A Bell & Howell Company*
Columbus    Toronto    London    Sydney

Published by Charles E. Merrill Publishing Company
*A Bell & Howell Company*
Columbus, Ohio 43216

This book was set in Palatino and Korinna.
Copyediting: Frances Margolin
Cover Design Coordination: Will Chenoweth

**Photo Credits:**   Part I, Cynda Williams; Part II, Dan Unkefer; Part III, Dan Unkefer; Part IV, *Values in the Classroom,* CEM; Part V, Dan Unkefer.

Copyright © 1980, by Bell & Howell Company. All rights reserved. No part of this book may be reproduced in any form, electronic or mechanical, including photocopy, recording, or any information storage and retrieval system, without permission in writing from the publisher.

Library of Congress Catalog Card Number: 79-92794

International Standard Book Number: 0-675-08180-7

Printed in the United States of America

2 3 4 5 6 7 8 9 — 85 84 83 82 81 80

To our mothers


INGEBORG HEMMERSAM NIELSEN
MAE SEMEL FELDMAN

Without their love and support in our early years
this work could not have been conceived.

# FOREWORD

Many disciplines have contributed to the field of learning disabilities. The current controversies and confusion reflect this diversity of theoretical orientations, clinical experiences, and remedial and research emphases. Yet when the focus of concern is the ability of the learning disabled person to adapt to the demands of his or her environment and to contribute to the welfare of others, it becomes evident that the successful teacher/clinician/therapist integrates training not only across skill and content areas, but also across all basic psychological functions. This book exemplifies such integration.

Part I presents the impact of language disabilities on children's learning, particularly in reading, describes the characteristics of learning disabilities, and sets forth the developmental sequence of auditory-vocal and language skills.

Parts II and III discuss the characteristics, assessment, and remedial procedures for the major language components of morphology, syntax, and semantics. Both assessment and remediation of language deficits require consideration of the individual's level of functioning in sensory-motor abilities, perception (visual, auditory, and haptic), higher thought processes (such as making inferences and categorizing), and social and emotional development. The authors discuss the importance and the interdependence of these functions as they relate to language abilities.

Part IV discusses how short-term and long-term memory affect language functions. In Part V, the school curriculum, particularly at the upper elementary and secondary levels, is analyzed in terms of language requirements. The interdependence of basic psychological functions and the necessary integration of these functions in the complex activities of the school curriculum are again demonstrated.

The book contributes to interdisciplinary integration also. We believe it will prove useful not only for professionals in the fields of speech, language, and communication disorders, but also for resource and program specialists for the learning handicapped, school psychologists, developmental psychologists, and reading and curriculum specialists—indeed, for all those concerned with furthering language development.

The authors concentrate on analysis of language behaviors and various methods to ameliorate language deficits. These are practical concerns, yet the reader is constantly aware of the authors' thoughtful synthesis of theory and recent research applied to assessment and intervention. Material is based on such theorists as Piaget, Luria, and Chomsky, among others. There is depth as well as breadth. Research and practice are integrated.

Although the book is clinically oriented, it fosters a structured and reasoned approach to observation, testing, and remediation. The authors' discussion of standardizd tests for various subareas of language, for example, presents not only descriptions and facts about a particular test or subtest, but also clarifies what can be learned from its use and its specific strengths and weaknesses. In other words, the book provides data for the decision-making processes when assessment tools or remedial methods are to be selected. It is not a "how to" book; it is that much rarer and much more valuable aid to good therapy/ education—an attempt to answer the additional questions, "For what purpose?" and "Why?"

Because it is so comprehensive, because it integrates other basic psychological functions and school curriculum with language abilities and synthesized research and practice, and because it is designed for professionals trained in different disciplines, the book is syntactically and semantically complex (to use some of its concepts). The authors have, however, provided definitions of technical terms in the margins, a glossary, and excellent summary tables; they have also provided many verbatim language samples, examples of test items and training methods, and lists of materials. The overall organization is clear. Nevertheless, it is not a book which can be read without concentration and without some prior knowledge. Involvement of the reader is demanded.

Everyone, no matter how experienced in working with learning/ language disabled individuals, will discover new insights in this book. No one can assimilate its contents and interpret the definition of learning disabilities set forth in Section 5(b) or P.L. 94-142—"Specific learning disability means a disorder in one or more of the basic psychological processes involved in understanding or in using language, spoken or written . . ."—in any restricted or narrow sense. This book encourages a breadth of view which can contribute to fruitful cooperation among professionals, which is necessary if learning disabled individuals are to receive optimal assistance.

We have read this book with great interest, and we believe others will also find it of value.

*Phyllis Maslow, Ph.D.*
*Marianne Frostig, Ph.D.*

# PREFACE

This book seeks to put the day-to-day management of the learning disabled child with a language disorder squarely within the domain of the classroom teacher. We want to provide a bridge between classroom teachers and specialists such as the speech and language pathologist, the special educator, the learning disabilities specialist, the remedial reading teacher, the psychologist, the guidance counselor, and other concerned professionals.

Thus, we have focused on the language components of the curriculum and we discuss strategies for adapting and enhancing materials. Parts II, III, and IV cover syntax, semantics, and memory problems, respectively. For each type of problem, the book includes many examples and illustrations of the characteristics of the problems of learning disabled youngsters in understanding and using spoken language. These examples should help the teacher identify the student's specific difficulty. Again, for each type of problem, the book features detailed discussions of the diagnostic evaluation of language disorders in school-aged children and adolescents. We then provide systematic discussions of the bases and rationales for intervention. Intervention objectives, task formats, and sequences are presented with numerous illustrations and concrete examples to assist teachers and special educators as well as speech and language pathologists.

We are indebted to many people for encouraging and supporting this work. We express our special thanks to Tom Hutchinson for his focal role and continuing encouragement and understanding. Tom supported us when the pressure was on and the writing process seemed interminable. Students and professional colleagues with whom we have been in contact through courses, workshops, seminars, and in-service training programs have contributed significantly to this book. They asked for clarification, provided relevant references, and shared their knowledge and practical experiences and insights. We thank all of them. Our husbands, children, and parents supported our efforts unfailingly and gave us good counsel and love. We are grateful to them for their support. Special thanks go to Else Abele, Eleanor Kalter, Debbie Kavish, and Nancy Sinden, who assisted us at various stages; to the learning disabled children and youth who gave us the opportunity to learn from them; to the parents who entrusted their children to us; to the giants on whose shoulders we stand, Kurt Goldstein, Alesandr Romanovich Luria, Maria Montesorri, and Alfred Strauss; and last but not least to the "Big Five" in learning disabilities, William Cruickshank, Marianne Frostig, Newell Kephart, Samuel Kirk, and Helmer Myklebust, whose pioneering efforts paved the way for us all.

**Publisher's Note:**
For information on a complete language assessment program developed by the authors, *CELF: The Clinical Evaluation of Language Functions*, see page 452.

# CONTENTS

# The Language
# Problem
# of the
# Learning
# Disabled

# LANGUAGE DISABILITIES
## Impact, Ages, and Stages

Of all the problems experienced by children with learning disabilities, language may be the most pervasive. Using **language**—both **processing** other people's messages and **producing** one's own—is a uniquely human function. It affects all learning and all interactions. To help children who have deficits in language processing and production, the communication specialist or teacher needs to understand how language works and how various kinds of language deficits relate to each other. The communication professional also needs to understand what "learning disabilities" are and how being "learning disabled" affects a child—both academically and emotionally.

Understanding the extent of a child's language disabilities and the specific nature of his or her problems may help the professional:

(1) Understand the characteristics and severity of the **oral language** deficits which may underlie reading, writing, and spelling difficulties.
(2) Refine and develop diagnostic methods to identify and differentiate potential problems in reading, writing, and spelling.
(3) Determine alternative treatment procedures for the specific language disabilities identified by diagnoses.
(4) Understand the bases for learning difficulties in such diverse curriculum areas as social studies, science, and mathematics.
(5) Understand the bases for problems in family and social interactions and assist in academic and vocational counseling.

*See the glossary, pages 443-48, for definitions of terms found in boldface in this book.*

*Language processing refers to the act of listening to and interpreting spoken language.*

*Language production refers to the act of formulating and using spoken language.*

*Oral language is any spoken language. A child can have a problem processing (understanding) oral language and/or producing it (speaking).*

## THE IMPACT OF LANGUAGE DISABILITIES

Oral language deficits have a widespread impact on a child. They may affect other language abilities, including reading, a particularly critical skill. Reading depends upon both oral language and knowledge of the native language. The skilled reader understands both the **syntax** and the **semantics** of the language (Goodman, 1967, 1969; Kavanagh, 1968; Kolers, 1972; Levin & Kaplan, 1971; Mattingly, 1972; Mehler, Bever, &

Carey, 1967). Beginning reading depends upon accuracy in the deliberate analytical decoding of letters and upon conscious translation of these letters into their **auditory-vocal** equivalents, which the child has already learned. The syntax presented to the beginning reader at the primer level is designed to be highly familiar. It usually follows basic phrase-structure rules, with rare instances of more complex combinations.

*See the appendix, page 429, for definitions and examples of language structures such as phrases, clauses and sentences.*

To advanced readers, on the other hand, the visual decoding process becomes highly automatic. Interpretation may depend upon accurate processing of the meaning of phrases, clauses, and sentences and of the semantic content of phrase, clause, and sentence meaning. Interpreting or reading any printed or written language requires the reader to reduce an often syntactically and semantically complex and elaborate description of events, experiences, thoughts, or attitudes into a condensed and abbreviated inner meaning representation. A syntactically complex printed-read message may be spoken in a structurally less complex and more condensed format. In turn, these printed and spoken messages may be related to an even simpler and more condensed inner meaning representation, as illustrated below.

**Printed-read message**
All books shall be returned to the library within two weeks from the date stamped.

**Spoken message**
Bring the books back to the library in two weeks.

**Inner meaning representation**
Bring books back (in) two weeks.

A child's trouble in understanding spoken sentences may be related to difficulties in reducing the **surface structure** of printed messages into their inner meaning equivalents. A child's limitations in understanding specific spoken vocabulary, basic concepts, linguistic relationships, or **figurative language** may be related to deficits in the semantic interpretation of their printed equivalents. At an even lower level, **auditpry-visual** integration and **auditory discrimination** deficits may be related to inconsistencies or errors in translating printed letters and other symbols into their auditory-vocal equivalents.

Difficulties in processing or in producing oral language may have even more adverse effects upon written language expression. The relationship between oral language and written language expressed in writing has been described by Vygotsky:

> Writing . . . requires deliberate analytical action . . . of the child. In speaking, he is hardly conscious of the sounds he pronounces and quite unconscious of the mental operations he performs. In writing, he must take cognizance of the sound structure of each word, dissect it, and reproduce it in alphabetical symbols. . . . In the same deliberate way he must put words in a certain sequence to form a sentence. (1962, p. 99)

Furthermore, an inner representation (inner speech) links the spoken and written language forms:

> Written language demands conscious work because its relationship to inner speech is different from that of oral language: The latter precedes inner speech in . . . development, while written speech follows inner speech and presupposes its existence. But the grammar of thought is not the same. (Vygotsky, 1962, p. 99)

Vygotsky elaborates on the differences in the complexity and grammar of oral language, inner speech, and written language:

> Inner speech is condensed, abbreviated. . . . Written speech is deployed to its fullest extent, more complete than oral speech. Inner speech is . . . predicative because the situation, the subject of thought, is always known to the thinker. Written speech . . . must explain the situation fully. . . . The change from maximally compact inner speech to maximally detailed written speech requires what might be called deliberate semantics— . . . structuring of the web of meaning. (1962, p. 100)

While there are many specific language disorders found in learning deficits in disabled children, we will look at three general types of problems: deficits in word knowledge, in word and sentence formation, and in word finding.

### Deficits in Word Knowledge—Sample

Learning disabled children may learn selected vocabulary items later than their nondisabled age peers, and they may have problems recalling specific words when they are needed. The following responses from learning disabled children from grades 3 through 5 illustrate some of their difficulties in finding the right words.

*In this book, we shall use* **recall** *to mean to bring back from memory; to recollect or remember.* **Retrieve** *means to recover from memory for use in language production.*

When asked to complete the phrase "Jack, King, and _____," some of these children offered the following responses:

(1) Jack, King, and Princess.
(2) Jack, King, and Mike.
(3) Jack, King, and mother.
(4) Jack, King, and Crownprince.
(5) Jack, King, and Jill.
(6) Jack, King, and candle.
(7) Jack, King, and Knight.
(8) There are fifty-two cards in a deck. You have clubs, spades, hearts, and diamonds. And aces, and Jack, King, and Queen.

While all of these children played cards and could identify, match, and select cards from a deck on command, completing the phrase still posed problems for them. Most of their error responses involve substitutions of associated words for the intended vocabulary item. Their problems seem to reflect inefficient and inaccurate recall and retrieval of the required word, even though the required word was available in their **receptive** vocabulary. The responses suggest that some of these children identified one attribute of the intended concept—such as **gender**—in the responses "princess," "mother," and "Jill." Other children seemed to respond to the first word in the sequence, "Jack," and to form nursery rhyme associations with that word, as in the responses

*A child's receptive vocabulary includes all the words he can understand when they are spoken by other people.*

"Jill" and "candle." Only one response, "Knight," suggests that the child crossed semantic categories and retrieved from an associated semantic category, in this case, chess terms.

When asked to answer the question, "What is the opposite of add?" the same children responded by saying:

(1) I am adding.
   [*Teacher:* If you are not adding, you are _____.]
   [No response.]
   [*Teacher:* If you are doing the opposite of adding, you are _____.]
   I am not gonna add.
(2) Count.
(3) Numbers.
   [*Teacher:* If you don't add numbers, you _____.]
   Do them.
(4) Plus.

*See chapter 8 for a full definition of synonyms.*

In this case, the children seemed to provide **synonym** substitutions for the intended word. One of the children first formulated a sentence with the stimulus word.

When the same group of children were asked to answer the question, "What is the opposite of full?" they gave the following erroneous responses:

(1) Filling.
   [*Teacher:* If something is not full, what is it?]
   Milk.
(2) Full of candy.
   [*Teacher:* If something is not full, what is it?]
   Empty.
(3) Unfull.
   [*Teacher:* What word means *not full?*]
   It means it not full.
(4) A lot.
   [*Teacher:* What word means *not full?*]
   You don't eat too much.
(5) I am full.
   [*Teacher:* If it is not full, it is _____?]
   [No response.]
   [*Teacher:* If it is not going to be full, it is going to be _____?]
   It is gonna be in your mouth.

The error responses suggest that these children have several strategies for coping with their missing knowledge of the specific vocabulary item "empty." Some resort to formulating a phrase with the stimulus word in it, as in the responses "Full of candy," "I am full," and "It not full." Others provide alternative forms of the stimulus word, as in the responses "Filling" and "Unfull." Finally, when pressed to produce the exact word, some of the children resorted to remotely related responses such as "Milk," "You don't eat too much," and "It gonna be in your mouth."

**Word and Sentence Formation Deficits—Samples**

The problems of language and learning disabled youngsters in acquiring and using the rules for word and sentence formation are illustrated in the stories below. The vignettes provide examples of spontaneous discourse in response to specific general questions. The first sample was obtained from an 11-year, 8-months-old boy in response to the question, "Tell me what you saw on television last night."

(1) On the Waltons there was this boy and he won this contest.
(2) It's suppose to be a poem contest.
(3) And he thought that he was cheating his bigger brother John-boy.
(4) So he was scared to tell John-boy that he stoled his poem, but he didn't really.
(5) He just got an idea from John-boy's poem.
(6) And then John-boy was trying to figure out what who shot this man he knows.
(7) And then the man stole the chickens and then that night he bring 'em back.
(8) And then the guys going after them, he tripped and he fell and he shot himself in the leg.
(9) So he said that he wouldn't care who what happened, he just didn't wanna be called a fool because he tripped and shot himself.
(10) So the guy in jail got all his food from the neighbors.
(11) And then at the end Jim-bob told John-boy about the poem.
(12) John-boy said that he didn't really steal it, he just got ideas from it.

One striking feature of the sample is the frequency with which this boy uses the starters "and," "and then," and "so." They are used in two-thirds of the **utterances** and occur in clusters. The sample is also characterized by use of the indefinite form of the demonstrative pronoun "this" as in "this boy," "this contest," and "this man." This form seems to be used when a new person or what appears to be an unfamiliar concept is first introduced. The sample contains a total of 23 personal pronouns, and they are often used three or more times in any one utterance. The personal pronouns and the reflexive pronoun "himself" are used correctly in this sample, and generally the **referents** for the pronouns are indicated with appropriate frequency. This last feature indicates an area of strength in this youngster's use of the rules for introducing pronouns.

In this story, the child's difficulties in applying the word and sentence formation rules appear to affect primarily the verb forms. This boy uses a variety of primary verbs in his account but gets into problems with the irregular verbs "steal" and "bring." When he attempts to form the past tense of "steal," he first uses the form "stoled" and next the form "was stole." He uses "bring" when the past tense form "brought" should have been used, in the phrase "then that night he *bring*." He also has problems in forming the plural of the past participle of "to go" and omits the auxiliary verb "were [going]." Among the three secondary verb forms used, only one is formed incorrectly, in "It's *suppose to be*." Explicit negative sentences with contractions of "not" are formed correctly in this account, indicating another area of strength.

The account contains several correctly formed sentences with conjunctions featuring "and," "and then," "but," and "because." The rules for forming relative clauses are, however, not yet firmly acquired, as indicated by the reiterations of relative pronouns in the clauses, "to figure out *what who* shot" and "wouldn't care *who what* happened." Relative clauses are formed correctly by this youngster when the relative pronoun "that" is required, as indicated by the phrases, "thought *that*" and "to tell *that*."

The second sample was obtained from a 12-year, 2-months-old girl. The account was elicited in response to the question, "Can you tell me the story of the three bears?" She proceeded as follows:

(1)  Three little bears in the house.
(2)  They left the house and then this girl Goldilocks went into the house.
(3)  Then she went to the baby's food.
(4)  She went to the father's.
(5)  It was too hot.
(6)  Then she went to the momma's bear.
(7)  It was too cold.
(8)  So she ate the thing, sat down in the chair, the chair broke and she went to lay in bed.
(9)  While that, the bears were coming home.
(10) They came back into house, saw that the porridge was aten from the little bear and the chair was broken, went to their bedroom and saw Goldilocks.

The striking feature in this sample is the frequency with which subjects, objects, and verb phrases are omitted. The first and the tenth utterances contain no verb phrases. In the last utterance, the subject (agent) is missing in the sequence "the chair was broken, went to their bedroom." The fourth, sixth, and eighth utterances feature attempts to form prepositional phrases with objects and noun possessives. None of the attempts are successful. In the third utterance, this girl forms a correct noun possessive in the phrase "the baby's food." In the fourth utterance, the object of the prepositional phrase is omitted. In the sixth and eighth utterances, the noun possessives become entirely too much for her to handle. They deteriorate into the phrase forms "momma's bear" and "baby's bear." The objects of the prepositional phrases, "food" and "porridge," are omitted, and the constructions are formed as if "bear" was considered the object of the phrases. The difficulties in handling the structure of the prepositional phrases with noun possessives may in this case reflect problems in finding the word "porridge." This intended word is used in the last utterance.

When primary verbs are not omitted in the account, they are formed correctly, with one exception. The past participle of "to eat" becomes "was aten." The sample also features repetitive use of starters. In this case the child seems to favor the starters "then" and "so." When the overall quality of the account is considered, the girl's deficits in knowledge and use of word and sentence formation rules seem to be severe. They are also compounded by word-finding difficulties.

The third and last sample was obtained from a 12-year, 4-months-old learning disabled boy in response to the question, "What did you watch on television last night?" The boy's response was as follows:

(1) There was this boy who was going to the doctor's.
(2) He was taking drugs and he needed a good drug.
(3) And when he went to the doctor, he took the good drug.
(4) And then he went home and he started taking the bad drug.
(5) He took needles and pills and everything.
(6) Then the needles made him feel tired and made him stomach feel so painful.
(7) Then he started on pills.
(8) And he took a pill one at a time and each one hurt worse and worse.
(9) And then he went to the doctor's 'cause his knee was turning all red and blue.
(10) The doctor said it's 'cause of the pills.
(11) Then the doctor gave him another medicine and he went home and still took 'em.
(12) And about two weeks later he was dead.

The most striking feature in this boy's account, aside from the topic, is that two-thirds of his utterances begin with the starters "and," "then," and "and then." The sample also features an abundant occurrence of the conjunction "and." It is used either to **coordinate** phrases and clauses or to form conjunction deletions. Two utterances feature the conjunction " 'cause," and one contains a relative clause initiated by the relative pronoun "who."

The use of the third person singular possessive pronoun "his" is inconsistent in this sample. In one utterance it is used correctly in the phrase " 'cause his knee." In another, it is replaced by the objective case form "him" in the phrase "made him feel tired and made *him* stomach feel." The incorrect form may in this case represent a repetition of the objective case pronoun "him" featured in the preceding clause "made *him* feel tired." The account contains no explicit negative, passive, or interrogative sentences, making it impossible to know how they would be handled.

### Word Finding Deficits—Sample

Learning disabled children may have difficulties remembering and finding specific words when they are engaged in conversation or have to answer specific questions. Their word-finding efforts may result in spoken sentences which are not grammatical and which may contain an abundance of (among others) starters, place holders, indefinite references, word substitutions, **circumlocutions,** and **perseverative** repetitions of words, phrases, or clauses. The following sample was obtained from a 10-year, 8-months-old girl with learning disabilities in response to the question "Tell me what you saw on television last night." It illustrates the possible effects of word-finding problems on spontaneous spoken language.

(1)  First they had, they sang a song.
(2)  Then they had a commercial.
(3)  Then Cher was on top of the piano.
(4)  She was singing and went to all these things.
(5)  And once Chastity had a turn.
(6)  She's the little daughter.
(7)  And then Cher came back and she turn.
(8)  And then Dennis Weaver sang a song.
(9)  And then they had "Mr. and Mrs."
(10)  Cher was the wife and Sonny was the husband.
(11)  And then some guy, I forget what his name was, he comes in and he says "Barney Sue is drunk."
(12)  She says "I had a wonderful macaroni and cheese" something like that.
(13)  And all she does is she drank the wine sauce and she hit me in the face for no reason.
(14)  And then he comes in there.
(15)  And then she comes in and she says: "Oh there you are."
(16)  And then they say: "Will you do something about her?"
(17)  And then she starts kung fuin' everything.
(18)  And then sheriff tries to calm her down.
(19)  And then when she goes like that, she just touches like that, she falls down.
(20)  And then the guy says: "Look what you did."
(21)  And that was the end.
(22)  And they walked off.
(23)  And then they had "at the laundromat."
(24)  What they had was, they tell jokes like they were talking about what their husbands do.
(25)  And then after that they go into this thing like the wonder driers.
(26)  And then there's Cher and she's singing a song.

The most striking feature in this vignette is the frequent and perseverative use of the starters "and," "then," and "and then." These starters are used in 20 of the 26 sentences.

Another distinguishing feature is the frequent occurrence of the personal pronouns "they" (10 occurrences), "she" (14 occurrences), "he" (3 occurrences), "her" (2 occurrences), "his" (1 occurrence), "their" (2 occurrences), and "I" (1 occurrence). To sum up, 20 of the 26 sentences contain personal pronouns; of these, seven sentences contain two or more pronouns. The abundant use of pronominal phrases is associated with limited repetition of the referents for the various pronouns. As a result, it is unclear who performed the actions or experienced the events described.

The story also contains a relatively high proportion of the indefinite pronouns "some" (guy), "something," "everything," "this thing," (like) "that," and "all" as in "all these" and "all she." The only relative pronouns used in the sample are three occurrences of "what."

When we consider the use of main verbs, we see that "had" is used incorrectly as a substitute for another verb in the past tense in five of the

26 utterances. Reiteration of the main verb or verb phrase occurs in three of the utterances. Only two of the sentences contain secondary verbs, "tries to calm" and "starts kung fuin'."

The conjunction "and," which is acquired early in most children's vocabularies, is used in seven of the sentences. It is used for coordination of phrases and clauses in five of these. In the remaining two sentences, it is used to form conjunction deletions—in the verb phrase, "She was singing *and* went to all these things," and the noun phrase (direct object) of the verb phrase, "She says: 'I had a wonderful macaroni *and* cheese.'" There are no negations or interrogatives in the vignette.

The syntactic errors evident in this sample seem to reflect the girl's efforts to compensate when she is lost for words. When she has difficulties in recalling and retrieving specific words, her sentence formulation strategies appear to fall apart, and the resulting utterances violate the syntactic rules.

## CHARACTERISTICS OF LEARNING DISABILITIES

Children with specific learning disabilities show deficits in one or more of the processes basic to normal, efficient learning. They comprise a widely varied group, and the variations often make it difficult to pick out learning disabled children from a group of normal peers. They may have motor problems, including clumsiness and inadequate ability to perform movements in space. They may have perceptual problems that result in difficulties in analyzing what they see, hear, or touch. They may have problems in integrating information received from two or more differing sensory inputs, particularly vision, hearing, or touch. They may also have problems in storing information and in later retrieving specific information accurately. Any one child may have difficulties in all these areas or any combination of them.

In the area of language, they may have problems forming verbal abstractions and performing the logical operations required to interpret the complex relationships expressed in language. Their oral language problems may lead to deficits in perceiving and interpreting as well as in formulating and producing spoken language. The difficulties may also be reflected in academic retardation in subject areas such as reading, spelling, writing, mathematics, and other academic areas that require adequate language abilities.

The characteristic processing and production deficits of the learning disabled are not the primary effect of mental retardation, severe emotional disturbance, sensory impairments of hearing or vision, social maladjustment, cultural deprivation, or poor instruction. It is not unusual for the youngster with a learning disability to perform at *or above* normal levels in one or more skill areas. In fact, many definitions of "learning disabilities" include as one criterion the fact that the child must show a severe discrepancy between ability and achievement.

The youngster may learn to compensate for his disabilities with instruction. The discrepancies between the intact and the deficient

*For clarity, and because more males than females show learning disabilities, the masculine singular pronouns "he," "his," and "him" will be used in this book. However, many girls have learning and language disabilities; and all descriptions apply to girls as well as boys.*

processes and the interactions among his abilities and disabilities may, however, eventually result in deviant learning styles. The child may become frustrated and anxious, and may develop secondary behavioral-emotional disorders (Brutten, Richardson, & Mangel, 1973).

The language and communication deficits associated with learning disabilities are often subtle. They are, therefore, too frequently overlooked in the education of the youngster. Some observers suggest that the language deficits commonly associated with learning disabilities may be predicted on the basis of the youngster's rate of acquisition of the linguistic rules for word and sentence formation. The warning signs are very frequently overlooked or underrated, however. It is often not until after the learning disabled child has failed to acquire basic skills in reading, spelling, and writing that the question of whether he may have deficits in understanding and using spoken language arises.

Recent observations suggest that subtle language deficits associated with learning disabilities may persist into adolescence and young adulthood when the child does not receive appropriate clinical-educational intervention (Wiig & Semel, 1975; Wiig & Fleischmann, 1978). Another criterion in many definitions of "learning disabilities" is the need for special services—these children need help if they are to succeed. They cannot "make it" on their own. Against this background, it becomes critical to explore the relationships among language disabilities, developmental stages, and curriculum requirements. While not all learning disabled children will have all the characteristics and experiences we detail here, these descriptions do represent common patterns in the lives of many of these children.

## DEVELOPMENTAL STAGES AND AGES

### Infancy

The interaction among members of a family and a newborn infant may affect the infant significantly. Many learning disabled children are born at a disadvantage. They are often, but not always, the results of high-risk pregnancies or poor birth experiences. These may affect both the mother and the child. The mother may require a prolonged period of recuperation after the birth. The infant may also need prolonged medical attention. The family as a whole may be under enormous stress during a period when the parental bonds with the infant are normally strengthened through many positive interactions. The demands on the parents to tend to the physical well-being of the infant may channel their attention away from the infant's needs for sensory stimulation and social interactions. The subtle differences between the experiences of one infant and another—both in quality and quantity—can have significant long-term effects.

Parents often recognize that the learning disabled child is different early in life. He may have allergies, colic, and other physical problems that require his parents to handle him differently from their other children during the early months of infancy. Later the learning disabled child may show delays in reaching the standard milestones in perceptual and motor and/or speech and language development. Parents and other family members may unknowingly sabotage the infant's and toddler's listening and communication efforts. They may fail to support and encourage early auditory perception and language comprehension. The stimulation the child receives—both verbal and environmental—may be inconsistent and disorganized.

Developmental delays in the areas of early vocalization and language may become apparent when the child is late in babbling, imitating adult speech, and acquiring the first words. The child may then be slow in the acquisition of knowledge and use of word and sentence formation rules. He may stick to one- or two-word utterances for a longer period than his normally developing age peers. In many cases, one-word utterances predominate in the learning disabled child's speech past the expected age levels.

As a child who will later have a learning disability first develops auditory-vocal skills, he may show developmental delays and subtle differences from other children. The delays and differences may be in the acquisition of a specific skill or behavior. They may first manifest themselves in subtle differences in crying patterns (Swope, 1974). Since the delays appear to be circumscribed and specific rather than generalized, they may easily be overlooked or underestimated by the physician or psychologist.

*Tables 1.1 and 1.2 summarize the normal ages and stages in the early acquisition of auditory-vocal and language skills.*

**TABLE 1.1**

*The emergence of auditory-vocal skills from birth to 12 months of age*

| Age Range | Auditory Processing Skills | Vocal-Motor Production Skills |
|---|---|---|
| 0–1 mo. | Responds to mother's quieting efforts. Responds to sound of bell. | Vocalizes other than crying. |
| 1–3 mo. | Responds to sound of rattle. | Vocalizes once or twice during physical examination. |
| 1–4 mo. | Responds to sharp sounds such as the click of a light switch. | Responds with a social smile when an examiner talks or smiles. |
| 1–5 mo. (2.2 mo.) | Searches with eyes for sounds of a bell or a rattle. | Vocalizes at least 4 times during physical examination. |
| 1–5 mo. (2.3 mo.) | | Vocalizes 2 different sounds. |
| 1–6 mo. (2.7 mo.) | | Vocalizes to an examiner's social smile and talk. |
| 2–4 mo. | | Vocalizes with differentiated cries for hunger and pain. Coos with repetitions of one syllable. |
| 2–6 mo. (3.8 mo.) | Turns head to sound of bell. | |
| 2–6 mo. (3.9 mo.) | Turns head to sounds of a rattle. | |
| 3–4 mo. | Reacts to sudden noises. Heeds spoken voices. | Cries strongly. Sucks and swallows well. |

**TABLE 1.1** (*Continued*)

| Age Range | Auditory Processing Skills | Vocal-Motor Production Skills |
|---|---|---|
| 3–4 mo. | | Voice quality normalizes.<br>Responds with a meaningful smile.<br>Vocalizes back when talked to. |
| 4.6 mo. | | Vocalizes different attitudes such as pleasure, displeasure, eagerness, satisfaction, and anger. |
| 3–8 mo.<br>(4.8 mo.) | Discriminates strangers. | |
| 4–6 mo. | Turns to speaking voice.<br>Localizes source of sounds (bell, rattle, etc.).<br>Plays purposefully with noise-making toys.<br>Responds appropriately to friendly or angry voices. | Laughs aloud.<br>Tongue retracts in sucking.<br>Eats a cookie easily.<br>Babbles a series of syllable repetitions.<br>Babbles several sounds on one breath.<br>Babbles to people.<br>Vocalizes to mirror image.<br>Vocalizes to toys and for social contact. |
| 4–8 mo.<br>(5.8 mo.) | Listens with interest to sound productions of others. | |
| 5–12 mo.<br>(7.6 mo.) | | Vocalizes 4 different syllables.<br>Rings a bell purposefully. |
| 5–14 mo.<br>(7.9 mo.) | Listens selectively to familiar words such as "daddy," "dollie," "doggie." | Says "da-da" or equivalent. |
| 7–8 mo. | | Shouts for attention.<br>Sings tones.<br>Babbles with the inflectional patterns of adult speech.<br>Vocalizes in recognition of familiar people. |
| 6–14 mo.<br>(9.1 mo.) | Responds to verbal requests such as "Give me that." | |
| 6–13 mo.<br>(9.4 mo.) | Places objects on command, such as placing a cube in a cup. | |
| 8–15 mo.<br>(9.7 mo.) | Follows directions for simple actions such as stirring with a spoon. | |
| 7–16 mo.<br>(10.0 mo.) | Looks at pictures. | |
| 9–10 mo. | Responds to request to wave "bye-bye."<br>Responds to his or her name.<br>Responds to request to smile and pat a mirror. | Waves bye-bye.<br>Imitates a number of syllables after adults.<br>Plays peek-a-boo and patty-cake. |
| 7–13 mo.<br>(10.1 mo.) | Responds to inhibitory words such as "no-no." | Shakes head for no. |
| 7–17 mo.<br>(10.1 mo.) | | Inhibits action on commands such as "no, put it down" and "don't touch." |

TABLE 1.1 (*Continued*)

| Age Range | Auditory Processing Skills | Vocal-Motor Production Skills |
|---|---|---|
| 8–17 mo. (10.8 mo.) | Repeats actions which are laughed at or given verbal attention, such as imitations of adults talking on the phone. | |
| 9–18 mo. (11.8 mo.) | Responds to requests to put 3 or more cubes in a cup. | |
| 11–12 mo. | Understands meaningful gestures. Responds to requests for simple actions such as opening a small box or picking a pencil up. | Babbles monologues when alone. Imitates a variety of sounds. Says "Mama" and "Dadda" or other first word. Attempts new words such as "car," "milk," "shoe." |

**TABLE 1.2**

*The emergence of language skills from 12 to 36 months of age*

| Age Range | Language Processing Skills | Language Production Skills |
|---|---|---|
| 9–15 mo. (12.0 mo.) | | Says "mama" or "dada" or other first word. |
| 9–18 mo (12.5 mo.) | | Imitates words such as "baby," "apple," "more," and "up." |
| 13–14 mo. | | Tries to sing simple tunes as "Jack and Jill." |
| 10–23 mo. (14.2 mo.) | | Says 2 words in a single utterance as reported by mother or examiner. Uses meaningful gestures such as pointing to make wants known. |
| 15–16 mo. | Understands most simple questions. Points to own nose, eye, mouth, and other body parts on request. | Produces extensive vocalization and echoing responses. Has a speaking vocabulary of from 5 to 10 words. Uses 2-word phrases and short sentences. Uses expressive jargon. Speaks from 4 to 7 words with clear pronunciation. |
| 13–27 mo. (17.8 mo.) | | Names objects on confrontation of a ball, cup, pencil, watch, etc. |
| 14–26 mo. (17.8 mo.) | Responds to request for play actions such as "Put the doll in the chair," "Give the doll her milk," "Wipe the doll's nose." | |
| 14–27 mo. (18.8 mo.) | | Uses words and utterances to make wants known. |
| 17–18 mo. | | Speaks 10 words with clear pronunciation. |

**TABLE 1.2 (***Continued***)**

| Age Range | Language Processing Skills | Language Production Skills |
|---|---|---|
| | | Asks for desired objects by naming them ("cookie," "milk," etc.). |
| 15–26 mo. (19.1 mo.) | Points to parts of a doll such as "hand," "mouth," and "eyes" on request. | |
| 14–27 mo. (19.3 mo.) | | Names one pictured object such as a "shoe," "car," "dog," "cat", or "house." |
| 16–28 mo. (19.9 mo.) | Points to 2 pictures of objects such as a "dog," "shoe," "cup," "clock," "house," "flag," "star," "purse," or "book" on request. | |
| 16–20 mo. (20.6 mo.) | | Produces 2-word utterances (modifier and noun; operator and lexical item) such as "Here chair," "Fix it," "Want it," "Daddy home," "Eat cookie." |
| 16–30 mo. (21.4 mo.) | | Names 2 pictured objects in a series of pictures of a "shoe," a "doll," and an "apple." |
| 17–30 mo. (21.6 mo.) | Points to five pictures of objects such as a "cup," "chair," "table," "house," "flag," "star," "purse," or "book" on request. | |
| 21–22 mo. | | Attempts to describe experiences after the fact. Combines 3 words to describe ideas or events such as "Daddy go bye-bye." |
| 17–30 mo. (22.1 mo.) | | Names 3 pictured objects such as "shoe," "doll," "ball," "baby," and "apple." |
| 16–30 mo. (23.4 mo.) | Discriminates between 2 related requests such as "Give me the *cup;* Give me the *plate*." | |
| 17–30 mo. (24.0 mo.) | | Names 3 related objects such as "socks," "shoes," "pants," "shirt." |
| 23–24 mo. | Responds to simple requests for actions such as "Show me a dog," "Pick up the hat," "Give daddy the cup." Points to body parts such as a doll's nose, eye, and ear. Responds to questions for biographical and other information such as "What is your name?" and "What does the doggie say?" | Has discarded jargon. Shows marked decrease in sound and word repetition (echolalia). Refers to self by proper name. Produces sentences with from 2 to 4 words. |
| 22–30 mo. (28.2 mo.) | Understands 2 prepositions such as "in" and "on." | |

TABLE 1.2 (*Continued*)

| Age Range | Language Processing Skills | Language Production Skills |
|---|---|---|
| 23–32 mo. (30.0 mo.) | Understands 3 prepositions such as "in," "on," "under." | |
| 36 mo. | Identifies pictured objects on request when their function is indicated as in "Show me the one that you wear" or "Show me the one that you eat." | Tells his/her own sex. Indicates age by holding up fingers. Counts to 3. Repeats 5 to 7 syllable sentences, 2 to 3 nonsense syllables, 2 to 3 digits. Tells how common objects such as a fork, cup, shoe, or car are used. Produces phrases and sentences with personal pronouns, adjectives, prepositions, and/or adverbs. Uses regular noun plurals such as "dogs," "cups," "glasses." |

## Nursery School and Kindergarten

When the learning disabled child enters nursery school or kindergarten, he may not know the names of colors or be able to use scissors correctly, to tie shoe laces, to color within lines, or to arrange two or three objects in progression of size. In language skills, he may not be able to follow verbal directions, count in sequence, tell the names of the days of the week, or tell the names of items in the same semantic class or category. While all children develop mature **articulation** skills and **fluency** gradually, in the learning disabled child the period of normal articulation deviations and nonfluency may be extended. The learning disabled child may also have problems with discrimination between sounds, sequencing, and word finding during the preschool and kindergarten years. He may substitute or reverse sounds consistently. As a result, he may say "binglejells" when he intends to say "jingle bells," "buzgetti" for "spaghetti," and "aminals" for "animals." The normal period of baby talk may also be prolonged. He may have severe difficulties in remembering proper names and in finding specific words. Word-finding efforts may result in frequent word substitutions, circumlocutions, and use of **stereotyped** phrases.

The oral language of this child may be characterized by episodes of cluttering. The child may also have problems in differentiating and expressing the subtle distinctions in emotion and intention conveyed by **prosody**. This in turn may cause difficulties in interpreting imperatives, tag questions, and implied intentions and attitudes. Learning disabled children may also have other listening and language skill deficiencies. They may not be able to sit still while listening to a story and to learn the alphabet, word rhyming, finger plays, or songs. Significant to prereading skills, they may not be able to make one-to-one correspondences between sounds and letters.

*Cluttering refers to a disintegration of articulation with jerky and rapid spurts of speech, making the utterances difficult to understand. These episodes may break down the structure of sentences.*

*Prosody involves voice pitch, intensity, and juncture.*

*The secondary emotional problems that may be associated with learning disabilities have been discussed with eloquence by Brutten, Richardson, and Mangel (1973).*

In response to the learning disabled child's receptive and expressive language problems, he may be called slow to respond, confused, impulsive, inattentive, or even obstinate. Parents may react to their child's language and communication problems with guilt, overprotection, rejection, or genuine concern. If a child's parents' and peer's reactions are overwhelmingly negative or punishing, the learning disabled child may develop inappropriate emotional reactions or secondary emotional problems. These problems may cause the child to have continuing difficulties in interpersonal interactions and thus emphasize the learning disabilities.

The nursery school and kindergarten teacher is frequently able to identify the child who is academically at risk. Language disabilities among these children may often be discerned in their verbal interactions with their peers, parents, and teachers. Unfortunately, parents and teachers often limit their verbal approaches to these children. When they communicate with them, they frequently use restricted verbal forms. When they give them instructions, they often resort to motor or gestural demonstrations of the tasks rather than providing oral directions. As a result, the adults may inadvertently limit the child's chances to have experiences with and be rewarded for interpreting and using increasingly complex language.

Many learning disabled children who later will have language deficits acquire large early vocabularies with relative ease. This achievement often camouflages specific problems in processing, formulating, and producing spoken language. Thus, nursery school and kindergarten teachers often have great difficulty obtaining early assistance for the learning disabled child's language problems. Several investigations have found that a child who has learning disabilities in grades 3 and 4 was often detected and identified in kindergarten. As a result of the child's language deficits and the lack of early intervention, he may not acquire some of the preacademic skills necessary for first grade work. This may leave the child at an early disadvantage and open to academic and social failures and frustrations. Again, these problems may influence interpersonal relationships negatively during the school years (Bryan, 1974a; Bryan & Bryan, 1975; Bryan, Wheeler, Felcan, & Henek, 1976; Keogh, Tchir, & Wendeguth-Behn, 1974; Wender, 1971).

## The Early Grades

Learning disabled children who enter the first grade without adequate preacademic skills may have a multitude of failures. They frequently show limited ability to identify sounds in phonics work. They may have difficulties in same-different discriminations of sounds and words. They may find it hard to analyze and synthesize sound sequences, to form stable sound-letter associations, and to segment words into their smallest grammatical units. These difficulties may be reflected in limited or slow academic achievement in reading, spelling, writing, and mathematics.

In the first grade there is a heavy emphasis on phonics, word attack skills, and structural analysis. Temporal and spatial language concepts such as *before-after, second,* and *third* are also emphasized. In addition, the child must learn the meaning of more abstract words and linguistic concepts in mathematics, including *few, many, all-except, either-or, neither-nor,* and *some*. The acquisition of these language skills may pose severe difficulties for the language and learning disabled child.

The demands for processing and interpreting spoken language, formulating and producing language for oral presentations, and recalling verbal materials increase significantly in the second grade. Language problems which were present in the first grade tend to persist or increase in severity with these increased demands. At the same time, less classroom time is spent with manipulative materials. The child must be able to acquire new knowledge from the teacher's verbal presentations, and must accurately follow oral directions for action.

The length and complexity of the sentences spoken by the learning disabled child frequently appear to increase at this time. It may seem as if the child is catching up with his or her peers. Word-finding problems which earlier resulted in word and sound substitutions and circumlocutions seem to decrease. Early episodes of stuttering may also decrease, and the child's speech prosody and **intonation** may improve. All of these signs of growth may alleviate the teacher's concern for the child's language deficits.

## The Middle Grades

The delays demonstrated by learning disabled children in the acquisition of syntactic rules and abstract linguistic concepts limit their academic achievement significantly in the middle grades (Aiken, 1972; Wiig & Semel, 1974a). Basic skills in reading and mathematics are reviewed briefly in the third grade. It is at this stage that specific learning disabilities in children tend to become obvious. The early problems in formulating and producing spoken language may, however, appear to have decreased. In spite of this, subtle high-level deficits in both language processing and production may persist. These deficits may influence reading comprehension and mathematics skills, among others. Word substitutions may persist in oral reading, sentence recall and repetition, copying, and writing to dictation. When the language and learning disabled child is reading out loud, he may substitute words with greater than normal frequency. This may result in substituting a word such as "kitten" for "cat" or "knife" for "fork." The word substitution errors in reading, writing, and verbal recall tend to be somewhat predictable. Substituted words tend to belong to the same semantic class as the intended words, and **antonyms** and synonyms are frequently interchanged. Word substitution errors in oral reading appear most prevalent when the level of difficulty of the material is below the level of the child's reading achievement. They seem to decrease as the relative difficulty of the material increases. Visual discrimination errors in reading, on the other hand, appear to increase when the level of difficulty of the material is at or above the level of reading achievement.

The demands on children change drastically when they enter the fourth grade. From this point on, there is generally little or no skill building in phonics, vocabulary, number concepts, or language concepts. Specific deficits may receive very little attention in the large classroom. As a result, the learning disabled child may be lost in reading and mathematics sessions. The child's limitations in language processing, formulation, and production may go unnoticed but affect his achievement in all academic areas. Academic texts in areas such as social studies often contain vocabulary words which are well above the child's reading level. This feature may magnify the comprehension problems of the child with a language deficit. Problems in mathematics increase significantly in the level of difficulty of the vocabulary as well as in syntactic complexity. These features place greater demands upon the child's linguistic and cognitive processing skills.

In the fourth grade and later, adequate knowledge of word classes and relations, syntactic structures and **transformations,** and implied causes, effects, and relationships are prerequisites for academic achievement. There is an increasing emphasis on specificity as well as fluency, flexibility, and elaboration in vocabulary, sentence structure, and topic presentation. In order to process the complex materials used in education, the child must be able to perform simultaneous letter-sound, syntactic, semantic, and logical analyses and syntheses. The ability to process information at several levels and in more than one **modality** at the same time may be exceedingly weak among children with language and learning disabilities.

*A modality is a channel through which a child receives information. Examples include the auditory mode—listening—and the visual mode—seeing or reading.*

The educational implication seems to be that language and learning disabled youngsters may benefit from language therapy during the years from kindergarten through the fourth grade. Language intervention may provide increased opportunities for skill-building activities that will benefit later learning. Schools should make systematic efforts to identify language processing and production deficits among learning disabled children during the early and middle grades in order to provide appropriate intervention before the problems are compounded.

## The Upper Grades

During the middle and upper grades, learning disabled children become increasingly aware of their academic and social failures and of being different. During that period, they may show subtle emotional reactions including forms of aggression, anxiety, compulsiveness, frustration, ridgidity, lack of motivation, and withdrawal, with increasing frequency. These problems may go unnoticed by parents, teachers, or psychologists until overt acts like aggression, pilfering, or severe nightmares reveal the child's emotional turmoil. The learning disabled child may not be able to verbalize his reactions adequately till he enters the middle or upper grades. Generally, the child's native intellectual ability appears to determine the age when he will verbalize his emotional reactions. The greater the child's intellectual ability, the earlier he tends to have some insight into his problems and reactions and to verbalize his frustrations.

Learning disabled children often reveal the depth of their anguish when they are counseled. Language and learning disabled children in counseling have expressed feelings of guilt toward their parents for being "dumb," a sense of "being ugly and a polluter," and a wish to "be dead so nobody will bug me." These are serious reactions and deserve professional attention in the form of counseling along with specific skill-building activities.

In the upper grades, the language and learning disabled youngster shows an increasingly widening gap in academic achievement in comparison to his age peers. Language deficits that have been overlooked previously may come to the surface at this time. The youngster's learning disabilities may no longer seem specific and circumscribed but may encompass all subject areas.

In the area of nonverbal communication and social and interpersonal interaction, the language and learning disabled youngster in the upper grades may seem to grow increasingly insensitive and clumsy. He may give inappropriate social responses. He may get into trouble because he is unable to interpret other people's emotions and predict their intentions. In turn, he is liable to be rejected by his peers, and his emotional problems may increase.

### Adolescence and Young Adulthood

During prepuberty and puberty and into adolescence and young adulthood, verbal and nonverbal communication deficits may continue to influence the quality of a child's interpersonal interactions negatively. These deficits may also limit the person's potential for self-realization. Deficits in social perception, resulting in difficulties in perceiving and interpreting nonverbal communication cues, are often increased by the increasing social demands. Adult sexual identities and roles emerge and develop during this period and require children to adjust their body images and self-concepts. Sensitivity to the verbal as well as to the nonverbal cues of other people help children develop appropriate sexual identities.

The visual-perceptual and visual-motor organization problems that many individuals with learning disabilities have may impose further barriers to interpersonal interaction and social perception. Learning disabled adolescents may have difficulties and be confused in interpreting the emotions, attitudes, and intentions that other people communicate through facial expressions and body language. They may respond inappropriately to subtle nonverbal, social cues and may be rejected by peers of the opposite sex, by significant adults, and by strangers. Their lack of emotional sensitivity to expressions of love, affection, and approval may result in feelings of basic insecurity that may remain throughout life. Their inadequacies in using nonverbal cues may in turn result in deviant personality development (Sullivan, 1953, 1954, 1964).

*For a more detailed discussion of the social perception problems of the learning disabled, see Wiig & Semel (1976, pp. 297–319).*

The assumption that the learning disabled child will outgrow his deficits and be normal as an adolescent and young adult is proving erroneous. Language deficits which begin early in life and go untreated may persist into young adulthood and emerge again and again in later life. They tend to come out when new circumstances—perhaps a new line of study, a new job, or a promotion—place different and unexpected demands upon language processing and use in speaking or writing. Some learning disabled people may learn to skillfully avoid situations which tax their basic incapacities. Others may be open to failure all their lives. Some learn to compensate and to use adaptive strategies to find success in spite of their deficits. Some never acquire compensatory strategies and may need assistance in developing adaptive and efficient techniques for compensation even once they are past school age.

The barriers to adequate and rewarding verbal and nonverbal interpersonal interaction for the learning disabled child suggest we need to increase our efforts to monitor language skills throughout the school years. The subtlety of the language and communication deficits of the learning disabled further suggests that language abilities should be reassessed at several crucial stages in the formal education process. Among these crucial stages are the fourth grade, the transitions to junior and senior high school, and the freshman year of college or the beginning of vocational training. Increased attention to developing functional and adequate communication skills up to the child's potential may benefit the individual and society alike. Developing these skills may increase the learning disabled person's potential for self-realization and for a satisfying vocational or professional career.

*part* **II**

## Morphology
## and
## Syntax

# FORMING WORDS
## Characteristics and Assessment

English words are composed of one or more basic units of meaning called **morphemes,** and the rules for forming words out of morphemes are called *morphology.* Skilled English speakers use morphology to:

(1) Modify the meaning of root words and produce the semantic distinctions of:
   (a) Number and case, as in noun plurals (girl-girl*s*) and noun possessives (the girl'*s*),
   (b) Verb tense (walk*ed*) and aspect (has been walk*ing*) and third person singular of verbs (walk*s*),
   (c) Comparison, as in the comparative and superlative forms of adjectives (bigg*er,* bigg*est*).
(2) Derive nouns from verbs (teach*er*) and other word classes (great-*ness*), adjectives (spott*y*), adverbs (quick*ly*), and diminutives (book-*let*), and specify their syntactic roles in sentences,
(3) Extend or modify the meaning of root words by the addition of a prefix (*dis*cover, *anti*social).

*See the appendix for definitions of grammatical structures such as noun plurals.*

Derived words such as "teacher" and "quickly" contain two morphemes each (teach-er, quick-ly). When dividing the words "teacher" and "quickly" into their component morphemes, each of them is found to contain a root word, or **free morpheme**. A free morpheme has referential meaning; it can stand alone. They also each contain a **bound morpheme,** *-er* and *-ly,* which does not have referential meaning and which cannot stand alone in a sentence. The *bound morphemes* in English can be classified further as either:

(1) **Prefixes** such as *in-, dis-, un-, re-,* and *di-.*
(2) **Suffixes** such as *-er, -ly, -ed, -ness, -ing, -ate, -ine, -able, -tion,* and *-al.*
(3) **Infixes** such as *-ess* in **inflected** words such as steward*ess*es.

The English suffixes may belong to two categories. They may be used for **derivation,** to change the syntactic role of a word such as run (verb) into runn*er* (noun) and slow (adjective) into slow*ly* (adverb).

*An inflected word is a word to which an ending is added to modify its meaning; a derived word has an ending which changes its grammatical function.*

25

They may also be used to inflect root words (free morphemes) to form, among others:

(1) Noun plurals as in boy–boys, cat–cats, and dress–dresses.
(2) Noun possessives as in boy–boy's–boys', cat–cat's–cats', and dress–dress's–dresses'.
(3) Present progressive tense of verbs as in walking and running.
(4) Third person singular of verbs as in walks and runs.
(5) Past tense of verbs as in walked.
(6) Comparative and superlative forms of adjectives as in greater and greatest.

## Normal Development

Children with normal language development seem to learn the linguistic rules for word formation incidentally and effortlessly, and in most children the processing and production of words, phrases, and sentences soon becomes highly automatic. Several researchers have investigated the order in which morphological rules are acquired.

Carrow (1973) reports the order of and age ranges for the acquisition of selected word formation rules and applications in Table 2.1.

**TABLE 2.1**

*Order of acquisition of word formation rules (from Carrow, 1973)*

| Word Formation Rule | Application | Age Range of Acquisition | | |
|---|---|---|---|---|
| | | *by 75%* | | *by 90%* |
| Regular noun plurals. | balls | 3–6 | to | 6–0 years |
| | coats | 5–6 | to | 6–6 years |
| | chairs | 6–6 | to | 7–0+ years |
| Present progressive tense. | running, hitting | 3–0 | to | 3–6 years |
| Present progressive tense. | going | 3–6 | to | 5–6 years |
| Adjective forms. | | | | |
| Comparative. | smaller, taller | 4–0 | to | 5–0 years |
| Superlative. | fattest | 3–0 | to | 3–6 years |
| Noun derivation. | | | | |
| -er | hitter | 3–6 | to | 5–0 years |
| | painter | 4–0 | to | 6–0 years |
| | farmer | 5–0 | to | 6–6 years |
| -man | fisherman | 5–6 | to | 6–0 years |
| -ist | bicyclist, pianist | 7–0 | to | 7–0+ years |
| Adverb derivation. | | | | |
| -ly | easily, gently | 7–0+ | to | 7–0+ years |

*3–6 = 3 years, 6 months*

Drawn from Carrow, E. *Test of auditory comprehension of language.* Austin: Urban Research Group, 1973.

Berko (1958) investigated the knowledge of word formation rules by 4- to 7-year-old children in an ingenious research design. The children applied a variety of inflectional and derivational word endings to nonsense words associated with nonsense pictures. Figure 2.1 shows the format used to test the children's ability to apply the noun plural endings.

FIGURE 2.1
*The Plural Allomorph in /-Z/*

THIS IS A WUG.

NOW THERE IS ANOTHER ONE.
THERE ARE TWO OF THEM.
THERE ARE TWO _____.

Source: Berko, Jean. The child's learning of English morphology. *Word*, **14**, 150–77. Reprinted by permission of the author.

By using nonsense words, Berko could evaluate the children's knowledge of English morphology rather than their rote memory of the inflections and derivations of actual words. Comparison of the responses by preschoolers in the age range from 4 to 5 years and of first graders in the age range from 5 years, 6 months to 7 seven years demonstrated that the children acquired the knowledge of word formation rules in an orderly and predictable fashion. The responses also showed that the children first learned a general rule and later refined their knowledge by acquiring the more specific rules. In general, the children were best able to apply inflectional word endings that are highly regular and frequent and that have the fewest variants.

In the study, boys and girls performed at similar levels. First graders performed consistently better than preschoolers, with significant differences being recorded for about 50% of the test items. The first graders demonstrated significant improvements over the preschoolers, which indicated that they had perfected their knowledge of the rules for forming regular noun plurals and possessives and present progressive tense. At age 7, children were still refining their knowledge and application of the rules for forming the comparative and superlative of adjectives, for deriving nouns, and for deriving adverbs.

Several more recent studies have explored the acquisition of inflectional word endings as evidenced by their use in spontaneous speech. Thus, Brown (1973) ranked the order of acquisition of a set of 14 selected morphemes by three children who were studied extensively. He observed a stable order of acquisition by these children when he used a criterion of 90% correct use in required contexts. The order of acquisition was as follows:

(1) Present progressive tense ending (morpheme) "-ing."
(2) Prepositions "in" and "on."
(3) Regular noun plural.
(4) Past tense irregular, e.g., "came," "went."
(5) Noun possessive, e.g., "Adam's chair."
(6) Uncontractible **copula** forms of *to be* ("am," "is," "are," "was," "were").
(7) Articles "a" and "the."
(8) Past tense regular, e.g., "Sarah walked."
(9) Third person regular ending (morpheme) "-s," e.g., "Eve walks."
(10) Third person irregular forms "does" and "has."
(11) Uncontractible auxiliary, e.g., "will," "can."
(12) Contractible copula forms of "to be," e.g., "It's a gun."
(13) Contractible auxiliary, e.g., "I'll do it."

*A copula is any word which expresses the relationship between the subject and predicate of a sentence.*

*Allomorphic variation is a change in a morpheme required by a change in environment; thus "be" changes to "am" in the environment of "I" ("I am") (Pei & Gaynor, 1975).*

Brown comments that "when the effects of allomorphic variation are partialled out, Berko's data support the order we found" (1973, p. 292). Brown concludes that both semantic and grammatical complexity determine the order of acquisition. He also says that the order is *not* related to the frequency order of the word endings and morphemes in the parents' speech.

In a related study, deVilliers and deVilliers (1973) obtained cross-sectional data from 24 children ranging in age from 16 to 40 months on the acquisition of the word endings and morphemes which Brown studied. Their results agreed with the order of acquisition Brown reports, and they also agreed that semantic and grammatical complexity determine the sequence in which the word formation rules are acquired.

Several investigations of the knowledge of the general and specific word formation rules by school-age children indicate that the development proceeds from the application of the most general rules to finer and finer differentiation of the rules. Menyuk (1963a, 1964) established that significantly more children of nursery school age than of grade school age omit the irregular past tense forms of verbs and substitute regular past tense formed by adding -*t*, -*d*, or -*ed*. Children of kindergarten age also used immature forms in forming the third person singular and plural of the present tense of verbs, past tense of verbs, singular and plural nouns, possessive pronouns, and adjectives.

Koziol (1973) found that the period of major learning of the rules for forming noun plurals occurs between kindergarten and grade 1. The accurate use of the plural forms of regular nouns appears to be delayed by about one grade level, while the accurate formation of irregular noun plurals is delayed by two or three grade levels. Until about grade 3, the children have problems in forming the plurals of nouns which end in -*sk* and -*st* clusters.

## The Learning Disabled Child

Learning disabled children characteristically show a number of difficulties with morphology. They may have trouble with the semantic distinctions of number, case, tense, aspect, and comparison and the distinctions in the syntactic roles of words. Their problems suggest that they do not acquire the rules for word formation at the same rate and with the same degree of sophistication as peers do. The problems seem to reflect language delays or disabilities. We should not forget, however, that some learning disabled children may show language differences due to dialectical variations or bilingual backgrounds.

*See pages 45–48 in this chapter for more on dialectical variations in word formation rules.*

## CHARACTERISTICS OF WORD FORMATION DEFICITS

Studies of learning disabled children indicate that they may experience significant delays in the acquisition of morphological rules (Golick, 1976; Vogel, 1974; Wiig & Semel, 1976; Wiig, Semel, & Crouse, 1973). There are many possible reasons why some learning disabled children have problems with morphology. Their difficulties in processing and applying the word formation rules accurately may relate to:

(1) Perceiving and processing parts of phrases, clauses, and sentences that are unstressed (articles, prepositions, auxiliaries, modals).
(2) Perceiving and inferring word endings that tend to blend and be reduced in rapid conversation.
(3) Focusing on the perceptually highlighted parts of speech in phrases, clauses, and sentences.
(4) Focusing on the highly information-loaded words (nouns, verbs, adjectives) in phrases, clauses, and utterances and disregarding units that carry little information and appear redundant and irrelevant (auxiliaries, modals, prepositions, pronouns, conjunctions).
(5) Leaving out parts of words and phrases in speaking, which leads them to delete unstressed syllables, reduce consonant clusters, and neutralize final consonants and inflectional endings.
(6) Abstracting and applying the rules for distribution of inflectional and derivational suffixes.
(7) Abstracting the meaning of prefixes and using prefixes to extend word meanings.

The learning disabled child who expresses sophisticated ideas in relatively complex sentence structures may still have difficulties using the accepted rules for word formation. These difficulties at times occur to the same extent in both spoken and written language. Problems in perceiving and interpreting the inflectional word endings used by others also occur both in spoken and read language forms.

The difficulties in perceiving, identifying, processing, and using the inflectional and derivational word endings may be attributed to, among other causes, auditory-perceptual deficits and limitations in short-term memory for spoken utterances and sentences. Plagued by these limitations, learning disabled children often develop inefficient processing strategies; they may ignore hard-to-hear words or parts of words. They may fail to perceive and process whole words such as auxiliaries and function words, which generally receive low stress. Instead, the learning child may tend to focus on and retain words that stand out because of their stress or their high information content. As a result, many learning disabled children favor root words such as nouns, verbs, and adjectives. The efficiency of their processing strategies is in turn influenced by factors such as the context in which an utterance occurs as well as the speaker's style, speed, and intonation and stress patterns.

Learning disabled children also have trouble with parts of words, especially word endings. The information load of the derivational and inflectional endings in a spoken sentence is relatively low. As a result, these word endings may appear redundant and irrelevant to the learning disabled child—especially because the child can follow much of what is said accurately without focusing on word endings. The habit of not attending to spoken word endings is often reflected in the children's speech, where they may manage to make their intentions clear without using the appropriate word formation rules.

Skousen (1974) states that the induction of rules depends upon the word forms that are actually heard. Due to auditory-perceptual problems, learning disabled children may not hear the spoken word and sentence forms consistently and clearly enough to abstract and induce the grammatical regularities of the word formation rules. Their errors in forming words resemble those of the much younger normal child. Some of their errors may be similar to forms which are acceptable in dialectical variations or Nonstandard English, even though the children may have been exposed to Standard English exclusively.

Brown (1973) points out that, in children with normal language development, the order of acquisition of the inflectional and derivational word endings (morphemes) depends in part upon their semantic complexity. Learning disabled children may fail to grasp or differentiate the underlying meaning of the various word endings and prefixes. In turn, the intended meaning of their utterances and sentences may be so limited that they may not need to use word endings or prefixes to modify or elaborate the basic semantic content. This tendency may be further reinforced if they feel that they manage to convey their semantic intentions and the listener can interpret the utterances because they occur in a certain context.

## Specific Morphological Deficits

The morphological deficits of learning disabled children may be reflected in:

(1) The formation of noun plurals, especially the irregular forms (-*s*, -*z*, -*ez*, vowel changes, -*ren*, etc.).

(2) The formation of noun possessives, both singular and plural (-*s*, -*s'*).

(3) The formation of third person singular of the present tense of verbs (-*s*).

(4) The formation of the past tense of both regular and irregular verbs (-*t*, -*d*, -*ed*, vowel change).

(5) The formation of the comparative and superlative forms of adjectives (-*er*, -*est*).

(6) The cross-categorical use of inflectional endings (*-s*, *'s*, *s'*).
(7) Noun derivation (*-er*).
(8) Adverb derivation (*-ly*).
(9) The comprehension and use of prefixes (*pre- post-*, *pro-*, *anti-*, *di-*, *de-*).

We will now look at each of these types of deficits in more detail.

*Noun Plurals*

Children with normal language development show significant increases in the acquisition of the rules for forming noun plurals between the ages of 4 to 5 and 6 to 7 years. At 5 to 6 years of age, they may still form irregular noun plurals using the rules for forming regular noun plurals and produce such forms as "peopleses," "mouses," and "sheepses." Of the three inflectional morphemes for forming regular noun plurals, the forms requiring addition of /ez/ proved the hardest to learn (Berko, 1958; Menyuk, 1969; Wiig, Semel, & Crouse, 1973). Learning disabled children may have several different types of problems in forming noun plurals:

(1) They may have problems in perceiving and discriminating among the various pronunciations of the plural morpheme *-s* and perceiving and understanding how the immediately preceding speech sounds affect the choice of which ending to use. As a result, they may have an inconsistent and unclear perception of the features of words which determine whether an **unvoiced** /s/, **voiced** /z/, or /ez/ should be added to the root word to form the plural. Often learning disabled children add the plural endings inconsistently, sometimes saying "the boys" and sometimes "the *boyses*." They may also overgeneralize the use of a plural ending and use, for example, /ez/ to form all plurals, resulting in utterances such as the "the *boyses*," "the *catses*," and "the *dressesses*." They may also omit plural endings of nouns which require the addition of /ez/ and produce utterances such as "They eated *their sandwich*."

**Voiced** *speech sounds are produced with vibrations of the vocal fold chord; they include the vowels and consonants such as* b, d, *and* g. **Unvoiced** *speech sounds without that vibration include* p, t, *and* k.

(2) They may show prolonged use of the rules which children normally acquire early for forming noun plurals in which the plural endings /s/ and /z/ are generalized to inappropriate root words. This habit may result in the omission of plural endings for nouns which already end in either /s/ or /z/ and produce utterances such as "The *two nurse* went home" and "Their *nose were* cold."

(3) They may have problems in memorizing the individual occurrences of rules for forming irregular noun plurals. As a result, learning disabled children may generalize the rules for forming regular noun plurals to the irregular noun forms and produce utterances such as "The *childs* have" for "The children have," "He hurt his *foots*" for "He hurt his feet," and "The *mouses* played" for "The mice played."

*Noun Possessives*

Children who develop language normally seem to acquire the singular and plural forms of noun possessives at about the same time. Even 4- to 5-year-olds seem to have learned the singular and plural forms of the possessive for root words which end in voiced and unvoiced conso-

**FIGURE 2.2**
*Omission of Plural Endings*

nants other than /s/ and /z/. They seem to have the greatest problems in acquiring the rules for forming possessives of nouns which end in /s/ and /z/ (Berko, 1958). The formation of noun possessives, both singular and plural, may pose one or more of the following problems for children with learning disabilities.

(1) They may fail to perceive and discriminate the noun possessive endings and may omit the ending in forming the noun possessive singular. As a result, they may produce utterances such as "It is the *boy hat*" for "It is the boy's hat" or "That's the *nurse bag*" for "That's the nurse's bag."

(2) They may have problems in perceiving and acquiring the rules which determine whether the unvoiced /s/, voiced /z/, or /ez/ should be added to the root word to form the singular possessive. Often learning disabled children add these endings inconsistently, sometimes saying "It's the *catses* hat" for "It's the cat's hat." At other times, they generalize one ending to all forms of the singular possessive and may produce utterances such as "It's the *nurseses* bag," "It's the *boyses* cat," and "It's the *manses* hat."

(3) They may show prolonged use of the early acquired rules for forming noun possessives in which the noun possessive singular endings are generalized to the plural forms. As a result, they produce plural possessives such as "The two *catses* hats were blue" for "The two cats' hats were blue."

## Third Person Singular of Verbs

Learning disabled children may have control of the most common rules for subject-verb agreement in the third person singular. But in spite of this, they may fail to add the inflectional suffix /s/, /z/, or /ez/ to irregular verbs in the third person singular. This omission may result in idiosyncratic sentence forms such as "Jane never *go* to the movies," "Then my father *come* home and *eat* his dinner" and "He *take* sugar in the coffee." Their error patterns in subject-verb agreement for person

and number rarely involve overgeneralization of the rule for forming third person singular of verbs. Even then, learning disabled children may add -*s* to the present tense forms which do not require this ending and may produce utterances such as "They always *walks* to school" and "We never *likes* to wear our boots."

*Verb Tenses*

Learning disabled children may have several types of difficulties in differentiating and forming verb tenses.

(1) Some show delays in acquiring the rule of forming the present progressive tense of verbs which require addition of the ending -*ing* to the root verb and insertion of the copula "be" between the subject and the primary verb. Learning disabled children may learn a partial rule for forming the present progressive in which they add the ending -*ing* to the root verb but fail to insert the copula "be" in the verb phrase. As a result, they may say things like "Jack *walking* to school" for "Jack is walking to school" and "I *goin'* to do it" for "I am going to do it."

(2) Learning disabled children may also have problems perceiving and acquiring phonological conditioning rules for the regular past tense of verbs which determine whether the unvoiced /t/, voiced /d/, or /ed/ should be added to the root verb. As a result, they may use these endings inconsistently and sometimes produce utterances such as "She *walkded* to school" and at other times "She *walked* to school." They may also overgeneralize the use of one of the past tense endings to form inappropriate verb forms such as "She *sleeped* in the bed" and "She *sob-b'ed* because she was sad."

(3) A third problem is deficits in perceiving, acquiring, and recalling the rules for the internal vowel changes that are appropriate for the individual irregular verbs. As a result, learning disabled children may overgeneralize the rules for forming regular past tense to irregular verbs and produce utterances such as "The dog *runned* real fast" for

"The dog ran real fast," "The man *ringed* the bell" for "The man rang the bell," and "He *thinked* very hard and then he got a good idea." They may also use the present tense of verbs for intended past tense forms, especially if the past is indicated by phrases such as "yesterday," "after that," and "when that" and the inflection therefore appears redundant or if a series of past tense verbs occur in the same sentence. These tendencies may lead them to say things like "He sat down and then he *take* the book and *read* it."

(4) Learning disabled children may have deficits in perceiving, acquiring, and recalling the rules for the use of forms of the copula "to be" and of auxiliary verbs such as "to do," "to have," "can," "will," "shall," "may," and "must." As examples, they may substitute the present, past, and future tense forms and produce idiosyncratic utterances such as "I *do* it last week" and "Tomorrow I *did* it." They may also substitute forms of the copula *to be* for other auxiliaries and say "I *am* have my bike tomorrow" for "I will [shall/may] have my bike tomorrow." In a similar vein, they may confuse forms of the copula "to be" and say "They *been* very surprised when they got the presents" and "I *were* happy when mammy came."

(5) Deficits in perceiving, differentiating, and expressing the time and sequence denoted by the tenses are common. As a result, they may produce utterances such as "Yesterday I *builded* a plane and tomorrow I *finished* it," in which the actual sequence of the actions is communicated only by the terms "yesterday" and "tomorrow."

**FIGURE 2.4**

*Confusion of Present and Future Tenses*

The **aspect** *is the characteristic of a verb which indicates whether the action is completed or in progress, momentary or habitual, etc. The perfective aspect expresses a one-time, nonhabitual action (Pei & Gaynor, 1975). Thus "have been seeing" is the perfective aspect of "to see."*

(6) Learning disabled children show deficits in perceiving, interpreting, and expressing the **perfective aspect** denoted by the forms "have -en." They may omit forms of "to have" in these constructions and produce utterances such as "The car *been* fixed so we can use it now" for "The car has been fixed so we can use it now" and "We *been* waiting for you" for "We have been waiting for you." They may also substitute forms such as "were gonna wait," "have waiting," or "were waiting" for "have been waiting" and forms such as "is fixed," "was fixed," or "has fixed" for "has been fixed."

*Comparative and Superlative Forms of Adjectives*

The comparative and superlative forms of adjectives may pose problems for children with learning disabilities.

(1) Some may have difficulties in differentiating the meaning of the inflectional ending -*er* used to form the comparative of adjectives, as in "big–bigger" and the derivational suffix -*er* used to derive nouns from verbs, as in "sing–singer." As a consequence, they may be confused when asked a question of comparison such as "Which one is bigger?" They may interpret the inflectional ending -*er* to indicate the person who performs an act and may search for the act referred to by the word "big."

(2) They may not easily discern that the inflectional ending -*er* used to form the comparative implies a comparison of identical qualities or attributes in two objects, persons, events, or ideas. They may also have trouble dealing with a comparison between a concrete quality such as size and an abstract quality such as character as in the statement, "John is *bigger than* Bill [size], but Bill is a *bigger person than* John [stature or character]."

(3) Learning disabled children may have problems in grasping the underlying **ordinal** relationships and multiple stage comparisons implied by the superlative forms of adjectives. When he hears a statement such as "Jane is *smaller than* Betty, who is the *tallest* girl in the class," the learning disabled child may interpret the sentence to state that *Jane is small* and *Betty is tall.* He may totally fail to grasp the underlying ordering of the girls in the class according to size, as well as the implied comparison of Jane and Betty to all the other girls.

(4) They may have difficulties in labelling and expressing the underlying order when three or more objects, persons, events, or ideas are compared. As a result, they may describe three or more objects of increasing size like this: "This one is *big.* This one is *also big,* and this one is *very big.*"

(5) They may show delays in acquiring the rules for forming irregular comparatives and superlatives of adjectives such as "good" ("better–best") or "courageous" ("more courageous–most coura-

**FIGURE 2.5**

*Difficulty in Making Appropriate Comparisons for Three or More Objects*

geous"). The regular endings for comparatives and superlatives of adjectives may be generalized to irregular adjectives, resulting in forms such as "gooder–goodest" and "courageouser–courageousest." In a similar vein, the modifiers "more" and "most" may be used with all irregular adjectives, resulting in forms such as "more good" and "most good."

(6) Some may have problems with comparisons where the same quality or attribute is compared even though the root adjective has been changed. An example would be "This girl is *tall*. This girl is *shorter,* and this girl is the *shortest."*

(7) Learning disabled children may be confused when a statement of comparison progresses in the negative (subtractive) rather than in the positive (additive) direction as in the commands "Point to the basket with *fewer* apples than this one" and "Point to the basket with the *fewest* apples" (subtractive) rather than "Point to the basket with *more* apples than this one" and "Point to the basket with the *most* apples" (additive).

### Cross-Categorical Use of Inflectional Endings

A special problem arises for learning disabled children because the same inflectional endings are used for several word classes. As an example, the inflectional suffix -s may be used to denote:

(1) Noun plural as in "boys" and "cats."
(2) Third person singular of verbs as in "speaks" and "walks."
(3) Contractible copula or auxiliary as in "He's small" (He *is* small) and "He's a dog" (He *has* a dog).
(4) Singular forms of noun possessives such as *the man's* and *the horse's*.
(5) Plural forms of noun possessives when the root word does not end in /s/ as in "the men's" and the "children's."

The difficulties learning disabled children have in differentiating the underlying meaning of the various uses of the same inflectional endings are further complicated by the variations in the articulation of the inflectional -s. These variations are determined by the characteristics of the preceding speech sounds. Thus, -s is pronounced as an unvoiced /s/ after unvoiced consonants only. It is pronounced as a voiced /z/ after voiced consonants and all vowels. In turn, it is pronounced as /ez/ after all final /s/ and /z/ speech sounds. Table 2.2 shows an overview of the cross-categorical use of the same inflectional endings.

### Noun Derivation

Learning disabled children may experience difficulties in acquiring and applying the rules for noun derivation.

(1) They may compound two root words to form a label for the person who performs a specific act or function longer than other children. For example, learning disabled children may use the terms "joggerman" and "workman" to refer to males who jog and work. When interpreting spoken or read language, they may expect compound nouns to be used to refer to persons involved in specific actions

**TABLE 2.2**
*Inflectional endings*

| **Inflectional Ending** | **Variations** | | |
|---|---|---|---|
| *-s* | /s/ | /z/ | /ez/ |
| Noun plural. | cats | boys | dresses |
| Singular possessive of nouns. | cat's | boy's | dress's |
| Plural possessive of nouns. | cats' | boys' | dresses' |
| Third person singular of verbs. | speaks | runs | buzzes |
| Contraction of the copula "is." | The cat's big | The boy's big | The dress's big |
| Contraction of the auxiliary "has." | The cat's a ball | The boy's a ball | The dress's a pocket |

or functions. When these expectations are not met, they may act confused and fail to interpret the derived nouns that are used as labels.

(2) Learning disabled children may become confused by the use of the derivational endings *-er, -or,* or *-ist* in forming labels for people who perform a novel action or function. The inconsistencies in the use of the derivational endings *-er* and *-or* may best be observed in written expressions, where these endings may be consistently misspelled. In a similar vein, the derivational endings may be applied incorrectly, resulting in words such as the "laboror," the "machiner," and the "jewelist" for the "laborer," "machinist," and "jeweler."

(3) They may show deficits in perceiving and abstracting the relationship in meaning between a derived noun such as "physicist" and its root word "physics." Learning disabled children may therefore consider each derived noun to have a novel meaning which is not directly related to the meaning of the root word. As a result, they may have difficulty grasping the relationships in meaning among several derived nouns such as "nationality," "nationalist," and "nationalism," all of which are derived from the root word "nation."

(4) Difficulties in differentiating the various uses of the word ending *-er* to derive nouns are common. This derivational ending may be used to:

(a) Derive a noun to describe a person who takes part in an action, as in the word "baker."
(b) Derive a noun to describe a place of origin, as in the word "villager."
(c) Derive a noun which describes a special characteristic, as in the word "six-footer."
(d) Derive a noun which describes the frequency of an action or process, as in the word "flicker."
(e) Derive a noun which denotes the outcome of an action or process, as in the word "remainder."

Many learning disabled children interpret all nouns derived by adding the word ending *-er* to indicate the person who performs an action. This uniformity in interpretation leads to misunderstandings of both spoken and read language and keeps them from making finer distinctions in the meaning of derived nouns.

(4) Learning disabled children show delays in acquiring the less common and more abstract suffixes such as *-ess, -ist, -ity, -ism, -cracy,* and *-graphy*, which can be used to derive nouns. They also show delays in acquiring the rules for their application. As a result, they may have difficulties in dividing novel and relatively uncommon nouns into their basic units of meaning. This problem in turn may affect their ability to acquire and interpret high-level vocabulary items and may limit their comprehension of both spoken and read language.

## Adverb Derivation

Learning disabled children may have problems in perceiving, abstracting, and applying the adverbial endings *-ly* and *-y*. Their problems may relate to the position of adverbial phrases in sentences and the stress they receive in rapid speech. Adverbial phrases tend to occur at the end of sentences, and they do not generally receive much stress. In addition, many people do not pronounce the final phrases in sentences vigorously and clearly, especially in rapid conversation. These factors would make it easy for the learning disabled child to miss the adverbial phrases and to have difficulties in inducing the rules for adverb derivation.

The difficulties in interpreting and using adverbial phrases and in acquiring the rules for adverb derivation may also be related to the more generalized problems in interpreting and using terms which denote direction, degree, or manner with respect to time. Learning disabled children may not perceive the intended modification of the meaning of a verb or verb phrase such as "walking" or "was walking" by the adverbs "slowly," "happily," or "obliquely." In speaking, these children may omit the adverbial endings and say things such as "I walk *slow*" and "He drives *quick*." Selected suffixes are listed in Table 2.3.

**TABLE 2.3**
*Overview of selected suffixes*

|  |  | Additional Examples | |
|---|---|---|---|
| **Suffixes Beginning with a Consonant** | | | |
| -ful | Means *full of* as in "careful." | helpful | hopeful |
|  | Means *tending to* as in "harmful." | wasteful | useful |
|  | Means *as much as will fill* as in "spoonful." | | |
| -less | Means *without* as in "hopeless." | helpless | homeless |
|  | | useless | childless |
|  | | careless | |
| -ly | Used to form adverbs as in "glad–gladly." | lovely | quickly |
|  | Means *per* as in "weekly." | lonely | lightly |
|  | Means *like* as in "manly." | | |
| -ment | Denotes an action as in "abridgement." | movement | replacement |
|  | Denotes a product as in "fragment." | engagement | equipment |
|  | Denotes a means as in "ornament." | basement | pavement |
|  | Denotes a state or condition as in "amazement." | | |
| -ness | Denotes a quality as in "kindness." | coolness | politeness |
|  | Denotes a state as in "darkness." | | |

**TABLE 2.3 (*Continued*)**

| | | Additional Examples | |
|---|---|---|---|
| -some | Indicates a tendency as in "quarrelsome." <br> Used collectively as in "twosome." | lonesome <br> handsome | threesome |

**Suffixes Beginning with a Vowel**

| | | | |
|---|---|---|---|
| -able <br> -ible <br> -ble | Denote ability, tendency or likelihood, as in "teach-able," "perishable," and "obtainable" (base words usually add -*able*). | suitable <br> comfortable | acceptable <br> washable |
| -al | Means *of* or *pertaining to, like,* or *befitting* as in "parental"; *action* or *process,* as in "bestowal." <br> Used to form nouns from verbs. | directional <br> accidental | economical <br> additional |
| -ance <br> -ence | Added to nouns and verbs to denote action, state or quality, as in "clearance" and "accordance." | acceptance <br> allowance | difference <br> attendance |
| -ation | Used to form nouns denoting action, as in "transportation." | plantation | presentation |
| -ant | Denotes instrumentality, as in "resistant." | important | accountant |
| -ent | Denotes performing a specified action, or being in a specified condition, as in "absorbent." | different | |
| -ed | Used to form past tense and past participle. | talked <br> counted | worked <br> poisoned |
| -en | Used to form verbs from adjectives, as in "sweeten." <br> Used to indicate material, as in "golden." <br> Used to form plurals, as in "children." | harden <br> soften | sharpen |
| -er | Used as an agent ending, as in "baker." <br> Used to show comparative degree, as in "higher." | | |
| -or | Used as an agent ending, as in "sailor." | | |
| -est | Used to show superlative degree, as in "highest." | | |
| -ing | Used to form present participles as in "going." <br> Used to form nouns from verbs as in "covering." | requesting <br> shadowing | studying |
| -ish | Means *belonging to* as in "Danish." <br> Means *like* as in "girlish." <br> Means *somewhat* as in "sweetish." | feverish <br> foolish | youngish |
| -ism | Denotes a doctrine, state or practice as in "realism." | criticism | |
| -ist | Denotes one who does something as in "dramatist." | realist <br> violinist | tourist <br> soloist |
| -ity | Used to form abstract nouns as in "civility." | similarity | absurdity |
| -ive | Denotes tendency or connection as in "destructive." | protective <br> defective | possessive <br> collective |
| -ize | Denotes action or policy as in "mobilize" and "economize." | specialize <br> generalize | vocalize |
| -ous | Means *full of, having,* or *like* as in "glorious." | poisonous <br> dangerous | glamorous <br> humorous |
| -y | Means *inclined to* as in "chilly." | soapy | greedy |

Adapted from Childs, Sally B. and Ralph De S. *Childs spelling rules.* Educators Publishing Service, Cambridge, Massachusetts 02139 by Recille Hamrell, Chittenden South Supervisory District, Shelbourne, Vermont. Used with permission.

*Prefixes*

The interpretation and use of prefixes may present significant problems for the learning disabled child. Table 2.4 lists many English prefixes.

(1) Many learning disabled children are confused by prefixes of Latin origin. They may have trouble discriminating between similar-sounding prefixes and may assign the same meaning to them. This problem may affect prefixes such as *inter-* and *intra-* and *pre-*, *pro-*, and *per-*, among others.

(2) They may also be confused by similar-sounding prefixes such as *-in* and *-im*, *pre-* and *re-*, *under-* and *un-*, *com-* and *con-*, *em-* and *en-*, among others. This may result in inconsistencies in hearing the prefixes and accordingly in assigning meaning to them and in determining their distribution.

(3) Learning disabled children may have problems in understanding that the addition of a prefix changes the meaning of a word such as "cover," which may be changed in meaning by adding *un-*, *dis-*, or *re-*, as in "uncover," "discover," and "recover." As can be seen, the prefixed words may be more and more distantly related to the root word and may even act as synonyms for entirely different root words. In this example, "uncover" means the opposite of "cover." "Discover" may be used as a synonym for "find." "Recover" is the most complex in meaning, as it may function as a synonym for "find" in the sentence "She *recovered* her jewels," for "get well" in the sentence "I hope you will *recover* quickly from your illness," and for "cover again" in "The upholstery on my couch was just *recovered*."

(4) Learning disabled children may have problems in perceiving and retaining the sequence of the prefix and the root word; they may, for example, perceive the word "recover" as "covere" and interpret the word to mean *recovery*.

(5) Difficulties in retaining, differentiating, and interpreting prefixes of Greek origin, such as *micro-* and *macro-*, among others, are common. Like the problem with Latin prefixes, this may hinder the child's acquisition of advanced and high-level vocabulary. It may eventually affect academic achievement in science courses and in advanced reading.

## ASSESSMENT OF WORD FORMATION

### Currently Used Formats for the Assessment of Morphology

To assess a child's ability to use the rules for how to inflect and derive basic meaning units of base-words, we use rule extension. That is, we present a stimulus word and see if the child can use the rules for its inflection correctly. The child's ability to extend specific inflectional and derivational rules to a new and unfamiliar base-word can only be evaluated in pure form when nonsense words are used as the stimuli. Unfortunately, the currently standardized and commercially available tests of morphology evaluate the extension of rules with **lexical** items.

Whether the base-words used to elicit rule extension are nonsense words or lexical items, the format best suited to the task is a sentence

*A lexical item is a word that is part of the vocabulary of a specific language.*

**TABLE 2.4**
*Overview of prefixes*

| | | Additional Examples | |
|---|---|---|---|

**Selected Prefixes Ending in a Vowel**

| | | | |
|---|---|---|---|
| a- | Means *on*, *in*, *into*, *to*, *in such a manner or condition*, as in "afoot," "abed," "ashore," "aloud." Means *of*, as in "akin." Is a variant of *ab-* meaning *off*, or *away from*. | afire | arise |
| de- | Means *separation*, *negation*, *descent*, or *reversal*, as in "dethrone," "demerit," "deduce," or "detract." | demerit | dethrone |
| pre- | Means *prior to* or *before*, as in "prewar." | preheat prejudge | premature |
| pro- | Means in favor of, as in "proslavery." Is used figuratively to indicate priority in time or space, as in "provision." | protest | proclaim |
| re- | Indicates repetition or backwards motion, as in "reprint," or "retract." | repay revisit | rewrite reform |

**Less Common Prefixes Ending with a Vowel**

| | | | |
|---|---|---|---|
| bi- | Means *twice* or *two*, as in "bilateral." | biweekly biplane | bicycle bifocal |
| se- | Indicates withdrawal, as in "seclude." | secret | separate |
| semi- | Means *half*, as in "semicircle." | semidarkness semifinal | semiannual |
| tri- | Means *three*, as in "tricycle." | triangle tricolor | triweekly |
| ex- | Means *out of*, *from*, *thoroughly*, as in "export." | extend excuse | except |
| inter- | Means *between*, *reciprocally*, or *together*, as in "intermarry." | intermission | interact |
| mis- | Means *ill*, *wrong*, *negation* as in "mistrust." | misspell misplace | misprint misfire |
| out- | Means *extra*, *beyond*, or *not in* as in "outside." | outlaw outdoors | outline outboard |
| over- | Means *over* as in "overcome." | overact overthrow overboard | overwork overnight |
| post- | Means *behind* or *after*, as in "postgraduate." | postscript postwar | postgraduate |
| super- | Indicates superiority over, as in "superman." | superheat | supernatural |
| trans- | Means *across* or *beyond*, as in "transverse." | transport transplant | transmit |
| un- | Means *not*, or indicates reversal, as in "unfair" or "unkind." | unroll unpin | unfold |
| under- | Indicates place or position below, as in "underbrush." | underwear underestimate | underpass underneath |

Adapted from Childs, Sally B. and Ralph De S. *Childs spelling rules.* Educators Publishing Service, Cambridge, Massachusetts 02139 by Recille Hamrell. Chittenden South Supervisory District, Shelbourne, Vermont. Used with permission.

completion or cloze format. In this format, the base-word is featured in an introductory sentence that sets the topic. Then in an incomplete sentence, the base-word is omitted and must be supplied by the child in an inflected or derived form. Figures 2.1 and 2.6 show examples of two items which follow this format. One item uses nonsense words and associated cartoons (Figure 2.1). The second item uses a lexical item and black-line real situational drawings to assess the application of the same rule (Figure 2.6).

**FIGURE 2.6**

*Item 1 from ITPA Grammatic Closure Subtest*

Source: ITPA, Rev. Ed. Reprinted by permission of the University of Illinois Press.

The second item evaluates the child's actual familiarity with and ability to use noun plural forms for a familiar word. In contrast, the first item requires the child to use the noun plural inflectional ending /-z/. Given this limitation in current test design, the clinician may well decide to use an adaptation of the Berko Experimental Test of Morphology (Berko, 1958) for extension testing. The extension testing is used to determine whether a child's error on a test of morphology that uses real word stimuli reflects unfamiliarity with the rule being tested or with the lexical item used.

*Extension testing is simply further testing of a child who seems to have a problem.*

## Selected Tests of Morphology

*Illinois Test of Psycholinguistic Ability (ITPA): Grammatic Closure*

*Other subtests of the ITPA are reviewed elsewhere in this book (see the index for specific subtests).*

This subtest of the ITPA (Kirk, McCarthy, & Kirk, 1968) evaluates the child's ability to apply inflectional and derivational morphological rules to real words. In addition, it assesses the child's knowledge of the rules for selecting personal pronouns and prepositions. The subtest contains 35 items, each of which follows a sentence completion format. Each of the items is associated with one or more pictorial presentations of the sentence meaning. The illustrations are designed to facilitate the recall and formulation of the inflected or derived forms of the target words.

Analysis of the morphological or selection rules featured in the items indicates the following distribution:

(1) *Regular noun plurals* are featured in three items (Items 1, 5, 30).
(2) *Irregular noun plurals* are featured in seven items (Items 17, 19, 22, 23, 28, 31, 32).

(3) *Noun possessive singular* is featured in one item (Item 8).
(4) *Noun derivation* is featured in one item (Item 12).
(5) *Present progressive tense* is featured in one item (Item 4).
(6) *Regular past tense* forms are featured in two items (Items 6, 18).
(7) *Irregular past tense* forms are featured in three items (Items 9, 26, 27).
(8) *Past participle* ("eaten") is featured in one item (Item 13).
(9) The adjective "any" is featured in one item (Item 14).
(10) *Comparatives of adjectives* are featured in three items (Items 15, 20, 24).
(11) *Superlatives of adjectives* are featured in three items (Items 16, 21, 25).
(12) *Adverbs* of place and time are featured in two items (Items 10, 11).
(13) *Prepositions* are featured in two items (Items 2, 7).
(14) *Personal and reflexive pronouns* are featured in three items (Items 3, 29, 33).

The ITPA was standardized on 962 children residing in midwestern suburban towns, ranging in age from 2 to 11 years. Normative data for the Grammatic Closure subtest are available for the age range from 2 years, 2 months to 10 years, 4 months. **Test-retest reliability coefficients** range from .46 to .86 as a function of age. The reported **internal reliability coefficients** range from .60 to .74.

Among the assets of this subtest are:

(1) Relative ease of administration and scoring.
(2) Clarity of the stimulus pictures, which are black-and-white and shaded line drawings.
(3) The reported positive correlations among performances on this subtest and tests of reading and writing achievement (Newcomer, Hare, Hammill, & McGettigan, 1975).

Among liabilities of the subtest are:

(1) The geographic, socioeconomic, and racio-ethnic biases of the standardization sample. The clinician should be cautious in generalizing the norms to children from widely differing backgrounds.
(2) The variability in the test-retest reliability measures as a function of age from inadequate (.46) to acceptable (.87). The clinician should be careful when interpreting the significance of a child's deviation from the norm at the lower age levels.

*Test Of Linguistic Development (TOLD): Grammatic Completion*

The TOLD Grammatic Completion subtest (Newcomer & Hammill, 1977) was designed to evaluate the child's use of selected morphological rules with real words. The items are designed to use a sentence completion format to elicit responses. The items are presented verbally by the examiner without associated pictorial cues. Completion of an item therefore requires accurate interpretation and recall of the stimulus sentence, as well as knowledge of the morphological rule tested.

*Other subtests of the TOLD are reviewed elsewhere in this book.*

The subtest contains 30 items. Each of the items consists of from one to three sentences. The first sentence in an item defines the topic and presents the word which forms the basis for a subsequent inflection or derivation. The last sentence in a sequence is incomplete. An example of an item is:

THE DRESS BELONGS TO THE WOMAN. WHOSE DRESS IS IT? IT IS THE _____

Analysis of the distribution of the morphological rules assessed by the items indicates that:

(1) *Noun plurals,* regular and irregular, are featured in five items (Items 1, 20, 23, 27, 29).
(2) *Noun possessives,* singular and plural, are featured in four items (Items 3, 7, 9, 10).
(3) *Present progressive tense* is featured in four items (Items 2, 4, 6, 14).
(4) *Present tense, third person singular* is featured in two items (Items 5, 12).
(5) *Past tense,* regular and irregular, is featured in five items (Items 8, 13, 22, 24, 28).
(6) *Noun derivation* with *-er* is featured in three items (Items 11, 16, 18).
(7) *Comparatives of adjectives,* regular and irregular, are featured in three items (Items 15, 17, 26).
(8) *Superlatives of adjectives,* regular and irregular, are featured in three items (Items 19, 21, 25).
(9) *Past perfect tense* is featured in one item (Item 30).

The TOLD was standardized on a sample of 1014 children, ranging in age from 4 years, 0 months to 8 years, 11 months. The demographic features of the sample closely matched the 1970 Census of Population and Housing (U.S. Department of Commerce). Normative data are presented in Language Ages in which raw scores on each of the subtests are converted to age equivalents. Scaled Score equivalents for raw scores are presented for each 6-month interval throughout the age range from 4 years, 0 months to 8 years, 11 months.

The test-retest reliability coefficient reported for a sample of 21 children tested with a 5-day time interval is extremely high, .96. **Concurrent validity** coefficients for the relationship with the ITPA Grammatic Closure subtest range from .79 at 8 years to .89 at 6 years of age.

Among the assets of the TOLD Grammatic Completion subtest are the following:

(1) The representative characteristics of the standardization sample, which permits the clinician to compare the performances of a variety of children against the normative data.
(2) The relative clarity of the instructions for administration and scoring.
(3) The relative ease and speed of test administration and scoring.
(4) The representativeness and relative evenness in the distribution of the morphological rules tested.

It is a liability of the subtest that the test-retest reliability measures were obtained with such a short time interval and on a relatively small sample. Thus the reliability coefficient may be spuriously high, and it may not adequately represent the stability of performances over time.

Summary overviews of these tests of morphology are presented in Table 2.5.

**TABLE 2.5**
*Characteristics of selected standardized tests of morphology*

| Name | Purpose | Age Range | Stimuli | Responses | Scoring |
|------|---------|-----------|---------|-----------|---------|
| ITPA: GRAMMATIC CLOSURE | Evaluates the knowledge of basic word formation rules and grammatic structures, using real word stimuli. | 2 yr. 2 mo. to 10 yr. 4 mo. | 33 items. Each is an incomplete sentence with associated pictorial stimuli. The stimulus sentences are spoken while pictorial counterparts are presented. | Child completes the stimulus sentences with the inflected or derived word forms or grammatic structures, using the verbal and pictorial stimuli as cues. | Responses are recorded verbatim. Raw scores may be converted to age levels or scaled scores. |
| TOLD: GRAMMATIC COMPLETION | Evaluates the knowledge of basic word formation rules, using real word stimuli. | 4 yr. 0 mo. to 8 yr. 11 mo. | 30 items. Each features an incomplete sentence. Only verbal stimuli are used to elicit responses. | Child completes the stimulus sentences with the appropriate inflected or derived word forms, using the verbal stimuli only as cues. | Responses are recorded verbatim. Raw scores may be converted to Language Age equivalents or to scaled scores. |

## Dialectical Variations

The learning disabled child's use of the word formation rules must always be evaluated against his dialectical background in order to determine which of his deviations must be attributed to dialectical differences and which to delays in his acquisition of the standard rules. The account of dialectical variations in Table 2.6 in the use of word formation rules is adapted from Jeter (1977).

**TABLE 2.6**
*Characteristics of dialectical variations of morphology*

| Dialect-Rule | Characteristics | Sample Utterances |
|--------------|-----------------|-------------------|
| **Noun Plural** | | |
| Black English. | Absence of the noun plural endings -s or -es may occur occasionally. | She got five *dollar*. The other *teacher*, they went home. |
| Appalachian English. Southern White Nonstandard. | Absence of the noun plural endings for nouns that denote weights and measures, especially when these are preceded by a numeral. | She bought 2 *pound* of apples. He moved 10 *year* ago. He ran 50 *yard*. |
| Black English. Southern White Nonstandard. | Addition of the regular -s plural ending to irregular nouns. | He saw two *deers*. She looked at her two *foots*. |

**TABLE 2.6 (Continued)**

| Dialect-Rule | Characteristics | Sample Utterances |
|---|---|---|
| **Noun Possessive** | | |
| Black English. | Noun possessives of common nouns indicated by word order. Speakers from northern urban communities may alternate between using 's and relying on word order. | It the *girl* book.<br>It the *man* car. |
| | Double possessive marking may be used in compound personal names. | It *Jim's Brown's* car. |
| **Third Person Singular Present Tense Marker** | | |
| Black English. | Suffix -*s* or -*es* used in standard English to mark the third person singular is absent. | She *walk*.<br>The man *walk*.<br>The dog *run*. |
| | Third person forms of "to do" and "to have" are absent. | The man *have* a car.<br>The teacher *do* silly things. |
| | Third person -*s* and -*es* may be overgeneralized to other persons. | I *walks*.<br>You *runs*.<br>The boy, they *runs*. |
| Nonstandard. | Use of the auxiliary "do" in negative constructions. | The man *don't* cook.<br>The girl *don't* drive. |
| **Forms of "To Be"** | | |
| Black English. | Copula "is" may be absent in all contexts where it is contractible in Standard English. | She a bad girl.<br>He running home. |
| Black English.<br>Southern White Nonstandard. | Copula "are" tends to be used less often than "is" in dialects with copula absence. It may be absent in all contexts where "are" is contractible in Standard English. | You nice.<br>They bad. |
| Nonstandard. | Utterances with "to be" may not show person number agreement in both present and past forms. | You *was* at school.<br>They *is* at home. |
| **Verb Phrases with Modals** | | |
| Black English.<br>Southern White Nonstandard.<br>Appalachian English. | Verb phrases with the modals "might," "should," "could" may contain two modals. | You *might should* do it.<br>He *might could* come.<br>She *used couldn't* do it. |
| **Past Tense** | | |
| Black English. | The past tense word ending -*ed* is not pronounced due to consonant reduction. | He *finish* dinner.<br>He *crack* the nut. |
| Nonstandard. | Past tenses of irregular verbs are formed by adding -*ed*. | She *knowed* the boy.<br>He *drinked* the milk. |

**TABLE 2.6 (*Continued*)**

| Dialect-Rule | Characteristics | Sample Utterances |
|---|---|---|
| | Uninflected forms of irregular verbs may be used instead of the inflected forms. | He *come* home yesterday.<br>She *begin* school last week. |
| | The past participle form of irregular verbs with different past and past participle forms may be used for the past tense. | He *seen* her this morning.<br>She *done* it.<br>They *drunk* the coffee. |
| **Perfective Construction** | | |
| Black English. | The form "been" may be used to indicate that an action took place in the distant past. | I *been had* the measles 10 years ago. |
| Black English.<br>Southern White Nonstandard.<br>Appalachian English. | The form "done" may be combined with a past tense form to indicate that an action was started and finished at some point in the past. | She *done tried* that.<br>He *done fixed* the car. |
| **Future** | | |
| Black English.<br>Southern White Nonstandard. | "Is" and "are" may be deleted when the future indicator "gonna" is used. | I *gonna* do it.<br>He *gonna* drive.<br>They *gonna* have trouble. |
| | The future indicator "gonna" may be reduced to the forms "mana," "mon," and "ma." | I *'mana* go.<br>I *'mon* go.<br>I *'ma* go. |
| Nonstandard. | The contracted form of "will ('ll)" may be omitted in future forms. | I see you tomorrow.<br>They bring you on Sunday. |
| **Invariant Be** | | |
| Black English. | The form "be" may be used as a main verb. | I *be* home at noon.<br>Today she *be* busy. |
| | The form "be" may be used without specification of tense to indicate an intermittent act or event. This form carries social stigma. | You *be* good (sometimes). |
| Nonstandard.<br>Black English. | The forms "will" and "would" may be omitted when followed by "be." | He *be* at school soon.<br>They *be* happy if you gave them some money. |
| **Participle Forms** | | |
| Appalachian English.<br>Black English. | The prefix *a-* may be added to participles when they serve as progressives or adverbials. | I heard he was *a-singing* the song.<br>They went *a-hunting*. |
| **Comparative and Superlative** | | |
| Nonstandard. | The word endings *-er* and *-est* may be added to polysyllabic words or to irregular adjective forms. The adverbs "more" and "most" may also be used in these forms. | She is *beautifuller* than her sister.<br>It was the *awfullest* thing.<br>They are the *baddest* boys.<br>It was the *most awfullest* day. |

**TABLE 2.6 (*Continued*)**

| Dialect-Rule | Characteristics | Sample Utterances |
|---|---|---|
| **Intensifying Adverbs** | | |
| Black English. Southern White Nonstandard. Appalachian English. | The intensifying "right" may precede adjectives, adverbs, and the word "smart." The intensifier "plumb" may be used to indicate completeness. | She is *right* pretty. They came *right* quick. He is *right* smart. That is *plumb* foolish. |
| **Adverb Derivation** | | |
| Nonstandard. | The derivational adverb ending -*ly* may be omitted optionally, particularly in southern dialects and Appalachian English. | He came running *quick*. He missed her *terrible*. |

Adapted from Feter, I. K. (Ed.) *Social dialects: Differences vs. disorder.* Rockville, Maryland: American Speech and Hearing Association, 1977.

# FORMING WORDS Intervention 3

The morphological elements of English modify the meaning of root words and produce semantic distinctions of, among others, number, case, and tense. They are also used to derive new words from other word classes and define their syntactic roles. The morphological elements used to modify or extend word meaning or to derive new words take the forms of suffixes and prefixes. These elements cannot stand alone, even though they are basic elements of meaning. They must be bound to root words to function. These bound morphemes are used to:

(1) Produce the semantic distinctions of number and case for noun plurals and noun possessives.
(2) Produce the semantic distinctions of verb tense and aspect and of the third person singular in the present tense.
(3) Produce the semantic distinctions for comparative and superlative forms of adjectives.
(4) Derive nouns, adverbs, and diminutives, and specify their syntactic roles.
(5) Extend or modify word meaning by addition of a prefix.

Learning disabled children may have a number of problems in interpreting and expressing the semantic distinctions of number, case, tense, aspect, and comparison. They may also have difficulty in discerning and expressing the distinctions in the syntactic roles of words indicated by suffixes. Their problems suggest that they do not acquire the word formation rules at the same rate and with the same degree of consistency and sophistication as their normally developing age peers. Normally developing children seem to acquire the rules for forming words incidentally. Their interpretation and use of word formations in phrases, clauses, and sentences become automatic and accurate during the early school years.

The difficulties of language and learning disabled children in applying the accepted rules for forming words may be evident even when they express relatively sophisticated ideas. They are often observed to the same extent in spoken and in written language. They seem to affect the irregular forms more significantly than the regular word forms.

Furthermore, the children's problems in perceiving and interpreting the functions of inflectional and derivational word endings usually appear the same for language that the children hear and language that they read.

Investigations of learning disabled children's acquisition of morphological rules indicate that the order in which the various rules are learned is similar to that observed among other children. It follows, then, that the rules should be taught in an intervention program in a normal developmental sequence. In addition, word formation rules that share common properties should be introduced together to help the child transfer and generalize the established rules. On this basis, here is a suggested sequence for introducing word formation rules in intervention programs.

(1) Regular noun plurals.
(2) Noun-verb agreement for singular and plural forms of regular nouns and verbs in the present tense.
(3) Regular noun possessives in the singular and plural forms.
(4) Irregular noun plurals.
(5) Irregular noun possessives.
(6) Regular past tense of verbs.
(7) Irregular past tense of verbs.
(8) Adjectival inflections for comparative and superlative forms.
(9) Noun and adverb derivation.
(10) Prefixing.

The sections below focus on difficulties which may arise in establishing rules for the various morphological categories. They also focus on applicable formats for intervention, with illustrations. For basic principles and discussions of formats, see pp. 97–101 in chapter 5.

## CROSSCATEGORICAL USE OF SUFFIXES

*You may wish to review Table 2.2.*

As we have seen, a special problem may arise for language and learning disabled children in learning the rules for all the different inflectional endings with -s. This complexity should be taken into account in intervention, so the child learns to differentiate and use the various forms within and across categories.

## SPECIAL AREAS OF DIFFICULTY

### Noun Plurals and Noun-Verb Agreement

There are many formats and activities available for teaching the word formation rules for regular and irregular noun plurals. Initially, the children may be required to identify which among several spoken regular or irregular singular and plural nouns mean *only one* and which mean *more than one*. This procedure permits the clinician to identify the noun categories—regular or irregular—that present problems.

The formats which may be used to establish and consolidate the rules for forming regular and irregular noun plurals include:

(1) Recognition and judgment of correct grammar.
(2) Classification of regular and irregular singular and plural nouns.
(3) Sentence completion.
(4) Oral cloze.
(5) Directed rule application.

Regardless of the format used, regular nouns should be introduced first. Nouns that share the same phonological conditioning rules for plurals and apply either /s/, /z/, or /ez/ should be introduced together. Irregular noun plurals should be introduced last. Forms which share the same rule should be featured together to help the children categorize and recall the irregular forms. It is also important that the singular and plural noun forms be introduced with a range of markers to permit generalization of the rules. Among markers which should be used are *a, an, the, this, that, these, those, all,* and *some.* The examples below illustrate some of the formats applied to regular and irregular noun forms.

*Sentence completion and oral cloze with multiple choices*

| | |
|---|---|
| Mary takes two _____. | (book/books) |
| Sometimes she takes only one _____ to school. | (book/books) |
| Is the _____ she takes very heavy? | (book/books) |
| No, it is a very small _____. | (book/books) |
| Why doesn't she take all her _____ to school? | (book/books) |

*Recognition and judgment of correct grammar*

| | |
|---|---|
| The boy carries several newspaper. | (right/wrong) |
| All the children carried their lunch. | (right/wrong) |
| The girl carried all the apple. | (right/wrong) |
| She gave me these glove. | (right/wrong) |

*Classification of singular and plural forms*

| | | |
|---|---|---|
| **Sample:** | one | more than one |
| **Nouns to be Classified:** | | apples, book, newspaper, lunches, gloves, desserts, shoe, foot, mice, children, moose, bills, wallet |

*Directed rule application*

The cat climbs the tree.
*Now say the same sentence, but with two of them.*

The sheep sleep in the barn.
*Now say the same sentence, but with only one of them.*

The mouse eats the cheese.
*Now say the same sentence, but with two of them.*

## Differentiating Verb Inflections and Tense

Learning disabled children frequently have problems acquiring the rules for forming tense by inflection. Several verb tenses and numbers are indicated by adding inflectional suffixes to root words. Among inflected verb forms are:

(1) The present progressive tense, formed by adding the suffix *-ing* to the root word.

(2) The third person singular of present tense verbs, formed by adding /s/, /z/, or /ez/ to root words.
(3) The past tense, formed by adding the suffix /t/, /d/, or /ed/, to regular verbs and by internal vowel changes for irregular verbs.

Language and learning disabled children may have a variety of problems in mastering the rules for inflected verb forms. Their difficulties may reflect a limitation in perceiving and applying the phonological conditioning rules that determine which variation of a specific inflectional suffix to use; for example, whether to use "builded" or "built." These difficulties would especially affect the regular past tense forms and the third person singular of the present tense of verbs. The children's problems may also reflect difficulties with differentiating and expressing the distinctions of duration and time that the various verb forms denote. This problem would especially affect the distinction between the present progressive and present tense forms and among the past, present progressive, present, and future tenses. Another difficulty which may arise involves the irregular verb forms and forms of the copula "to be," auxiliaries, and modals. These verb forms must be learned in part by rote memory, which is a problem for some learning disabled children.

Intervention to improve the perception, acquisition, and expression of verb inflections and tenses should follow the normal developmental sequence or order of difficulty for the various rules and forms. Table 3.1 shows the order of difficulty, from easiest to hardest, for selected verb inflections and tenses, suggested by normal developmental data and clinical observation.

**TABLE 3.1**
*Order of difficulty of verb inflections and tenses*

| Inflected Form or Tense | Example |
| --- | --- |
| Present progressive tense (*-ing*). | The boy is runn*ing*. |
| Third person singular of the present tense (/s/, /z/, /ez/). | The boy hop*s*. The boy run*s*. The boy dress*es*. |
| Regular forms of past tense (/t/, /d/, /ed/). | The boy talk*ed*. The boy phon*ed*. The boy select*ed*. |
| Irregular forms of past tense. | The boy *ran*. |

Discrimination and differentiation among present progressive and present tense verb forms may be taught with sentence completion or oral cloze formats, either with or without multiple choices. The examples below illustrate these formats applied to forms of the verbs "walk" and "sleep."

| The boy is _____. | (walking/walks) |
| The boy _____ every day. | (walking/walks) |
| The boy is _____. | (sleeping/sleeps) |
| The boy _____ every night. | (sleeping/sleeps) |

Right now the boy is _____.
During the night the boy _____.
He often _____ through class.
He often _____ in the park.
Right now he _____ in the park.

To work on the temporal aspects denoted by verb tenses, the clinician can use sentences which feature references to either a time in the past or future or to the present. Initially, these time cues may be placed first in the sentence, to highlight the temporal aspect. Later, they may be placed at the end of sentences; and finally they may be deleted. Several formats may be used with verb tenses. Among them are judgment of correct grammar, classification of time of action, identification and naming of times of action, sentence completion and oral cloze with or without multiple choices, and reformulation of sentences to reflect past, present, and future tense. The examples below illustrate how these formats can be applied.

*Judgment of correct grammar*

| Yesterday the boy walks home. | (right/wrong) |
| Tomorrow the girl was in town. | (right/wrong) |
| Right now John is at school | (right/wrong) |
| Every day John walks. | (right/wrong) |

*Classification of verb forms*

**Samples:**              yesterday    now    tomorrow

**Verb Forms to be Classified:**    is walking, walked, will walk
is sleeping, will sleep, slept
ate, will eat, is eating
will run, ran, is running

*Classification of sentences*

**Samples:**              yesterday    usually    now    tomorrow

**Sentences to be Classified:**    Joe was reading his book.
Joe will read his book.
Joe is reading his book.
Joe read his book.
Joe reads his books.

*Sentence completion and oral cloze*

| Yesterday Sue _____. | (walked/ walks/ is walking/ will walk) |
| Right now Sue _____. | (slept/ is sleeping/ sleeps/ will sleep) |
| Tomorrow Sue _____. | (travels/ travelled/ will travel/ is travelling) |
| Sue often _____ home. | (ran/ will run/ runs/ is running) |

*Directed reformulation of sentences*

**Sample:** Usually the boy eats cereal.
Yesterday _____.
Tomorrow _____.
Right now _____.

**Sample:** The girl drove the car yesterday.
Tomorrow _____.
Usually _____.
Right now _____.

Irregular verb forms and auxiliaries may be taught in similar formats. Working on knowledge of the rules for verb phrases which express mood and aspect follows naturally after auxiliaries have been established. The forms "must," "have to," "shall," and "ought" combine with various verb forms to express subtle differences of mood. The forms "have," "will," and "am" may combine with verbs to express aspect. To help the child understand the subtle meaning of expressions of habitual aspect, inferences, or obligations in verb phrases, the clinician can use formats which call for identification of deep structure identity and paraphrase. The examples below illustrate these formats.

*Deep structure refers to the underlying meaning of sentences; it contrasts with surface structure, or actual syntactic form of a sentence.*

*Identification of deep structure identity*

| | |
|---|---|
| I *shall* go to London. | |
| I *am determined to* go to London. | (<u>same</u>/different) |
| I *may* go to London. | |
| I am sure I will go to London. | (same/<u>different</u>) |
| I *must* go to London. | |
| I *am obliged to* go to London. | (<u>same</u>/different) |
| I *may* fly to London. | |
| I *will probably* fly to London. | (<u>same</u>/different) |
| I *will* fly to London. | |
| I *am sure* to fly to London. | (<u>same</u>/different) |
| I *will* go to London next week. | |
| I might go to London next week. | (same/<u>different</u>) |

*Paraphrase*

| | | |
|---|---|---|
| I *will probably* leave tomorrow. | *Say it another way.* | (will/<u>may</u>) |
| I am *ordered to* be home for dinner. | *Say it another way.* | (will/<u>must</u>) |
| I am *sure to* win the bet. | *Say it another way.* | (<u>will</u>/may) |
| I *have to* go now. | *Say it another way.* | (might/<u>must</u>) |
| I am *determined to* go now. | *Say it another way.* | (<u>shall</u>/may) |
| I *have to* go but I *don't want to.* | *Say it another way.* | (might/<u>ought</u>) |

## Comparative and Superlative Forms of Adjectives

Learning disabled children with language deficits may be delayed in the acquisition and use of comparative and superlative forms of adjectives. The delays may be caused by problems in perceiving and applying the rules for adding suffixes to regular forms and differentiating regular forms from irregular forms. There may, however, be other causes for their delays. Some language and learning disabled children do not easily discern the ordinal or comparative basis which underlies the use of the inflected adjective forms. If this is the case, the child must first develop a cognitive understanding of comparisons. In other words, the youngster may need to compare two or three objects which differ in only one dimension. The dimension of difference may be size, length, weight, volume, or any other quality or attribute. The youngster may be asked to compare qualities of highly familiar objects and of tokens or designs. The comparisons may be made in response to specific questions with or without objects or pictures being present. The examples below illustrate the format.

*Questions of comparison*

Show me the *big* apple.       (one large and one small apple present)
Show me the *small* apple.
Which apple is *bigger*?
Which apple is *smaller*?
Now, show me the *big* apple.       (add a larger size apple to display)
Now, show me the *small* apple.
Which apple is the *biggest*?
Which apple is the *smallest*?
This apple is small. This apple is _____. This apple is the _____. (line apples up
    according to size and point)
Which is *bigger,* an apple or a pumpkin?
Which is *smaller,* a cat or a tiger?
Which is the *biggest*—a mouse, a cat, or an elephant?
Which is the *smallest*—a baby, a boy, or a man?

Once the child understands the concept of comparison, formats which may be used to establish and consolidate comparative and superlative forms of adjectives, regular and irregular, include: judgment of correct grammar, sentence completion and oral cloze, and directed sentence transformations. These formats are illustrated below.

*Judgment of correct grammar*

Jane is nicest than Sue.       (right/wrong)
Bob is taller than Jane.       (right/wrong)
Joan ran the faster of all.       (right/wrong)

*Sentence completion and oral cloze*

Cars are fast but planes are _____.       (faster/fastest)

Jack is five feet tall. Joe is six feet tall.
Joe is _____ than Jack.
Jack is _____ than Joe.
George is six feet five inches.
George is _____.       (taller/smaller/the smallest)

Sue has five apples. Jane has six apples.
Jane has _____ apples than Sue.
Sue has _____ apples than Jane.
Iris has ten apples.
Iris has _____.       (more/the most/fewer)

*Directed sentence transformation*

Jorge has four cars. Mike has two cars.
*What can you say about Mike? What can you say about Jorge?*

Sue is four years old. Ellen is six years old.
*What can you say about Ellen? What can you say about Sue?*

Parents are older than their children.
*What can you say about children?*

Trucks are more expensive than cars.
*What can you say about cars?*

Grandparents are older than parents. Parents are older than children.
*What can you say about grandparents? What can you say about children?*

## Derivation and Derivational Suffixes

Derivational suffixes are morphemes which are used to derive new words from already existing bases. Our word "teacher" is an example of a derived noun. It is formed by adding the suffix *-er* to a common verb base, "teach." The derivational rules that may cause problems for the language and learning disabled child include those for deriving nouns, diminutives, and adverbs.

Language and learning disabled youngsters may not realize that a derived word is related in meaning to its base word. As a result, they may not readily identify the root words or bases in derived nouns or adverbs. One of the objectives in intervention is, therefore, to improve the recognition of root words in derived words. A related objective is to improve the identification of the smallest meaningful units—root word and suffix—in common derived words by segmentation. A third objective is to establish the ability to analyze and synthesize the meanings of base and suffix combinations and to determine the grammatical function of the derived word.

In an intervention program, derived nouns and noun derivation should precede adverb derivation. Among the procedures which may be used in intervention are segmentation tasks, sentence completion and oral cloze with or without multiple choices, and identification of identity or similarity of underlying sentence meaning. The examples below illustrate these formats.

*Segmentation*

(a) Find the hidden word in each of these words:
    happiness, happily, happier    (happy)
    thoughtful, thoughtless    (thought)
    scientist, scientific    (science)
    patriotic, patriotically    (patriot)

(b) Find the parts in these words. Each part must have its own meaning.
    beginning, beginner    (begin, -ing, -er)
    shopper, shopping    (shop, -er, -ing)
    buyer    (buy, -er)
    thoughtful, thoughtless    (thought, -ful, -less)

(c) Tell me what each of the parts in these words mean.

| | |
|---|---|
| jogger | (jog, -er) |
| painter | (paint, -er) |
| decorator | (decorate, -or) |
| slowly | (slow, -ly) |
| windy | (wind, -y) |
| fearless | (fear, -less) |

*Sentence completion and oral cloze*

(a) **Occupations**

Mrs. Jones teaches. She is a _____.

Mr. Welch paints. He is a _____.

Ms. Porter works on science projects. She is a _____.

Jonah climbs mountains. He is a _____.

(b) **Characteristics**

Ted gave his mother a present. He is a _____ person. (thoughtless/thoughtful)

Jane is not usually afraid. She is a _____ person. (fearful/fearless)

Christopher is goodlooking. He is a _____ guy. (handsome/ugly)

Ilona is full of thanks. She is a _____ person. (busy/grateful)

The wind blew hard. It was very _____. (windful/windy)

(c) **Multiple Derivations**

Mother took her _____ list to go _____. She buys very carefully. She is a good _____.

Jorge took his skis. He went _____. He skis very well. He is a good _____.

Mona worked on a science project. She made a _____ discovery. Now she is a _____.

*Identification of identity or similarity in meaning*

Larry did his job without thought.
Larry did his job thoughtlessly. (same/different)

Sue finished her work in a hurry.
Sue finished her work slowly. (same/different)

Mark walked to school at a slow pace.
Mark walked to school slowly. (same/different)

**Prefixing**

Like suffixes, prefixes are meaningful units which cannot stand alone. They always precede the base word, and modify or expand it and sometimes change its meaning. They do not, however, change the grammatic function of the base word. In that respect they are unlike derivational suffixes and like inflectional suffixes.

Prefixed words are not always closely related to their bases; and, in fact, some prefixed words are only distantly related in meaning to their root words. Sometimes prefixed words function as synonyms for entirely different root words, as we saw in the example of "cover" (base), "uncover," "recover," and "discover."

Prefixes and prefixed words may present a range of difficulties for the language and learning disabled youngster or youth. The difficulties may reflect the child's confusion among the meaning of various prefixes and lack of differentiation among the meanings of similar-sounding or related prefixes. The problems may also relate to a problem of remembering that the addition of some prefixes may change the meaning of the base word. An early problem with prefixed words seems to relate to difficulties in recalling the sequence for the prefix and the base. Among the objectives in intervention are to establish consistent understanding of the meaning of prefixed words and differentiation among the meanings of root words and prefixed word forms. These objectives may be reached by using a variety of formats in intervention, including judgments of equivalence in meaning, identification of differences in meaning, reformulation with a lexical paraphrase, and directed prefixing. The examples below apply these formats.

### *Judgment of equivalence in meaning*

Lock the door.
Unlock the door.                        (same/different)

Have you discovered the chair?
Have you recovered the chair?           (same/different)

Mother planted the shrubs.
Mother replanted the shrubs.            (same/different)

She restated her thoughts.
She stated her thoughts again.          (same/different)

### *Identification of differences in meaning*

Mother discovered the old chair in the attic.
*What happened?*

Mother recovered the old chair in the attic.
*What happened? How do the words "discover" and "recover" differ?*

### *Reformulation of sentences with lexical paraphrase*

When dad came home he opened the door with his key.
*Say the same thing using the word "unlock."*

Jane took the cover off the new chair.
*Say the same thing in a different way. You can use the word "uncover."*

He told the same story again.
*Say the same thing in a different way. You can use the word "retell."*

*See Table 2.4 for an overview of selected prefixes you may want to feature in intervention.*

In an intervention designed to establish the sequence of prefixes and their bases, printed color-coded cue cards may be used. Each prefix should be printed in the same color on a separate card. All bases should be printed in the same color and on separate cards. The initial task may require the youngster to combine bases and prefixes in the right sequence. Next, the youngster may be asked to tell what each prefixed word means. Subsequently, the prefixed words may be used in the formats described above, or they may be used to formulate as many sentences as possible that incorporate the prefixed words.

This chapter has focused on establishing knowledge of specific word formation rules in spoken language. Some learning disabled children may handle these word formation rules easily and accurately in spoken language. But they may, nonetheless, have problems applying the rules for reading comprehension or in writing. If this seems to be the case, the child may need intervention to help learn to transfer the word formation rules from the spoken-heard language code to the written-read language code.

# 4

# FORMING SENTENCES
## Characteristics

## BACKGROUND

Learning disabled children and adolescents may have significant difficulties with the rules for forming sentences. According to Johnson and Myklebust (1967),

**Ideation** *refers to the process of forming ideas and relating them to each other.*

> Disorders of formulation and syntax vary in nature and severity. In some instances the greatest problem is in **ideation** and productivity, while in others it is primarily syntactical. In the majority, however, both are present. (p. 228)

We have increasing evidence that deficits in processing and producing sentence structure can persist in adolescence and young adulthood. As Johnson and Myklebust (1967) stress eloquently,

> In high school, grammar and English are the most difficult subjects for students with learning disabilities. Those who enroll in college also are in need of supplementary tutoring or help in grammar and English. The reasons for this difficulty are numerous, but of primary significance are the problems of memory and abstraction. Learning the parts of speech, types of phrases or clauses, and grammar rules assumes that the students can use symbols to talk about symbols.

To better understand these difficulties, we need to discuss how sentences are made in English—the rules native speakers use. Then we will look at the specific difficulties experienced by many learning disabled children. The next chapter will discuss how to identify and assess these problems, and chapter 6 will cover intervention with the individual child.

### English Sentence Formation

*The structural components of English, such as Noun Phrase, Verb, and Adverbial Phrase, are described and illustrated in the Appendix.*

The infinite variety of sentences in the English language may be traced back to five basic sentence patterns. All sentences are developed from one of these patterns, through a process of applying various transformations. These transformations allow us to form sentences such as negatives, passives, interrogatives, and imperatives, to mention only a few. The five basic sentence patterns are illustrated in the sentences below:

(1) "Boys run home," consisting of a Noun Phrase ("boys"), a Verb ("run"), and an Adverbial Phrase ("home").
(2) "Boys play games," consisting of a Noun Phrase ("boys"), a Verb ("play"), and a Noun Phrase ("games"). An Adverbial Phrase such as "sometimes," "often," or "endlessly" may be added.
(3) "The boy is my brother," consisting of a Noun Phrase ("the boy"), Copula *to be* ("is"), and a second Noun Phrase ("my brother").
(4) "The boy is tall," consisting of a Noun Phrase ("the boy"), Copula *to be* ("is"), and an Adjective ("tall").
(5) "The boy became ill/a student," consisting of a Noun Phrase ("the boy"), a Verb ("became"), and either an Adjective ("ill") or a second Noun Phrase ("a student").

According to **transformational grammar** (Chomsky, 1957), these five sentences may be generated by applying **Phrase-Structure rules.** Each of the five sentences ($\Sigma$) may be divided into two units: (1) a Noun Phrase (NP) ("the boy") and (2) a Verb Phrase (VP) ("ate the cake"), according to the **rewrite rule:**

$$\Sigma \rightarrow NP + VP$$

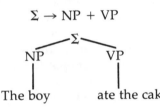

The Noun Phrase in the last three sentences listed may be divided into: (1) a determiner (T), "the," and (2) a noun (N), "boy," according to the rewrite rule:

$$NP \rightarrow T \text{ (determiner)} + N \text{ (noun)}$$

The Verb Phrases (VP) in sentences 2, 3, 4, and 5 may be further subdivided into a Verb (V) and a Noun Phrase (NP) or Adjective (Adj), according to the rewrite rule:

$$VP \rightarrow V \text{ (verb)} + NP \text{ (noun phrase)/Adj. (predicate adjective)}$$

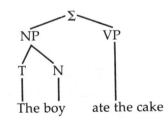

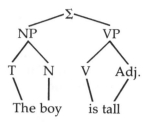

The example sentences contain a variety of verbs in the Verb Phrase. The first sentence features the present tense of an irregular verb ("run"), the second sentence features the present tense of a regular verb ("play"), the third and fourth sentences feature the third person singular of "to be" ("is"), and the last uses the past tense of the verb "become." The five basic sentence patterns listed are all simple; affirmative, active, and declarative; they are called **kernel** sentences.

*See pages 132–33 for more on the kernel sentence and its components.*

Transformational grammar also contains a set of supplementary rules (the transformational component) that may be applied to transform the kernel sentences. These rules indicate the changes required in the surface structure to transform kernel sentences from (1) active to passive, (2) affirmative to negative, (3) declarative to interrogative, or (4) combinations of these. Among the transformational rules are rules for forming negative, passive, interrogative, conjoined (compound), and relative clause embedded (complex) sentences.

Transformational grammar also distinguishes between the surface structure of a sentence and its **deep structure**. The surface structure reflects the syntactic properties of the sentence; the deep structure reflects the meaning. Thus you could understand the surface structure of a sentence but not its deep structure, if you were unfamiliar with the words used; or you could understand the deep structure—know what ideas are being discussed—but not understand the surface structure—how the different words relate to each other. Let us now turn to the order in which normal children learn to use these rules.

**FIGURE 4.1**
*Surface/deep structure*

## Normal Acquisition and Use of Sentence Structures

The sequence of the normal acquisition and use of syntactic structures, operations, and transformations has been the object of considerable attention and research. Investigations of the development of the rules for forming sentences during the preschool and early elementary years have provided evidence of the sequence in which normally developing children learn the rules for forming grammatical sentences.

Menyuk (1969) reports that the normally developing child uses all the classes in the phrase structure rules for forming sentences by 3 years of age. Thus, 3-year-old children understand and express the functional relationships among subjects, predicates (verbs), and objects in sentences. They also appear to understand the rules that define these functional relationships and are able to expand a simple subject into a noun phrase, a simple predicate or main verb into a verb phrase with auxiliaries or modals, and a simple object into a noun phrase and a verb phrase. According to Menyuk, the order of development of the various sentence types during the period before 3 years of age progresses as follows:

*Classes refer to the phrases and elements (such as Noun Phrase) used in sentences.*

(1) Conjoining elements or words into rudimentary sentences.
(2) Developing sentences with subjects and predicates (verbs).
(3) Expanding the simple verb phrase to include forms of the copula *to be*, auxiliaries, and modals.
(4) Embedding an element within a sentence and attaching the element to the verb.
(5) Changing the order of elements within a sentence, such as the tense markers, auxiliaries, and modals.

While the children produced completely well-formed active declarative, negative, and interrogative sentences before 3 years of age, some of them showed deviations in the application of the basic rules. For example, they would violate the rules that determine the words and phrases that can appear in certain contexts. They would also produce redundancies within the grammatical classes by using two auxiliaries, (*Did was* the boy tall?), modals (*Can could* I go?), or tense markers (The boy *is was* jumping.). Menyuk interpreted these redundancies to indicate that the young child wanted to insure that the listener would understand the utterance or to provide greater definition of the forms. The children learned to use syntactic operations to formulate completely grammatical sentences in the following order:

(1) **Addition,** resulting from adding an element in an utterance.
(2) **Deletion,** resulting from omitting elements in an utterance.
(3) **Substitution,** resulting from using a similar element.
(4) **Permutation,** resulting from rearranging the word order.
(5) **Embedding,** resulting from inserting an element in a phrase.
(6) **Nesting,** resulting from inserting a series of elements in a phrase or utterance.

First graders also produced sentences which were not completely grammatical. Their grammatically incorrect utterances also involved

**TABLE 4.1**

*Percentages of first graders who produced well-formed sentences (From Menyuk, 1969)*

| Percentage | Sentence Type | Examples |
|---|---|---|
| 100 | Infinitival complement. | I want *to have it*. |
| 100 | Adjective, nominal compound and possessives. | The *boy and girl* danced. It is the *boy's* hat. |
| 97 | Adverb inversion. | *Sometimes* boys like to cook. |
| 95 | "And" conjunction. | The boy ran *and* the girl jumped. |
| 90 | Imperative sentences. | *Go* to the cafeteria! |
| 89 | Conjunction deletion. | The boy *drank* the tea *and ate* the pie. |
| 89 | Separation with verb and particle construction. | The boy *took* the dog *out*. |
| 87 | Relative clauses. | That's the boy *who lives next door*. |
| 69 | Reflexive structure. | The man shaved *himself*. |
| 66 | Substitution and embedding. | The man *who was sick* went home. |
| 64 | Passive construction. | The car *was bought by* the man. |
| 41 | Pronominalization. | *You* take it. |
| 35 | "Cause" conjunction. | She ate it *cause* she was hungry. |
| 29 | Nominalization. | They went *fishing*. |
| 20 | Participle complement. | The *roaring* river disturbed me. |
| 20 | "If" conjunction. | *If* it rains, I won't play outside. |
| 19 | "So" conjunction. | She bought it *so* she could play with it. |

redundancies. They would reiterate a particular grammatical class, as in the utterance "He'll *might* get in jail," in which the auxiliary is followed by a modal—perhaps for good measure. The first graders were still expanding the basic sentence structures and adding new structures to their repertory of sentences. Table 4.1 on p. 64 shows the percentages of correct usage for various sentence types by the first graders (Menyuk, 1969).

The sequence in which children learn to comprehend sentences containing selected syntactic structures has also been investigated. Table 4.2 on p. 65 shows the sequence of the development of comprehension that Carrow (1973) reports.

Higher level linguistic constructions include sentences in which the subject-object relationship in a sentence is stated by the verb and not by the sequence of the noun phrases in the surface structure. Verbs such as the pairs "ask"/"tell" and "promise"/"tell," adverbial phrases such as "easy to"/"eager to," and verbs such as "know," "feel," and "believe" require specification in a relative clause. They make it difficult to infer from the sentence structure who is the agent and who is the object.

**Pronominalization** is the process of using a pronoun to refer to a previously stated noun or proper name.

Chomsky (1969) assessed the interpretation of four constructions: (1) "ask"/"tell," (2) "promise"/"tell," (3) "easy to see," and (4) **pronominalization,** by 5- to 10-year-olds. The four syntactic structures share one feature—the grammatical relationships they express are not explicit in the surface structure of the sentences. The developmental sequence for the four selected constructions was found to be:

(1) "Pronominalization," as in "Pluto knew that Mickey was tired. *Who was tired?*" was acquired earliest. It was interpreted correctly by all

**TABLE 4.2**

*Sentence of development of comprehension of sentence types (from Carrow, 1973)*

| Syntactic Structure | Sentence | Age of Comprehension By 75% | | By 90% |
|---|---|---|---|---|
| Simple imperative. | Go! | 4–6* | to | 6–0 years |
| Negative imperative. | Don't cross! | 5–6 | to | 7–0+ years |
| Active declarative. | | | | |
| Regular noun and present progressive. | The girl is jumping. | 3–0 | to | 3–0 years |
| Irregular noun and present progressive. | The sheep is eating. | 6–6 | to | 7–0 years |
| Past tense. | The man painted the house. | 5–6 | to | 7–0+ years |
| Past participle. | The lion has eaten. | 6–0 | to | 7–0+ years |
| Future. | He will hit the ball. | 7–0 | to | 7–0+ years |
| Reversible. | The car bumps the train. | 6–6 | to | 7–0+ years |
| Perfective. | The man has been cutting trees. | 7–0+ | to | 7–0+ years |
| Interrogative. | | | | |
| Who . . . | Who is by the table? | 3–0 | to | 3–0 years |
| What . . . | What do we eat? | 3–6 | to | 5–0 years |
| When . . . | When do you sleep? | 3–6 | to | 5–6 years |
| Negation. | | | | |
| Explicit. | The girl isn't running. | 5–6 | to | 7–0+ years |
| Inherent. | These two are different. | 6–6 | to | 7–0+ years |
| Reversible passive. | The boy is chased by the dog. | 5–6 | to | 6–0 years |
| Conjunction. | | | | |
| If . . . | If you're the teacher, point to the dog; if not, point to the bear. | 7–0+ | to | 7–0+ years |
| . . . then | Look at the third picture; then point to the baby of his animal. | 7–0+ | to | 7–0+ years |
| neither . . . nor | Find the one that is neither the ball nor the table. | 7–0+ | to | 7–0+ years |

* 4–6 = 4 years, 6 months.

children at or above 5½ years, but with consistent failure before that age.

(2) "Easy to see," as in "The doll is *easy to see*," was interpreted correctly by all children at age 8½ years and older, and the pattern of development suggested a potential learning period of from 3 to 4 years of duration.

(3) "Promise"/"tell," as in "Bozo *promises/tells* Donald to do a somersault," were interpreted correctly by all 9-year-olds and showed a mixed pattern of acquisition in 6-, 7-, and 8-year-olds.

(4) "Ask"/"tell," as in the sentence "*Ask/tell* Joe what to feed the doll," were interpreted with considerable variation in the age of acquisi-

tion. The general pattern of development suggested a gradual improvement in comprehension with age, up to age 10.

Researchers studying language acquisition have also studied the maturation of syntactic structures and the attainment of syntactic maturity. Hass and Wepman (1974) analyzed the structure of spoken sentences in school children ranging in age from 5 to 13 years. Analysis indicates that the spoken sentences could be characterized by five factors: (1) fluency, (2) embeddedness, (3) finite verb structure, (4) noun phrase structure, and (5) qualified speech. Of these, only the factor embeddedness, determined by the mean number of embedded clause components per sentence, increased with age. This result suggests that children learn to elaborate surface structure as they grow older. They use relatively more complicated noun phrases and sentence structures which are independent of the total number of words or the proportion of words used.

## Problems Experienced by Learning Disabled Children

Rosenthal (1970) observes that learning disabled children have increasing problems processing spoken sentences when the sentences increase in structural complexity and in **syntactic compression**. Examples would include possessive clauses such as "It is *my sister's hat*" and relative clause transformations such as "The baby *that fell* cried loudly." Semel and Wiig (1975) observe that learning disabled children may have significant problems in understanding and interpreting *wh*- questions; sentences with the demonstrative pronouns *this, that, these,* and *those;* passive sentences; sentences that express relationships between direct and indirect objects such as "Mother showed *the girl the baby*"; and sentences with relative clauses. Learning disabled children may also have difficulties interpreting and recalling adjective sequences and discerning the rules for adjective order in modifier strings. They often have trouble interpreting elements of conjoined sentences and syntactically ambiguous sentences.

Observations of learning disabled children suggest that they may have problems integrating the surface structure and the deep structure. When asked to repeat sentences, they are often unable to recall the structure of the sentences, but they *can* recall key words with information and meaning. This indicates that they depend upon the meaning properties of sentences when they have to recall them. They also have problems recalling sentences with unexpected or less than meaningful underlying deep structure. For example, one group of learning disabled adolescents found it extremely hard to repeat sentences such as *"She washed plastic, red, small, eight cups"* and *"Wasn't the fat ceiling robbed by the tired pen?"* (Wiig & Roach, 1975).

Some learning disabled children appear to perceive and interpret the words used in sentences easily, but fail to interpret the relationships among the individual words, as expressed by the sentence structure. In other words, they seem to process the deep structure with minimal reference to the surface structure. They may correctly understand the isolated words *cat, dog,* and *bite* in a sentence such as "The dog was bitten by the cat," but may fail to understand the agent-action-object relationship because of the word order required in passive sentences. As a result, they may assume that the cat was bitten by the dog (which is a much more probable event).

Other learning disabled children seem to process the surface and deep structures in sequence rather than simultaneously and may therefore need extra time to interpret a sentence. As an example, it may take a long time before a learning disabled child responds to a relatively simple question such as "Did you go to school today?" He may first have to process the meaning of each word, then process the question transformation, and finally integrate the two. This kind of sequential processing usually results in accurate interpretation of sentences if the sentence is not too long or complex. Longer and more complex sentences, such as "John, who was the boy that had the birthday party, opened his present over there" may be lost in the process. As a frequently used strategy, sequential processing of spoken sentences is not adequate. The interpretation is not a real-time process. The child's processing of a sentence may be interrupted at various points because it is out of step with the input. That is, the speaker does not stop to let the child process each sentence as he goes along. This strategy may result in errors and confusion when the spoken messages are long, complex, or incomplete, as frequently happens in rapid conversation, class presentations, or lectures. The child simply does not have time to keep up.

The problems learning disabled children have in processing sentences and abstracting the rules for sentence structure are reflected in the sentences they speak. Sample sentences spoken by children with learning disabilities are presented below. These utterances were produced by a group of 12- to 14-year-old learning disabled children who were asked to talk about ice cream in response to an item in an experimental version of the Clinical Evaluation of Language Functions (Semel & Wiig, 1980).

*For information on problems of written language, see Myklebust (1965, 1973).*

(1) I like ice cream *when* I *get* my tonsils out.
(2) Ice cream lasts long, long, long.
(3) People buy ice cream at the store and they eat it for a party or something.
(4) I eat ice cream *on* my birthday party and I eat it everyday and I want to stop eating.
(5) I *like* a whole big *cream*, big ice cream, big ice cream and it *was* good.
(6) Jay *went* to the shop and *asked* the man for a strawberry one, vanilla one, butter pecan and chocolate and I *like* to eat it.
(7) Mother *go* to the store and *take* Phillip with Charles and Rodney and *buy* some of the big, big ice cream sundae; don't forget to buy me a big ice cream sundae with a strawberry short cake.
(8) Me, my friends had ice cream and then we went home and then his mother said: Go get more ice cream. And then his father *said get himself* ice cream too. It was delicious and say do you know we had a *Thanksgiving for turkey*.
(9) My mother has a giant bowl of ice cream and full of cake.

The problems learning disabled children have with sentence structures may reflect limitations in the:

(1) Acquisition of the sentence formation rules (syntax).
(2) Immediate recall of sentences, due to limitations in short-term **auditory memory**.
(3) Internal **reauditorization** of heard sentences.
(4) Temporal sequencing and sequential recall of words and word order.
(5) Range of acquired and available sentence structures and transformations.
(6) Processing and abstracting word meaning with adequate and appropriate reference to sentence structure.
(7) Simultaneous analysis, synthesis, and integration of the surface and deep structures of sentences, resulting in relatively slower and sequential processing of meaning and structure.
(8) Speed and accuracy of recall of sentence structures and transformations for sentence formulation.

**Auditory memory** *is the process of remembering something which has been perceived through the auditory channel, such as a sound of a spoken word or phrase.*

**Reauditorization** *refers to the process of rehearsing spoken sentences or messages internally in the "mind's ear," as it were.*

## CHARACTERISTICS OF SPECIFIC SYNTACTIC DEFICITS

### The Noun Phrase

The Noun Phrase may contain definite and indefinite articles that function as noun determiners. There is only one definite article, *the*, in the English language, while there are two indefinite articles, *a* and *an*. The specific indefinite article required in a Noun Phrase depends upon the sound of the noun or adjective that follows it. Thus, we use the form *an* when the following word starts with a vowel and the form *a* when the following word begins with a consonant.

Learning disabled children may have problems learning the rules for using the two indefinite articles, *a* and *an*, and applying the rules in spoken language. In general, those children with problems differentiating the use of the two forms of the indefinite articles will use one of the forms exclusively. Frequently the chosen form is *a*, resulting in utterances such as "A apple tastes good" and "The car had a accident."

In discourse, they may also have problems acquiring the rules for using the definite and the indefinite articles. Mature speakers use an indefinite article (*a* or *an*) to introduce a noun the first time it occurs in the conversation. When they use the same noun again, the definite article (*the*) is used. Some severely involved, learning disabled children and adolescents may continue to use the definite article when a noun is first introduced in discourse past the ages expected. In contrast, 9-year-old children with normal language development approximate the adult use of the rules for articles in discourse (Warden, 1976).

### The Verb Phrase

The verb of the Verb Phrase may present difficulties for the learning disabled child in both processing and production. The child who has problems in the interpretation and use of verbs from a structural point of view may confuse verb tenses and aspects, modal auxiliaries, and perfective constructions, among others.

Learning disabled children frequently have difficulties distinguishing among the temporal aspects denoted by the verb tenses. These may result in:

(1) Failure to differentiate the nonpast aspects from the past aspects of verb use. For instance, learning disabled children may not grasp the distinction between the two sentences "I walk all the time" (nonpast) and "I walked all the time" (past). They may assume that both sentences express an action of the past, or that they both express an on-going activity. In a similar vein, they may use the expression "I walk all the time" in combination with the adverbial phrase "last week," indicating that the past tense was intended.

(2) Failure to distinguish the nonfuture aspects of the sentence "I walk all the time" from the future aspects of the sentences "I will walk all the time" or "I shall walk all the time." In this case, they may assume that the two sentences express the same temporal aspects, and interpret the sentences to mean either that in the future the action of walking will be repeated consistently or that the action of walking is on-going. They may not differentiate the nonfuture and future aspects of verbs and produce utterances such as "I walk all the time next summer," indicating that the future tense is intended.

These confusions seem to suggest that the temporal and spatial reference points of the sentences may not be shared by the speaker and the listener. Thus, learning disabled children often give the impression that the *now*, the zero point of reference for the time expressed by the verb, is fluid. In normal speaker–listener interactions, both people understand that the zero point to be used in determining tense is the *now*. This shared zero point of reference can be illustrated on a time line.

| PAST | NOW | FUTURE |
|---|---|---|
| ◄ · · · · · · · · · · · · · · · · · · · · · · · · · | · · · · · · · · · · · · · · · · · · · · · · · · · · · · · · · · · · · · | ► |
| Past tense | Present progressive | Future tense |
| Perfective constructions | Present tense (habitual) | |

The utterances produced by learning disabled children and their responses to questions that express temporal aspects suggest that their zero reference point, which determines their use of tense, may move around on the time line. At times, the *now* for the learning disabled child seems to be located at some point in the past. At other times, the *now* appears to be located somewhere in the future. We can infer this instability in the time reference from statements made, such as "Last Sunday I'll build a plane and then I finished it tomorrow" and "When I get twelve, I bees a grown-up."

Learning disabled children seem to have similar problems when auxiliaries are used in the verb phrase to denote distinctions *within* either the past or the future. They may have great problems in dif-

**FIGURE 4.2**

*Verb Tense Confusion*

PAST

FUTURE

PRESENT

ferentiating, let alone expressing, the distinctions denoted by the present perfective, as in "The boy *has jumped* the rope," and the past perfective, as in "The boy *had jumped* the rope." Similarly they may find it impossible to distinguish among the subtle durational features denoted by the progressives in verb phrases such as "The boy *had been jumping*," "The boy *would have been jumping*," "The boy *will be jumping*," and "The boy *will have been jumping*." They may also have difficulties in perceiving the distinction between an on-going activity, as expressed by the present progressive in sentences such as "I *am running*," and a habitual activity, denoted by the present tense in utterances such as "I *run*" or the emphatic "I *do run*." This difficulty usually shows up in both the spoken and the written expressions of learning disabled children.

Problems in interpreting the subtle distinctions in mood (habitual aspects, inferences, or obligations) expressed by the modals *must, have to,* and *ought to* are prevalent among learning disabled children. As a consequence, they may interpret the sentences "I have to go to Boston," "I *must go* to Boston," and "I *ought to* go to Boston" to mean that I *will be going* to Boston for sure. They may have similar problems differentiating between and interpreting the respective levels of probability expressed in the sentences "You *will get* the ball," "You *shall get* the ball," and "You *may get* the ball."

Learning disabled children also frequently misinterpret and misuse perfective constructions with *have -en -ing,* as in *have been waiting* and *have been running,* they may interpret a sentence such as "I have been waiting for you for an hour" to mean that I *will wait* or *am going to wait* for yet another hour or that *a long time ago I waited* for an hour. When they attempt to use *have been* constructions, they may omit either the auxiliary *have* or the form of *to be* or both, and produce utterances such as "I *waiting* for you for an hour," "I *have waiting* for you an hour," or "I *been waiting* for you an hour."

Learning disabled children's difficulties in forming verb phrases with forms of *to be,* auxiliaries, and modals may be further compounded when they attempt to produce direct and indirect quotations, as in the sentences "Mother *said: 'I am* going to the store' " and "Mother *said that she was* going to the store." They may confuse the rules for the verb phrases in the two sentence types, and produce utterances such as "Mother *said that I am going* to the store" or "Mother said: *'I was going* to the store.' "

In summary, the difficulties experienced by learning disabled children in interpreting and using verb phrases with forms of *to be,* auxiliaries, and modals may relate to:

(1) Problems in perceiving the generally unstressed auxiliaries and modals in complex verb phrases and in recalling their order in the verb phrase.
(2) Problems in perceiving and abstracting the rules for the use of *to be,* auxiliaries, and modals in complex verb phrases.
(3) Problems in perceiving, abstracting, and recalling the subtle durational and intentional features denoted by complex verb phrases.
(4) Problems in labelling subtle durational features and in expressing intentions and probabilities which may not be clearly understood.

## Negative Sentences

The interpretation of negative sentences depends upon accurate identification of the stressed, negated word or phrase, as well as upon the appropriate logical subtraction of the negated feature. Therefore, learning disabled children with auditory perception deficits or with logical processing problems seem especially prone to have difficulties with negative sentences. The ease with which children with learning disabilities comprehend explicit negative sentences that contain *not* is related to:

(1) The proximity of and the relationship between the negation *not* and the negated word or phrase.
(2) The immediate relevance of the negated feature or features to the child.
(3) The prominence of the stress placed on the negated word or phrase.
(4) The complexity of the logical operation of subtraction required.

As an illustration, the sentence "The ball is not on the table" may be interpreted to mean somewhere other than *on* the table (under, next to, etc.) or on something *other than* the table (the floor, a chair, etc.), depending upon the stress in the sentence. The logical process of deduction the child must use will depend on variables such as whether or not the ball is located within his range of vision, so he can verify a hypothesized location. Table 4.3 shows a tentative order of difficulty for the comprehension of some explicit negative statements and questions. It is based on the relationship among (1) the importance of the negated aspect, (2) the proximity and the sequential relationships between *not* and the negated aspects, and (3) the complexity of the logical operation of deduction the child is required to use.

The interpretation of negative sentences will occasionally pose problems for some learning disabled children. They seem to have trouble

**TABLE 4.3**
*Tentative order of difficulty of explicit negative sentences featuring **not***

---

**Importance of Negated Word.**
1. The ball is not *red*.
2. The ball is not *round*.
3. The ball is not *jumping*.
4. The ball was not *hit*.

**Proximity, Sequence, and Function of Negated Word or Phrase.**

| | |
|---|---|
| 1. The ball is not *big*. | The boy is not *tall*. |
| 2. The ball is not *rolling*. | The boy is not *walking*. |
| 3. The ball is not *on* the table. | The boy is not walking *on* the log. |
| 4. The ball is not on the *table*. | The boy is not walking on the *log*. |
| 5. The *ball* is not on the table. | The *boy* is not walking on the log. |
| 6. The ball is not on the table *by the window.* | The boy is not walking on the log *by the road.* |

**Logical Complexity.**
1. This ball is not *big*.
2. This ball is not the *biggest*.
3. This ball is not *bigger than* that ball.
4. Throw the ball that is not *red*.
5. Do not *throw the ball that is red*.
6. Throw the ball that is not *red and blue*.
7. Do not *throw the ball that is red and blue*.
8. Do not *throw the ball that is not red*.
9. Do not *throw the ball that is not red and blue*.

---

processing the surface structure while also performing the logical operation of subtraction or deletion that is required for interpretation of the deep structure. That is, in an explicit negative sentence which contains the word *not*, one of the expressed attributes, actions, or outcomes must be subtracted by logical processing. Consider the utterance, "The ball is *not* red." If this sentence is heard out of context, it would be hard to decide what the color of the ball might be. Now consider the utterances, "The ball is *not* red. It is blue." In this case, the color red, which was subtracted from the concept of the ball in the first sentence, is replaced by a second color, blue, in the following utterance. As a result, the last pair of utterances is easy to interpret. The explicit negation of the first sentence of the pair may almost be disregarded, since it provides only temporary and redundant information.

Learning disabled children may, however, have problems understanding even comparatively evident utterances in which an explicit negation is followed by a true statement of affairs. They may fail to process the relatively unstressed *not*, or they may not perceive the stress placed on the word which is negated. They may, therefore, have problems identifying whether or not the sentence contained an active declarative positive statement and which word was negated. As a result, they may interpret the utterances "The ball is not red. It is blue" to say that someone has a red ball and a blue ball or a ball that is red and blue.

Wiig, Florence, Kutner, Sherman, & Semel (1977) assessed and compared the perception of selected explicit negative sentences by learning disabled children and adolescents and their academically achieving age peers and adults. The sentences contained from five to ten words and from three to six critical semantic elements. All sentences were built on the basic sentence pattern Noun Phrase + Verb Phrase. In sentences with action verbs, the negated elements included subject, direct object, indirect object, locative preposition, and object of the preposition. In sentences with the copula *is*, the negated elements included subject, locative preposition, object of the preposition, and predicate adjective. The results indicate that the order of difficulty in interpreting the explicit negative sentences was similar for all subjects. The function of the negated semantic element as well as sentence length appeared to influence the ease of comprehension. The order of difficulty from easiest to hardest is shown in Table 4.4.

**TABLE 4.4**

*Order of difficulty in interpreting explicit negative sentences*

| Negated Element | Example |
| --- | --- |
| 1. Predicate adjective. | The girl is not *tall*. |
| 2. Object of the preposition (copula verb). | The man is not at *home*. |
| 3. Predicate. | The girl is not *sitting* on the chair. |
| 4. Preposition. | The man is not walking *down* the steps. The cup is not *on* the table. |
| 5. Indirect object. | The boy is not giving the cake to the *woman*. |
| 6. Subject. | The *woman* is not washing the dishes. |
| 7. Object of the preposition. | The boy is not standing under the *umbrella*. |
| 8. Direct object. | The boy is not giving the *package* to the girl. |

Carrow (1973) observes that an explicit negative sentence in which the predicate adjective denoting color was negated, "It's not black," was interpreted correctly by 90% of a sample of normal children by age 5 years. Two explicit negatives with negation of an action verb in the present progressive form, "The girl is not swimming" and "The girl isn't running," were understood by 90% of the children by age 7 years as was a negative imperative, "Don't cross," and an inherent negative, "These two are different." The ages reflect the time when the negative sentences could be interpreted without a facilitating context. When the context facilitated their understanding children at much earlier ages could understand these sentences.

## Passive Sentences

Passive sentences are often misinterpreted by learning disabled children. Their interpretation appears to take at least two steps: (1) processing the surface structure and (2) performing the logical operation of identifying and comparing the expressed subject for the interpretation of the deep structure. The problems encountered by learning disabled children seem to relate to their expectations about the order of the subject and object in English sentences. They expect the first noun of the sentence to function as the subject of the action expressed by the

verb phrase. And they expect the second noun encountered in a
sentence, following the verb phrase, to function as the object of the
action. When hearing a passive sentence they appear to form an
immediate hypothesis that the first noun is the subject and the last the
object of the action. Learning disabled children seem to disregard the
presence of the preposition *by* in the sentence structure, which should
signal that an alternative hypothesis is required. Their problems in
processing passive sentences may be further compounded by difficulties in retaining and recalling the order in which the nouns were
presented. Either process would result in misinterpretations.

Based on investigations of the immediate recall of various passive
sentences, the normal order of difficulty seems to progress as follows
(Savin & Perchonock, 1965):

(1) Active declarative: "The girl drove the car."
(2) Passive: "The car was driven by the girl."
(3) Passive question: "Was the car driven by the girl?"
(4) Negative passive question: "Wasn't the car driven by the girl?"
(5) Emphatic passive: "The car *was* driven by the girl."
(6) Negative passive: "The car was not driven by the girl."

Learning disabled children seem to experience the order of difficulty
of passive sentences differently. Their sequence agrees with observations by Slobin (1963, 1966) and Turner and Rommetveit (1967a, 1968). It
progresses as follows:

(1) Active declarative: "The mailman sorted the packages."
(2) Passive: "The packages were sorted by the mailman."
(3) *Wh-* passive question: "What was sorted by the mailman?"
(4) Passive question: "Were the packages sorted by the mailman?"
(5) Negative passive: "The packages were not sorted by the mailman."
(6) Negative passive question: "Weren't the packages sorted by the
    mailman?"
(7) Emphatic passive: "The packages *were* sorted by the mailman."
(8) Emphatic negative passive: "The packages *were not* sorted by the
    mailman."

The fact that mention of the actor may be deleted in passive sentences such as "Mail is delivered every day" or "The paper is printed
every day" appears to cause special problems for children with learning disabilities. When they encounter these passives, they may search
for the subject, assume that the direct object is the subject, or infer an
incorrect subject for the deep structure. Typically, they interpret passive
sentences in which the actor is not mentioned in a concrete fashion and
overlook the abstract and indefinite aspects of the sentences. As a
result, they may interpret a sentence such as "Mail is delivered every
day" to mean that the speaker gets letters every day.

Learning disabled children have been observed to understand irreversible passive sentences more easily and correctly than reversible
passive (Wiig & Semel, 1973, 1974b). In an irreversible passive sentence, the meaning of the words makes only one interpretation logi-

**FIGURE 4.3**
*Passives*

**FIGURE 4.4**
*Passives (girl-boy)*

cally possible. An example would be "The door was closed by the man." Anyone who understands the words will know that a man can close a door, but a door cannot close a man. On the other hand, in a reversible passive sentence, the interpretation can go either way. For instance, in "The girl was kicked by the boy," the child could believe that either the girl was the actor or the boy was the actor; either one is capable of kicking. The two interpretations have equal probability of occurrence and are equally logical. Learning disabled children seem to experience the greatest problems in processing and interpreting the meaning of reversible passive sentences that contain proper nouns, such as "Mary was followed by Joe." In an irreversible passive sentence, such as "The ball was kicked by the boy," the interpretation is facilitated by the logic and commonness of the act. The learning disabled child may be able to understand the sentence, even though he may not have perceived and processed its structure accurately. To accurately process and interpret reversible passive sentences, the child must know the rules for the passive transformation and accurate processing of the surface structure.

The problems of learning disabled children in perceiving, processing, and interpreting passive sentences may be related to:

(1) Deficits in retaining and recalling the surface structure characteristics of passives, reflecting limitations in short-term memory and immediate recall.

(2) Tendencies to form the hypothesis that the first noun heard must be the subject of the sentence, in direct analogy with the structure of the affirmative active declarative sentence. For example, the passive "Jane was picked up by Mary" may be interpreted as if it were the active declarative counterpart, "Jane picked Mary up."

(3) Deficits in retaining the sequence of the critical nouns in passive sentences while recalling the surface structure characteristics. As a result, the passive sentence "Jane was picked up by Mary" may be recalled and processed as if the original sentence were "Mary was picked up by Jane."

(4) Deficits in perceiving and recalling the relatively unstressed critical words which signal the passive transformation. In the sentence "Jane was picked up by Mary" the presence of the auxiliary "was" and the preposition "by" signal to the listener that the sentence is in the passive voice. These signal words are relatively unstressed in comparison with the remaining words of the sentence, and may therefore be overlooked or disregarded by learning disabled children.

(5) Delays in the acquisition of the rules for the passive sentence transformation, reflecting deficits in auditory perception, short-term auditory memory, and recall of sequences, among others.

## Interrogative Sentences

Many learning disabled children have problems in processing and interpreting questions that require either (1) transposing of the subject and the predicate, as in the interrogative "*Has Daddy* finished dinner?" (*Daddy has* finished dinner), (2) addition of an auxiliary, as in the interrogative "*Did* daddy *finish* his dinner?" (Daddy *finished* his dinner), or (3) preposing of a *wh-* form as in *wh-* questions such as "*When* did daddy finish his dinner?" (Daddy finished his dinner *two minutes ago*) or "*Where* did daddy go?" (Daddy went *to the store*) (Semel & Wiig, 1975).

Language and learning disabled children tend to find tag questions the easiest question form to interpret and use. Tag questions allow them to follow the subject-predicate-object sequence in active declaratives and clearly identify the question status at the end.

Yes/no interrogatives such as "Are you ready to go to school?" are generally next easiest to process and interpret, if the active declarative counterpart contains an auxiliary or a form of *to be*, as in the sentence "You are ready to go to school." These interrogatives are formed by shifting the position of the auxiliary or copula (*to be*) to the initial position in the sentence. Interrogatives that are transformed from active declarative sentences that do not contain auxiliaries or forms of *to be* tend to be relatively harder for the learning disabled child to process and use. These question sentences require· the child to add an auxiliary or modal at the beginning of the sentence and change the tense of the main verb. As an example, the declarative "The boy baked these cookies" may be transformed into the interrogative forms *"Did the boy bake these cookies?"* and *"Has the boy baked these cookies?"* The following auxiliaries and modals may be used to form interrogatives of declarative sentences which do not contain an auxiliary or a form of *to be:*

(1) Do, does . . . did as in *"Did you go the movies?"*
(2) Have, has . . . had as in *"Have you gone to the movies?"*
(3) Can . . . could as in *"Could you go to the movies?"*
(4) Will . . . would as in *"Would you go to the movies?"*
(5) May . . . might as in *"Might you go to the movies?"*
(6) Shall . . . shall as in *"Shall you go to the movies?"*
(7) Must . . . must as in *"Must you go to the movies?"*

Learning disabled children appear to have difficulties perceiving and learning the rules for the changes required to transform a declarative sentence into a yes/no interrogative. In spontaneous speech, these questions do not occur very often. When learning disabled children do use them, they tend to substitute other question forms such as tag questions or questions with a preposed and obvious question word. Some examples of the questions asked by learning disabled students are:

(1) "I turned the stove off, did I?" in which a *to do* tag question is added to a statement. The tag question may be incorrectly formed, as in this example, in which the required tag would be "didn't I?"
(2) "I turned the stove off, have I?" in which a *to have* tag question is added to a statement. The tag question may or may not be incorrectly formed, as in this example in which the tag should have been "haven't I?" When the *to have* tag is added, learning disabled children generally forget the rule that the statement must contain the auxiliary *to have*. The accurate form of this tag question would be "I *have* turned the stove off, *haven't I?"*
(3) "I turn the stove off, can I?" in which a *can* tag question is added to a statement which may occur in its correct form, "I can turn the stove off," or in an incorrect form, as in the example. Frequently, the *can* tag is formed incorrectly as in the question above. It may also occur in its correct form, "can't I?"
(4) "I hope I turned the stove off?" in which a question word or phrase is preposed to indicate that it is a question. Generally this question form is spoken with rising inflection to further specify the interrogative intent.

Often, a learning disabled child will select one type of tag question or a specific question word or phrase to form his questions. The interrogatives used by these children, therefore, tend to have idiosyncratic characteristics. Among the question words or phrases that may be chosen by learning disabled children to precede their questions are "I hope," "I wish," "I wonder," "I don't know," and "Say," to mention only a few.

Yes/no interrogatives are relatively easier to interpret and use when their active declarative counterparts contain forms of *to be* or auxiliaries. The questions "Is Peter at the movies?" and "Can Peter go to the movies?" may serve as illustrations. The first question is derived from the active declarative counterpart, "Peter is at the movies," by reversing subject and predicate. The second question is derived from the active declarative "Peter can go to the movies" by reversing subject and auxiliary order. Compare these interrogatives to the question "Did the boy bake these cookies?" The active declarative counterpart is "The boy baked these cookies." The question transformation required two changes. An auxiliary, "did," was added and placed before the subject. Furthermore, the form of the main verb was changed from past tense to the infinitive form.

Interrogatives that feature forms of "can," "will," "must," and "should" may involve direct or indirect questions. In some cases, questions with "can," "will," "must," and "should" do require a yes/no answer. They may ask for answers to questions about ability ("can"), future plans or intentions ("will"), or imposed demands or restrictions ("must," "should"). As examples, the questions "Can you lift that box?" "Will you leave for Paris tomorrow?" "Must we take the garbage out?" and "Should we stop playing now?" ask direct questions. Language and learning disabled youngsters may be quite confused between these kinds of literal uses and the pragmatic uses of indirect requests. These indirect requests are not to be interpreted literally and answered by yes/no. They are to be interpreted on the basis of relational and contextual cues.

When "can," "will," "must," and "should" are used in indirect requests, the listener must react nonverbally rather than verbally. For instance, the interrogative "Can you stop playing?" does not ask whether it is possible. It requests the listener to stop in an indirect, polite, nonauthoritative fashion. The interpretation of the request depends *entirely* upon the context in which it is spoken. More examples of interrogatives that may serve as indirect requests are given below.

| Indirect request | Interpretation |
|---|---|
| Can't you open the door? | Open the door. |
| Must you play piano right now? | Stop playing. |
| Will you pick it up now? | Pick it up. |
| Should you wear a coat? | Put a coat on. |
| Shouldn't you take your bag? | Take your bag. |

Language and learning disabled youngsters may answer indirect requests with yes/no. They may not perceive or integrate the contextual and relational cues that signify a request for a change in action. The pragmatic meanings elude them. Or they may disregard indirect requests completely because they have always failed to respond appropriately to them.

According to some observations, normally developing children deal equally well with affirmative and negative indirect requests (Leonard, Wilcox, Fulmer, & Davis, 1978). Affirmative and negative indirect requests that feature "can" and "will" proved easier to interpret than those which feature "must" and "should." The confusion in responding to these requests, in either the affirmative or negative forms, appeared to be related to the expected actions. The indirect request "Must you play the piano?" is a request to cease the action. "Mustn't you play the piano?" is a request to perform the action. Clearly the rules for interpreting and using some indirect requests defy the most common rules of English—that a predicate indicates or demands the action, while a negated predicate indicates that the action has either stopped or is absent.

When learning disabled children are asked *wh-* questions, they may also have problems interpreting them. Their difficulties suggest the following order of increasing complexity for the *wh-* forms:

(1) "What," as in *"What* did you get for your birthday?"
(2) "Who," as in *"Who* said so?"
(3) "Which," as in *"Which* shoes do you like best?"
(4) "Where," as in *"Where* did you put your shoes?"
(5) "When," as in *"When* do you get home from school?"
(6) "Why," as in *"Why* did you buy those shoes?"
(7) "How," "how many," "how much," as in *"How* did you do that?" *"How many* apples do you have?" and *"How much* did they cost?"
(8) "Whose," as in *"Whose* mother said that?"

**FIGURE 4.5**
*Wh- questions*

**WHEN DID COLUMBUS LAND ?**
The Nina, The Pinta, The Santa Maria
**WHY DID COLUMBUS GO ?**
Queen Isabella's palace in Spain
**WHERE DID COLUMBUS GO ?**
In 1942

With learning disabled children it is frequently necessary to paraphrase a question of place, time, or method into a corresponding *what* form. For example, learning disabled children may be able to answer questions formed with "what place," "what time," and "in what way," even though they may not respond to questions with the expected *wh-* forms "where," "when," and "how." When they form *wh-* questions, they may leave out required auxiliaries or retain the word order of the corresponding declarative sentence and prepose a *wh-* for good measure. The resulting questions may sound like this:

(1) "What time you going?" in which the *wh-* form "what time" is used to replace the form "when" and the auxiliary "are" has been omitted.
(2) "Where you going?" in which the auxiliary "are" has been omitted but the expected *wh-* form occurs.
(3) "What time you are going?" in which the declarative word order has been retained and the *wh-* form "what time" has been placed at the beginning to signal the intended question.

Children with normal language development appear able to answer questions with preposed "who," "what," and "where" at about age 3. They are, however, not able to answer "when" and "how" questions at that age (Brown, 1968; Brown, Cazden, & Bellugi, 1968). Lee (1974) suggests that "what . . . do" questions may be acquired later than "who" or "what" questions and that "where," "when," and "why" questions are acquired even later.

## Conjunction of Clauses

Sentences may contain several clauses that may either be coordinated by the use of one of the coordinate conjunctions "and," "but," "or," and "nor" or subordinated by one of the subordinating conjunctions, such as "because," "if," "before," and "after." Coordination and retention of complete clauses results in compound sentences such as:

(1) "Jane plays the piano *and* John plays the flute" in which the original independent clauses "Jane plays the piano" and "John plays the flute" are coordinated.
(2) "Jane plays the piano *but* she does not like to play Beethoven" in which the clauses "Jane plays the piano" and "Jane does not like to play Beethoven" are coordinated.
(3) "Jane could play the piano *or* she could play the guitar" in which the clauses "Jane could play the piano" and "Jane could play the guitar" are coordinated.
(4) "Jane cannot play the flute *nor* can she play the saxophone" in which the clauses "Jane cannot play the flute" and "Jane cannot play the saxophone" are coordinated.

If the clauses to be coordinated share the same subject, verb, direct object, indirect object, or predicate subject, parts of the original clauses may be omitted to form simple sentences with conjunction deletion. The following are examples of sentences with conjunction deletion:

(1) "Jane plays *the piano* and *the guitar*" in which the subject and predicate are shared, as in "Jane plays the piano" and "Jane plays the guitar," resulting in a compound direct object.
(2) "Jane plays the piano for *her mother* and *her aunt*" in which the subject, predicate, and direct object are shared in the original clauses "Jane plays the piano for her mother" and "Jane plays the piano for her aunt," resulting in a compound indirect object.

(3) *"Jane* and *John* play the piano" in which the predicate and the direct object are shared in the original clauses "Jane plays the piano" and "John plays the piano," resulting in a compound subject.

(4) "Jane is *creative* and *smart*" in which the original clauses shared the subject and the copula as in "Jane is creative" and "Jane is smart," resulting in a compound predicate adjective.

Learning disabled children may have difficulties in recalling, interpreting, and using sentences with coordinated clauses or with coordination of phrases by conjunction deletion. Their difficulties may reflect:

(1) Problems in recalling the two independent coordinated clauses in compound sentences: These sentences tend to be relatively long and may tax the child's short-term auditory memory. As a result, the learning disabled child may remember only one of the coordinated clauses, either the first or the last.

(2) Problems in retaining and recalling the coordinated phrases in sentences with conjunction deletion such as "John and Mary play the piano." The difficulties may arise from the children's expectations that each sentence should have only one subject. They may subsequently disregard the second subject in the noun phrase. In a similar fashion, learning disabled children may expect only one predicate adjective, verb, direct object, or indirect object in each sentence. If there are several conjunction deletions in one sentence, as in *"The man* and *the woman hopped* and *skipped* joyfully across *the lawn* and *the meadow,"* they may be unable to retain the individual phrases and may be totally unable to tell what they heard.

(3) Problems in associating two subjects with one expressed action (verb) and direct or indirect object. For example, learning disabled children may interpret the sentence *"Jane* and *John* play the piano" to mean that they sit next to each other and play on the piano at the same time. Thus they may disregard the interpretation as being totally improbable. They may have similar problems of association in sentences with one subject and a compound predicate, predicate adjective, direct object, or indirect object. For example, they may think that the sentence "Jane *hops* and *skips* across the lawn" means that Jane combines a hop and a skip, a feat which does not make sense and therefore does not warrant attention.

(4) Problems in identifying and recalling the referent or referents for personal pronouns in compound sentences such as "Eric shot the ball, and *he* scored the basket." Learning disabled children may attribute the second action to someone other than Eric and therefore misinterpret the sentence.

When subordinating conjunctions are used to combine two clauses, learning disabled children may have trouble discerning which clause is the main clause and which one is subordinated. They may also have difficulties interpreting the meaning of the subordinating conjunction and may therefore not understand the relationship between the clauses in the sentence. The fact that the order of the main clause and the subordinated clause changes may confuse them further. As an example of the options we have in the order of the clauses in a subordinated conjunction, consider a sentence containing the conjunction *"before."* We may choose the order in which we wish to describe a sequence of actions and say "Before I went to the movies, I ate dinner" or "I ate dinner *before I went to the movies.*" In the first sentence, the order in which the actions are described does not correspond to the actual sequence of events. In the second sentence the description and the actual sequence of the acts coincide.

The difficulty of interpreting sentences with coordinated conjunctions relates to the following variables (Clark, 1973):

(1) Order of mention. Sentences in which the sequence of mention and the sequence of action coincide, as in the sentence "I opened the door before I went out," are easier to interpret than sentences in which the order of action is violated or reversed, as in "Before I went out, I opened the door."

*The number of derivational transformations in a sentence is the number of transformations applied to the Kernel sentence to form the new sentence. For instance, the sentence "Wasn't the truck followed by the police car?" is three steps removed from the Kernel sentence "The police car followed the truck." The transformations involved are (1) declarative to interrogative, (2) affirmative to negative, and (3) active to passive.*

(2) Derivational simplicity. Sentences with fewer derivational transformations are easier to interpret than those with relatively more transformations. For example, the sentence "He got up from *the chair when* he saw the door open" is considered somewhat easier to interpret than the derivationally more complex sentence "*When* he saw the door open, he got up from *his chair.*"

(3) Choice of theme. Sentences which contain clauses in which there is a shared theme ("The boy was reading a *book* since it told him how to fix cars.") are simpler than sentences in which there is little or no continuity between the two successive utterances ("The boy was reading a book since the weather was balmy.")

According to Clark (1973):

> Of the three principles, choice of theme basically makes the speaker use one syntactic construction rather than the other. Developmentally, it directly affects the order in which a child will learn to use certain syntactic structures. The two other principles are equally important; psychologically, there is a strong preference for mentioning events in chronological order unless there is some (pragmatic) reason not to, and linguistically, there is a preference for using the subordinate clause in second position. (p. 604)

According to Lee (1974, p. 40), the normal acquisition of subordinating conjunctions progresses in the following sequence: (1) "because," (2) "so," (3) "if," (4) "until," (5) "after," (6) "since," (7) "although," and (8) "as." The complex relationships expressed among clauses when they are combined by subordinating conjunction are summarized in Table 4.5. When the structural and derivational complexity of sentences with subordinated conjunctions is kept as closely equal as possible, learning disabled children experience the following order of difficulty in interpreting and using conjunctions.

(1) "cause/because" as in "Charlotte went out *because* she was bored."
(2) "if" as in "Charlotte goes out *if* she wants to."
(3) "so" as in "Charlotte goes out *so* she can meet Lauren."
(4) "when" as in "Charlotte goes out *when* she wants to."

(5) "after" as in "Charlotte went out *after* Lauren called."
(6) "before" as in "Charlotte went out *before* Lauren called."
(7) "until" as in "Charlotte did not go out *until* Lauren called."
(8) "since" as in "Charlotte went out *since* she was bored."
(9) "although" as in "Charlotte went out *although* she was tired."
(10) "as" as in "Charlotte went out *as* she was bored."

**TABLE 4.5**

*Relationships expressed by subordinating conjunctions*

| Relationship | Concept | Conjunctions |
|---|---|---|
| Outcome. | Cause-effect. | 'cause, because, as, since, in order that, so that. |
| Time. | Temporal. | when, after, before, until, as soon as, while. |
| Condition. | Conditional. | if, unless, although. |

The difficulties in processing, interpreting, and using sentences with subordinated clauses may reflect:

(1) Problems in perceiving and interpreting the cause-effect relationships that are signalled by the use of subordinating conjunctions such as "cause/because," "since," "in order that," and "so that," as in the sentences:
  (a) Julie drank the water quickly *because* she was very thirsty.
  (b) We will not ask John to go fishing with us *since* he does not like to fish.
  (c) You must bring your license *in order* to drive my car.
  (d) She brought her swimsuit *so that* she could take a swim.
(2) Problems in perceiving and interpreting the temporal relationships signalled by the subordinating conjunctions "when," "after," "before," "until," "while," "as soon as" as in the sentences:
  (a) The dog barked *when* the mailman came.
  (b) I went out to play *after* I drank my milk.
  (c) You may not play outside *until* you have finished your work.
  (d) The girl set the table *while* her mother cooked dinner.
  (e) We will eat the cake *as soon as* it is baked.
(3) Problems in perceiving and interpreting the conditions signalled by the subordinating conditional conjunctions "if," "unless," and "although," as in the sentences:
  (a) We shall stay home *if* it rains.
  (b) I cannot buy the ice cream *unless* you give me money.
  (c) He bought the car *although* he did not have cash.
(4) Problems in perceiving, recalling, and interpreting the order of events described in sentences with subordinating temporal conjunctions when the actual sequence is not reflected in the surface structure, as in the sentences:
  (a) *Before* he went out, he opened the door.
  (b) He opened the door *after* he got up from the chair.

(5) Problems in perceiving which clause reflects the main idea and which the subordinated, when the subordinated clause precedes the main clause, as in the sentences:

   (a) *Unless you give me the money,* I cannot buy the ice cream. (conditional)

   (b) *Although he did not have cash,* he bought the car. (conditional)

   (c) *As soon as it is baked,* we will eat the cake. (temporal)

   (d) *While the mother cooked dinner,* the girl set the table. (temporal)

   (e) *Since it is raining,* we will stay home. (cause-effect)

   (f) *Because it rained,* she stayed inside. (cause-effect)

As a result, learning disabled children may disregard the information given in the subordinated clause and react only to the meaning of the main clause. For instance; they may interpret the sentence "If it rains, we will stay home" to express the verdict that we will stay home regardless of conditions.

(6) Problems in the retention of the sequence of the main and the subordinated clause due to sequential memory deficits. As a consequence, spoken sentences such as "Since John does not like to go fishing, we will not ask him to go with us" may be processed and interpreted as if it had been heard as "Since we will not ask John to go with us, he does not like to go fishing," a rather confusing statement.

## Complex Sentences

Complex sentences may contain, among other elements, relative clauses, noun phrase complements, and adverbial clauses. Learning disabled children and adolescents may have difficulties in both processing and producing sentences with:

(1) Adverbial clauses which express aspects of location, distance, speed, time, etc., as in the sentence "Jack put his new bike *where it would be safe.*"

(2) Embedded noun phrase complements, as in the sentence "The fact *that all the children knew their multiplication tables* pleased the teacher."

(3) Nonembedded relative clauses, as in the sentence "Huck Finn ran away from Pap, *who had treated Huck like a piece of property.*"

(4) Embedded relative clauses, as in the sentence "The children *who lived in Boston* left by plane this morning."

(5) Coordinated relative clauses, as in the sentence "The boy *who did not score the winning touchdown* or *get carried off the field* but *who played an outstanding defensive game* was named the best player of the year."

(6) Nested relative clauses, as in the sentence "The boy *who is sitting under the big tree eating an ice cream sundae he bought at the drugstore* is my brother."

Normal children acquire relative clause transformations at about the same time as *wh-* questions (Miller, 1973). The four most commonly used relatives in young children's speech are "what," "where," "when," and "that." "When" was used earlier in relative clauses than in questions. Among learning disabled and academically achieving college students, the order of difficulty of relativized sentences seems to follow the sequence from easy to hard shown in Table 4.6 (Wiig & Fleischmann, 1978):

**TABLE 4.6**
*Order of difficulty of relative pronouns*

| Relative Pronoun | Sentence Category | Example |
|---|---|---|
| Whose | Appended, object-related relative clause. | He saw the girl *whose* leg was broken. |
| What | Free relatives. | He ate *what* his mother cooked. |
| Which | Appended, object-related relative clause. | The boy ate the bananas *which* he bought. |
| Who | Appended, object-related relative clause. | The dog chased the girl *who* had on the red dress. |
| Who | Embedded, subject-related relative clause. | The man *who* bought the dog chased the woman. |
| Deleted. | Appended, object-related relative clause with pronoun deletion. | She saw the man she liked. |

*Sentences with Adverbial Clauses*

The difficulties experienced by learning disabled children and adolescents in processing, interpreting, and using sentences with adverbial clauses may reflect problems in:

(1) Perceiving the relationship between an adverbial clause which denotes subtle aspects of space and time and the primary clause. As a result, these children may search for the specification of the location or time denoted by the *where* and *when* in the adverbial clauses in sentences such as "Jack put his bike *where* it was safe" and "Charlotte came *when* it was convenient." In turn, they may answer questions such as "Where did Jack put his bike?" by saying "In the garage, of course" or "I don't know. You did not tell me."

(2) Perceiving and interpreting the subtle indefinite and relative space, time, or quality relationships denoted by the adverbial clauses in sentences such as:

   (a) She sat down *where she could be warm.*   (indefinite relative spatial reference)

   (b) She waited *while they ate dinner.*   (indefinite relative temporal reference)

   (c) She talked *as loud as she could.*   (indefinite relative quality reference)

   The problems in interpreting and describing these sentences appear similar to those learning disabled children have in grasping other terms or clauses with spatial or temporal references. The problems seem compounded by the relative and therefore nebulous aspects denoted by the adverbial clauses.

(3) Retaining and recalling the critical words or elements in a sentence with an adverbial clause. As an example, when the learning dis-

abled child hears a sentence such as "The truck was parked where it could not be seen," he may focus on and retain only a limited number of the words—perhaps "truck" or "could not be seen." He may fail to recall that the main ideas of the sentence focused on the words "was parked" and therefore his interpretation of the sentence meaning may be incomplete and/or inaccurate.

## Sentences with Noun Phrase Complements

In most active declarative sentences, the noun phrase which contains the subject is followed immediately by the verb phrase. Noun phrase complements occupy a position that interrupts that common sequence of phrases. Placement of a noun phrase complement between the noun and the verb phrases, as in the sentence "The thought *that I might win in the lottery* made me delirious," causes the normal sequence used in processing to be disrupted. It necessitates a change in the child's perceptual strategy for processing the sentence. The noun phrase complement also increases the length of the sentence disproportionately, placing a greater burden on short-term auditory memory. Because the surface structure is so complex, the listener must be able to form appropriate perceptual-conceptual chunks (the constituent clauses), as well as repeat processing to integrate and synthesize the meaning of the noun phrase complement with that of the noun.

Since sentences which contain noun phrase complements tax both the short-term auditory memory capacity and its efficiency, it is a small wonder that they may cause problems for children with learning disabilities. Their difficulties with this structural transformation may reflect primarily short-term auditory memory deficits. These deficits may result in:

(1) Partial retention and recall of the words and phrases in the sentence. Typically, the initial noun phrase or subject and its associated verb phrase tend to be recalled, while the noun phrase complement is lost. Some learning disabled children may perceive a sentence such as "The fact that you finished your work pleases me" as if it had been spoken "The fact pleases me," leaving the complement out. As a consequence, they may wonder about what fact the speaker is referring to and may not even perceive the speaker's intended encouragement. Other learning disabled children may recall only the noun phrase complement of the sentence and interpret it as a factual statement, "You finished your work." While this statement may be heartening to the child, it is hardly a reward of the magnitude intended.

(2) Adherence to one perceptual strategy for processing sentences and limited ability to shift processing strategies when required. For example, the learning disabled child may adhere to a processing strategy that follows the rule for active declarative sentences and expect that the initial noun phrase will be followed immediately by the verb phrase. As a result, the sentence "The fact that you finished your work pleases me" may be interpreted as if "fact" were followed by its associated verb phrase "finished," as in the rather meaningless combination "The fact you finished."

(3) Incomplete or missing integration of the meanings expressed in the noun phrase and in the noun phrase complement. When hearing a sentence such as "The fact that you finished your work pleases me," learning disabled children may fail to form a complete and expanded meaning of the concept *fact*. They may integrate and synthesize the meaning of only parts of the complement, such as "that you finished" or "your work" with the meaning of the noun phrase. As a consequence, the interpreted sequences could be "The fact that you finished pleases me" or "The fact your work pleases me," both of which convey a different meaning than the original sentence.

*Sentences with Nonembedded Relative Clauses*

Nonembedded relative clauses follow the main clause of a sentence. They provide added meaning for the object stated in the main clause. The nonembedded relative clause may be introduced by one of the relative pronouns *who, which, that,* or *whose*. Sentences with nonembedded relative clauses that follow patterns such as the sentence "Mother gave the cake to the woman *who* lives next door" may be processed in part by using the perceptual strategy appropriate for active declarative sentences. The main clause "Mother gave the cake to the woman" follows the rule that the noun phrase that contains the subject of the action precedes the verb phrase. It also follows the rule that the verb precedes the second noun phrase, which contains the direct and indirect objects. It is not until the relative clause "who lives next door" has to be processed and its meaning integrated with that of the main clause that the children need to change strategies. In order to integrate and synthesize the meanings of the two clauses, the children must identify the reference for the relative clause. They must also reprocess the main clause in order to arrive at an expanded and specified meaning. The appended relative clause also adds to the length of the sentence and may therefore tax the short-term auditory memory.

Learning disabled children may find it difficult to:
(1) Retain and recall the appended relative clause.
(2) Retain and recall the main clause after hearing the relative clause.
(3) Integrate the meaning of the relative clause with that of the main clause to form an expanded and better specified meaning.
(4) Associate the meaning of the relative clause with the intended reference.

When learning disabled children and adolescents hear the sentence "Mother gave the cake to the woman who lives next door," some may recall and process only the main clause "Mother gave the cake to the woman," resulting in a partial, indefinite, and unspecified interpretation of the meaning of the original sentence. Other learning disabled children and adolescents may no longer remember the main clause once they hear the relative clause, and therefore only interpret the phrase "who lives next door." They may believe that what was intended to function as a relative clause in a larger context is actually a question, as in "Who lives next door?" or that it expresses uncertainty in the speaker.

Some learning disabled children and adolescents may recall both the main and relative clause accurately, but may fail to integrate and synthesize the meaning of the two clauses. Essentially, they may hear two disconnected messages, one "Mother gave the cake to the woman" and the next "Who lives next door?" Others may associate the relative clause with the wrong reference. In the sentence "Mother gave the cake to the woman who lives next door," they may associate the meaning of the relative clause with the subject, leading to the interpretation that "Mother, who lives next door, gave the cake to the woman."

### Sentences with Embedded Relative Clauses

Embedded relative clauses follow the subject of the main clause. They occupy a position between the subject and the predicate and add meaning to the stated subject. The embedded relative clause may be introduced by one of the relative pronouns *who, which,* or *that*. When you hear a sentence with an embedded relative clause, as in the sentence "The children *who live in Boston* left by plane this morning," the perceptual strategy used with active declarative sentences must be changed to allow you to recall, interpret, and synthesize the meaning of the relative clause with that of the main clause. The problems learning disabled children and adolescents have with sentences with one embedded relative clause are similar to those they have with noun phrase complements positioned between the noun and the verb phrase and with sentences with nonembedded relative clauses. Their difficulties may again be attributed primarily to short-term memory deficits, which may lead to partial and incomplete recall and retention and subsequent interpretation of selected words, phrases, and clauses. The problems in remembering all of the sentence when it contains an embedded relative clause may result in:

(1) Recall and interpretation of the main clause only, as in processing the clause "The children left by plane this morning" and disregarding the specification intended by the relative clause.
(2) Recall and interpretation of the embedded relative clause only, as in processing the clause "who live in Boston" in isolation and out of context.
(3) Recall and interpretation of unrelated words and phrase segments, as in processing the sequence "The children live in Boston by plane."
(4) Partial or missing integration and synthesis of the meaning of the main clause and the embedded relative clause. This may result in interpreting the two as independent sentences, as in "The children left by plane this morning" and "Who live(s) in Boston?"

In addition, learning disabled children may show inaccurate perception and association between the embedded relative clause and the referent. This occurs especially when the sentence contains two **animate** nouns, as in "The *children* who live in Boston left with their *aunt* on a plane this morning." In this case, they may associate the meaning of the relative clause with the noun "aunt," misinterpreting the sentence meaning. A similar problem may arise if the noun clause contains a coordinated subject, as in the sentence *"The children and their aunt who live in Boston left by plane this morning."* In that case, they may associate and synthesize the meaning of the relative clause with only one of the subjects—either *children* or *aunt*. Either process would result in an incomplete interpretation of the sentence meaning.

Unfortunately for learning disabled children and other people with memory problems, sentences may contain more than one embedded relative clause. They may be coordinated, as in the sentence "The boy *who did not score the winning touchdown* or *get carried off the field* but *who played an outstanding defensive game* was named the best player of the year." They may also be nested, as in the sentence "The boy *who is sitting under the big tree eating an ice cream sundae* (which) *he bought at the drugstore* is my brother."

When a sentence contains multiple embeddings of relative clauses, its sheer length may surpass the listener's short-term auditory memory span. It may also tax his or her ability to form coherent perceptual-conceptual units such as phrases and clauses. In addition, the task of forming and retaining accurate associations among the relative clauses and their many referents may become staggering in sentences with two or more embedded or nested relative clauses.

Learning disabled children and adolescents may feel the effects of these conditions with extra force if their short-term memory abilities are not up to par to the task. When hearing sentences with multiple embedded relative clauses, they may be overwhelmed. They may be totally unable to retain, recall, or interpret any of the words, phrases, or clauses contained in the sequence. If pressed, they may invent an interpretation related to the general context of the conversation. They may also invent silly, nonsense, wild, and sometimes naughty interpretations. Some learning disabled children withdraw their attention and stop listening to the speaker as soon as they realize that they cannot cope with the length or complexity of the sentence. They may never refocus their attention and may move on to other activities such as fidgeting, doodling, or grooming. Their problems in processing and interpreting spoken sentences with multiple embedded or nested relative clauses tend to be duplicated in reading, speaking, and writing and may adversely influence all activities which require higher level language functions.

## Ambiguous Sentences

Ambiguous sentences have more than one possible meaning or interpretation. This may lead to uncertainty and confusion in their interpretation, unless they are tied directly to an immediate context which can clarify the vagueness. When confronted with an ambiguous sentence, the learning disabled child may focus on one interpretation only. If that interpretation does not match the intended meaning of the speaker, the child may become more and more confused while attempting to reconcile the inconsistencies. For instance the sentence "The restaurant even serves crabs" spoken and heard out of context may mystify a child. The child may interpret the statement to tell that in the restaurant in question they serve not only people, but also that ferocious crabs with big claws may be seated at the tables and be served dinner. Puzzled by this unusual image, the child may react as if he had heard a joke, and he may fail to hear the next statements. He may also be slowed down by his processing of the ambiguous sentence, and that delay may make him out of phase in listening to further comments by the speaker.

Ambiguity in the interpretation of English sentences may arise when:

(1) One or more words in a sentence has dual or multiple meanings, as in the sentence "She wiped her *glasses*."
(2) The surface structure can be resolved into alternative clauses by changes in bracketing. For example, the sentence "She told *her baby stories*" has two alternative interpretations arising from different resolutions of the clause "her baby stories." On one level, this phrase can be interpreted as the indirect object, "her [personal] baby stories," meaning that she told stories from her early childhood. On a second level, the phrase can be interpreted to contain reference to a direct object, "stories," and an indirect object, "her baby"; or "She told stories to her baby."
(3) The deep structures of the two interpretations share little in common and differ in the subject-predicate-object relationships, as in the sentence "Flying planes can be dangerous." On one level, the phrase "flying planes" functions as the agent or subject of the condition. On the second level, "flying planes" can be resolved into "flying," the predicate or action, and "planes," the object of the action.

Chomsky (1965) postulates that the steps in processing and interpreting logical sentences proceed as follows:

(1) Appreciation of the underlying meaning (deep structure).
(2) Resolution of the sentence structure (surface structure).
(3) Interpretation of the words (lexical content).

Based on this model of sentence processing, ambiguities involving the underlying structure should be discovered and processed more readily than ambiguities involving the syntactic or lexical (word) levels. Lexical ambiguities should be the most difficult to interpret.

However, several subsequent investigations of the resolution of ambiguous sentences have reported results that contradict Chomsky's early model. In fact, lexical ambiguities have been observed to be perceived and interpreted most easily, followed by syntactic (surface structure) ambiguities and then ambiguities involving the underlying structure. Three major theoretical models for processing ambiguities have been proposed in the literature. They are:

(1) The oblivion hypothesis (MacKay, 1966).
(2) The exhaustive computation hypothesis (Fodor & Garrett, 1966).
(3) The unitary perception hypothesis (Carey, Mehler, & Bever, 1970).

The *oblivion hypothesis* proposes that the meaning of an ambiguous word or phrase may not be seen until the ambiguity is resolved on the basis of the nonambiguous context of a sentence. The presence of an ambiguity interferes with the assignment of any interpretation to an ambiguous sentence, thus preventing processing of the utterance for some period of time. According to this hypothesis, an ambiguous sentence such as "The man kept the watch" would not be resolved unless the content of the surrounding sentences specified that the man was either (1) visiting a jeweler to buy a watch or (2) on the bridge of a ship on the look-out.

The *exhaustive computation hypothesis* postulates that all possible readings of an ambiguity are computed by the listener and that only pragmatic and syntactic biases result in the selection of a single reading for attention and recall afterwards. According to this hypothesis, the listener who heard the sentence "The man kept the watch" would immediately interpret all alternative meanings and select the appropriate one later, on the basis of information presented subsequently that clarified the context of the ambiguous statement.

The *unitary perception hypothesis* states that "under certain syntactic and pragmatic circumstances, only those semantic and syntactic relations [of ambiguous sentences] pertaining to a single structural description will be perceived and processed" (Carey, Mehler, & Bever, 1970, p. 244). In support of this theory, Foss, Bever, and Silver (1968) observe that when a picture displayed after the presentation of an ambiguous sentence was appropriate to the most probable interpretation of an ambiguity, there was no difference in the reaction time to ambiguous and nonambiguous control sentences. According to this hypothesis, the listener who heard the sentence "The man kept the watch" would think of only the most probable meaning. In this case, it might be that a man who bought a new watch decided to keep it rather than exchange it.

Schultz and Pilon (1973) observe that, in normally developing children, the detection of word level (lexical) ambiguities was superior to that of surface structure (syntactic) ambiguities at about age 10 (grade 4). The detection of surface and deep structure ambiguities improved sharply at about age 12 (grade 6) and showed less changes during the period from 12 to 15 years.

Wiig, Gilbert, and Christian (1978) observed a similar developmental sequence in spite of differences in methodology. The greatest increase in the interpretation of word level (lexical) ambiguities by normally developing children was observed at about age 10 (grade 4). The greatest improvement in the interpretation of surface and deep structure ambiguities occurred at or about age 12 (grade 6). The normal developmental sequence and age levels for the interpretation of sentence ambiguities is outlined in Table 4.7 on p. 92.

Children with learning disabilities may feel uncertain in resolving the intended meaning of sentences with surface and deep structure ambiguities. Typically, learning disabled children misinterpret the syntactic ambiguities in which there is no one-to-one relationship between the surface structure and the meaning (deep) structure (Wiig, Semel, &

**TABLE 4.7**

*Development of ability to interpret sentence ambiguities*

| Type of Ambiguity | Example | Approximate Age of Acquisition |
|---|---|---|
| Word level (lexical). | She wiped her glasses. | 10 yr. |
| Surface structure (syntactic). | She told her baby stories. | 12 yr. |
| Deep structure (underlying). | Flying planes can be dangerous. | 12–15 yr. |

Abele, submitted for publication). As a result, they may misinterpret sentences such as "Jane saw Tom walking across the street," "John found a book on Broadway," or "Mary saw the skyscrapers flying over New York." The problems of learning disabled children when they encounter ambiguous sentences may be reflected in:

(1) Rigid focusing on the concrete interpretation of syntactically ambiguous sentences, in spite of previous experience with the alternative and more abstract interpretations.

(2) Failure to perceive the alternative interpretations of syntactically ambiguous sentences.

(3) Difficulties in reauditorizing and rephrasing (rebracketing) sentences with surface structure ambiguities.

(4) Difficulties in reauditorizing, perceiving, and interpreting the alternative subject-predicate-object relationships possible in sentences with deep structure ambiguities.

(5) Impulsive fixation on an incorrect interpretation and failure to verify the intended meaning on the basis of existing contextual cues.

(6) Partial, incomplete interpretation of a syntactic ambiguity as a result of substitutions of key words.

(7) Difficulties in deciding upon any one of the alternative interpretations of an ambiguous sentence.

(8) Failure to perceive the significant features of stress, pitch, and juncture that may serve as cues to the interpretation of an ambiguity.

(9) Difficulties in finding the appropriate words for rewording syntactically ambiguous sentences to clarify structural uncertainties.

# FORMING SENTENCES
## Assessment

# 5

Assume that I, the author, were given the task to evaluate your, the reader's, knowledge and use of the English word and sentence formation rules. You might want to ask me a series of questions about the procedure I would use. You might want to ask me some of these questions:

- When do you feel it is most appropriate for you to observe me?
- Where, in what situations, and with whom do you want to observe me, in order to get the best estimate of my knowledge and use of English?
- How long do you feel you need to observe me in order to get the best estimate of my linguistic competence?
- How do you plan to analyze the language used in the interactions you will observe?

In asking these questions, you would have identified some of the major concerns of the clinician-educator who is involved in the evaluation of linguistic abilities. Specifically, you would have addressed yourself to the questions of:

(1) The best timing of a language evaluation.
(2) The situational context of the evaluation.
(3) The presence or absence of interpersonal interactions in the evaluation and the naturalness of the language observed.
(4) The time required for the evaluation or the size of the language sample needed for a valid judgment of the linguistic competence.
(5) The critical linguistic structures that should be evaluated or the structural nature of the language sample needed for an evaluation.
(6) The adequacy of the linguistic analysis used to evaluate the language observed.

Ideally, we might say, an experienced observer should follow you around for at least a week to get an accurate picture of your linguistic knowledge and performance. You must be observed while you interact and talk with your peers, parents, superiors, and with strangers. You should be observed while speaking, while taking class notes, and while writing letters, essays, or term papers. You should be observed at a time of day when you feel at your best as well as at a time of day when you are tired. You should be observed when happy as well as when angry or frustrated. All of these comments would tell you that I recognize that external factors influence your linguistic performance and the way in which you reflect your knowledge of the structural rules of English. They would also reflect my awareness that:

(1) The length of the observation and of the language sample influences the probability that it reflects actual linguistic knowledge and competence.
(2) The surface structure of spoken language may change as a function of the social or interpersonal context and constraints.
(3) The modality of expression, that is, whether it is spoken or written, may influence the surface structure **elaboration** of sentences.
(4) Fatigue may influence the linguistic performance negatively and therefore lower the chance that the estimate of linguistic competence will be accurate.
(5) Emotional state may influence the surface structure of sentences and the degree of structural and topical elaboration.
(6) The knowledge and application of linguistic rules is reflected in listening comprehension, in speaking in a monologue or in a dialogue, in reading, and in writing.
(7) The demands placed on auditory memory may limit the application of linguistic rules; excessive demands may decrease your performance in recalling sentences and paragraphs.

Returning to the task at hand, let us now consider some of the practical limitations faced by the clinician-educator involved in evaluating a child's or adult's knowledge and use of linguistic rules. The limitations are related to *time* and *location*. The educator-clinician is constantly faced with the need to evaluate a child's linguistic abilities and provide a differential diagnosis of linguistic deficits within a short time period, generally limited to 1 or 2 hours. Frequently the evaluation must be performed at a specified location, whether adequate or not, and with possibilities for interactions between the examinee and the examiner only. No one else is around. It is rarely possible to observe a child referred for language evaluation in a variety of settings and interactions, at different times of day, and over a prolonged period of time. Given these constraints, the clinician must select procedures for sampling and analysis that maximize both the information obtained within a limited time and the chance that he or she will obtain valid and reliable estimates of linguistic competence. This chapter discusses the assets and liabilities of many of the sampling and analysis procedures available to the clinician-educator.

# EVIDENCE OF KNOWLEDGE OF SYNTAX

As we have just discussed, a variety of factors—both external and internal to the speaker—may influence linguistic performance. As a result, a child's or adult's knowledge of the rules of language or his competence cannot be reliably inferred only from his or her perform- ance in using the language for speaking. To assess someone's actual knowledge of linguistic rules, the variables that influence performance should be recognized and controlled as carefully as possible.

Research studies on the sequences in which children learn the lin- guistic rules have used several different techniques to tap the child's generalizations about the language; in other words, his linguistic com- petence. These generalizations are developed through multiple expe- riences with the environment and verbal interactions with other people. They reflect the child's judgments about the form and structure of sentences and of their meanings. These generalizations, the rules the child uses, are reflected in his ability to perform one or more of the following tasks.

(1) Judge the grammaticality of sentences and differentiate well- formed sentences from grammatically incorrect utterances.
(2) Identify two sentences with the same underlying meaning which have surface structure differences by retrieving the shared underly- ing meaning, or deep structure.
(3) Differentiate sentences that are similar in their surface structure but differ in underlying meaning or deep structure.
(4) Perceive and resolve syntactic or deep structure ambiguities in sentences with more than one interpretation.

We assume that the normal adult speaker of a language reaches a level of linguistic maturity and competence that is reflected by accurate generalizations about the language. Let us consider each of the tasks listed above and relate them to actual judgments about language. Competent adult speakers find it easy to judge whether utterances are acceptable, grammatical sentences or not. They find it easy to judge and differentiate the grammaticality of utterances such as:

(1) She has washed plastic red small eight cups. (Violates adjective order)
She has bought five large brown leather cases. (Follows adjective order)

(2) Were the flowers delivered by the messenger? (Interrogative transfor- mation)
Were delivered the flowers by the messenger? (Violates phrase order)

(3) Pale luminous feelings blithely painted the ocean. (Follows syntactic rules but violates semantic rules)

**Adjectives** *and other words naming English structures are defined and illustrated in the Appendix.*

Competent adult speakers are also able to decide whether two sen- tences of different structure share the same meaning. As a result, the adult is able to tell that each of the sentence pairs below shares the same underlying meaning.

(1) The car followed the train. (Active declarative)
The train was followed by the car. (Passive)

(2) Did the police follow the car? (Interrogative)
Was the car followed by the police? (Passive interrogative)

(3) Didn't the rhinoceros cross the river? (Negative active interrogative)
Wasn't the river crossed by the rhinoceros? (Negative passive inter- rogative)

Sentences that are similar in surface structure but differ widely in underlying meaning are also easily distinguished by the adult speaker. For example, the competent adult immediately distinguishes the differences in the grammatical relationships between the noun "man" and the verbs in the two sentences below.

(1) The *man* was eager to please. (Subject)

(2) The *man* was easy to please. (Object)

Structural ambiguities in sentences are readily perceived and resolved by the competent adult speaker when they occur within a context. A sentence contains a structural ambiguity when a listener can interpret it in more than one way by processing the surface structure according to different conceptual structures. The following sentences feature structural ambiguities.

(1) She likes small dogs and cats.
   **Interpretations:**    She likes small dogs and all cats.
                           She likes all cats and small dogs.

(2) She told her baby stories.
   **Interpretations:**    She told stories to her baby.
                           She told her stories about babies.
                           She told stories of her early childhood.

(3) Flying planes can be dangerous.
   **Interpretations:**    It can be dangerous to fly planes.
                           Planes that are flying can be dangerous.

There are other methods of tapping linguistic competence that have been used by linguists investigating language development and language disorders. For example, some linguists observe and describe the rules or the grammar reflected in young children's spontaneous speech. Their observations have resulted in detailed grammars for child language (Brown, 1973; Slobin, 1971). A different and more stringent method of investigating rule learning assesses the child's ability to use a linguistic rule in an unfamiliar context. This method was used by Berko (1958) to explore developmental sequences for acquiring word formation rules (morphology). Berko created nonsense words that were associated with cartoons. The children had to form plurals, possessives, progressive and past tenses, and comparatives and superlatives of these nonsense words by extending the English inflectional rules. They were also asked to derive nouns and adverbs by rule extension.

Yet another method of uncovering the child's knowledge of linguistic rules uses self-corrections as evidence. In this method, the child's monitoring of his spoken sentences and his resulting corrections give examples of the structural models he has learned. In a related method, the child is given a model sentence and asked to paraphrase it. Finally, the speaker may be asked direct questions about the structural aspects of language to evaluate his linguistic awareness. This method attempts to uncover the child's or adult's ability to think about language and to comment on it, a skill which is developed relatively late in childhood.

At the present time, the standardized clinical-educational tests of linguistic development do not use any of the methods we have just described. Instead, to allow for the constraints of the clinical setting, they use one or more specific circumscribed tasks, from which the clinician evaluates the child's linguistic skill. Let us now look at some of the formats that are commonly used.

### Task Formats Used in Formal Assessment of Syntax

*The Spontaneous Speech Sample*

Analyzing the child's spontaneous language, as reflected in a speech sample, has several advantages over other methods of sampling language behavior. First, this method introduces fewer constraints on the child than do structured language tests. Second, children may produce syntactic structures in spontaneous speech that are not evident in elicited language samples (Prutting, Gallagher, & Mulac, 1975). Third, this sampling and the subsequent analysis provides the clinician with evidence of the child's productive language capacity in interpersonal interactions in natural settings. It may therefore be considered to be highly valid. A spontaneous speech sample may be the most suitable method for evaluating which morphological and syntactic rules and structures the child has learned well enough to use readily in his language.

Analysis of a spontaneous speech sample has limitations, however. Among them are the size of the sample required. In standard clinical situations, the spontaneous speech sample consists of 50 to 100 utterances. In contrast, the spontaneous speech samples analyzed in basic research studies of children's language acquisition will contain from 300 to 800 or more utterances. In these larger samples, situational cues such as the topic of conversation, the task at hand, the age, sex, and familiarity of the examiner, and the structure of the examiner's questions appear to have fewer negative effects. When a relatively small language sample is analyzed, these factors may influence the quantity as well as the structural qualities of the child's speech (Cazden, 1970b).

A second limitation of the clinical analysis of a spontaneous speech sample relates to the quality of the analysis. In research on syntactic development, the investigation will often come up with a full grammar for each child, based on the structural regularities in the language sample. In a clinical assessment, this task is not practical. The size of the sample and the training required to master the analytic technique, as well as the time required for the linguistic analysis of a large sample of utterances, may be prohibitive. The methods of analysis used in clinical settings have, therefore, usually focused on specific selected aspects of language structure. Among these measures are the mean length of utterance (MLU) and the developmental sentence scoring (DSS) techniques.

*See pages 101–4 for more on these techniques.*

*Grammatical Contrasts*

A method of evaluating a child's ability to understand and produce phrases and sentences that contain minimal grammatical contrasts was introduced in experimental tests of syntax (Fraser, Bellugi, & Brown, 1963). It has since been applied in a series of standardized and commercially available tests of syntactic development. In this method, a sentence or a sentence-pair is presented in association with two or more pictorial choices. The child is required to identify the picture or pictures which best represent the meaning of the sentence or sentences presented. The pictorial choices are designed so that at least one of the pictures illustrates the meaning of a sentence that contains a minimal grammatical contrast when compared to the stimulus sentence. The item below illustrates a sentence comprehension test designed to assess the ability to differentiate minimal grammatical contrasts (Semel & Wiig, 1980). The stimulus sentence for the item is *Mother asked: "Who is that?"* The three pictorial foils, shown in Figure 5.1, illustrate the following grammatically contrasting sentences:

(1) Mother asked: *"What* is that?"

(2) *Father* asked: *"What* is that?"

(3) *Father* asked: *"Who* is that?"

**FIGURE 5.1**

Source: Semel, E. M., & Wiig, E. H. *Comprehensive Evaluation of Language Functions: Processing Word and Sentence Structure.* Columbus, Ohio: Charles E. Merrill, 1980.

Adequate performance on this kind of phrase and sentence comprehension test depends upon acquisition of several basic skills. First,
the vocabulary used in the items must be familiar to the child. Second,
the child must be familiar with and have learned strategies for processing the syntactic-grammatic contrasts featured. Third, the child must
have adequate auditory memory for the length and structure of the
spoken sentences. Fourth, the child must be able to differentiate minimal grammatical contrasts that depend upon phoneme discrimination
or differences in word order. To do this requires both phonemic discrimination skills and sequential memory ability.

When using a test of the differentiation of grammatical contrasts, the
clinician should be aware that the design of the test itself affects the
probability that the child will respond correctly. When four pictorial
choices are given, the child has a 25% chance of choosing the right
answer at random. If the number of choices is reduced to three, the
probability of a chance correct response increases to 33%. If there are
only two choices, the probability of a chance correct response is 50%
and there is an additional complication. One of the pictorial choices in a
set of three may be an easily detected decoy or unrelated sentence
(Carrow, 1973). In that case, if the child eliminates the decoy, the
probability of a correct response is no longer 33%, but closer to 50%.
Therefore, the educator-clinician should consider the relative probabilities of a chance correct response to each and the contents of the
pictorial choices when he or she evaluates a test of grammatical contrasts. Unfortunately, most tests of grammatical contrasts do not provide an adequate overview of the contrasts featured in each test item.
This limitation makes the examiner's calculations of the probability of a
correct response more difficult. It is also more difficult to analyze the
bases for error responses.

*See pages 104–10 for reviews
of specific tests which use
this format.*

*Sentence Imitation*

The child's knowledge and control of syntactic rules and structures
may also be assessed using sentence imitation tasks. In this procedure,
the examiner reads selected sentence structures and transformations.
The child is asked to immediately recall and repeat the sentences.
Sentence imitation has been used extensively to assess the linguistic
competence of children, adolescents, and adults. It has been found to
differentiate, among others, language disordered and normally developing children, learning disabled and academically achieving adolescents, and brain-damaged **aphasic** and normal adults (Menyuk,
1964; Menyuk & Looney, 1972a; Newcombe & Marshall, 1967; Rosenthal, 1970; Wiig & Roach, 1975).

The question for the clinician-educator is whether the structures that
the child can imitate are also part of the child's spontaneous language
repertory. Early studies suggested that the child's grammar is the same
in spontaneous speech as in the spontaneous imitations of the speech
of adults (Ervin, 1964). In contrast, Menyuk (1964) observed that children are able to control more syntactic structures in elicited sentence
imitation than in spontaneous speech. The conflict in these two studies
may be related to the difference between spontaneous imitation and

elicited imitation. When a child spontaneously repeats sentences produced by adults, the child controls the structures that will be imitated. When the child is asked to repeat model sentences spoken by an experimenter, the structures to be imitated have been selected for him. He may be able to imitate a larger proportion of selected structures than he would produce on his own.

Experimental evidence consistently indicates that there are interactions between syntactic structure, semantic aspects, and memory for sentences. The surface structure of sentences appears to be processed in short-term auditory memory; and the memory for sentence structure is, therefore, not long lasting. In contrast, memory for the meaning, or deep structure, of sentences can be preserved over time; it appears to be processed in long-term memory. It has also been found that syntactic structures that are not directly related to the meaning tend to be omitted in the imitation of sentences (McNeill, 1970). This relationship between short-term auditory memory and sentence structure suggests that the educator-clinician should evaluate the child's memory capacity for verbal stimuli that are not related by linguistic structure. The individual child's memory capacity should be considered in interpreting his responses to a sentence imitation task. The best technique is to increase the length of the model sentences introduced to the child to the point where the child's memory capacity is stretched. If the clinician does not do this, the child may be able to repeat the sentences correctly, even though he has not learned the featured syntactic structures and transformations well enough to use them in spontaneous speech. Sentence imitation tests should, therefore, feature sentences of increasing length as well as complexity.

The sentences should contain familiar and unfamiliar lexical items. When the words in the model sentences are of relatively low frequency or are unfamiliar to the child, his imitations may indicate how well he used his syntactic knowledge to facilitate sentence recall.

Most sentence imitation tasks feature only syntactically accurate and semantically meaningful sentences. In these sentences, the child can use word and underlying sentence meaning (deep structure) to help recall the surface structure. Newcombe and Marshall (1967) increased the information available from the sentence imitation task by including grammatical sentences in which the word choices violated the semantic rules. They thereby kept the child from depending on word or underlying sentence meaning for recall. They also included sentences which were not grammatical but where the word choices followed semantic rules. In addition, they included random strings of words in which neither the structure nor the words nor the underlying meaning could facilitate the child's recall. Newcombe and Marshall found that the task of recalling utterances that violated either the syntactic, semantic, or syntactic-semantic rules for sentence formation differentiated left-hemisphere damaged, aphasic adults from right-hemisphere damaged and nonbrain-damaged adults. In a related study, recall of these sentences was also found to differentiate learning disabled and academically achieving adolescents (Wiig & Roach, 1975). With these findings as a background, Semel and Wiig (1980) have developed a

*For discussions of formats to use for informal or supplementary testing of a child's knowledge of syntax as well as for intervention, see pages 116–20 and Table 5.2.*

sentence imitation test that features meaningful as well as syntactically and semantically varied sentences. The rest of this chapter reviews selected standardized tests of morphology and syntax, with emphasis on content analysis, validity, and reliability.

*See pages 110–16 for reviews of specific tests which use the sentence imitation format.*

## SELECTED TESTS OF SYNTAX

### Analysis of Spontaneous Speech Samples

*Mean Length of Utterances (MLU)*

This method of analyzing a spontaneous speech sample was introduced by Nice (1925) and has since been used extensively in studies of language development (Brown, 1973; McCarthy, 1930; Templin, 1957). The MLU measure is obtained from a spontaneous speech sample of 50 consecutive utterances. The examiner counts the number of words in each of the utterances of the sample, totals the count, and divides by 50 to obtain the mean length for the utterances. This measure, although relatively simple, has been found to be the best single measure of length of utterances for assessing language development. It correlates positively (.80) with psychological scale values of degree of language development (Shriner & Sherman, 1967). Furthermore, specific aspects of syntactic development correlate with MLU measures based on the mean number of morphemes used (Brown, 1973). Normative data for MLU based on mean number of words used have been reported for the age range from 1 year, 9 months to 9 years, 5 months based on the results of nine developmental studies (Johnson, Darley, & Spriestersbach, 1963).

Shriner (1969) discusses the assets and liabilities of Mean Length of Utterances (MLU) as a measure of expressive language development. MLU can vary as a function of manipulations by the examiner and certain situations. Furthermore, with age the density of ideas in a single sentence increases, along with the number of embeddings (Cazden, 1972; Hass & Wepman, 1974). MLU does not reflect these changes in the "quality" of the utterances. Therefore, it provides very little information about changes in control over morphology and syntax as a function of age, past the early stages of language development.

Among assets of this method of analyzing a spontaneous speech sample are:

(1) The relative ease of obtaining a spontaneous speech sample of the size needed for the analysis.
(2) The naturalness and therefore the validity of the language sample.
(3) The extreme ease of analysis and scoring.

These assets are counterbalanced by limitations. Among them are:

(1) The variability of the reliability of the MLU measure, caused by external factors.
(2) The inability of MLU to reflect the structural characteristics of the child's productive language past the early stages of development.

## Developmental Sentence Analysis

This method of analyzing a spontaneous speech sample is designed to provide a quantitative measure of the use of syntactic structures in spontaneous language formulation and production (Lee, 1974). Eight grammatical form categories were selected to provide an index of syntactic development. These grammatical categories have the most significant developmental progression in children's language. They are:

(1) Indefinite pronouns and noun modifiers.
(2) Personal pronouns.
(3) Main verbs.
(4) Secondary verbs.
(5) Negatives.
(6) Conjunction.
(7) Interrogative reversals.
(8) *Wh-* questions.

A spontaneous speech sample consisting of 50 complete sentences is analyzed and scored to obtain quantitative measures, called *Developmental Sentence Scores* (DSS). The spontaneous speech sample is recorded on audio tape for subsequent transcription and analysis. The manual (Lee, 1974) discusses methods for obtaining a representative spontaneous speech sample in a clinical setting. Among stimulus materials that can be used to stimulate the child's verbalizations are toys, pictures, and illustrations for a familiar story. Specific stimulus pictures are suggested from a preprimer series and from a rendition of the story "The Three Bears" (Robinson, Monroe, & Artley, 1962a; Utley, 1950).

*There are many techniques which can be used to elicit a spontaneous speech sample. They include asking a youngster to (1) retell a story, (2) tell about a television program he watched, (3) describe an illustration of a complex or humorous situation, (4) tell about a hobby, pet, or sports event, (5) tell about a special event such as his last birthday or a vacation, or (6) complete an open-ended story.*

The manual provides comprehensive guidelines for the analysis of the sentences in the spontaneous speech sample. They make allowances for articulation errors, nonfluencies, grammatical reformulations, and word-finding incidences. The data subjected to the analysis must consist of a block of 50 consecutive utterances in the form of complete sentences. The analysis technique allows the examiner to exclude incomplete and fragmentary sentences, stereotyped repetitions, unintelligible utterances, and echoed utterances.

In the Developmental Sentence Scoring (DSS) procedure, each grammatical form is scored independently using a weighted scoring system. The weighted scores represent a progressive sequence of grammatical growth for each category. The weighted scores range from 1 to 8 points for most of the eight grammatical form categories. In addition, a "sentence point" score of 1 is added for each sentence that meets adult English standards. The child does not receive this sentence point for semantic irregularities, omissions or confusions of syntactic rules and structures, and word order changes. A reweighted DSS scoring system and samples of analyzed spontaneous speech are presented (Charts 8, 10, 12, 14, 15). In addition, the scoring criteria for each grammatical form category are described in detail (pp. 138–163). The final Developmental Sentence Score (DSS) reflects the mean value or the sum of the individual sentence scores divided by the number of sentences analyzed.

The DSS procedure was standardized on a sample of 160 middle-class children, ranging in age from 3 years, 0 months to 6 years, 11 months. All resided in a Midwestern suburban area. Normative data are presented in the form of selected percentiles for DSS for the age range from 3 years, 0 months to 6 years, 11 months at 1-year age intervals. The DSS of an individual child may also be judged against the mean score for a lower age group to obtain an estimate of language delay. Successive DSS measures may be used to evaluate the child's progress during language training. The author stresses that the analysis measures the degree of delay in the acquisition of syntactic structures in spontaneous speech. It does not purport to provide a differential diagnosis of **etiology** or handicapping condition. An adaptation of the Developmental Sentence Analysis method has been developed for Spanish-speaking children (Toronto, 1972).

**Etiology** is the cause of a disease or handicapping condition.

The performances by the standardization group have gone through extensive statistical analysis. The evidence indicates significant increases in syntax usage, as indicated by DSS measures, as a function of age. The most discriminating DSS categories were Main Verbs, Conjunctions, and Indefinite Pronouns-Noun Modifiers. The rank order of the remaining DSS categories from the most to the least discriminating was: personal pronouns, secondary verbs, negatives, sentences points, *wh-* questions, and interrogative reversals. Measures of length of utterances and DSS increased progressively with age.

Analysis of the internal consistency of the DSS indicated increasing consistency among components of the test and the total test as a function of age, with an overall reliability coefficient of .71. The **split-half reliability** coefficient was .73, indicating good internal consistency of measures. The DSS measures did not vary significantly as a result of changes in stimulus materials for four of the grammatical categories. However, there were significant differences in DSS with changes in stimuli for indefinite pronouns, personal pronouns, secondary verbs, and interrogative reversals. When the DSS measures for four repeated applications within 2-week period were compared, there was a significant trial effect. This suggests that the technique should be used only for the evaluation of long-term changes.

*In a trial effect, the subject learns the material or skill being tested during the test process.*

Lee (1974) has also suggested a separate analysis for Developmental Sentence Types (DST) for presentence utterances that are fragmentary and incomplete. This analysis is appropriate for preschoolers with significant language delays. In contrast, the Developmental Sentence Scoring (DSS) method is suggested for the analysis of syntactic structures that involve elaboration of the basic subject–predicate construction or sentence transformation.

Among the assets of the Developmental Sentence Analysis procedure and the DSS measures are:

(1) Analysis of a spontaneous conversational speech sample provides a natural measure of the syntactic structures that the child can use in expressive language.
(2) Analysis of conversational speech may reflect the child's linguistic performance in verbal interactions with peers, parents, teachers, and other significant adults.

(3) The results of the analysis may be used to formulate immediate prescriptive teaching goals.
(4) The results of the analysis may be applied directly in language training using Interactive Language Development Teaching as a procedure for intervention (Lee, Koenigsknecht, & Mulhern, 1975).

Among the liabilities of the Developmental Sentence Analysis are:

(1) The geographic, socioeconomic, and racio-ethnic bias of the standardization sample limits the use of the normative data to children of middle-class, standard American dialectical backgrounds.
(2) The test-retest reliability measures for intervals less than 4 months suggest that the normative data should be applied with caution.
(3) There is evidence of variations in the test scores due to variations in transcription and sampling procedures.
(4) The method of analysis and scoring of the spontaneous speech sample is time-consuming.

Other, more complex methods of analyzing a spontaneous language sample have been proposed by Crystal, Fletcher, and Garman (1975) and Tyack and Gottsleben (1974).

## Grammatical Contrasts in Sentence Comprehension

*Assessment of Children's Language Comprehension (ACLC)*

The ACLC was designed to assess basic receptive language skills (Foster, Giddan, & Stark, 1972). It attempts to determine the child's ability to process, recall, and interpret lexical items and syntactic sequences of increasing length. The purpose of the test is to assist the clinician-educator in determining the appropriate length of the syntactic sequences to teach in language intervention.

The test contains four separate sections which evaluate:

(1) The comprehension of 50 vocabulary items (30 nouns, 10 verbs, 5 adjectives, and 5 prepositions) introduced in the subsequent test sections.
(2) The comprehension of 10 sequences of 2 lexical items each.
(3) The comprehension of 10 sequences of 3 lexical items each.
(4) The comprehension of 10 sequences of 4 lexical items each.

The test format requires the child to point to the one pictorial choice from an array that best illustrates the meaning of the word or word sequence presented by the examiner. Each item is associated with an array of from three to five pictorial choices. For example, with the test item "CAT BEHIND THE BED" (Item 23), the child is given the following array of choices:

(1) A cat *on* a bed.
(2) A cat *behind* a bed.
(3) A cat behind a *table*.
(4) A *ball* behind a bed.

An analysis of the syntactic relationships implied in the word sequences indicates the following distribution:

(1) Subject-predicate (noun-verb) relationships are featured in 4 items (Items 11, 14, 17, 20).

(2) Modifier-noun (noun phrase) relationships, as in "little tree," are featured in 4 items (Items 13, 15, 18, 19).

(3) Coordination by "and" as in "car and balloon," is featured in 2 items (Items 12, 16).

(4) Expanded subject (modifier + noun)–predicate relationships, as in "happy lady sleeping," are featured in 2 items (Items 22, 25).

(5) Subject-predicate-object relationships, as in "boy riding the horse," are featured in 2 items (Items 26, 27).

(6) Conjunction deletion with coordinated subjects is featured in 1 item (Item 24).

(7) An expanded subject (modifier + noun)–predicate adjective relationship, as in "big fence broken," is featured in 1 item (Item 30).

(8) Subject–prepositional phrase relationships are featured in 4 items (Items 21, 23, 28, 29).

(9) An expanded subject (modifier + modifier + noun)–predicate relationship, as in "happy little girl jumping," is featured in 1 item (Item 31).

(10) Conjunction with coordination of two subject–predicate sequences is featured in 1 item (Item 32).

(11) Conjunction deletion with coordination of objects, as in "boy pulling wagon and car," is featured in 1 item (Item 36).

(12) An expanded subject–predicate–object (modifier + noun) sequence is featured in 1 item (Item 37).

(13) Subject–predicate–prepositional phrase relationships are featured in 5 items (Items 33, 34, 38, 39, 40).

The ACLC was standardized on 365 nursery school and kindergarten children from the West Coast. Normative data in the form of mean scores are presented for the age range from 3 years, 0 months to 6 years, 5 months.

Among the assets of the ACLC are:

(1) Administration and scoring are relatively easy and quick.

(2) The stimulus pictures (shaded drawings) are clear.

(3) A pre-test of the vocabulary featured in the items is provided.

(4) A group test form that permits screening of more than one child at a time is available.

(5) Suggestions for intervention procedures according to the child's assessed level of functioning are given.

However, the test does not provide measures of internal consistency of the items, test-retest reliability, and concurrent and diagnostic validity.

*Northwestern Syntax Screening Test (NSST)*

The Northwestern Syntax Screening Test is designed to screen for the ability to process and reproduce selected syntactic structures and transformations (Lee, 1971). The test contains two sections, Receptive and Expressive. Each section features 20 items, consisting of two semantically and syntactically contrasting sentences each. The items are associated with four pictorial choices each for the Receptive section and two pictorial choices each for the Expressive section.

An analysis of the grammatical contrasts featured in the sentence pairs in both the Receptive and Expressive subsections indicates the following contrasts:

 (1) Affirmative–negative.
 (2) Gender (male–female) of the third person subjective case pronoun.
 (3) Singular–plural forms of verbs marked by "is" and "are."
 (4) Noun singular–plural.
 (5) Present–past tense marked by inflectional endings.
 (6) Subject–object in the active voice.
 (7) Singular–plural of third person (noun-verb agreement).
 (8) Noun modification–noun possessive.
 (9) Present progressive–future tense.
(10) Animate–inanimate forms of the relative pronoun.
(11) Affirmative–interrogative marked by "is" and "has."
(12) Singular–plural marked by inflections.
(13) *Wh-* interrogatives ("where," "who").
(14) Subject–object in the passive voice.
(15) Demonstrative pronouns "this" and "that."
(16) Indirect object–direct object.

The examiner reads the Receptive items out loud. The child is required to identify the pictorial choices that best represent the two sentences read from among four choices. The examiner reads the Expressive items without indicating which of the two sentences in a pair is associated with each of the pictorial choices. Then the examiner points to each of the pictorial representations of the sentences, while asking "What is this one?" and "What's that one?" Only verbatim repetitions of the original sentence forms are scored as correct. Responses that are not grammatically identical are not acceptable even though the child has retained the intended grammatical distinction between the sentence pair. For example, Item 20 consists of the sentences "The man brings *the girl the boy*" and "The man brings *the boy the girl*." The responses "The man brings the boy *to* the girl" and "The man brings the girl *to* the boy," while grammatically identical, would be scored as incorrect. This procedure is justified on the basis that the grammatical structure being tested "may have introduced enough complexity to cause the [specific structure] to be dropped." The NSST was standardized on 242 children, ranging in age from 3 years, 0 months to 7 years, 11 months. All came from middle- and upper-class suburban communities. Normative data are presented for scores which fall at the 90th, 75th, 50th, and 10th percentiles for each age level. Critical cut-off points (10th percentile) are presented at 1-year intervals. The cut-off points indicate the need for language training. Test-retest reliability and concurrent validity measures are not reported. A Spanish version of the test is available (Toronto, 1973).

The limitations of the NSST as a critical indicator for language training needs at the present time outweigh its assets. Among the most severe negative features are:

(1) The bias of the standardization sample, which restricts generalization of the normative data to standard American English speaking, middle- or upper-class suburban children.
(2) The lack of measures of test-retest reliability, internal consistency, and concurrent validity in the presence of the clinical-diagnostic claims.

*Test for Auditory Comprehension of Language (TACL)*

This test is designed to provide an in-depth assessment of the child's ability to process linguistic structures and analyze error response patterns according to grammatical categories (Carrow, 1973). The test contains 101 items grouped by grammatical category. Each item is associated with three pictorial choices. The test items are grouped in major categories to permit the examiner to analyze error responses according to structural category. The featured grammatical categories include:

(1) Vocabulary (Items 1 to 41).
(2) Morphology (Items 42 to 88 and 98).
(3) Syntax (Items 89 to 101).

The vocabulary items featured include (1) 12 nouns, (2) 18 adjectives denoting color, quantity, and quality, (3) 7 verbs, and (4) 3 adverbs. The morphological and selectional rules assessed under Morphology are (1) noun derivation (6 items), (2) noun plural (4 items), (3) superlative forms of adjectives (3 items), (4) verb forms (18 items), (5) pronouns (8 items), (6) prepositions (6 items), and (7) *wh-* interrogative forms (3 items). The syntax items feature (1) 2 simple, 4 complex, and 1 compound imperatives, (2) 2 phrases that assess noun–verb agreement, (3) 2 noun phrases with 2 modifiers each, and (4) 1 direct–indirect object transformation.

The pictorial choices associated with each item are three black line drawings. One of the choices for each item illustrates the meaning of the word or morphological or syntactic structure being tested. The foils illustrate either two semantic or grammatical contrasts of the stimulus word, phrase, or sentence, or one grammatical contrast and one decoy. The child is required to point to the picture which best represents the meaning of the word, phrase, or sentence spoken by the examiner.

The test was standardized on a sample of 200 middle-class Black, Anglo, and Mexican-American children residing in the Southwest. The children ranged in age from 3 years, 0 months to 6 years, 11 months. The reported 2-week test-retest reliability coefficients are .94 for the English version of the test and .93 for a Spanish version. Concurrent validity has been established with several clinical groups, ranging from deaf children to children with diagnosed language disorders. Mean and median performance scores and percentile ranks are presented for each of eight age levels in the age range from 3 years, 0 months to 6 years, 11 months. Age expectations in percentiles (75th and 90th) are also presented for each of the items.

There are both English and Spanish language versions of the TACL. A Screening Test for Auditory Comprehension (STAC) was developed in 1972. It consists of 25 of the items featured in the comprehensive test. The screening test may be administered to groups of children. Cut-off scores, generally the 10th or 20th percentile, are provided to determine the need for in-depth assessment of language comprehension.

Among the assets of the TACL are the:

(1) Relative ease of administration.
(2) Analysis form provided to discern error response patterns within grammatical categories.
(3) Availability of grammatical category subscores and percentiles for each of the items. This feature permits easy assessment of a child's gains as a result of maturation and/or intervention.

Among the limitations of the test are the:

(1) Geographic and socioeconomic biases of the standardization sample.
(2) Relatively small sample size (25 children at each age level) upon which the norms are based.
(3) Short time-interval employed in assessing test-retest stability, which may have resulted in spuriously high reliability measures.
(4) Lack of consistency and clarity of the directions given to the child.
(5) Dependence of the performance on morphology and syntax items upon specific vocabulary knowledge.
(6) Ambiguity in the classification scheme used to categorize items into grammatical categories.
(7) Uncommon contexts in which some concepts, such as *left*, *up*, and *middle*, are introduced.

Specific limitations of the Spanish version of the TACL are discussed by Rueda and Perozzi (1977). They include the fact that a negative correlation was obtained between performances on the Spanish version of the TACL and the Screening Test of Spanish Grammar (STSG). These authors concluded that, since the Spanish TACL uses a direct translation of English, its validity is dubious. The syntactic structures featured in the Spanish screening test are, in contrast, derived directly from the Spanish idiom, increasing its validity.

## *Test of Language Development (TOLD): Grammatic Understanding*

The TOLD Grammatic Understanding subtest is designed to evaluate the child's ability to process selected syntactic structures (Newcomer & Hammill, 1977). The child is required to listen to spoken sentences and to identify pictorial representations of the underlying meaning of each of them. Each sentence is associated with a vertical array of three pictorial choices, black line drawings. Of the three pictorial choices, one represents the deep structure or underlying meaning of the stimulus sentence. One represents the meaning of a semantically–grammatically contrasting sentence. The third choice represents either the meaning of a semantically–grammatically contrasting or of a related but not contrasting sentence.

The subtest contains 25 sentences. An analysis of the critical grammatical contrast featured in each item indicates the following distribution according to phrase structure or transformation:

(1) Adverbial phrase, predicate adjective, and complement contrasts are featured in 3 items (Items 1, 3, 8).
(2) Prepositional phrase contrasts are featured in 3 items (Items 4, 7, 15).
(3) Verb phrase contrasts are featured in 9 items (Items 11, 12, 16, 17, 19, 21, 23, 24, 25).
(4) Noun singular–plural and count noun contrasts are featured in 3 items (Items 9, 10, 12).
(5) Negative–affirmative contrasts are featured in 5 items (Items 2, 5, 6, 13, 14).
(6) Conjunction with coordinated clause contrast is featured in 1 item (Item 18).
(7) Embedded relative clause contrast is featured in 1 item (Item 20).
(8) Indirect object contrast is featured in 1 item (Item 22).

The TOLD was standardized on a sample of 1014 children, ranging in age from 4 years, 0 months to 8 years, 11 months. The demographic features of the sample closely matched the 1970 Census of Population and Housing (U.S. Department of Commerce). Normative data are presented in Language Ages in which raw scores on each of the subtests are converted to age equivalents. Scaled score equivalents for raw scores are presented for each 6-month interval throughout the age range from 4 years, 0 months to 8 years, 11 months. Measures of internal consistency, test-retest reliability, concurrent validity, and diagnostic validity are presented for each subtest.

The test-retest reliability coefficient reported for a sample of 21 children with a 5-day interval is .87. Concurrent validity coefficients for the relationship with the Northwestern Syntax Screening Test: Receptive (Lee, 1971) range from .33 at 8 years to .67 at 6 years.

The greatest asset of the TOLD Grammatic Understanding subtest is the demographic representativeness and the size of the standardization sample. This feature permits the examiner to apply the norms to a wide range of children. There are several liabilities of the subtest, however. Among them are:

(1) The small sample and the short time-interval used to assess test-retest reliability, which may have produced spuriously high correlation coefficients.
(2) The relatively high probability of a correct response (33% for most items, and higher for some).
(3) The minimal pictorial contrasts are often associated with sentence meaning representations that do not feature minimal grammatical contrasts in the surface structure.

*Clinical Evaluation of Language Functions (CELF): Processing Word and Sentence Structure*

*Other subtests of the CELF
are reviewed elsewhere in
this text.*

This subtest of the CELF is designed to assess the ability to process and interpret selected word and sentence structures and transformations (Semel & Wiig, 1980). The subtest contains 26 items. Each item features a sentence associated with four pictorial choices. One of the choices provides a pictorial representation of the meaning of the stimulus sentence. The three other choices feature pictorial representations of sentences with minimal grammatical contrasts. The word and sentence structures featured in the items are outlined below.

(1) Four items feature prepositional phrases with the prepositions "behind," "at," "between," and "from" (Items 1, 7, 8, and 15).
(2) Four items feature pronominalization with the pronouns "themselves" (reflexive), "her" (objective case), "mine" (possessive replacive), and "hers" (possessive) (Items 2, 19, 24, and 26).
(3) Three items feature verb phrases with the verb forms "is eating" (present progressive), "have dressed" (past participle), and "will build" (future) (Items 5, 6, and 20).
(4) One item features a noun plural, "tires" (Item 9).
(5) One item features a noun possessive (Item 22).
(6) Two items feature modifier (adjective) sequences (Items 11 and 18).
(7) Two items feature explicit negations ("not") (Items 23 and 25).
(8) Two items feature passive transformations (Items 10 and 25).
(9) Three items feature *wh-* interrogatives ("how much," "where," and "who") (Items 4, 14, and 17).
(10) One item features an indirect object transformation (Item 12).
(11) Four items feature relative clause transformations with embedding (Items 3, 13, 16, and 21).

Test-retest reliability was established with 30 randomly selected children in the age range from 8 years, 3 months to 8 years, 6 months. The subtest was readministered with a 6-week time interval. The test-retest correlation coefficient was .96, indicating good stability over time. Concurrent validity was established with the Northwestern Syntax Screening Test: Receptive (Lee, 1971). The concurrent validity coefficient was .53. Normative data have been established for the lowest 20 percent of children, as identified by the CELF Screening tests. The Clinical Evaluation of Language Functions is a criterion-referenced language test with criteria scores for each grade level from K through 10.

## Sentence Imitation

*Carrow Elicited Language Inventory (CELI)*

The CELI is designed to provide a systematic analysis of the child's knowledge and productive control of transformational rules and of the syntactic and semantic markers inherent in lexical items (Carrow, 1974). The test uses a sentence imitation procedure in which the child is required to repeat spoken model sentences verbatim. This procedure allows the examiner to analyze the grammatical forms and syntactic structures the child may be imitating but may not yet use in spontaneous speech.

The CELI contains 52 model utterances, of which one is a phrase and the remaining are complete sentences. The model sentences were chosen to include basic sentence types and specific grammatical morphemes and sentence transformations. The 51 complete and grammatical sentences have been cross-categorized as follows:

(1) 47 are in the active and 4 in the passive voice.
(2) 37 are affirmative and 14 are negative.
(3) 37 are declarative, 12 interrogative, and 2 imperative.

The grammatical categories and features include: nouns (59), noun plurals (8), verbs (103), adjectives (9), adverbs (12), pronouns (41), articles (41), negatives (13), prepositions (14), demonstratives (2), conjunctions (7), and contractions (12). Here are two examples of the items.

**Item 1.** Big girl (phrase).

**Item 52.** If it rains, we won't go to the beach.

An analysis of the structural and transformational characteristics of the items indicates the following distribution:

(1) A noun phrase is featured in 1 item (Item 1).
(2) Active declaratives with variations of basic Noun Phrase + Verb Phrase constructions are featured in 6 items (Items 2, 8, 9, 11, 32, 36).
(3) Active declarative with conjunction deletion is featured in 1 item (Item 3).
(4) Nominalization and complements are featured in 3 items (Items 4, 21, 23).
(5) Yes/no interrogative transformations are featured in 3 items (Items 5, 40, 41).
(6) Yes/no negative interrogative transformations are featured in 3 items (Items 22, 42, 43).
(7) Negative tag questions are featured in 2 items (Items 15, 16).
(8) Negation is featured in 6 items (Items 12, 13, 14, 17, 18, 19).
(9) *Wh-* interrogatives are featured in 3 items (Items 34, 38, 39).
(10) One *wh-* negative interrogative is featured (Item 44).
(11) One emphatic is featured (Item 6).
(12) Imperatives are featured in 3 items (Items 7, 37, 48).
(13) Comparative construction is featured in 1 item (Item 10).
(14) Intransitives, adverbial and prepositional phrases are featured in 4 items (Items 28, 29, 30, 31).
(15) Active declaratives with future tense markers, perfective constructions, and multiple auxiliaries and/or modals are featured in 5 items (Items 24, 25, 26, 27, 35).
(16) Conjunction with subordinated clauses is featured in 3 items (Items 20, 49, 52).
(17) Reversible passives are featured in 2 items (Items 45, 46).
(18) Direct–indirect and indirect–direct object transformations are featured in 2 items (Items 33, 47).
(19) Ask/tell transformations are featured in 2 items (Items 50, 51).

The child's imitations of the model phrase and sentences are recorded on audio tape to permit analysis of responses and of error patterns. The responses to each of the items are scored for error types as either substitutions, omissions, additions, transpositions, or reversals. The scoring and analysis forms that accompany the test provide a detailed scoring section and verb protocol that may prove of value in determining areas for educational or clinical intervention. The verb protocol classifies each verb as either modal, auxiliary, copula, verb, infinitive, or gerund. The structure of the sentences in which the verbs occur is specified as either declarative, interrogative, negative, or affirmative. The error type may be specified to reflect incorrectly formed tense, person, or number. The responses to the test items are scored to provide total error scores and subscores for each grammatical category and error type.

The CELI was standardized on a sample of 475 white, middle-class children residing in the Southwest. Two-week test-retest data indicate a test-retest reliability coefficient of .98 and an intertester reliability coefficient of .99 for a sample of 20 children. Concurrent validity was established with performances on the Developmental Sentence Scoring (Lee, 1974) of spontaneous speech. The concurrent validity coefficient was .79. Normative data for mean total error scores and mean subcategory error scores are provided at 1-year intervals for the age range from 3 years, 0 months to 7 years, 11 months. Percentile rank scores and **stanine scores** (normalized standard scores) are also provided to determine an individual child's relative performance in relation to the standardization sample.

The author describes the inventory as a diagnostic tool which may be used to (1) identify children with language problems, (2) determine which linguistic structures contribute to the child's inadequate linguistic performance, and (3) quantify language status. She cautions that performance problems may reflect auditory memory deficits and suggests that other tests need to be used for differential diagnosis.

Among assets of the CELI are:

(1) The relative ease and speed of administration.
(2) The availability of a detailed method of analysis for error response patterns.
(3) The availability of rules for scoring the responses by children with mild articulation disorders.

Among liabilities of the test are the following:

(1) The biases in the geographic, socioeconomic, and racio-ethnic characteristics limit generalizations beyond groups of children that share the characteristics of the standardization sample.
(2) There are no discussions of dialectical variations in morphology and syntax provided to assist the examiner in evaluating the appropriateness of a structurally deviant response against the standards of his background.
(3) The analysis of the model sentences does not include a breakdown by sentence transformation, limiting the immediate cross-referencing with other language samples and language tests.

*Test of Language Development (TOLD): Sentence Imitation*

The TOLD Sentence Imitation subtest was designed to evaluate the child's recall and productive control of syntactic structures (Newcomer & Hammill, 1977). The design focuses specifically upon the recall and retention of word order and grammatic markers. The child is required to repeat spoken model sentences verbatim. The two following items illustrate the format and contents.

**Item 3.** After the party, the boys fixed the car.

**Item 27.** Yesterday, we were saved from the clutches of an angry teacher.

The test contains 30 model sentences, ranging in length from 5 to 12 words. An analysis of the structural characteristics of the sentences indicates the following distribution:

(1) Affirmatives are featured in 7 sentences (Items 1, 2, 4, 16, 21, 27, 29).
(2) Negation is featured in 2 sentences (Items 8, 9).
(3) Negative tag questions are featured in 3 sentences (Items 13, 14, 15).
(4) Yes/no negative interrogatives are featured in 2 sentences (Items 7, 20).
(5) Conjunction with clause subordination is featured in 9 sentences (Items 3, 5, 10, 17, 18, 19, 22, 23, 28).
(6) Relative clause transformation is featured in 4 sentences (Items 11, 25, 26, 30).

The TOLD was standardized on a sample of 1014 children, ranging in age from 4 years, 0 months to 8 years, 11 months. The demographic features of the standardization group closely matched the 1970 Census of Population and Housing (U.S. Department of Commerce). Normative data are presented in Language Ages. Scaled score equivalents for raw scores are presented for each 6-month interval throughout the age range from 4 years, 0 months to 8 years, 11 months. The test-retest reliability coefficient obtained for a sample of 21 children with a 5-day interval between tests is .98. Concurrent validity coefficients for the relationship with the Detroit–Related Syllables (Baker & Leland, 1967) subtest range from .77 at 4 years to .89 at 6 years.

The strongest asset of the TOLD Sentence Imitation subtest is the representativeness and size of the standardization sample. Among liabilities of the subtest are:

(1) The short time-interval and the relatively small sample used to establish test-retest reliability, which may have resulted in a spuriously high correlation coefficient.
(2) The selection of vocabulary and the idiom seem slightly contrived.

*Detroit Tests of Learning Aptitude (DTLA): Auditory Attention Span for Related Syllables*

This subtest of the DTLA evaluates the immediate recall and imitation of 43 model sentences (Baker & Leland, 1967). The model sentences featured in the subtest range in length from 5 words (6 syllables) to 22 words (27 syllables). The length of sentences is increased by controlling the number of words as well as the number of syllables. The model sentences are not controlled or sequenced for syntactic complexity. Analysis of the structural characteristics of the model sentences indi-

*Other subtests of the DTLA are reviewed elsewhere in this book.*

cates that in most cases increases in length are accompanied by linear expansions of structure rather than by embedding. The distribution of structural characteristics among the test items is as follows:

(1) Pronominalization is featured strongly in the test, with representation in 28 of the sentences (Items 1 to 5, 8, 9, 11 to 16, 19 to 21, 23, 24, 27 to 30, 32 to 35, 37, 40).
(2) Imperative is featured in 1 item (Item 6).
(3) Coordination of clauses with "and" or "but" is featured in 9 items (Items 6, 13, 22, 24, 29, 31, 33, 35, 38).
(4) Conjunction with subordination of one or more clauses is featured in 7 of the sentences (Items 9, 11, 17, 21, 25, 32, 36).
(5) Relative clause transformation is featured in 7 of the sentences (Items 19, 27, 28, 37, 41, 42, 43).
(6) Embedded noun complements, adverbial clauses, and subject-related relative clauses are featured in 3 of the sentences (Items 25, 28, 39).
(7) Preposed prepositional phrases are featured in 12 of the model sentences (Items 8, 9, 19, 22, 24, 30, 33, 34, 38, 40, 41, 42).
(8) Negative, passive, and interrogative transformations are not featured.

The model sentences are spoken by the examiner, and the child is required to repeat the sentences verbatim. Repetitions with more than three errors in the form of omissions, substitutions, or additions are scored as incorrect.

The DTLA was standardized on samples of 150 children at each age level in the age range from 3 years, 0 months to 19 years, 0 months. All children in the standardization sample attended the Detroit Public Schools. Test-retest reliability was measured initially using a sample of 48 children and a 5-month interval between tests. The resulting correlation coefficient was .96, indicating a high degree of stability over time. A second reliability coefficient of .68 was reported for a 2- to 3-year time interval when a group of 792 students in the age range from 7 to 10 years was tested. Correlations among subtest performances within the test battery were reported to range between .2 and .4.

Among the assets of this sentence repetition test are:

(1) The clarity of the instructions and the ease of administration and scoring.
(2) The wide age range for which normative data are available.
(3) The level of the vocabulary featured in the items and the length of the model sentences, which increases to a point where a child's memory capacity is severely stretched.

The assets of the test are offset by limitations in standardization and in reliability. They relate to:

(1) The geographic and residential biases of the sample.
(2) The lack of specification of socioeconomic and racio-ethnic characteristics of the sample.

(3) The age of the normative data, collected before 1958.
(4) The variability in the test-retest reliability coefficients obtained from a relatively small sample (48) and a relatively large sample (792).

*Clinical Evaluation of Language Functions (CELF): Producing Model Sentences*

This subtest of the CELF is designed to assess the child's ability to control sentence structures and transformations in a sentence imitation task (Semel & Wiig, 1980). The subtest contains 30 items. Of these, 23 are sentences that are structurally acceptable and meaningful. Seven of the items are sentences in which the structural rules have been violated and the meaning deviates from the acceptable. The subtest taps aspects of language production related to (1) knowledge of the rules for forming sentences, (2) retention and immediate repetition of sentences and word strings, (3) dependence on consistency in sentence meaning for sentence recall, and (4) resistance to deviations in meaning and structure in the immediate recall of word sequences.

The sentences and word sequences featured in the 30 items range in length from 6 to 20 syllables, with a mean length of 11 syllables. The word length ranges from 5 to 17, with a mean length of 8 words per item. The items may be broken down for structural characteristics as indicated below.

(1) Three items feature active, affirmative, declarative sentences of increasing length determined by the addition of adjectives and adjective sequences (Items 1, 17, and 25).
(2) One item features an explicit negative sentence transformation (Item 5).
(3) Four items feature passive sentence transformations, of which one is a negative passive, one a passive interrogative, and one a passive negative interrogative (Items 6, 7, 11, and 18).
(4) Five items feature interrogative sentence transformations with one passive interrogative, one negative interrogative, and one passive negative interrogative (Items 2, 3, 4, 7, and 18).
(5) Two items feature compound sentences with coordination of clauses (Items 10 and 22).
(6) Four items feature sentences with conjunction deletion (Items 9, 12, 19, and 30).
(7) Two items feature "if" conjunction (Items 8 and 15).
(8) Four items feature relative clause transformations (Items 21, 24, 27, and 28).
(9) Seven items feature structural and semantic variations in word sequences (Items 13, 16, 20, 23, 24, 26, and 29).

The items are sequenced in approximate order of difficulty. The vocabulary used is of increasing difficulty. Sentence length and complexity is also increased with the progression in items.

Test-retest reliability of the subtest was established with 30 randomly selected children in the age range from 8 years, 3 months to 8 years, 6 months. The test was readministered with a 6-week time interval between administrations. The test-retest correlation coefficient was

.86, indicating good stability of the performances over time. A concurrent validity correlation coefficient of .67 was established with the ITPA Verbal Expression subtest (Kirk, McCarthy, & Kirk, 1968). Normative data were established for the lowest scoring 20% at each age level, as identified by the CELF Screening tests. The Clinical Evaluation of Language Functions is a criterion-referenced language test with criteria scores for each grade level from K through 10.

## Other Test Formats

*Clinical Evaluation of Language Functions (CELF): Producing Formulated Sentences*

This subtest is designed to evaluate the ability to formulate and produce sentences which incorporate specific given words (Semel & Wiig, 1980). The subtest taps aspects of language production related to (1) recognizing the word selection constraints imposed by specific words and concepts, (2) recognizing the structural constraints imposed on sentences by specific word selections, (3) identifying and formulating sentences that are complete, meaningful, and grammatical.

The subtest contains 12 items, each of which requires the child to say a sentence that incorporates a stimulus word. The twelve words to be

**TABLE 5.1**

*Characteristics of selected standardized methods of analysis of spontaneous speech*

| Name | Purpose | Age Range | Stimuli | Responses | Scoring |
|------|---------|-----------|---------|-----------|---------|
| MEAN LENGTH OF UTTERANCES (MLU) | Evaluates the average length of the child's spontaneous utterances. Provides an indirect estimate of early syntactic growth. | 1 yr. 9 mo. to 9 yr. 5 mo. | Stimulus objects, toys, or illustrations of a familiar story are used to elicit a spontaneous speech sample of 50 consecutive utterances. | The child's spontaneous speech is recorded on audio tape for later transcription and scoring. | The number of words in each utterance are counted, totaled, and divided by 50 to obtain the mean word length. |
| DEVELOP-MENTAL SENTENCE ANALYSIS | Evaluates the child's knowledge and expressive use of selected syntactic structures in spontaneous speech. | 3 yr. 0 mo. to 6 yr. 11 mo. | Stimulus objects, toys, or illustrations of a familiar story are used to elicit a spontaneous speech sample of 50 consecutive utterances. | The child's spontaneous speech in response to the stimuli is recorded on audio tape for later transcription and scoring. | Each utterance is scored to reflect which of eight grammatical form categories are used. Each grammatical form is given a weighted score. The total weighted score is divided by 50 to obtain a Developmental Sentence Score (DSS). The DSS may be converted to a percentile or a mean age level. |

incorporated in the formulated sentences are: (1) car, (2) yellow, (3) children, (4) nothing, (5) what, (6) belongs, (7) because, (8) slowly, (9) after, (10) tell, (11) herself, and (12) if.

Each formulated sentence is scored for grammaticality and level of structural complexity by using a given set of scoring criteria. Sentences are assigned a point score that reflects the structural quality of the sentence.

The test-retest reliability of the subtest was established with 30 randomly selected children ranging in age from 8 years, 3 months to 8 years, 6 months. The subtest was given to the children with a 6-week interval between administrations. The test-retest reliability coefficient was .84, indicating adequate stability of the items and scoring of performances over time. The subtest performances were compared with performances on the ITPA Verbal Expression (Kirk, McCarthy, & Kirk, 1968) subtest. The resulting coefficient of concurrent validity was .94. Normative data are presented for the lowest scoring 20% of children at each age level, as identified by the CELF Screening tests. The Clinical Evaluation of Language Functions is a criterion-referenced language test.

Summaries of these tests of syntax are presented in Tables 5.1, 5.2, and 5.3.

**TABLE 5.2**

*Characteristics of selected tests for the differentiation of grammatical contrasts*

| Name | Purpose | Age Range | Stimuli | Responses | Scoring |
|------|---------|-----------|---------|-----------|---------|
| ACLC | Evaluates the ability to interpret sequences of critical words without grammatical markers. | 3 yr. 0 mo. to 6 yr. 5 mo. | 50 items; 20 single words, 10 two-, 10 three-, and 10 four-word sequences. Examiner says the word sequences while presenting from 3 to 5 pictorial choices for each item. | The child points to the picture among the choices which best represents the meaning of the spoken word or word sequence. | Responses are scored as either correct or incorrect. The total score may be converted to mean age equivalents. |
| NSST: RECEPTIVE | Screens for the ability to differentiate and interpret sentences of increasing syntactic complexity. | 3 yr. 0 mo. to 7 yr. 11 mo. | 20 sentence pairs, each associated with four pictorial choices. Examiner says a sentence pair. Each sentence is repeated for identification of the appropriate pictorial representation of the sentence meaning. | The child points to the pictorial choices which best reflect the meaning of the two grammatically contrasting sentences in each item. | Each correct sentence interpretation receives a score of 1 point. The total score for the test may be converted to age level or pertile equivalents. Cut-off points (10th percentile) are presented for each age level. |

**TABLE 5.2 (*Continued*)**

| Name | Purpose | Age Range | Stimuli | Responses | Scoring |
|------|---------|-----------|---------|-----------|---------|
| NSST: EXPRESSIVE | Screens for the differentiation of grammatical contrasts in the delayed repetition of sentences of increasing syntactic complexity. | 3 yr. 0 mo. to 7 yr. 11 mo. | 20 sentence pairs associated with 2 pictorial choices each. The examiner says each sentence pair, then points to each of the pictures while asking, "What's this one?" | The child is required to repeat verbatim the original stimulus sentence associated with each of the pictures. | Each verbatim sentence imitation receives a score of 1 point. The total score may be converted to age level or percentile equivalents. Cut-off points (10th percentile) are provided. |
| TACL | Evaluates the ability to interpret class and function words and word and sentence structure. | 3 yr. 0 mo. to 6 yr. 11 mo. | 101 items, each associated with 3 pictorial choices. Examiner says items while presenting the pictorial choices. | The child points to the pictorial stimulus which best represents the meaning of each word, phrase, or sentence. | Each correct identification receives a score of 1 point. The total score may be converted to mean, median, or percentile rank equivalents. |
| TOLD: GRAMMATIC UNDERSTANDING | Evaluates the ability to interpret sentences of increasing syntactic complexity. | 4 yr. 0 mo. to 8 yr. 11 mo. | 25 items, each associated with 3 pictorial choices. Examiner says each item while presenting the associated pictures. | The child points to the pictorial choice which best represents the meaning of each sentence. | Each correct response receives a score of 1. The total score may be converted to Language Age or scaled score equivalents. |
| CELF: PROCESSING WORD AND SENTENCE STRUCTURE | Evaluates the ability to interpret sentences of increasing syntactic complexity. | K to 10 | 26 sentences, each associated with 4 pictorial choices representing grammatical contrasts. Examiner says each sentence while presenting the associated pictorial choices. | The child points to the pictorial choice which best represents the underlying meaning of each stimulus sentence. | Each correct choice receives a score of 1. A criterion point score is presented for each grade level. |

## Dialectical Variations in the Use of Sentence Structure

The rules for forming sentences are subject to dialectical variations that must be taken into account when the syntactic ability of a learning disabled child is evaluated. The deviant sentence forms produced by some children with learning disabilities may reflect the standards of

**TABLE 5.3**

*Characteristics of selected standardized tests of sentence imitation*

| Name | Purpose | Age Range | Stimuli | Responses | Scoring |
|---|---|---|---|---|---|
| CARROW ELICITED SENTENCE INVENTORY | Evaluates the immediate recall and repetition of sentences of increasing syntactic complexity. | 3 yr. 0 mo. to 7 yr. 11 mo. | 52 items, 1 phrase and 51 sentences. Examiner says the phrase and sentences for the child to repeat. | The child is required to repeat each stimulus sentence verbatim. | Each verbatim repetition receives a score of 1. Error scores are converted to age level, percentile rank, or stanine scores. Detailed analysis of errors is provided. |
| TOLD: SENTENCE IMITATION | Evaluates the immediate recall and repetition of sentences of increasing length and complexity. | 4 yr. 0 mo. to 7 yr. 11 mo. | 30 sentences, ranging in length from 5 to 12 words. Examiner says each sentence for repetition. | The child is required to repeat each sentence verbatim. | Each accurate repetition receives a score of 1. The total score may be converted to Language Age or scaled score equivalents. |
| DTLA: AUDITORY ATTENTION SPAN FOR RELATED SYLLABLES | Evaluates the immediate recall and repetition of sentences of increasing length. Structure is not controlled. | 3 yr. 0 mo. to 19 yr. 0 mo. | 43 sentences, ranging in length from 5 to 22 words. Examiner says each sentence for immediate repetition. | The child is required to repeat each sentence verbatim. | Each repetition with fewer than three substitutions, omissions, or additions receives a weighted score. The total score may be converted to age level equivalents. |
| CELF: PRODUCING MODEL SENTENCES | Evaluates the immediate recall and repetition of sentences and semantically and syntactically varied sequences of increasing length and complexity. | K to 10 | 30 items, 23 sentences and 7 semantically and syntactically varied sequences. Items range in length from 5 to 17 words. Examiner says the sentences and sequences for immediate repetition. | The child is required to repeat each item verbatim. | Responses are recorded and assigned a point score. A criterion point score is presented for each grade level. |

their dialectical backgrounds and may not indicate problems in acquiring the rules for sentence formation in Standard English. Table 5.4 summarizes syntactic variations that may be attributed to various dialects.

It can be very difficult to differentiate between language or dialectical differences, deficits, and delays. A child may well have several things

**TABLE 5.4**
*Dialectical syntactic variations (adapted from Jeter)*

| Dialect-Rule | Characteristics | Sample Utterances |
|---|---|---|
| **Negation.** | | |
| Black English. | The form *ain't* may correspond to the Standard English form *didn't*. | She *ain't* do it. |
| | A negative indefinite pronoun may be used in the noun phrase. | *Nobody didn't* do it. |
| Black English. Southern White Nonstandard. | A negative auxiliary such as *can't, wasn't,* or *didn't* may be used at the beginning of sentences with indefinite pronouns. | *Didn't nobody* do it. *Can't nobody* do it. *Wasn't nobody* there. |
| Nonstandard. | The form *ain't* may be used for *has/have* and *am/are*. | She *ain't* done it. They *ain't* gonna take it. |
| | Double negatives may be used in sentences with indefinites. | She *didn't* do *nothing*. He *didn't* see *nobody*. |
| | An adverb which expresses negation, such as *hardly,* may be featured, resulting in double negation. | She *never hardly* saw him. *Hardly nobody* thought so. |
| Black English. Southern White Nonstandard. | Negative concord may occur across clauses in sentences such as "There *isn't much* I *can* do now." | There *isn't* much he *can't* do now. There *wasn't* much they *couldn't* do. |
| **Interrogatives.** | | |
| Black English. Southern White Nonstandard. | The indirect question form may be identical in structure to the direct question form. | I asked *where was she going*. I wonder *was she driving*. |
| **Relative clauses.** | | |
| Black English. Southern White Nonstandard. Appalachian English. | The relative pronoun which introduces the relative clause may be omitted. | That the boy *hit me*. There's the man *walks downtown*. |
| Nonstandard. | The relative pronoun *which* may be featured as an associative or conjunction. | He saw me talk to this boy *which* he doesn't like. |
| | The forms *what* and *those* may be used as substitutes for the relative pronouns *who, which, that,* or *whom*. | The boy *what* lives next door is nice. The car *what* I bought won't run. |

working simultaneously. The sentence structures used may, for instance, combine Black English, Nonstandard, and deficient patterns, or any two of those. It is important, however, that the clinician-educator try to determine the basis for the child's language problems, because different intervention objectives and strategies might apply. Chapter 6 will discuss intervention for syntax difficulties.

# FORMING SENTENCES
## Intervention

**6**

## BASIC PRINCIPLES FOR INTERVENTION

The clinician who needs to plan or select intervention strategies and sequences for establishing a child's knowledge of word and sentence formation rules should consider several characteristics of learning disabled children. First, the morphological and syntactic deficits of language and learning disabled children seem to be quantitative rather than qualitative. That is, the order of difficulty for the various word and sentence formation rules is basically the same for language and learning disabled and for normally developing children and adolescents. It follows, then, that an intervention program should introduce unfamiliar or unestablished word and sentence formation rules according to normal developmental sequences or established order of difficulty.

Second, investigations indicate that learning disabled children and youth tend to depend heavily upon word, phrase, and clause meanings for processing and recalling sentences. This dependence on familiarity and predictability of word, phrase, and clause meanings has direct implications for intervention. Vocabulary selections must be carefully controlled and highly familiar when the objective is to work on morphology and syntax.

Third, clinical and diagnostic observations suggest that many learning disabled children have problems with the immediate auditory memory for spoken sentences. These limitations may drastically shorten the number and length of phrases and clauses which the child can recall. Therefore phrase and clause length should be carefully controlled in intervention programs to establish and consolidate morphology and syntax. Initially, the number of phrases and clauses should be kept to an absolute minimum. Similarly, the number of words in each phrase and each clause should be kept to a minimum.

Fourth, language and learning disabled children and youth may be limited in their use of imagery. They may be inefficient in recoding words, phrases, and clauses into perceptual (visual) representations or images of their meanings. These youngsters tend to show **perceptual**

**Perceptual adherence**
*involves attending to one di-*
*mension of stimuli, the*
*visual-perceptual features, in*
*problem solving, rather than*
*using verbal strategies to ar-*
*rive at a solution.*

**adherence** in problem-solving tasks. They appear to use and depend upon visual-perceptual rather than verbal-symbolic cues or approaches to problem solving. Thus the materials and procedures used in intervention should feature pictorial representations of word, phrase, or clause meanings. If pictorial representations are commercially unavailable, hard to find, or impossible to produce, printed versions may be used instead. The pictorial representations may be used to highlight the underlying, referential meaning of words, phrases, or clauses. Function words without a referential meaning base should be presented in printed form. When printed words, phrases, or clauses are used, they may be color-coded to feature critical words, grammatical markers, and phrases. The color helps to focus the child's attention on the critical cues. Pictorial or printed representations focus attention, permit rehearsal, and help the child recode internal images, and recall the structure later.

Clinical observations suggest that language and learning disabled children and youth benefit from multiple presentations and repetitions of word and sentence structures and transformations. At least 10 presentations or repetitions appear to be needed when unfamiliar or unestablished rules or transformations are introduced. Last, but not least, observations indicate that processing precedes production of morphological and syntactic structures. The task requirements in intervention should emphasize first recognition, then differentiation, interpretation, and finally formulation of sentences.

From these conclusions, we can derive a set of general clinical principles for selecting and designing materials for working on a child's knowledge and use of morphology and syntax. These principles are applicable primarily to rules and structures for which the interpretation does not depend upon pragmatic or contextual cues for accurate interpretation. The approaches to structures that do need pragmatic references vary considerably and will be discussed separately.

*Principle 1*

Unfamiliar word and sentence formation rules should be introduced and sequenced according to normal developmental sequences or established orders of difficulty.

*Principle 2*

The word selections featured in phrases, clauses, and sentences used for intervention should be highly familiar. They may be selected from vocabulary lists for age or grade levels at least 3 years or grades below the child's current vocabulary age or grade level.

*Principle 3*

Sentence length in number of words should be kept to an absolute minimum. This may be achieved by limiting sentence length to 5 to 10 words and phrase or clause length to 2 to 4 words. Minimum sentence length will depend upon the syntactic complexity of the units for which the rules apply.

*Principle 4*

Pictorial or printed representations of words, phrases, or clauses should be given for all spoken sentences. Pictures of referents for content words with referential meaning may be used in association with printed representations of nonreferential or function words.

*Principle 5*

Unfamiliar word or sentence formation rules should be introduced in at least 10 illustrative examples. The examples should feature different word selections.

*Principle 6*

Knowledge of word or sentence formation rules should be established first in recognition and comprehension tasks and then in formulation tasks.

*Principle 7*

The knowledge and control of word and sentence formation rules should be established first with highly familiar word choices. It should then be extended to contexts with higher level or less familiar vocabulary or with unfamiliar concepts.

*Principle 8*

The knowledge and use of word and sentence formation rules should be tested in at least 10 examples that feature vocabulary not previously used.

# SELECTED TASK FORMATS FOR INTERVENTION

There are a variety of formats to use in intervention programs focusing on word and sentence formation rules. Each format differs in task requirements. The formats also differ in the range of application and in the degree of difficulty for the youngster. This section describes 12 selected formats and the task requirements and range of application of each. The formats are not necessarily discussed in order of relative difficulty. They will be discussed again in later sections that focus on intervention for specific components of morphology or syntax.

## 1. Recognition and Judgment of Correct Grammar

This format may be applied to a wide range of word and sentence formation rules. It may require the child to recognize and judge whether word and sentence formations are grammatical (right) or not grammatical (wrong). It may also require the child to differentiate and identify grammatical from grammatically incorrect structures. When the task requirement is to judge whether or not a structure is grammatical, one structure is presented at a time. The youngster may be instructed to say "yes" or "right" if the structure is grammatical and "no" or "wrong" if it is not. The examples below illustrate the format applied first at the level of morphology and then at the level of syntax.

*Example A. Morphology*

Yesterday the boy *goes* to school.      (right/wrong)

*Example B. Syntax*

The boy went to school yesterday, *hadn't he?*      (right/wrong)

When the task requirement is to differentiate and identify grammatical structures from ones that are not grammatical, several structures are presented at one time. The youngster may be asked to raise a hand when he hears a sentence that is wrong (not grammatical) in a spoken paragraph or in a sequence of unrelated sentences. The youngster may also be instructed to listen to two sentences and identify which was grammatical afterwards. The examples below illustrate that task requirement at the levels of morphology and syntax.

*Example C. Morphology*

Yesterday the boy *goes* to school.
Yesterday the boy *went* to school.
*Which one was right?*

*Example D. Syntax*

The boy went to school yesterday, *didn't he?*
The boy went to school yesterday, *wasn't he?*
*Which one was right?*

## 2. Classification and Categorization of Structures

This format may be used for both morphology and syntax. It requires directed categorization of selected sentences according to structural identities. Sentences that belong to identical morphological or syntactic categories may feature critical word selections that are identical. For example, in certain passive sentences "is"/"was" or "are/"were" . . . "by" are critical for structure, as in the sentences "The boy *was* brought *by* his mother" and "The girl *was* called *by* her friend." They may also feature semantically related but unidentical word selections or semantically unrelated word selections, depending upon the level of intervention. The sentence pair *"Have* you finished cleaning up your room?" and *"Did* you finish cleaning up your room?" is an example of a pair of structures where the structurally critical words are not identical. The critical word formations featured at the level of morphology may follow identical rules or mix both regular and irregular formations. The structural categories to be used may be identified by providing printed examples of each. The task may require the child to categorize spoken and/or spoken and printed sentences. The examples below illustrate the format used with both morphology and syntax.

*Example A. Morphology*

| **Samples:** | Yesterday | Tomorrow |
|---|---|---|
| | . . . walked . . . | . . . will walk . . . |

**Selected Structures:**      He will walk his dog.
                              He walked his dog.
                              She talked about her dog.
                              She will talk about dogs.

> She took her dog to the kennel.
> She will take her dog to the kennel.
> He went for a walk with his dog.
> He will go for a walk with his dog.

*Example B. Syntax*

|  | ACTIVE | PASSIVE |
|---|---|---|

**Samples:** The boy baked the cake.  The cake was baked by the boy.

**Selected Sentences:**
> The dog was walked by the girl.
> The girl walked the dog.
> The dress was cut by the boy.
> The boy cut the dress.
> The train pushed the car.
> The car was pushed by the train.
> The horse pulled the wagon.
> The wagon was pulled by the horse.

### 3. Sentence Completion

The sentence completion format lends itself to teaching rules for words and phrases that are located at the end of sentences. The child may complete the sentence by selecting a target structure from among several choices. He may also be asked to make up the target structure. In either case, the child must use the available syntactic and semantic cues in the sentence frame to select or formulate the target word, phrase, or clause. In this format, a lead-in sentence may be used to set the topic and give a base word or relationship to be modified. The examples below illustrate the use of a multiple choice format to develop the ability to choose the correct word and the correct clause.

*Example A. Morphology*

The bus was slow. It drove very _____.    (fast/ slowly/ slower)

*Example B. Syntax*

First John saw Jeff. Then John saw his father.
John saw Jeff _____.  (after he saw his father/ when he saw his father/ before he saw his father)

### 4. Cloze Procedure

The cloze format is related to the sentence completion format. It features one or more sentences in which one or several target words are deleted. The cloze format may be presented in oral, printed, or combined oral and printed forms. This format lends itself well to teaching the selectional and distributional rules for, among others, auxiliaries, personal and reflexive pronouns, prepositions, and relative pronouns. The format requires the child to identify, select, and formulate target words on the basis of syntactic and semantic cues in the sentence frame. The cloze sentence frame may be preceded by one or more complete sentences that set the topic and define relationships among words. The format may be used with or without multiple choices for the selection of target words. The following examples illustrate the multiple choice cloze format for morphology and syntax.

*Example A. Morphology*

John is five feet tall. Charles is six feet tall. Charles is _____ than John.     (shorter/ taller/ tallest)

John is _____ than Charles.     (shorter/ taller/ shortest)

*Example B. Syntax*

He gave the book to the boy _____ lives next door.     (what/ who/ which)

## 5. Normalization of Scrambled Sentences

In this format, the youngster is presented with printed or spoken sentences in which the order of words, phrases, or clauses is violated. The format lends itself to working on the rules for word and phrase order in kernel sentences, for adjective order in expanded noun phrases, and for phrases and clauses in sentence transformations. When printed representations of the scrambled sequences are introduced, each word, phrase, or clause should be printed on a separate card to permit the child to manipulate the units and arrange the parts in the correct sequence. Among sentence transformations that lend themselves to this format are passives, yes/no and *wh-* interrogatives, conjunctions, and relativization. The examples below illustrate the format applied at the levels of a phrase, a kernel sentence, and a sentence transformation.

*Example A. Noun phrase*

the     dog     brown     small
The small brown dog.

*Example B. Phrase structure*

the steak     the boy     ate
The boy ate the steak.

*Example C. Sentence transformation*

eat     the steak     the boy     did     ?
Did the boy eat the steak?

## 6. Recognition and Identification of Deep Structure Identity

This format requires the child to identify and select sentence transformations that share the same underlying meaning or deep structure in the presence of surface structure differences. The format may require the child to judge whether two spoken or printed sentences have the same meanings or different meanings. He may be required to select a sentence transformation that shares a meaning from among several choices. Examples of sentences which mean the same in spite of their differences in structure include:

*Example A*

The truck followed the police car.     (active)
The police car was followed by the truck.     (passive)

Did the truck follow the police car?     (interrogative)
Was the police car followed by the truck?     (passive interrogative)

The examples below illustrate same/different and multiple choice tasks:

*Example A. Same/different judgment*

The truck followed the police car.
The truck was followed by the police car.     (same/different)

*Example B. Multiple choice*

**Sample:**     Was the police car followed by the truck?

**Choices:**     The police car was followed by the truck.
Did the truck follow the police car?
Did the police car follow the truck?

## 7. Paraphrase

The paraphrase format requires the youngster to rephrase or state the underlying sentence meaning while using a different structure. This format lends itself well to extending the range of the obligatory and optional sentence transformations the child is able to produce. The format may introduce a sentence transformation and require a paraphase of less syntactic complexity. It may introduce a relatively simple sentence structure and require a paraphrase at a higher level of syntactic complexity, a relatively more difficult task. The examples below illustrate the paraphrase format for reduction and increase of syntactic complexity, respectively.

*Example A. Make active*

**Stimulus sentence:**     The bus was followed by the police car.

**Paraphrase:**     The police car followed the bus.

*Example B. Conjunction*

**Stimulus sentence:**     First the girl combed her hair, and then she went to the movies.

**Paraphrase:**     The girl combed her hair before she went to the movies.

## 8. Directed Sentence Transformation

In this format the child applies a specific sentence transformation to a kernel sentence upon verbal request. This format lends itself to intervention on obligatory transformations such as negatives, yes/no interrogatives, negative interrogatives, or imperatives. The format requires the child to know the function of a specific transformation. In this format a kernel sentence is presented initially in either oral, printed, or oral and printed forms. The examples below illustrate the format applied to specific sentence transformations.

*Example A. Interrogative*

         The girl is driving the car.
         Ask a question with the same words.

*Example B. Negative*

         The girl is driving the car.
         Now, use *not* to tell just the opposite.

*Example C. Imperative*

         The girl is driving the car.
         Now, tell the girl to do what the sentence said.

## 9. Sentence Formation with Incorporation of Selected Key Words

Several sentence transformations feature critical grammatical markers which determine and signal the structural features. Among words which signal a sentence transformation are initial *wh-* forms ("what," "who," "which," "where," "when," "how," "why"), conjunctions ("before," "after," etc.), relatives ("that," "who," "which," "whose"), and reflexive pronouns ("herself," "himself," "themselves," etc.). These words may be used to elicit the formulation of specific sentence transformations. The examples below illustrate the format for *wh-*interrogative, reflexivization, and conjunction with clause subordination.

*Example A*

         Make a sentence with the word "where" to ask a question.

*Example B*

         Make a sentence with the word "himself."

*Example C*

         Make a sentence with the word "if."

## 10. Resolution of Complex Sentences into Component Sentences

This format requires the child to identify and resolve sentences with two or more clauses into their component sentences. The format may be applied to sentences with conjunction deletion, conjunction of clauses, adverbial clauses, noun phrase complements, and relative clause transformations. The task may require the youngster to identify component sentences from among several choices or spontaneous resolution into component sentences. The examples below illustrate the format applied to a sentence with conjunction deletion and one with a relative clause transformation.

*Example A. Conjunction deletion*

         **Sample:**      Jack and Harry play the piano.
         **Choices:**     Jack plays the piano.
                       Jack plays with Harry.
                       Harry plays the piano.
                       Harry plays with Jack.

*Example B. Relative clause transformation*

**Sample:**   The boy who lives next door found my cat.

**Choices:**   The boy found the cat.
The cat found the boy.
The cat lives next door.
The boy lives next door.

## 11. Synthesis of Component Sentences into Complex Sentences

This format requires that two related sentences be joined to form a complex sentence. The format may be applied to the same sentence transformations as the resolution format discussed above. The task may require the child to identify a complex sentence from among several choices or to spontaneously synthesize and formulate a complex sentence. The examples below illustrate this format with multiple choices applied to conjunction with clause subordination and to relative clause transformation with deletion of the relative pronoun.

*Example A. Conjunction with clause subordination*

**Sample:**   Ellen carries her umbrella. It is raining.

**Choices:**   Ellen carries her umbrella after it is raining.
Ellen carries her umbrella because it is raining.
Ellen carries her umbrella then it is raining.

*Example B. Relative clause transformation*

**Sample:**   Iris met her aunt. She likes the aunt.

**Choices:**   Iris met the aunt who she likes.
Iris met the aunt what she likes.
Iris met the aunt she likes.

## 12. Recognition and Identification of Deep Structure Differences

This format requires the child to identify differences in the underlying meaning of sentences that appear alike because they share surface structure characteristics. The format lends itself to limited numbers of sentences and transformations. The task may require same/different judgments of equivalence in meaning or identification of the agent of the action or the recipient of the action (subject–object). The examples below illustrate the formats in sentence pairs that differ in underlying meaning (deep structure) despite the apparent similarities in surface structure.

*Example A*

The man was happy to please.
The man was eager to please.   (same/different)

*Example B*

The man was easy to please.
The man was eager to please.   (same/different)

*Example C*

The woman was happy to leave.
It made the woman happy to leave.   (same/different)

*Example D*

> The woman was happy to go.
> Did the woman feel happy?      (yes/no)

*Example E*

> The woman was urged to go.
> Did the woman urge to go?      (yes/no)

*Example F*

> Jack told Mary to pick up the groceries.
> Jack promised Mary to pick up the groceries.      (same/different)

*Example G*

> Jack promised Mary to pick up the groceries.
> Was Mary to pick up the groceries?      (yes/no)

The formats described in this section are summarized for easy reference in Table 6.1. The spontaneous speech sample and discourse, both of which have already been described, can also be used.

**TABLE 6.1**

*Intervention formats for syntax*

| Format | Task Requirements | Example | Applicability |
|---|---|---|---|
| Recognition and judgment of correct grammar. | To recognize and judge whether word or sentence formations are grammatical (right) or agrammatical (wrong). | Yesterday the boy *goes* to school.      (right/wrong) | Any word or sentence formation. |
| Classification and categorization of structures. | To categorize selected sentences on the basis of structural identities. | Categories: *Yesterday    Tomorrow* Sentences:  He will walk his dog.  He walked his dog. | Any word or sentence formation. |
| Sentence completion. | To complete an incomplete sentence with a critical word, phrase, or clause. | The bus was slow. It was driving very _____. (fast/slowly/slow) | Limited to structures that occur at the end of sentences. |
| Cloze procedure (oral or written). | To provide a critical word, phrase, or clause which was deleted within a sentence. | Jane saw the woman _____ lives next door. (who/what/which) | Any word or sentence formation. |
| Normalization of scrambled sentences. | To rearrange critical words, phrases, or clauses presented in a scrambled sequence into grammatic sentences. | Wore    because    the boy    a coat    it rained. | Passives, yes/no and *wh-* interrogatives, conjunction, relativization. |
| Recognition and identification of deep structure identity. | To indicate if two sentences with different structures mean the same. | The boy followed the ice cream truck. The ice cream truck was followed by the boy. | Active/passive, yes/no interrogative, conjunction, relativization. |

**TABLE 6.1 (*Continued*)**

| Format | Task Requirements | Example | Applicability |
|---|---|---|---|
| Paraphrase. | To rephrase or state the underlying meaning of a sentence while using a different structure. | First the girl combed her hair and then she went to the movies. The girl combed her hair before she went to the movies. | Active/passive, yes/no interrogative, conjunction, relativization, indirect object transformation, etc. |
| Directed sentence transformation. | To transform a kernel sentence into specific sentence transformation such as negative, passive, interrogative, imperative. | The girl is driving the truck. Ask a question with the same words. | Any sentence transformation. |
| Sentence formation with incorporation of selected key words. | To form a sentence with a given word which signals the structure. | Make a sentence with the word:<br>Because<br>Which<br>Themselves | Any sentence transformation which features critical words. |
| Resolution of complex sentences into component sentences. | To identify the component sentences in complex sentences with two or more clauses. | The boy who lives next door found my dog. | Any sentence which features combinations of two or more clauses. |
| Synthesis of component sentences into complex sentences. | To combine two or more related sentences into one complex sentence. | Iris met her aunt. She likes her aunt. | Any related sentence pair or triplet. |
| Recognition and identification of deep structure differences. | To identify when two structurally similar sentences differ in underlying meaning or in subject/object relationship. | The girl was *easy* to please. The girl was *eager* to please. (same/different) | Any sentence pair with words such as easy to/eager to, promise/tell, or learn/teach. |

# IMPROVING KNOWLEDGE OF SYNTAX

Sentence structure or syntax provides a predictable and limited framework for embedding content words and word formations. Because the number of grammatical structures and sentence transformations is finite and limited, sentences are grammatically redundant. This redundancy becomes fully apparent only when the child has learned to use syntactic structures and sentence transformation rules easily in both processing and production. At that point the child's processing of the structural characteristics of sentences becomes highly automatic, rapid, and efficient and can be performed in short-term memory.

As we saw in Chapter 4, the infinite variety of spoken sentences we may encounter in English have their bases in five basic sentence patterns. Every sentence may be traced back to one or more of these

*See pages 60–62 as well. We will recap some of that information here.*

patterns. The basic sentences are all simple, affirmative, active, declarative—so-called *kernel* sentences. They express the basic underlying relationships that comprise the deep structure of the message. Here are five basic sentence patterns in English:

(1) Boys run.
(2) Boys play games.
(3) The boy is my brother.
(4) The boy is tall.
(5) The boy became ill.

The word sequences or strings, which we often call *phrases*, that underlie each kernel sentence are all formed according to a rather simple set of rules. They can be considered basic rules and are called *phrase-structure rules (PS rules)* (Chomsky, 1957). Once an utterance is described in terms of its phrase structures, we cannot describe it at a lower or simpler structural basis. There are 11 kinds of word strings that combine to make up the kernel sentences (Chomsky, 1957).

(1) Sentence ⟶ Noun phrase (NP) + Verb phrase (VP)
(2) VP ⟶ Verb (V) + Noun phrase (NP)
(3) NP ⟶ Noun phrase singular (NPsing)
                    or
                    Noun phrase plural (NPpl)
(4) NPsing ⟶ Article (T) + noun (N) + zero morpheme ending (Ø)
(5) NPpl ⟶ Article (T) + noun (N) + plural morpheme ending (S)
(6) T ⟶ the
(7) N          boy, game, brother, etc.
(8) Verb ⟶ Auxiliary (Aux) + Verb (V)
(9) V ⟶ run, play, etc.
(10) Aux ⟶ C (M) (have + en) (be + ing)
                    where: C (to be) + S for NPsing present tense.
                         or
                         C (to be) + Ø for NPpl present and past tense.
(11) M ⟶ will, can, may, shall, must.

*An elaborate sentence is derived from a kernel sentence by adding additional structures or changing the presentation of the basic structure.*

*Transformational grammar describes how the users of a language combine and change basic phrase structures to derive elaborate and/or complex sentences.*

Most of the sentences we encounter in mature spoken and written English are elaborate rather than simple. These more elaborate constructions may be generated by applying a limited set of transformational rules. This set of rules, the transformational grammar, supplements the phrase-structure rules. Among English transformational rules are those for forming passives, interrogatives, conjunctions and relativization. All of these transformations emphasize changes in word order.

Language and learning disabled children have a range of difficulties in processing and using sentence structure. Some of them seem to have problems integrating the surface structure, which reflects the syntactic properties, with the deep structure, which reflects the underlying meaning. Some appear to interpret the individual words in sentences easily but seem to be unable to understand the relationships among words expressed by structure. In other words, they seem to interpret word meanings with minimal reference to the meaning added by the structural characteristics of the sentence. When a sentence transformation rearranges the basic elements, language and learning disabled youngsters tend to have problems. It is as though they expect all sentences to feature the actor (subject) first, followed by the action (verb-predicate), and then the recipient of the action (direct and indirect objects). When this order is changed in the surface structure, they may fail to reverse it when they interpret the underlying meaning.

Other language and learning disabled youngsters seem to require more time to process and understand a sentence than is given in normal conversation. They appear to need extended time to process the surface structure and then to integrate the surface structure with the word meanings. Longer and more complex sentences seem to get lost in their minds and may remain unprocessed. This problem may occur as a result of limitations in immediate auditory memory, in internal reauditorization and **rehearsal**, or in recursive (repeated) processing ability. The limitations in the processing of surface structure may result in misinterpretations of a wide range of sentence transformations and misuse of certain structures. Among them are the following:

*Rehearsal is the process of saying something over again to yourself in order to remember it.*

(1) Noun phrases ("The car had an accident.")
(2) Verb phrases ("I am going to the store.")
(3) Negative sentences ("The ball is not red.")
(4) Passive sentences ("Jane was picked up by John.")
(5) Interrogative sentences and indirect requests ("Where are you going?" "Can't you turn the light off?")
(6) Sentences with coordinated clauses or conjunction deletion ("Turn the light off and open the door." "Paul and Jean play the flute.")
(7) Sentences with subordinated clauses and conjunction ("It snows because it is cold.")
(8) Sentences with adverbial clauses ("Jack put his bike where it was safe.")
(9) Sentences with noun phrase complements ("The fact that you finished the homework pleases me.")
(10) Sentences with subject- and object-related relative clauses ("The woman who lives next door went to Florida." "She gave it to the woman who lives next door.")
(11) Sentences with surface or deep structure ambiguities ("She told her baby stories." "Flying planes can be dangerous.")

*These sentence types and the kinds of problems learning disabled children have with them are discussed in more depth in chapter 4. You may wish to review.*

In addition, learning disabled children may have problems with word order in even simple sentences. Let us now turn to specific procedures that can be used to help a child who has problems with these various structures. Because problems with forming verb phrases are largely problems with forming words, they have been dealt with in chapter 3. You may wish to review pages 50–59.

## Establishing Word Order in Simple Sentences

Without specific instruction, some language and learning disabled children may not learn the rules for sequencing words implicit at the phrase-structure level. Several formats and activities may be used to help teach the sequential patterns for kernel sentences. Two of them are illustrated in these examples.

*Judgment of correct grammar*

| | |
|---|---|
| She in the yard played. | (right/wrong) |
| She played in the yard. | (right/wrong) |
| Karen wanted to play the game. | (right/wrong) |
| Jack the game played. | (right/wrong) |

*Normalization of scrambled spoken and printed sentences*

| | | | | |
|---|---|---|---|---|
| jumps | Jack | | | Jack jumps. |
| good | taste | bananas | | Bananas taste good. |
| Jane | my | sister | is | Jane is my sister. |
| red | is | the | car | The car is red. |
| ill | Sue | became | | Sue became ill. |

It may also be necessary to teach the child to differentiate between sentence fragments (incomplete sentences) and complete sentences. Activities designed to teach this differentiation may act as a transition to working on sentence transformations. Imperatives should be included at this stage, as learning disabled children often judge them to be fragments rather than complete sentences. The examples below show two formats that may be used.

*Judgment of correct grammar*

| | |
|---|---|
| The boys are. | (right/wrong) |
| The boys run. | (right/wrong) |
| The girl became. | (right/wrong) |
| Come here! | (right/wrong) |
| Go! | (right/wrong) |

*Sentence completion and oral cloze*

The girl ate _____.
The woman _____ tall.
The boy is _____.
_____ walked home.
The man _____ the car.

## The Noun Phrase

Without instruction some younger children with language and learning disabilities may use the indefinite and definite articles *a* and *an* inconsistently. They may not have discerned and internalized the rules which determine their use. Their problems may be compounded by the fact that the indefinite articles are often unstressed and articulated as if they were a part of the noun in rapid speech. The rules for the indefinite articles for singular nouns must be abstracted and become automatic so that the child can apply them in both speaking and writing. The objective in intervention is to help the child to perceive and internalize the obligatory rules that the indefinite article *a* is used before singular nouns that begin with a consonant and *an* is used before singular nouns that begin with a vowel. Several formats and activities may be used to assist in establishing these rules. Among applicable formats are judgment of correct grammar, classification of nouns by the beginning sound, phrase or sentence completion, oral cloze, and visual confrontation naming. The formats are illustrated in these examples, some of which feature adjectives.

*Judgment of correct grammar*

| | |
|---|---|
| I have an brother. | (right/wrong) |
| I have a sister. | (right/wrong) |
| I have an aunt. | (right/wrong) |
| I have a uncle. | (right/wrong) |
| I have a older brother. | (right/wrong) |
| I have a smart uncle. | (right/wrong) |
| I have an elderly aunt. | (right/wrong) |
| I have an younger sister. | (right/wrong) |

*Classification of nouns by beginning sound*

**Samples:** a an

**Nouns to be Classified:** egg, orange, lemon, hamburger, apple, steak, avocado, hotdog, ice cream, popsicle

*Phrase completion*

| | | | |
|---|---|---|---|
| _____ boy | (a/an) | _____ old boy | (a/an) |
| _____ brother | (a/an) | _____ smart brother | (a/an) |
| _____ aunt | (a/an) | _____ young aunt | (a/an) |
| _____ alligator | (a/an) | _____ wild alligator | (a/an) |
| _____ cow | (a/an) | _____ brown cow | (a/an) |
| _____ owl | (a/an) | _____ little owl | (a/an) |

*Sentence completion*

Yesterday I saw a _____.
Last week I heard an _____.
I want to buy a _____.
I want to eat an _____.

*Oral cloze*

Everybody has a body.
Everybody has _____ ear. Everybody has _____ eye. Everybody has _____ nose.
Everybody has _____ knee. Everybody has _____ ankle. Everybody has _____ arm.
Everybody has _____ hand. Everybody has _____ jaw. Everybody has _____ elbow.

*Visual confrontation naming*

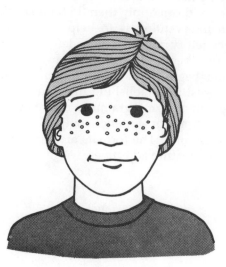

This is (a/an) 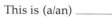.

This is (a/an) _____.

This is (a/an) _____.

This is (a/an) _____.

Some learning disabled children may have to be taught to be aware of the correct use of indefinite and definite articles for singular nouns in discourse. Accurate use of the indefinite and definite articles in discourse depends upon awareness of the *listener's* perspective in relation to the topic. When a new topic is introduced in the noun phrase in discourse, it is unknown to the listener. Discourse rules, therefore, require that the noun phrase must contain the indefinite article if the topic is indicated by a singular noun form. When the same topic is mentioned again, it is assumed to be familiar to the listener. Discourse rules now require that the noun phrase must contain the definite article if the topic is indicated by a singular noun form. As an illustration, consider the use of indefinite and definite articles in this conversation.

> "Yesterday when I went downtown. I saw *an* old horse. It was standing by *a* lamppost."
> "What was it doing there?"
> "*The* horse was eating oats from *a* bag. *The* bag was made of leather. It was brand new."
> "Where was that lamppost?"
> "*The* lamppost was on the corner of North and Main streets."

Among formats which may be used to establish awareness and use of the rules for using indefinite and definite articles in discourse are oral cloze and discourse with immediate or delayed feedback. The examples here illustrate these formats.

*Oral cloze*

I have _____ cat and _____ dog. _____ cat is brown and _____ dog is spotted.

I hear _____ bird outside. _____ bird is sitting in _____ tall tree. _____ tree is next to my window.

We have _____ great new car. _____ car gets 30 miles to _____ gallon.

*Discourse with feedback*

Tell me about your vacation/birthday party/new pet/baby brother/the circus/or the like.

Immediate feedback may be provided by using a buzzer or a red/green light combination to indicate success or errors. Noun phrases that contain incorrect articles should be corrected and repeated immediately. Delayed feedback may be provided by audio taping, followed by listening to identify and correct errors.

## Negative Sentences

Some of the younger children with language and learning disabilities may misinterpret negative sentences because they do not perceive the stress placed on the negated word accurately and consistently. The objective in intervention in that case is to make the child aware of the stress pattern and accurate perception and differentiation of the stress patterns in negative sentences. Among formats which may be used in intervention to meet these objectives are same/different judgment of sentence pairs, identification of the stressed, negated word in sentences, and generating of alternative hypotheses about the actual situation or implied meaning. The examples below illustrate these formats.

*Same/different judgment*

*Listen to these sentences. Tell me if they are the same or not the same (different).*

The girl is not *sitting* on the chair.
The girl is not sitting on the *chair*.      (same/different)

The man is not walking to the *store*.
The man is not *walking* to the store.      (same/different)

The woman is not washing the *dishes*.
The *woman* is not washing the dishes. (same/different)

*Identification of the stressed, negated word*

*Listen to this sentence. Tell me which of the words is stressed.*

The boy is not *sitting* at the table.
The boy is not sitting at the *table*.
The *boy* is not sitting at the table.

The man is not washing the *car*.
The *man* is not washing the car.
The man is not *washing* the car.

The girl is not *running* to school.
The *girl* is not running to school.
The girl is not running to *school*.

*Generating alternative hypotheses*

*Listen to these sentences. Each of them tells that something is not true. I'll ask you a question after each of the sentences.*

The ball is not *red*.
*What do you think the ball looked like?*

The book was not on the *shelf*.
*Where do you think the book was?*

The lamp was not *on* the table.
*Where do you think the lamp was?*

Eat the apple that is not *green*.
*Which apple should you not eat? Which color apple could you eat?*

Do not *throw the ball* that is not *red*.
*Which color ball could you throw?*

Do not *skate* when the river is not *frozen solid*.
*When can you skate?*

## Passive Sentences

Passive sentences are often misinterpreted by children with language and learning disabilities. These sentences require the child to process the surface structure to discern the relationship between the expressed subject and object. They also require the child to integrate the surface structure and the deep structure in spite of the differences in subject–object order. Language and learning disabled youngsters seem to approach passives with the expectation that the first noun must be the actor (subject) and the last the recipient of the action (object). They seem to fail to revise that hypothesis in spite of the structural cues in the passive. Normally, English speakers hear the verb phrase "was . . . by" as the cue for reversing the object-subject sequence when interpreting the passive. Language and learning disabled children may not perceive the structural cues, act appropriately when they hear them, or recall the object-subject in a passive. Their problems increase when the subject and object may both serve as actors or recipients. This is the case in reversible passive sentences such as "Paul was phoned by Bob." In reversible passives, it is not immediately obvious who did what and to whom.

Passive sentences come in a variety of forms. They may be questions, they may be negative, or they may be emphatic. When designing intervention, the clinician should introduce irreversible passives before reversible passives, which are more difficult to master. Irreversible passives feature subject-object combinations in which it is clear who performed the act and who was acted upon. The logic of the actor–recipient relationship may stand out if one noun is an animate noun and the other, inanimate. For example, it is clear who did what to whom in an irreversible passive such as "The cake was eaten by the girl." The relationship may be less clear when both nouns are animate, as in "The dog was walked by its master." Finally, there is very little logic in reversible passives that feature proper names, as in "Jill was brought by Ellie." Either person may be the actor or the recipient of the act.

Among formats which may be used to establish knowledge of the passive transformations are recognition of deep structure identity, paraphrase, directed sentence transformations, sentence completion and cloze procedures, and normalization of scrambled sentences. These formats are illustrated in the examples below.

*Identification of deep structure identity*

The girl read the book.
The book was read by the girl.                    (same/different)

The book was given to the girl by the boy.
The girl gave the book to the boy.                     (same/different)

The book was given to the boy by the girl.
The book was not given to the girl by the boy.    (same/different)

Didn't the girl give the book to the boy?
Wasn't the book given to the boy by the girl?      (same/different)

*Identification of actor–recipient (subject–object)*

The book was bought by the man.
*Who did the buying?*

The cat was stroked by the boy.
*Who received the stroking?*

Susan was driven by her aunt.
*Who drove the car?*

The shot for distemper was given to my dog by the veterinarian.
*Who got the shot? Who gave the shot?*

*Paraphrase*

The bone was eaten by the dog.
*Say it another way. Start with "The dog."*

The car was not driven by the small boy.
*Say it another way. Start with "The small boy."*

Wasn't the traffic directed by the policeman?
*Say it another way. Start with "Didn't the."*

*Directed sentence transformation*

The policeman directed the traffic.
*Make it into a passive. Start with "The traffic."*

Did the policeman direct the traffic?
*Make it into a passive question. Start with "Was the traffic."*

Didn't the policeman direct the traffic?
*Make it into a negative passive question. Start with "Wasn't the traffic."*

*Normalization of scrambled sentences*

was hit      by the boy      the ball
The ball was hit by the boy.

?      the car      driven      by my father      was
Was the car driven by my father?

## Yes/No Interrogatives and Indirect Requests

Language and learning disabled children and youth may have problems in interpreting and using yes/no **interrogatives**. These interrogatives may be formed in several ways. They may be formed by adding a **tag question** to an active declarative, as in "Daddy finished dinner, didn't he?" They may be formed by reversing the subject and predicate, as in "Was dinner good?" Finally, they may be formed by adding and **preposing** an auxiliary, as in "Did daddy finish dinner?"

In intervention, tag questions formed correctly may be used as a reference form or as a starting point. Yes/no interrogative transformations should be introduced according to order of difficulty, and the specific functions should be stressed. The following objectives are sequenced to provide guidelines for intervention.

*Objective 1*

Interrogatives with forms of *to be*, formed by reversing the subject and the predicate, should be introduced and established before other yes/no interrogatives.

*Objective 2*

Interrogatives in which an existing auxiliary ("do," "have," "can," "will") is preposed and which serve as direct yes/no requests should be introduced and established next in the sequence.

*Objective 3*

Interrogatives which require selection and addition of an auxiliary and which serve as direct yes/no requests may be introduced and established next.

*Objective 4*

Negative forms of direct yes/no interrogatives should be introduced after their affirmative counterparts have been established.

*Objective 5*

Indirect requests should be introduced last in the sequence of remediation. Affirmative forms of indirect requests should be introduced before negative forms. Intervention should stress the perception and interpretation of contextual cues and relations for discerning the pragmatic meaning.

*Teaching Yes/No Interrogatives*

Among formats which may be used to establish knowledge and use of yes/no interrogatives are differentiation and classification of interrogatives, identification of deep structure identity, paraphrase, directed sentence transformation, and normalization of scrambled sentences. These formats are illustrated in the examples below.

*Classification and differentiation of interrogatives*

(a) Classification of declaratives and interrogatives
   **Samples:**     Eric is tall.     Is Eric tall?
   **Sentences**
   **to be**        I am tired.     Are you tired?
   **Classified.**  The dog is old.     Is the dog old?
                    Children are noisy.     Are children noisy?
                    Dogs can jump.     Can dogs jump?     Do dogs jump?
                    Planes can fly.     Do planes fly?     Can planes fly?

(b) **Identification of interrogatives**

| | | |
|---|---|---|
| Charlotte can go to the movies. | (question? | yes/no) |
| Can Charlotte go to the movies? | (question? | yes/no) |
| Did Charlotte go to the movies last night? | (question? | yes/no) |
| Charlotte will go to London this summer. | (question? | yes/no) |

Might Charlotte go to Paris next year?    (question?   yes/no)
Would you like to go to London?    (question?   yes/no)
Mike likes to go to London.    (question?   yes/no)

## Directed interrogative transformation

Bob is Jack's best friend.
*Ask a question with the same words.* Is _____?

Bob and Jack are ten years old.
*Ask a question with the same words.* Are _____?

Bob and Jack went on a canoe trip.
*Ask a question with the same words.* Did _____?

Mommy will be home next week.
*Ask a question with those words.* _____ mommy _____ home next week?

## Identification of deep structure identity

Did you buy the new car?
Have you bought the new car?    (same/different)

Can you go to the theatre tonight?
Are you allowed to go to the theatre tonight?    (same/different)

Will you go downtown tomorrow?
Do you plan to go downtown tommorow?    (same/different)

## Paraphrase

Have you finished your homework?
*Ask the same question in another way.*

Are you allowed to stay up late?
*Ask the same question in another way.*

Do you plan to leave tomorrow?
*Ask the same question in another way.*

## Normalization of scrambled interrogatives

today    home    did    come    daddy    ?
Did daddy come home today?

will    next week    be    home    mother    ?
Will mother be home next week?

you    like    to have    would    a new bike    ?
Would you like to have a new bike?

## Teaching Indirect Requests

The children must be able to differentiate indirect requests from direct requests. This differentiation depends upon accurate perception of the speaker's intentions in relation to a total context or situation. It is best taught in demonstrations, short skits, or role-playing activities. In the demonstrations and short skits, the children can witness humorous examples of the incorrect, literal interpretation of the indirect requests. The language and learning disabled child needs repeated demonstrations and examples to learn how indirect requests deviate from the common English rules. Activities such as those described for yes/no interrogatives do not give the child the verbal and the contextual cues he needs to pick out the pragmatic meaning of an indirect request.

Role-playing activities, with associated discussions and explanations and revisions or error responses, may help the child learn to correctly respond to and ask indirect questions.

*Teaching Wh- Interrogatives*

*Wh-* questions form a prominent part of most school curricula. Reading comprehension, for example, is often assessed primarily by asking a set of *wh-* questions that ask for specific information from the materials the child has read. In other curriculum areas, such as social studies and the sciences, knowledge and acquisition of information are also commonly assessed by asking *wh-* questions. It is therefore essential for academic achievement and performance to be able to respond rapidly and accurately to various forms of *wh-* questions.

A variety of formats may be used in intervention to establish the selectional rules for *wh-* forms in interrogatives. Among these formats are classification of affirmative and interrogative forms, matching *wh-* forms to words and phrases, identification of matched affirmative and *wh-* interrogative forms, identification of deep structure identity, sentence completion and oral cloze, paraphrase, and responding to *wh-* questions for details. The examples below illustrate each of these formats.

*Classification of affirmatives and wh- interrogatives*

| **Samples:** | statement question |
| --- | --- |
| **Sentences to be Classified:** | The girl lives next door. |
| | Who lives next door? |
| | Joan has a kitten. |
| | What does Joan have? |
| | Jill went to school. |
| | Where did Jill go? |
| | Dinner is at 6 o'clock. |
| | When is dinner? |

*Matching wh- forms to words and phrases*

*Tell me if these tell us "where" or "when."*
at the movies    on the table    outside    inside

*Tell me if these tell us "who" or "which."*
Santa Claus    George Washington    My mother    The boy    A man

*Tell me if these tell us "how" or "why."*
because we are moving    since it rains    as I am hungry

*Identification of matched affirmatives and wh- interrogatives*

| **Affirmative:** | They went to my house. |
| --- | --- |
| **Wh- interrogatives:** | *Tell me which one of these asks that question.* |
| | When did they go? |
| | Where did they go? |
| **Wh- interrogative:** | When did they leave? |
| **Affirmatives:** | *Tell me which statement goes with this question.* |
| | They left home. |
| | They left last week. |

*Identification of deep structure identity*

**Sample:**    *Who* said that?        *Tell me which question asks the same thing.*
**Choices:**    What animal said that?
                What person said that?

**Sample:**    *When* are you leaving? *Tell me which question asks the same.*
**Choices:**    What person are you leaving?
                What place are you leaving?
                What time are you leaving?

**Sample:**    *Why* are you happy? *Tell me which question asks the same.*
**Choices:**    How much are you happy?
                For what reason are you happy?

*Sentence completion and oral cloze*

**Statement:**    The circus came to town last week. It will stay till next Tuesday.
**Question:**     When _____?
                  How long _____?

**Statement:**    Daddy bought two tickets for the circus. Mary and John are going next week.
**Question:**     Who _____?
                  How many _____?
                  When are _____?

**Statement:**    Last week Joe and his friends went to the movies. They saw a western. After the movies they had pizza. They went home at 10 o'clock.
**Question:**     _____ did Joe and his friends go to the movies?
                  _____ did they see?
                  _____ did they eat after the movies?
                  _____ did they go home?

*Paraphrase*

*What person lives next door? Ask the same question another way.*
**Paraphrase:**    *Who* lives next door?

*What animal do you like best? Ask the same question another way.*
**Paraphrase:**    *Which* animal do you like best?

*What place do you live at? Ask the same question another way.*
**Paraphrase:**    *Where* do you live?

*What time do you get out of school? Ask the same question another way.*
**Paraphrase:**    *When* do you get out of school?

*What way do you get home from school? Ask the same question another way.*
**Paraphrase:**    *How* do you get home from school?

*For what reason do you like ice cream? Ask the same question another way.*
**Paraphrase:**    *Why* do you like ice cream?

*Responding to wh- questions for details*

The flowers mother planted in the garden in the spring are red and pink.
*What did mother plant?*
*When did mother plant the flowers?*
*Where were the flowers planted?*
*What colors were the flowers?*

He is somebody you see at the circus. He wears old clothes and big shoes. He hops when he walks and he has a red nose. He does funny things. He makes people laugh.
*Who is he?*
*What does he wear?*
*How does he walk?*
*Who laughs at him?*

## Conjunction

Language and learning disabled children and adolescents often have trouble understanding and producing sentences that use coordinating or subordinating conjunctions. In selecting or designing intervention materials, the principles of order of mention in the sentence, derivational simplicity, and choices of theme should be considered. Both school children and adults prefer conjunctions in which the order of mention of the clauses agrees with the order of action or occurrence (Clark, 1973). As a consequence, conjunction sentences in which the order of mention matches the chronological order of occurrence should be introduced before those in which the two aspects do not agree.

The principle of derivational simplicity relates to the relative number of transformations that must be applied to the deep structure to form the conjunction. Based on this principle, the conjunction "He got up from his chair *when he saw the door open*" is easier than the sentence "*When he saw the door open*, he got up from his chair." It follows that with the exception of conjunctions with "before" and "after," conjunctions with the subordinated clause last should be introduced before conjunctions with the subordinated clause first in the sequence.

The third principle, choice of theme, suggests that conjunctions in which there is rhematic-thematic continuity in the clauses are simpler than conjunctions in which there is no apparent continuity in the clauses.

### Coordinated Conjunctions

Conjunctions with "and" in which the clauses are coordinated and have equal status appear easier for language and learning disabled children to use than other conjunctions. The children need to be able to use "and" to go on to sentences with conjunction deletion. The rules for conjunction deletion may be taught in formats which require the child to resolve the sentence into its components or combine the components into conjunctions with deletion. These formats are illustrated below.

#### Resolution of conjunction deletions into component propositions

John and Mary play the flute.
John plays the flute.
Mary plays the flute.

The mailman sorts and delivers the letters.
The mailman sorts the letters.
The mailman delivers the letters.

Mary plays the piano and the flute.
Mary plays the piano.
Mary plays the flute.

*Synthesis of components into conjunction deletions*

The boy ate the cake.      The girl ate the cake.
The boy and girl ate the cake.

John cut the logs.      John carried the logs.
John cut and carried the logs.

The boy ate the hamburger.      The boy ate the french fries.
The boy ate the hamburger and french fries.

Conjunctions that feature "or, "either . . . or," and "but" with deletions may also be taught using these formats. Here are examples for each of these conjunctions.

*Resolution of conjunctions into component propositions*

John rides a motorcycle *or* drives a car.
John rides a motorcycle.
John drives a car.
**Inferred:**      John cannot do both at one time.

Sue can eat *either* cake *or* pie.
Sue can eat cake.
Sue can eat pie.
**Inferred:**      Sue has a choice of one of these.

I do not like coke *but* I like ice cream.
I do not like coke.
I like ice cream.

*Synthesis of components into conjunctions*

Mary travels by train.      Sometimes Mary travels by plane.
**Inferred:**      Mary cannot do both at the same time.
Mary travels by train *or* by plane.

Bob can choose hamburgers.      Bob can choose hotdogs.
**Inferred:**      Bob has a choice of one of these.
Bob can choose *either* hamburgers *or* hotdogs.

Sam does not want milk.      Sam wants orange juice.
Sam does not want milk *but* orange juice.

Oral cloze procedures may be used to teach the selectional rules for the coordinating conjunctions "and," "or," "either . . . or," and "but." The examples below illustrate this format with and without multiple choices.

*Oral cloze*

For dinner you can have steak _____ hamburger.      (but, or)

Dan likes cake _____ he likes ice cream better.      (and, but, or)

I don't want salad _____ I would like a vegetable.      (or, and, but)

You can have one of these. You can have _____
ginger ale _____ coke.      (and, or, either . . .
                                                        or)

The waitress said: You can have salad, potato, _____ vegetables with that. What kind of dressing would you like on your salad, French, Russian _____ Italian? For your potato, you can have _____ French fries, scalloped, _____ baked potato. For your vegetable, you can have carrots _____ broccoli, _____ you cannot have both.

*Subordinated Conjunctions*

Most learning disabled children learn to use "because" at approximately the normal age. As a result, conjunctions with "because" may be used as reference examples to demonstrate the principles involved in combining two related propositions into conjunctions. They may also be used to help the child learn to automatically resolve and synthesize simple subordinated clause conjunctions. "Because" conjunctions may serve as logical reference examples for establishing "if" and "when" conjunctions. These conjunctions should be introduced with the subordinated clause following the main clause. When this pattern is mastered, sentences with the subordinated clause first can be introduced. The examples below illustrate one progression the clinician can use in working on "if" and "when" conjunctions.

| | |
|---|---|
| **Reference conjunction:** | John wears a raincoat *because* it rains. |
| **If conjunction:** | John wears a raincoat *if* it rains. |
| | (condition) |
| **When conjunction:** | John wears a raincoat *when* it rains. |
| | (time) |
| **Clause reversal:** | *Because* it rains, John wears a raincoat. |
| | *If* it rains, John wears a raincoat. |
| | (condition) |
| | *When* it rains, John wears a raincoat. |
| | (time) |

Several of the subordinating conjunctions, including "since" and "as," are used as synonyms for more common forms. A substitution format may be used to establish the less frequent synonyms of conjunctions. The following examples illustrate a possible progression for intervention.

| | |
|---|---|
| **Reference conjunction:** | John wears a raincoat *because* it rains. |
| **Since conjunction:** | John wears a raincoat *since* it rains. |
| **As conjunction:** | John wears a raincoat *as* it rains. |
| **Clause reversal:** | *Because* it rains, John wears a raincoat. |
| | *Since* it rains, John wears a raincoat. |
| | *As* it rains, John wears a raincoat. |

The conjunctions "although," "though," and "even though" may be introduced after the conjunctions "since" and "as" have been learned. The clinician should keep the word selections the same as in the earlier conjunctions. The next sentences illustrate a possible progression for introducing "although," "though," and "even though." The actual progression should depend upon which of the three forms is the preferred and most common in the youngster's environment.

| | |
|---|---|
| **Reference example:** | John wears a raincoat.     It does *not* rain. |
| **Although conjunction:** | John wears a raincoat *although* it does not rain. |

| **Though conjunction:** | John wears a raincoat *though* it does not rain. |
| **Even though conjunction:** | John wears a raincoat *even though* it does not rain. |
| **Clause reversal:** | *Although* it does not rain, John wears a raincoat. |
| | *Though* it does not rain, John wears a raincoat. |
| | *Even though* it does not rain, John wears a raincoat. |

Among formats that lend themselves to invention programs on conjunctions with subordinated clauses are resolution of conjunctions into their components, sentence transformation with incorporation of conjunctions, recognition of deep structure identity, paraphrase, normalization of scrambled sentences, and synthesis of component sentences into conjunctions. The examples below illustrate each of these formats with the conjunctions "because," "since," and "as."

*Resolution of conjunctions into component propositions*

John ate a hamburger because he was hungry.
John was hungry.
John ate a hamburger.

Since he was tired, Dad went to bed.
Dad was tired.
Dad went to bed.

Sally ran as she was late.
Sally ran.
Sally was late.

*Sentence transformation with incorporation of conjunctions*

Make a sentence with the word "because."

Make a sentence with the word "as."

*Recognition of deep structure identity*

Because I am thirsty, I want some water.
I want some water because I am thirsty.     (same/different)

Since it rains, I will not leave now.
I will not leave now as it rains.           (same/different)

*Paraphrase*

| **Sample conjunction:** | Jane went home because it was late. |
| **Paraphrase:** | Because _____. |
| | Since _____. |
| | As _____. |

*Normalization of scrambled conjunctions*

Jane     since     was     she     late     ran

Jane ran since she was late.
Since Jane was late, she ran.
Since she was late, Jane ran.

*Synthesis of component sentences into conjunctions*

Jorge is in bed.     Jorge is ill.
Jorge is in bed *because/since/as* he is ill.
*Because/since/as* Jorge is ill, he is in bed.

Neva went to London.     Neva wanted to visit her uncle.
Neva went to London *because/since/as* she wanted to visit her uncle.
*Because/since/as* Neva wanted to visit her uncle, she went to London.

## Complex Sentences

Indefinite adverbial clauses, noun phrase complements, and embedded and nonembedded relative clauses can all be taught with the same techniques in an intervention program. Among formats for intervention that lend themselves to working on these rules are: judgment of correct grammar, resolution of complex sentences into their components, normalization of scrambled sentences, and synthesis of component sentences into complex sentences. These formats must be used along with repeated reiteration of the rules that govern the selection of specific relatives and the placement of the relative clause, indefinite adverbial clause, or noun phrase complement. The clinician should also explain the underlying meaning and the relationships among words, phrases, and clauses. Here are examples of each of the formats for intervention suggested above.

*Judgment of correct grammar*

The man, which lives next door, is in Europe.     (right/wrong)
The dog, which is barking, is my neighbor's.     (right/wrong)

*Resolution into component propositions*

The girl, who is wearing the red dress, is my sister.
The girl is my sister.
The girl is wearing a red dress.

The men, who are carrying the furniture, are the movers.
The men are carrying the furniture.
The men are the movers.

*Normalization of scrambled sentences*

the boy     is     who     is wearing     my brother     jeans
The boy, who is wearing jeans, is my brother.

*Synthesis of component sentences*

The boy is angry.     The boy lost his bike.
The boy, who is angry, lost his bike.

The horse was kicking furiously.     The horse was my uncle's.
The horse, that/which was kicking furiously, was my uncle's.

## Ambiguous Sentences

Learning disabled children and adolescents may not have problems with ambiguous sentences as long as the sentences occur in a familiar context. The child can then use experiential and contextual cues to resolve the ambiguity and help interpret the sentence accurately. Problems in perceiving and interpreting ambiguous sentences may become evident, however, in rapid conversation, where the context or topic may suddenly change. These problems also show up in understanding isolated sentences or in reading comprehension where the context may not be obvious.

Ambiguities in sentences may arise at the semantic level, when one or more of the words in a sentence has several meanings. The perception and resolution of a semantic ambiguity depends upon adequate knowledge of the range of possible meanings of the featured word as well as upon adequate use of the available contextual cues. Intervention strategies aimed at establishing adequate knowledge of multiple-meaning words and therefore indirectly of semantic ambiguities are described in chapter 9.

Ambiguities in sentences may also arise at the syntactic level. A sentence can be syntactically ambiguous because one of its clauses can be interpreted both concretely and idiomatically. For example, the sentence "He laughed at the car" can be interpreted concretely as "He laughed while standing at the car" or idiomatically as "He laughed because the car was funny looking." Syntactic ambiguity may also arise when one of the clauses in a sentence can be resolved into two different structures. For example, in the sentence "He fed her dog bones" the clause "her dog bones" can be interpreted to contain an indirect object ("her"), a direct object ("bones") and a modifier ("dog") and to mean "He fed her the kind of bones you feed to a dog." It can also be interpreted to contain an indirect object ("her dog") and a direct object ("bones") and to mean "He fed bones to her dog."

Sentences may also be ambiguous at the level of the underlying meaning (deep structure). These ambiguities arise when the same word may function either as the subject or the object of the stated action. As an example, in the sentence "The duck is ready to eat," the word "duck" may be used to refer to the subject of the action, as in the paraphrase "The duck is about to eat its food." The word "duck" may, however, also be interpreted to refer to the object of the action of eating, as in the paraphrase "You can eat the duck now; it is cooked and ready."

Fortunately, the range of sentence transformations and word choices which can lead to syntactic or deep structure ambiguities in sentences is limited. The ambiguous sentences given above are typical illustrations. The objective in intervention may therefore be to develop the child's awareness of the sentence structures and word choices that can lead to ambiguity. A second goal is to teach the child to find alternative interpretations for these sentences. Sentence transformations that should be featured in intervention are (1) sentences with idiomatic use of prepositional phrases, (2) sentences with indirect object transformations ("He told *his navy stories*"), (3) sentences that feature verb phrases such as "is"/"are ready to," and (4) sentences with nominalization of verbs in the noun phrase ("*Visiting relatives* can be a nuisance"). Among formats which may be used in intervention are sentence or paragraph paraphrase and picture identification. Before these formats are introduced, you may, however, need to establish basic awareness of the fact that some sentences may have more than one meaning. The examples below illustrate possible intervention formats.

*Establishing awareness of multiple sentence meanings*

(a) **Prepositional phrases**
*Listen to this word: "laugh." Show me how you do it.*
*There are many ways in which you can laugh. Tell me how you can laugh. You can laugh* loudly.
You can laugh _____.
You can laugh _____.
You can laugh _____.

*There are many places where you can laugh. Tell me some places where you could laugh. You can laugh* at school.
You can laugh at _____.
You can laugh at _____.
You can laugh at _____.
You can laugh at _____.

*There are many things that are funny and make you laugh. Tell me some funny things that make you laugh. You could laugh at* a clown.
You can laugh at _____.
You can laugh at _____.
You can laugh at _____.

*Now listen to this sentence.*
The boy laughed at the car.
*Tell me what that means. Could it mean something else? Tell me what else it could mean.*

(b) **Indirect object transformation**
*Listen to this sentence.*
The man saw a walking stick.
*Could it mean a stick was walking by itself along the road?* (yes/no)
*Could it mean the man saw a stick he could use to support himself while walking?* (yes/no)

(c) **Nominalization**
*Listen to this sentence.*
Visiting friends can be a pain.
*Could it mean that when you visit your friends it is sometimes unpleasant? (yes/no)*
*Can you think of something else it could mean?*

*Paraphrase format*

*Listen to this sentence.*
Eating apples cost more than cooking apples.
*Can you say what that means in a different way?*
*Can you give me another meaning for the sentence?*

*Picture identification*

*Listen to this sentence.*
The duck is ready to eat.
*Point to the pictures that show what it could mean* (on page 152).

# THE DUCK IS READY TO EAT.

## SELECTED INTERVENTION PROGRAMS AND RESOURCES

### Interactive Language Development Teaching

Lee, Koenigsknecht, and Mulhern (1975) introduced a syntax development program that is appropriate for youngsters with language delays and disabilities in preschool settings, nursery school, kindergarten, and the early elementary grades. The program was developed on the basis of **psycholinguistic** findings and principles. It uses a conversational setting that closely resembles the setting for normal language development. The format centers around storytelling. It features short stories that incorporate key word formations and sentence structures. The child is required to respond to specific questions or prompts that relate to the plot line of each story. The format emphasizes interpretation while it helps the child learn to abstract, recall, and use specific syntactic and transformational rules.

The narrative materials featured in these lessons reflect the experiences and backgrounds of young children. They are concrete and describe everyday activities involving typical families. Each lesson is preceded by an overview of the materials needed, the concepts and vocabulary featured, and the grammatical structures that receive primary or secondary emphasis in the lesson. Guidelines are provided for the verbal interactions between the educator-clinician and the child (pages 19–23). The guidelines suggest how responses may be elicited and emphasize model sentence imitation, sentence completion, expansion, self-correction, and rephrasing of requests.

The language training program is divided into two levels. Level I emphasizes the acquisition and productive control of basic sentence structures, coordination of clauses, and simple transformations. Level II features grammatical structures that develop later. It stresses elaboration of the verb phrase, secondary verb forms, conjunction, and more complex transformations. The program may be used with individual children or with small groups.

The efficacy of the Interactive Language Development Teaching program has been assessed with a group of 25 children ranging in age from 3 years, 2 months to 5 years, 9 months. After a treatment period of 8.3 months, these language delayed children showed significant gains in both receptive and expressive language abilities. Clinically significant gains in the control of syntax in language production were observed on several formal measures. Their Developmental Sentence Scores (DSS) (Lee, 1974) indicated a mean gain of 10.8 months. Performances on the ITPA Grammatic Closure subtest (Kirk, McCarthy, & Kirk, 1968) indicated a mean gain of 15.0 months. The mean gain on the Northwestern Syntax Screening Test: Expressive (Lee, 1971) was 6.8 months. These results support the use of the method and program.

*See chapter 5 for a discussion of these assessment measures.*

## Semel Auditory Processing Program

The Semel Auditory Processing Program (SAPP) (Semel, 1976) is designed to enable classroom teachers or specialists to remediate problems in processing spoken language. The program contains three levels. The Beginning Level is designed for developmental ages 3 to 7 years; the Intermediate Level, for developmental ages 7 to 11 years; the Advanced Level, for developmental ages 11 years and up. Each level features a teacher's manual, a student's response book, and a set of 96 activity cards. The teacher's manual contains an introduction to aspects of auditory processing, a description of the program at the level, assessment guidelines, and suggestions for use. The student's response book provides for paper-and-pencil responses for each of the units. The activity cards provide additional opportunities for work in all areas of processing.

The three levels of the SAPP are identical in format, but they differ in the difficulty of the words presented and of the structures and activities featured. Sections and activities that focus on linguistic skills emphasize morphological and syntactic rule learning while using a variety of formats. The task requirements stress segmentation of words into morphemes, analysis and synthesis of structures, sentence completion, and oral clozure.

The efficacy of the SAPP has recently been evaluated by Semel and Wiig (1980). It was administered to a group of 45 language and learning disabled youngsters in the age range from 7 years, 6 months to 11 years, 0 months. A significant proportion of these youngsters made gains on the following tests: Detroit Tests of Learning Aptitude: Auditory Attention Span for Unrelated Words and Verbal Absurdities subtests (Baker & Leland, 1958), Illinois Test of Psycholinguistic Abilities: Grammatic Closure subtest (Kirk, McCarthy, & Kirk, 1968), and Carrow Elicited Language Inventory (Carrow, 1974). The mean performance gain on the Carrow Elicited Language Inventory was 12.57%. The mean performance gain on the DTLA Auditory Attention Span for Unrelated Words subtest was 15.73 months and on the Verbal Absurdities subtest 22.0 months. The mean gain on the ITPA Grammatic Closure subtest was 15.84 months. These gains were obtained over a training period equivalent to 15 weeks, during which intervention was provided for 30 minutes daily.

## Other Programs and Resources

1. *Developmental Syntax*(Coughran-Liles Syntax Program).
   Lila Coughran and Betty V. Liles. Learning Concepts, 2501 North Lamar, Austin, TX 78705.

2. *Language Lotto.*
   Lassar G. Gotkin. New Century Education Corporation, 440 Park Avenue South, New York, NY 10016.

3. *Monterey Language Program* (Programmed Conditioning for Language).
   Burl B. Gray and Bruce P. Ryan. Monterey Learning Systems, 900 Welch Road, Palo Alto, CA 94304.

4. *National Language Learning—English and Spanish.*
   Harris Winitz, James Reeds, and Paul Garcia. General Linguistics Corporation, P.O. Box 7172, Kansas City, MO 64113.

5. *Peabody Language Development Kit—Level P.*
   Lloyd M. Dunn, J. O. Smith, and Katherine B. Horton. American Guidance Service, Circle Pines, MN 55014.

6. *Peabody Language Development Kits—Levels 1, 2, and 3.*
   Lloyd M. Dunn and J. O. Smith. American Guidance Service, Circle Pines, MN 55014.

7. *Teaching the American Language to Kids (TALK).*
   Richard Dever. Charles E. Merrill Publishing Company, 1300 Alum Creek Drive, Columbus, OH 43216.

8. *Wilson Initial Syntax Program (WISP).*
   Mary S. Wilson. Educators Publishing Service, 74 Moulton Street, Cambridge, MA 02138.

9. *Wilson Expanded Syntax Program (WESP).*
   Mary S. Wilson. Educators Publishing Service, 74 Moulton Street, Cambridge, MA 02138.

10. *Fokes Sentence Builder.*
    Joann Fokes. Teaching Resources, 100 Boylston Street, Boston, MA 02116.

11. *Fokes Sentence Builder Expansion.*
    Joann Fokes. Teaching Resources, 100 Boylston Street, Boston, MA 02116.

12. *Developmental Language Lessons.*
    Charlane W. Mowery and Anne Replogle. Teaching Resources, 100 Boylston Street, Boston, MA 02116.

13. *Syntax Development: A Generative Grammar Approach to Language Development.*
    Mary S. Wilson. Educators Publishing Service, 74 Moulton Street, Cambridge, MA 02138.

14. *Syntax of Kindergarten and Elementary School Children.*
    R. C. O'Donnell, W. J. Griffin, and R. C. Norris. National Council of Teachers of English, 1111 Kenyon Road, Urbana, IL 61801.

## Selected Language Development Texts

1. *Language Development: Structure and Function,* 2nd edition.
   P. Dale. Holt, Rinehart, and Winston, New York, NY. 1976.

2. *Language Acquisition.*
   J. G. deVilliers and P. A. deVilliers. Harvard University Press, Cambridge, MA. 1978.

3. *The Acquisition and Development of Language.*
   P. Menyuk. Prentice-Hall, Inc., Englewood Cliffs, NJ. 1971.

4. *Language and Maturation.*
   P. Menyuk. The MIT Press, Cambridge, MA. 1977.

5. *Children and Communication: Verbal and Nonverbal Language Development.*
   B. S. Wood. Prentice-Hall, Inc., Englewood Cliffs, NJ. 1976.

*part* III

Semantics

# UNDERSTANDING WORDS AND WORD RELATIONSHIPS
## Characteristics

# 7

Without understanding specific word meanings and the meanings of relationships among words, a listener would get very little information from a sentence. The semantic component of language is concerned with the meanings of single words and word combinations, with multiple word meanings, with figurative language, and with the affect of structure and context on the nature of meaning. A word does not contain a unitary, unalterable, or static meaning. The meanings of words may shift as a function of time, cultural change, the social and experiential context, and arbitrary decision by a group of speakers. New words, phrases, and idioms are constantly added to the language as the need arises. And other words may fall out of use, as we can see in the development of slang. Understanding the nature of word meanings, how they can be affected by various relationships and contexts, and how to shift among word meanings and adapt to new meanings is necessary for precise verbal expression. Some language and learning disabled children and adolescents may have problems with some of the semantic aspects of language. Our current knowledge of their problems is in large part based upon clinical observation. The scientific knowledge we have about learning disabled children's problems in learning the significance of word meanings and relationships is scant. This chapter will describe some of the current observations and issues related to the acquisition and use of word meanings by learning disabled children and adolescents. In chapters 8 and 9 we will discuss some approaches to assessment and intervention.

While many language and learning disabled children earn normal vocabulary development scores on standardized tests such as the Peabody Picture Vocabulary Test (Dunn, 1959) or the WISC Vocabulary subtest (Wechsler, 1949) (Johnson & Myklebust, 1967; Wiig & Semel, 1976), others have striking gaps in their vocabularies. For example, they may fail the item of the Peabody Picture Vocabulary Test for "building." The picture associated with this vocabulary item is a small boy repairing a wagon. Many learning disabled children say that there is no picture of a "building," suggesting they have problems with words having multiple meanings. Other learning disabled children have difficulty with the meaning of action verbs, and others fail items which require knowledge of the meaning of adjectives. A detailed analysis of children's error patterns in vocabulary comprehension often indicates islands of specific deficits in selected word categories. They may have difficulties with the multiple meanings of nouns, verbs, adjectives, adverbs and prepositions. They may show specific delays, for example, in concept formation for words which denote parts of the body, with differentiated body actions and movements, spatial and temporal relationships, attributes of persons, objects and events, or kinship terms.

Because the specific vocabulary deficits of learning disabled children may be frustrating to them, these children may be loquacious and glib, perhaps in an effort to compensate for or mask their vocabulary deficits. Often the loquaciousness is reflected in overuse of nonspecific and indefinite words, in utterances such as "This thing that" or "I went over there to find that thing, whatever it is." When they cannot readily use appropriate vocabulary words, they often use semantically empty place holders such as "whatchama call it," "thing-a-ma-jig," or "whatever it is." They may also try to produce a specific word and end up with a deviant word stream, such as "It is over there, by the place over there. You know, right by the thing you sit on. You know, right there." They may use interjections abundantly as if to stall and delay, resulting in utterances such as "I, uh, kind of would like to, uhm, have something to drink, uhm, maybe, uh, a coke." They may indicate their hesitancy by filling pauses and repeating words, and may produce nonspecific and extraneous utterances such as "Well, Julie and what's her name? Jane, went to a sort of place in the mountains. I'm not sure where it was. Well, anyway. They went to this place in the mountains and they learned, well, you know, to ski."

Presented with the task of defining words, as on the WISC Vocabulary test, their responses may be correct but words that occur frequently in the definitions of other children may be conspicuously absent. For example, in defining the word "diamond," frequent responses are: "A precious stone," "A jewel," "It sparkles," or "It is very valuable." In contrast, learning disabled children may offer:

(1) Alternate definitions, such as "A place where you play baseball," or "A card like clubs, hearts, or spades in a deck of cards."
(2) An associated word substitution, such as "A spade" or "A shovel."
(3) A functional definition of either the target word or an associated word, such as "A diamond is a thing you wear on your finger" or "A spade is a thing that you dig with."
(4) Superordinate class names, such as "A diamond is a ring" or "A spade is a garden tool."
(5) An action in which the item or an associated item would be used as the instrument of the action, as in "If you have some glass, you could use it to cut with" or "If there was snow in your driveway, you could dig with it."

**FIGURE 7.1**
*Definition of Diamond*

In order to avoid words they are unsure of or to mask their imprecise use of words, learning disabled children may change the topic of conversation. When they are unsure of a target word, they may founder as they search for a substitute word. As a result, they may produce oblique responses such as "Well, fur. It is. Well, I like to go hunting for squirrels with my daddy. We have a new baby in our house. Did you eat turkey for Thanksgiving?" Table 7.1 presents an overview of the various characteristics of word use that may result from the specific vocabulary deficits of learning disabled children.

**TABLE 7.1**

*Characteristics of word use in the spoken utterances of language and learning disabled children*

| Characteristic | Content | Sample Utterances |
|---|---|---|
| Lack of specificity. | Overuse of indefinite words. | "This thing that"<br><br>"It's something like" |
| Effort to maintain topic. | Circumlocution around the topic. | "It's over there, by the place over there. Right by the thing over there." |
| | Overuse of functional definitions. | "You know, the thing that you sit on" |
| Hesitancy. | Overuse of interjections and place holders. | "You know, uhm, I would like, uh, well, er . . ., you know, uhm, a coke." |
| | Filling of pauses with word repetitions. | "Now, you see that. It's a building. Now, it's a a tall building." |
| | Filling of pauses with repetitions of phrases. | "I have a pencil, you know, and there's a book, you know." |
| | Overuse of meaningless starters. | "Now, you see; well, it's on my back." |
| Topical discontinuity. | Frequent changes in topic. | "What are feathers? Well. I like to go hunting with my uncle. Did you ever eat pheasant?" |

# DEFICITS IN SPECIFIC WORD CATEGORIES

Language and learning disabled youngsters may have difficulties in accurate and broad understanding of specific categories of words. They may have problems interpreting multiple-meaning words accurately. Words that belong to certain semantic–grammatic word categories may present problems of both processing and production. Among the word categories that may be involved are verbs (action references), adjectives (attribute references), adverbs (action modifiers), prepositions (spatial-temporal referents), and pronouns (substitute references for persons, quantity, space, and time). An overview of the characteristics and possible bases for the problems in understanding and using certain words and word categories is presented in Table 7.2. The problems that may be associated with each word category are discussed in greater detail in the next sections.

**TABLE 7.2**

*Characteristics and bases of semantic deficits among learning disabled children and adolescents*

| Semantic Category | Structural-Semantic Category Affected | Examples | Bases |
|---|---|---|---|
| Multiple-meaning words. | Nouns. | "glasses" (for seeing or drinking) | Problems in (1) shifting from one alternative interpretation to another, (2) differentiating the concrete and the abstract, generalized interpretations of words, phrases and sentences, and (3) differentiating differences in word meaning when they are determined by grammatical class membership, as in the utterances "He likes to *run*" and "There is a *run* in your stocking." |
| | Verbs. | "running" (person, water, engine) | |
| | Adjectives. | "short" (opposite of tall/long) | |
| | Adverbs. | "loudly" (intensely, garishly) | |
| | Prepositions. | "at" (location, time, idiomatic use) | |
| | Figurative language. Idioms. Metaphors. | "eyes" (sharp, dancing) "as . . . as . . ." (. . . white . . . snow) | |
| | Proverbs. | "Strike while the iron is hot." | |
| | Lexical ambiguities in sentences. | "She wiped her *glasses*." | |
| Action references. | Verbs. | "balancing," "bouncing," "tumbling," etc. "bring"/"ring," "driving"/"diving" | Problems in (1) learning labels for subtle differences in motor actions, and (2) auditory discrimination. |
| Attribute, affect, quantity, etc. | Adjectives. | "long"/"short," etc. | Problems in spatial discrimination and labelling. |
| | | "first"/"last," etc. | Problems in temporal discrimination and labelling. |
| | | "sweet"/"bitter"; "rough") "smooth"; "happy"/"sad"; "pretty"/"ugly," etc. | Problems in discriminating and labelling qualities of taste, texture, affect, attractiveness, etc. |
| Modification of actions. | Adverbs. | "somewhere"/"anywhere"; "quickly"/"slowly," etc./ | Problems in differentiating and labelling indefinite, relative spatial/temporal references. |

**TABLE 7.2 (*Continued*)**

| Semantic Category | Structural-Semantic Category Affected | Examples | Bases |
|---|---|---|---|
| Modification of actions. | Adverbs. | "The man is walking *proudly*"—"The *proud* man is walking." | Problems in understanding and perceiving the function of adverbs in relation to the deep structure. |
| Spatial-temporal referents. | Prepositions. | "in," "on," "under," "by," "at," "to" | Problems in the perception and internalized linguistic labelling of (1) definite and indefinite spatial references, |
| | | "before," "after," "around," "while," "during," | (2) definite and indefinite temporal references, |
| | | "run up," "down." | (3) directional or conditional changes. |
| | | "in"/"on," "behind"/ "beside"/"beneath" | Problems in auditory discrimination. |
| Substitute references for persons, animals, objects, etc. | Personal pronouns. | "he"/"she," "him"/"her" | Problems in differentiating gender. |
| | | "I"/"you," "we"/"us"/ "they" | Problems in differentiating number and person contrast. |
| | | "She," "her," "her," "hers" | Problems in differentiating case. |
| | | "*It* is a nice day." | Problems in the referentially neutral use. |
| | | "*You* (all) made a mess." | Problems in exclusive use of *you*. |
| | | "her"/"hers," "our"/ "ours," "my"/"mine" | Problems in differentiating possessive and possessive-replacive use of pronouns. |
| | | "*Her* mother lent *her her* car while *she* was waiting for *hers*." | Problems in recalling referents in extended discourse. |
| Shared subject-object reference. | Reflexive pronouns. | "Jack washed herself"; "He shaved hisself." | Problems in forming associations with (1) the references and (2) the corresponding personal pronouns. |
| Proximal-distant contrast references. | Demonstrative pronouns. | "this," "that," "these," "those" | Problems in (1) auditory discrimination and (2) perceiving and internalizing linguistic labels for differences in orientation in space and time. |
| Indefinite references to persons, quantity, space, time. | Indefinite pronouns. | "somebody," "anywhere," "everything" | Problems in identifying and interpreting the components of the compounded pronouns. |

**TABLE 7.2** (*Continued*)

| Semantic Category | Structural-Semantic Category Affected | Examples | Bases |
|---|---|---|---|
| | | "any-"/"no-" | Problems in differentiating concepts of inclusion/exclusion. |
| | | "somebody"/ "something" | Problems in differentiating pronouns within the same class. |

## Multiple-Meaning Words

The problems of learning disabled children in interpreting multiple-meaning words appropriately have been attributed to the following causes, among others:

(1) Tendency to remain concrete.
(2) Limitations in imagery.
(3) Limitations in use of symbols.
(4) Limitations in conceptualizing.
(5) Retention of narrow word meanings.
(6) Adherence to the most frequent and concrete word meanings.
(7) Limitations in the ability to shift from one grammatic-semantic category to another.
(8) Perceptual adherence to one reference (Johnson & Myklebust, 1967; Klees & Lebrun, 1972; Wiig & Semel, 1976).

Examples of learning disabled children's difficulties in interpreting multiple-meaning words appropriately are abundant. They may misinterpret sentences such as "She wiped the *glasses*" and "The bill is *large*," which are ambiguous because they contain dual or multiple-meaning words. They may have problems in responding promptly and correctly to a simple statement such as "The *nail* broke," if they fail to distinguish the two meanings of the word *nail*, to use the available contextual cues, to evaluate the alternatives logically, or to ask for further clarification. In general, they will adhere to one interpretation of dual or multiple-meaning words and are slow to shift from one alternative interpretation to another. There are similar problems in learning disabled children's interpretations of multiple-meaning action verbs, such as *go* as in the sentences "The car *goes* fast," "The engine wouldn't *go*," "She is always *on the go*," and "You can't *go by* what she says." Another common problem verb is *run*, as in the sentences "Can you *run*?" "The engine doesn't *run*," "The water is *running*," "I always *run into* your aunt downtown," and "You are *run down*."

Special problems seem to arise when the various meanings of a multiple-meaning word involve words which belong to different grammatical categories. For example, the word "run" belongs to the class of nouns, with reference to either a run in a stocking or a process of action, e.g., "on the run." "Run" also belongs to the class of verbs, with reference to (1) rapid body movement, e.g., "I can run," (2) the action of an engine or machine, e.g., "The car runs," "The sewing machine runs," or (3) an idiomatic use, e.g., "His thoughts run in circles," "His nose is running." In addition, the root word "run" may occur in a compound word such as "runway," adding to the child's confusion.

The learning disabled child may also not be able to accommodate for changes in word meaning and in the grammatical category of a word when these changes are determined by context or syntax. He may not understand the contrast in word meaning when a word such as "building" is used in the sentences "He was in the building" and "He was building." In a similar vein, the learning disabled child may misinterpret a common direction to "Go check it" and respond that he cannot write a check. The error responses of learning disabled children to multiple-meaning words suggest that they interpret these words according to their most common and/or concrete meaning and grammatical class membership.

## Verbs

The verbs that tend to cause difficulties for the learning disabled child describe complex actions or movements for which the child has not learned the motor or conceptual patterns. Examples of problem verbs include "balancing," "bouncing," "crawling," "crouching," "evading," "leaping," "passing," "punching," "swaying," "tossing," "tumbling," "twisting," and "vaulting." Outside the range of complex action verbs, the forms of the copula *to be* seem to cause special problems for learning disabled children, both in processing and producing spoken language. On one hand, they may fail to see that the meanings (deep structure) of the phrases "The tall man" and "The man is tall" are identical and that the two forms can be used interchangeably for stylistic variation. On the other hand, they may interpret the copula *to be* in "unmarked" sentences such as "The man is tall" and "Jane is pretty" to imply change over time, and conclude that the sentences state that yesterday the man was *not* tall and Jane was *not* pretty.

**Style** *is the arrangement of correct forms to achieve an effect or carry out a purpose.*

Learning disabled children may have peculiar problems in discriminating and differentiating verbs with similar sound sequences. Verbs that may cause confusion because of their similarities in sound and lead to problems of interpretation include:

(1) bring–ring
(2) spell–sell
(3) send–bend–lend
(4) driving–diving
(5) falling–feeling–filling
(6) smelling–smiling
(7) growing–groaning

Normal development patterns for the acquisition of selected verb meanings suggest the progression for some common action verbs shown in Table 7.3 (Carrow, 1973).

**TABLE 7.3**

*Order of acquisition of verbs (from Carrow, 1973)*

| | Age of Acquisition | |
|---|---|---|
| Verb Form | By 75% | By 90% |
| jumping | 3–0 yrs. | 3–0 yrs. |
| jump | 3–0 yrs. | 3–6 yrs. |
| running | 3–0 yrs. | 3–6 yrs. |
| hitting | 3–0 yrs. | 3–6 yrs. |
| sewing | 3–0 yrs. | 4–0 yrs. |
| giving | 3–6 yrs. | 4–0 yrs. |
| drawing | 3–6 yrs. | 5–0 yrs. |
| going | 3–6 yrs. | 5–6 yrs. |
| eating | 4–0 yrs. | 4–6 yrs. |
| catching | 5–6 yrs. | 6–6 yrs. |
| coming | 7–0+ yrs. | 7–0+ yrs. |

It is also possible to use the Peabody Picture Vocabulary Test (Dunn, 1959) as a source of information about the sequence and the approximate age range when normal children learn the differentiated meaning of certain verbs. Their sequence, with approximate age levels, is shown in Table 7.4.

This sequence suggests a progression along several dimensions. First, children progress from concrete and easily observable action

**TABLE 7.4**

*Order of acquisition of verbs (from Dunn, 1957)*

| Form A | Form B | Approximate Ages of Acquisition |
|---|---|---|
| blowing | climbing | 3–3 to  4–2 yrs. |
| digging | sitting | 3–3 to  4–2 yrs. |
| catching | pulling | 3–3 to  4–2 yrs. |
| tying | hitting | 4–3 to  5–5 yrs. |
| pouring | ringing | 4–3 to  5–5 yrs. |
| sewing | baking | 4–3 to  5–5 yrs. |
| building | peeking | 5–6 to  7–5 yrs. |
| picking | skiing | 5–6 to  7–5 yrs. |
| shining | balancing | 7–6 to  9–5 yrs. |
| yawning | pledging | 7–6 to  9–5 yrs. |
| tackling | gnawing | 9–6 to 11–5 yrs. |
| directing | filing | 11–6 to 13–5 yrs. |
| — | harvesting | 11–6 to 13–5 yrs. |
| assaulting | erecting | 11–6 to 13–5 yrs. |
| hoisting | soldering | 13–6 to 15–5 yrs. |
| wailing | — | 13–6 to 15–5 yrs. |
| — | dwelling | 15–6 to 17–5 yrs. |
| hovering | lubricating | 15–6 to 17–5 yrs. |
| probing | confiding | 17–6+ yrs. |
| angling | reclining | 17–6+ yrs. |
| appraising | frisking | 17–6+ yrs. |
| confining | — | 17–6+ yrs. |

references to abstract and subtle action and affect references. Second, they move from early acquired, **gross motor** and concrete actions to later acquired, **fine motor** and highly differentiated actions. Third, the relative frequency of the verbs in the English language and the origin of the verb forms seem to influence the developmental sequence. Verbs of Anglo-Saxon origin, such as "blow," "build," and "sew," seem to be acquired relatively early, while verbs of Romance origin, such as "confide," "confine," and "erect" tend to be acquired later.

When these two sets of developmental data are compared, we find inconsistencies in the reported ages of acquisition. Thus, while "catching" and "sewing" appear in both sets, they appear in opposite order of acquisition and with different ages of acquisition. These inconsistencies may reflect differences in the test items, but they should be considered when you use the normal data to develop expectations for a learning disabled child.

## Adjectives

Learning disabled children show several kinds of difficulties in interpreting adjectives, including:

(1) Problems in perceiving and differentiating the spatial meanings expressed by adjectives that denote length ("long," "short," etc.) height ("tall," "short,"), width ("thin," "wide," "narrow," etc.), or distance ("near," "far," "distant," etc.).
(2) Problems in perceiving and differentiating the temporal meanings expressed by adjectives that denote time, such as "early," "late," "first," "last."
(3) Problems in perceiving and differentiating the attributes and qualities expressed by adjectives that denote taste ("sweet," "sour," etc.), smell ("sweet," "pungent," etc.), attractiveness ("pretty," "ugly," etc.), texture ("rough," "smooth," etc.), and/or affect ("happy," "sad," etc.).
(4) Deficits in retaining and recalling adjective sequences (modifier strings) such as "The *small, vicious, grey* dog" or "He bought a *new, heavy, shiny, red* truck."
(5) Problems in interpreting dual or multiple-meaning adjectives correctly, as in ambiguous sentences such as "The bill is *large*" (size or amount).

Any statement which describes how a person perceives an event or object is necessarily abstract. Because everyone's perceptions are unique, their differences in the perception and interpretation of an event often result in variations in how they think about things, the words which they use to describe them, and the ease with which they understand other people's statements about them (Clark, Carpenter, & Just, 1973). For example, one person seeing a glass of water filled to the midline may think and say that the glass is half-empty. Another, seeing the same glass of water, may say that it is half-full. In turn, the first person may need additional time to interpret a statement about the event which describes the glass as being half-full. The second person would have similar problems hearing a statement to the effect that the glass is half-empty.

The ways learning disabled children understand and use adjectives seem closely tied to their perception and interpretation of auditory, visual-spatial, temporal, tactile, kinesthetic, and affective events. They often seem to be confused and to have perceptual deficits, resulting in variations in their initial interpretation and internalized description of events and objects. They then have difficulties in interpreting and using adjectives. For example, a learning disabled child who has a visual-perceptual deficit may not perceive the subtle differences in facial and body motions which differentiate emotions such as surprise and anger. As a consequence, this child may interpret and describe both emotions as anger and may not understand a statement such as "Here Jane is surprised and here she is angry."

Adjectives which denote attributes such as color, size, and shape seem to be more easily understood by learning disabled children than adjectives which denote spatial or temporal meaning. Adjectives which denote affective, quantitative, or qualitative meanings appear harder to grasp. Learning disabled children have a number of problems with adjectives, including the following:

(1) Problems in spatial-temporal perception are commonly reflected problems with adjectives that denote length, height, width, distance, time, affect, or age.
(2) Problems in olfactory, tactile, or kinesthetic perception are commonly reflected in problems in interpreting and using adjectives that denote smell, taste, texture, temperature, or pain.
(3) Problems in logical processing or seriation commonly affect the interpretation and use of adjectives that denote attractiveness or relative quality and the use of the comparative and superlative forms of adjectives.
(4) Problems in short-term auditory memory, simultaneous analysis and synthesis, and rule learning for the constraints on adjective order commonly cause difficulties in interpreting and using adjective sequences such as "big, heavy, shiny, grey," etc.

Many disabled children show discrepancies in interpreting and recalling adjectives as compared to their academically achieving peers. They have problems in recalling and interpreting a sequence of critical words such as "Happy little boy sleeping," in understanding comparative linguistic relationships such as "Are apples bigger than watermelons?" and in repeating sentences with adjective sequences such as "He has sold the long, heavy, grey, shiny car" (Semel & Wiig, 1975; Wiig & Roach, 1975; Wiig & Semel, 1973, 1974a).

The early, normal sequence of acquisition of adjective meaning has been reported as shown in Table 7.5 (Carrow, 1973). Table 7.6 shows the sequence and ages of acquisition for paired adjectives denoting size, quality, quantity, and position, as observed by Bangs (1975).

**TABLE 7.5**
*Order of acquisition of adjective meaning*

| Attribute | Adjective | Age of Acquisition | |
|---|---|---|---|
| | | By 75% | By 90% |
| Size. | little | 3–0 yrs. | 4–0 yrs. |
| | big | 3–6 yrs. | 4–6 yrs. |
| Color. | red | 3–0 yrs. | 3–6 yrs. |
| | black | 3–6 yrs. | 4–0 yrs. |
| | yellow | 3–6 yrs. | 5–0 yrs. |
| Size and color. | small, red | 4–0 yrs. | 6–0 yrs. |
| | large, blue | 5–6 yrs. | 7–0+ yrs. |
| Color sequence. | black and white | 4–6 yrs. | 6–6 yrs. |
| Speed. | fast | 4–0 yrs. | 6–0 yrs. |
| Height. | tall | 4–6 yrs. | 5–0 yrs. |
| Texture. | soft | 5–0 yrs. | 6–0 yrs. |

**TABLE 7.6**
*Sequence of acquisition of paired adjectives*

| Attribute | Aspect | Adjective | Age of Acquisition |
|---|---|---|---|
| Size. | Spatial. | big | 2–6 to 3–0 yrs. |
| Size. | Spatial. | little | 3–6 to 4–0 yrs. |
| Length. | Spatial. | tall | 2–6 to 3–0 yrs. |
| Length. | Spatial. | short | 4–0 to 4–6 yrs. |
| Width-volume. | Spatial. | fat | 4–0 to 4–6 yrs. |
| Width-volume. | Spatial. | thin | 4–6 to 5–0 yrs. |
| Quality-texture. | Tactile. | soft | 2–6 to 3–0 yrs. |
| Quality-texture. | Tactile. | hard | 3–0 to 3–6 yrs. |
| Quality-weight. | Spatial. | heavy | 2–6 to 3–0 yrs. |
| Quality-weight. | Spatial. | light | 3–6 to 4–0 yrs. |
| Quality. | Spatial, etc. | same | 3–0 to 3–6 yrs. |
| Quality. | Spatial, etc. | different | 4–6 to 5–0 yrs. |
| Quantity-volume. | Spatial. | empty | 3–0 to 3–6 yrs. |
| Quantity-volume. | Spatial. | full | 3–6 to 4–0 yrs. |
| Quantity. | Spatial, etc. | more | 3–6 to 4–0 yrs. |
| Quantity. | Spatial, etc. | less | 3–6 to 4–0 yrs. |
| Position. | Spatial. | high | 3–6 to 4–0 yrs. |
| Position. | Spatial. | low | 4–6 to 5–0 yrs. |
| Position. | Spatial-temporal. | first | 5–0 to 5–6 yrs. |
| Position. | Spatial-temporal. | last | 5–0 to 5–6 yrs. |

## Adverbs

Learning disabled children often misinterpret or fail to process adverbs, avoid them in their own language, and overlook them in reading. Their problems with adverbs seem to reflect:

(1) Difficulties with the grammatical classification and interpretation of adverbs derived from adjectives. These difficulties affect adverbs

derived from adjectives by adding -*ly*, in adverbs such as "quick*ly*," "slow*ly*," and "quiet*ly*."

(2) Difficulties in perceiving the function of adverbs in relation to the underlying meaning of the sentences. Learning disabled children may not know which word in the sentence is modified by the adverb. As a result, they may interpret a sentence such as "The man is walking proudly" to mean "The proud man is walking."

(3) Problems in understanding the attributes and qualities denoted by adverbs derived from adjectives. The problems these derived adverbs pose are similar to those caused by their adjective counterparts.

(4) Problems in understanding the reference points in space denoted by the situationally bound adverbs "here" and "there."

(5) Problems in understanding the indefinite spatial references denoted by situationally bound, indefinite adverbs such as "somewhere," "anywhere," or "nowhere."

Adverbs pose problems for learning disabled children in both understanding and repeating of sentences (Menyuk & Looney, 1972a; Semel & Wiig, 1975; Wiig & Roach, 1975). Both learning disabled children and adolescents show significant deficits in recalling adverbs in the final position of sentences, a position which generally facilitates retention and recall.

## Prepositions

Prepositions may denote (1) position, (2) direction, (3) manner, and (4) time. To be able to accurately internalize a linguistic description for and then interpret a preposition, the child needs adequate visual-spatial perception and understanding. The interpretation of prepositions is further complicated by their multiple meanings. For instance, the preposition "at" may be used to denote:

(1) A point or place in space, as in "*at* the door."
(2) A location or position in time or order in a time sequence, as in "*at* noon," "*at* age 60," and "*at* the beginning."
(3) Presence or location, as in "*at* home" and "*at* hand."
(4) Amount, degree, or rate, as in "*at* high speed" and "*at* great expense."
(5) Goal or objective, as in "look *at* me" and "aim *at* the spot."
(6) Occupation or involvement, as "*at* school" and "*at* work."
(7) State or condition, as in "*at* peace" and "*at* ease."
(8) Cause, as in "He was angry *at* her stubbornness."
(9) Method or manner, as in "The teacher explained *at* length."
(10) Relative quality or value, as in "*at* my worst" and "*at* cost."

The spatial prepositions may be classified according to the dimensions involved in defining the space or location. According to Takahaski (1969), the preposition "at," when used to express space, denotes a *point* (a dimensionless, conceptual space) and is understood by reducing all dimensions. The preposition "to" denotes the first dimension in space, a *line*, which is bound by two points. The preposition "on" denotes two dimensions in space, a *plane* or *surface*, bound by lines. The preposition "in" denotes the fourth dimension in space, a *three-dimensional body* enclosed by surfaces. In terms of this model, learning disabled youngsters seem to have fewer problems in interpreting prepositions which denote a space or location specified by two or three dimensions, as do the prepositions "on" and "in." But they may have significant difficulties with prepositions that denote the first dimension in space or a dimensionless conceptual space, as do the prepositions "to" and "at."

**FIGURE 7.2**
*Locative Prepositions (in-on)*

Clark (1968) distinguishes among the following components of meaning of prepositions: (1) direction, (2) position, (3) manner, and (4) time. This classification system encompasses several functions of prepositions. Prepositions may also have different objects—either something animate, inanimate, or abstract. The prepositions themselves seem to cluster according to these distinctions.

The problems of learning disabled children in acquiring and interpreting prepositions vary from child to child. Their difficulties may relate to:

(1) Problems with understanding the reference points in space indicated by the various prepositions of position or location, such as "in," "on," "under," "over," "in front of," and "behind."

(2) Problems with understanding the changes in direction or condition indicated by the prepositions of direction, as in the phrases "run *over*," "run *under*," "run *up*," "run *down*," "run *to the left*," "run *to the right*."

(3) Problems in differentiating the definite positions, locations, or directions indicated by prepositions such as "on" or "into" from the indefinite positions, locations, or directions indicated by prepositions such as "at" and "to."

(4) Differences in the understanding of prepositions that denote a point or period in time, such as "after," "before," and "during."

(5) Problems in differentiating the spatial and temporal uses of prepositions such as "on," "at," "from," and "around," as in the phrases *"on* Sunday," *"at* noon," *"from* Friday to Saturday," and *"around* noon."

(6) Problems in interpreting and using prepositions that are determined by syntactic structure, as in the sentences "He went *to* school" and "He is *at* school."

(7) Perceptual confusion among prepositions with similar combinations of speech sounds. As an example, the pair "in" and "on" are frequently confused by learning disabled children, but are usually firmly established in normal children by age 2 (Turton, 1966). Prepositions which share a prefix may also be confused, resulting in problems with prepositions such as "behind," "beside," "before," and "beneath." Auditory-perceptual confusion can also be observed with prepositions which share the same consonants, consonant clusters, or vowel combinations, resulting in confusion among the prepositions "before," "after," and "in front of" and "about," "around," and "without."

(8) Problems in understanding the meaning of prepositions when they are used in unusual contexts or structures. For example, the preposition "with" is most often used to indicate the instrument used for an action, as in the sentence "I write *with* a pen." When "with" is used to denote the concept *together with*, as in the sentence "He drove *with* his aunt," it may lead to confusion among learning disabled children. Instructions such as *"With* the red pencil mark the square" or *"With* the blue pencil mark the small circle" may not be understood because of their unusual surface structure. The problems may reflect difficulties in handling the unusual position of the prepositional phrase within the sentences.

(9) Problems in interpreting and using prepositions in idiomatic expressions. As an example, when the verb "look" is used idiomatically, it may combine with several prepositions, as in the sentences:

  (a) She looks *up* to me.
  (b) She looks *down* her nose.
  (c) She looked it *up*.
  (d) She looked *through* me.
  (e) She looked *toward* her vacation.
  (f) She looked *over* the field.
  (g) She looked *into* the matter.
  (h) She looked *out* for herself.

(10) Problems in differentiating among static and dynamic interpretations of prepositions. As an example, a learning disabled child, directed to "Crawl *under* the table" may remain under the table rather than emerge on the other side, if he does not perceive the alternative meaning.

Semel and Wiig (1975) report that learning disabled children may demonstrate significant deficits in interpreting prepositions such as "over," "under," and "behind" in isolation and when presented as part of a sequence of four critical words, as in the instruction "Point to: Monkey sitting *on* fence." Learning disabled children and adolescents may also show significant problems in understanding sentences which contain linguistic relationships such as "The dog fell *on* the cat. Who was on top?" (Wiig & Semel, 1973, 1974).

Normal developmental patterns indicate the progression and age levels for the acquisition of the meaning of selected prepositions shown in Table 7.7 (Bangs, 1975).

**TABLE 7.7**

*Order of acquisition of prepositions*

| Type | Preposition | Age of Acquisition |
|------|-------------|--------------------|
| Locative. | in | 2–0 to 2–6 yrs. |
| Locative. | on | 2–6 to 3–0 yrs. |
| Locative. | under | 2–6 to 3–0 yrs. |
| Directional. | off | 2–0 to 2–6 yrs. |
| Directional. | out of | 2–6 to 3–0 yrs. |
| Directional. | away from | 2–6 to 3–0 yrs. |
| Directional. | toward | 3–0 to 3–6 yrs. |
| Directional. | up | 3–0 to 3–6 yrs. |
| Directional. | down | 4–6 to 5–0 yrs. |
| Locative. | in front of | 3–6 to 4–0 yrs. |
| Locative. | in back of | 3–6 to 4–0 yrs. |
| Locative. | next to | 3–6 to 4–0 yrs. |
| Locative. | beside | 4–0 to 4–6 yrs. |
| Directional. | around | 3–6 to 4–0 yrs. |
| Locative. | ahead of | 5–0 to 5–6 yrs. |
| Locative. | behind | 5–0 to 5–6 yrs. |

## Personal Pronouns

The difficulties of learning disabled children in understanding and using the personal pronouns may be related to:

(1) Problems in differentiating gender for the third person singular pronouns "he" and "she" (subjective case), "him" and "her" (objective case), "his" and "her" (possessive), and "his" and "hers" (possessive replacive). Gender confusion may result in utterances such as "*John* went to the store and then *she* went to the park."

(2) Problems in differentiating the first and second person singular pronouns "I" and "you" (subjective case) and "me" and "you" (objective case) in interpersonal interchanges in which the speaker-listener roles change rapidly. This may result in the learning disabled child answering a question such as "Do you want ice cream?" with the response "Yes, *you* want ice cream."

(3) Misinterpretation of the exclusive use of the personal pronoun "you" as if it referred to only the listener. As a result, the learning

disabled child may interpret a generalized statement such as "You have made a terrible mess so you will have to stay after school to clean up," to refer to him alone.

(4) Overgeneralization of the referential application of the third person singular pronoun "it" to refer to persons, resulting in utterances such as, "The girl was unhappy. *It* started to cry."

(5) Misinterpretation of the referentially neutral pronoun "it" in utterances such as "It is snowing," "It is noon," "It is a beautiful day." In response to these utterances, the learning disabled child may search for a referent to explain who or what caused the stated condition.

(6) Confusions in the interpretation and application of case for the pronouns "I," "you," "he," "she," "it," "we," "you," "they" (subjective/**nominative case**) and "me," "you," "him," "her," "it," "us," "you," "them" (objective/**accusative case**). The confusion appears to result from a lack of firm associations between the corresponding subjective and objective case forms of the pronouns. Typical utterances which reflect this problem are: "*Me* go home," "*Them* didn't go," "Jane gave the ball to *they*," and "*Us* won't go home now."

(7) Confusion in the interpretation and application of the possessive ("my," "your," "his," "her," "its," "our," "their") and possessive **replacive** ("mine," "yours," "his," "hers," "its," "ours," "theirs") forms of the personal pronouns. Examples of utterances which reflect this problem are: "That is *mine* hat," "Those are *yours* apples," or "Them are *theirs* shoes." Problems in interpreting the possessive and possessive replacive forms may be reflected in failure to perceive that the two sentences "The pennies *belong* to *them*" and "The pennies *are theirs*" share the same meaning.

(8) Reiteration and correction of pronouns in spontaneous discourse. As a result of reiteration of pronouns, learning disabled children may produce sentences such as "*My, mine* hat is in the closet," "It's *hims, hers* hat," or "Then *her, she* went to the store."

(9) Problems in remembering and recalling the referents for the personal pronouns in extended discourse. As a result, learning disabled children may confuse or lose track of the referents in extended statements such as "Julie bought a new car. It now belongs to *her. Her* old car broke down. *She* needed a new car badly. *Her* mother lent *her her car* while Julie was waiting for *hers* to be delivered."

(10) Failure to identify the referents for pronouns consistently in extended discourse and confusion in the associations between referents and personal pronouns. These problems may result in extended statements such as "Julie bought a new car. It now belongs to *him. Her* old car broke down. *She* needed a new car badly. *His* mother lent *her his* car while *she* was waiting for *his* car to be delivered to *him*.

Studies of the normal acquisition of pronouns provide information about the relationships among the major stages in normal children's acquisition of syntax and selected pronouns (Brown, 1973; Chipman & deDardel, 1974; Moorehead & Ingram, 1973). The relationships are summarized in Table 7.8.

**TABLE 7.8**

*The acquisition of syntax and of selected pronouns*

| Pronoun-Case | | Linguistic Stage | Approximate Ages |
|---|---|---|---|
| **Subjective.** | | | |
| I | I: | Sentencelike word. | 12–18 mos. |
| you | I: | Sentencelike word. | 12–18 mos. |
| he | III: | Structure. | 24–36 mos. |
| she | III: | Structure. | 24–36 mos. |
| it | I: | Sentencelike word. | 12–18 mos. |
| we | IV: | Operational changes. | 30–48 mos. |
| you | IV: | Operational changes. | 30–48 mos. |
| they | IV: | Operational changes. | 30–48 mos. |
| **Objective.** | | | |
| me | II: | Modification. | 18–24 mos. |
| you | III: | Structure. | 24–36 mos. |
| him | IV: | Operational changes. | 30–48 mos. |
| her | V: | Categorization. | 36–60 mos. |
| it | I: | Sentencelike word. | 12–18 mos. |
| us | IV: | Operational changes. | 30–48 mos. |
| you | IV: | Operational changes. | 30–48 mos. |
| them | III: | Structure. | 24–36 mos. |
| **Possessive.** | | | |
| my | I: | Sentencelike word. | 12–18 mos. |
| your | III: | Structure. | 24–36 mos. |
| his | IV: | Operational changes. | 30–48 mos. |
| her | V: | Categorization. | 36–60 mos. |
| its | V: | Categorization. | 36–60 mos. |
| our | V: | Categorization. | 36–60 mos. |

## Reflexive Pronouns

The reflexive pronouns "myself," "yourself," "himself," "herself," "itself," "yourselves," "ourselves," and "themselves" may present comprehension problems for the learning disabled child. The difficulties seem to relate to problems in (1) identifying the referent or referents for these pronouns and (2) categorizing gender and number, especially for the third person singular and plural reflexive pronouns. The reflexive pronouns are used in constructions in which the subject and object refer to the same person or animal. They are also used to avoid ambiguities, as in sentences such as "Betty got herself a new coat" and "Father bought himself a new pipe." The difficulties in interpreting and using reflexive pronouns appear to be reflected as:

(1) Problems in perceiving and acquiring the rules for sentence structures in which the subject and object share the same referent. As a result, learning disabled children may interpret the reflexive pronoun to refer to a person other than the subject and invent a second person to fit the context. For example, a sentence such as

"Mary washed herself before she came downstairs" may lead to the misconception that Mary washed someone other than herself while she was upstairs.

(2) Problems in forming the associations between the personal and reflexive pronouns in the third person singular and plural. In spontaneous speech, learning disabled children may form the third person singular and plural reflexive pronouns by compounding the possessive forms of the personal pronouns "his" and "their" with "self" or "selves," resulting in utterances such as "He shaved *hisself*" and "They did it *theirselves*."

## Demonstrative Pronouns

The demonstrative pronouns "this," "that," "these," and "those" are frequently misinterpreted and misused by children with learning disabilities. Their difficulties may reflect:

(1) Auditory perceptual problems, resulting in confusion because of the relative similarities in the speech sound sequences. This confusion is most prevalent between the two members of the minimally paired pronouns "this" and "these," and "these" and "those."

(2) Problems in perceiving and interpreting differences in orientation or location in either space or time. As a result, they may confuse the pronouns "this" (near the speaker) and "that" (away from the speaker), and "these" (near the speaker) and "those" (away from the speaker).

(3) Problems in perceiving and internalizing the rules for speaker-listener uses and interpretations of the demonstrative pronouns as they denote near-distant contrasts. These problems may be further compounded by the fact that the point of reference in space shifts between the speaker and listener and that the speaker and/or the listener may move in space during a conversation. As a result, learning disabled children may fail to perceive any internal consistency in a conversation. They may have trouble with statements such as *"This* is the book *that* belongs over there" and *"Those* books belong to *these* girls over here."

Semel and Wiig (1975) have shown that the demonstrative pronouns "this" and "that" may pose significant problems in learning disabled children's interpretation of syntactic structures. In comparison, normally developing children seem able to differentiate the meaning of "these" in the age range from 3–0 and 4–0 years and of "that" in the age range from 3–6 to 5–0 years (Carrow, 1973).

## Indefinite and Negative Pronouns

Learning disabled children may have difficulties in processing and interpreting the **indefinite pronouns** ("any," "anybody," "anyone," "anything"; "some," "somebody," "someone," "something"; "everybody," "everyone," "everything") and negative pronouns ("nobody," "no one," "nothing"). Their difficulties in interpretation may coexist with seeming ease in using the indefinite and negative pronouns. This facility may mask vocabulary or word-finding problems. The problems

**FIGURE 7.3**
*Demonstrative Pronouns*

in understanding the indefinite and negative pronouns may be reflected as:

(1) Difficulties in differentiating the pronouns which express quantity and concepts of inclusion and exclusion ("any-," "some-," "every-," "no-"). Similar problems may be observed in the learning disabled child's ability to interpret other concepts of quantity, inclusion, and exclusion, such as "few," "most," and "several."

(2) Confusion among pronouns within the same class, such as "some," "somebody," "someone," and "something," and failure to grasp the subtle distinctions in the meaning of the various forms.

(3) Difficulties in understanding the difference between forms of the indefinite and negative pronouns such as "somebody"/"anybody" and "nobody"/"everybody."

(4) Difficulties in perceiving, identifying, and differentiating the components of the compounded forms of the indefinite and negative pronouns. As a result, they may fail to isolate and interpret the seperate meanings of the determiners "any-," "some-," "every-," and "no-" and of the nouns "body," "one," and "thing."

(5) Confusion in the references for indefinite and negative pronouns, since they do not refer directly to other nouns but occupy a noun-like position in sentences. As a result, learning disabled children may be totally confused upon hearing sentences such as "These days nobody gives anybody anything for nothing," since they may not be able to differentiate and identify the subject, direct and indirect objects, and the object of the preposition.

(6) Difficulties in reading comprehension at the early grade levels, due to problems in differentiating between the pronouns compounded with "some-" and "any-."

### Dialectical Variations in Pronoun Use

The personal, reflexive, and demonstrative pronouns are subject to dialectical variations which should be taken into account in considering the production of pronouns by children with learning disabilities. If a learning disabled child belongs to a community with a nonstandard social dialect, variations in pronoun use which reflect the dialect should not be considered to indicate the presence of a language disability. These variations must be interpreted to indicate a language difference. The dialectical variations shown in Table 7.9 may be observed in the use of the personal, reflexive, and demonstrative pronouns (Jeter, 1977).

**TABLE 7.9**
*Dialectical variations in pronoun use*

| Dialect | Characteristic | Sample Utterances |
|---|---|---|
| Nonstandard. | Nominative/objective neutralization in coordinate subject noun phrases. | *Me* and *him* will go.<br>*Her* and *me* play together.<br>*Him* and *her* like it. |
| | Addition of -*s* to the possessive replacive pronoun first person singular, resulting in the form *mines*. | That hat is *mines*.<br>It is *mines*.<br>Those are *mines*. |
| | Addition of "-self" to all personal pronouns and extension of the possessive form used for first and second persons ("myself," "yourself") to the third person ("hisself," "theirself"). | Mother gave it to *myself*.<br>*Herself* took it.<br>Father shaved *hisself*.<br>The boys washed *theirself*. |
| | Substitution of the demonstrative "them" for "those." | I want some of *them* apples. |
| | Addition of "here" and "there" in forming demonstratives with "these" and "them," resulting in the combinations "these here" and "them there." | I like *these here* apples better than *them there*. |
| Black English. | Nominative/objective neutralization; typical in preadolescence. | *Her* not going.<br>*Him* ain't home. |
| | Use of nominative or objective case of pronouns for possessives. | Jane told *she* mother.<br>Bill took *him* sneaker. |
| Southern White Standard. | Addition of a personal **dative** to the noun phrase (subject). | I got *me* a new car.<br>She cut *her* a slice of bread. |
| | Addition to the plural forms of "you," resulting in the forms "y'all," "youse," or "you'uns." | *Y'all* come over tonight.<br>*Youse* mad at me?<br>*You'uns* get the food. |
| Nonstandard. | Use of a pronoun in apposition to the noun subject of a sentence. | The teacher, *she* yell at the kids.<br>My father, *he* bigger than yours. |

# DEFICITS IN WORD RELATIONSHIPS AND FIGURATIVE LANGUAGE

## Basic Linguistic Concepts

Relationships among two or more words, phrases, or clauses in a sentence are often expressed by basic linguistic concepts such as *and*, *either . . . or*, and *if . . . then*. To interpret these concepts accurately, you must understand the logical operations and be able to perceive and interpret the relations expressed among the critical words, phrases, or clauses in the sentence. The basic linguistic concepts may be classified according to the logical operations required and the relationships expressed in Table 7.10.

**TABLE 7.10**

*Basic linguistic concepts*

| Logical Operation-Relationship | Basic Linguistic Concepts |
|---|---|
| Coordination. | and |
| Class-exclusion. | not, all . . . except, neither . . . nor |
| Class-inclusion. | all, many, some, any, few, several |
| Class-inclusion-exclusion. | either . . . or, all . . . some, all . . . none |
| Spatial-sequential. | first, last, middle, second, third, fourth |
| Temporal-sequential. | first, last, before, after, when, not . . . until |
| Cause-effect (conditional). | when . . . then, if . . . then |
| Instrumental. | with, without |
| Revision. | no . . . instead, rather |

The problems of learning disabled children in interpreting the meaning and intent of these basic linguistic concepts may best be seen when they are asked to follow oral directions. Their difficulties may also be revealed when they are questioned carefully after hearing a story or extended discourse which contains basic linguistic concepts. The difficulties in understanding and using the basic linguistic concepts may reflect:

(1) Delays in the acquisition and formation of basic concepts expressing quantity, spatial, or temporal relationships.

(2) Delays in learning to classify, with delayed ability to perceive and interpret class-inclusion and class-exclusion. These delays may manifest themselves in difficulties in understanding and using the basic linguistic concepts of inclusion and exclusion ("all," "many," "any," "some," "either . . . or," "all . . . except," etc.).

(3) Delays in learning to put things in sequence, along with delays in the perception and interpretation of one-to-one correspondence in the spatial or sequential aspects of ordinal relationships. These delays may be reflected in difficulties in understanding and using the basic spatial-sequential linguistic concepts ("first," "last," "second," "third," etc.).

(4) Delays in learning temporal seriation, resulting in difficulties in understanding and using the basic temporal-sequential linguistic concepts ("before," "after," "first," "last," "when . . . then," etc.).

(5) Delays in perceiving and learning cause-effect or conditional relationships, resulting in difficulties in understanding and using basic cause-effect linguistic concepts ("when . . . then," "if . . . then," etc.).

(6) Difficulties in perceiving and interpreting unusual relationships among actions and instruments, as expressed in the sentences "Eat your ice cream *with* the *fork*" and "Point to the window *with* your *pencil*."

**FIGURE 7.4**
*Linguistic Concepts:*
*Quantity, Spatial,*
*Temporal*

Table 7.11 presents the approximate order in which normal children learn the basic concepts. It is based on responses obtained from children in kindergarten and grades 1 and 2 (Boehm, 1970).

**TABLE 7.11**
*Approximate order of acquisition of selected basic concepts*

| Concept | Context Category | Concept Category |
|---|---|---|
| some but not many | Quantity. | Inclusion-exclusion. |
| a few | Quantity. | Inclusion. |
| the most | Quantity. | Inclusion. |
| the second | Space-time. | Serial order; spatial or temporal. |
| several | Quantity. | Inclusion. |
| after | Time. | Serial order; temporal. |
| as many . . . as | Quantity. | One-to-one correspondence in number. |
| not the first nor the last | Space-time. | Exclusion. |
| zero | Quantity. | Exclusion. |
| every | Quantity. | Inclusion. |
| a pair | Quantity. | Inclusion. |
| equal (numbers) | Quantity. | One-to-one correspondence in number. |
| in order | Space. | Serial order; spatial. |
| third | Space-time. | Serial order; spatial or temporal. |
| the least | Quantity. | Inclusion. |

## Linguistic Relationships

Logical relationships among two or more critical words may be expressed in sentences which contain:

(1) Comparative relationships, as in the sentence "Watermelons are *bigger* than apples."

(2) Passive relationships, as in the sentence "The boy was *brought by* the woman."

(3) Possessive or familial relationships, as in the sentence "My cousin Joe is my *uncle's son*."

(4) Spatial relationships, as in the sentence "The elephant sat *on* the mouse."

(5) Temporal or temporal-sequential relationships, as in the sentence "Does December come *before* November?"

(6) Analogous relationships, as in the statement "A *key* is to a *door* as a *dial* is to a *telephone*."

(7) Figurative relationships, as in idioms such as "My father *hit the roof*," metaphors such as "Lisa is *sharp as* a tack," and proverbs such as, "*Strike while the iron is hot*."

FIGURE 7.5
*Spatial Relationship*

The relative difficulties learning disabled children have in interpreting and using these linguistic relationships may be related to both their content and their format, in the following ways:

(1) The number of critical items which are to be compared or related influence the ease of interpretation. Thus, relationships which compare or relate two critical items are relatively easier to interpret than relationships which contain three or more critical items. Similarly, the ease of understanding decreases in direct proportion to increases in the number of critical items.

(2) Whether or not the relationship is expressed in positive or negative terms will influence the ease of understanding. Relationships which are expressed in positive terms and feature words such as "*bigger* than," "*warmer* than," or "*taller* than" are generally easier to interpret than those which feature negative terms such as "*smaller* than," "*colder* than," or "*shorter* than." It is also easier to interpret or verify a question expressed positively, such as "Is Florida *warmer* than Maine?" than a question expressed negatively, such as "Is Maine *colder* than Florida?"

(3) Whether or not the relationship expressed is true or false will influence the ease and speed of understanding. Sentences which

express true, logical, and valid relationships are generally easier and faster to interpret than sentences which contain false, illogical, or invalid relationships. As a consequence, the question "Are watermelons *bigger* than apples?" is more easily answered than the question "Are apples *bigger* than watermelons?" Both of these questions require the child to compare the sizes of the two objects. In one question, "Are watermelons bigger than apples?" the two fruits are mentioned in a sequence progressing from big to little. That sequence appears logical when the word "big" is featured. In the other question, "Are apples bigger than watermelons?" the sequence from little to big appears less logical, because the word "big" is featured. Relationships in which the critical elements to be compared are featured according to our logical preferences tend to be easier to interpret than those which violate our preferences.

(4) The syntactic structure of an expressed relationship will influence the ease of interpretation. The structure of linguistic concepts may vary from simple to complex. The same comparative relationship may be expressed in a simple sentence structure, such as "May is bigger than Joan," or in a complex sentence structure, such as "Yesterday I heard May say that she was bigger than Joan." While the logical relationship in the comparison of May and Joan is the same in the two sentences, the syntactic complexity of the second sentence complicates the task.

(5) The reversibility of the critical items featured in an expressed relationship will influence the ease of understanding. For example, irreversible passive relationships, such as "The car was driven by John" (it would be inconceivable that the car would drive John), are relatively easier to interpret than reversible passive relationships, such as "John was pushed by Jane" (John may just as well have pushed Jane).

The difficulties experienced by learning disabled children in perceiving and interpreting linguistic relationships may relate to:

(1) Problems with the simultaneous analysis and synthesis of the critical concepts and words contained in the relationship. Learning disabled children may interpret each of the critical items or words correctly but may fail to grasp the overall meaning expressed by the relationship. These deficits may affect the perception and interpretation of all of the linguistic relationships. As a result, they may answer a question such as "Are apples bigger than watermelons?" inconsistently, saying "Yes" (apples are big) or "Yes" (watermelons are big) without having compared the two fruits for size.

(2) Deficits in forming or reconstructing internal images of the objects or events which are compared or related and in revisualizing the implied ordinal relationship. These deficits may affect the child's interpretation of the linguistic relationships selectively. The ability to revisualize the objects or events and their ordinal or spatial relationship seems critical in understanding comparative and spatial relationships such as "Are parents *older than* their children?" and "The elephant sat *on* the mouse. Was the mouse on top?"

(3) Deficits in the retention and recall of word order. The accurate perception and interpretation of comparative, passive, spatial, temporal, familial, and analogous relationships may depend upon accurate retention of word order. Learning disabled children may not retain the sequence of the critical words in the relationship accurately or may recall only one of the items, resulting in misinterpretations. For example, they may accept a statement such as *"Children* are older than their *parents"* because they may fail to retain and recall the sequence of presentation of the two critical words *children* and *parents*, they think they heard the statement *"Parents* are older than their *children."* Similarly, they may focus on and recall only one of the critical words featured in a passive relationship such as "Jane *was pushed by* John." If the word which the child recalls happens to be the first in the sentence, *Jane*, he may alter the interpretation of the passive to indicate that Jane pushed someone or something and not understand subsequent statements such as "Luckily she was not hurt badly. She scraped her knee a little but was very angry at John after that."

(4) Narrow and rigid word meanings. This problem may affect the understanding of spatial, temporal, analogous, and figurative relationships.

(5) Narrow, rigid, or irrelevant associations between words and concepts. These deficits may affect the perception and interpretation of analogous relationships. Learning disabled children may not perceive the basis for the relationships between the word pairs in the expressed analogy. As an example, learning disabled children may have formed strong and rigid associations between the words "feathers" and "indians," or "feathers" and "chickens" or "turkeys." They may not generalize the association to "birds," the category. As a result, they may fail to perceive the analogy expressed in a statement such as *"Birds* have *feathers* and *mammals* have *hair."*

Learning disabled children have been reported to follow the normal developmental sequence but with significant delays in learning selected linguistic relationships (Wiig & Semel, 1973, 1974a). They had the most severe difficulties in interpreting familial relationships, followed in order of decreasing difficulty by spatial relationships, temporal-sequential relationships, passive relationships, and comparative relationships. Their problems seemed to persist into adolescence when they were not provided with remediation.

*Normal Developmental Sequences*

Children with normal language development have been found to show significant increases in the comprehension of comparative, passive, spatial, temporal, and familial relationships during the age period from 7 to 11 years (Wiig & Semel, 1974a). Between the ages of 11 and 13 years, however, the comprehension of these linguistic relationships remains stable.

*Piaget describes the following stages of normal cognitive growth: (1) sensorimotor stage, from birth to about 2 years of age, (2) preoperational stage, from about 2 to about 7 years of age, (3) concrete operational stage, from about 7 to about 11 years of age, and (4) formal operational stage, after about 11 years.*

In terms of theories of cognitive and logical growth, the comprehension of sentences which express linguistic relationships between words is said to improve throughout the concrete operational stage of development (Inhelder & Piaget, 1964; Piaget & Inhelder, 1969). When children go through the normal period of transition from the concrete operational to the more abstract, formal operational stage of development, their learning of linguistic relationships stabilizes.

Developmental data suggest an order of difficulty for the linguistic relationships which agrees with Piaget's theory of logical growth. In the early grades (1 through 3), the comparative relationships were most easily interpreted, followed in order of difficulty by the passive, temporal, spatial, and familial relationships. Comparative relationships require logical operations normally acquired at the preoperational level of development. Spatial and temporal relationships, however, are acquired during the concrete operational stage.

## Verbal Analogies

The perception, interpretation, and use of verbal analogies by learning disabled children appears to be directly affected by (1) the type of analogy expressed or required (whole-part, part-whole, antonym, etc.) and (2) the relative complexity of the format in which the analogy is presented. Verbal analogies may express one or more of the following relationships among word pairs:

(1) Whole-part relationship: "A *dog* is to *hair* as a *bird* is to *feathers*."
(2) Part-whole relationship: "A *key* is to a *door* as a *dial* is to a *telephone*.
(3) Part-part relationship: "A *toe* is to a *finger* as a *foot* is to a *hand*."
(4) Action-object relationship: "*Driving* is to a *car* as *flying* is to a *plane*."
(5) Object-action relationship: "A *steak* is to *broiling* as a *cake* is to *baking*."
(6) Purpose relationship: "A *bat* is to *baseball* as a *racket* is to *tennis*."
(7) Spatial relationship: "The *United States* is to *Canada* as *South America* is to *North America*."
(8) Temporal relationship: "*Morning* is to *breakfast* as *noon* is to *lunch*."
(9) Temporal-sequential relationship: "*April* is to *May* as *June* is to *July*."
(10) Cause-effect relationship: "*Lightning* is to *thunder* as *fire* is to *smoke*."
(11) Familial relationship: "A *brother* is to a *sister* as an *uncle* is to an *aunt*."
(12) Numerical relationship: "*Fourteen* is *to seven* as *twenty* is to *ten*."
(13) Degree relationship: "*Meters* are to *kilometers* as a *millimeter* is to a *meter*."
(14) Antonym relationship: "*Big* is to *little* as *night* is to *day*."
(15) Synonym relationship: "*Laugh* is to *giggle* as *crying* is to *sobbing*."
(16) Grammatical relationship: "*Boy* is to *boys* as *child* is to *children*."

In general, learning disabled children find part-whole, whole-part, action-object, object-action, and antonym relationships easier to perceive and interpret than the other relationships. Spatial, temporal, temporal-sequential, familial, numerical, degree, and cause-effect relationships appear to be influenced by visual-perceptual deficits and by delays in learning the logical operations that are required to resolve the associative relationship among the words and concepts. Synonym and grammatical relationships appear to be influenced, in turn, by delays in syntactic development.

The format in which a verbal analogy is presented may facilitate its understanding by learning disabled children. The analogous relationships among the concepts *trees, leaves, flowers,* and *petals* may be expressed in several formats, such as:

(1) Leaves *grow* on trees and petals *grow* on flowers (part-whole analogy).
(2) Trees *have* leaves and flowers *have* petals (whole-part analogy).
(3) Leaves *are* to trees as petals *are* to flowers (part-whole analogy).
(4) Trees *are* to leaves as flowers *are* to petals (whole-part analogy).

In the two first formats, the verbs "grow" and "have" facilitate the perception and interpretation of the analogous relationships. In contrast, the empty form of the copula, "are," causes the two last formats to be relatively harder to understand. In general, verbal analogies that contain verbs or other structures that add redundancy in meaning are easier for learning disabled children to interpret than the same analogies expressed without the extra cues for interpretation.

## Figurative Language

Our language is rich in idioms, metaphors, and proverbs. If they are taken literally, they may be meaningless or the interpretation may be incorrect. In order to understand figurative relationships, changes in meaning, significance, and use of specific words, phrases, or sentences have to be discerned and the concrete word meanings must be translated into generalized, abstract concepts. The process used in interpreting figurative relationships is similar to that used in interpreting dual or multiple-meaning words. The words must be accurately categorized and reclassified, semantically and grammatically, in order to arrive at the various possible interpretations. Although dual and multiple-meaning words have referential bases (that is, they refer to objects, actions, events, or ideas), the words in idioms, metaphors, and proverbs must be translated into nonreferential, abstract, and generalized concepts. With learning disabled children, the abstract and generalized meaning of the various idioms, metaphors, and proverbs may need to be taught separately, with little transfer from one to the next. They may need to learn the meaning of common idioms, metaphors, and proverbs one-by-one in order to be able to distinguish when language is used figuratively rather than literally.

### Idioms

Idioms often contain dual or multiple-meaning words which may be known to the learning disabled child. Many idioms tend to use the same words in various combinations. Parts of the body, for example, are featured in a large number of idioms. As an illustration, the body part "eye" is used in a variety of idioms such as "sharp eyes," "eyes popped," "eyes danced," "to have eyes for," and "to eye." Typically, learning disabled children perceive and interpret only the literal, concrete meaning of the words when they encounter idioms such as "He hit the roof" or "I'm all tied up at the office." Figure 7.6 illustrates the confusion which may be experienced by learning disabled children when they encounter an idiom.

**FIGURE 7.6**
*Literal and Abstract Interpretations of the Idiom*

SHE JUST FELL APART.

*Metaphors*

Metaphors such as "It was white *as* snow" express comparisons between the actual subject of the utterance and a descriptive image. The two things being compared are generally widely different in spite of the fact that they share some common, highlighted aspect. Although the images created by the two are the same in similes and metaphors, these two formats can be differentiated by featured words. Metaphors feature the combination "as . . . as" while similes feature the verb "like," as in the expression "Bob eats *like* a bird." Learning disabled children commonly interpret metaphors and similes according to the literal and concrete meaning of each word and may be confused at the outcome.

*Proverbs and Platitudes*

Proverbs and platitudes share the same imagery as metaphors and similes. In addition, they include a piece of moral advice which can be discerned only when the generalized, abstract meaning of the utterances is understood. The proverb "Strike while the iron is hot," for instance, may be interpreted at the concrete level to mean that you should never let the iron get cold before you strike something, a practical admonition. At the abstract level of interpretation the general moral advice "Don't delay until it is too late" is apparent. Unfortunately, the abstract and generalized meaning of proverbs may continue to elude the learning disabled child. He may remain at the concrete level of interpretation and fail to understand why people bother to tell him something so obvious. At the extreme, he may miss the differentiated meanings of proverbs and platitudes in literature and fall prey to a pedestrian view of life and some of its more attractive facets.

# 8

# UNDERSTANDING WORDS AND WORD RELATIONSHIPS
## Assessment

## BACKGROUND

Assume that I ask you, "What does *building* mean?" You might just respond by asking me to clarify my question. Specifically, you might ask, "Do you want to know the meaning of the label used for the *object* building, that is, a noun, or the meaning of the *action* building, which is a verb?" Or you may not have immediately thought my question through; you may forget that the word "building" can have several meanings, depending upon its environmental or its verbal context. As a result, you may have started to explain either the meaning of the noun "building" or the meaning of the verb "building." And you could explain the verb "building" either by action or with words. Your explanation—whether you used actions or words—would reflect not only some commonly agreed-upon meaning for "building"; it would also reflect some things about you. Among these might be:

(1) Your sex and age,
(2) Your racio-ethnic background,
(3) Your educational or professional background,
(4) Your socioeconomic background,
(5) The social and environmental context of the discussions, and
(6) Your familiarity or experience with the structures we label "build-ings" and the actions we call "building."

Thus, to assess a child's competence in processing and producing word meaning, we need to understand something of how words relate to the objects, actions, or ideas he labels. We need to know some ways words can relate to each other and how those relationships communicate messages that the sounds of the words and structure of the sentence alone do not communicate. Then we can see and understand possible ways to assess whether a child has learned certain word meanings and relationships.

# REFERENTIAL MEANING

Most of the words and phrases we use are easily recognizable as labels for observable **referents**. For example, a proper noun such as "Daniel" may be used to refer to a particular person. The noun "chair" may be used to refer to a particular piece of furniture. The adjective "blue" may be used to refer to a particular item that has a certain attribute—its color is blue. The verb "walk" may be used to refer to a particular motor action. We say that words that are related directly to persons, objects, actions, attributes, feelings, relationships, or events, and serve as their labels, carry *referential meaning*.

*A referent is the real person, object, quality, event, or idea represented by a label word.*

The concept of referential meaning may sound simple, but it is not. First, many different—even widely different—referents may share the same word label. Second, many different word labels may be used for the same referent. That is, there is not a one-to-one relationship between a word with referential meaning and its referent.

Let us look at some examples. "Daniel" can be a Biblical character, or my next-door neighbor. "Blue" can be the color of the sky, or Daniel's mood after his cat died. The pronoun "you" may refer to anyone or to everyone present at any one time. The only condition for its appropriate use is that all the persons referred to by "you" must be listening to the speaker. The personal pronoun "I," on the other hand, is reserved for the speaker to refer to himself. But speaker and listener roles change back and forth rapidly in a conversation, and the referents for the "you" and the "I" change accordingly. And consider how we label coins. We say either a "penny" or "one cent," a "nickel" or "five cents," a "dime" or "ten cents," a "quarter" or "twenty-five cents." For still another example, we refer to a certain liquid served in a social setting as a "drink," a "cocktail," or a "martini."

We have said that words that label persons, objects, events, qualities, and relationships carry referential meaning. An alternative way of describing those same words is to call them *labels for semantic categories*. Thus we can say that the word "chair" refers to the category of objects that all share the feature that they may be used for one person at a time to sit on or in. The word "blue" can be said to refer to the category of items that share the feature of color we arbitrarily label "blue." The word "walk" may be said to refer to the category of motor actions that share the essential feature of ambulation at an arbitrarily chosen speed.

*Semantic categories are groups of words for objects, actions, relationships, or events that share an essential feature.*

We can also label the members of a given category by other category names. To mention a few of the objects fit for the act of sitting by one person, we say "stool," "high chair," "settee," "recliner," or "lounger." Each of these word labels refers to a subcategory of chairs within the broader category of objects for one person to sit on. And each subcategory may be a category in itself, and its members may form further subcategories.

Therefore we see that assessing a child's use of a word with referential meaning, or semantic category if you prefer, is a complex task. The child may correctly say "flower" to label a rose, but she may also say "flower" to refer to the front lawn. And she may not be able to produce the verb "to flower," experienced by certain "trees." To fully evaluate a child's acquisition of the meaning of a word, you may need to explore the limits of all the *categories* of *referents* the child relates to that word.

# RELATIONSHIPS AMONG WORD MEANINGS

Our discussion of the multiple relationships among words and their referents or semantic category relationships involves the concept of *associative relations* among words and word meanings. That is, words may relate to other words in several different ways. One way to assess a child's acquisition of the meaning of a word is to look at these relationships. For instance, does the child understand the relationship between "half-dollar" and "fifty-cent piece," between "hot" and "cold."

## Synonymy

*Perfect synonyms are two terms that label* identical *referents.*

*Synonyms are two terms that label referents that are quite similar, but not necessarily identical.*

We find one relationship among word meanings when an object, action, event, or idea is referred to interchangeably with two or more different word labels. With our coin names, two words have identical meanings in reference to an amount of money. We say that the two terms used to label a coin are perfect synonyms. This does not happen often, however. It is more common that the words that we use interchangeably for reference have some overlap, but do not refer to identical referents. They are *synonyms,* or words that are related by similarity in meaning. An example is the words "house," "home," and "residence," "drink," "cocktail," and "martini."

When the relationship among synonyms is expressed in sentence form, we can state that "A house *is* a home, and a home *is* a residence." The relationship based on overlap in meaning may be diagrammed as in Figure 8.1.

**FIGURE 8.1**
*Partial Overlap in Meaning among Words which May Be Used as Synonyms in Some Contexts*

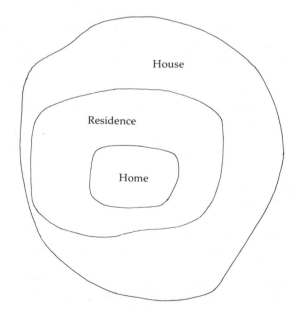

Two words may be associatively related because they refer to extremes of the same continuum of meaning. That is, they are related by extreme difference in degree while referring to the same quality. Words that refer to the opposite extremes of a continuum are called verbal opposites or *antonyms*. For example, assume that the shared quality referred to by two words is distance. In that case, you may refer to the two extremes by the word labels "short"/"long" or "near"/"far," depending upon your perspective. The speaker who is surveying the continuum of distance depicted in Figure 8.2 can use several different descriptions. When viewing point A on the continuum, he may say either, "It is *near*," "It is a *short* distance away," or "It is *not far*." In reference to Point B, he may say either, "It is *far*," "It is a *long* distance away," or "It is *not near*."

*Antonyms are two words with reverse or opposite meanings that share a concept or quality.*

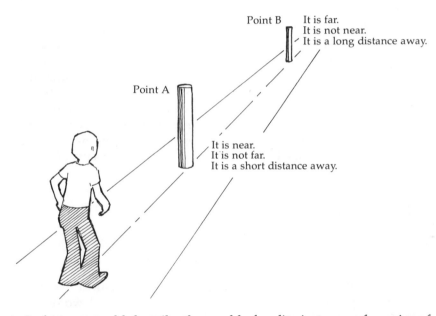

**FIGURE 8.2**

*Word and Sentence Choices Available for Describing Identical Distances from a Viewer*

In fact, we could describe the world of reality in terms of a series of these continua, each of which gives rise to a pair of opposites, that is, to an antonym pair. Common among these continua are qualities that can be measured and quantified, including:

(1) Distance ("near"/"far"),
(2) Height ("tall"/"short"),
(3) Weight ("light"/"heavy"),
(4) Temperature ("hot"/"cold"),
(5) Time ("early"/"late").

Other continua are more qualitative. They may reflect/affect ("happy"/"sad") or value judgments ("good"/"bad").

To further complicate matters, while most words have only one antonym, some words refer to more than one quality and thus may have more than one antonym. Consider the attribute label "short," which can form one extreme of at least two continua of meaning. If the dimension referred to is distance, its opposite is "long." If the dimension is height, however, its antonym differs; it is "tall."

If you understand an antonym relationship, you can perceive the shared meaning in sentences that may otherwise appear unrelated. For example, the sentences in the following dialogue might appear completely unrelated in meaning to someone who did not correctly understand the antonyms and their application to both space and time.

Tourist:   Is the village near here?
Local:   No, it is far away.
Tourist:   How far?
Local:   About two hours and thirty minutes away.
Tourist:   That's not far. That's near. I've driven 600 miles in the last 12 hours already.

## Reciprocity

*Reciprocity is the process indication of a give-and-take relationship between two participants in an action. Other examples include "teach"-"learn," "give"-"take," "send"-"receive."*

Some words share another type of opposite relationship. For instance, I may "buy" a car or I may "sell" a car. In the first instance, I would *acquire* a car and *give* money in return; in the second instance, I would *acquire* money and *give* a car in return. The mature speaker knows that the outcome of the two actions is not the same, nor are they extremes along some continuum of meaning. Instead, the words "buy" and "sell" refer to reciprocal actions; they are related by **reciprocity**. Only verbs feature reciprocal or give-and-take relationships between actions. Other verb pairs that are associated by reciprocity of action include:

(1) Ask–tell,
(2) Borrow–lend,
(3) Give–receive,
(4) Add–subtract,
(5) Multiply–divide.

You can better understand the reciprocity of these pairs of verbs by considering pairs of sentences featuring the reciprocal words. For instance, "Jane *told* John to leave" is identical in meaning to "John *was asked* to leave by Jane." The sentence pairs below give more examples. In each sentence pair, one of the reciprocal verbs is used in the active form (subject-predicate-indirect object). The other is used to form the passive (indirect object-predicate-subject).

**(1)** Jane *lent* John the money.
John *borrowed* the money from Jane.

**(2)** Jane *gave* John the money.
John *received* the money from Jane.

A mathematical example of reciprocity would be

**(3)** 13 equals 5 + 8 (add)
13 − 8 (subtract) equals 5

If you understand the reciprocity of action implied by reciprocally related words, you can perceive the shared meaning of sentences that differ in surface structure. Without this knowledge, the exchange below might be meaningless. The relationship among the meanings of these sentences is held together by the reciprocity of the verbs.

John: Jane, did you *give* the money to Jack?
Jane: No, he *received* it from Joe.
John: Well, did Joe *receive* the money from his father?
Jane: No, his mother *gave* him the money.

**Inclusion**

Two words may be related to each other in meaning through semantic class membership. For example, the meanings of the words "lion" and "tiger" are related because they both belong to the semantic class "wild animals." If the word "whale" were added to form the grouping "lion," "tiger," "whale," the relationship in meaning among the words shifts; it would now come from shared membership in the semantic class *mammals*. A second example of relationship in meaning by class inclusion involves the relation between the terms "to boil" and "to bake." These two terms both mean *to cook* in a certain way. A diagram of the relationship between the words *truck, bus, plane,* and *boat* is presented in Figure 8–3. A further differentiation of the relationship among the words is presented in Figure 8–4 on p. 194.

**FIGURE 8.3**
*A Relationship in Word Meaning by Inclusion in the Same Semantic Class*

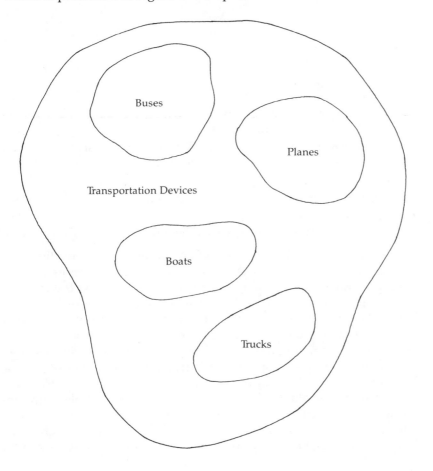

Buses

Planes

Transportation Devices

Boats

Trucks

**FIGURE 8.4**

*Shared and Different
Word Meanings by
Semantic Subcategory
Inclusion and Exclusion*

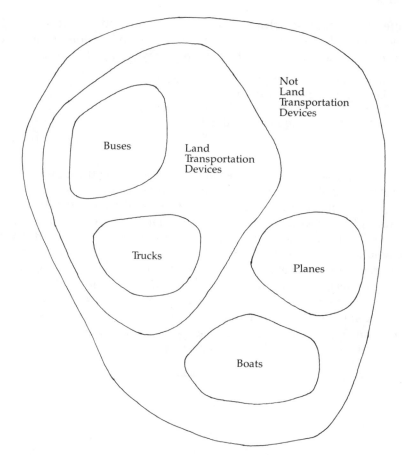

If you understand relations among word meanings by inclusion, you can understand the implied meaning expressed in sentences that would otherwise appear unrelated. For example, consider the potential for thinking that the following exchanges make no sense at all.

**Question:** Have you seen any tigers?
**Answer:** No, there are no wild animals here.

**Question:** Is the turkey baking?
**Answer:** I haven't begun to cook yet. Sorry.

Clearly, defining the meaning of words and of the relationships between words is a complex process. Word meaning serves as a system for segmenting reality (Bolinger, 1968) or reflecting how the child organizes the world and provides labels for categorizing or separating elements (Lenneberg, 1967). In other words, the child uses words to separate and give meaning to his observations and experiences and keep various elements apart in his thinking. These views directly affect the clinical-educational process of evaluating the acquisition and knowledge of word meaning. The child's knowledge of word meanings should be evaluated when he is in the process of observing the world around him and thinking and talking about it. If we are to adequately observe what a word or category label means to a child, we must observe how the child uses the word to interpret aspects of his world and to express his actions and those of other people within that reality. But these observations would require a long period of time, and may therefore be impossible for the clinician involved in diagnosis.

Therefore, in clinical-educational evaluations the alternative is to sample the child's knowledge of a variety of words and relations. The sample is used as evidence of the child's knowledge of referential and relational word meanings, and of his ability to integrate word meaning across phrases and sentences. The validity of the sampling procedure depends on both the format and the content of the tests that are used to assess word meaning and vocabulary knowledge. The next section describes test formats that have been used in research and in the clinical evaluation of the acquisition of word meaning. Later sections review selected commercially available, standardized tests, with emphasis on their formats and contents.

## TASK FORMATS FOR INFORMAL ASSESSMENT AND EXTENSION TESTING

### Identification and Selection

The task most widely used for evaluating a child's acquisition of word meaning is identification and selection. This task has been employed extensively both in research into meaning in child language and in formal, standardized tests of word meaning. A stimulus word or phrase is spoken to the child. In response, the child must choose either an object or a picture that corresponds to the spoken word from among several choices. For example, the child may be requested to select "the big one" from among two choices, each rectangles that differ from each other in both width and height (Maratsos, 1973).

Usually, either two, three, or four object or picture choices are presented for each spoken word or request. The foils for the target item may be widely different from and not at all related to the meaning of the spoken stimulus. Or they may be very similar and closely related to the meaning of the stimulus, and therefore require subtle discriminating. The examples below illustrate possible relationships among a stimulus item and the foils used with the item.

(a) **Unrelated Foils**

    Stimulus word:    tall

    Foil labels:    happy, blue, girl

(b) **Related Foils**

    Stimulus word:    tall

    Foil labels:    short, long, wide

In research on children's acquisition of word meaning, identification and selection has been used to assess the acquisition of:

(1) Meaning of dimensional terms ("big," "tall," "short," "long," "high," "low," and so on) in both the base form and in the comparative and superlative forms of adjectives (Brewer & Stone, 1975; Donaldson & Wales, 1970; Townsend, 1974).

(2) Idioms ("He broke her heart") (Lodge & Leach, 1975).

(3) Perception and resolution of lexical ambiguities in sentences ("He wiped the glasses") (Schultz & Pilon, 1973; Wiig, Gilbert, & Christian, 1978).

## Acting Out Meaning

The task of acting out word and sentence meaning requires the child to recognize and interpret significant word meanings and relations among words. In addition, it requires motor planning to act out a meaning either through body actions or by manipulating objects. For example, the child may be required to act out by manipulating a boy and a girl doll appropriately upon hearing a sentence such as "The boy hits the girl" (Bellugi-Klima, 1971). Or children may be required to act out a sequence among events after hearing sentences such as "The elephant jumps before the dog sits down" and "After the elephant jumps, the dog sits down" (Clark, 1971).

The task of acting out has been employed extensively in research on the development of word and sentence meaning, but it has not been employed widely in formal standardized language tests. Exceptions are the formats used in the Token Test Part V (DeRenzi & Vignolo, 1962) and the Clinical Evaluation of Language Functions: Processing Linguistic Concepts (Semel & Wiig, 1980). Both of these tests evaluate the child's comprehension of relational words and of temporal, conditional, and inclusion-exclusion relationships. In research on child language, acting out has been used to establish, among others, the acquisition of:

(1) Spatial and temporal relational terms ("right," "before," "after," "until") (Barrie-Blackley, 1973; Beiswenger, 1968; Clark, 1971; Johnson, 1975; Long & Looft, 1972).
(2) Reciprocally related terms ("pay," "trade," "buy," "sell," "ask"/ "tell") (Chomsky, 1969; Gentner, 1975).
(3) Presuppositions with **factive** ("know"), **nonfactive** ("said"), and **counterfactive** ("wished") verbs (Harris, 1975).
(4) Conditional relationships ("if . . . , " "unless . . . ," "don't . . .") (Beiswenger, 1968).
(5) Passive relationships and constructions (Maratsos, 1974a).

## Judgment of Acceptability and Preference

Another way to evaluate a child's knowledge of word meaning is to ask the child to make a judgment about a statement or question. The judgments may take two forms. First, you can require the child to judge the *acceptability* of a word, statement, or question; second, you can ask for the child's *preference* for a specific word, statement, or question. Both formats have been used widely in research on child language. They are, however, not often featured in formal, standardized tests of language .

In judging acceptability, the child listens to a word, statement, or question. He then judges whether the word, semantic relationship, statement, or question was right (its meaning was consistent with its context) or wrong (its meaning was inconsistent with its context). Here are two examples of judgment of acceptability test items (Wiig & Semel, 1974a).

Are trains faster than planes?          (Yes/No)

Are parents older than their children?          (Yes/No)

In the judgment of preference, the child listens to two or more words, semantic relationships, statements, or questions. He then decides which stimulus he prefers. This decision requires the child to judge the consistency of word or sentence meanings in relation to a context. Waryas and Ruder (1974) present rationales for the clinical-educational use of preference judgments in evaluating language abilities.

These two types of judgment tasks have been employed in research on child language to establish, among others, the acquisition of:

(1) Comparative relationships ("bigger," "faster") (Lumsden & Poteat, 1968; Wiig & Semel, 1974a).
(2) Spatial and temporal relationships ("in front of," "in the middle," "to the right," "before," "after") (Coker, 1975; Wiig & Semel, 1974a).
(3) Familial relationship terms ("sister," "brother," "aunt," "uncle," "grandmother," "grandfather") (Chambers & Tavuchis, 1976).
(4) Conditional and inclusion-exclusion relationships ("both . . . and," "or," "if . . . then") (Paris, 1973).
(5) Metaphors ("as gigantic as a skyscraper") (Gardner, Kircher, Winner, & Perkins, 1975).
(6) Evaluation ("good"/"bad"), potency ("strong"/"weak"), and activity ("moving"/"still") judgments for lexical items (DiVesta & Stauber, 1971).

### Recognition of Lexical Paraphrases

One way to evaluate the child's knowledge of synonymy is to use lexical paraphrases. In this task two sentences with the same surface structure but with a difference in one word are presented to the child. The child listens to two spoken sentences that differ by only one word choice. He is then asked to indicate whether they mean the same thing or are similar in meaning, or if they are different. The sample sentence pairs below could be used for the recognition of a lexical paraphrase.

Jane has a small dog.
Jane has a tiny dog.

The old woman sat on the porch.
The aged woman sat on the porch.

The cat was lying on the couch.
The cat was lying on the sofa.

This format has been used in research comparing language-disordered and normally developing children (Hoar, 1977). It is not currently featured in any formal, standardized test of language abilities.

## Instructional and Descriptive Communication

Another means of evaluating the knowledge of specific word meanings and semantic relationships is instructional communication (Glucksberg, Krauss, & Weisberg, 1966). With this task, two children can be assessed. One is designated the speaker and the other the listener. Each child has a set of visual stimuli available; the two sets of stimuli are identical. The children cannot see each other's stimulus arrays. The stimuli could, for instance be wooden blocks that differ in color, shape, and size. The speaker is required to describe his visual stimulus array to the listener. That is, the speaker must select words and word combinations that best describe an array of stimuli in order for the listener to re-create that array correctly without seeing it. The speaker might say "The small blue circle is first" and so on. This technique has been used extensively to assess the knowledge, use, and comprehension of referent-distinguishing adjectives (Fishbein & Osborne, 1971; Ford & Olsen, 1975; Garmiza & Anisfeld, 1976; Glucksberg & Kraus, 1967; Kraus & Rotter, 1968).

The development of role-taking and communication abilities has also been discussed by Flavell, Botkin, Fry, Wright, and Jarvis (1968). In their tasks, a speaker describes combinations and rules for games, drawings, locks, and so on, on the basis of information available to only the speaker. Both techniques of assessing communication abilities lend themselves to the informal assessment of word knowledge and use. Neither is featured in currently standardized tests.

## Spontaneous Use of Words

The spontaneous use of words to describe objects, actions, conditions, sequences, and relationships, gives insight into the meanings of certain words for the speaker. Sampling word meaning simply by listening to "ordinary" conversation provides more detailed assessment than any other method. It also takes into account that language and communication occur naturally in a social context, for purposes of interpersonal communication. It acknowledges that word selections and **registers** in language use can be influenced by the speaker's background, by his perceptions of his audience, and by the environment of the interchange (Ellis & Ure, 1969; Fishman, 1971). While this sampling method has been used extensively in sociolinguistic research, it has not been featured in formal, standardized tests of language assessment.

**Register** *is a stylistic variation used by a speaker to fit the style or requirements of the listener.*

# TASK FORMATS IN FORMAL ASSESSMENT

## Identification and Selection: Format

A format commonly used in the formal assessment of referential or relational word meanings requires the child to identify a pictorial representation of the meaning of a word. A series of from three to five choices may be provided. The task is to select the best representation of the meaning of the word from among the choices given. The Peabody

Picture Vocabulary Test (PPVT) uses this format (Dunn, 1965). The stimulus word for Item 27 of the PPVT is "building." As we saw at the beginning of this chapter, when you hear this word in isolation, there are two immediate possibilities for its meaning. The word may refer to an object labelled "building" or to an action labelled "to build." In this case the choice of the grammatic-semantic category is determined by the four pictures provided. All four show action, so the meaning of the word must be *to build*.

Having figured out that the word "building" denotes an action in this case, the next task is to decide which of the actions pictured it labels. This decision might be made by process of elimination. If the child knows the names of all actions except the one at the lower left, he may point to that choice after eliminating all the others. His decision was, then, made without any actual knowledge of the label for the pictured action. Of course, a correct decision may be based upon actual knowledge of the meaning of the word *to build*, which can include reference to fixing certain objects. The difference between two decision processes is generally reflected in the child's response time. The process of elimination usually takes more time because more decisions have to be made. In fact, each decision to eliminate a picture may involve **verbal mediation** in that a label may have to be evoked for each action.

**Verbal mediation** *is the process of using internal verbal labels or descriptions to assist in problem solving or in remembering.*

A third method children use in selecting a pictorial representation is guessing. In this example, a guess would have a 25% chance of being correct. Often you can detect guessing responses by watching the location of the pictures the child selects. Some youngsters will choose the pictures in the same location on the plates for several responses in a row. Others use a pattern for four responses that moves from the upper left to the upper right, proceeds to the lower left, and ends with the lower right picture.

The task required in responding to the PPVT Item 27 has other subtleties. A child's entire experience with the verb "to build" may have been in the context "to build a house," or it may have been in the context "to build a tower" (with blocks). If the child has not had any experience with the word "building" in the context of repairing something, he may not respond at all or he may say that there is no building on the page. This same child may have adequate knowledge of the meaning of "to build" in common, everyday situations in his life. He may even use the word "to build" correctly in telling what he is doing while he is stacking a series of blocks to form a tower or constructing a model airplane.

Thus we can see that the specific pictures provided in any test of word meaning may interfere with the probability that a certain child will respond correctly. The specific choices determine the visual differentiations that have to be made and the problem-solving strategies the child will use for identification and selection. Any clinical-educational interpretation of a child's performance on a vocabulary test should reflect this dilemma. Extension testing may be required to determine the contexts in which the child has internalized the meaning of a word or word category. Several informal methods and formats lend themselves to extension testing for word meaning. Among them are:

(1) Judgment of the acceptability of or preference for a specific verbal label for selected objects or pictured objects and events
(2) Acting out of word meanings
(3) Lexical paraphrase techniques

## Identification, Selection, and Labelling of Referents: Tests

*Peabody Picture Vocabulary Test (PPVT)*

The PPVT (Dunn, 1965) was designed to evaluate the knowledge of the meaning of single words using a picture selection format. The test contains 150 items, each of which consists of a single word stimulus associated with four pictorial choices. The vocabulary items are presented in increasing order of difficulty. The examiner says each word. The child is then required to point to the one picture among the four possible choices that best represents the meaning of the word.

The PPVT is published in two parallel forms, each featuring 150 vocabulary items. An analysis of the grammatical word categories featured in the items indicates that the predominant group of the lexical items may function as subjects-objects in sentences (nouns). The second largest group of lexical items may function as predicates in sentences (verbs). The verbs featured in the test are presented in the present progressive form. The smallest group of lexical items may function as noun modifiers in sentences (adjectives).

The Peabody Picture Vocabulary Test was standardized on a sample of 4012 children in the age range from 2 years, 3 months to 18 years, 5 months. All youngsters in the standardization sample were white and resided in and around Nashville, Tennessee. The socioeconomic characteristics of the sample are not specified.

The reliability of the PPVT has been established in several studies. Test-retest reliability coefficients for both forms of the test are high (.97), indicating excellent stability of the performance measures over time. Alternate form measures of reliability range from .67 for 6-year-olds to .84 for 17- to 18-year-olds. Performances on the PPVT have been found to correlate positively with performances on the Stanford-Binet (.71) and with WISC Full-Scale I.Q. (.61).

Among the assets of the Peabody Picture Vocabulary Test are:

(1) Ease and speed of administration and scoring.
(2) Perceptual clarity and minimal ambiguity of the pictorial choices for the vocabulary tested.
(3) Wide age range for which the test is applicable.
(4) Availability of alternate test forms for repeated administration of the test over short time intervals.

The limitations of the test relate to:

(1) The racio-ethnic biases of the standardization sample. This aspect suggests caution and perhaps that the norms should not be generalized to nonwhite children.
(2) The lack of specification of the socioeconomic backgrounds of the standardization sample. This aspect further limits the generaliza-

tion of the norms and suggests that they should be applied only to children with middle-class backgrounds.

(3) The pictorial representations of word meanings are in several instances outdated; they feature racial and sexual biases.

(4) The implication that the PPVT may be used to assess verbal intelligence. This implication should be disregarded in the use of the test by speech-language clinicians and special educators. Measures of concurrent validity with tests of mental abilities are low, ranging from .58 to .61.

*Test of Language Development (TOLD): Picture Vocabulary*

This subtest of the TOLD (Newcomer & Hammill, 1977) was designed to assess the child's knowledge of word meaning in a picture identification task. The subtest contains 25 vocabulary items. Each item is a spoken word associated with four pictorial choices in the form of black line drawings. The child points to the correct drawing. An analysis of the grammatical categories and functions of the items featured indicates the following distribution:

(1) Lexical items that may function as subject-object in sentences (nouns) are featured in 19 items (Items 1–7, 9, 12, 14–20, 22, 25).

(2) Lexical items that may function as noun modifiers in sentences (adjectives) are featured in 6 items (Items 8, 10, 11, 21, 23, 24).

The TOLD was standardized on a sample of 1014 children, ranging in age from 4 years, 0 months to 8 years, 11 months. The demographic features of the standardization sample closely matched the 1970 Census of Population and Housing (U.S. Department of Commerce). Normative data are presented in Language Ages, in which raw scores on each of the subtests are converted to age equivalents. Scaled score equivalents are presented for each of six age intervals throughout the age range from 4 years, 0 months to 8 years, 11 months. Measures of test-retest reliability for the subtest were obtained on a sample of 21 children, tested with a 5-day interval. The test-retest coefficient of correlation was .95. Concurrent validity coefficients for the relationship with the Peabody Picture Vocabulary Test ranged from .76 at 4 years old to .95 at 6 years old.

The strongest asset of this test is its recent standardization and the size of and representativeness of the standardization sample. These features permit the examiner to generalize the norms to a relatively wide variety of children. Because the format requires only a pointing response, children with severe organic disorders of articulation, limited expressive vocabulary, or dysnomia can be tested. This vocabulary test is part of a larger battery of language tests. This feature permits comparison of performances by an individual child across tasks and ability areas.

Among the limitations of the subtest are:

(1) The relatively narrow age range for which the test is applicable.

(2) The small size of the samples and the short inter-test time interval, which may have resulted in spuriously high measures of test-retest reliability.

(3) The contrived word choices.

*Toronto Tests of Receptive Vocabulary*

The Toronto Tests of Receptive Vocabulary (English/Spanish) (Toronto, 1977) were designed to assess knowledge of the meaning of spoken vocabulary in Mexican-American children. The tests consist of two independently developed sections, one designed to evaluate vocabulary knowledge in English-speaking and one in Spanish-speaking Mexican-American children.

Both the English and the Spanish test versions contain 40 vocabulary items. Each item features a word to be spoken by an examiner. Each word is associated with three pictorial choices, black line drawings. One of the three choices features a pictorial representation of the word meaning. Two serve as foils. The foils for each item were designed to represent either visually or functionally associated objects, actions, or attributes.

The vocabulary items featured in the English and the Spanish versions of the test are not identical. In each language, the vocabulary items were selected to reflect cultural and attitudinal differences and biases within the different communities. The distribution of the vocabulary items according to grammatic word category is, however, similar in the two language versions. The distribution of the vocabulary items in the English version is as follows:

(1) 23 items are nouns that denote persons, objects, or characteristics.
(2) 13 items are verbs that denote actions.
(3) 3 items are adjectives that denote attributes and attitudes.

The TTRV was standardized on a sample of 1276 children, distributed about equally at 3-month intervals in the age range from 4 years, 0 months to 10 years, 11 months. The children were selected to represent three ethnic-language backgrounds. They were: (1) English-speaking Anglo-American, (2) English-speaking Mexican-American, and (3) Spanish-speaking Mexican-American. Children were assigned to the Spanish-speaking group when Spanish was spoken in the home at least 75% of the time.

Normative data in the form of percentile ranks (10th, 25th, 50th, 75th, 90th) are presented for each age level at one year intervals in the range from 4.0–4.11 to 10.0–10.11 years. Test-retest reliability for each of the tests was established with appropriate language-ethnic groups with a time interval of 1 month between tests. The correlation coefficients obtained were .92 for a group of 55 Anglo-American children, .91 for 52 English-speaking Mexican-American children, and .82 for 45 Spanish-speaking Mexican-American children. Measures of correlation for the homogeneity of the items within each of the tests ranged from .80 to .81 for the three ethnic-language groups, indicating acceptable internal stability. The validity of the test was reported to be supported by a positive correlation (.66) between chronological age and performance scores.

The author cautions that the Spanish version of the test discriminates between age groups only between the ages of 4 and 8 years. It does not discriminate adequately between age levels in the range from 8 to 10 years. The English version, on the other hand, does not provide adequate age discrimination among English-speaking Mexican-American children between 7 and 8 years.

Among assets of the TTRV are the following:

(1) The vocabulary items were selected to reflect cultural and attitudinal biases in the ethnic-language groups for which the tests were designed.
(2) The test-retest reliability measures indicate adequate stability of performances over short time intervals.
(3) Each of the tests in relatively easy and fast to administer (about 10 minutes) and score.
(4) The pictorial stimuli associated with the items are relatively clear and unambiguous.

The liabilities of each of the tests include the following:

(1) The socioeconomic characteristics of the standardization samples are not accounted for. As a result, the norms should be generalized only with caution.
(2) The geographical and cultural-ethnic biases of the standardization sample suggest caution in generalizing the norms to children of other than Mexican-American, Spanish-speaking backgrounds.
(3) The age range for which the tests are standardized and provide age discriminating norms is limited to a 4- to 5-year span.
(4) The tests have not yet been validated against similar, commonly used tests of receptive vocabulary.
(5) The children in the standardization sample were selected to reflect an age continuum within an age level. They were not selected to reflect discontinuous age levels. This factor may obscure the performance indices of growth in receptive vocabulary knowledge.

### Definition of Word Meaning: Format

An alternate format for assessing the knowledge of the referential or relational meaning of a word is to ask for a definition. Depending upon your perspective, you may see this method as tapping three different types of knowledge. It may be said to indicate whether a child has internalized a specific word as a label for a category rather than for a specific instance. From this perspective, the child is using words as a tool in the process of the cognitive organization of his world. A second perspective suggests that a definition indicates whether a child has internalized the central features of a concept or a category (Rips, Shoben, & Smith, 1973; Rosch, 1973). Finally, the method of definition may be said to tap the internalization of relations among meaning features (Norman, Rumelhart, *et al.*, 1975). This internalization shows up when the child creates definitions in sentence form which reflect the semantic relationships among the words. If the child gives a definition in the form of synonyms or a dissembled array of words to describe the meaning features of the stimulus word, you might conclude that he has not yet integrated and internalized the relations among the word's semantic features.

It is necessary for a clinician to understand which aspects of meaning are tapped in a word definition task in order to understand the rationales for evaluating and scoring the responses. In word definition tests, the responses are usually scored on a point scale. Comparing the scoring criteria for three recently standardized tests for word knowledge through definition, we can see several similarities (McCarthy, 1970; Newcomer & Hammill, 1977; Wechsler, 1974). Table 8.1 summarizes the similarities in the Scoring Criteria.

**TABLE 8.1**

*Scoring criteria used by selected tests of word definition*

| Criteria for Scoring | WISC-R Vocabulary | McCarthy: Word Knowledge | TOLD: Oral Vocabulary |
|---|---|---|---|
| Highest point score. (2/1) | Synonyms. Major uses. Primary, definitive features. Classification. Figurative use. Cumulative definition in sentence. Example of action or causal relationship. | Major uses. Salient characteristics. Synonyms. | Precise definition by classification, synonym, or one definitive characteristic. A combination of two, less definitive descriptions. |
| Lowest point score. (1) | Vague synonym. Minor use. Nondefinitive attribute. Inclusion of word in sentence. Concrete instance. Definition of related word form. | Minor uses. Nonsalient characteristics. Vague synonyms. | *Not used.* |
| No score. (0) | Obviously wrong. **Verbalism.** Vague, trivial response with poverty of contents. | Obviously wrong. Verbalism. Vague or trivial response. | Vague or trivial response. One, less definitive characteristic. Obviously wrong. |

The differences in the scoring criteria among the three tests may relate to the age range for each test. Of the three tests compared, the WISC-R Vocabulary subtests cover the widest and the oldest age range, from 6½ to 16½ years. The McCarthy Scales of Children's Abilities: Word Knowledge subtest covers the next widest age range and also the youngest, from 2½ to 8½ years. The TOLD: Oral Vocabulary subtest, in contrast, covers only the age range from 4 to 8 years. This difference may explain why the WISC-R Vocabulary subtest scoring guide includes more elaborate and abstract word definitions than the other two tests.

If a youngster is unable to perform at age expectations on a word definition task due either to delays in the acquisition of word meaning, word finding, and retrieval difficulties, or to motor or sensorimotor impairments of speech, extension testing is indicated. Among possible formats that may be used for extension testing are:

(1) Selection of a pictorial representation of the meaning from among a series of choices.
(2) Judgment of the acceptability of a word definition provided by the examiner.
(3) Judgment of the preference of a word definition from among two or more choices.
(4) Acting out of the meaning of a word by gestures, gross motor or fine motor actions, or manipulation of objects.

## Definition of Vocabulary: Tests

### *McCarthy Scales of Children's Abilities: Word Knowledge*

This subtest of the McCarthy Scales of Children's Abilities is designed to evaluate the child's understanding of the meaning of selected lexical items by identification of referents and by definition (McCarthy, 1970). The subtest constitutes one of six which comprise the Verbal Scale. The subtest contains two parts, for the evaluation of the (1) selection and labelling of pictured vocabulary items and (2) definition of oral vocabulary.

*The other subtests of this scale are Pictorial Memory, Verbal Memory I and II, Verbal Fluency, and Opposite Analogies. These subtests are discussed below.*

The Picture Vocabulary subsection features nine vocabulary items in association with five cards of the pictorial referents. The initial five vocabulary items ("apple," "tree," "house," "woman," "cow") are associated with a single picture card showing their referents. The examiner says the word, and the child is required to identify the appropriate pictured representation of the referent. Four additional vocabulary items ("clock," "sailboat," "flower," "purse") are featured along with one picture representation each. The child is asked to say the name of each of the pictured references. The test manual provides a range of the verbal labels that are acceptable in response to each of these items.

The Oral Vocabulary subsection features ten words ("towel," "coat," "tool," "thread," "factory," "shrink," "expert," "month," "concert," "loyal") to be defined by the child. The examiner says each word. The child must give a verbal explanation of the meaning of each of the lexical items. Each of the definitions is scored on a three-point scale. The test manual provides detailed examples of definitions for each item and for each score point.

The McCarthy Scales of Children's Abilities were standardized on a sample of 1032 children ranging in age from 2 years, 6 months to 8 years, 6 months. The sample was distributed evenly within 10 age groups at 6-month intervals. The standardization sample was selected to match the demographic characteristics of the general population, closely based on the 1970 U.S. Bureau of the Census, Census of Population. Test-retest reliability for each of the six scales of the test battery (Verbal, Perceptual-Performance, Quantitative, General Cognitive, Memory, Motor) was established using a sample of 125 children. Test-retest measures were obtained at a 1-month interval. The reliability coefficients for the Verbal Scale ranged from .82 at 7½ to 8½ years to .89 at 3 to 3½ years. Correlations of the relationship with performances by 35 children with WPPSI Verbal Scale and Stanford-Binet IQ were .51 and .66, respectively, indicating limited overlap.

Normative data in the form of Scale Index Equivalents of raw scores are available for each of the six scales. The normative data are presented for 25 age levels at 3-months intervals in the age range from 2 years, 6 months to 8 years, 6 months.

Among assets of the Word Knowledge subtest are:

(1) Demographic representativeness of the standardization sample. This feature permits you to generalize the norms to a wide range of children.
(2) Recent standardization and norms.
(3) Ease and speed of administration.
(4) Clarity of directions and criteria for scoring.

The limitations of the subtest relate to the following aspects:

(1) Normative data in the form of Scale Index quivalents are not available for each of the subtests.
(2) Test-retest reliability measures are not provided for each of the subtests.
(3) This subtest should be administered in conjunction with the remaining subtests of the Verbal Scale to provide a valid measure of the child's word knowledge, verbal memory, and verbal recall.
(4) The age range for which this test is appropriate is relatively limited.

*Test Of Language Development (TOLD): Oral Vocabulary*

This subtest of the TOLD assesses the child's vocabulary knowledge in a verbal definition task (Newcomer & Hammill, 1977). The subtest contains 20 vocabulary items, each consisting of a word which is to be defined by the child. The examiner says each word. The child is in turn required to give a verbal account of the meaning of each word either by one precise definition or by two descriptive characteristics. As an example, the stimulus word "cow" (Item 5) may be described by one of several precise definitions such as: a bovine, a heifer, a beef, or a female moose, buffalo, or elephant. It may also be defined by a combination of two descriptive characteristics, such as "gives milk and has horns."

Analysis of the vocabulary items by grammatical category and function indicates the following distribution:

(1) Lexical items which may function as subject-object in sentences (nouns) are featured in 12 items (Items 1, 3–10, 13, 14, 18).
(2) Lexical items which may function as predicates in sentences (verbs) are featured in only 1 item (Item 2).
(3) Lexical items which may function as noun modifiers in sentences (adjectives) and which denote height, affect, age, and/or status are featured in 5 items (Items 11, 12, 15, 16, 19).
(4) A lexical item which denotes location (preposition) is featured in 1 item (Item 17).

(5) A lexical item denoting the direction of action (adverb) is featured in 1 item (Item 20).

The TOLD was standardized on a sample of 1014 children ranging in age from 4 years, 0 months to 8 years, 11 months. The demographic features of the sample closely matched the 1970 Census of Population and Housing (U.S. Department of Commerce). Normative data are presented in Language Ages in which raw scores are converted to age equivalents. Scaled Score equivalents are presented for each 6-month age interval in the range from 4 years, 0 months to 8 years, 11 months. Measures of test-retest reliability for the TOLD subtests were obtained using a sample of 21 children tested with a 5-day interval. The test-retest reliability coefficient for the Oral Vocabulary subtest was .93. Concurrent validity coefficients for the relationship with the WISC Vocabulary subtest ranged from .84 at 8 years to .91 at 6 years.

Among the assets of the TOLD Oral Vocabulary subtest are:

(1) A relatively large, demographically representative sample used for standardization.
(2) The strength of the relationship of performances to WISC Vocabulary subtest scores.
(3) The possibility of comparison of performances across subtests of the TOLD and across tasks and ability areas.
(4) The availability of this subtest in the domain of the special educator.

Among liabilities and limitations are:

(1) The relatively narrow age range for which this subtest is applicable.
(2) The fact that the small sample size and the short time interval between tests may have resulted in spuriously high measures of test-retest reliability.

*Wechsler Intelligence Scale for Children–Revised (WISC-R): Vocabulary*

This subtest of the WISC-R is designed to evaluate the child's knowledge of word meaning through definition (Wechsler, 1974). The Vocabulary subtest is one of six which comprise the Verbal Scale. The remaining subtests of this scale are: Information, Similarities (page 215), Arithmetic, Comprehension, and Digit Span (page 302). The Vocabulary subtest features 32 lexical items, sequenced in order of difficulty, which are to be defined by the child. A detailed point scoring guide is provided for each item. Responses receive a score of 2 if they are synonyms, describe a major use, define primary features, provide general classification, or provide a definitive example of action or causal relationship. Responses which reflect poverty of content or are partial and incomplete receive a score of 1.

An analysis of the grammatical category and function of the lexical items indicates the following distribution:

(1) Lexical items that may function as subject-object in sentences (nouns) are featured in 19 items (Items 1–9, 12, 17, 18, 21, 23–27, 29).
(2) Lexical items which may function as predicates (verbs) are featured in 7 items (Items 10, 13, 15, 20, 22, 28, 30).

(3) Lexical items which may function as noun modifiers (adjectives) are featured in 5 items (Items 11, 16, 19, 31, 32).

(4) One lexical item may function as either subject-object or noun modifier (Item 14).

The WISC-R was standardized on a sample of 2200 children distributed evenly in 11 age groups, ranging from 6 years, 6 months through 16 years, 6 months. The demographic characteristics of the sample closely match reports of the 1970 United States Census. Normative data are presented in the form of Scaled Scores for each of the 11 age levels sampled. In addition, IQ equivalents are presented for the sum of the scaled scores on the Verbal, Performance, and Full-Scale. Split-half reliability coefficients are presented for each subtest. For the Vocabulary subtest, the coefficients range from .70 at 7 years, 6 months to .92 at 16 years, 6 months.

The WISC-R Vocabulary subtest has a recent standardization and norms and a representative standardization sample. These assets permit the user to generalize the norms to a wide range of children. In addition, the subtest is applicable for a relatively wide age range.

However, this test is designed to be administered by a psychologist with extensive training in giving the test. After the psychologist has the results of the test, the special educator or speech-language pathologist may examine the results to obtain information about the child's knowledge of word meaning and his relative verbal ability.

*Detroit Tests of Learning Aptitude (DTLA): Social Adjustment*

This subject of the DTLA is designed to assess the knowledge of socially significant vocabulary through definition (Baker & Leland, 1967). If the child can accurately define the featured vocabulary, the clinician can assume the child has broad knowledge of the meaning of words related to the social environment. The subtest contains 20 items, each of which features a word or concept which must be defined verbally. The lexical items featured are:

> Jail, money, fireman, policeman, school nurse, grocery store, knife, library, red light, janitor, party, stamps, letter, post office, flag, laws, courthouse, board of health, committee, quarantine.

The child's definition of each word is scored to reflect whether it is:

(1) Beside the point or incorrect.
(2) Vague, too general or very limited.
(3) Specific, brief, correct, but limited in expression.
(4) Generalized, offers explanation, or uses superior vocabulary.

Examples of responses within each scoring category are given in the test manual. The responses permit the user to analyze the child's knowledge of the meaning of words with social relevance along a simple-concrete to complex-abstract continuum.

The Detroit Tests of Learning Aptitude were standardized on 150 children at each age level ranging from 3 years, 0 months to 19 years, 0 months. All children in the standardization sample attended the Detroit public schools. Test-retest reliability was measured initially using a sample of 48 children and a time interval of 5 months. The correlation coefficient obtained was .96, indicating high stability of performances over time. A second test-retest correlation coefficient of .68 was reported for a 2-year time interval between tests, using a sample of 792 students in the age range from 7 to 10 years. Normative data are provided for the age range from 3 years, 0 months to 19 years, 0 months.

Among the assets of this subtest is the vocabulary content. The words which are featured here are not highlighted in other tests of vocabulary knowledge. These lexical items are especially relevant to the experiences of children and adolescents in urban settings. They are not appropriate for the experiences of rural children, however.

The primary asset of the test—its relevance for urban children—is also its primary drawback. The standardization sample is demographically biased. Since the racio-ethnic and socioeconomic characteristics of the standardization sample are not indicated, the norms should be generalized only to urban, white children. In addition, the norms are dated, and therefore should not be applied inflexibly. Rather than using the norms alone, the clinician should look for significant performance discrepancies from age expectations (18 months of age below expectations or more) for a more appropriate indication of intervention needs.

### Identification and Expression of Antonymy and Reciprocity of Meaning: Format

Currently standardized tests use two basic models for the assessment of knowledge of antonymy and reciprocity. One format uses word association. One member of a word pair related by either antonymy or reciprocity is presented by the examiner. The stimulus word is expected to provoke a verbal response that features the exact opposite (Baker & Leland, 1967). Here is an example:

**Item 4.**   Stimulus:      Brother.
             Expected response:      Sister.

The second format uses an incomplete verbal analogy to bring forth an antonym or a semantically related term (Kirk, McCarthy, & Kirk, 1968; McCarthy, 1970). In this format, a carrier phrase is used to express the relationship between two words. A second incomplete phrase features a word that belongs to the same semantic-grammatic category as the first word in the carrier phrase. The youngster is to say the word that completes the second phrase to form a verbal analogy. The example below illustrates the format of verbal analogy items (Kirk, McCarthy, & Kirk, 1968).

**Item 12.**   Carrier phrase:      A rabbit is fast.
              Incomplete phrase:      A turtle is _____.
              Expected response:      Slow.

While the two formats differ, they share some task requirements. To provide the expected verbal response, the child must have learned a group of words that are related in meaning by antonymy, reciprocity, or semantic class membership. The child must also be able to recall, retrieve, and produce the specific word called for. As a result, the accuracy of the responses may be influenced negatively by (1) delays in learning an adequate repertory of antonymns and reciprocally related terms, (2) word finding and retrieval deficits, or (3) motor and sensorimotor impairments.

When the test features incomplete analogies, the youngster must also be able to perceive and abstract, an expressed semantic relationship between two words and use that relationship in a second context. This format therefore taps the child's relational thinking ability as well as word knowledge. If a child is unable to perform at the expected level for his age, extension testing to discern the nature and extent of the problem is indicated. Among possible formats which may be used for extension testing are:

(1) Judgment of the acceptability of word pairs related or unrelated by antonymy or reciprocity.
(2) Judgment of preference for word pairs among a series of related and unrelated pairs.
(3) Selection of an antonym or reciprocally related term from among a series of verbal choices or pictorial representations of meaning.
(4) Completion of *visual* analogies to evaluate the child's relational thinking ability with nonverbal stimuli.

## Identification and Expression of Antonymy and Reciprocity: Tests

*McCarthy Scales of Children's Abilities: Opposite Analogies*

This subtest of the McCarthy Scales of Children's Abilities is designed to evaluate the child's knowledge and expression of antonymy and his relational thinking ability (McCarthy, 1970). It constitutes one of the subtests of the Verbal Scale. The remaining subtests of this scale are: Pictorial Memory, Word Knowledge I and II (page 205–6), Verbal Memory I and II (pages 303–4), and Verbal Fluency (page 339).

The subtest contains nine statements in the form of a verbal analogy to be completed by the child. Each of the analogies follows this format:

**Item 1.** The sun is *hot*, and ice is _____.

The examiner reads each statement out loud. The child is required to complete the verbal analogy by saying the appropriate antonym. Of the nine analogies, five may be completed with one of several synonyms listed in the test manual. Only four items require a specific antonym. An analysis of the grammatical category and function of the antonym pairs indicates that eight items—the antonyms for "hot," "big," "fast," "soft," "sour," "light" (weight), "thick," and "rough"—require the child to know, recall, and produce verbal labels for attributes that may function as noun modifiers (adjectives). One item—the antonym for "up"—requires the child to know and recall a label for a direction (preposition).

The McCarthy Scales of Children's Abilities were standardized on a sample of 1032 children ranging in age from 2 years, 6 months to 8 years, 6 months. The sample was distributed evenly within 10 age groups at 6-month intervals. The standardization sample was selected to match the demographic characteristics of the general population, closely based on the 1970 U.S. Bureau of the Census. Test-retest reliability for each of the six scales (Verbal, Perceptual-Performance, Quantitative, General Cognitive, Memory, Motor) was established for a sample of 125 children with a 1 month test-retest interval. The reliability coefficients for the Verbal Scale ranged from .82 at 7½ to 8½ years to .89 at 3 to 3½ years. Correlations of the relationship of performances by 35 children on the Verbal Scale with WPPSI Verbal-Scale and Stanford-Binet IQ were .51 and .66, respectively.

Normative data in the form of Scale Index Equivalents of raw scores are available for each of the scales and for 25 age levels at 3-month intervals. The normative data cover the age range from 2 years, 6 months to 8 years, 6 months.

Among the assets of the Opposite Analogies subtest are:

(1) It is easy and quick to administer and score.
(2) The criteria for scoring responses are clear.
(3) The standardization sample is demographically representative, which permits the clinician to generalize the norms to a wide range of children.
(4) The standardization and norms are recent, which suggests their validity with today's children.

The subtest's limitations relate to the following characteristics:

(1) Normative data are not available for individual subtests. As a result, the Opposite Analogies subtest must be administered in conjunction with the other subtests of the Verbal Scale to provide a valid measure.
(2) The age range for which the subtest is applicable is relatively limited.

*Illinois Test of Psycholinguistic Ability (ITPA): Auditory Association*

The Auditory Association subtest is designed to evaluate the child's ability to perceive and produce verbal analogies which feature antonyms and lexical items which are related by inclusion of meaning (Kirk, McCarthy, & Kirk, 1968). The subtest contains 42 items, sequenced according to progressive level of difficulty. The following example illustrates the format of the items.

**Item 12.** A rabbit is fast; a turtle is _____.

The grammatical categories and functions of the items featured in the word pairs are distributed as follows:

(1) Lexical items that may function as subject-object (nouns) are featured in 23 of the items (Items 2, 5, 7, 8, 10, 13, 14, 19, 22, 24, 26, 28–31, 33–35, 38–42).
(2) Lexical items that denote actions and may function as predicates (verbs) are featured in 6 items (Items 1, 3, 6, 9, 16, 27).

(3) Lexical items that denote attributes and may function as modifiers (adjectives) are featured in 12 items (Items 11, 12, 15, 17, 18, 20, 21, 23, 25, 32, 36, 37).

(4) A lexical item that denotes direction (preposition) is featured in item 4.

To respond accurately to the test items, the child must understand antonymy and inclusion of meaning. In addition, he must be able to perceive the logical relationships between the members of the first word pair and extend it to the second word pair to complete the analogy. Inadequate performance on the test may therefore reflect one or more of several limitations: (1) limitations in the available vocabulary of antonyms and semantically related terms, (2) difficulties in reasoning by analogy, and (3) problems in word recall and retrieval. To make a differential diagnosis of the contributing difficulties, the clinician will need corroborative results from other tests.

*A differential diagnosis involves listing all the possible causes of a condition and eliminating those that do not fit the situation, one-by-one, until only one probable cause is left.*

The ITPA was standardized on 962 children in the age range from 2 years, 0 months to 10 years, 11 months. All resided in midwestern suburban towns in Illinois and Wisconsin. The racial-ethnic characteristics of the sample are not given, but the test implies that the children came from middle-class backgrounds. Normative data for the Auditory Association subtests are available in the age range from 2 years, 4 months to 10 years, 11 months. Five-month test-retest stability coefficients for the subtest range from .83 to .90, suggesting good consistency of the performances over time. The internal consistency of the subtest is adequate, with split-half correlation coefficients ranging from .74 to .85.

Among the assets of the ITPA Auditory Association subtest are its relative ease and speed of administration and scoring, stability of performances over short time intervals, and wide age range with normative data.

Weaknesses of the subtest relate to the geographic and socioeconomic biases of the standardization sample. The clinician should be careful in generalizing the norms to children of other than suburban middle-class backgrounds. Because of the implied racial-ethnic biases, the norms should not be generalized to any minority child.

*Detroit Tests of Learning Aptitude (DTLA): Verbal Opposites*

The Verbal Opposites subtest is designed to assess the child's knowledge of antonyms and reciprocal terms and the ability to recall and produce exact opposites and reciprocates (Baker & Leland, 1967). The subtest contains 96 items, each of which features a member of an antonym or reciprocal word pair. The examiner says each stimulus word. The child is required to recall and say the word which forms the other member of the pair. The vocabulary items were selected so that generally only one word satisfies the criterion. The vocabulary items are sequenced according to relative frequency and reading level and along a continuum from concrete to abstract.

Analysis of the stimulus words by grammatical category and function indicates the following distribution:

(1) Lexical items that may function as agents-objects (nouns) are featured in 20 items (Items 1, 2, 4, 29, 33, 44, 45, 50, 58, 59, 62, 70, 75, 83, 84, 87, 88, 91, 92, 96).
(2) Lexical items that may function as labels for actions or predicates (verbs) are featured in 17 items (Items 26–28, 33, 35, 46, 51, 56, 60, 67, 68, 73, 76, 77, 79, 82, 94).
(3) Lexical items that may function as labels of attributes or noun modifiers or predicate adjectives (adjectives) are featured in 56 items (5–19, 21–24, 30–32, 35–41, 43, 47–49, 52–55, 57, 61, 63–66, 69, 71, 72, 74, 78, 80, 81, 85, 86, 89, 90, 93, 95).
(4) A lexical item that may function to modify an action or a predicate (adverb) is featured in 1 item (Item 25).
(5) Lexical items that may function to define spatial or temporal relationships are featured in 3 items (Items 3, 20, 42).

The Detroit Tests of Learning Aptitude were standardized on 150 children at each age level in the range from 3 years, 0 months to 19 years, 0 months. All children in the standardization sample attended the Detroit Public Schools. Test-retest reliability was measured initially using a sample of 48 children and a time interval between tests of 5 months. The resulting correlation coefficient was .96, indicating high stability over time. A second correlation coefficient of .68 was reported for a sample of 792 children in the age range from 7 to 10 years, tested with a time interval of 2 to 3 years. Normative data are provided for the age range from 3 years, 0 months to 19 years, 0 months.
Among the assets of the Verbal Opposites subtest are:

(1) The administration and scoring are easy and quick.
(2) The contents and the task requirements are unique among standardized clinical-educational tests.
(3) The contents and the task requirements are very good for identifying associative word substitutions and delays in the acquisition of antonymy and reciprocity.
(4) The subtest is applicable for a wide age range.

Among liabilities and limitations of the subtests are the datedness of the norms and the demographic biases of the standardization sample. These aspects suggest that the norms should not be applied to nonurban or nonwhite children, and should be applied with caution and flexibility to urban white children because of their datedness. The Verbal Opposites subtest is not recommended for children in the age range from 3 to 6 years.

### Inclusion of Word Meanings: Format

Among current standardized tests, two formats are employed in assessing the knowledge of inclusion of word meaning. One requires the child to formulate and express essential shared meanings (similarities); the other, essentially different meanings (differences), in a pair of words that belong to the same grammatic-semantic category (Baker & Leland, 1967; Wechsler, 1974). In the first case, the examiner says a word pair orally. The youngster must abstract and describe the most essential aspect, feature, or characteristic that is shared by the two terms in the pair. The responses are generally scored on a three-point scale. The highest score (2) may reflect a classification response that gives the name of the semantic category to which both terms belong. A lower point score (1) may reflect a specific property or function that is a relevant similarity in meaning. Failure on an item receives a score of zero. This score may reflect irrelevant perceptual features, properties, or functions, vague generalizations, or clearly wrong responses. Here is an example of a similarities item and the criteria used for scoring (Wechsler, 1974).

> **Item 5.**   Apple–Banana.
> *Classification response* (2 points):      Both are fruits.
> *Property or function response* (1 point):      Both are foods/sweet/used for cakes or pies/etc.
> *Irrelevant or erroneous response* (zero points):      Both are good for you/ small/round/soft/yellow etc.

The second way to assess knowledge of inclusion of meaning requires the child to describe essential differences in meaning between the members of a related word pair. Thus the child must exclude all the meanings that are shared or included in the terms and describe only essential differences. In currently standardized tests, this task is usually required after the child describes the essential similarities between the two word labels or concepts; that is, the child describes both similarities and differences for a given word pair (Baker & Leland, 1967). The responses to this task are also scored on a point scale. The following example (Baker & Leland, 1967) illustrates both format and criteria for scoring likenesses and differences in word meaning.

> **Item 10.**   Telescope–Microscope
> *Essential likeness:*      Devices to aid vision.
> *Essential difference:*      *Telescope* is for distant objects.
>                                       *Microscope* is for small or nearby objects.
> *Point score for combined response:*      3 points.

Still another format for tapping inclusion and exclusion of word meaning is featured in the Clinical Evaluation of Language Functions: Word Classes subtest (Semel & Wiig, 1980). This test features several word series consisting of either three or four words. After hearing a word series, the youngster must recall, abstract, and repeat the two words in the series that are the most strongly associated by inclusion of meaning. The task requires the child to exclude the words in the series that are unrelated or distantly related in meaning. It taps the child's ability to perceive and recall which spoken words share essential meanings or relations. The example below illustrates the format.

> **Item 13.**   *Before–In–Under–After*.

If a child does not perform at age expectations on tests of inclusion and exclusion of word meaning, he needs extension testing. The formats which may be used to tap knowledge of inclusion of meaning and semantic categorization ability include:

(1) Categorization and classification of pictured objects according to semantic categories, such as fruits, liquids, meats, vegetables, furniture, tools, toys, and transportation.
(2) Hierarchical classification of attribute blocks according to first one, then two, and three specified attributes such as color, color and size, color and size and shape, etc.
(3) Identification of a pictured object and/or word which does not belong in a semantic category in a word series, such as "apple-lemon-meat-banana."
(4) Judgment of the acceptability of or preference for paired words.

## Inclusion of Meaning: Tests

*Wechsler Intelligence Scale for Children–Revised (WISC-R): Similarities*

This subtest of the WISC-R is designed to assess the child's ability to abstract and define shared meanings or similarities among verbal concepts which denote objects, measures, values and ideas, and quantitative relationships (Wechsler, 1974). It is one of six subtests which comprise the Verbal Scale. The remaining subtests are Information, Arithmetic, Vocabulary (pages 207–8), Comprehension, and Digit Span (page 302).

The subtest contains 17 items, each of which consists of a word-pair related by inclusion of meaning. The items are presented in increasing order of difficulty. The examiner says each word pair. The child is required to identify and describe the quality or dimension shared by the concepts. Guidelines are provided for scoring each of the definitions. A weighted point score is assigned to each response. The highest score (2) reflects whether the description features an essential similarity, such as identification of the semantic category of which the concepts are members. A score of 1 is assigned if the child provides a functional or perceptual characteristic. An example of an item and scoring of the responses is provided below.

**Item 4.** Piano–Guitar
*Response:* "Both are string or musical instruments." Score: 2
*Response:* "You play them both." Score: 1
*Response:* "They both have strings." Score: 1

The WISC-R was standardized on a sample of 2200 children distributed evenly in 11 age groups in the age range from 6 years, 6 months to 16 years, 6 months. The demographic characteristics of the standardization sample closely matched reports of the 1970 United States Census. Normative data are presented in the form of Scaled Scores for each of the 11 age levels. In addition, IQ equivalents are presented for the sum of the scaled scores on the Verbal, Performance, and Full-Scale. Split-half reliability coefficients are presented for each subtest. For the Similarities subtest, they range from .74 at 15½ to .87 at 6½ years of age.

The WISC-R has a relatively recent standardization and norms and a representative standardization sample. Thus the norms can be generalized to a wide variety of children. In addition, the subtest is applicable for a relatively wide age range. The results allow the clinician to compare the child's abilities across skill areas and tasks. Unfortunately, administration and interpretation of the test require extensive training, and are usually done by a psychologist. The special educator and speech-language pathologist will need to examine the psychologist's results to find out about the child's learning of the inclusion of meaning among concepts.

*Detroit Tests of Learning Aptitude (DTLA): Likenesses and Differences*

This subtest of the DTLA is designed to assess the ability to abstract and describe ways in which verbal concepts which denote objects, qualities, or ideas share essential characteristics or are essentially different (Baker & Leland, 1967). The subtest contains 32 word pairs, related in meaning by inclusion. The word pairs are sequenced according to difficulty. An analysis of the grammatical category and function of the lexical items indicates the following distribution:

(1) Lexical items that may function as subject-object (nouns) and that are related by semantic class or by spatial and temporal relationship are featured in 31 items.
(2) A lexical item that may function as a label for actions (verb) is featured in only 1 item (Item 3).

The examiner says each word pair. The child is then required to tell first how the two members of the word pair share a meaning and second how they differ. The scoring key provided in the test manual specifies the most essential shared characteristics and differences of each word pair. Responses are scored for correctness on a four-point scale. The highest point score (3) is given for responses with essential (determining or limiting) similarities and differences. The first item of the subtest illustrates the comparison required and the scoring guide.

**Item 1.** Morning–Afternoon
*Likeness:* Part of a day.
*Difference:* Early—before noon.
Late—after midday.    Score: 3

The DTLA was standardized on a sample of 150 children at each age level in the range from 3 years, 0 months to 19 years, 0 months, and normative data cover this entire range. All children in the standardization sample attended the Detroit Public Schools. Test-retest reliability was measured initially with a time interval of 5 months, using a sample of 48 children. The resulting correlation coefficient was .96, indicating high stability over time. A second correlation coefficient of .68 was reported for a sample of 792 students tested with a 2 to 3 year time interval.

The Likenesses and Differences subtest has the following advantages:

(1) It is applicable over a wide age range.
(2) The words and concepts featured include operative items (manipulative reference such as "spoon"–"fork") and figurative items (vis-

ually established reference such as "canal"–"river") as well as abstract concepts.

(3) The test allows the examiner to compare the child's performances on subtests which tap different aspects of knowledge of word meaning (Verbal Opposites and Likenesses and Differences).

However, the norms of this test are dated, and the standardization sample is not representative. Therefore, the norms should be applied only to urban, white children, and they should be flexibly applied. In addition, the directions for examiner questioning are vague, and scores depend upon individual examiner judgments.

*Clinical Evaluation of Language Functions (CELF): Processing Word Classes*

The Processing Word Classes subtest of the CELF was designed to evaluate the ability to perceive relationships between words and verbal concepts and to identify related words (Semel & Wiig, 1980). The subtest contains 22 items. Each of the items features three or four verbal concepts of which two are associated. Each item contains one or two verbal concepts that act as foils. The foils were chosen from different but related semantic classes. For example, the two foils for the word pair featured in item 2, "dog" and "bark," were chosen from a related animate class ("boy") and from a class of actions ("crumble").

The items on the subtest may be classified according to the relationship between the members of each word pair, as outlined below.

(1) Eight items feature two words related by semantic class membership (Items 1, 2, 3, 8, 9, 10, 11, 18).
(2) Nine items feature two words related by antonym relationship (Items 5, 6, 7, 12, 13, 15, 20, 21, 22).
(3) One item features two words related by spatial relationship (Item 17).
(4) Two items feature two words related by temporal relationship (Items 14, 19).
(5) One item features two words related by agent-action relationship (Item 4).
(6) One item features two words related by superordinate-subordinate relationship (Item 16).

The test-retest reliability of the subtest was established with 30 randomly selected children in the age range from 8 years, 3 months to 8 years, 6 months. The subtest was administered twice with a 3-month interval between administrations. The test-retest reliability coefficient was .85, indicating adequate stability over time. Concurrent validity was established against the ITPA Auditory Association subtest; the correlation coefficient obtained was .46. The Clinical Evaluation of Language Functions is a criterion-referenced language test. Criterion raw scores have been established for each grade level from K through 10.

**Interpretation of Relational Terms: Format**

Knowledge of specific relational terms for (among others) spatial and temporal relations among words, phrases, and clauses is assessed in two different formats in currently standardized tests. In one type the child judges the acceptability of statements and associated questions. The stimuli express comparative, passive, spatial, temporal, familial, and figurative relationships among words. The following example illustrates this format for each of the relationships featured in the test (Semel & Wiig, 1980).

*Comparative relationship*

**Item 1.**    Are parents older than their children?

*Passive relationship*

**Item 13.**    Judy was pulled by Sue. Was Sue pulled?

*Analogous relationship*

**Item 16.**    Is big to little as night is to day?

*Spatial relationship*

**Item 26.**    Mike walked to the right of Russell. Was Russell on the right side?

*Temporal-sequential relationship*

**Item 23.**    Does December come before November?

*Familial relationship*

**Item 24.**    If Lillian's mother has a sister, could Lillian's sister be called Lillian's aunt?

*Figurative relationship*

**Item 27.**    My Father hit the roof. Does it mean:
My father slapped his hand on the roof?

To judge the acceptability of the stated relationships, the child must master several tasks. He must be able to identify and recall the critical terms involved in the relationship. He must also be able to perform the logical operations required to either accept or reject the expressed relationship. Finally, he must perceive and interpret the abstract meanings of the figurative relationships and reject the concrete interpretations.

A second format uses oral command for action to assess the knowledge of relational terms that conjoin sentences and result in either coordination or subordination of clauses. Current tests that feature linguistic concepts of time ("when"/"then"), condition ("if"/"then"), or inclusion-exclusion ("all"/"except") use a format in which the vocabulary is controlled and limited to highlight the critical relational terms (DeRenzi & Vignolo, 1962; Semel & Wiig, 1980). They use tasks in which oral commands have to be carried out either by manipulating tokens or by pointing to simple pictorial displays of colored lines.

Accurate performance in response to an oral command like this one depends upon several abilities. Because these commands use the same vocabulary over and over again and the correct action cannot be inferred from the context, it is critical that the child has learned the meaning of the relational term. In addition, the youngster must be able to recall the action sequence accurately. If a youngster does not execute a command accurately, you cannot automatically assume that he does not know the meaning of the featured relational term in other contexts. The incorrect performance indicates only that the meaning of the concept may not be firmly enough established without contextual and logical cues, or that the child has a short-term memory deficit. As a result, extension testing should be done to determine which contextual cues help the child perform accurately. Among formats that may be used for extension testing are:

(1) Rephrasing the oral commands to include familiar vocabulary along with pictorial representations or actual objects and events. As examples, a command such as "Point to all the lines except the blue one" may be restated as "Take all the cars except the blue one." A command such as "Point to a line that is neither yellow nor red" may be restated two ways. It may be paraphrased "Point to a line that is not yellow and not red" or "Take a car that is not yellow and not red."

(2) Acting-out oral commands with familiar objects and in familiar settings. For example, a command such as "Point to a blue line before you point to a yellow line" may be restated in the form "Pick your book up before you open it."

### Interpretation of Relational Terms: Tests

*Boehm Test of Basic Concepts*

This test is designed to evaluate the knowledge and understanding of basic concepts of quantity and number, space (dimension, direction, orientation), time, and combinations of these (Boehm, 1970). The test has two forms, each of which contains 50 items arranged according to increasing difficulty. The items in the two forms of the test follow the same formats and feature the identical terms for the basic concepts. Each item features an oral direction associated with either a set of three horizontally displayed pictorial choices or with a composite picture. All pictures are black line drawings. The instructions for the items are available in both English and Spanish.

The BTBC may be administered as a group or as an individual test. In either case, the child is given a pencil and a response booklet which contains the pictorial choices for three or four items on each page. The examiner says each statement or oral direction. The child either identifies the best representation of the featured concept or completes the action indicated in the oral direction. The concepts featured in the items were selected from curriculum materials for grades K–1. Analysis of the concepts featured in the test indicates the following distribution, according to semantic category:

(1) Spatial concepts are featured in 17 statements and directions (Items 1–3, 5, 10, 11, 18, 20, 21, 26, 28, 34, 38, 39, 41, 44, 48).

(2) Temporal concepts ("never," "always") are featured in 2 oral directions (Items 33, 36).

(3) Spatial-temporal concepts are featured in 7 statements and directions (Items 4, 7, 9, 14, 16, 23, 29).

(4) Concepts of quantity are featured in 15 statements and directions (Items 6, 8, 12, 13, 15, 19, 24, 25, 27, 37, 40, 42, 45, 47, 50).

(5) Spatial-temporal-quantitative concepts are featured in 3 oral directions (Items 17, 32, 49).

(6) Miscellaneous concepts such as *skip, separated,* and *matches* are featured in 6 directions (Items 22, 30, 31, 35, 43, 46).

The BTBC was standardized on a sample of 9737 children attending grades K, 1, and 2. The children in the standardization sample resided in five cities in the West, Midwest, Southeast, and Northeast. The socioeconomic status of the sample ranged from low to high. The racial-ethnic characteristics are not specified. Alternate form reliability coefficients range from .72 at K to .88 at grade 2. Normative data are presented by percentile rank for each item, grade, and socioeconomic level (low, middle, high).

The Boehm Test of Basic Concepts had several assets, including:

(1) Ease and speed of administration and scoring.

(2) Ease of error pattern analysis according to semantic concept category.

(3) Availability of alternate test forms.

(4) Possibility for individual and group administration.

(5) Availability of a Spanish and an English version of the test items.

(6) Availability of a class record form by individual concept and concept category, for easy identification of children in need of follow-up, diagnosis, and/or intervention.

(7) Suggestions for the selection of remediation sequences and strategies within the test manual.

(8) Standardization sample which is recent and geographically and socioeconomically representative.

(9) The extraordinary size of the standardization sample, which suggests that minority children were included proportionately.

Among the weaknesses and limitations of the BTBC are:

(1) Limited value of the mean norms for first graders of middle or high socioeconomic backgrounds, since these overlap with the means for second graders.

(2) Disproportionate frequency of spatial concepts.

(3) Lack of individual score sheets.

(4) Although instructions are available in Spanish, the vocabulary selections in that language may be questioned.

(5) Lack of cut-off points or levels for determining the difficulty of a given item by grade level.

(6) Tenuous test-retest comparisons of the performances of an individual child; the difference scores have been reported to be statistically unreliable (Boehm, 1970, p. 16).

*Token Test: Part V*

The Token Test is designed to evaluate the ability to process and recall verbal directions of increasing length and complexity (DeRenzi & Vignolo, 1962). This test has been used extensively in research and in clinical work with adults with acquired aphasia. It has been revised and adapted for use with children (Noll, 1970).

The Token Test is designed so that the linguistic structures are minimally redundant in order to assure that the meaning of each word or relationship among words is grasped and retained. The oral commands featured in the test are executed by manipulating tokens according to the directions given by the examiner. There are 20 tokens in the set. They combine features of color (red, blue, green, yellow, white), shape (circle, square), and/or size (big, little). The test contains five parts. The first four parts of the test contain 10 commands each. They are presented in the form of imperatives, with either the form "Take . . ." or "Show me . . ." The length of the items increases from 4 to 10 words. Conjunctions and coordination of clauses are introduced in parts II, III, and IV of the test.

Part V of the Token Test contains 21 items. The items feature particles, complex syntactic structures, compound oral commands, and basic linguistic concepts. An analysis of the critical concepts and relationships featured in the original form of the Token Test indicates the following distribution according to semantic category:

(1) *Spatial* concepts (prepositions) are featured in 7 commands (Items 1, 2, 7, 8, 12, 14, 20).
(2) Concepts of *inclusion* ("and," "or," "together with") are featured in 3 commands (Items 5, 6, 18).
(3) Concepts of *exclusion* ("except") are featured in 2 commands (Items 10, 15).
(4) *Temporal* concepts and relationships ("when," "after," "before") are featured in 3 commands (Items 11, 19, 21).
(5) Concepts denoting *space-time* dimensions ("slowly," "quickly") are featured in 1 command (Item 13).
(6) *Conditional* concepts and relationships ("if," "no," "instead of") are featured in 3 commands (Items 9, 16, 17).
(7) *Instrumental* concepts and relationships ("with") are featured in 2 commands (Items 3, 4).

The Token Test: Part V has been found to identify subtle, high-level language processing deficits among adults with aphasia and adolescents with learning disabilities (Lapointe, 1976; Wertz, Keith, & Custer, 1971; Wertz & Perkins, 1972). It has unique features and assets, including:

(1) The control of the action-object vocabulary, which highlights comprehension of the specific critical linguistic concepts and relations in the commands.
(2) Analysis of the error response patterns may help the clinician identify concepts and relations which have not been adequately mastered when the contextual and semantic cues are reduced to a minimum.

The assets are offset by the extremely limited standardization information and by the absence of measures of test-retest reliability. Furthermore, the appropriate use and interpretation of test results require careful understanding of the task and of the functions of the concepts.

*Clinical Evaluation of Language Functions (CELF): Processing Linguistic Concepts*

This subtest of the CELF was designed to evaluate the ability to process, interpret, and remember oral directions which contain basic linguistic concepts such as "and," "either . . . or," and "if . . . then" (Semel & Wiig, 1980). The accurate interpretation of the basic concepts featured depends upon accurate perception and interpretation of the logical relationships expressed among the remaining words and concepts in the sentence.

The subtest contains 22 items, each of which is associated with a series of colored lines. In order to feature the basic linguistic concepts in the items, the vocabulary in the oral directions is restricted and controlled, as is the word length. The vocabulary featured in the sentences, other than the linguistic concepts, is limited to the following words: (1) "point to," (2) "line," (3) "red," "blue," and "yellow." The linguistic concepts featured in the items were selected to represent a range relative to the time of acquisition. The linguistic concepts and logical relationships they express are listed in Table 8.2.

**TABLE 8.2**

*Common linguistic concepts*

| Linguistic Concept | Logical Relationship | Item Number |
|---|---|---|
| "not" | Exclusion. | 1 |
| "and" | Coordination. | 2 |
| "all . . . except" | Inclusion-exclusion. | 3 |
| ". . . with" | Instrumental. | 4 |
| "after . . ." | Temporal. | 5, 21 |
| "no instead" | Exclusion-revision. | 6 |
| ". . . after" | Temporal. | 7, 22 |
| "when . . ." | Temporal. | 8 |
| ". . . before" | Temporal. | 9, 21 |
| "if . . ." | Temporal-conditional. | 10 |
| "don't . . . till" | Temporal-conditional. | 11 |
| "either . . . or" | Inclusion-exclusion. | 12 |
| "before . . ." | Temporal. | 12, 22 |
| "with . . ." | Instrumental. | 14 |
| "some, all . . . some" | Inclusion. | 15, 19 |
| "anyone, any . . . all" | Inclusion. | 16, 20 |
| "without" | Instrumental-exclusion. | 17 |
| "neither . . . nor" | Exclusion. | 18 |

The examiner says the oral direction featured in each of the items. The youngster points to the colored lines required by the oral direction in response.

The test-retest reliability of the subtest was evaluated with 30 randomly selected children in the age range from 8 years, 3 months to 8 years, 6 months. The test was readministered after an interval of 6 weeks. The test-retest correlation coefficient for the subtest was .96, indicating good stability. The concurrent validity was established by comparing the performances with those on the Token Test: Part V. The correlation coefficient for the relationship was .62. The Clinical Evaluation of Language Functions is a criterion-referenced language test. Criterion raw scores have been established for each grade level from K through 10.

*Clinical Evaluation of Language Functions (CELF): Processing Relationships and Ambiguities*
This subtest of the CELF is designed to evaluate the ability to process and interpret sentences with comparative, passive, spatial, temporal-sequential, familial, and analogous relationships, idioms, metaphors, and proverbs (Semel & Wiig, 1980). The subtest taps aspects of language processing related to perceiving logical and figurative relationships among words and going beyond the concrete, nominative function of words to grasp the abstract word meanings in figurative language.

The subtest contains 32 items, divided equally into subgroups of four items. The sentences in the spoken items are presented in a statement-question format. After listening to each statement and associated questions, the youngster responds with a yes or a no. The items may be categorized as indicated below.

(1) Four items express comparative relationships ("older," "heavier," "taller," "shorter") among words and concepts (Items 1, 2, 12, 19).
(2) Four items express passive relationships ("was chosen," "was pushed," "was caught," "was followed") in sentences (Items 5, 10, 13, 14).
(3) Four items express spatial relationships ("on," "in," "between," "to the right of") among objects and persons (Items 4, 20, 26, 28).
(4) Four items express temporal-sequential relationships among days of the week, months of the year, and times of day (Items 7, 21, 23, 25).
(5) Four items express familial relationships (Items 6, 15, 22, 24).
(6) Four items express analogous relationships among words and concepts. The relationships featured in the analogies are opposite (antonym), part-whole, action-implement, and cause-effect (Items 3, 9, 16, 18).
(7) Four items feature idioms and metaphors (Items 8, 11, 17, 27).
(8) Four items are commonly used proverbs (Items 29, 30, 31, 32).

The test-retest reliability of the subtest was evaluated with 30 randomly selected children in the age range from 8 years, 3 months to 8 years, 6 months. The test-retest interval was 6 weeks. The resulting correlation coefficient was .77, indicating adequate stability over time. Concurrent validity was established with subtests of the ITPA, DTLA, and the Northeastern Syntax Screening Test. The coefficients of concurrent validity were .58 for the NSST: Expressive, .42 for the ITPA Auditory Association subtest, .46 for the ITPA Auditory Sequential Memory subtest, .43 for the ITPA Grammatic Closure subtest, and .47 for the DTLA Verbal Opposites subtest. The Clinical Evaluation of Language Functions is a criterion-referenced language test. Criterion raw scores have been established for each grade level from K through 10.

## Integration of Word Meaning Across Clause and Sentence Boundaries: Format

The ability to integrate the meanings of specific words across clause and sentence boundaries and to detect inconsistencies is not generally assessed in current language tests. Formal tests that focus on this ability are, however, available in the intelligence and learning aptitude testing. Both the Stanford-Binet and the Detroit Tests of Learning Aptitude feature Verbal Absurdities subtests that tap the ability to integrate word meaning and detect absurdities. An item from the Stanford-Binet illustrates the format of an item. This item requires the child to integrate, make a logical comparison, and accept or reject the quantitative relationships that are expressed by critical word choices.

YEAR 10 (a)      In the year 1915 many *more women than men got married* in the United States.

## Integration of Meaning Across Phrases, Clauses, and Sentences: Tests

*Detroit Tests of Learning Aptitude (DTLA): Verbal Absurdities*

This subtest of the DTLA is designed to evaluate the child's ability to perceive and identify absurdities in verbal statements (Baker & Leland, 1967). The subtest contains 20 items, each featuring a statement consisting of one or two sentences. Each of the statements contains a word, phrase, or clause which contradicts the topic of the statement. The absurdity in the statements can be discerned only when the child can integrate word meanings accurately within a sentence or across phrase, clause, and sentence boundaries. The following statements illustrate the format of the items.

**Item 4.**      One cold snowy day *last summer,* a woman wearing a heavy fur coat passed my house.

**Item 19.**      A boy with a *pound of meat* said, "This package is *too heavy.* Next time I shall ask for a *pound of feathers.*"

An analysis of the bases for the absurdities or incongruences in meaning indicates the following distribution, according to the logical comparisons of word meaning required for accurate judgment:

(1) Integration and comparison of terms for *attributes* such as speed, weight, altitude, and geographical characteristics are required in 5 statements (Items 1, 16, 17, 19, 20).

(2) Integration and judgment of terms and *human potential for concurrent action* are required in 2 statements (Items 2, 3).

(3) Integration and sequencing of terms for *temporal events* such as times of day, seasons of the year, and dates are required in seven statements (Items 4–7, 9, 11, 14).

(4) Integration and judgment of terms for *cause-effect relationships* are required in 3 statements (Items 10, 12, 13).

(5) Integration and comparison of terms for *cause-action relationships* are required in 2 statements (Items 8, 18).

(6) Integration and comparison of *numerical terms* are required in 1 statement (Item 15).

The Detroit Tests of Learning Aptitude were standardized on 150 children at each age level between 3 years, 0 months and 19 years, 0 months. All children in the standardization sample attended the Detroit Public Schools. Test-retest reliability was measured initially with a 5-month time interval and with a sample of 48 students. The correlation coefficient was .96. A second correlation of .68 is reported for 792 children tested with a 2- to 3-year time interval. Normative data are provided for each subtest for the age range from 3 years, 0 months to 19 years, 0 months.

Among the assets of the DTLA Verbal Absurdities subtest are:

(1) The design of the subtest makes it especially applicable for the special educator and speech-language pathologist.
(2) The subtest is applicable for a wide age range.
(3) The test has high test-retest reliability for short time intervals.

These assets are somewhat offset by the severe limitations in standardization. The geographic, socioeconomic, and racial-ethnic biases of the standardization sample limit the generalization of the norms to urban, white children. In addition, the fact that the norms are dated suggests that they should be applied with great caution and flexibility.

**TABLE 8.3**

*Selected tests for the identification, selection, and labelling of referents*

| Name | Purpose | Age Range | Stimuli | Responses | Scoring |
|---|---|---|---|---|---|
| PPVT | Evaluates knowledge of the referential meaning of single words (receptive vocabulary). | 2 yr. 3 mo. to 18 yr. 5 mo. | 150 lexical items, each associated with 4 pictorial choices. Two parallel forms are available. Examiner says each word in sequence. | Upon hearing each word, the child selects its pictorial representation from among 4 choices. | Each correct response receives a score of 1. Raw scores may be converted to MA, IQ, standard scores, and percentile ratings. |
| TOLD: PICTURE VOCABULARY | Evaluates knowledge of the referential meaning of single words (receptive vocabulary). | 4 yr. 0 mo. to 8 yr. 11 mo. | 25 lexical items, each associated with 4 pictorial choices. Examiner says each word in sequence. | Upon hearing each word, the child selects its pictorial representation from among the 4 choices. | Each correct response receives a score of 1. Raw scores are converted to Language Ages and Scaled Score equivalents. |
| TORONTO TESTS OF RECEPTIVE VOCABULARY | Evaluates knowledge of the referential meaning of single English and Spanish words. | 4 yr. 0 mo. to 10 yr. 0 mo. | 40 English and 40 Spanish lexical items, each associated with 3 pictorial choices. English and Spanish word choices are not identical. | Upon hearing each word, the child selects its pictorial representation from among the 3 choices. | Each correct response receives a score of 1. Raw scores are converted to percentile ranks at 1-year intervals. |

**TABLE 8.3 (*Continued*)**

| Name | Purpose | Age Range | Stimuli | Responses | Scoring |
|---|---|---|---|---|---|
| McCARTHY SCALES OF CHILDREN'S ABILITIES: WORD KNOWLEDGE | Evaluates the knowledge of word meaning by identification of referents and by definition. | 2 yr. 6 mo. to 8 yr. 6 mo. | 9 words, each associated with a pictorial representation; 4 words to be labelled; 10 words, each of which must be defined. The examiner says each of the words in sequence or presents pictures for labelling. | Upon hearing a word, the child either points to its referent or defines the word verbally. When a picture of a referent is presented, the child says its name. | Each correct identification or labelling of a pictured referent receives a score of 1. Definitions are scored on a 3 point scale. Raw scores are totalled for the Verbal Scale. They may then be converted to Scale Index Equivalents. |
| TOLD: ORAL VOCABULARY | Evaluates the knowledge of word meaning by definition. | 4 yr. 0 mo. to 8 yr. 6 mo. | 20 words, each of which must be defined by the child. The examiner says each of the words in sequence. | Upon hearing a word, the child defines it verbally. | Each correct and acceptable definition receives a score of 1. Raw scores are converted to Language Ages and Scaled Score equivalents. |
| WISC-R: VOCABULARY | Evaluates the knowledge of word meaning by definition. | 6 yr. 0 mo. to 16 yr. 10 mo. | 32 words, each of which must be defined by the child. The examiner says each word in sequence. | Upon hearing a word, the child defines it verbally. | Each response is scored on a 3-point scale. Raw scores are converted to Scaled Score Equivalents. The sum of the Scaled Scores for each scale may be converted to IQ. |
| DTLA: SOCIAL ADJUSTMENT | Evaluates the knowledge of word meaning by definition. | 3 yr. 6 mo. to 17 yr. 9 mo. | 20 words from the social environment which must be defined. Examiner says each of the words in sequence. | Upon hearing each word, the child defines it verbally. | Each definition is scored on a 4-point scale to reflect a concrete-abstract continuum. Raw scores are converted to age level equivalents. |

**TABLE 8.4**

*Selected tests for the identification and expression of antonymy and reciprocity*

| Name | Purpose | Age Range | Stimuli | Responses | Scoring |
|------|---------|-----------|---------|-----------|---------|
| McCARTHY SCALES OF CHILDREN'S ABILITIES: OPPOSITE ANALOGIES | Evaluates the child's knowledge of antonymy and his relational thinking ability. | 2 yr. 6 mo. to 8 yr. 6 mo. | 9 items, each of which forms a verbal analogy to be completed by the child. The examiner says each incomplete analogy in sequence. | Upon hearing an incomplete analogy, the child says the word which accurately completes it. | Each correct response receives a score of 1. Raw scores are totalled for the Verbal Scale. They may then be converted to Scale Index Equivalents. |
| ITPA: AUDITORY ASSOCIATION | Evaluates the child's knowledge of antonymy and reciprocity of meaning. | 2 yr. 4 mo. to 10 yr. 11 mo. | 40 items, each of which is an incomplete analogy. The examiner says each analogy in sequence. | Upon hearing an incomplete analogy, the child says the word which accurately completes it. | Each correct response receives a score of 1. Raw scores are converted to scaled scores and to age equivalents. |
| DTLA: VERBAL OPPOSITES | Evaluates the child's knowledge of antonyms and reciprocal terms. | 6 yr. 0 mo. to 19 yr. 0 mo. | 96 words, all members of an opposite or reciprocal word pair. The examiner says each of the words in sequence. | Upon hearing a word, the child says its exact opposite or reciprocal. | Each correct response receives a score of 1. Raw scores are converted to age level equivalents. |
| WISC-R: SIMILARITIES | Evaluates the child's knowledge of shared meanings (inclusion of meaning) among words and concepts. | 6 yr. 2 mo. to 16 yr. 10 mo. | 17 word pairs which are related by semantic class membership. The examiner says each word pair in sequence. | Upon hearing a word pair, the child describes the essential quality or dimension shared by the concepts. | The responses are scored on a 2- or 3-point scale. Raw scores are converted to Scaled Score Equivalents. The sum of the scaled scores for each scale may be converted to IQ. |
| DTLA: LIKENESSES AND DIFFERENCES | Evaluates the child's knowledge of shared and essentially different meanings among words and concepts. | 6 yr. 0 mo. to 19 yr. 0 mo. | 32 word pairs which are related by semantic class membership but which differ in some quality or dimension. The examiner says each word pair in sequence. | Upon hearing a word pair, the child describes first the essential quality or dimension shared by the concepts and then the essential difference. | The responses are scored on a 3-point scale. Raw scores are converted to age level equivalents. |

**TABLE 8.4** (*Continued*)

| Name | Purpose | Age Range | Stimuli | Responses | Scoring |
|------|---------|-----------|---------|-----------|---------|
| CELF: PROCESSING WORD CLASSES | Evaluates the child's knowledge of inclusion of meaning among words and concepts. | Grades K to 10. | 22 sequences of 3 or 4 words, 2 of which are related by inclusion of meaning. The examiner says each word series in sequence. | Upon hearing a word sequence, the child says the 2 words in the sequence which are related by inclusion of meaning. | The responses receive a score of 1 point each if correct. Criterion raw scores available for K-10. |
| BOEHM TEST OF BASIC CONCEPTS | Evaluates the knowledge of relational terms for quantity, space, and time. | Grades K to 2. | 50 items in each of 2 test forms. The items are commands or statements with associated pictoral choices. The examiner says each statement or command in sequence. | Upon hearing a statement or command, the child either selects a pictorial representation from among 3 choices or completes the command for action. | Correct responses receive a score of 1. Raw scores are converted to percentile rank for item, grade, and socioeconomic level. |
| TOKEN TEST: PART V | Evaluates the knowledge of relational terms and linguistic concepts. | Inclusive. | 21 oral commands for action with tokens. The examiner says each command in sequence. | Upon hearing a command, the subject completes the action requested using the tokens as objects. | Correct responses receive a score of 1. Normative data for children have been reported by Noll (1970). |
| CELF: PROCESSING LINGUISTIC CONCEPTS | Evaluates the knowledge of relational terms and linguistic concepts. | Grades K to 10. | 22 oral commands for pointing responses. The examiner says each command in sequence. Each item is associated with a series of six colored lines. | Upon hearing a command, the child points to one or more of a series of colored lines. | Correct responses receive a score of 1. Criterion raw scores available for K-10. |
| CELF: PROCESSING RELATIONSHIPS AND AMBIGUITIES | Evaluates the knowledge and interpretation of linguistic relationships and ambiguities. | Grades K to 10. | 32 items, each consisting of one or more yes/no questions. The items contain comparative, passive, spatial, temporal, familial, idiomatic, and proverbial relationships. The examiner says each item in sequence. | In response to each question, the child answers yes if the relationship stated is true. He answers no if it is false. | Correct responses receive a score of 1. Criterion raw scores available for K-10. |

# UNDERSTANDING WORDS AND WORD RELATIONSHIPS Intervention

# 9

## BASES FOR INTERVENTION

To develop or select intervention strategies and materials for a child with a problem in understanding words and word relationships, the clinician-educator should consider several observations drawn from research and clinical work. First, language and learning disabled youth retain narrow and concrete word meanings. They may therefore depend on context for the interpretation of specific words and relationships among words. Thus the meaning and functions of specific words and concepts may need to be established in a wide variety of semantic and referential contexts. These contexts should range from being highly familiar, expected, and prototypical to being unfamiliar, abstract, and unexpected. This implication holds for establishing knowledge and use of unfamiliar labels for agents and objects (nouns), actions (verbs), attributes (adjectives and adverbs), and location and time (prepositions). They also hold for establishing knowledge of antonyms, synonyms, and relational terms.

The normal sequence of acquisition of word knowledge must also be considered in planning intervention. The factors which should be considered include: (1) the use of prototypical or "best" exemplars and referential contexts, (2) the progression from general to specific application, (3) the relative semantic complexity, (4) the **unmarked-marked** distinction in relation to referential context, and (5) the frequency of use by parents and other significant people in the youngster's life. We will now look at each of these factors in more detail.

## Referential Contexts

The same word may occur in a wide range of semantic and environmental contexts. Some of the referential contexts for a word seem more natural than others. Take as an example the word "kick." The "best," most natural and socially acceptable context for featuring this word would be in relation to *kicking a ball*. Less acceptable, if not socially unacceptable, contexts for featuring the work "kick" would be in relation to *kicking a dog* or *kicking people around*. As a second example, the superordinate name bird is "best," most naturally, and prototypically featured in relation to a "robin" in this society. It seems less natural or even atypical to feature it in relation to a "goose," an "emu," or a "ptarmigan." In other societies, on the other hand, the protypical example of a bird may be a ptarmigan (in Greenland). The principle that word meanings are learned earlier in prototypical contexts than in atypical contexts holds across age levels from childhood to adulthood. A second principle also seems to hold in child- and adulthood. It is that specific words tend to be identified and associated with their "best" or prototypical referents (Anglin, 1977; Bowerman, in press). These observations have direct implications for intervention. Unfamiliar words, concepts, and relations should be introduced in a prototypical semantic-referential context. The range of their application may then be extended to include less typical and finally atypical semantic contexts.

## Generality of Application

Each word or concept can be said to be composed of a combination of critical meaning (semantic) features. Consider, for example, the critical meaning features in adjectives such as "big," "tall," and "wide." All of them refer to a dimension in relation to space. "Big" may refer to the general size of a person, animal, or object. Something can be called "big" if it has a large volume (a "big" box), is relatively tall (a "big" building), or is relatively long, voluminous, or wide (a "big" truck). In comparison, the word "tall" has a much narrower and more specific range of application. It contains the critical meaning feature *relative height* (vertical). In the same vein, the word "wide" has a specific application. The critical semantic feature in that word is *relative width* (horizontal). The normal order of acquisition of word meanings suggests that whether a word is general or specific influences the time of acquisition. Words with relatively general features of meaning are acquired earlier than words with relatively more specific features of meaning and application (Clark, 1973). However, some exceptions to this principle have been observed. Three-year-olds and adults were asked to judge which of two animals and rectangles was "big." They used height and width combinations as a basis for judging. When 4-year-olds were asked the same questions, they concentrated on the relative height (tall) (Maratsos, 1973). These observations suggest that the salience or relative value of a dimension, reference, or context to a person must be considered in planning intervention. Whether or not a specific word contains general or specific features of meaning must at times be judged by the person's preferences. We can summarize the implications of these findings for intervention. Words, concepts, and relations with general meaning features should be introduced in intervention before related words with more specific meaning features are introduced.

## Semantic Complexity

Words such as "give" and "pay" are related by inclusion of meaning. They share a critical feature or component of meaning which we can call *possession*. They differ, however, in other aspects of meaning as well as in the relative complexity or number of meaning (semantic) features. "Give" may be used to refer to a simple act of transfer of something from one person to another. In comparison, "pay" is used to refer to a more complex act of transfer. In the transfer denoted by "pay," there is an *obligation* to return something (money, etc.) in exchange for what was given. Due to the added feature of meaning, we can consider "pay" relatively more complex semantically than "give." We can compare words and concepts that are related in meaning to one another in terms of relative semantic complexity. In general, the word in a related word series which contains the largest number of semantic features is the most complex. The word in the series which contains the smallest number of semantic features is the least complex. Observations of normal language development indicate that words with relatively fewer meaning features (lesser semantic complexity) are acquired earlier than words with relatively more meaning features (greater semantic complexity) (Anglin, 1977; Clark, 1973; Gentner, 1975). The implications for intervention point to the sequence for introducing semantically related words. In a series of related words (labels for agents-objects, actions, attributes, synonyms, etc.) the least semantically complex term should be introduced first. Related words should be introduced according to the order of increasing complexity.

## Unmarked and Marked Words

The distinction between unmarked and marked words applies to antonym pairs in all semantic fields (space, time, order of occurrence, etc.). Intuitively, people show a preference for one word in an antonym pair over the other. In general, the intuitively preferred word seems to be the "positive" or greater member of the pair. If asked which of the two words "more" or "less" they prefer, most people would choose the word "more." This seems to be the case especially when the antonyms are presented in isolation and out of context. Consider now what would happen if these two words were presented in different referential contexts. Assume that the same people were asked which one they prefer, either "We can expect *more* rain tomorrow" or "We can expect *less* rain tomorrow." Intuitively, we know the relative values of the two words have changed due to the contexts. Now most people may prefer the last sentence ("We can expect *less* rain tomorrow"), unless they had been subjected to drought for a while. Now assume that the following two sentences were presented to a group of avid skiers, "We can expect *more* snow tomorrow" and "We can expect *less* snow tomorrow." It is not hard to predict which sentence would be preferred. Observations of normal language development indicate that the meaning of preferred, expected, greater, or "positive" (*unmarked*) members of antonym pairs are generally established first. The meaning of the less preferred, unexpected, smaller, or "negative" (*marked*) member is acquired later (Clark, 1974, 1975). This principle is subject to exceptions. Some people tend to consistently prefer the lesser, unexpected, or "negative" member of an antonym pair over its "positive" (greater or expected) opposite (Eilers, Oller, & Ellington, 1974). Other observations suggest that the same word in an antonym pair may be "positive" (*unmarked*) in relation to some objects or referential contexts and "negative" (*marked*) in relation to others. Consider as an example the antonym pair "up"/"down." It seems that "up" is generally positive in relation to "balloons," "planes," and possibly "elevators." "Down," on the other hand, seems to be positive or expected in reference to objects such as "yo-yos." In turn, "up" is generally negative in reference to yo-yos and "down" is negative in reference to balloons, planes, and elevators. Based on these observations, it has been hypothesized that the first to be acquired in an antonym pair should be the one which represents a *change* from the normal state or condition (Greenfield & Smith, 1976, p. 218). Until additional evidence is presented, this hypothesis may be used in intervention. The combined implication for intervention is that the positive expected member of an antonym pair which denotes a change from the normal state should be introduced first. If it is already well established, it may be used as reference for contrasting the meaning of the negative member of the pair, which does not denote a change in the normal state.

## Frequency of Use

The frequency with which a specific word occurs in the speech of the child's caregivers seems to determine the order in which the child uses words. This active use of a word does not always signal that the meaning of the word is fully understood (Anglin, 1977). The child may not have a full understanding of some of the meaning features contained in a word or know the full range of its application. The word may have been learned in relation to familiar and concrete referential contexts and be used in a narrow range of contexts. More specific or abstract uses of the word may not have been discerned and learned. It follows that the degree of familiarity with the meaning features (general and specific) of words and concepts should be assessed among language and learning disabled youth before the scope of intervention is planned. Intervention should be provided when the child's familiarity with the critical meaning features of words is inadequate, based on age, sex, grade, curriculum, or social expectations or demands.

Observations of normal developmental patterns in the acquisition of word meaning and of the characteristics of the semantic deficits among language and learning disabled youth suggest some principles for intervention. Some of the principles are summarized and outlined below. They are not necessarily presented in order of priority.

## Summary of Principles

*Principle 1*

Unfamiliar or unestablished words, concepts, or relational terms should be introduced in intervention in a sequence which follows normal developmental patterns and/or age or grade expectations and sequences.

*Principle 2*

Unfamiliar words, concepts, and relationships should be introduced in their prototypical or "best" semantic and referential contexts. (The *balloon* goes *up*. The *yo-yo* goes *down*.) The range of application of the words and concepts should then be extended to include less typical and finally atypical semantic and referential contexts.

*Principle 3*

Semantically related words and concepts should be taught in a sequence which introduces words with relatively more general meaning features before words with relatively more specific meaning features ("big"/"tall"/"wide").

*Principle 4*

Semantically related words and concepts should be taught in a sequence which introduces relatively less semantically complex words before the relatively more complex ones ("give"/"pay"/"trade").

*Principle 5*

Antonyms should be introduced in a sequence in which the expected, positive member which denotes a change from the normal state is presented first. (Turn the light *on*.) The negative opposite should be presented next, to provide the contrast. (Turn the light *off*.)

*Principle 6*

Sentences (semantic contexts) used to feature unfamiliar or unestablished words, concepts, and relationships should be controlled for phrase and clause length and syntactic complexity. The sentence length should be kept to a minimum (5 to 10 words). Phrase and clause length should also be kept to a minimum (2 to 4 words). The syntactic complexity should be kept to a minimum by controlling transformations and the complexity of the verb phrase.

*Principle 7*

Materials and methods should feature pictorial referents and representations of referential contexts and relationships wherever possible.

*Principle 8*

Pictorial representations of the referential contexts should be designed to emphasize the critical components of meaning or contrast in meaning features. For example, the pictorial representations of the referential contexts for antonyms should differ only along a single dimension (color, size, length, height, etc.). Pictorial representations which differ along several dimensions (color and size, etc.) should be used relatively late in efforts to extend the range of new words and concepts.

*Principle 9*

Unfamiliar or unestablished words, concepts, and relationships should be introduced in at least 10 familiar, typical, but different semantic-referential contexts. Pictorial representations of meaning should be featured along with the spoken labels. Verbal definitions and elaboration of meaning features should be provided for the concepts in each of the different contexts.

*Principle 10*

The range of application of each new concept should be extended to less familiar and typical and more specific and abstract semantic contexts in at least 10 examples. A variety of task formats may be used. Selected task formats are described below.

*Principle 11*

Descriptive communication tasks and role-playing activities should be used to extend the range of application and control of newly established words, concepts, and relationships and to consolidate communicative competence.

*Principle 12*

Contexts with minimal redundancy and highly controlled vocabulary may be used to extend the range of application and control of specific concepts to topic areas such as mathematics and the sciences. These contexts and tasks may require action on tokens or on attribute blocks, commonly used in mathematics. Conditional, cause-effect, spatial, temporal, and inclusion-exclusion concepts may need to be taught.

## SELECTED TASK FORMATS FOR INTERVENTION

Several different formats and tasks may be used in working on knowledge of the meaning and use of specific words and semantic concepts and relations. The formats differ in the associated task requirements and may also differ in the range of application and in the degree of difficulty for the youngster. This section will describe selected task formats for intervention, discuss the task requirements and range of application, and illustrate each format with examples. The selected formats are not necessarily presented according to relative order of difficulty. These formats will be illustrated repeatedly in the next section of this chapter, which discusses intervention for specific word meanings and semantic relations.

### Identification, Differentiation, and Verbal Elaboration of Components of Meaning (Semantic Features)

This format may be used to teach knowledge of the meaning of a wide range of concepts and relationships. It may be used to define and differentiate the meanings of antonyms, synonyms, and words related by inclusion of meaning. The format requires the child to identify and compare similarities and differences in components of meaning (semantic features). We will use the synonyms "trousers," "pants," "slacks," "jeans," and "britches" to illustrate the isolation of similarities (shared components) and differences (not shared components) of meaning. Table 9.1 compares and contrasts the synonyms.

To teach the child to differentiate the components of meaning of related words, you can use verbal definition, comparison, or elaboration. The definition, comparison, and verbal elaboration of the mean-

**TABLE 9.1**

| | | | Components of Meaning | | | |
|---|---|---|---|---|---|---|
| Synonym | Category | Location | Parts | Users | Occasion | Other |
| Trousers. | Outerwear. | Lower body. | Leg portions. | Males. | Formal. | Part of suit. |
| Pants. | Outerwear. | Lower body. | Leg portions. | Males/females. | Either. | |
| Slacks. | Outerwear. | Lower body. | Leg portions. | Males/females. | Informal. | |
| Jeans. | Outerwear. | Lower body. | Leg portions. | Males/females. | Informal. | Made of denim. |
| Britches. | Outerwear. | Lower body. | Leg portions. | Males. | | 17th, 18th century |

ing components may be elicited in response to a series of *wh-* questions. The *wh-* questions may ask for verbal elaboration of, among others, function, users, parts, composition, and semantic category membership. The child may answer the *wh-* questions spontaneously or in sentence completion, multiple word choice, or labelling formats. Here is an example of one way to proceed with the intervention.

*Step 1*

**Pictorial Representations:**   boy wearing jeans    same boy wearing formal suit with pants

**Questions**
Look at this boy.
In this picture (1), he is wearing jeans.
In this picture (2), he is wearing trousers.
In what way (how) are jeans and trousers alike?
Do you wear jeans?
When do you wear jeans?
Do you ever wear trousers?
When do you wear trousers?
What are your jeans made of? What color are they?
What are trousers made of?
What other word can you use for trousers?      (pants)

*Step 2*

**Pictorial Representations:**   boy in jeans    man in slacks    man in suit
woman in slacks

**Questions:**
What can you say about all of these?
They are all wearing _____.      (jeans/pants)
Tell me in what way their pants are alike?
Tell me in what way the pants are different?
Let's compare two pairs of pants at a time.
When would a man wear a suit?
When would he wear slacks?
What would you call these pants?      (pointing to one picture at a time)

## Judgment of Consistency of Meaning

This format requires the child to decide whether or not there is consistency of meaning either within a single phrase, clause, or sentence or across several sentences. The child must identify words, phrases, or clauses which violate the topic or semantic-referential context. This format lends itself well to working on the selectional rules for, among others, pronouns, prepositions, antonyms, and synonyms. The task format may require the child to correct the inconsistencies in word choices. This may be achieved either by selecting the appropriate word from among several choices or by spontaneous word substitution and revision. The examples below illustrate this format applied to pronouns and prepositions.

*Pronouns*

*Do these sentences make sense?*
John went outside. *She* picked up the newspaper.          (right/wrong)
*Can you correct the last sentence?*

The girl washed *itself*.                                                       (right/wrong)
*Can you correct it?* The girl washed _____.

*Prepositions*

*Do these sentences make sense?*
The cat was sitting *in* the table.                                       (right/wrong)
*Can you correct it?*

Lilly thought *against* her sister.                                       (right/wrong)
*Can you correct it?* Lilly thought _____.

## Semantic Classification and Categorization

This format lends itself well to working on inclusion of meaning or semantic class membership. It may require the child to classify and categorize pictorial referents and then name the semantic class and the members in the class. It may also feature printed words and require the child to classify and name each class and its members. As a third alternative, it may require the child to name as many members of a given semantic class as possible. The youngster may be asked to name as many animals, foods, furniture items, or clothing items as he can think of. The task format may be applied to a wide range of words and concepts. It may be applied to words with referential meanings, such as labels for actors and objects (nouns), actions (verbs), or attributes (adjectives). It may also be applied to more abstract words and concepts such as "history," "freedom," and "democracy." The examples given below illustrate this format.

*Classification of foods*

**Materials:**          picture cards featuring a variety of foods
**Procedure/task:**     spontaneous/directed classification of foods and subsequent labelling of each subgroup and of members of each subgroup

*Classification of animals*

**Materials:**          printed labels or cards with animal names (pets, farm animals, wild animals, etc.)
**Procedure/task:**     spontaneous/directed classification of animals with subsequent naming of each subgroup and of members of each subgroup

*Controlled association and naming of animals*

Tell me the names of as many animals as you can think of.
First tell me the names of some pets.
Now, tell me the names of some farm animals.
Next, tell me the names of some wild animals.

## Matching and Categorization on the Basis of Person, Place, and Time Deixis

This task format is related to semantic classification. It requires the child to categorize words and concepts on the basis of **deictic** features and contrasts of person, place, and/or time. This format is applicable only to words and concepts that denote distinctive contrasts of person ("I"/"you"), place ("here"/"there"), or time ("now"/"then"). You can present the concepts for matching and categorization in minimally paired sentences which provide references to typical contexts or occurrences. The format may require the child to judge whether two sentences with contrasts in person, place, or time go together. It may ask for matching of sentence pairs which share features of person, place, or time. It may also require the child to categorize sentences along a given dimension with respect to person, place, or time. After matching and categorizing words or sentences with deictic contrasts, the child should be asked to define and demonstrate the contrast featured. The definition and demonstration may be conducted in listener-speaker interactions and in role-playing activities. The following examples illustrate this format for contrasts in person, place, and time.

**Deixis** *refers to the process of denoting the shifting perspective in place or time of the speaker or of the speaker and listener in verbal interaction.*

*Judgment of contrasts in person, place, and time*

Listen to these sentences. Tell me if they go together.

| | | |
|---|---|---|
| *This* is my hat. | *That* is your hat. | (yes/no) |
| *There* is your hat. | *Here* is my hat. | (yes/no) |
| I want to eat *now*. | I want to eat *last week*. | (yes/no) |
| Dad gave the money to *us*. | Dad gave the money to *them*. | (yes/no) |
| *We* got the money. | *He* got the money. | (yes/no) |

*Matching of contrasting sentence pairs by deixis*

Here are some sentences. Two of them go together because they contrast. Find the two sentences that go together.

*I* listen to the radio.
*He* listens to the radio.
*You* listen to the radio.
*They* listen to the radio.　　(I-you)
*Those* are mine.
*This* is mine.
*These* are mine.
*It* is mine.　　(these-those)

*Definition of contrasting meaning features by actions and answers*

If I say, "*Come* over here," what do I want you to do?
If I say, "*Go* over there," what do I want you to do?
If I say, "*Bring* the book," what do I want you to do?
If I say, "*Take* the book with you," what do I want you to do?
If I say, "*Those* are mine," how many are there? One or many? Where are they?
Near or far away?

If I say, "*That* is mine," how many are there? One or many? Where are they? Near or far away?

## Sentence Completion

This format lends itself to working on the semantic rules for selecting words, concepts, and relations which are placed last in sentences. You may introduce either a single incomplete sentence or two or more related sentences, the last of which is incomplete. In both cases the child must use the semantic and syntactic cues presented in the sentences to select an appropriate word or phrase to complete the sentence. The format may use incomplete verbal analogies designed to elicit antonyms and other associatively related words. It may feature concrete, "best," or prototypical referential contexts that are incomplete. Multiple choices may be provided to help the child with the selection and completion. The examples below illustrate the sentence completion task first with prototypical contexts and then with verbal analogies.

*Prototypical referential contexts*

| | |
|---|---|
| I take my coat _____. | (off/on/over) |
| I put my shoes _____. | (in/on/over) |
| I turned the water _____. | (in/on/over) |
| I held the door _____. | (open/off) |

*Verbal analogies*

| | |
|---|---|
| Trees have leaves and birds have _____. | (feathers) |
| John is my uncle and Sally is my _____. | (aunt) |
| I drive a car and I fly a _____. | (plane) |
| It is warm in the South and it is cold in the _____. | (North) |

## Oral or Written Cloze

This format resembles the sentence completion format. If differs, however, in that the missing word can be found at any point in a sentence. The cloze format requires the child to select one or more missing words in sentences or paragraphs on the basis of the available syntactic and semantic cues. Thus it has a wider range of application than sentence completion. In oral or written cloze, words may be deleted selectively. The deletions may include one or more syntactic-semantic categories, such as labels for actors-objects (nouns), actions (verbs), or attributes (adjectives). Word categories such as prepositions and pronouns may also be the focus of the deletions. Cloze sentences and paragraphs may be presented with or without multiple choices for the selections. The paragraph below illustrates the cloze format (oral or written) with deletion of prepositions.

*Cloze paragraph with deletion of prepositions*

Peter loves his room. He has a blue rug _____ the floor. There is a lion poster _____ the wall _____ his bed. He has a desk _____ to the window. _____ the desk is a lamp which hangs _____ _____ the ceiling. _____ his table he has two tanks _____ fish _____ them.

The lexical paraphrase format lends itself well to working on synonymy and antonymy. In this format, the youngster hears a spoken sentence. He is then asked to rephrase the sentence by substituting one or more words by either a synonym or an antonym. Pictorial representations or objects may be used to provide contexts for the task. The examples below illustrate lexical paraphrase applied to selected antonyms and synonyms.

*Antonymy*

There is no milk in this glass. It is *not full*.
*What can you say about this glass with a different word? Use the word opposite of "full."*

*Synonymy*

This boy is wearing pants. The pants go only to the knee.
*What can you say about the boy? Use a different word for his pants.*

## Identification of Words Based on Descriptive Definitions (Riddles)

This format may require the child to name a specific word or identify a pictured object on the basis of the descriptive definition given about it. It lends itself best to establishing and consolidating the labels for persons, animals, or objects. In other words, it may be used to teach vocabulary items with referential meaning. The format may require active participation from the youngster. In that event, the youngster would be asked to provide the descriptive definitions. A peer or adult would either name the referent or identify a picture of the referent, a descriptive communications task. The examples below illustrate the descriptive definition task with an adult as the speaker. The descriptive communication task in which the youngster provides the definitions is described in more detail later.

*Identification from descriptive definitions*

You can eat it. It is made of ground beef. It is served in a bun. You may want ketchup with it. It is a _____.
You can ride on it. It rides on tracks. It has an engine. It has a caboose. It is a _____.

## Twenty Questions

The twenty-questions format is familiar to most people as a party game. It lends itself well to intervention when the purpose is to establish verbal specificity and ability to narrow the field by semantic class or shared meaning features. It requires the youngster to use his knowledge of meaning features and of inclusion of meaning to zero in on the intended referent. The task may feature an array of from 10 to 20 pictured objects or references. The youngster must identify the target object or reference by asking a series of yes/no questions. The actual number of items presented will depend upon the youngster's skill at the task. It will also depend upon the relationships among the items. The questions asked by the youngster may be guided and modified by the adult while the task is being mastered.

## Descriptive Communication

This format has been used in investigations of children's ability to use appropriate words and structures to communicate information to others (Glucksberg, Krauss, & Weisberg, 1966). In this task the youngster is required to communicate specific information about objects or pictured references to a listener—an adult or another child. The speaker and listener are given the same set of objects or pictured references. They are seated so that they cannot see the items the other one has or what the other person does. The speaker describes an object or pictured reference. The listener identifies the object or reference described or performs an action described. The materials used and the descriptions required can be manipulated to feature a wide range of references, attributes, or actions. As a concrete example, the speaker and listener may each be given a set of blocks of different colors and sizes. The speaker (youngster) may be asked to describe one block at a time. The listener must select each block as it is described. The speaker may also ask the listener to arrange the blocks in a special array or configuration or to perform various actions with them. The task gives the youngster an opportunity to take an active, communicative role during the intervention process. It provides a chance for him to participate in interpersonal communicative interaction. It provides immediate feedback to gauge the success with which the information was communicated. It also provides for transfer of word knowledge to and consolidation of expressive communication skills or communicative competence. The task requirements may be expanded as the youngster gains competence and skill. Descriptive communication tasks have been described by, among others, Longhurst and Reichle (1975), McCaffrey (1975), and Rees, Kruger, Bernstein, Kramer, and Bezas (1974).

## Role Playing

The role-playing format resembles descriptive communication in that the youngster may assume an active, participatory role in communicating information. The role-playing task may be manipulated so that it requires use of specific vocabulary as well as of a range of syntactic structures. With young children, the role-playing activities may incorporate objects and puppets that interact. The role-playing activities may focus on everyday situations, activities, and demands for communication. With older children or adolescents, role playing may center around planning social activities. They may also feature social interactions in which conflicts need to be resolved. They may focus on situations which require persuasion from one of the speakers. The possibilities are endless. Role-playing activities may be designed to focus on establishing flexibility in the use of social register. In that event, the status of the participant roles would be varied to elicit more or less formal expressive language forms. For example, the role-playing activities may simulate an interview for a job such as a paper route. In that case, the applicant (youngster) must use words and structures (register) that will be accepted by the interviewer based on his status. As another example, role playing may simulate an adult party in which the youngster is a participant. The object is for the youngster to adapt his word choices and sentence structures to the relative status of several listeners (adults). The possibilities are again infinite. The text *Let's Talk* by Sathre, Olson, and Whitney (1973) may serve as a source for role-playing activities with pre-adolescents and adolescents.

Table 9.2 summarizes the intervention task formats we have just discussed.

**TABLE 9.2**

*Selected intervention formats for word meaning*

| Format | Task Requirement | Example | Range of Application |
|---|---|---|---|
| Identification, differentiation, and elaboration of meaning. | To identify and compare similarities and differences in components of word meaning. | In what way are jeans and trousers alike? In what ways are they different? | May be used to define and differentiate the meanings of antonyms, synonyms, and words related by inclusion of meaning. |
| Judgment of consistency of meaning. | To identify words, phrases, or clauses which violate a topic or a semantic-referential context. | Is this sentence right or wrong? "The girl sat over the table." What is wrong about it? | May be used to establish the selectional rules for pronouns, prepositions, synonyms, and antonyms, etc. |
| Semantic classification and categorization. | To classify and categorize pictured objects or events or words and to name the semantic class. | Tell me the names of some animals. Which ones are farm animals? Which ones are wild animals? | May be used to classify words with referential meaning for agents, objects, actions, or attributes, among others. |
| Matching and categorizing by deixis. | To classify and categorize by shifting perspectives in person (I/you), place (here/there), or time (now/then). | If I say, "Come over here," what do I want you to do? If I say, "Go over there," what do I want you to do? | May be used only to establish deictic terms of person, place, or time. |
| Sentence completion. | To select an appropriate word or phrase to complete a sentence. | Complete this sentence. "I held the door_____." | May be used to establish selectional rules for words or phrases placed last in a sentence. |
| Oral or written cloze. | To select one or more missing words in a sentence on the basis of semantic and syntactic cues. | Complete this sentence by filling in the missing words. "Peter loves his room. _____ has a blue rug_____ his_____." | May be used to establish the selectional rules for any word category in sentences or paragraphs. |
| Lexical paraphrase. | To rephrase a sentence by substituting one or more words in it. | Listen to this sentence. "The boy walked up the street." Give me another word for "street." | May be used for establishing synonyms and antonyms, among others. |
| Identification based on descriptive definition (riddles). | To name a specific word on the basis of a descriptive definition or riddle. | You can ride on it. It goes on tracks. It has an engine and a caboose. It is a_____. | Any word with referential meaning. |

**TABLE 9.2** (*Continued*)

| Format | Task Requirement | Example | Range of Application |
|---|---|---|---|
| Twenty questions. | To identify a target object or word by asking yes/no questions. | I am thinking of something you find in the kitchen. Ask me questions about it and find out what it is. | Any word with referential meaning. |
| Descriptive communication. | To communicate specific information about objects or pictured objects or events. | Tell me about one of these things. I'll find the one you are telling me about. | May be used to establish the use of any word category or attribute label, describing color, size, function, action, location, or possession, etc. |
| Role playing. | To use specific words or phrases in various sentence types in a pretend communication situation. | Let's pretend you are applying for a paper route. I'll pretend I'm the boss. You'll apply for the job. What are you going to say? | May be used to establish the use of appropriate words, phrases, or sentences in a social communication situation. |

# INTERVENTION CONTENTS: BACKGROUND

As we have seen so far in Part III, the problems of language and learning disabled youngsters in interpreting the meanings of specific words, concepts, and word relationships have been attributed to many factors. Here are some of the factors which contribute to problems with semantics:

(1) Limited ability to abstract and categorize.
(2) Tendency to be concrete and literal.
(3) Limited imagery, symbolization, and conceptualization.
(4) Retention of narrow word meanings.
(5) Perceptual adherence to one reference for words and concepts.
(6) Adherence to the most frequent, expected, and prototypical interpretations of words and relations.
(7) Limited ability to shift from one semantic-grammatic category to another in order to identify alternative interpretations of multiple-meaning words.
(8) Limited ability to perform the simultaneous analysis and synthesis and logical operations required to interpret relationships (spatial, temporal, etc.) among words, phrases, and clauses.

The contents and formats used in intervention should be selected to respond to these limitations in order to help the youngster overcome them. We will now look at specific intervention goals in the realm of semantics, and at some of the formats that can be used with each goal.

# WORKING ON SPECIFIC WORD CATEGORIES

**Action Verbs**

Verbs may label overt actions that can be observed in others and experienced by oneself. In other words, they may have obvious referential meanings and occur in concrete referential contexts. Other verbs refer to feelings, attitudes, intentions, and subtle emotional or value judgments. In that case they define reactions or relations that are not readily observable. Action verbs with concrete referential meanings are generally among the easiest kinds of words to teach to children with language and learning disabilities. Nonetheless, it may be necessary to broaden the child's knowledge of action verbs and range of application. It may also be necessary to teach the child to distinguish among the meanings of action verbs with subtle differences in meaning.

You can teach the child to differentiate among the meanings of action verbs by having him experience and label motor actions. This procedure may be used to teach the subtle meaning differences among action verbs such as *pushing, pulling, bending, stretching, twisting*, and the like. The overt experiences with the actions permit the child to learn the motor, **proprioceptive**, and **kinesthetic** patterns associated with the action and label. It allows the child to have a broader understanding of the meaning base for verbs and may facilitate their later recall and use. Specific activities such as acting out given verbs, labelling motor activities, and following oral commands for motor actions may be used in an intervention program. These activities may be performed in the classroom or in the gym. They may be directed by the gym teacher and carried out in group activities. The children may be actively involved in the act of communication by asking them to give the oral commands for the various actions.

Some verbs may cause problems when they are used in oral commands for actions because they have counterparts which sound similar. The children may be confused by the similarity of sound for verbs such as "bring"/"ring" and "bend"/"send"/"lend." It may be necessary to provide very structured opportunities to teach the language and learning disabled child to discriminate among similar-sounding verbs. One approach is to use minimally paired sentences in oral commands, requiring the child either to make a same/different judgment of the meaning of the commands or to act out the meanings. The examples below illustrate these task formats.

*Judgment of identity in meaning*

Bring the bell.     Ring the bell.     (same/different)
Walk fast.     Talk fast.     (same/different)

*Acting out meaning*

Show me how you walk fast.
Show me how you talk fast.
Show me how you would ring the bell.
Show me how you would bring the bell.

Auxiliaries and infinitives may cause problems for the child in interpreting the meaning of the verb phrase in sentences. You can teach accurate interpretation of the meaning of the main verb in complex verb phrases by discussing the rules for the use of auxiliaries and infinitives. Language and learning disabled children seem to believe that the auxiliary or infinitive changes the meaning of the main verb. If that appears to be the case, it is necessary to teach the selectional rules for secondary verbs and the grammatic-semantic functions. Several procedures may be used. They are described in detail in sections on intervention for syntax.

## Adjectives

*Intervention to deal with the meaning of adverbs is much the same as intervention for adjectives.*

The problems of language and learning disabled youngsters in processing and producing adjectives seem to reflect several bases. They seem to relate to the salience, immediate value, or relevance of the dimension or attribute denoted by the adjective in question. They seem to relate further to the nature of the youngster's perceptual abilities and deficit. The youngster with problems in interpreting facial expressions and body language cues may not interpret or use adjectives which denote feelings or attitudes. The youngster with problems in perceiving and interpreting relationships in space may not accurately interpret or use adjectives which denote spatial features or relations. In intervention, each youngster's perceptual strengths and weaknesses should be considered and accounted for. In addition, the relative salience of dimensions among normally developing children at various age levels may be used as a guide. There are several sources to consult to find the age appropriateness of specific dimensional terms and contrasts. Among them are tests of cognitive and intellectual development and receptive vocabulary, and vocabulary lists for various age and grade

**TABLE 9.3**

*Suggested sequence for the introduction of adjectives in language intervention*

| Dimension-Attribute | Sample Adjectives |
| --- | --- |
| 1. Size. | big, little, small |
| 2. Color. | red, blue, green |
| 3. Color and size. | big red, small blue |
| 4. Shape. | round, square |
| 5. Length. | long, short |
| 6. Temperature. | hot, cold |
| 7. Height. | tall, short |
| 8. Width. | wide, narrow, thin |
| 9. Age. | new, old, young |
| 10. Taste. | sweet, sour |
| 11. Odor. | clean, sweet, pungent |
| 12. Attractiveness. | pretty, ugly, nice |
| 13. Time. | first, last, early, late |
| 14. Speed. | fast, slow |
| 15. Texture. | hard, soft, smooth, rough |
| 16. Affect. | happy, sad, angry, fearful |
| 17. Distance. | near, far, distant |

levels. The sequence suggested for introducing adjectives in language intervention is based in part upon developmental data (Table 9.3). It is also based upon clinical observations of the relative order of difficulty of adjectives experienced by language and learning disabled youth.

Since adjectives denote aspects of dimensions, many of them have opposites and form antonym pairs. Specific intervention formats for establishing antonymy are described later in this section. Adjectives *See page 264.* can also be clustered in related groups or families by similarity of meaning or synonymy. Specific intervention formats for establishing synonymy are also discussed below. *See page 265.*

Here are some specific intervention task formats which may be used to teach the child to differentiate adjective meanings.

*Identification on the basis of description of attributes*

Find an object that is big, blue, and round and can bounce.     (ball)
Show me a boy with brown shoes.
Show me a girl with a red skirt and a blue blouse.

*Sentence completion with or without multiple choices*

An apple is _____.          (blue/red)
A car is _____.             (light/heavy)
A lion is _____.            (wild/tame)

*Identification of specific attributes in adjective sequences*

*Listen to these sentences. I will ask you questions about them.*

The girl had two big green apples.
*How many apples did she have? What size were they? What color were they?*

The man washed the dented old heavy grey car.
*What color was the car? What age was the car? What weight was the car? What did the body of the car look like?*

*Categorization by dimension and application*

*Listen to these words. Tell me which of these each goes with.*

**Samples:**                   it looks . . .      it smells . . .

**Words to be Categorized:**   good, sweet, nice, pungent, sour, spicy, new, old, pretty, used, broken

*Listen to these words. Tell me which one of these they describe best.*

**Samples:**                   a car     an apple     a tiger

**Words to be Categorized:**   fast, big, sweet, old, round, long, shiny, angry, wild, hungry, roomy, broken, new

*Identification and elaboration of meaning features*

*Listen to these three sentences.*
The girl was *nice*. The girl was *pleasant*. The girl was *pretty*.
*Do they tell the same thing about the girl? What is the difference between saying "The girl is nice" and "The girl is pretty"?*
*What is the difference between saying "The girl is nice" and "The girl is pleasant"?*

There are also a variety of formats available to teach the child to use adjectives, once he has learned their meaning. The applicable formats include the lexical paraphrase, twenty questions, sentence completion and oral cloze, and descriptive communication tasks. These are illustrated in the examples below.

*Lexical paraphrase*

The boy was *little*.
*Use a different word to say the same thing about the boy.*

The kitten was *nice*.
*Use a different word to say the same thing about the kitten.*

*Twenty questions*

**Target:**                 kitten
**Possible questions:**     Is it alive/not alive?
                            Is it small/big?
                            Is it a person/animal?
                            Is it a wild animal/farm animal/pet?
                            Does it bark/purr/meow?
                            Is it a mother/baby cat?

*Oral cloze*

**Title:**    SUSAN'S FAVORITE TOYS

Susan is my _____ friend. She is a very _____ girl. She has so _____ toys. All of her toys are _____. She has a _____ doll. The doll is wearing a _____ dress. It is also wearing a _____ apron. She has a _____ stuffed zebra. It has _____ stripes on it. On her bed she has a _____ dog. It has _____ fur and a _____ collar around the neck. Her _____ toy is a Spanish doll. She can dance. She is wearing a _____ and _____ dress. The dress has a _____ skirt with a _____ fringe at the bottom. Susan got it from her mother.

*Descriptive communication*

Select two sets of identical pictured objects, persons, events, or the like. They must be familiar to the youngster. Place one set in front of the youngster and keep one set. Ask the youngster to describe one of the pictured items without giving its name. Ask the youngster to tell about its characteristics (size, shape, color, etc.) and uses. Select the item described when the child has given you sufficient attributes and uses. The pictured items may belong to one or to several semantic classes. Items that share essential characteristics but differ along several dimensions (size, color, shape, sound, movement pattern, etc.) lend themselves well to descriptive communication. Among possible sets of related pictured items are:

**Fruits:**      Apple, pear, banana, orange, lemon, lime, grapes, etc.
**Vegetables:**  Carrots, peas, beans, potatoes, cabbage, beets, cauliflower, etc.
**Animals:**     Tiger, lion, leopard, cougar, ocelot, polar bear, grizzly bear, black bear, koala bear, panda bear, etc.
**Flowers:**     Roses, tulips, mums, gardenias, violets, etc.

# Prepositions

Prepositions are functors or grammatical morphemes. They carry components of meaning (space) determined in part by the external reality or context to which they refer. Some meaning components and functions are, however, determined by the structural and semantic characteristics of the sentences in which they occur. The same preposition may function to denote a spatial relationship ("at the door"), a temporal relationship ("at noon"), or an idiomatic use ("laughed at me").

The number of prepositions used in English is relatively large. Fortunately, nine prepositions comprise about 90% of the prepositions used in written language (Fries, 1952). They are "at," "by," "for," "from," "in," "on," "to," "of," and "with." These nine prepositions may, however, carry about 250 possible meanings and functions. It follows that, of the repertory of prepositions listed in Table 9.4, the nine most common ones (underlined) should receive special attention in intervention.

**TABLE 9.4**
*Prepositions*

| | | | | |
|---|---|---|---|---|
| about | behind | down | of | to |
| above | below | during | off | toward |
| across | beneath | except | on | under |
| after | beside | for | out | until |
| against | besides | from | outside | up |
| along | between | in | over | upon |
| among | beyond | inside | past | with |
| around | but (except) | into | since | within |
| at | by | like | through | without |
| before | concerning | near | | |

Streng (1972) points out that most of the common prepositions may be used as idioms and that there are few patterns to indicate which ones are appropriate. For example, consider the sentences below. In these sentences several prepositions are used in conjunction with the verb "ran." The combinations function as idioms.

Jane *ran for* Mayor this year.
Julie *ran into* her friend at the store.
Joan *ran across* some old letters.
Jessica *ran through* her lines in the play.
Jen *ran up against* a wall when she tried her plan.

*Developmental sequences*

The normal order of acquisition of prepositions may suggest a sequence for introducing prepositions in intervention. Brown (1973) reports that "in" and "on" are the first prepositions learned. In early language these prepositions are used to denote spatial position. In contrast, they may be used to denote abstract aspects in adult speech, in phrases such as "in time" and "on target." Clark (1972) observes the following relative order in learning spatial and temporal prepositions that form antonym pairs.

In front-in back
Up-down

In-out
On-off
Over-under
Above-below
Ahead-behind
Before-after

Hunt (1965) investigated the control of prepositions in writing by analyzing written language samples by children in grades 4, 8, and 12. Prepositional phrases were the third most frequent modifiers of nouns. Only half the prepositions used by each grade indicated place. The number of prepositional phrases used in sentences correlated with clause length. These observations suggest the following guidelines for intervention.

(1) *Definite spatial prepositions* such as "in" and "on" should be introduced before other prepositions.
(2) *Indefinite spatial prepositions* such as "at" and "by" should be introduced next.
(3) Spatial prepositions used to denote *temporal* aspects of meaning such as "in" and "at" may be introduced next in the sequence.
(4) *Instrumental prepositions* such as "with" and "without" should be introduced after definite and indefinite spatial and temporal prepositions have been established.
(5) *Idiomatic uses* of specific prepositions should not be introduced until the spatial and temporal uses of the same preposition have been firmly established.

*Intervention objectives and task formats*

Language and learning disabled youngsters have been observed to confuse:

(1) Similar sounding prepositions such as "in" and "on," "off" and "of," "for" and "from," and "before," "behind," "below," "beneath," and "beside."
(2) Members of antonym pairs such as "on"/"off," "in"/"out," and "before"/"after."
(3) Definite and indefinite spatial aspects of prepositions such as "in," "on," "under" (definite spatial) and "at," "by," "beside" (indefinite spatial).
(4) Locative and directional uses of prepositions such as "sit *under*" and "crawl *under*" (direction) and "hold *over*" and "jump *over*" (directional).
(5) Spatial and temporal uses of prepositions such as "at," "in," and "on."
(6) Literal (spatial) and idiomatic uses of prepositions such as "at," "in," "on," and "into" ("She ran *into* her friend").

Based on the observed patterns of problems learning disabled children have in interpreting and using prepositions, here is a sequence for the objectives in intervention.

*Objective 1*

To teach adequate discrimination and differentiation among similar-sounding prepositions.

*Objective 2*

To teach antonym pairs among prepositions.

*Objective 3*

*See page 250 for specific procedures.*

To teach differentiation of the meaning and use of the definite and indefinite spatial prepositions.

*Objective 4*

To teach the child to differentiate the spatial and temporal uses of prepositions.

*Objective 5*

To teach the selectional rules for temporal prepositions.

*Objective 6*

To teach the child to differentiate the instrumental and noninstrumental uses of the prepositions "with" (". . . the knife"/". . . my aunt") and "without" (". . . using my hands"/". . . my aunt").

*Objective 7*

To teach the literal and idiomatic uses of common spatial prepositions such as "across," "around," "at," "by," "in," "into," "on," and "to."

Boehm (1969), Frostig (1975), and Semel (1970) provide sequences for the presentation of prepositions, which can be used in planning intervention programs.

(1) Introduce spatial relationships expressed by the common prepositions in relationship to the child's body.
(2) Introduce the spatial concept and relationship expressed by prepositions of space, using concrete manipulative materials and motor actions.
(3) Teach specific verbal labelling of the spatial references for the various prepositions.
(4) Use each of the spatial prepositions in several concrete situations with associated motor actions, to facilitate internalization and generalization.
(5) Represent the spatial prepositions by pictures, drawings, photographs, and verbal descriptions and labels.

You may need to use direct and concrete physical experiences to teach the differences in location or direction in space denoted by the various prepositions. This may be accomplished by having the child act out various verbal commands and contrast and label various placements of persons, animals, or objects in space. The verbal commands which follow the initial demonstrations may require the child to place an object in a specified location. They may also ask him to move in space and to place himself in first one and then another location. Here are some examples of oral commands which may be used, in a suggested sequence:

*Oral commands for definite locations in space*

Sit *on/under/behind* your chair.
Stand *on/behind/in front of* your desk.
Put your pencil *on the chair/under* the chair.
Put the chair *in front of/behind* the desk.
Put the pencil *on top of/under* your book.
Put the pencil *under/beneath* the paper.
Put the chalk *between* the book and the pencil.

*Oral commands for indefinite locations in space*

Put the chair *by/next to* my desk.
Put the chair *by/against* the wall.
Put the chair right *at/by* the door.
Put the chair close *to* your desk.
Put the pencil *by/beside/next to* the book.
Hold the pencil *above* your head.
Push the pencil *beyond* your reach.

*Oral commands for placements and movements in space*

Sit *on* the desk/the floor/the chair/the window sill.
Sit *in front of* the desk/the closet/the door.
Hide *behind* the desk/the door.
Crawl *under* the desk/the chair/the table.
Jump *over* the book/the line/the chalk.
Walk *outside*.
Look *inside* the closet.
Run *to* the door/the window/the desk.
Run *from* the window *to* the door.

Language and learning disabled children may confuse prepositions with similar speech sounds. In intervention, you can use verbal commands which juxtapose and contrast these prepositions. The oral commands may feature some or all of the prepositions listed in Table 9.5.

The comprehension of spatial prepositions may be further taught by associating a known location with activities or events that occur there. Among the task formats which may be used to work on the associations among prepositions, activities and events, and locations are sentence completion, questions for location, and descriptive communication tasks. These formats are illustrated below.

*Sentence completion with or without multiple choices*

At the *zoo* you can . . .        (go swimming/catch fish/feed the elephants)
At the *beach* you can . . .        (see tigers/go swimming/feed the elephants)
At the *circus* you can . . .        (catch fish/see the tigers/go swimming)

**TABLE 9.5**
*Prepositions used in oral commands*

| Similar-Sounding Prepositions | Oral Commands |
|---|---|
| on-off | Put your coat *on*. Take your coat *off*. |
| in-on | Put the coat *in* the closet.<br>Put the coat *on* the closet. |
| behind, below, beneath, beside, between | Put the pen *behind/below/beneath* the desk.<br>Put the pen *between* the desks. |
| above, across, against, around | Hold your hands *above/against* you.<br>Move your hands *across* the desk.<br>Move your hands *around* the edge of the desk. |
| in, inside, into | Put the pen *in* your shirt pocket.<br>Put the pen *inside* your shirt.<br>Put the pen *into* your shirt pocket. |

*Questions for location*

Where can you go swimming?
Where can you see tigers and monkeys?
Where can you see clowns?
Where can you build sand castles?

*Descriptive communication tasks*

*Provide a series of pictures in which the same or a few familiar objects are placed in different locations in a room. Have the child describe the location of an object. Select the pictured object on the basis of the description of location or differences in location.*

*Present the child with a complex picture of a location and an associated event (a fair, a street scene, a circus scene, etc.). Keep a copy of the same picture for yourself. Tell the child to point to various objects, animals, persons, or events when you tell him their location in relation to other objects, persons, animals, or events. Reverse the task and have the child tell a location, and you pick out the object, person, animal, or event to be found there.*

When common spatial prepositions are used to denote a point in time, the specific preposition to be used is determined by selectional rules. These rules are usually learned automatically by the normally developing child. However, they may have to be explained and taught for the language and learning disabled youngster before he can interpret and use phrases with temporal prepositions accurately. Here are some of the selectional rules that determine which specific temporal preposition to use:

(1) "At" denotes specific times during the *day* ("at lunch," "at two o'clock," "at noon," "at dinner").
(2) "On" is used to denote specific days of the week ("on Tuesday"/ "Saturday"/ . . .).
(3) "In" is used to denote specific months of the year or seasons of the year ("in February/March"/ . . . ; "in the winter/fall"/ . . .).
(4) "During" or "in" may be used to denote seasons of the year. Their selection is optional ("in the summer"/"during the summer").

*Selected Materials, Approaches, and Programs for Teaching Prepositions*

Several sources discuss educational procedures and present programs for improving the comprehension and use of prepositions and prepositional phrases. In particular, Bangs (1968) suggests concrete situations and activities to improve the young child's (3- to 4-year-old's) comprehension of prepositions. Johnson and Myklebust (1967) suggest that intervention for prepositions should begin at the concrete level by asking the child to put his hand "on"/"under" a table and/or to manipulate a ball by putting it "in"/"on" a box. In subsequent steps, they suggest using pictured objects. They emphasize that the prepositions must be used in a variety of contexts to help the child learn to generalize. They also emphasize sentence patterning, where one feature of a sentence is changed at any one time. For example, the preposition may be changed while the object of the preposition and the action are kept constant. The object of the prepositional phrase may then be changed while the action and prepositions are kept constant. Finally, combinations of verbs, prepositions, and objects of prepositional phrases may be changed.

Semel (1970, 1976) introduces a wide range of prepositions in a variety of task formats. The S-O-S and SAPP programs use judgment of correct grammar and sentence completion and oral cloze tasks with and without multiple choices among others.

Wilson (1972) has a program in which the prepositions "in," "on," "under," "in front of," "behind," "next to," and "over" are used and compared at both the concrete and abstract levels. Different settings and referential contexts are provided for teaching the same concept or preposition.

## Personal and Reflexive Pronouns

Language and learning disabled youngsters often find it hard to interpret and use personal pronouns. They seem to have difficulties learning the referential and selectional rules. Intervention should therefore be designed to teach the rules for noun-pronoun substitutions and the relationships among person references and pronoun references in sentences.

Pronouns are grammatical morphemes or functors. Their use is determined in part by the structural characteristics of a sentence or discourse sequence. Their use is also determined by the persons and referential contexts to which they relate. We can therefore say that pronouns have major structural as well as major meaning (semantic) functions. The personal pronouns in English can be categorized on the basis of three major features: person, number and case. These classes are labelled and outlined in Table 9.6.

In the normal sequence of acquisition of personal pronouns, "he," "she," and "it" appear in spontaneous speech from around 2 years, 4 months of age (Chipman & deDardel, 1974). Children's acquisition of pronouns has been related to linguistic levels in the age range from 1 year, 7 months to 3 years, 1 month (see page 175).

**TABLE 9.6**
*Personal pronouns*

| Person-Number | Case | | | Possessive-Replacive |
|---|---|---|---|---|
| | Subjective | Objective | Possessive | |
| 1st person. | | | | |
|   Singular. | I | me | my | mine |
|   Plural. | we | us | our | ours |
| 2nd person. | | | | |
|   Singular. | you | you | your | yours |
|   Plural. | you | you | your | yours |
| 3rd person. | | | | |
|   Singular | he | him | his | his |
|   (has gender). | she | her | her | hers |
| | it | it | its | its |
|   Plural. | they | them | their | theirs |

The interpretation of personal pronouns is complicated by the fact that stress for emphasis may indicate different references for the same pronoun. Consider these examples:

John hit Harry and then *Sarah* hit him. (Harry is also hit by Sarah)
John hit Harry and then Sarah hit *him*. (John is hit by Sarah)

When the personal pronoun is unstressed, the grammatic and semantic roles of the actors are determined by word order. When the personal pronoun receives emphatic stress, the listener must perceive the implied change of roles in the actor-recipient relationship. Young children (3, 4, and 5 years old) interpret references for unstressed personal pronouns much better than for stressed pronouns. The interpretation of stressed personal pronouns improves with increasing age. Language and learning disabled youngsters may not discern the changes in grammatic-semantic roles denoted by spoken stress differences. They may need to be made aware of the significance of stress in structured examples. Thus the differentiation of unstressed-stressed pronoun references should probably be the focus of one aspect of intervention.

Language and learning disabled children may also fail to grasp the rules for pronominalization in sentences with two identical noun phrases, as in "*John* came to dinner and *he* stayed a week." They may not recognize that some of their own sentences, such as "He came to dinner and John stayed a week" violate syntactic, distributional rules.

Personal pronouns are classified within the system of communication on the basis of person deixis or contrast. They may refer to either the speaker, listener, or other/others (nonspeakers/nonhearers). In order to differentiate third person singular pronouns, referents that are nonspeakers and nonhearers must be further specified as either human or nonhuman. Those third person singular pronouns that have human referents must be further specified as either male or female (gender).

When the child has learned to specify the referent(s) of a personal pronoun in semantic terms, it must be specified according to its structural roles in sentences. This specification results in the identification of either (1) subject marking (speaker), " I," (2) reflexive marking, "myself," (3) possessive marking, "my," or (4) replacive pronoun marking "mine." The objective case is chosen when the pronoun features contain none of the four markings. Waryas (1973) provides the suggestions below for the design of intervention procedures for pronoun interpretation and use.

*For further discussions of deixis, consult DiPietro (1973), Fillmore (1975), Ingram (1971), and Lyons (1968).*

(1) *Semantic* features (speaker/listener/other; human/nonhuman; male/female) should be emphasized before *syntactic* features (case) are introduced.
(2) Pronominalization of the *speaker* and *listener* roles should begin early in intervention.
(3) Control of the *singular* forms of pronouns should be established before the *plural* forms are introduced.
(4) The *referents* for pronouns should be established first if the child seems to be confused about the potential referents for noun-pronoun substitutions.

Combining our knowledge of the normal order of acquisition of pronouns and pronominalization with Waryas' ideas, we can make the following suggestions for intervention.

*Principle 1*

The referents for the singular pronouns "I" (speaker), "you" (listener), "he," "she," "it" (other) in the subjective case should be taught first if the youngster seems to be confused between pronoun referents and noun-pronoun substitutions.

*Principle 2*

Pronominalization of the speaker and listener roles in interactions and dialogue should be introduced next in order to teach the child to differentiate the semantic feature speaker ("I") and listener ("you") in verbal interchange.

*Principle 3*

The referents for the plural personal pronouns in the subjective case should be taught next.

*Principle 4*

Pronouns in the objective case and with possessive markings may be introduced next. The singular forms of pronouns should be introduced and established before the plural forms. The emphasis in intervention at this stage should be on differentiation of the semantic features (*subject/object; possessor*).

*Principle 5*

The possessive-replacive personal pronouns ("mine," "yours," etc.) should be introduced last in the sequence.

If needed, differentiation of the stressed and unstressed forms of the same pronoun should occur late, if not last, in the intervention sequence.

Referents for personal pronouns may be established in activities or games. Objects may be featured in the interactions. For example, the educator-clinician may pass an object such as *a ball* from him or herself to one or more children in a group, saying:

> I gave the ball to Joe. Joe has the ball. *He* has the ball.
>
> I gave the ball to Ann. Ann has the ball. *She* has the ball.
>
> I gave the balls to Jane and Mary. Jane and Mary have the balls. *They* have the balls.

Subsequent activities may emphasize the semantic differentiation of speaker-listener-other. The task formats may require the youngsters to judge whether or not the pronouns used are correct (right/wrong). They may be asked to select appropriate personal pronouns from several choices or to provide the desired pronoun spontaneously. These task formats are illustrated below.

*Judgment of correct grammar/semantic consistency*

I gave the car to Peter.
*She* has the car now.                      (right/wrong)

I gave the pencil to Mary.
*She* has the pencil now.                    (right/wrong)

I gave the blocks to Jack and Phyllis.
*I* have the blocks now.                      (right/wrong)

*Oral cloze with multiple choices*

| | | |
|---|---|---|
| I gave the cards to Jane. _____ has the cards now. | (they/she) |
| I gave the cards to Bob. _____ has the cards now. | (she/he) |
| I gave the bone to the dog. _____ has the bone now. | (we/it) |

*Spontaneous pronominalization*

I gave the ring to David. Who has the ring now?
I gave the shoes to you, Ann, and Julie. Who have the shoes now?

Similar activities and task formats may be used to teach the child to differentiate objective, possessive, and possessive case pronouns. The examples below illustrate selected formats.

*Judgment of correct grammar*

I gave the matches to Bill.
The matches now belong to *her*.           (right/wrong)

I gave the penny to Jane.
The penny now belongs to *it*.             (right/wrong)

I gave the candy to Bob and Erik.
The candy now belongs to *them*.           (right/wrong)

The penny belongs to Mary.
The penny is *mine*.                       (right/wrong)

*Sentence completion*

I gave the paper to Joan. The paper now belongs to _____.
The pencil belongs to Angel. It is _____.
The pencils belong to you and me. The pencils are _____.
The letters belong to Ann and Jane. The letters are _____.

*Oral cloze*

Jack bought a new car. _____ old car broke down. The new car now belongs to _____. It is _____ car to do with as he wants.

The boy gave the girl a flower. _____ liked the flower. It was _____ favorite flower. The rose is now _____.

*Identification of deep structure (meaning) identity*

The apple belongs to me.
The apple is mine.            (same/different)

The pennies belong to them.
The pennies are ours.         (same/different)

The car is ours.
The car belongs to us.        (same/different)

The sneakers are yours.
The sneakers belong to us.    (same/different)

To teach the child to differentiate the meaning and referents for unstressed and stressed personal pronouns, you may use tasks which require judgment of identity in meaning. This task format may be followed up by role-playing activities and acting out the meaning of sentences.

*Judgment of deep structure (meaning) identity*

George yelled at Bob and then
Joe yelled at *him*.
George yelled at Bob and then
Joe yelled at him.              (same/different)

Iris gave a present to Lita and then
Tony gave a present to her.
Iris gave a present to Lita and then
Tony gave a present to *her*.   (same/different)

## Demonstrative Pronouns

The demonstrative pronouns "this," "that," "these," and "those" express differences in the location of persons or objects in space. An intervention program to teach the child to distinguish the contrasts in location (place deixis) denoted by these demonstratives may involve direct observation of spatial relationships among objects, animals, or persons. Acting out oral directions which use a demonstrative may help. The activities can use one or more objects, placed in different locations around the room. They may be moved from one location to another. Each location or move should be labelled and described in sentences that use demonstratives. Here is a sample activity.

You and the child throw a ball back and forth between you. Label the ball *"this* ball." Place the ball at the far side of the room away from you and the child. Tell the child, "The ball is over there." Look at the ball and say, "See that ball over there. Go get that ball." When the child brings the ball say, "Now the ball is over here. You brought me *this* ball."

You may also use two balls. Place one near you and the child. Place one at the far end of the room. Call the ball near you "this ball" and the one away from you "that ball." Move with the child to a position close to the ball at the other end of the room. Tell the child, "Look at *this* ball." Point to the ball you left and say, "Look at *that* ball." Now move back to the first ball. Tell the child, "*This* ball is close to us. That ball is far away." "Bring me *that* ball over there." When the child has brought the ball, place it next to the ball already in the location. Tell the child, "Now we have two balls. They are close to us. Look at *these* balls." Place two other balls in the location far away from you. Tell the child, "Now there are two balls over there. Look at *those* balls." Move with the child to the far end of the room next to the two balls you placed there. Now tell the child, "Now we are close to *these* balls. We are far away from *those* balls."

When the child grasps the concept of place deixis denoted by "this"/ "that," "these"/"those," you may introduce other objects. If the child transfers the concept of place deixis readily to new objects, move around the room away from the child. Ask the child to point to various objects in the room on oral command. First ask the child to point to an object (ball) close to him. Ask him if he can tell you where the ball is. Then ask him to tell you if it is "this ball" or "that ball" to him. Next point to an object away from him (chair). Ask him if it is "this chair" or "that chair" to him. Extend this activity to two or more objects ("these"/"those").

Many language and learning disabled children seem to have trouble with the demonstrative pronouns either because they sound alike or because they change form ("this"/"that," "these"/"those") in relation to the speaker. Their problems are further confounded when the speaker-listener roles are interchanged, and the demonstratives change accordingly. It is essential that the youngster understand that the demonstrative pronoun form is determined by the relationship in space between a speaker and the object he is talking about. You must train the youngster to take the perspective of the speaker in space himself. Taking the perspective of others may remain a problem for some language and learning disabled youngsters unless they are specifically trained, with actual experiences. The youngster should remain in the same location while the adult moves from one location to another. The adult may first ask the youngster whether a specific object is close to or far away from him (the adult). When the youngster has indicated the relative distance of objects from the adult, he may be asked to use a demonstrative which would be used by the *other* person in speaking. The interaction may proceed as follows. The adult points to an object and says, "Is it near to me or far away from me? What word could I use about it to tell you it is close to/far away from me?"

Other formats may also be used to teach demonstrative pronouns. They include judgment of correct grammar-semantic consistency, sentence completion and oral cloze, categorization by place deixis, and directed requests. The examples below illustrate these formats with

singular and plural forms of the demonstratives. The tasks are performed with two sets of three pencils each. One set is placed on a table
next to the youngster ("this," "these"). The other is placed away from
the youngster ("that," "those"). Each set is arranged so that one pencil
is placed to one side ("this," "that"). The two other pencils are placed
next to each other on the other side ("these," "those"). The adult is
seated next to the youngster.

### Judgment of correct grammar-semantic consistency

*Pointing to the single pen nearest the youngster.*
I want *those* pens.                                                                    (right/wrong)
*Pointing to the single pen farthest away from the youngster.*
I want *that* pen.                                                                      (right/wrong)
*Pointing to the two pens nearest to the youngster.*
I want *these* pens.                                                                    (right/wrong)
*Pointing to the two pens farthest away from the youngster.*
I want *that* pen.                                                                      (right/wrong)

### Sentence completion and oral cloze

I want the pen that is closest to us. I want _____.
I want the pen that is farthest away from us. I want _____.
I want the two pens that are closest to us. I want _____.
I want the two pens that are farthest away from us. I want _____.
_____ pen is close to me. _____ pen is far away from me.
_____ pens are close to me. _____ pens are far away from me.

### Categorization of sentences by place deixis

**Samples:**                                    Near              Far Away
                                                close to . . .    away from . . .

**Sentences to be Categorized:**                That pen is yours.
                                                This car is mine.
                                                Those pens are ours.
                                                Those dogs are mine.
                                                That coat looks new.
                                                These gloves are the nicest.
                                                I shall take those cakes.
                                                You will take this cake.
                                                Did you see these rings?
                                                I saw those rings.
                                                I want that ring.
                                                She bought a ring just like this one.

### Directed requests

*Pointing to the single pen farthest away from the youngster and adult.*
How would you ask me for the pen I am pointing to?                                      (that)
*Pointing to the two pens closest to the youngster.*
How would you ask me for the pens I am pointing to now?                                 (these)
*Pointing to the two pens farthest away from the youngster.*
How would you ask me for the pens I am pointing to now?                                 (those)
*Pointing to the single pen closest to the youngster.*
How would you ask me for the pen I am pointing to now?                                  (this)
*Now ask me to give you all of the pens, one at a time.*
*Use the words "this," "that," "these," or "those" when you ask.*

The indefinite and negative pronouns "someone," "somebody," "something," "somewhere," "anyone," "anybody," "anything," "anywhere," "no-one," "nobody," "nothing," and "nowhere" may cause problems for learning disabled students. Each features a component of meaning of either class inclusion or exclusion that must be interpreted accurately. In intervention, the concepts of inclusion ("some" and "any") and of exclusion ("no") must be taught first. Intervention procedures appropriate for this task are discussed below, on pages 268–71. You can then teach the meanings of the root words "-body," "-one," "-thing," and "-where." The child must learn that they are references to persons ("-body," "-one"), objects ("-thing"), and places ("-where").

# WORKING ON SEMANTIC CLASSIFICATION AND CATEGORIZATION

In order to understand a variety of vocabulary items, such as antonyms, synonyms, homonyms, and multiple-meaning words, a child must be able to classify and categorize words and concepts. Differentiating the shades of meaning among words also depends upon adequate as well as flexible classification and categorization of the words and concepts involved. For instance, to differentiate between the words "newspaper" and "magazine" you must be able to abstract and contrast similarities and differences in their meaning features. You must also be able to classify and reclassify the two related words according to their various characteristics of meaning.

Language and learning disabled children may have problems in abstracting either similarities or differences in word meanings or both. They may find it difficult to classify and reclassify words and concepts by meaning features. They seem to experience special problems with inclusion of meaning and the related aspects of classification (Klees & Lebrun, 1972). Some may be able to categorize words and concepts into specific concrete classes. They may categorize words on the basis of size, color, or function. They may, however, not understand that the same word may belong to several semantic classes or to subclasses of a larger word class. Their problems in shifting from one semantic class to another in classifying words by meaning components may be associated with a certain degree of inflexibility in verbal thinking and reasoning. To counteract these limitations, some language and learning disabled youngsters may need to develop basic nonverbal classification.

Inhelder, Sinclair, and Bovet (1974) describe nonverbal training procedures for class inclusion and seriation. They describe a series of logical exercises to teach the cognitive operations necessary to internalize compensatory or inclusive relationships. They emphasize the mental operations basic to class inclusion and the associated use of the relational statement ". . . but . . ." ("long *but* thin," etc.).

Extension testing may be necessary to decide whether a youngster's nonverbal classification abilities are adequate when his verbal semantic classification ability is not. The educator may use a set of picture cards of, for example, foods, animals, or furniture. The youngster is asked to sort the cards in groups so that the ones that are alike go together. Often language and learning disabled children and youth sort by visual-perceptual characteristics (color, size, shape, etc.). Sometimes they form small classes that share a characteristic and form a semantic subclass. They may, however, fail to carry the classification through the whole set of pictured objects, and they may be inconsistent in the basis for their classification from one card to the next. In the event that the child does not have nonverbal classification skills, they must be introduced and strengthened before verbal classification tasks are introduced.

Other materials may also be used for extension testing. One appropriate set of materials is the Attribute Blocks which are often used in teaching math. The Attribute Blocks lend themselves to comparing how well the youngster can categorize by a single dimension and by multiple (two, three, or four) dimensions. They may be used to test the child's hierarchical classification skills and flexibility in forming subgroups or subclasses and in shifting strategies for classification. Some language and learning disabled youngsters may not be able to use several dimensions for classification at the same time. Others may be slow or inadequate in shifting strategies for their classifications. In either case, it may be beneficial to use nonverbal classification procedures to strengthen the logical operations involved and increase the child's flexibility. For younger children, the early childhood curriculum by Lavatelli (1970) may be used to work on their nonverbal classification abilities. For older children, the Attribute Blocks may be more appropriate.

Once the child has mastered nonverbal classification, he can move on to verbal classification. This may be facilitated if you verbally specify the critical meaning components of the semantic classes involved. You can begin with two familiar semantic classes. Later, you can expand to include other and less familiar semantic classes. The steps outlined here may be used.

Step 1.   Take a deck of picture cards of two classes (foods, animals, furniture, clothing, tools, toys, etc.).

Step 2.   Show one card of a pictured object A to the youngster.

Step 3.   Name the pictured object or have the child name it.

Step 4.   Describe and elaborate on the critical characteristics of the object to demonstrate the task. You may describe its use, function, shape, color, location, or ownership.

Step 5.   Show a second card, a pictured object B, to the youngster.

Step 6.   Ask the youngster to name it.

Step 7.   Ask the youngster a series of *wh*- questions to elicit verbal elaboration of the critical characteristics ("what . . . use," "where," "when," "who has," "what else").

Step 8.   Ask the youngster how A and B are different. Then ask how they are alike, if appropriate.

Step 9.    Show the youngster a third picture card of an object C.
Step 10.    Repeat steps 6, 7, and 8.
Step 11.    Ask the child to place item C with either A or B.
Step 12.    Proceed with the classification, item by item, until verbal elaboration of the characteristics of the pictured objects and of their likenesses and differences in relation to the other objects has become automatic.

Here are example procedures to use in strengthening verbal classification skills.

*Association of semantic class name and names of class members*

Is a lion an animal or a bird?
Is tag a game or a toy?
Which of these is an animal: A robin, a dog, or a car?
Which of these is a fruit: A carrot, a potato, a pineapple?

*Identification of an item which does not belong to the semantic class*

Which of these does not belong: Apple, pear, shoe, banana?
Which of these does not belong: Tiger, dog, lion, cougar?

*Categorization of words by meaning components*

*Listen to these:* bread and butter, socks and shoes.
*Which are things you eat? Which are things you wear?*

*Listen to these:* hat, dress, pants, socks, coat.
*Which are things you wear when you go outside? Which are things you would wear in the house?*

*Listen to these:* candy, lemons, cookies, limes.
*Which of these are sweet? Which of these are sour?*

*Naming the semantic class*

*Listen to these:* red, white, and blue.
*What are they?*                                    (shapes/colors)

*Listen to these:* tea, coffee, and hot chocolate.
*What are they?*                                    (soups/beverages)

*Listen to these:* marbles, checkers, and playing cards.
*What are they?*                                    (clothes/games)

*Listen to these:* winter, summer, and fall.
*What are they?*                                    (months/seasons)

*Elicited verbal elaboration of differences*

Tell me all the differences you can think of between *summer* and *winter*.
Tell me all the differences you can think of between a *plane* and a *helicopter*.

*Elicited verbal elaboration of similarities*

Tell me all the things that are alike about *apples* and *oranges*.
How are *cars* and *trains* alike?
What are some ways that *cows, goats,* and *sheep* are alike?

*Elicited verbal elaboration of similarities and differences*

> *Listen to these:* bed, couch, and chair.
>
> *Tell me how they are alike. Tell me in what ways they are different.*
>
> *Listen to these:* plane, helicopter, and rocket.
>
> *Tell me how they are alike. Tell me in what ways they are different.*

*Twenty questions*

> *Place pictures of from 10 to 20 food items in front of you and the youngster. Direct him to think of a food. Ask yes/no questions till you can identify the food the youngster thought of. When the youngster understands the task requirements, reverse the task. Tell the youngster that you are thinking of a food. Tell him to ask you questions till he can find the food you are thinking of.*

| | | |
|---|---|---|
| **Target item:** | Baked beans. | |
| **Potential questions:** | Is it a fruit? | (yes/no) |
| | Is it a meat? | (yes/no) |
| | Is it a vegetable? | (yes/no) |
| | Is it a vegetable you cook? | (yes/no) |
| | Do you serve it plain? | (yes/no) |
| | Do you serve it stewed? | (yes/no) |
| | Do you serve it baked? | (yes/no) |
| | Are they baked beans? | (yes/no) |

*Descriptive communication tasks*

> *Place pictures of five groups of objects with three items in each group in front of you and the youngster. Ask the youngster to think of one item in one of the semantic classes or groups (clothes, furniture, toys, games, kitchen utensils, tools, etc.). Tell the youngster to describe the item to you by use, function, possession, size, color, taste, location, and class membership.*

## WORKING ON ANTONYMS, SYNONYMS, HOMONYMS, AND MULTIPLE-MEANING WORDS

The difficulties some language and learning disabled children have in differentiating word meanings may be especially blatant when they encounter antonyms, synonyms, **homonyms**, and multiple-meaning words. In intervention, you may need to begin at the level of already established nonverbal and verbal abilities. As a concrete example, intervention to teach the antonym "empty" should not proceed until the child is able to contrast an object which is full and one which is empty in nonverbal matching tasks. And the label "empty" should not be introduced until the child is able to respond to the verbal label "not full." The child must understand the concept of antonymy before the popular labels can be attached. Similarly, the child must understand the concept of synonymy before specific synonyms can be taught. At a basic verbal level, the youngster may know that people can be called by several names. They may be called by their first names, their last names, or by a kinship term—Suzie, Ms. Whalen, or Mommy. The already established concepts and labels may be used as reference points in intervention to expand the child's repertory of antonyms, synonyms, homonyms, and multiple meaning words.

An intervention program to develop an age-appropriate repertory of antonyms should progress from concrete, early acquired, and frequent antonym pairs to the less frequent, later acquired, and relatively more abstract ones. The vocabulary items used in verbal opposites tests are usually sequenced according to developmental order, relative frequency, and reading level. They tend to be arranged from relatively concrete and highly familiar to relatively more abstract and less familiar. These tests may be used as guidelines for selecting and sequencing antonym pairs by frequency and level of abstraction. Investigations of the normal development of antonymy (Clark, 1972) and curriculum materials in English and Language Arts can also be used for sequencing antonyms.

Here are some principles to consider when selecting or designing intervention materials, nonverbal or verbal. First, the unmarked or preferred member of an antonym pair ("big," "tall," "kind," etc.) should be taught and established before the marked or less preferred member is introduced ("small," "short," "cruel," etc.). The unmarked member of the antonym pair can then be used as a reference for the meaning and label of the verbal opposite. The unmarked member of an antonym pair is generally, but not always, the positive word (kind) and the marked, the negative word (cruel). But as an example of an exception to the rule, small children seem to prefer the antonyms "tiny" or "small" over their opposites "huge" or "big."

Second, the antonyms should be featured in the most common, normal, expected, or prototypical referential contexts. For example, the antonym "outside" may be considered unmarked (preferred) or marked (less preferred) depending upon the context in which it is used. Assume that the learning and referential context for the word "outside" is the statement "Let's go outside." If it is said after a week of being cooped up inside while it rained, "outside" should be perceived as unmarked (preferred). If it is said at a time when it is cold and raining outside, it may be perceived as marked or less preferred. Consider the verbal opposite, "inside," in the same contexts. If the statement is "Let's go inside" after a long, cold walk in the snow, "inside" may well be perceived as the unmarked (preferred) term. If it is said to a child who is having a wonderful time at the playground, the term "inside" may be perceived as marked (less preferred). From these examples, it should be clear that antonyms should be taught in a variety of contexts.

Third, use unambiguous pictures or objects to establish knowledge of the meaning of antonym pairs. They should differ only along the critical dimension featured in the meaning of the antonym pair. For example, pictures associated with the antonyms "wet"/"dry" should be of the same person in the same clothes so that only the presence or absence of wetness differs. If you need to use pictures which differ along several dimensions, you should use them with caution or relatively late in intervention. They may be used at a relatively advanced stage to consolidate and extend the range of application of the antonyms. When they *are* used, the objective may be to teach the child to generalize to contexts which are not prototypical and relatively natural, since nature favors multidimensional differences.

The processing and production of antonyms may be taught with a variety of task formats, including verbal elaboration, sentence completion or oral cloze responses, or answers to direct questions. The examples below illustrate these formats.

*Verbal elaboration, labelling, and extension of antonyms*

| **Pictorial Stimuli** | A | B |
| --- | --- | --- |
| | full glass | same glass empty |

| **Verbal Elaborations** | | |
| --- | --- | --- |
| | What is in this picture? (A) | (a glass) |
| | What is inside the glass? | (milk/juice/etc.) |
| | What can you say about a glass with a lot of milk in it? | (it's full) |
| | What is in this picture? (B) | (a glass) |
| | What is in the glass? | (nothing) |
| | What can you say about a glass with nothing in it? | (it's not full) |
| | What is another word for "not full"? | (don't know) |
| | Empty. This glass (B) is _____. | (empty) |
| | This glass (A) is _____. | (full) |
| | This glass (B) is _____. | (empty) |

*Extension of the range of full-empty*

| **Pictorial Stimuli** | A | B |
| --- | --- | --- |
| | a vase with flowers | a vase without flowers |
| | full glass | empty glass |

| **Verbal Elaborations** | | |
| --- | --- | --- |
| | What can you say about this vase? | (A) |
| | What can you say about this vase? | (B) |
| | How are this vase and this glass alike? | (A) |
| | How are this vase and this glass alike? | (B) |

*Judgment of consistency of meaning*

The *sun* shines at *night*.                (right/wrong)
*Elephants* are very *small*.               (right/wrong)
*Bob* said he was Nancy's *sister*.         (right/wrong)
She *drank* the coffee till the cup was *full*.   (right/wrong)

*Sentence completion and oral cloze*

The present made Joe _____.              (happy/sad)
Tigers are _____.                        (tame/wild)
The boy loved his birthday present. He _____ it.   (accepted/refused)
The father was tall and heavy. The little boy was _____ and _____.
Mother said, "I sent the letter to you." Bill answered, "I never _____ it."

The new car was *not big*. What size do you think it was?
The glass was *not full*. What could you say about the glass?
Bob did *not* leave *during the day*. When do you think Bob left?
The teacher said to Mary, "Don't multiply those numbers." What was Mary to
do instead?

## Synonyms

An important point to teach in developing adequate comprehension
and use of synonyms is that they are rarely identical in meaning.
Synonyms are generally related by meaning and may convey approximately the same intent. Some synonyms change meaning, however,
depending upon the context. These synonyms may be especially difficult for language and learning disabled youngsters to differentiate and
use. As an example of a change in synonym meaning, consider the
word "bold." It may serve as a synonym for the word "courageous" in
the context "The soldier was very bold." It may also be used as a
synonym for "shameless" in the context "The boy's behavior was
bold."

At times a word may be substituted by one or more synonyms. Often
the synonyms differ in the degree to which their meanings overlap
with the original word. For example, an "angry" man may be described
as "furious," "outraged," "infuriated," or "villainous." While these
synonyms differ in shades of meaning, they share a negative connota-
tion. Synonyms which share a connotative meaning base are often
used in popular writing, advertising, news, and sports announce-
ments. They add variety to language, but they frequently confuse the
language and learning disabled youngster. He may think that each
synonym denotes an unrelated and totally new meaning or characteristic.

The primary objective in an intervention program to develop a repertory of synonyms should be to alert the youngster to the varied interpretations and uses of common synonyms. This may be achieved by
extended verbal elaboration of both shared and different meaning
components through direct *wh-* questioning. In intervention, a series
of prompts for the similarities and differences in meaning may be used
to help.

*Verbal elaboration and definition*

| | |
|---|---|
| **Pictorial stimuli** | people wearing trousers (suits), pants (suits), slacks, jeans, and britches (navy uniform) |
| **Potential questions** | These people are all wearing pants. |
| | The pants they wear are not all the same. |
| | Let's look at each of the pictures, *one at a time*. |
| | I'll ask you some questions, you answer them. |

(1) What color are this man's/woman's pants?
What are they made of?
Where would they wear that type of pants?
Where would you buy that type of pants?
What would you call that type of pants?
(trousers/pants/slacks/jeans/britches)

(2) What can you say that is the *same* about all the pants you see here? (outer garments, worn on lower body, long legs, made of cloth)

What can you say about *jeans* that is special? (made of denim, range of blue colors)

What can you say about *britches* that is special? (part of navy uniform)

What can you say about both *slacks* and *jeans* that is special? (casual wear)

What can you say about *trousers* and *pants* that is special? (usually worn with a jacket, part of suit, formal wear)

### Judgment of identity and similarity of meaning

Sally *giggled* when she heard the joke.
Sally *laughed* when she heard the joke.           (same/different)

Burt was *infuriated* when the boys teased him.
Burt was *happy* when the boys teased him.           (same/different)

### Direct questions

Sally *giggled* when she heard the joke. *What did Sally do when she heard the joke? What is another word for "giggle"?*

Burt was *infuriated* when the boys teased him.
*How did Burt feel when the boys teased him? What is another word for "infuriated"?*

## Homonyms

Homonyms are words that sound the same but are spelled differently and have widely different meanings. They may belong to the same or to different semantic-grammatical classes or parts of speech. For example, the meanings of the homonyms "sail" and "sale" can generally be figured out from the semantic or referential contexts in which they occur. When planning an intervention to teach the child to recognize homonyms, the variables that influence their perception and interpretation must be considered. First, one important factor in the intelligibility of spoken words on auditory perception tests is frequency of word usage. The context and experience with similar-sounding words also help determine the perception and interpretation of homonyms. The three factors that determine homonym interpretation when they are presented in isolation are (1) word frequency, (2) cultural patterns of use, and (3) salience or immediate relevance to the listener.

The primary objective in teaching a child to accurately perceive and interpret homonyms is to get him to use grammatic-semantic and contextual cues. Among the formats which may be used in working on homonyms are those which require judgment of identity of meaning, answers to direct questions, and sentence formulation. These formats are illustrated below.

### Judgment of identity of meaning

Mary went *to* a sale.
Mary went *for* a sail.           (same/different)

There *was* lots of mail here today.
There *were* lots of males here today.           (same/different)

*Direct questions*

Sally and her mother went *to* a sale last week.
*Did Sally and her mother go sailing on a boat?*    (yes/no)
*Did they go shopping?*    (yes/no)

When the *mail* arrived, the boys went to get it.
*Did the boys go to pick the man up?*    (yes/no)
*Did they pick the letters and magazines up?*    (yes/no)

*Sentence formulation*

Make a sentence with the word "sail" (spoken).
*Present SAIL (printed).*

Now make a sentence with the word "sale" (spoken).
*Present SALE (printed).*

## Multiple-Meaning Words

Multiple-meaning words are words which are spelled the same and sound the same but may function as different parts of speech depending upon the context. For example, consider the words "run," "table," "over," "go," and "mark." They may function as nouns, verbs, adjectives, and/or prepositions, depending upon the semantic-grammatic contexts in which they occur. Here are some direct illustrations.

> **RUN.**
> There is a *run* in my stocking.    (Noun)
> There is enough time to *run*.    (Verb)
> Let's take a long *run*.    (Noun)
> In the long *run*, it does not count.    (Idiomatic)

Based on clinical experiences, skill in semantic classification and some knowledge of morphology and syntax help a child differentiate multiple word meanings. Specific intervention procedures to facilitate semantic classification and categorization are discussed above. Intervention programs for knowledge and use of morphology and syntax are discussed in chapter 6.

*See pages 259–62.*

## WORKING ON WORD RELATIONSHIPS

As we know, a sentence may contain two or more words, phrases, or clauses that are related to each other. Consider, for example, the relationship expressed between the words "parents" and "children" in the statement "Parents are *older* than their children." The relationship expressed here is one of age. In other sentences, the relationships expressed may be cause-effect ("because"), condition ("if"), space ("between"), or time ("when, before"), to mention a few.

Relationships among words, phrases, or clauses in sentences may be expressed or signalled in one of several ways. First, they may be expressed by basic linguistic concepts such as "because," "if," "when," "all except," "none," and the indefinite and negative pronouns, including "somebody," "anything," "nobody," and "no-one." Some of these concepts function in sentences to join two related clauses, and are called *conjunctions*. Others function as modifiers, and some as indefinite and negative pronouns. The relationship may also be expressed in comparative, spatial, temporal, or familial sentences. Other relationships among words may be expressed in the form of analogies. In all these cases, the ability to interpret sentences that feature relationships among words, phrases, or clauses depends upon several skills and competencies. You must accurately identify the critical words, phrases, or clauses featured in the relationship. Then you must identify and interpret the words which signify the expressed relationship. You must use logical problem solving skills to perceive and interpret the nature of the relationship. Processing sentences which contain logical relationships, therefore, depends on syntactic, semantic, and logical problem-solving skills and competencies.

## Basic Linguistic Concepts

*See page 178 for a summary of these concepts and the words used to express them.*

Sentences that contain linguistic concepts of cause, condition, time, inclusion, or exclusion may be difficult to grasp for children with language and learning disabilities. They may not discern the critical words or concepts in these sentences. They may misinterpret the nature of the relationship among words. Their difficulties become especially obvious when they are asked to follow oral directions in the classroom or when they are asked questions about materials they have heard or read.

We can outline several principles for selecting or designing intervention programs for understanding linguistic concepts. These principles relate to establishing a logical basis for interpretation of the concepts. Principles for working on the functions of these concepts in the sentence structure are described above.

*See page 145.*

*Principle 1*

Introduce the basic linguistic concepts according to their relative order of acquisition or of difficulty. Table 9.7 lists an observed order of difficulty for selected linguistic concepts.

*Principle 2*

The basic linguistic concepts should be featured first in prototypical, exemplar, or expected contexts.

*Principle 3*

Associate unfamiliar linguistic concepts with physical demonstrations or motor actions as well as labelling and questioning.

*Principle 4*

Pictorial representations used to illustrate the meaning of basic linguistic concepts should be unambiguous and feature prototypical situations with familiar cues.

*Principle 5*

Verbal statements which describe the basic linguistic concepts should be controlled for length, syntactic complexity, and level of difficulty of vocabulary. The order-of-mention should agree with the order-of-action when your purpose is to establish accurate and logical interpretation.

*Principle 6*

Introduce the linguistic concepts in simplified contexts with minimal contextual cues and redundancy. Manipulative materials such as colored sticks of varying lengths or Attribute Blocks may be used to consolidate the logical interpretation of sentences with basic linguistic concepts.

**TABLE 9.7**

*Observed order of difficulty of selected linguistic concepts for children with learning disabilities (Semel & Wiig, 1980)*

| Linguistic Concept | Logical Operation |
| --- | --- |
| not | Exclusion. |
| and | Coordination. |
| all . . . except | Inclusion-exclusion. |
| . . . with | Instrumental. |
| after . . . | Temporal-sequential. |
| no . . . instead | Exclusion-revision. |
| . . . after | Temporal-sequential. |
| when . . . | Temporal-sequential. |
| . . . before | Temporal-sequential. |
| if . . . | Conditional. |
| don't . . . till | Conditional-temporal. |
| either . . . or | Inclusion. |
| before . . . | Temporal-sequential. |
| with . . . | Instrumental. |
| some, all . . . some | Inclusion. |
| any, anyone . . . all | Inclusion. |
| without | Instrumental. |
| neither . . . nor | Exclusion. |

The next examples apply these principles to the linguistic concepts "when . . . (then)" and "if . . . (then)."

**STEP 1.** *Practical demonstration and labelling*

**Q.** What happens *when* I turn this light switch ? (turns the switch)
**A.** The light goes on.
**R.** That is right. *When* I turn the switch, *then* the light goes on.

**Q.** What will happen *when* I turn the light switch now? (turns the switch)
**A.** The light goes off.
**R.** That is right. *When* I turned the switch, the light went off.

**Q.** What will happen *if* I turn this faucet? (does not turn the faucet)
**A.** Water will run.
**R.** That is right. *If* I turn the faucet, *then* the water will run.

**Q.** What will happen *if* I push this button? (does not push button)
**A.** The bell will ring.
**R.** That is right. *If* I push the button, the bell will ring.

**STEP 2.** *Extension of range of application*

| Pictorial Stimuli: | a picture of a rain scene without people (A) |
|---|---|
| | same scene with people in rainwear and carrying umbrellas (B) |

| Statements: | Here it is raining. (A) |
|---|---|
| | Here are some people in the rain. (B) |

**Q.** What do people wear *when* it rains?
**A.** When _____.

**A.** What else could people do when it rains?
**A.** When it rains _____.

**Q.** What would you wear *if* it started to rain?
**A.** If _____.

**Q.** What would your friends do *if* it started to rain?
**A.** If _____.

| Pictorial Stimuli: | a camp fire with *no* smoke (A) |
|---|---|
| | a camp fire *with* smoke (B) |

| Statements: | Here is a fire. (A) |
|---|---|
| | Here is a fire with a lot of smoke. (B) |

**Q.** What happens *when* there is a fire?
**A.** When _____.

**Q.** What tells you *if* there is a fire in a house.
**A.** If _____.

**STEP 3.** *Verbal formulation of cause-effect relationships*

| Pictorial Stimulus: | an exaggerated situation; water is flowing over the sides of a bathtub |
|---|---|

**Q.** Tell me what happened here. Use some sentences to tell me that begin with the word *when*.
**A.** When _____.

**Q.** What can you learn from this situation? Use some sentences to tell me that begin with the word *if*.
**A.** If _____.

**STEP 4.** *Extension of concepts to contexts with minimal redundancy*

| Stimuli: | a set of colored tokens of different sizes or shapes or Attribute Blocks |
|---|---|

**Verbal Commands:**

*When* I take a red square, you take a small circle.

*If* I point to a red circle, then you point to a blue triangle. (points to several tokens before pointing to a red circle)

You point to a small, blue circle *when* I point to a small, red square.

Point to a big, blue triangle only *if* I point to a blue square. (points to several tokens but not to a blue square)

**STEP 5.** *Extension of range of application in verbal elaborations*

Susan is planning a picnic this Sunday.
Suppose it begins to rain on Sunday.
Where could Susan have her picnic?               (inside)
When could she have the picnic?               (earlier/later)
What else could Susan do *if* it were to rain?

Suppose Peter saves fifty dollars.
What could he buy for himself?
What could he buy for his room?
What could he buy for his mother?
What would you buy *if* you had saved fifty dollars?

## Linguistic Relationships

Among the linguistic relationships which may cause difficulties for the language and learning disabled youngster are sentences which express (1) comparative and superlative relationships, (2) passive relationships, (3) spatial relationships, (4) temporal-sequential relationships, and (5) familial relationships. In the following sections, the difficulties associated with each of these types of relationship and the principles for intervention are discussed.

## Comparative Relationships

The relative level of difficulty of comparative sentences is determined by several factors.

(1) Sentences which compare two words (*"Apples* are bigger than *cherries"*) are relatively easier to interpret than sentences which compare three or more words (*"Apples* are bigger than *cherries*, and cherries are bigger than *raisins"*).
(2) Statements and questions which express true relationships ("Are elephants bigger than tigers?") are relatively easier to interpret than those which express false relationships ("Are tigers bigger than elephants?").
(3) Sentences which express a positive comparison (*"bigger* than," "*taller* than") are relatively easier to interpret than those which express negative comparisons ("*smaller* than," "*shorter* than").

It follows that in intervention programs, positively stated, true comparisons of two critical words should be introduced before other comparisons. Negatively stated, false comparisons of more than two words should be brought in later in the sequence. Tasks which require judgment of validity (true/false), sentence completion and oral cloze responses, and descriptive communication may all be used.

## Passive Relationships

Interpretation of passive sentences is dependent upon the presence or absence of semantic-referential and logical cues. *Irreversible* passives, in which the agent-object relationship is perceived immediately by logic, are the easiest to interpret ("The car was driven by John"). Reversible passives, in which either noun may serve as the agent or object, are relatively harder to interpret ("Mary was driven by John"). Therefore logical cues to interpretation should be included in the first part of the intervention. The cues may then be reduced gradually to increase the child's dependence upon structure and structural (syntactic) cues. The primary objective in intervention should be to teach the child the association between the surface structure and the deep structure representations. To do this, you can use substitution in which an affirmative, active, declarative sentence is presented first. This sentence is then associated with its passive counterpart. You can gradually modify the nature of the active and passive sentences you use from irreversible to reversible. The sequence is illustrated with the judgment of identity of meaning format.

*Judgment of identity of meaning (deep structure)*

The man drives the car.
The car is being driven by the man.              (same/different)

The man walked the dog.
The dog was being walked by the man.          (same/different)

The man brought the boy.
The boy was being brought by the man.        (same/different)

The man brought John.
John was brought by the man.                      (same/different)

Charles brought John.
John was brought by Charles.                       (same/different)

*See page 139.*

To process and produce passive sentences, you need to know the transformational rules. Strategies, sequences, and task formats for improving knowledge and use of the passive transformation are described in chapter 6.

## Spatial Relationships

To process and produce sentences which involve spatial relationships, you must know the meaning of the spatial prepositions and prepositional phrases. For intervention sequences and strategies, see pages 246–52.

## Temporal-Sequential Relationships

To process and produce sentences that involve temporal-sequential events, you need to understand event sequence and serial order. Among sequential series that are used heavily in sentences with temporal relationships are days of the week, months of the year, seasons of the year, holidays, and times of day. Before you begin a program of intervention to improve the interpretation of sentences with temporal relationships, you should evaluate the child's recall of time series (Semel & Wiig, 1980).

Sentences that involve relationships among temporal events in their true sequence are relatively easier to interpret than those in which the logical or expected sequence of events has been altered. For instance, it is relatively easier to respond to the question, "Does February come before March?" than to the question "Does March come after February?" In the first question, the order-of-mention matches the expected order of the events. It is also relatively easier to interpret a correctly stated sequence than a falsely stated sequence. For example, the question "Does summer come before fall?" is relatively easier to interpret and answer than the question "Does fall come before summer?" Based on these principles, here is a sequence for the procedures and tasks.

(1) Sentences that feature adjacent temporal events in their serial or expected order should be introduced first (Tuesday–Wednesday; January–February).
(2) Sentences that feature adjacent events in reverse order may be introduced next (Wednesday–Tuesday).
(3) Sentences that feature nonadjacent temporal events should be introduced last in their expected order and then in reversed order (Tuesday–Thursday; January–March).

The task formats that may be used to work on temporal-sequential events include judgment of temporal consistency, sentence completion and cloze, categorization by time deixis, descriptive communication, and role playing. These formats are illustrated below.

*Judgment of temporal consistency*

Judy arrived on Tuesday and Jane arrived the next day.
Jane arrived on Thursday. (right/wrong)

Sam left before the weekend and Jack left on Sunday.
Sam left on Monday. (right/wrong)

*Sentence completion and oral cloze*

We have arts on Mondays and gym two days later.
We have gym on _____. (Wednesday)

We have math two days after we have gym.
Math is on Thursdays.
Gym is on _____. (Tuesdays)

Jonathan cooks Sunday dinner a day ahead.
He cooks Sunday dinners on _____. (Saturdays)
The day before that he cleans the house.
On _____ he cleans his house. (Fridays)

*Categorization by time deixis*

| **Samples:** | Sunday and after Sunday | Thursday and after Thursday |
|---|---|---|
| **Sentences for categorization:** | She arrived on Monday. | |
| | She left on Friday. | |
| | She went to Boston on Wednesday. | |
| | She came home on Saturday. | |
| | She went to New York on Tuesday. | |
| | She met me in San Francisco on Sunday. | |

*Descriptive communication tasks*

**Materials:** two sets of from 5 to 10 identical theatre tickets, train tickets, or other dated materials

**Task:** Ask the youngster to describe one of the events or ticket dates by relating it to others in time (day of week, month of the year, season, etc.). The youngster should be instructed that he cannot tell the exact date, day, month, or year of the ticket.

**Familial Relationships**

Kinship terms may not be very significant in the modern-day youngster's daily life. Family structures tend to be fluid; some youngsters may not have a consistent and intact family structure to relate these terms to. Kinship terms may nonetheless become significant in the child's academic experiences. In subject areas such as the social sciences, family relationships are important in the study of historical events. Kinship terms are also featured prominently in the classical literature and therefore in English and Language Arts. The objective in intervention may therefore be to teach the child to recognize expressed family relationships in spoken and written language. These kinship terms should be established in relation to a person other than the child himself. The labels for direct and immediate family members (father, mother, sister, and brother) should be established before the labels for more remote and distant relatives (grandfather, grandmother; uncle, aunt; cousin). Photographs may be used to provide a concrete analogy and help relate kinship terms to features of age, gender, etc. A family tree may be used as a point of departure. It may include pictures and should include proper names and kinship terms. If a family tree is used, the organization should be similar to that used in historical or classical novels or texts.

## Verbal Analogies

*The relationships which can be expressed by verbal analogy are listed on page 184.*

Verbal analogies are commonly used in teaching and in texts to provide new information and insights about shared relationships. The objective in an intervention program for a learning disabled child may be limited to recognizing verbal analogies and accurately interpreting the expressed relationships. In an intervention program, the sequence in which analogies are introduced must be controlled. Clinical observations of the relative order of difficulty for the various types of verbal analogies suggest the following sequences.

(1) Whole-part analogies should be introduced in intervention before part-whole analogies are introduced.
(2) Agent-action analogies should be introduced before action-agent analogies.
(3) Action-object analogies should be introduced before object-action analogies.
(4) Antonym analogies should be taught in the same sequence as verbal opposites.
(5) Spatial analogies should be taught before temporal or temporal-sequential analogies.
(6) Temporal-sequential analogies should be introduced in the expected order of occurrence or sequence before reversals in the sequence.
(7) Verbal analogies should be introduce in active, affirmative, declarative sentence formats when possible and before the formal construction, . . . is to . . . as . . . is to . . . , is featured.

In an intervention program with the limited objective of teaching the child to recognize and interpret verbal analogies, specific task formats seem appropriate. Among the appropriate task formats are judgment of the consistency of the relationships expressed in the analogy and sentence completion with or without multiple choices. The examples below illustrate these two formats.

|  | *Judgment of consistency of the expressed relationship* |
|---|---|
| A dog has paws and a boy has hair. | (right/wrong) |
| You can bake a cake and you can broil a steak. | (right/wrong) |
| We swim in the summer and we ski in the mountains. | (right/wrong) |
| A boy can be a brother and a girl can be an uncle. | (right/wrong) |

*Sentence completion*

A dog has a mouth and a bird has a _____. (beak/trunk)

After lightning you can hear thunder and after a fire you can see _____. (wind/smoke)

You use a racket to play tennis and you use a bat to play _____. (soccer/baseball)

Monday comes before Tuesday and Saturday comes before _____. (Monday/Sunday)

A horse is big but an elephant is bigger.
A butterfly is small but a mosquito is _____. (bigger/smaller)

## WORKING ON FIGURATIVE LANGUAGE

Clinical observations indicate that language and learning disabled youth may have problems recognizing and interpreting figurative language. They frequently interpret figurative expressions literally and concretely. Their misinterpretations may result in confused actions and statements. These may be quite humorous to everyone else, but not to the learning disabled youngster. They may not perceive the abstract intentions of idioms, metaphors, or proverbs. These youngsters may need help in recognizing and learning the meaning of even the most common figurative expressions. Unfortunately, figurative language is used extensively in English, and each example cannot be taught to the language and learning disabled youngster. The objective in intervention may therefore be to teach the child to recognize figurative language usages and to interpret the more commonly used idioms, metaphors, and proverbs.

Figurative language is interpreted by discerning changes in word meanings and translating the word meanings into abstract and generalized concepts. The words and phrases that are used as elements in idioms, metaphors, and proverbs do not have a referential meaning. In fact, the abstract meanings of the various idioms, metaphors, and proverbs may be totally unrelated to the usual referential meanings of the words, and may therefore have to be taught separately, with little transfer from incidence to incidence.

The ability to classify, define, and redefine multiple-meaning words is basic to the comprehension of figurative language. Procedures designed to improve semantic classification have been discussed in previous sections. They may be used as a point of departure to lead into intervention procedures with figurative language.

*See pages 259–62.*

### Idioms

Idioms often use words that may be very familiar to the language and learning disabled child or youth. In many cases, several idioms use the same words in different combinations. Parts of the body seem, for example, to be used in a large number of idioms. As an illustration, the word "eye" is featured in a variety of idioms, such as "have eyes for," "sharp eyes," "eyes popped," "eyes danced," and "to eye it." In intervention, you can accentuate the humor which comes from interpreting literally. Consider the idiom "I am all tied up at the office" and the confusion which would ensue from a literal interpretation. To teach this idiom, you could place illustrations of the concrete and literal interpretation and of the abstract and general interpretation side by side. The youngster can be required to identify the literal and then the abstract interpretations of spoken idioms. You can vary this procedure featuring only the abstract interpretations and asking the youngster to match spoken and illustrated idioms. Commercially available language materials use similar procedures (Newby Visualanguage).

*See Figure 7.1.*

Another appropriate format involves a spoken idiom in association with two or more choices for a match of interpretations. Here are some examples.

Bill caught a cold. *Does it mean:*
Bill was able to catch a cold with his hands.
Bill became sick with a cold.

The advertising business is a real jungle. *Does it mean:*
The advertising business is very competitive.
The advertising business has trees and wild animals in it.

## Metaphors

Metaphors express comparisons between an actual object or person and a descriptive image, using the word "as" as a connective between the two. The two things being compared in metaphors are usually widely different but share some common aspect which is highlighted through the descriptive image. An example of a metaphor is "It was white as snow." Metaphors can be distinguished from similes, another type of figurative expression. While the images created by metaphors and similes are the same, the simile features the word "like" as a connective. An example of a simile is "Bob eats like a bird."

Metaphors and similes may be introduced in intervention with an explanation of the structural principles of each one. You should emphasize the youngster's recognition and identification of the connectives. Stress that these connectives signal the figurative use of words and concepts which follow them. You can then present sentence pairs in which one states a fact and the other uses an image. The youngster may be asked which sentence states a fact. He may then be asked to identify the words in the metaphor or simile which signal the figurative use of language. Next, ask the youngster to tell which words were used to create the image rather than describe a fact. At a later stage, metaphors and similes may be introduced with or without multiple choices for interpretation. The examples below illustrate the two formats.

*Identification of factual statement and of figurative use*
Listen to these sentences.
They drank punch.
They were pleased *as* punch.

*Which sentence stated a fact?*
*Which sentence created an image and was not a fact?*
*Which word was used to signal the image?*
*What word described the image in the sentence?*

They worked *like* beavers.
They liked the beavers.
*Which of these sentences states a fact?*
*Which sentence contains an image?*
*Which word was used to signal the image?*
*What word was used to describe the image in the sentence?*

*Interpretation of metaphors and similes*

Sally is busy *as a beaver. Does it mean:*
Sally is busy taking care of her beaver.
Sally is very busy with something.

When Bill got the award, he was pleased *as* punch. *Does it mean:*
Bill looked like a bowl of punch when he got the award.
Bill was very happy when he got the award.

Mary's eyes shone *like* stars. *Tell me what that means*.

## Proverbs and Platitudes

Proverbs and platitudes share the same imagery as metaphors and similes. They also contain generalized moral advice which can only be discerned when the abstract meaning is perceived. For instance, the proverb "Strike while the iron is hot" may be interpreted as a practical admonition which says that the blacksmith should not let his iron get cold before he strikes. But at the level of abstract interpretation, the generalized moral advice "Don't delay until it is too late" is evident. In intervention, you may use formats which require (1) matching a spoken proverb with its abstract interpretation, based on selection from among two or three choices, (2) matching spoken proverbs to short stories such as fables, and (3) spontaneously matching a proverb to a short story or fable.

In daily life, modern children are rarely faced with a need to interpret proverbs. The youngster may, however, become more sensitive to abstract, figurative language if proverbs are introduced in intervention. Television commercials, advertisements, and propaganda frequently employ figurative language to persuade the consumer of the value of a product. The ability to perceive logic and validity of verbal imagery and general claims of excellence may constitute a valuable skill in daily living and practical decision making.

## WORKING ON IMPLIED AND PRAGMATIC MEANING

Language and learning disabled youngsters may have significant problems in perceiving hidden, unstated verbal meanings and in grasping their implications. In order for a youngster to grasp the full meaning of a monologue, dialogue, conversation, or read materials he must interpret each concept and relationship accurately. In addition, he must perceive and discern the causes, conditions, or consequences that are implied but not stated. The ability to discern implied but not explicitly stated aspects of a verbal or written message constitutes a valuable academic and social skill or competence. If a child cannot already do this, he should be taught to develop this ability to its maximum potential.

In order to interpret implied cause-effect relationships, the youngster must be familiar with causes and their potential consequences. He must also know which consequences can result from which potential causes. If the child is told that it may rain, he should immediately grasp the implied, unspoken message. In this case, there could be several different intended messages. It may be an admonition to wear a raincoat or an admonition to stay inside so that he won't get wet. If the child were to be told that the family car needs to be fixed, he should be able to guess potential causes for the repair. An initial objective in an intervention program may be to become familiar with a variety of cause-effect relationships to help the child recognize implied messages and their pragmatic meaning.

When the youngster has formed associations among a variety of causes and plausible outcomes, and outcomes and their potential causes, he must be guided to perceive when cause-effect relationships are implied. You can use verbal materials of increasing length and complexity to help him learn to recognize implicit messages. At first, use simple sentences. As the youngster's ability to detect implied meanings improves, paragraphs, short stories, recorded dialogues, or role-playing activities may be added. The task formats used in intervention may require the child to detect absurdities and ambiguities, spontaneously correct inconsistencies, predict outcomes and causes, and role play. Some of these are illustrated in the examples below.

## Detecting inconsistencies and absurdities

He hit the baseball with a racket.
*Was anything wrong in this statement?*
*What was wrong?*

Mr. Adams lived 30 miles from his work. After 4 years, he decided to buy a new bicycle to get there faster and to save money.
*Was anything wrong in this statement?*
*What was wrong?*

It was raining so hard yesterday that Phil took off his shirt to get a suntan.
*Was anything wrong in this statement?*
*What was wrong?*

It was a beautiful summer day and Leila decided to go swimming. She put on her bathing suit and drove into the warm water of the lake. After half an hour of swimming, she dried herself off on the shore and lay in the hot summer sun. Then she looked at the water and said: "Gee, I think I'll go ice skating. The ice is perfect today."
*What was wrong in this story?*

*Correcting inconsistencies and absurdities*

*Listen to these sentences. You can correct them by changing words.*

Charlie drank the hamburger.
*What word would you change?*

Brian liked the book so much he burned it.
*What word would you change?*

Ted was going to Europe. He didn't know whether to go by boat or bus.
*What word would you change?*

The weather was atrocious. First we heard the thunder and then we saw flashes of lightning.
*What words would you change?*

*Predicting outcomes and inferring causes*

Sue was hanging a picture on the wall. She tried to use a thumb tack. The thumb tack bent against the wall. She thought and thought about what she could do. Finally, she . . . .
*Can you finish the story?*
*What could she do?*     (use tape/give up/find another tack)

When I got to the corner, there was a big commotion. There were apples, pears, potatoes, and other vegetables all over. People were picking the fruits and vegetables up. Cars were stopped. In the middle of the road was the reason for it all . . .
*Can you finish the story?*

The implied meaning of a message is often signalled by features of intonation (pitch, intensity, duration, rate, juncture). The sentence "Give that to me!" can take on a variety of meanings, depending upon the intonation and differences in the context. If I say "Give that to *me*," I express that *I* am the person who wants it. "*Give* that to me," on the other hand, is intended to imply that I want it given to me. I do not want it thrown to me and I do not want to come and get it myself. "Give *that* to me" may be associated with my pointing at an object. The implied and intended message is that I want a particular object—not just any object. "Give that to me?" implies insecurity and asks if it can be possible that I am or will be given a particular object.

Language and learning disabled youngsters may have severe difficulties in picking up the nuances of meaning implied by differences in intonation patterns. Intervention is indicated in that case. The objective is to increase the child's awareness of the superimposed intonation patterns in statements and questions and to develop his ability to interpret the nuances of meaning. The task formats uses for intervention may require identification of stress in sentences or oral commands, judgments of identity of meaning, interpretations of the implied meanings, and role playing. The examples below illustrate some of these formats.

*Identification of stress*

*Listen to these sentences. Tell me which word is stressed in each of them.*
Give the pencil to *me*.                    (me)
Bring the *book* to Jane.                   (book)

*Run* to the blackboard.                        (run)

Put the *blue* pencil on the *big* table.        (blue, big)

*Judgment of identity of the implied message (pragmatic meaning)*

*Yesterday* Mrs. Jones went to the hospital.

Yesterday Mrs. Jones went *to the hospital*.        (same/different)

Tomorrow *Paul* must go to school.

Tomorrow Paul must go to *school*.        (same/different)

*Interpretation of the implied messages (pragmatic meaning)*

When I say, *"Run* to the door," what do I want you to be sure to do?

When I tell you, "Last year we *drove* to Los Angeles," what do I want you to be sure to know?

When I say, "I can't *read* the paper *in the dark*," what do I want you to do for me?

When I say, "Shouldn't you *clean* your desk," what do I want you to be sure to do?

# SELECTED PROGRAMS AND SOURCE MATERIALS

1. *Associations. Categories. Compound Words. Functions. Parts and Wholes. People, Places, and Things. Preposition Concepts Picture Cards. Seasonal Sequence Cards. Sequence Picture Cards.* Esther Brown. Teaching Resources, 100 Boylston Street, Boston, MA 02116.

2. *Newby Visualanguage. Adjectives, Prepositions, Idioms.* Newby Visualanguage Inc., Box #121 A, Eagleville, PA 19408.

3. *Peabody Language Development Kit—Level P.* Lloyd M. Dunn, J. O. Smith, and Katherine B. Horton. American Guidance Service, Circle Pines, MN 55014.

4. *Peabody Language Development Kit—Levels 1, 2, and 3.* Lloyd M. Dunn and J. O. Smith. American Guidance Service, Circle Pines, MN 55014.

5. *Semel Auditory Processing Program.* Eleanor M. Semel. Follett Educational Publishing Company, Chicago, IL.

6. *Sound-Order-Sense: A Developmental Program in Auditory Perception.* Eleanor M. Semel. Follett Educational Publishing Company, Chicago, IL.

7. *The World of Language Books.* R. A. Bennett, N. Mysliewiec, and B. Beckman. Follett Educational Publishing Company, Chicago, IL.

*part* # IV

## Memory:
## Retention and
## Retrieval

# REMEMBERING SPOKEN MESSAGES
## Characteristics and Assessment

# 10

The skilled use of language depends upon memory, both long and short term. You use your memory to process and understand spoken language, to recall other people's messages. And memory serves as a link between the language you hear and read and the language you speak and write. Thus problems with memory—either short or long term—can show up in problems with processing language and producing it. These different language skills rely on different memory skills. Language processing can be considered to be based primarily on **recognition**, while language production requires recall and retrieval (Winitz, 1973). Of course, language production depends on more than simple memory; it also is affected by the person's past experiences, current feelings, and the setting for the communication (Ahmann & Glock, 1971).

We can classify memory in several ways. First we can distinguish between short-term and long-term memory abilities in processing verbal, nonverbal, and visual input, among others. To process the structure of a sentence, we depend heavily upon short-term memory. To interpret the meaning (deep structure) of a sentence, we depend upon long-term memory (Miller & Chomsky, 1963).

Research on memory has led to a variety of conclusions about specific memory capacities. Nonverbal memory has been distinguished from verbal memory, and visual memory from verbal memory. In the area of verbal memory, two separate abilities—**associative memory** and **span memory**—have been recognized (French, 1951).

In memory span experiments, Miller (1956) observed invariances which indicate that short-term memory capacity is of the magnitude of about "seven, plus or minus two" familiar units or chunks of any kind (digits, words, etc.). That is, we can hold from five to nine chunks of information in short-term memory. The existence of chunks or coherent memory units in language processing and recall has been supported extensively. Fodor and Bever (1965) found that the major syntactic breaks between clauses in sentences influence the perception

*We can distinguish between these skills. Recognition refers to the process of realizing that you have heard something (a word, phrase, or sentence) before and matching what you heard to the memory of the language you have heard before. Recall refers to the process of remembering, reconstructing, and activating language stored in memory. And retrieval is the process of restoring and bringing back language from storage in memory for production and use in spoken language.*

*Associative memory refers to the recall of words that are related through association. Span memory refers to the recall of unrelated digits or word series.*

of the location of pauses in speech. This suggests that the parts of sentences marked by pauses, which help the listener analyze what he is hearing, may function as perceptual-conceptual units. In the absence of other contextual cues and in isolation from sentences, pauses in speech can induce structural organization (chunking) of the message (Bollinger & Gerstman, 1957). Several authorities share the view that verbal memory is used in constructing and producing language (Bartlett, 1932; Cofer, 1973).

Piaget and Inhelder (1973) classify memory in another way. They define *memory* as the conservation of acquired reactions, which in the strict sense encompasses reactions associated with recognition or recall. However, they modify this definition by referring to *memory* in its wider sense, reflecting the ability to reproduce whatever can be generalized in a system of actions or operations, either habitual, sensorimotor, or conceptual.

Piaget and Inhelder (1973) differentiate three major hierarchical *types* of memory, each of which is considered to contain several subclasses. Their memory types are:

(1) *Recognitive memory*, where the individual assimilates acquired data into organized structures or schemata.
(2) *Mnemonic reconstruction*, where the individual intentionally produces an action or its results.
(3) *Mnemonic recall*, where the individual reconstructs a thought on the basis of memory images.

According to Piaget and Inhelder, memory develops with age in the same way that cognitive abilities develop. In the developmental sequence, recognition memory develops before recollection memory, which depends upon the use of figurative symbols and conceptual representation or representative images. Here is how Piaget and Inhelder describe the relationship between memory and cognition:

> Once we realize that, in order to discover an organization, we must either construct it or at least reconstruct it, things begin to look quite different; and once we consider the memory adequate to this construction or reconstruction, we must also grant that it has an inner capacity for organization or reorganization, isomorphous with that of intelligence. But, in that case, there is no reason for separating the two; rather must we consider the memory as part of intelligence, though differentiated and specialized to perform a precise task; namely, the structuring of the past. (1973, pp. 400–401)

To repeat, we can distinguish between short-term memory, used to process other people's messages, and long-term memory, used to recall and retrieve words and sentence structures to be used in language production. This chapter and the next one discuss the problems many learning disabled children have with short-term auditory memory, as evidenced by their ability to repeat spoken utterances. The following two chapters focus on problems with the recall and retrieval of specific words or concepts or, in other words, with recollection memory.

# CHARACTERISTICS OF SHORT-TERM MEMORY DEFICITS

When you present someone with model sentences or word sequences for repetition, the immediate responses reveal which parts of the structures or sequences the listener retains and recalls. The imitations do not, however, tell you whether he· has understood the underlying meaning of the sentences or the words in a series. The immediate repetitions reflect the listener's short-term memory *capacity* in the number of units (chunks) which are retained and memory *efficiency* in the size of the units. What the listener will be able to repeat will depend upon the characteristics of the words and sentences, including:

(1) The number of perceptual-conceptual units (chunks) to be retained.
(2) The size of the perceptual-conceptual units (chunks) to be retained.
(3) The syntactic complexity of the sentences, as indicated in the complexity of the phrases and the transformations.
(4) The relative frequency of occurrence of the words used and the relative age and level of acquisition of the vocabulary and concepts.
(5) The associations among the words used.
(6) The position of stress in relation to critical words in the sentence structure and the superimposed intonation patterns.
(7) The serial position of individual words in phrases, sentences, and word sequences.
(8) The salience of the words and the content and topic to the individual.

Learning disabled children and adolescents have been found to consistently have short-term memory deficits which may show up as limitations in the number of units (digits, words, phrases, or clauses) they can retain as well as in the size of the units. However, their retention deficits may be masked by the ability to hang onto and recount the underlying meaning (deep structure) of phrases and sentences. As a result, the adults responsible for the child may disregard the implications of the immediate memory deficits for language learning and academic achievement.

When we consider learning disabled children's ability to recall and reproduce sentence (surface) structure, their responses suggest that they may experience especial difficulties in retaining and recalling certain types of sentences. The difficult structures include:

(1) Sentence structures in which the sequence of the main phrases (Noun Phrase + Verb + Noun Phrase/Predicate adjective) has been changed or reversed, as in:
   (a) Passive sentences in which the Noun Phrases which contain the subject and object have been reversed (*"The cat* was chased by *the dog"*).
   (b) Interrogative sentences in which the first Noun Phrase and the Verb have been reversed (*"Are you* going to school?") or the first Noun Phrase is preceded by an auxiliary (*"Did you* go to school?").

(c) Indirect object transformations in which the order of the direct and indirect objects have been reversed ("The woman showed *the baby the cat*").

(d) Relative clause transformations with embedded relative clauses in which a relative clause is inserted into the main clause ("The man *who lives next door* went to Europe").

These structures may cause problems because the child expects the subject of the sentence to precede the predicate and the object to follow the predicate. When this sequence is changed, the child must change his initial hypothesis and perform a repeated process of resolving the surface structure. This process requires adequate short-term memory capacity and efficiency and internal reauditorization ability.

*Again, internal reauditorization is the ability to repeat a message you have heard "in your head."*

(2) Sentences which contain phrases and clauses with unstressed auxiliaries, prepositions, and other words where the listener must remember the sequence and form for structural accuracy. For example, they may have difficulties in recalling sentences with:

(a) Complex verb phrases such as "I *have been going* to the beach this last week" or "They *should have been taking* their bikes."

(b) Prepositional phrases such as "They were walking *on top of* the roof *of* the house *next to* ours."

(c) Adverbial phrases such as "The man lives in the house *intermittently*."

(3) Sentences which contain words or phrases which could be moved within the structure and must therefore be recalled in their presented rather than their alternative position. For example, they may have difficulties recalling sentences with moveable:

(a) Adverbial phrases, as in "*Yesterday* I went downtown to go shopping" and "I went downtown *yesterday* to go shopping" and "I went downtown to go shopping *yesterday*." Some learning disabled children will find the first construction easiest to recall, while others will have the most success with the last.

(b) Subordinated clauses, such as "They went inside *because it rained*" or "*Because it rained*, they went inside."

(4) Sentences which contain phrases or clauses with noun, verb, or modifier sequences or multiple prepositions, such as:

(a) The *man*, the *woman*, and the *driver* went to the restaurant (conjunction deletion with multiple subjects).

(b) The girl *hopped, skipped,* and *jumped* from joy (conjunction deletion with multiple action verbs).

(c) The *big brown* dog chased the *red* ball across the *huge, soft green* lawn (adjective sequences).

(d) The woman went *out of* the door *to the left of* the reception desk *next to* the window (multiple prepositions).

When you are asked to repeat sentences immediately after you have heard them, the ability to recall and repeat accurately depends upon the interaction between the form of the sentence (surface structure) and the word and sentence meaning (deep structure). If you take away some or all of the underlying meaning from a sequence of words arranged according to accepted grammatical rules, as in the word string "Colorless green ideas sleep furiously," recall depends primarily upon memory for structure and upon short-term memory capacity and efficiency. You can also remove the structure of a sentence and string a set of words together at random, as in the utterance "Walk some by hard of clearly table very." In this case, recall depends heavily upon short-term memory capacity and upon the number of units which can be retained. Looking at learning disabled children's repetitions of model sentences that violate the rules for word selection and therefore do not make sense but that do follow the structural rules can provide insight into the nature of their difficulties in retaining and recalling sentences. For instance, when presented with the model sentence *"Pale luminous feelings blithely painted the ocean,"* learning disabled preadolescents repeated it with:

(1) Omissions of words and phrases at either the middle, beginning, or end of the sentence, as in the responses:
    "Pale" (omission: adjective + noun) "painted the ocean."
    "Plan luminous" (omission: noun + adverb) "covered the ocean, paled the ocean."
    (Omission: adjectives + noun) "Paint the ocean with . . . I forgot."
    (Omission: adjectives + noun + adverb + verb + noun) "The ocean. An ocean can be water. You can drink water."
    "Pale lucient failing pilely licken" (omission: noun).
    "Pale luminous feelings lightly" (omission: verb + noun).
    "Pale luminous feelings" (omission: adverb + verb + noun).
    (Omission: adjectives + noun) "Lightly" (omission: verb + noun).
    The pattern of word omissions suggests that learning disabled children do not recall words or sequences which make little sense or are unfamiliar, while they tend to recall words and sequences with meaning.

(2) Substitutions of words by similar words or neologistic words, as in the responses:
    "Pale luminous feelings *brightly* painted the ocean."
    "Pale luminous feeling *black* painted the ocean."
    "Pale luminous feelings *lightly*."
    "Pale *lucient failing pilely licken*."
    *"Plan* luminous *covered* the ocean, *paled* the ocean."
    *"Plan aluminum covered* the ocean."
    *"Point* the ocean with."
    Here the pattern of word substitutions suggests that, when a word was not well known or familiar, the children substituted a similar-sounding real or invented word. In the example, the meaning of the adverb "blithely" did not seem well-established, and it was therefore substituted by better known and similar sounding adverbs such as "lightly" and "brightly" or by a similar-sounding invented word, "pilely." The adjectives "luminous" and "pale" were substituted by similar-sounding words "lucient" and "aluminum" and "plan," respectively, possibly for similar reasons.

When a group of learning disabled adolescents were asked to repeat a set of sentences with less drastic changes in meaning, they showed similar patterns of word and phrase omissions and word substitutions (Wiig & Roach, 1975). Presented with the interrogative sentence "Wasn't the fat ceiling robbed by the tired pen?" they responded as follows:

(1) Ten of the adolescents obtained relative consistency in the meaning of the sentence by substituting for one or more of the words "fat," "ceiling," "tired," and "pen" and repeated the sentence as follows:
"Wasn't the fat ceiling *painted* by the tired *men*?"
"Wasn't the *tall* ceiling robbed by the tired *men*?"
"Wasn't the fat ceiling *painted* by the *big pen*?"

(2) One omitted the last word of the sentence, and three others omitted from five to seven words at either the beginning, middle, or end of the sentence, resulting in repetitions such as:
"Wasn't the fat ceiling robbed by the tired?" ("pen" omitted)
"Wasn't the fat ceiling robbed?" ("by the tired pen" omitted)
"Wasn't robbed by the tired pen?" ("the fat ceiling" omitted)
"Robbed by the tired pen." ("Wasn't the fat ceiling" omitted)

When the same group was given another sentence, "The sky that the dream thought jumped cheaply," which contains an embedded relative clause, they repeated with:

(1) Omission of from one to four words by seven of the adolescents, resulting in responses such as:
"The sky jumped cheaply." (embedded relative clause omitted)
"That the dream thought." (main clause omitted)
"The dream jumped cheaply" (noun of the main clause and verb of the relative clause omitted)
"The sky thought cheaply." (noun of the relative clause and verb of the main clause omitted)
"The sky that the dream thought jumped." (adverb omitted)

(2) Substitutions of one or more of the words "sky," "dream," "thought," or "cheaply" as if to obtain relative semantic consistency, as in the responses:
"The *cow* that the *man saw* jumped *quickly*."
"The *cow* that the dream thought jumped cheaply."
"The sky that the *man saw* jumped *quickly*."
"The sky that the *moon* thought jumped *quickly*."

In contrast to these learning disabled adolescents, their academically achieving age peers were generally able to recall these two sentences accurately and only two omitted one word each, indicating that they used the structure of the sentences to facilitate recall. The responses by the learning disabled adolescents, on the other hand, suggested that they did not use the sentence and clause structures efficiently and adequately and that they did not tend to form coherent perceptual units to facilitate recall. They seemed to depend on consistencies in word and sentence meaning for their recall; when they ran into inconsistencies, they changed the words to improve the meaning. It is noteworthy that their word substitutions were chosen from within the same grammatical class as the presented words and that some of their word substitutions suggested strong associations with a nursery rhyme, "the cow jumped over the moon."

The difficulties experienced by the learning disabled children and adolescents when they were asked to recall and repeat sentences with noun strings are illustrated in their immediate repetitions of the following sentences:

(1) Jack likes *hamburgers* with *ketchup*.
(2) Jack likes *hamburgers* with *relish, mustard,* and *ketchup*.
(3) Jack likes *french fries* and *hamburgers* with *ketchup, onions, mustard,* and *relish*.

The three sentences were presented in sequence after it had been ascertained that all the nouns were known and understood by the youngsters. The sentences were designed to keep the subject and verb constant and to expand the noun phrase of the verb phrase, containing the direct object. The repetitions of the first sentence "Jack likes hamburgers with ketchup," were characterized by the following errors:

(1) Reversal of the sequence of the nouns "hamburgers" and "ketchup," as in "Jack likes ketchup with hamburgers."
(2) Substitutions of the preposition "with" by either "and" or "on" (his), as in "Jack likes hamburgers and ketchup" or "Jack likes ketchup on his hamburgers."
(3) Omission of word endings such as the third person plural verb ending -*s* ("likes") and the noun plural -*s* ("hamburgers"), resulting in sentences such as "Jack like hamburgers with ketchup" or "Jack likes hamburger with ketchup."

The repetitions of the second sentence," Jack likes hamburgers with relish, mustard, and ketchup," were characterized by similar errors. Among them were:

(1) Reversals of the sequence of the three or four last nouns, resulting in repetitions such as :
"Jack likes *mustard* with *relish, ketchup* with a *hamburger*."
"Jack like hamburgers with *mustard, relish,* and ketchup."
(2) Substitution of the noun "onion" for the noun "relish," as in "Jack like mustard with *onion*, ketchup, and hamburger."
(3) Concurrent omissions of the word ending -*s* in the verb "likes" and the noun plural "hamburgers."
(4) Omission of the last three nouns, resulting in the sentence "Jack likes hamburgers."

The third and last sentence, "Jack likes french fries and hamburgers with ketchup, onions, mustard, and relish," was not repeated correctly by anyone of the learning disabled adolescents. Their repetitions were characterized by generalized and multiple errors. In order of the frequency, they were:

(1) Multiple reversals of the nouns associated with substitutions, omissions, additions, and/or repetitions of the conjunction "and," the preposition "with," or the nouns, resulting in sentences such as:

"Jack likes *french fries, ketchup, relish, mustard,* and *onions.*"

"Jack likes *hamburgers* with *mustard, ketchup,* and relish."

(2) Omissions of from one to three nouns, the most frequently omitted nouns being "onions" and "mustard."

(3) Perseverative repetitions of the nouns or of the conjunction "and," as in the sentences:

"Jack likes *ketchup,* hamburgers with *ketchup, and* mustard, *and* relish, *and* french fries."

"*Jack likes hamburgers and french fries with mustard, relish,* ketchup, *relish,* and onions."

(4) Substitution/addition of nouns, as in the sentences:

"Jack likes hamburgers with french fries with *hot dogs* and *beans.*"

"Jack likes french fries with hamburger and *peanut butter.*"

(5) Substitution by one youngster of a rhyming word sequence, "Relish, relish, delish, drink of water."

The responses suggest that even a sentence with a sequence of only two nouns within one of its phrases may be difficult for some learning disabled children and adolescents to recall accurately. As the size of the word sequence increases, their problems become more and more evident and the order of the words in the sequence appear most vulnerable and subject to change. When the number of words in a sequence seems to surpass the memory capacity, the errors in retaining and recalling the sentences appear most common and most blatant, resulting sometimes in distortion of the sentence meaning.

The difficulties experienced by learning disabled adolescents in recalling sentences that contain noun sequences seem to hold for other sentences which contain a sequence of words within one phrase. When a group of 30 learning disabled adolescents were asked to repeat two sentences with adjective sequences, their repetition errors also indicated omissions and reversals of the elements in the sequence (Wiig & Roach, 1975). The sentence, "She has bought five large brown leather cases," was repeated by 12 of the adolescents with omission of one or more of the adjectives. Four changed the sequence of the adjectives to "five *brown large* leather cases" and one substituted the adjective "big" for the adjective "large."

The sentence "She has washed plastic red small eight cups," in which the usual order of the adjectives was violated, caused similar problems. Eleven of the adolescents changed the adjective sequence, but only one of them normalized the sequence to "eight small red plastic cups." Nine omitted from three to six words in the sentence. In comparison, their academically achieving peers tended to normalize the sequence of the adjectives, and only four omitted words from the sequence.

Clearly, some learning disabled children and adolescents have more difficulty remembering what they have heard and repeating it than do their academically achieving peers. Their short-term auditory memory problems do not only affect the ability to repeat sentences, a task that you are rarely called upon to perform in real life. They also affect the ability to remember and follow spoken directions accurately and to rehearse and recall details and sequences of information accurately. As a result, some learning disabled children may leave out words, phrases, or clauses in spoken directions. If the child were asked to "feed the dog, put out the cat, take off your boots, don't touch the stove if it is hot, and make yourself a tuna fish sandwich," he may omit the direction to put out the cat and take off his boots. Other learning disabled children may substitute word opposites or associated words in spoken directions. They may respond to the direction to "feed the dog, put out the cat, take off your boots, don't touch the stove if it is hot, and make yourself a tuna fish sandwich" by feeding the cat, putting out the dog, and making a peanut butter and jelly sandwich. Their problems in recalling spoken directions may result in confusion and frustration, as shown in Figure 10.1.

**FIGURE 10.1**
*Following Directions*

Spoken directions may involve a sequence of actions that has to be followed in exact order to arrive at a logical goal. Take, for example, recipes and lab assignments, directions for arts and crafts assignments, or directions for travelling. In all of these it is imperative to follow the directions in the sequence in which they were presented or according to the sequence indicated by terms such as "before" and "after." Some learning disabled children may not retain the sequence given in oral directions for critical actions. Others may not interpret the spatial or temporal sequential terms correctly. On hearing a direction such as the one featured in Figure 10.2, they may go left when the direction says right, confusing spatial terms. They may confuse first and last, indicating problems with words that indicate serial order. In addition, they may leave out parts of the direction, substitute words, and change the sequence.

*For a discussion of problems with understanding spatial, temporal, or linguistic concepts, see pages 167–73; assessment and intervention for these problems are discussed on pages 217–23, 244–52, and 269–75.*

It is important in differential diagnosis to determine the basis for a child's problems in following oral directions and to determine how accurate recall can be facilitated. Some children may be able to remember and follow directions accurately if they are allowed to immediately repeat them out loud. Other children may need to write the directions down or to jot down the key words. Yet others may need to read the directions while they listen to them. In some cases, pretend acting out or gesturing of actions by the child is a good idea.

**FIGURE 10.2**

*Directions with Spatial, Sequential Concepts*

Spoken directions, statements, or questions often contain details of place, time, quantity, proper names, and other specifics. Some learning disabled children find it especially hard to remember people's names. Some may not remember numbers for dates, prices, distances, speeds, and other measurements. Some may have problems in remembering letters when they need to, and others may show combinations of all these problems.

In real life, spoken directions and information often contain extraneous words, such as "what I mean is actually," "the real point is that," and "when all is said and done," to mention only a few examples. Learning disabled children may have problems discerning the important elements in spoken directions and information when they are embedded in lots of extra words. If this is the case, if may be necessary to design an intervention program to assist the child to learn to separate significant from unessential information and extraneous verbiage. The next section of the chapter describes formats available to assess the specific memory problems experienced by an individual child.

## TASK FORMATS FOR ASSESSMENT

### Number Sequences

The most commonly used format for evaluating immediate auditory memory span requires the child to repeat a digit series. In this format, the examiner says a random sequence of digits which varies in length. The sequence must be retained, recalled, and repeated immediately by the child either exactly as the examiner said it or in the reverse order of presentation.

The number of digits which can be retained and repeated in forward order increases consistently with age throughout childhood. Normative data suggest the following relationship between chronological age and the mean number of digits which can be recalled in the order of presentation (Terman & Merrill, 1960).

| Chronological Age | Mean Number of Digits Forward |
|---|---|
| 2½ yrs. | 2 |
| 3    yrs. | 3 |
| 4½ yrs. | 4 |
| 7    yrs. | 5 |
| 10    yrs. | 6 |
| Adult | 7 |

Formal tests designed to assess forward digit recall use digit sequences which range in length from two to eight or nine digits. This range accounts for normal developmental increases in immediate memory span over a wide age range. It also allows for an account of individual differences and deficits.

Digit series in currently standardized tests are composed so that either (1) no digit is repeated in a specific digit sequence or (2) digits may be repeated in a specific sequence. Digit series in which digits are not repeated in an item are generally featured in comprehensive tests for cognitive abilities and intelligence (McCarthy, 1970; Terman & Merrill, 1960; Wechsler, 1974). Digit series in which digits are repeated are featured in one widely used clinical-educational test, the Illinois Test of Psycholinguistic Ability (ITPA) (Kirk, McCarthy, & Kirk, 1968). This design facilitates the immediate recall of digit series on a relative scale. Often an individual child will have variable performances on items with digit sequences of identical length. The two items below illustrate this design of test items.

**Item 20.**    3–6–1–9–2–7–7

**Item 21.**    5–3–6–9–7–8–2

The rate of presentation of the spoken digits also varies in different tests. The most frequently stipulated rate of presentation is one digit per second. This rate is generally stipulated in comprehensive tests of cognitive abilities and intelligence (McCarthy, 1970; Terman & Merrill, 1960; Wechsler, 1974). The rate of presentation differs in one notable instance, in the ITPA (Kirk, McCarthy & Kirk, 1968). The ITPA Auditory Sequential Memory subtest stipulates that digits are to be spoken at the rate of two digits per second, or at twice the usual rate. The authors suggest that this higher rate is more sensitive in identifying children's auditory memory span deficits. In the same vein, Aten and Davis (1968) observed that digit spans obtained with a rate of presentation of one digit per second did not differentiate learning disabled children from matched controls.

As we have seen, memory span tests may feature digit series which are to be recalled in the order of presentation (forward) only (Kirk, McCarthy, & Kirk, 1968). They may also feature digit series which are to be recalled and repeated in the reverse order of presentation (backward) (McCarthy, 1970; Terman & Merrill, 1960; Wechsler, 1974). When asked to repeat a digit series backwards, the child must use some active strategy to help him recall the digits. There are at least two strategies that can be used. In one, the child retains and reverses the sequence of the digits by continuous internal auditory rehearsal. That is, he rehearses the digit series over and over again in the original order of presentation. Each time, he recites or calls off the last digit in the rehearsal. With this method of recall, there are noticeable pauses between each digit recitation. Because of its relative slowness, it is an inefficient strategy. If the child who uses it has deficits in immediate sequential memory and internal auditory rehearsal, they will show up.

An alternative strategy involves recoding the spoken digits into an equivalent internal perceptual (visual) unit, which may be retained in the original order of presentation. With this pictured "number line," the child can read off the digits in the reverse order of presentation. This strategy appears to allow both fluent and rapid backwards recitation of a digit series.

The contrast between the memory abilities tapped by digits forward and digits backward recall have been discussed by, among others, Glasser and Zimmerman (1967). They consider the digits forward series to measure a "more passive auditory immediate recall," while digits backward series are considered examples of "more active auditory recall items" (p. 99). These authors also caution that performances on digit series recall can reflect the child's concentration, attention, and anxiety about being tested. The diagnostic value of digit span recall subtests seems to come from the potential to identify discrepancies between digit forward and backward memory. If the child shows a wide discrepancy (more than two digits) between the two, in favor of digits forward recall, he may be thinking only concretely. He may have limitations in the ability to shift his response set and to perform the mental abstractions necessary to perform the digit reversal. Furthermore, deficits in rote memory may indicate organic as well as functional disorganization.

Memory span for digits has in some instances been reported to correlate *poorly* with measures of intelligence and learning. Cohen (1959) reported that factor analysis indicates that digit span tests such as the WISC Digit Span subtest (Wechsler, 1949) do not measure general intelligence or memory or freedom from distractibility. Cronbach (1970) stressed this limitation in the statement that "Digit span has low correlations with other parts of the Wechsler, with school marks, and with other learning measures" (p. 294). In contrast, Whimby and Fischhof (1969) and Whimby and Ryan (1969) reported direct relationships among poor digit memory span and poor mental addition and logical problem-solving abilities in college students.

A second format for assessing immediate auditory memory span requires the child to repeat sequences of unrelated words (Baker & Leland 1967; McCarthy, 1970). This task has been observed to differentiate learning disabled and academically achieving children (Aten & Davis, 1968). The length of the word series used may range from two to eight words. The words used in current tests are both monosyllables and polysyllables. The items below illustrate the format and contents of unrelated word series of increasing length (McCarthy, 1970).

**Item 1.**     Toy  –  Chair  –  Light
**Item 3.**     After  –  Color  –  Funny  –  Today

The requirements of digit recall and word recall tests differ in one essential aspect. In all digit recall tests, forward or backward, the child must recall the order of presentation of the digits to receive any points for an item. Transpositions of digits are scored as failures. In current word recall tests, the order of presentation of the words need not be perfect for the child to obtain any score for the item. The responses are scored to reflect the number of words recalled, regardless of sequence. In one test, one point is subtracted from the total score for an item if the sequence has been altered (McCarthy, 1970).

Clinical observations suggest that regrouping the individual words may facilitate the recall of a series of unrelated words. This reorganization can result in word repetitions in which closely or loosely associated words are recalled together. For example, many children repeat the items above as follows:

**Item 1.**     (repetition)     Light  –  Toy  –  Chair
**Item 3.**     (repetition)     After  –  Today  –  Funny  –  Color

Some children seem to spontaneously use an alternative strategy. These youngsters form mental images of either the individual word meanings or of interactions among the word meanings. Taking Item 1 above, they may form an image of a toy on a chair with a light shining on it. This has been used in paired associate learning (Paivio, 1971). For example, people learned the word pair "shark-crib" relatively faster when they were instructed to form an interactive mental image of the word meanings. They may have visualized a shark in a crib or a shark in the process of eating a crib.

To gain qualitative information about the strategies a child has available for word recall, you must record the responses verbatim. Analysis of the sequence in which words are repeated in a given item may suggest whether the child is using active regrouping of words as a strategy. Extension testing may be needed to find out if telling the child to form interactive mental images among the word meanings would result in improved recall.

**Oral Directions**

The formats used in current tests of the recall of oral directions are generally variants of the formats used to tap auditory retention span.

The basic purpose of these tests is to evaluate the number, size, and complexity of the units of directions for actions which the child can retain and recall. Oral directions may be analyzed to reflect the number of actions to be executed. This analysis results in determining the level of the commands. Oral directions which contain only one request for action are called *one-level commands*. If two actions are required, the oral direction is said to contain a *two-level command*. The oral directions below illustrates a one-level command for action (Semel & Wiig, 1980).

**Item 1.**    Point to the last circle.

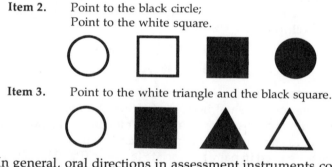

In this oral direction, the words "last circle" identify the object of the action. They form a perceptual-conceptual unit. Since this unit contains two elements, one word which defines shape and one which defines an attribute of the shape, it is called a *chunk*. Oral directions may be expanded in actual word length by adding units or chunks. When units or chunks are added, they may be connected by compounding with the word "and." They may also be added by repeating the action and defining a new object of the action. The oral directions below illustrate the two possible ways to add units and chunks (Semel & Wiig, 1980).

**Item 2.**    Point to the black circle;
                       Point to the white square.

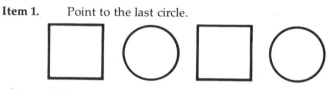

**Item 3.**    Point to the white triangle and the black square.

In general, oral directions in assessment instruments contain up to more than five units of action (Baker & Leland, 1967). Expansion by adding units or chunks of equal size will tap memory capacity or retention span. Oral directions may also be increased in difficulty by adding words to individual units and thereby increasing the size of chunks. Expansion by increasing the size of the chunks taps memory efficiency, the ability to synthesize words into perceptual-conceptual units. The oral directions below illustrate an increase in item difficulty resulting from adding a modifier (adjective) to each unit and increasing the size of the chunks (Semel & Wiig, 1980).

**Item 3.**    Point to the white triangle and the black square.

**Item 11.**    Point to the big black triangle and the first white square.

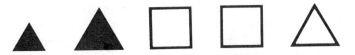

The oral directions featured in different formal tests may be associated with a variety of visual displays and/or actions. One formal test, the Token Test (DeRenzi & Vignolo, 1962), uses a set of tokens as objects for an action of identification defined by the verb "take . . . ." The oral directions featured in another test, the Detroit Tests of Learning Aptitude (DTLA) (Baker & Leland, 1967), require several different actions from item to item and within items. They also feature a variety of visual displays for the execution of the actions.

The actions required in the DTLA differ from items on other tests in one clinically important dimension. In some items, the actions require the child to identify visual-graphic stimuli by either underlining or crossing out. Other items require the child to form and produce forms and symbols. In the first instance, the listener can identify the visual stimuli to be acted upon while he hears the directions. In the second instance, the listener must turn the directions into internal perceptual (visual) units and reproduce the result in visual-graphic forms.

The sequence of actions in response to oral directions is generally not considered critical. In this respect, the task requirements differ from those for digit recall items, in which the order of presentation must be retained. In the same way, this task requirement in formal tests is different from everyday commands and directions. Oral directions and commands given in the home, the classroom, or in social and work settings may allow no flexibility in order of execution. The order of recall and execution may indeed be crucial to success. Consider as examples such everyday directions as:

> Turn to page 47 and find the second paragraph. I want you to copy it in your workbooks and underline all the words which contain consonant blends.

> When you get to the next corner turn right. Go to the second light and turn left. Go five blocks and you'll see the school on the right hand side.

There are several strategies that may be used in completing the oral directions featured in formal tests. If the oral directions request the child to identify one or more tokens, shapes, digits, letters, or other visual-graphic stimuli, the efficient listener may identify the objects by looking at them as they are mentioned. When the oral direction has been completed, the child can then use visual memory in pointing to or taking specific objects.

If the oral directions require active recoding, the task is harder. Active recoding is required when the oral directions tell the listener to write specific visual-graphic symbols in assigned spaces. For example, an oral direction may request the listener to write "a six in the diamond, the letter L in the first circle, a number four in the triangle." In that case, the most efficient strategy seems to be to transform the verbal messages into an internal perceptual (visual) code as they are spoken. Subsequently, the child can follow his internal perceptual representations in completing the task. It is also possible, though less efficient, to complete the oral direction above by internal auditory rehearsal. Internal auditory rehearsal may not be an effective strategy, however, if the oral directions contain requests for computations or manipulations of automatic series. For example, an oral direction may ask the listener to "cross out the number that is three times five; cross out every number that is five times four; cross out the largest number." In that case, internal auditory rehearsal may interfere with the ability to calculate the two products. Active recoding of the verbal messages into internal perceptual (visual) representations appears to be the only truly efficient strategy in recalling this kind of oral direction.

As a result, in assessment the task requirements of each oral direction featured in a formal test must be considered. This can give you some insight into the quality of the memory strategies a listener is using. It will also allow you to identify his limitations in memory strategies.

Extension testing may be used to identify the variables that facilitate recall of oral directions. It may assess whether using labels for everyday objects will help the child form chunks. For example, the oral directions featured in the Clinical Evaluation of Language Functions (Semel & Wiig, 1980) may be adapted to use pictured or real objects instead of geometric designs. The items below illustrate how an item is adapted.

**Item 3.**     Point to the white triangle and the black square.

**Item 3.**     Adapted with pictured objects.     Point to the white car and the black shoe.

Oral directions may also be adapted by reducing the number of chunks or units to find the point when the number of units tax the child's memory capacity. As an example, a five-level oral command may be broken down into five separate commands. First you test the child's interpretation and recall of each of the five commands. Then the individual units would be combined at random to form two-, three-, four-, and five-level commands. Each level command would be tested to find the point of breakdown. Here is an oral direction (Baker & Leland, 1967) and possible adaptations.

**Item 16.**     Put the third letter of the alphabet in the third figure, a six in the diamond, the letter *L* in the first circle, a number four in the triangle, and the first letter of the alphabet in the last figure. Do it now!

### Two-level commands

(1) Put a six in the diamond, and a number four in the triangle.

(2) Put the letter *L* in the first circle, and the third letter of the alphabet in the third figure.

(3) Put the first letter of the alphabet in the last figure, and a number four in the triangle.

### Three-level commands

(1) Put a six in the diamond, a number four in the triangle, and the letter *L* in the first circle.

(2) Put the third letter of the alphabet in the third figure, a six in the diamond, and the first letter of the alphabet in the last figure.

(3) Put a number four in the triangle, the first letter of the alphabet in the last figure, and the letter *L* in the first circle.

### Four-level commands

(1) Put a six in the diamond, a number four in the triangle, the letter *L* in the first circle, and the third letter of the alphabet in the third figure.

(2) Put the first letter of the alphabet in the last figure, a number four in the triangle, the third letter of the alphabet in the third figure, and a six in the diamond.

(3) Put the third letter of the alphabet in the third figure, a six in the diamond, the letter *L* in the first circle, and a number four in the triangle.

## Details in Spoken Paragraphs

When we listen to a story, a lecture, or a discourse, we retain only the meaning or deep structure of sentences, paragraphs, and larger units. We can perhaps retain the meaning of even relatively long lectures or discourses for extended periods of time if the content has immediate relevance. If it is episodic and of little relevance, on the other hand, we may forget what was said almost immediately.

Significant details such as proper names, place names, or dates which are embedded in sentences and paragraphs may also be retained and recalled verbatim for relatively long periods of time. These details must, however, be either repeated several times or rehearsed internally or overtly to allow transfer to long-term memory. Some details may be so episodic or of so little relevance that they are not even identified consciously or considered worthy of rehearsal and storage.

Unfortunately, children and adolescents in school settings are rarely asked if the details they have to remember for later examinations are of any relevance to them. They are expected to recall episodic information every day. They must recall details such as proper names, place names, dates, and other numerical details in a variety of subject areas such as history, social sciences, and physical sciences. It is therefore relevant for the clinician-educator to evaluate the youngster's ability to recall ideas, events, relationships, and specific details in spoken materials such as stories and paragraphs.

The recall of information presented in spoken paragraphs is featured in formal tests of reading abilities and deficits such as the Durrell Analysis of Reading Difficulty (Durrell, 1955). The purpose of evaluating listening skills in a reading assessment is to compare the child's relative levels of performance in comprehending and in recalling details in spoken and read paragraphs. The paragraphs presented for listening comprehension are graded. While the number of sentences may remain the same from paragraph to paragraph, the length and complexity of the sentences tend to increase with grade level. In the same vein, the nature of the details to be recalled changes as a function of grade level. At early grade levels, the paragraphs tend to feature details, events, and relationships that are within the child's range of experiences. At higher grade levels, the events and details may not be related to the youngster's experiences. The emphasis in the recall of these paragraphs may be on names, places, and dates and other numerical details. Spoken paragraphs with similar changes in the level of complexity of structure and detail are featured in formal tests of acquired language disorders in adults (Eisenson, 1954; Schuell, 1965). They are not generally featured in standardized tests of children's language abilities.

Spoken paragraphs presented to assess the recall of events, relationships, and specific details may identify a variety of deficits in listening and recall. The accurate recall of specific information in short spoken paragraphs which have been designed to match the child's syntactic and semantic development may give evidence of the child's ability to:

(1) Sustain auditory attention for the length of the presentation.
(2) Focus attention selectively and identify relevant ideas, events, relationships, or person, place, or time references.
(3) Recall and retrieve specific information after short time delays.

The primary bases of deficits in the recall of information presented in spoken paragraphs cannot be interpreted without corroborating evidence from other language tasks. The clinician-educator should consider the child's relative levels of functioning in other language areas, such as knowledge of word meaning, morphology, and syntax, and immediate recall of words and sentences.

Extension testing may be indicated to identify the specific nature of the information or details as well as the number and combinations of details which present difficulties. To obtain this evidence, paragraphs may be designed or adapted from existing materials. Spoken paragraphs used for extension testing may include the following:

(1) Proper and place names may be featured as the only details to be recalled. Graded paragraphs may be constructed which feature first one, then two, three, and/or four names of persons and places.
(2) Dates may be featured as the only details to be recalled. Graded paragraphs may be constructed which contain first one, then two, three, and four dates for years and days of the months.
(3) Numerical data may be featured as the only details to be recalled. Graded paragraphs may be constructed which contain from one to four numerical facts such as prices, measures of distance, speed, height, weight, and volume, and/or combinations of these.
(4) Combinations of names, dates, and numerical data may be featured for recall.

Selected, standardized tests for the recall of information presented in spoken paragraphs are reviewed and discussed below.

# TESTS OF RETENTION OF SPOKEN MESSAGES

This section describes currently available standardized tests that assess a child's ability to retain spoken messages. Tables 10.2, 10.3, and 10.4 at the end of the section summarize this information.

## Number Sequences

*McCarthy Scales of Children's Abilities: Numerical Memory*

The Numerical Memory subtest of the McCarthy Scales of Children's Abilities (McCarthy, 1970) is designed to assess the child's ability to recall and repeat digit series forward and backward. This subtest is one of four which comprise the Memory Scale. The subtest is also considered a part of the Quantitative Scale, the remaining subtests being Number Questions and Counting and Sorting.

The subtest contains six-digit sequences (Part I) designed to evaluate the immediate recall of series forward. The sequences increase in length from two to seven digits. Part II of the subtest features five-digit sequences for backward recall. An alternative digit series is provided for all subtest items. These are to be used if the first trial is either invalidated or failed by the child.

The digit series were designed so that digits are not repeated within a sequence. The manual stipulates that the digits are to be spoken at a rate of one digit per second.

The McCarthy Scales of Children's Abilities were standardized on a sample of 1032 children, ranging in age from 2 years, 6 months to 8 years, 6 months. The sample was distributed evenly within 10 age groups at 6-month age intervals. The standardization sample was selected to match the demographic characteristics of the general population closely based on the 1970 U. S. Bureau of the Census, Census of Population. Test-retest reliability for the six scales (Verbal, Perceptual-Performance, Quantitative, General Cognitive, Memory, Motor) was established for a sample of 125 children, tested with a 1-month interval. The reliability coefficients for the Memory Scale ranged from .77 at 3 to 3½ years to .83 at 7½ to 8½ years. Intercorrelations between Memory and Verbal Scale Indices averaged .80 for the 10 age levels in the standardization sample. Normative data for 25 age levels are reported in the form of Scale Index Equivalents of the raw score totals for each of the scales.

Among the assets of the subtest are:

(1) The standardization and norms are recent.
(2) The standardization is demographically representative, which permits generalization of the norms to a wide range of children.
(3) The directions for administration and the criteria for scoring are clear.

The limitations of the test relate to the following aspects:

(1) Normative data for the 25 age levels are not available for individual subtests.

(2) Test-retest reliability measures are not provided for individual sub-tests.

(3) The Numerical Memory subtest should be administered in conjunction with the remaining subtests of the Memory Scale to provide a valid index of the child's memory capacities.

(4) The age range for which the subtest is appropriate is relatively limited.

### *Wechsler Intelligence Scale for Children–Revised (WISC-R): Digit Span*

The Digit Span subtest of the WISC-R (Wechsler, 1974) evaluates the immediate memory for digit series forward and backward. The subtest contains two parts. Part I requires retention, recall, and repetition of digit series of increasing length in the order of presentation (forward). Part II requires reversal of spoken digit series of increasing length and repetition. Each part includes seven items. An alternate digit series is provided for each item. The alternate series are to be used if a series is either failed or invalidated.

The digit forward series (Part I) contains seven items which range in length from three to nine digits. The digit backward series (Part II) contains seven items which range in length from two to eight digits. All items are to be spoken by the examiner at a rate of one digit per second. The digit series are designed so that digits are never repeated within a series.

The WISC-R was standardized on a sample of 2200 children distributed evenly in 11 age groups, ranging from 6 years, 6 months to 16 years, 6 months. The demographic characteristics of the standardization sample closely matched reports of the 1970 Census of Population. Normative data are presented in the form of Scaled Scores for each of the 11 age levels sampled. In addition, IQ equivalents are presented for the sum of the scaled scores on the Verbal, Performance, and Full-Scale. Test-retest reliability coefficients are presented for this subtest. For the digit span subtest, the coefficients range from .71 at 10½ years to .84 at 7½, with an average of .78 for all age levels.

The WISC-R Digit Span subtest uses a recent standardization and norms and a demographically representative standardization sample. These factors permit the clinician-educator to generalize the norms to a wide range of children. In addition, the subtest is applicable for a relatively wide age range. The subtest may provide a rapid measure of auditory memory span and attention. It may also provide clinical insight into the strategies available for immediate recall and active recoding of auditory verbal stimuli.

However, this test is within the domain of the psychologist. Its administration and interpretation presuppose extensive training.

### *Illinois Test of Psycholinguistic Ability (ITPA): Auditory Sequential Memory*

The Auditory Sequential Memory subtest of the ITPA (Kirk, McCarthy, & Kirk, 1968) evaluates the child's ability to recall and repeat digit series forward. The subtest contains 28 digit series. They range in length from two to eight digits. The distribution of the items according to digit length is as follows:

(1) Two items feature two-digit sequences.
(2) Three items feature three-digit sequences.
(3) Four items feature four-digit sequences.
(4) Five items each feature five-, six-, and seven-digit sequences.
(5) Four items feature eight-digit sequences.

The digit series are to be spoken by the examiner at a rate of two digits per second. This relatively fast rate compared to other digit span tests is considered to be sensitive to immediate auditory memory deficits. The child is required to retain, recall, and repeat the spoken digits in the exact order of presentation. Digits may occur more than once in a series.

The ITPA was standardized on a sample of 962 children in the age range from 2 to 10 years. All children resided in suburban towns in Illinois and Wisconsin. The racial-ethnic characteristics of the children are not described, but it is implied that the children came from middle-class backgrounds. Normative data for the Auditory Sequential Memory subtest are available in the age range from 2 years, 0 months to 10 years, 3 months. Raw scores are converted to Age Scores and Scaled Scores. Five-months test-retest reliability coefficients range from .75 to .89 with an increase in stability as a function of age. Split-half correlation coefficients, indicating the internal consistency of the items, range from .74 to .95 and increase with age.

Performances are considered to indicate the number of unrelated units which the child can retain for immediate sequential recall and repetition. Sequencing difficulties may be indicated by digit reversals and transpositions. However, performances on this subtest cannot be translated directly to predict performances on measures of immediate sentence recall (McCarthy & McCarthy, 1969).

Among the assets of this test are the reported sensitivity of the items and rate of presentation to immediate auditory sequential deficits and the relatively wide age range for which the subtest is appropriate. These assets are offset by liabilities in the standardization. Among the specific limitations are (1) the demographic biases of the standardization sample, which limit generalizations of the norms to racial-ethnic minorities and to children who are not from middle class backgrounds, and (2) the inadequacy of the stability of performances for the younger age levels for which norms are provided.

**Word Sequences**

*McCarthy Scales of Children's Abilities: Verbal Memory Part I*

The Verbal Memory subtest, Part I, of the McCarthy Scales of Children's Abilities (McCarthy, 1970) features word series and sentences designed to assess the immediate recall of unrelated and structurally related words. It is one of four subtests which comprise the Memory Scale. The remaining subtests of this scale are Pictorial Memory, Tapping Sequence, and Numerical Memory. Since a child's score on the Verbal Memory subtest has been found to relate directly to his overall verbal skills, the subtest is also included in the Verbal Scale of the test.

Part I of the Verbal Memory subtest contains six graded items, four of which evaluate the immediate recall of unrelated word series. The other two items evaluate the immediate recall of words embedded in the structure of a sentence. Of the four unrelated word series, two contain the labels for three concrete concepts. These items are:

**Item 1.**     Toy  –  Chair  –  Light
**Item 2.**     Doll  –  Dark  –  Coat

Two items feature two-syllable words with more abstract meanings. These items are:

**Item 3.**     After  –  Color  –  Funny  –  Today
**Item 4.**     Around  –  Because  –  Under  –  Never

The last two items are sentences. Each sentence contains 14 words. The examiner says each of the featured word series and sentences. The child is required to repeat each item. The repetitions of the word series are scored to reflect the number of words recalled and repeated. A point is subtracted if the sequence of the words is altered.

The McCarthy Scales of Children's Abilities were standardized on a sample of 1032 children, ranging in age from 2 years, 6 months to 8 years, 6 months. The sample was distributed evenly within 10 age groups at 6-month intervals. The standardization sample was selected to match the demographic characteristics of the general population, closely based on the 1970 Census of Population. Test-retest reliability for each of the six scales (Verbal, Perceptual-Performance, Quantitative, General Cognitive, Memory, Motor) was established for a sample of 125 children tested with a 1-month interval. The reliability coefficients for the Memory Scale range from .77 at 3 to 3½ years to .83 at 7 to 7½ years. For the Verbal Scale, they ranged from .89 to .82 for the same age levels, indicating a decrease in stability with age. Normative data in the form of Scale Index Equivalents of raw scores are available for each of the scales. Norms are reported for 25 age levels at 3-month intervals in the age range from 2½ to 8½ years.

For the assets and liabilities of the subtest, see pages 301–2. In addition, the subtest should be administered in conjunction with the remaining subtests of both the Memory and the Verbal Scales to provide a valid measure of the child's memory capacities and verbal abilities.

*Detroit Test of Learning Aptitude (DTLA): Auditory Attention Span for Unrelated Words*

The Auditory Attention Span for Unrelated Words subtest of the DTLA (Baker & Leland, 1967) evaluates the short-term auditory memory span for unrelated words. The subtest contains 14 word series which increase in length from two to eight words. The words featured in the items are primarily nouns which label persons, animals, objects, and directions. The word series below illustrate the format and contents of the items.

**Item 5a.**     Head   Milk   Dress   Oats   Night
**Item 5b.**     Pipe   West   Fence   Coat   Mule

The DTLA was standardized on a sample of 150 children at each age level in the range from 3 years, 0 months to 19 years, 0 months. All children in the sample attended the Detroit Public Schools. The test-retest reliability coefficient for a sample of 48 children tested with an interval of 5 months was .96, indicating high stability over short time intervals. A second correlation coefficient of .68 was reported for a group of 792 children in the age range from 7 to 10 years, tested with a 2- to 3-year time interval. Normative data in the form of age level equivalents (Mental Age) are reported for the age range between 3 years, 0 months to 19 years, 0 months.

Observations indicate that the performances on this subtest will not directly indicate performances on the DTLA subtest for sentence recall. Johnson and Myklebust (1967) comment that language and learning disabled children may perform better on the word series than on the sentence recall subtest of the DTLA. McCarthy and McCarthy (1969) report observations of the opposite relationship between the performances. Their observations suggest that the meaning and structure of sentences may facilitate the immediate recall.

Among the assets of this DTLA subtest are the wide age range for which the test is applicable and the adequacy of the total test scores over short time intervals. These assets are offset by significant limitations, including the following:

(1) The sample used for standardization has strong geographical and residential biases. This factor limits the generalization of the norms.
(2) The lack of specification of the racial-ethnic and socioeconomic backgrounds of the children in the standardization sample further limits generalizations of norms.
(3) The normative data are dated, suggesting further caution in interpreting the norms.

## Oral Directions

*Detroit Tests of Learning Aptitude (DTLA): Oral Directions*

The Oral Directions subtest of the DTLA (Baker & Leland, 1967) is designed to evaluate the youngster's ability to retain, recall, and execute a series of actions in response to oral commands. The oral directions require the child to identify and/or produce selected visual-graphic stimuli and symbols. The subtest contains 17 oral directions, each associated with a visual-graphic stimulus display. The visual displays associated with the items are arranged in horizontal arrays on an 8 x 11 page. The oral directions are grouped in four sections, with increasing time allowed for the child to complete the actions required.

The first six oral directions are to be completed by the youngster within 10 seconds each. The six directions range in length from 13 to 23 words. The directions are sequential two- and three-level commands in which the order of presentation corresponds to the left-right orientation of the visual displays. The following item illustrates the format.

**Item 4.**     See the three circles. Put a number two in the first circle, a cross in the second circle, and draw a line under the third circle. Do it now!

The next three oral directions are to be completed within 15 seconds each. These directions are all three-level commands. Two items feature directions for sequential left-to-right commands. Two items feature directions for sequential left-to-right actions. In one, the order of presentation of the auditory and visual-graphic stimuli do not match. The following item illustrates the commands. It is associated with a display of the alphabet from A to Q.

**Item 9.**     Draw a line under the letter *F*. Cross out the letter *K*, and draw a line above *Q*. Do it now!

The next three items are given a time allowance of 20 seconds each. One is a three-level command which requires active numerical computation for the completion. Two items are four-level commands. Item 10 illustrates the computational requirements in one of the commands.

**Item 10.**    Cross out the number that is three times five; cross out every number that is in the thirties;. and cross out the largest number. Do it now!

The child is allowed 30 seconds to complete each of the last five items. Of the items, two are three-level and three are five-level commands. In all five items, active computation or recoding is required. In addition, four of the items feature a mismatch in the auditory-sequential and the visual left-to-right orientation of stimuli. The item below illustrates how complex the last items are.

**Item 16.**    Put the third letter of the alphabet in the third figure; a six in the diamond; the letter *L* in the first circle; a number four in the triangle; and the first letter of the alphabet in the last figure. Do it now!

The DTLA was standardized on a sample of 150 children at each age level in the range from 3 years, 0 months to 19 years, 0 months. All children attended the Detroit Public Schools. A test-retest reliability coefficient of .96 was reported for a sample of 48 children tested with a 5-month time interval. A second correlation coefficient of .68 was reported for a sample of 792 students in the age range from 7 to 10 years tested with a 2-year time interval. Normative data in the form of age level equivalents (Mental Age) are reported for the age range from 3 years, 0 months to 19 years, 0 months.

The DTLA Oral Directions subtest has the following advantages:

(1) The items are clinically sensitive to immediate auditory memory deficits and problems in recoding, internal imagery, and concurrent reconstruction of information.
(2) The items allow item analysis and extension testing with adaptation of the visual stimulus displays so that one display is presented at a time.

These qualities of the subtest are offset by the limitations in the sample used, which affect the interpretation and generalization of the norms.

*Token Test Parts I–IV*

The Token Test (DeRenzi & Vignolo, 1962) is designed to assess receptive language skills in adults with acquired aphasia. The test design measures the ability to retain, recall, and execute a set of oral directions with minimal redundancy and of increasing length and complexity. The test contains five parts. In the first four parts (Parts I-IV), one- and two-level commands are presented for immediate action. In the last part (Part V), the oral directions feature spatial, temporal, and conditional linguistic concepts and complex syntactic structures.

*See pages 220–21.*

The oral directions featured in the Token Test are executed by either identifying or manipulating one or more of a set of 20 tokens. The tokens are circles and rectangles which vary in size (large/small) and/or color (red/blue/green/yellow/white).

Part I of the Token Test features 10 oral commands which define the action ("Pick up . . .") and the object of the action. The object is defined by a modifier, a color label, and a noun ("circle" or "rectangle"). An example of an item is:

Pick up the yellow rectangle.

In Part II, the length of the oral directions has been increased by adding a second modifier for size ("large" or "small"). Ten oral commands are presented in which the object of the action ("Pick up . . .") is defined by two modifiers (color and size) and a noun ("circle" or "rectangle"). An example of an item is:

Pick up the large blue circle.

Part III features 10 oral commands, all two-level. Each command defines two different tokens. Only large size tokens are presented. The objects of each action ("Take . . .") are defined by a modifier, a color label, and a noun. The item below illustrates the 10 oral directions.

Take the red circle and the green rectangle.

Part IV contains 10 two-level commands expanded in length by adding modifiers for size ("large" or "small"). The objects of each action ("Take . . .") are defined by each two modifiers (color and size) and one noun. The item below illustrates the format.

Take the white large circle and the small green rectangle.

The Token Test has certain unique features and assets. Among these are:

(1) The action-object vocabulary is controlled for contents to highlight the specific concepts, units, and relationships.
(2) Analysis of the error response patterns may help the clinician identify the number and length of units which the subject can retain for immediate recall when contextual and logical cues are reduced.

The assets are somewhat offset by the extremely limited standardization information and by the absence of measures of test-retest reliability. The appropriate administration of the test requires understanding of the tasks and functions of the commands.

*Clinical Evaluation of Language Functions (CELF): Processing Oral Directions*

This subtest of the CELF (Semel & Wiig, 1980), is designed to evaluate the ability to process, interpret, and remember oral commands of increasing length and conceptual difficulty. The subtest taps aspects of language processing related to (1) the immediate recall and execution of spoken directions for action and (2) the interpretation and recall of adjective sequences, serial order, and left-right position.

The subtest contains 25 oral directions, ranging in length from 5 to 18 words. The visual displays associated with the oral commands feature arrays of black or white circles, squares, and/or triangles in two or three different sizes. The number of geometric shapes presented in the visual displays ranges from 5 to 15. The oral commands require pointing responses. The vocabulary used in the oral directions is controlled, containing only the following words: (1) "point to," (2) "circle," "square," "triangle," (3) "black," "white," (4) "small," "smallest," "big," "biggest," (5) "first," "last," "second," "fourth," "fifth," and (6) "to the right of," "to the left of." Analysis of the items for the level and number of adjective modifiers indicates the distribution below.

(1)  Nine of the items are one-level commands (Items 1, 7, 9, 12, 20, 21, 23, 24, 25).
(2)  Ten items are two-level commands (Items 2, 3, 4, 5, 6, 8, 11, 13, 14, 15).
(3)  Six items are three-level commands (Items 10, 16, 17, 18, 19, 22).
(4)  Eleven items contain one adjective modifier for each noun (Items 1, 2, 3, 4, 6, 7, 10, 16, 17, 18, 20).
(5)  Eight items contain two adjective modifiers for each noun (Items 5, 8, 9, 11, 13, 19, 22, 24).
(6)  Six items contain three adjective modifiers for each noun (Items 12, 14, 15, 21, 23, 25).

Table 10.1 shows the level of command, serial order, length of adjective sequences, and left-right orientation.

**TABLE 10.1**

| Level of Command | Number of Adjectives | No. Orientation | | | Serial Order | | | Right-Left Orientation | | |
|---|---|---|---|---|---|---|---|---|---|---|
| | | 1 | 2 | 3 | 1 | 2 | 3 | 1 | 2 | 3 |
| One-level | | — | 9 | — | 1,7 | | 12,21 | 20 | 24 | 23,25 |
| Two-level | | 2,3 | — | — | 4,6 | 5,8 11,13 | 14,15 | — | — | — |
| Three-level | | 16,17 | 19,22 | — | 10,18 | 11 | | — | — | — |

Digit indicates item number.

The test-retest reliability of the subtest was evaluated with 30 randomly selected children ranging in age from 8 years, 3 months to 8 years, 6 months. The children were retested with a 6-week interval between tests. The correlation coefficient obtained was .95, indicating good stability of the performances over time. Concurrent validity was established by comparison with performances on the Token Test, Part

IV. The resulting correlation coefficient was .58. The Clinical Evaluation of Language Functions is a criterion-referenced language test. Criteria raw scores have been established for Grades K through 10.

## Details in Spoken Paragraphs

*McCarthy Scales of Children's Abilities: Verbal Memory Part II*

The Verbal Memory subtest, Part II, of the McCarthy Scales of Children's Abilities (McCarthy, 1970) is designed to assess the recall of essential elements or ideas in a spoken story. The story highlights an event of high probability in everyday life. It describes a boy who helps a woman gather letters which have been scattered by the wind. The story contains eight sentences. They range in length from 7 to 13 words, with a mean length of 10.5 words. The sentences are primarily affirmative active declarative. They contain prepositional phrases, complements, and conjunction of clauses with deletions. One of the sentences features a direct quote.

The examiner reads the story to the child. The child is then asked to retell the story. The recount of the story is scored to reflect whether the child recalled essential relationships, elements, or ideas featured in the story. The story is arbitrarily divided into 11 items to facilitate scoring. Each item recalled receives a score of one if the main idea or event is reproduced according to a specified set of criteria. The criteria for scoring each item and examples of responses are presented in the examiner's manual.

The McCarthy Scales of Children's Abilities were standardized on a sample of 1032 children ranging in age from 2 years, 6 months to 8 years, 6 months. The sample was distributed evenly within 10 age groups at 6-month age intervals. The standardization sample was selected to match the demographic characteristics of the general population closely based on the 1970 Census of Population.

Test-retest reliability coefficients for each of the 6 scales (Verbal, Perceptual-Performance, Quantitative, General Cognitive, Memory, Motor) were established with a sample of 125 children, tested with a 1-month time interval. The reliability coefficients for the Memory Scale, of which this subtest is a part, ranged from .77 at 3 to 3½ years to .83 at 7 to 7½ years. For the Verbal Scale, of which the subtest is also a part, they ranged from .89 to .82 for the same age levels. Normative data in the form of Scale Index Equivalents are reported for each of the scales. Norms are available for 25 age levels at 3-month intervals in the age range from 2½ to 8½ years.

This subtest has several assets, including:

(1) The demographic representativeness of the standardization sample. The sample permits the norms to be generalized to a wide range of children.
(2) The relative recency of the norms.
(3) The fact that story recall is not tapped in a number of current language tests.
(4) The relative clarity of the directions for administration and of the criteria for scoring.

These assets must be considered in relation to limitations. Among these are the facts that:

(1) Normative data are not reported for each individual subtest for each of the 25 age levels.
(2) Test-retest reliability measures are not reported for each subtest.
(3) The subtest should be administered in conjunction with the remaining subtests of both the Memory and the Verbal Scale to obtain a valid measure of the child's relative capacities.
(4) The age range for which the subtest is appropriate is relatively limited.

*Clinical Evaluation of Language Functions: Processing Spoken Paragraphs*

This subtest (Semel & Wiig, 1980) is designed to evaluate the ability to process, interpret and remember details in spoken paragraphs. The subtest taps aspects of language processing related to the recall of details such as proper names and numerical and geographical data.

The subtest contains four paragraphs of increasing length and complexity. Paragraph I contains three sentences, which range in length from six to eight words. Each sentence is an active, affirmative, declarative sentence. The recall of the central figure in the paragraph, a cat, its color, and origin are elicited by three *wh-* questions.

Paragraph II also contains three sentences, ranging in length from 8 to 14 words. One of the sentences features a demonstrative pronoun, "this." Another features a relative clause transformation. The recall of the central object, its trade name, origin, and price are elicited by three *wh-* questions.

Paragraph III contains three sentences, ranging in length from 14 to 17 words. Two of the sentences feature relative clause transformations, one with an embedded clause. The recall of the central object, its origin, trade name, and price are elicited by four *wh-* questions.

Paragraph IV contains three sentences which range in length from 13 to 16 words. The paragraph features numerical data and names of geographical locations in a weather report format. The recall of the date of the report, the weather, and temperatures in different locations, and the weather forecast are elicited by seven *wh-* questions.

The test-retest reliability of the subtest was evaluated with 30 randomly selected children in the age range from 8 years, 3 months to 8 years, 6 months. The children were tested with an interval of 6 weeks between tests. The correlation coefficient obtained for the subtest was .84, indicating adequate stability of performances over time. The concurrent validity was established by comparison with performances on subtests of the ITPA and the Northwestern Syntax Screening Test. The coefficients of correlation obtained were .59 for the ITPA Verbal Expression subtest, .52 for the ITPA Auditory Association subtest, .46 for the ITPA Auditory Sequential Memory subtest, and .57 for the NSST Expressive subtest. Normative data have been established for the lowest 20% of children at each age level as identified by the CELF Screening tests. The Clinical Evaluation of Language Functions is a criterion-referenced language test.

**TABLE 10.2**
*Selected tests for the immediate recall of unrelated units (digits and words)*

| Name | Purpose | Age Range | Stimuli | Responses | Scoring |
|---|---|---|---|---|---|
| McCarthy Scales: Numerical Memory | Evaluates the immediate recall of digit series forward and backward. | 2–6 to 8–6 | (1) 6-digit series for forward recall which range from 2 to 7 digits and (2) 5 series for backward recall which range from 2 to 6 digits. Digits are spoken at a rate of 1 per second. | The child must repeat the series in the forward or reverse order of presentation. | Responses are scored to reflect accuracy in sequential recall. Raw scores are incorporated in the Memory Scale total. Scale Index Equivalents of raw scores are reported for each scale at 3-months age intervals. |
| WISC-R: Digit Span | Evaluates the immediate recall of digit series forward and backward. | 6–0 to 17–0 | (1) 7-digit series for forward recall which range from 3 to 9 digits and (2) 7 series for backward recall ranging from 2 to 8 digits. Digits are spoken 1 per second. | The child must repeat the series in the forward or reverse order of presentation. | Responses are scored to reflect accuracy in sequential recall. Raw scores are converted to Scaled Scores and to MA and IQ. Scores are incorporated in the Verbal-Scale total. |
| ITPA: Auditory Sequential | Evaluates the immediate recall of digit series forward. | 2–0 to 10–3 | 28 digit series which increase in length from 2 to 8 digits. Digits are spoken at a rate of 2 per second. | The child must repeat each digit series, retaining the forward order of presentation. | Responses are scored to reflect accuracy in sequential recall. Raw scores are converted to Age Equivalent and/or Scaled Scores. |
| McCarthy Scales: Part I | Evaluates the immediate recall of unrelated and structurally related words. | 2–6 to 8–6 | (1) Four 3- and 4-word sequences and (2) 2 sequences in which words are embedded in the structure of sentences. | The child must repeat each word sequence and sentence verbatim, retaining the order of presentation. | Responses are scored to reflect the number of words recalled. A point is subtracted for changes in sequence. Raw scores are incorporated in the Memory and the Verbal Scale totals. Raw scores are converted to Scale Index Equivalents. |

**TABLE 10.2 (*Continued*)**

| Name | Purpose | Age Range | Stimuli | Responses | Scoring |
|---|---|---|---|---|---|
| DTLA: Auditory Attention for Unrelated Words | Evaluates the immediate recall of word series of increasing length. | 3–0 to 19–0 | 2 sets of 7 series of unrelated words, increasing in length from 2 to 8 words. The word series are spoken at the rate of 1 word per second. | The youngster must repeat each word series verbatim in the order of presentation. | Responses are scored for the total number of words recalled in each series (simple score) and for the relative number of words recalled in each series (weighted scores). The scores are converted to age level equivalents (Mental Age). |

**TABLE 10.3**

*Selected tests for the recall of oral directions*

| Name | Purpose | Age Range | Stimuli | Responses | Scoring |
|---|---|---|---|---|---|
| Token Test Parts I–IV | Evaluates the retention and recall of oral directions which increase in length and size of units. | Childhood and adulthood | 4 parts each featuring 10 one- or two-level oral commands. The commands require identification of 1 or more colored large or small tokens. | The subject is required to identify the token or tokens defined in each oral direction. | Responses are scored to reflect the accuracy in the execution of each command. Qualitative analysis of the response patterns may suggest the level which results in difficulties in the recall. |
| CELF: Processing Oral Directions | Evaluates the retention and recall of oral directions which increase in length and size of units. | K to 10 | 25 one-, two-, and three-level commands. The commands are executed by identifying colored geometric designs of different sizes. | The child is required to identify the designs defined in each of the oral directions. | Responses are scored to reflect the accuracy in the execution of each command. Criteria scores are given for K to 10. |

**TABLE 10.3** *(Continued)*

| Name | Purpose | Age Range | Stimuli | Responses | Scoring |
|------|---------|-----------|---------|-----------|---------|
| DTLA: Oral Directions | Evaluates the retention, recall, and execution of oral directions which increase in length and size of units. | 6–3 to 19–0 | 17 oral directions of increasing length from 2 to 5 units. Time allowances for items increase from 10 to 30 seconds. The commands are executed by identifying or producing visual-graphic symbols on associated visual displays. | The youngster must complete the directions in each item within the time allowed. The sequence of the actions need not be retained. | Responses are scored for accuracy and speed in the recall and execution. Scores are converted to age level equivalents (Mental Age). |

**TABLE 10.4**

*Selected tests for the recall of details in spoken paragraphs.*

| Name | Purpose | Age Range | Stimuli | Responses | Scoring |
|------|---------|-----------|---------|-----------|---------|
| McCarthy Scales: Verbal Memory Part II | Evaluates the recall of essential elements and ideas in a spoken story. | 2–6 to 8–6 | A paragraph with 8 sentences which tells a simple story. | The child is required to retell the story in his own words. The recount must contain essential relationships, elements, and ideas from the original story. | Responses are scored to reflect whether 11 arbitrary items are reproduced. Raw scores are incorporated in the Verbal and the Memory Scale totals. Scale Index Equivalents are reported at 3-month age intervals. |
| CELF: Processing Spoken Paragraphs | Evaluates retention and recall of details (proper names and numerical data) in spoken paragraphs. | K to 10 | 4 paragraphs with 3 sentences each. Sentences are of increasing length and complexity in details. | The child is required to recall proper names, geographical names, and numerical data in response to a set of *wh-* questions. | Responses are scored to reflect whether the details were recalled verbatim and/or accurately. Criteria scores are given for K to 10. |

# 11 REMEMBERING SPOKEN MESSAGES
## Intervention

## IMPROVING RETENTION AND RECALL

The efficient listener can retain and recall detailed information or directions for a long time after hearing them. He participates actively in the process of listening and of storing the information for later recall. He may rehearse the spoken message by internal reauditorization. He may recode the heard messages into internal images or visual-perceptual representations and use these images in later recall of the information. He may ask the speaker to repeat the message so that he can store it better. He may also ask the speaker to talk more slowly to facilitate storage of the information. The efficiency of transfer of heard messages (verbal information) from immediate memory to long-term memory is known to be influenced by the rate of presentation, internal auditory rehearsal, repetition, and internal recoding, to mention only a few factors.

Language and learning disabled youngsters may have difficulties in retaining and recalling details in spoken messages or in recalling oral directions. They may not be able to rehearse the messages internally by reauditorization. They may be inefficient in recoding spoken language into internal images or representations. They are often reluctant to ask for repetition. They may not even know to ask for a slowed down rate of presentation. Finally, they may not discern what information in spoken messages is significant and what is not. As a result, they may recall irrelevant details and miss the significant information.

In intervention to improve the retention and delayed recall of spoken messages and information, one objective is to facilitate and improve internal rehearsal strategies. A second objective is to facilitate accuracy in focussing on and recalling the significant details or information. A third objective is to strengthen the association between meaning and action in oral commands and directions. These objectives are best met if the content of the verbal messages or oral directions presented in an intervention program is controlled.

**Facilitating Variables for Delayed Recall**

The delayed as well as the immediate recall of spoken (verbal) information may be facilitated by several variables. Some of these can be controlled in intervention; others cannot. Among the facilitating variables are word frequency, associative strength, linguistic structure, logical relationships, length, serial position, intonation, and salience or immediate relevance. Some, if not all, of these variables may and should be controlled in designing intervention materials. And there are other factors to be considered, including the intensity of the attention, the interest in the subject, and the amount of drill or overlearning provided. Some of these facilitating variables will be discussed in more detail below. The discussions focus on those variables which are best controlled in the design and contents of the verbal messages used in intervention.

*Word Frequency*

Word frequency may affect the ease of recall of verbal materials in that high frequency words—commonly used words—tend to be more easily recalled than low frequency words. The relative frequency of words used in intervention materials may be determined and controlled for by consulting word counts and indices of frequency in spoken or written English. Among source materials are reference texts authored by Caroll, Davies, and Richman (1971), Rinsland (1945), and Thorndike and Lorge (1944).

*Association Strength*

The strength of the association between and among words may affect the retention and recall in that sequences with strong association among the critical words are easier to recall than those with weak association. For instance, the word sequence "knife, fork, and spoon" has strong association among the words. The word sequence "dog, car, and apple" has relatively weak association. The relative degree of association strength among words may be determined by consulting free and restricted association norms. These norms have been presented by, among others, Palermo and Jenkins (1964) and Riegel (1965).

*Linguistic Structure*

The surface structure characteristics of statements, questions, and commands (imperatives) is known to influence their immediate retention and recall. It has also been established that form and structure which is not relevant to the meaning of sentences is not retained over time (Sachs, 1967). Changes in the surface structure of sentences appear to go unrecognized if the original and the changed sentences are presented with an interval of more than about 25 to 30 seconds. In contrast, changes in the words used in the sentences seem to be recognized over longer intervals between the original and the changed forms. Changes that affect the meaning of a sentence were recognized consistently with intervals up to about 45 seconds. The relative order of

*See pages 131-52.* difficulty for various syntactic structures and transformations has been discussed in previous sections.

In intervention to facilitate and improve the retention and recall of verbal information, the order of presentation of the various sentence structures and transformations should be controlled. Recall of sentence structure should only be required immediately after the presentation, within a period of no more than 15 to 25 seconds. Recall of semantic details or of sentence meaning may be required with longer delays.

## Semantic-Logical Relationship

The semantic and logical relationships among critical words in sentences and oral commands will influence their immediate as well as the delayed recall. Critical words that are related by semantic class membership tend to be easier to recall than words that are related by spatial (where) or temporal (when) relationships. For instance, it is relatively easier to recall a direction for action that asks you to buy "apples, pears, bananas, and oranges" (fruits) than one that asks you to buy "sour cream, eggs, butter, and crescent rolls" (in the dairy case).

## Length of Sequences

The number of critical elements (words, phrases, or clauses) included in sentences and oral directions will influence the ease of retention and recall. Length or the number of critical elements featured is a determining variable in recalling and repeating both digits or unrelated word sequences. Sentence recall, on the other hand, seems more sensitive to structure than to length. As a result, the educator-clinician must consider structural aspects and length together when designing verbal materials for an intervention program to facilitate and improve retention and recall. When sentence structure is minimal or absent and the critical words or elements have minimal association strength or semantic relationship, length may become a critical consideration. The number of critical words, phrases, clauses, or details featured in sentences or oral directions should be determined both by the maximum number of units (digits or words) and the size of the units or chunks that can be retained.

## Intonational Features

Features of intonation such as phrasing and stress patterns may facilitate or hamper sentence recall. Normal phrasing or phrasal cueing as in the sentence, "The baby/who ate the food/drank the milk," helps children recall. It is also easier to recall digit series such as seven-digit telephone numbers or license plates when the digits are divided into two or more chunks divided by pauses with each group held together by common phrasing: 555/12/12. Sentences, digit sequences, or word series spoken in a monotone without normal phrasing or stress are harder to recall than identical sequences spoken with normal intonation. It follows that phrasal cueing and normal intonation should be used in presenting spoken materials for later recall of meaning or details.

The relative position of words or critical elements in a sentence or word or digit sequence affects recall directly. Final words or critical elements tend to be easier to recall than beginning or initial elements, and the middle elements are the hardest to recall. However, there *are* individual differences in whether the last or the first words or critical elements in a series or sentence are recalled best. In intervention, the serial position of critical elements, words, phrases, or clauses should be considered and controlled. Both the normal pattern of facilitation and the individual child's preference should be considered.

The relevance or immediate value of a word or detail to an individual can be critical in influencing the ease of retention and recall. Words and terms that are immediately relevant and of value to a person tend to be recalled more readily than those that are of lesser value or salience. The relevance or salience of words, details, and sentences is a subjective variable and must therefore be established for each youngster when planning his intervention program. Some items or topics seem to have relatively high salience at some age levels, and the sex of the child is an issue in many cases. To some youngsters, dolls and clothes may be of high salience. To others, cars and mechanical tools may be valued highly. Some youngsters seem to prefer foods. In order to establish the salience of a topic to the youngster, the educator-clinician can ask him about his hobbies and favorite activities or preferences. The content, topic, and vocabulary selected for the intervention materials should reflect the immediate values or preferences of the individual youngster.

## Oral Commands and Directions

Oral commands and oral directions may be used in intervention to facilitate and improve delayed auditory recall. Language and learning disabled youngsters often find it relatively easy to follow oral commands that require gross motor actions and involve body parts. For instance, they may find the command "Raise your hand" relatively easy to follow and execute. The command "Raise the flag" may be harder to follow, even though the object involved—the flag—may be highly familiar. In responding to both gross and fine motor commands, language and learning disabled youngsters may find it difficult to retain certain types of details. They may find it hard to execute commands for actions if the commands contain adjective sequences, prepositional phrases, right-left directions, number facts, or linguistic concepts of time or condition. They may find it relatively easier to respond to commands if the components or steps are separated by pauses or by "and."

Based on clinical observations, the oral commands presented to language and learning disabled youngsters in intervention programs should be carefully sequenced and controlled. First, commands for gross motor actions or actions which involve body parts should be used before commands for fine motor actions or manipulations are introduced. Second, the vocabulary selections, length, syntactic structure, association strength, and semantic-logical relationships among items and the serial position of critical items should be controlled using the guidelines discussed above. Third, the rate of presentation of the oral directions and the phrasing and phrasal cueing should be controlled to facilitate recall. Initially, the rate of presentations should be slower than normal, and phrasal cueing may be exaggerated. The rate of presentation and the phrasing can be modified gradually till they approach those of normal conversation. Fourth, one-level commands should be introduced before two-, three-, or four-level commands. Fifth, the two-, three-, or four-level commands should feature the word "and" between components at first. This connective should then be replaced by a long pause between elements or components, and gradually the pauses should approximate normal length. Sixth, difficult prepositional phrases, adjective sequences, linguistic concepts, number facts, and right-left directions should be introduced late in the sequence.

Here is one possible sequence for using intervention materials and tasks designed to facilitate, control, and improve the delayed recall or oral directions.

STEP 1. *Following patterned oral commands for gross motor actions*

**Sample commands:** Go to the blackboard.

Go to the blackboard *and* take a piece of chalk.

Go to the blackboard *and* take a piece of chalk *and* write your name.

Go to the blackboard *and* take a piece of chalk *and* write your name *and* then go to your desk.

STEP 2. *Following unpatterned oral commands for gross motor actions*

**Sample commands:** Go to the door.

Walk to the desk *and* pick up the book.

Run to the closet *and* get your coat *and* put it on.

Skip to the blackboard *and* take a piece of chalk *and* bring it to your desk *and* put it down.

STEP 3. *Following patterned and unpatterned oral commands for gross motor actions*

**Sample commands:** Go to the door. (pause) Open it.

Go to the door. Open it. (pause) Close the door.

Go to the door and open it. (pause) Then close it and run to your desk.

Run to the window. Close it. Take the book on the desk. Sit down on your chair.

STEP 4. *Following oral commands for fine motor actions*

**Materials:** Paper dolls and paper clothes.

**Sample commands:** Put on the dress.

Put on the skirt *and* the blouse.

Put on the hat *and* the shoes *and* the coat.

Put on the skirt *and* the blouse *and* the scarf *and* the coat.

STEP 5. *Following oral commands for fine motor actions*

**Materials:** Paper and crayons.

**Sample commands:** Draw a red circle.

Draw a yellow flower. (pause) Draw a shining sun.

Draw a blue bird. (pause) Take a green crayon.
(pause) Draw a tree.
Draw a black triangle. (pause) Take the yellow
crayon. (pause) Draw a yellow circle. (pause) Write
your name.

### STEP 6. *Following oral commands which contain adjective sequences*

**Materials:** Colored tokens (size; shape; color).
**Sample commands:** Touch the blue circle.
Touch a small yellow circle.
Touch a big blue triangle.
Touch the big red circle *and* the small blue circle.
Touch the small blue triangle, the big red square, *and* the
big red triangle.
Touch the blue circle, the yellow square, *and* the red
triangle.
Touch the small blue circle, the big yellow square, *and*
the big green triangle.

### STEP 7. *Following oral commands which contain prepositions*

**Materials:** Books, pencils, crayons, paper, desk, chair.
**Sample commands:** Pick the book *up*.
Pick a pencil *up* and put it *on top of* the book.
Stand *on* your chair, turn *around*, and jump *down*.
Pick up a red crayon and put it *next to* the book.
Take a piece of paper and put it *on top of* the chair.
Put the pencil *next to* the paper, the book *on top of* the
paper, and the red crayon *under* the table.
Hold the pencil *over* your head *in your left* hand.
Take a pencil *with your right* hand and point to the
window *to the right of* the door.

### STEP 8. *Following oral commands which contain number facts*

**Materials:** A deck of cards.
**Sample commands:** Find an ace. Find a King.
Find a heart. Find a two. Find a nine.
Find two aces. Find a nine of hearts. Find a
seven of spades.
Find the six, seven, and eight of spades, the ten of
hearts, and the two of diamonds.

### STEP 9. *Following oral commands which contain linguistic concepts*

**Sample commands:** Pick up *all* the crayons.
Pick up *some* of the books.
Pick of *any* of the pencils and *all* of the paper.
Pick up *some* of the crayons, *all* of the books, a *few* of
the pencils, and *several* pieces of paper.
*When* I pick up a pencil, you pick up a crayon.
*If* I pick up a book, you pick up a pencil.
*After* I write my name, you write yours.
Write your name *before* I write mine.
Point to the pencil that is *shorter* than this line.
Point to the *longest* pencil, the *smallest* piece of chalk,
and the *biggest* book.

If the youngster finds it hard to follow any but one-level commands, it may be necessary to emphasize strategies that facilitate delayed recall. One strategy is to ask the youngster to repeat each of the components of the command immediately after he hears it. This may be followed up by asking the youngster to repeat the complete command aloud before he starts to execute it. Any errors in the overt repetitions of the components of the commands or of the complete commands should be corrected, and the command repeated until correct. A second strategy is to ask the youngster to repeat the oral commands silently as he hears them and to repeat or rehearse them while he executes the actions. In the beginning, the rehearsal may be overt and done aloud. As the youngster improves in his ability to repeat and rehearse, the reauditorization should be done internally and silently. At times, the educator-clinician may spot check if the youngster is rehearsing internally by asking him to say the words or the command out loud.

A third strategy which may be used is to print the critical words in all commands. The critical words may then be placed in front of the child as they are spoken in the oral command. The child may pick the printed words cards up and carry them with him to help him recall and execute the command. An advanced strategy would be to ask the youngster to write down the critical words in oral commands and directions as they are spoken. He may then be asked to reconstruct the command and say it out loud before it is executed. This strategy may help with note taking in the classroom and with focussing the youngster's attention on the critical elements in the directions.

Yet another strategy is available, and it may be the one the child uses already. The child can look at and "mark" the objects involved in the directions as they are said. This strategy has its limitations, however. It can only be used for directions that feature objects or actions in the immediate environment. It does not generalize to directions in which the immediate environment is surpassed. It is therefore a strategy that does not facilitate later recall of directions or information in the classroom.

## Recalling Semantic Details

Language and learning disabled youngsters may demonstrate strengths as well as limitations in long-term memory and recall of details. They may have exceptionally good memory for and recall of telephone numbers, car names, or unessential detail. This strength may be associated with specific limitations. These same youngsters may have poor long-term memory and recall of proper names, details presented in conversations, stories, or curriculum materials, or number facts and monetary terms. When their limitations are blatant, the educator may try to teach them mnemonic techniques. These may work for some youngsters, but for others they are of no avail as they cannot match the right mnemonic rule to the appropriate occasion. They may confuse rules and mesh two separate rules into one that is obviously nonfunctional.

Procedures designed to facilitate and improve the delayed auditory recall of verbal information should emphasize the recall of semantic details of various types. In an intervention program, it may be necessary to begin with paying attention. Many language and learning disabled children and youth are inactive listeners. They have never acquired active listening skills. These strategies may need to be introduced in listening tasks and activities. The first and immediate objective may be to establish the ability to identify the critical details in spoken materials and to disregard unessential information. This objective may be met by reading short paragraphs and stories and requiring the youngster to press a red light or raise his hand when he hears a critical detail (word, phrase, or clause). In this procedure, it is important that the youngster receive *immediate* feedback and that there is a way to chart his progress at the task. This task may be adapted for advanced readers. They may be given a text to follow as the story is being read and asked to underline words that express critical and relevant details.

A second and related objective is to establish internal rehearsal and other strategies such as internal imagery to facilitate the later recall of detail. The youngster with strong visual memory and revisualization ability may be asked to form internal images as he hears the relevant details. The youngster who does not have strong internal perceptual (visual) imagery may be asked at intervals to rehearse details out loud. With repetition of this strategy, the periodic rehearsal of details should become internalized. A third objective may be to establish the ability to write down relevant details or to take notes while listening to spoken information. This last strategy is especially important for youngsters in the upper grades and in high school. It generalizes well to classroom activities and may therefore increase the child's academic achievement. Actual note taking or writing down key words and phrases may be preceded by the activity described above, in which the listener underlines critical details as he hears them read to him.

Among materials and task formats which may be used to facilitate and strengthen delayed auditory recall of semantic details are oral directions, paragraphs, and stories. Each of these may be associated with direct questions for the recall of relevant details. Spatial and temporal data and number and quantity facts should be emphasized in intervention. The examples below illustrate task formats and materials.

*Oral directions with questions for semantic details*

Listen to these directions.

Go to the corner and take a right turn.
*Where (what place) do you take the turn?*
*In what direction should you turn?*

Go half a mile up Highland Park and bear left at the park entrance.
*How far up Highland Park should you go?*
*Which direction should you go at the park entrance?*

Drive 25 miles till you get to Exit 9. Take that exit and follow Route 17 for about 10 miles.
*How far is it to Exit 9?*
*Which Route do you follow when you get off at Exit 9?*
*How far do you go on Route 17?*

*Oral paragraphs (newscasts, weather reports, newspaper articles, etc.) with questions for details*

Today temperatures will be in the upper twenties, with rain probable this morning, clearing in the afternoon. Tomorrow will be sunny and in the lower thirties.

*What will the temperature be today?*
*What will the temperature be tomorrow?*
*When is it supposed to rain?*
*When is the rain expected to stop?*

A 100,000-ton oil tanker broke up off the coast of Miami this evening, spreading a slick that extends for 28 miles. Clean-up operations have begun on the slick, which has not yet reached the shore.

*Where did the tanker break up?*
*How large was the oil slick it spread?*
*What was the condition at shore when clean-up was started?*

# WORD FINDING, FLUENCY, AND FLEXIBILITY
## Characteristics and Assessment

BACKGROUND

In spontaneous conversation, you generally have the freedom to choose your words and use the sentence types which best reflect your thoughts, ideas, and feelings. The limitations placed on your selections are relatively light. Nonetheless, you are controlled by both semantic (selectional) and linguistic constraints that determine your choice of words, phrases, and sentences. For example, if you were to begin one of your sentences with the word "yesterday," you would automatically be obliged to use a verb form in the past tense or in some other form which indicates that the action described by the verb occurred in the past.

Similarly, the characteristics of the objects, persons, events, ideas, or feelings you want to describe impose certain constraints on your selection of words from the lexicon. When you ask a child to name a pictured object such as a red ball or to give the verbal opposite for a word such as "night," you impose semantic constraints that govern the child's word selections. The child must retrieve and use words which are appropriate and accurate in the specific context and that best describe the characteristics you want him to emphasize. Let's now return to the example of the picture of the red ball. If you ask the child to tell what it is, he would be expected to say "a ball" or "It's a ball." If you ask the child what color the ball is, the expected response would be "red" or "It's red." In this situation, the child is obliged to function under relatively rigid constraints; in fact, there may only be one word which will satisfy the verbal request. In order to speedily and accurately recall and retrieve a specific word upon request, you must have an organized long-term memory and be efficient in locating and retrieving the stored words from it.

When you attempt to find a word which is not automatically and rapidly available to you, you direct your consciousness toward filling a shape or finding a part which you may vaguely perceive. In the process, you guide your attempts at finding the desired word by an image of its structure, either visual, auditory, or motor-kinesthetic. Word-finding difficulties are not uncommon among normal children and adults, but they seem to occur with less frequency than among children, adolescents, and adults with language and learning disabilities.

Brown and McNeill (1970) suggest that association by either prefix and/or suffix seems to play a role in normal word recall. They also note that adults are able to determine the number of syllables in an intended word even though they are unable to retrieve it. Association by similarities in speech sounds also aids recall. For example, adults gave the following phonologically related words while searching for the word "sampan:" (1) "saipan," (2) "siam," (3) "sarong," (4) "sanching," and (5) "sympoon." First and last sounds in words appeared to be more easily recalled than middle sounds. This suggests that the attention to the initial speech sounds in words may be strongest and may be followed by attention to the final sounds and finally to the medial sounds.

Freud (1971) describes the psychodynamics of "slips of the tongue" in his early work. In a similar vein, Fromkin (1973) reports on the phonologically, morphologically, and semantically based slips of the tongue among normal adults. She uses the response "There's a small Chinese . . . I mean Japanese restaurant" to illustrate a semantically or meaning-based word substitution. Another example of a semantically based word substitution is the use of the word "Dachshund" for "Volkswagen." This slip of the tongue is considered to result from the erroneous selection of a word which shares several semantic features (small, German, animate) with synonyms such as "beetle" or "bug" for the intended word "Volkswagen." Transposition errors may result from misuse of word endings, as in substituting the words "ambigual" for "ambiguous," "motionly" for "motionless," and "intervenient" for "intervening."

Learning disabled children may have difficulties in recalling and retrieving specific words accurately and speedily when they are asked to name pictures or objects, find proper names, or describe past experiences or events, or in spontaneous conversation. For example, a learning disabled child confronted with a series of pictures of common objects such as a key, a comb, a pencil, a cup, a pen, and a ring may call them a "door," a "brush," a "pen," a "glass," a "pencil," and a "finger," respectively. The responses indicate that each intended label or word was replaced by the name of an associated object. If asked to tell whether it is night or day, the same child may say "night" with conviction even though it is actually day. He used the opposite for the intended word. When asked if it is night, the child may answer "no," which shows that he actually knew the time of day. Similarly, the child may point to a picture of a television and say that it is a "telephone" or to a picture of a moon and say "noon." This pattern suggests similarities in sounds between the intended and the substituted words caused the errors of retrieval.

Learning disabled children's patterns of word substitution errors suggest that they may retrieve erroneous words which are related to the intended word by:

(1) Semantic class membership and associative relationship, as in substituting the word "banana" for "orange" (fruits) or "tiger" for "lion" (wild animals).

(2) Opposition, as in substituting the word "hot" for "cold" (temperature) or "brother" for "sister" (kinship).

**FIGURE 12.1**
*Antonym Relationship*

(3) Speech sound (phonological) composition, as in substituting the word "blue" for "brown" (color), "sing" for "sting" (action), or "television" for "telephone" (media). Sound substitutions generally occur within the same semantic class. However, they may cross semantic categories if the intended word is relatively new and unfamiliar.

**FIGURE 12.2**
*Phonological Relationship*

(4) Perseveration, as in repeating a previously produced word used in naming objects or pictures, naming antonyms, or completing verbal analogies. For example, the child may recite the names for a

series of common objects such as a key, a comb, a pencil, a cup, a pen, and a ring as follows: *"key*, comb, pencil, *key*, pen, *key."*

The word-finding problems of learning disabled children also show up when they are asked to form verbal associations, like saying as many words as they can think of in a predetermined time or naming as many animals as they can think of in a short period. When confronted with these tasks, the child with word-finding problems may be slow, may repeat words over and over, or may say a few words rapidly and then get totally stuck. The result is that these children have a restricted range of available words because of their recall and retrieval deficits.

Johnson and Myklebust (1967) call the problem of finding specific words when required **dysnomia**. They describe the problem as being "a deficit primarily in reauditorization and word selection" (p. 114). They state that the learning disabled child with dysnomia understands and recognizes the intended word but is unable to retrieve it on demand. When the child searches for a target word, he may resort to gestures. Johnson and Myklebust describe a learning disabled girl who, searching for the word "crash" to describe an accident, doubled her fists, hit them together, and covered her ears to indicate the loud sound the impact made (p. 115).

Learning disabled children may do other characteristic things when searching for a specific word they need to get their ideas across but cannot find. They may produce idiosyncratic hand movements, such as moving one hand in rotation. They may respond with facial grimaces or ticks. They may hit a table or their thigh with a hand, swing a leg, or repeatedly tap a rhythm with one foot. We will now look in more detail at the types of word-finding problems experienced by learning disabled children.

## CHARACTERISTICS OF WORD-FINDING DEFICITS

Word-finding problems, including **anomia,** dysnomia, and **amnestic aphasia**, have been described extensively in the literature in cases of adults with acquired brain lesions and aphasia. Geschwind (1972) defines *anomia* as "the inability of the patient (aphasic) to name things shown to him" or failure to name specific items on confrontation. He identifies several types of naming errors. In *classical anomia*, the word-finding difficulties tend to be general in nature and to involve both the sound and meaning of words. They also tend to cross sensory input modalities (visual and tactile) and occur in speaking, oral reading, and writing. In *disconnection anomia*, the errors tend to occur only with input from a specific modality. For example, a person may name a visually presented object, but he may be unable to name the same object when it is placed in his hand and he is blindfolded and cannot see it.

Goldstein (1948) differentiates anomia and amnestic aphasia. In anomia, proper names are difficult to recall and retrieve. Anomia is similar to but more severe and more frequent than the common situation in which you are introduced to a large number of people at a cocktail party and come away without remembering more than one or two of the people by name. In amnestic aphasia, the person cannot recall and retrieve the appropriate labels for objects, events, actions, or qualities.

Schuell and Jenkins (1972) relate the degree of difficulty in finding specific words to the frequency of occurrence of the words in the language. Thus, infrequently used words are harder for aphasics to recall than commonly used words. Wiig and Globus (1971) found relationships between the ease with which aphasics identify words and the associative strength and logical relationships between the words.

The word-finding difficulties of learning disabled children and adolescents appear to cross input modalities. They may have trouble naming objects or pictured objects or events, naming objects to be identified by touch, and reading. Their problems also seem to encompass both the recall and retrieval of proper names and of names for objects, animals, actions, attributes, and other characteristics. The problems occur even when the words the children are trying to recall and retrieve are familiar to them and easily recognized on picture vocabulary tasks. As a result, these naming errors and word-finding problems cannot be attributed to limited vocabulary development. In rapid conversation, the continuous search for specific words may cause idiosyncratic patterns of expression, including:

(1) Prolonged pauses appropriately or inappropriately placed in the utterances, as in "I went to the (pause) store to buy (pause) some (pause) delicious (pause) something."

*Table 12.1 summarizes this information.*

(2) Repeated use of semantically empty place holders such as "uh," "uhm," "err," "now err," "ah," and "well," as in the utterance "I *err, ah,* went to *err, uhm,* the *uhm* store to buy *uh* some *err* delicious *well err* something."

(3) Interjection of stereotyped meaningless phrases, such as "thig-a-ma-jig," "watcha'ma call it," "look," "you know," "you see," "that thing," or "right," as in the utterance "*You see,* I went to the *watch'-ma call it* store to buy *that thing, you know.*"

(4) Repeated use of starters such as "and," "and then," "then," "now," and "well" to begin sentences, phrases, and clauses, as in the utterance "*And then* I went to the store *and then* I bought something *well* that was delicious."

(5) Overuse of indefinites such as "something," "somewhere," "somehow," "this," and "that" as substitutions for content words, in utterances such as "*Somehow* I went to *this place somewhere* to buy *something* delicious."

(6) Frequent round-about descriptions or definitions which may tell, among others, the form, color, function, or location of an object without giving its name, as in the utterance "I went to *a place where you can buy things you can eat* and I bought *something to eat* that *tasted like something very sweet.*"

(7) Overuse of words which lack specificity, such as "thing," "junk," "stuff," or "place," used to replace a wide range of nouns, in utterances such as "I went to this *place* to buy some *stuff,* and I got some *junk* that tasted delicious."

**FIGURE 12.3**
*Lack of Specificity*

(8) Restricted range and imprecise use of verb choices containing forms such as "get," "make," and "put" in utterances such as:
  (a) I *got* the window open (opened).
      I *got* my dress on (dressed).
      I *got* the fish (caught).
      I *got* the fire out (put out).
  (b) I *made* a cake (baked).
      I *made* a tower (built).
      I *made* a picture (drew).
      I *made* a hem (sewed).
  (c) I *put* the eggs in the batter (mixed).
      I *put* a ribbon on it (tied).
      I *put* the flowers in (planted).
      I *put* the letter in the box (dropped).
(9) Borrowed word formations in which words and expressions are invented or extended by analogy, as in utterances such as "I got this, you know I'm sick, I got *volcano craters* all over" (chicken pox) or "The doctor was using his *earphones*" (stethoscope).
(10) Redundancies by repetition of phrases, as if the child were not sure of the appropriateness of an expression, as in utterances such as "I'm *confident,* I'm *positive,* I'm *sure* we will find out" or "He *told me,* he *said,* he *did say* he'd do it."
(11) Perseverative repetitions of sounds, syllables, words, phrases, clauses, or ideas, as in the utterances:
  (a) "I am going to have *cream, ice cream, vanilla ice cream, chocolate ice cream,* a big *ice cream sundae.*"
  (b) "I *said to him,* and then I *said to him* that I couldn't come, and I *said to him* I was sorry, and then I *said to him* I'll come next Sunday."
  (c) "I bought that candy for *five cents* last year; it now costs *ten cents,* I should have bought more, I bought it for *five cents* and now it costs *ten cents,* I got it cheap. I got it for *five cents* and now it costs *ten cents* [ad nauseam] . . ."

(12) Borrowing words which are appropriate in other contexts to fill the immediate need for a label, as in the utterances:
    (a) The baby is all *topsy turbie* (fell down).
    (b) They had this big *hullabaloo* for his birthday (party).
(13) Substitutions of prefixes and suffixes, as in the utterances:
    (a) My mother *dis*covered the bed (uncovered).
    (b) She talked so kind*ness* (kindly).
    (c) They did a lot of *pro*pollution demonstrations (antipollution).

Though the expressions of learning disabled children may contain blatant evidence of word-finding problems to the trained ear, parents, educators, psychologists, and physicians may not be aware of the indicators. Because the expressions often occur in a context in which the listener can reconstruct the child's intended message, the substitu-

**TABLE 12.1**

*Idiosyncratic language expression patterns among learning disabled children and adolescents*

| Category of Overuse | Characteristic Expressions | Sample Utterances |
|---|---|---|
| Prolonged pauses. | pause | I went to (pause) the store to buy (pause) some (pause) delicious (pause) something. |
| Semantically empty place holders. | uh, uhm, err, ah, well . . . | I err ah went to err ah the uhm store to buy uh some err delicious well err something. |
| Stereotyped phrases. | whatcha'ma call it, you know, you see . . . | You see, I went to the whatcha'ma call it store to buy that thing, you know. |
| Starters. | and, then, and then, now, well, etc., used to begin sentences, phrases, and clauses | And then I went to the store and then I bought something well that was delicious. |
| Indefinites. | this, that, something, some-where . . . | Somehow, I went to this place some-where to buy something delicious. |
| Circumlocutions. | descriptions rather than labels such as "things you can eat/drink/play with," etc. | I went to this place where you can buy things to eat and I bought some-thing to eat that tasted delicious. |
| Words lacking specificity. | thing, junk, stuff, place . . . | I went to this place to buy some stuff and I got some junk that tasted deli-cious. |
| Imprecise and restrictive verb use. | got, made, put . . . | I got the fish. (caught) I made the dress. (sewed) I put the bulbs near the tree. (planted) |
| Borrowed word forma-tions. | invented or extended word use | I got volcano craters all over. (chicken pox) |
| Redundant repetitions of assertive phrases. | I'm confident/positive/sure, He said so, He told me . . . , etc. | I'm confident, I'm sure he will come. He told me so. He said he will come. |
| Perseverative repetitions. | repetitions of sounds, syllables, words, phrases, clauses, or ideas | I'm going to have cream, ice cream, vanilla ice cream. |
| Borrowing of words. | use of words, often slang, which are appropriate in other contexts | The baby is all topsy turbie. (fell down) |
| Substitution of prefixes and suffixes. | *dis-* for *un-*, *-ness* for *-ly*, *pro-* for *anti-* . . . | They did a lot of propollution demon-strations. (antipollution) |

tions may be accepted as appropriate and their idiosyncratic characteristics overlooked. The pressure and frustration felt by the learning disabled child when he is obliged to produce a response but cannot find the precise words to express his ideas or to answer a question may have detrimental effects. He may not only lapse into idiosyncratic language patterns but may lose his ideas, change the topic, invent fictitious stories, become fidgety or overactive, laugh inappropriately, or stare vacantly at a fixed point in space in an attempt to avoid what for him may appear to be a catastrophy. After repeated frustrations, the child may find refuge in silence. Since adults may consider the child's silence a relief, they may inadvertently reinforce this behavior and foster the child's passivity.

## FLEXIBILITY AND ELABORATION IN LANGUAGE FORMULATION

A child's or adult's language abilities are judged in part by his facility in producing a variety of vocabulary items and sentence structures to describe the past and the present. The ease with which the individual can produce different types of verbal responses (words, phrases, or sentences) to describe objects, persons, events, ideas, feelings, or attitudes indicates his flexibility and his ability to elaborate in formulating and using language. There are several specific abilities which contribute to facility and diversity in language formulation and production. They include (1) verbal fluency, reflected in ready availability of words, phrases, and sentences, (2) flexibility, reflected in willingness to shift from one set and type of words, phrases, and sentences to another, either spontaneously or adaptively to accommodate to external changes or constraints, (3) creativity, reflected in unusual responses, and (4) elaboration, reflected in attention to descriptive details and embellishment of phrases and sentences.

Creativity, elaboration, flexibility, and fluency are all revealed by variety in the selection of vocabulary, phrases, clauses, and sentences. They are also revealed by how well the speaker can expand on a topic and how well he can focus and refocus a listener's attention on shared information. For instance, a person with superior language production abilities would be able to describe fog in a variety of ways, ranging from the terse and prosaic "The fog is grey" or "Fog is a type of weather" to the poetic "The fog rolled in, isolating everyone in his own sphere of existence, creating echoes of loneliness."

In educational and academic settings, creativity, elaboration, flexibility, and fluency in language are rewarded in such subject areas as English composition, history, and foreign languages. Learning disabled children and adolescents may have difficulties in meeting these educational standards. Typically, they will have problems in providing specific descriptions and directions. Their choice of vocabulary and sentence structures may not be full and rich; many have no ornamentation in their descriptions.

On the other hand, creative language production may be an area of relative strength in some learning disabled children and adolescents.

They often give unusual solutions to both nonverbal and verbal problems, and they may show extraordinary originality in selected areas. These children can describe some events and experiences and solutions to problems quickly, accurately, and with highly elaborate utterances. They may also express wild, silly, and sometimes naughty ideas and intentions. This facility may, however, mask underlying language problems. Their abilities in spontaneous language production may be limited by specific deficits, which may reduce the speed and accuracy with which these youngsters can retrieve related words, phrases, sentences, or expressions.

In addition, word-finding difficulties, reflected in the overuse of indefinites, placeholders, and word substitutions, seem to interfere with the use of spoken or written language. Many learning disabled children and adolescents lack fluency when asked to perform on standard verbal tasks (Bannatyne, 1971; Johnson & Myklebust, 1967; Lerner, 1971; Wiig & Semel, 1976b). Their responses on word association tasks often show that they shift from one group or class of words to another in trying to retrieve a series of words and that they may not use efficient grouping or associative clustering strategies for retrieval. In descriptions of objects, events, ideas, or intentions, learning disabled youngsters may neglect details and provide terse, stereotyped, and concrete responses. For example, they may fail to describe attributes of objects such as their form, size, or composition, possessive relationships or ownership, and relationships between objects and their functions or potential actions. These limitations may show up when they are asked to:

(1) Name items that belong to a class or group when they are given its name or the common properties. The task may involve naming games, articles of clothing, farm animals, wild animals, etc.
(2) Give unusual uses for objects or materials such as orange juice, which may be used for baking bread.
(3) Construct a variety of sentences which incorporate a specific word, such as "car," or which follow a specific rule of structure, such as being questions.
(4) Tell jokes, puns, or riddles.
(5) Use language to mediate movements, plan or execute actions, or elaborate on a point.
(6) Explain multiple cause-effect relationships, as among clouds, rain, thunder, lightning, and people carrying umbrellas.
(7) Complete stories such as "The little red hen" in which the implications of actions must be verbalized.
(8) Formulate alternative responses to metaphors such as "It rained like cats and dogs" and proverbs such as "A stitch in time saves nine."
(9) Formulate alternative titles to a story.

Several of these deficits have been the focus of formal investigation. Wiig and Semel (1975) investigated and compared the speed and accuracy with which learning disabled adolescents and academically achieving adolescents named the members of the classes foods, animals, and toys during a 1-minute period. The learning disabled adolescents produced significantly fewer names of foods during the interval than their academically achieving age peers. Their responses also indicated that they did not employ obvious grouping or associative clustering strategies. They would name foods at random, shifting from one food category to another, perhaps naming first a type of meat and then a type of dessert. In contrast, their academically achieving age peers used obvious associative clustering strategies. They grouped foods either by categories such as fruits, vegetables, or meats or in relationship to meals such as breakfast, lunch, dinner, or dessert.

The responses given by the learning disabled adolescents were also distinguished by immediate or delayed repetitions of already named foods. The frequency of their repetitions suggested that they had problems remembering which foods they had already named. This suggests difficulties in using groupings for their selections of items from long-term memory and holding the items they had named in short-term memory. The learning disabled adolescents tended to recall and name foods one at a time, with a considerable interval between items. They did not name the foods in series with intervals between each series, as did their peers. This contrast suggests that the academic achievers recalled foods in larger units or conceptual chunks, a strategy which facilitates retrieval and recollection of related items (Simon & Chase, 1973).

The combined findings of the study suggest that learning disabled adolescents may be significantly delayed in learning to associate or group items to facilitate retrieval and recall from long-term memory. This suggestion has been supported by investigations of how learning disabled children react to the organization of input (Freston & Drew, 1974; Parker, Freston & Drew, 1975). When given a list of words to recall, the learning disabled children were unaffected by the organization of the list. Instead, their recall of the listed words depended on the frequency of the words. In contrast, their academically achieving age peers recalled significantly more words when they were grouped according to conceptual categories such as animals, flowers, foods, or geometric shapes. This finding indicates that the academic achievers took advantage of the input organization, while the learning disabled children did not. Furthermore, the authors concluded that this deficiency could be attributed to deficits in short-term auditory memory.

There have been suggestions that learning disabled adolescents may have similar difficulties in recalling and producing a variety of sentence types. Wiig and Semel (1975) observed that learning disabled adolescents produced mostly relatively short, positive, active, declarative sentences, such as "I have a coat," "I have a new coat," "I want a car," and "The car belongs to my daddy" when they were asked to form sentences which incorporated the words "coat," "new," "want," and "belongs." In contrast, their academically achieving age peers produced a variety of relatively longer and more complex sentence types, such as negatives, interrogatives, and conjoined sentences. Their responses reflected their relative superiority in recalling and formulating a variety of linguistic structures and sentence types.

# TASK FORMATS FOR ASSESSING WORD RETRIEVAL

The process of retrieving a specific word to name an object or event and suit a specific semantic-syntactic context may break down at one or more spots. In some cases, the intended word eludes your mind totally, and there is a long pause and no response. In other cases, you may feel that you have the word on the tip of your tongue, and you can vaguely remember some of its sounds or syllables (Fromkin, 1973). In that case, you may substitute a word that resembles the intended word in either sound structure or in meaning.

A different situation exists when you substitute an associated word because you have difficulty retrieving a specific word. For example, you could say "brother" when the intended word was "sister" or "shoes" when the intended word was "socks." Associated word substitutions reflect a retrieval system in which you identify the semantic class to which the intended word belongs. The error is thought to occur because several words in a class may have equal probabilities of occurring in a certain context (Luria, 1966, 1973). Associated word substitutions occur with greater than expected frequency among some children with dyslexia and some language and learning disabled adolescents (Denckla & Rudel, 1976; Wiig & Semel, 1975).

A different manifestation of word retrieval deficits occurs when only the speed of retrieval is affected. In that case, a specific naming response may be accurate, but it may be significantly delayed. The slowness may be especially obvious when the speaker has to shift rapidly from word to word when the words belong to the same semantic class. It may be obvious in counting, in naming days of the week or months of the year, or in naming colors. The requirement to shift rapidly from one word to the next in a series or within a semantic class may result in perseverative repetitions of words or word sequences.

In diagnosis, it is important to differentiate vocabulary deficits from word-finding and retrieval problems. You can make this differentiation only on the basis of significant discrepancies between vocabulary age and age-equivalent level of performances on tests of word retrieval. It is also important to differentiate deficits in accuracy, speed, fluency, and flexibility. To provide an in-depth assessment of word retrieval abilities and/or deficits, the test formats selected should feature a variety of task requirements. Currently used formats for the evaluation of word recall and retrieval deficits include tasks which require:

(1) Rapid naming upon confrontation of visual stimuli.
(2) Rapid naming of automatic-sequential series.
(3) Rapid naming of words in either free or controlled association.

The following sections discuss the characteristics of each of these recall and retrieval tasks. Selected formal tests for word recall and retrieval will be reviewed in detail later.

## Naming on Confrontation

The ability to retrieve a specific word upon confrontation with a visual stimulus may be assessed using pictured objects, actions, or attributes.

This format is used in a formal test of aphasia in adults (Goodglass & Kaplan, 1972). It has also been used in investigations of word retrieval abilities among children and adolescents with language and learning disabilities (Denckla & Rudel, 1976; and Wiig & Semel, 1975). Picture naming lends itself to evaluating the accuracy as well as the speed of word retrieval. It also lends itself to evaluating and comparing word retrieval abilities for words in different semantic-grammatic classes and categories. The format allows the clinician to analyze the qualitative characteristics of the error responses. The analysis may tell whether the errors reflect predominantly:

(1) Associated word substitutions.
(2) Perceptually related word substitutions, in which the substituted words define visually similar objects or events.
(3) Phonologically related word substitutions or rhyming responses.
(4) Perseverative repetitions of previous words or names.
(5) Bizarre or neologistic naming responses.

An alternative design for evaluating word retrieval speed and accuracy uses colored geometric forms to elicit rapid responses (Semel & Wiig, 1980). In that design, the task is to first name a limited number of colors upon confrontation with a stimulus card with arrays of colored circles. Second, the child must name a limited number of geometric forms upon confrontation with a stimulus card with arrays of outlined geometric designs. Finally, the child must name color-form combinations in response to a stimulus card which features arrays of colored geometric forms. This format lends itself to tapping deficits in the speed of word retrieval and in the ability to shift rapidly from word to word within the same semantic category. It may discern whether the child's word retrieval deficits reflect primarily:

(1) Limitations in the speed of retrieval of single words which are semantically related.
(2) Limitations in the speed of retrieval of word combinations which contain words from semantically restricted word categories.
(3) Limitations in accuracy and verbal agility in producing words when rapid shifts are required within the same semantic word category.
(4) Perseverative word repetitions of previous items, single labels, or word combinations.

## Automatic-Sequential Language Series

A rapid recitation of an established series which is highly automatic to efficient speakers may also be used to assess word retrieval deficits. Among automatic-sequential language series which can be used are the alphabet, serial counting, days of the week, and months of the year. These series have been used extensively in assessing acquired language disorders in adults (Eisenson, 1954; Goodglass & Kaplan, 1972; Schuell, 1965). The ability to recite serial language serves as an excellent index of the severity of the language loss in adult aphasia.

When this recitation test is used in evaluating the language abilities of children, the results will depend upon several factors, including:

(1) Whether the child has learned the meaning of the specific words featured in a series.
(2) Whether the child can recall and retain the sequence of the labels or events featured in a series.
(3) How much automaticity the child has acquired in the recital of the series.

Recitation of automatic-sequential language series is not featured frequently in tests of language abilities in children. This task is, however, included in one current test of language abilities, the Clinical Evaluation of Language Functions (Semel & Wiig, 1980). In that test, the child is required to recite the names of the days of the week and the months of the year as rapidly as possible. The responses are scored for accuracy in sequential recall and retrieval, as well as for the speed of retrieval. Analysis of the response patterns can show that the child has:

(1) Limitations in the acquisition and automatization of automatic-sequential language.
(2) Problems with the sequential recall of automatic series.
(3) Problem with the speed of retrieval, in spite of accurate recall.
(4) Perseverative repetitions of words or word sequences.

### Free and Controlled Word Association

The fluency, flexibility, and speed of word retrieval in word association tasks depends in part on the efficiency of the child's internal organization and storage. Words and concepts seem to be organized and stored internally in cross-referenced categories or semantic classes. The internal organization appears to be amazingly similar among adult speakers of the same language who share similar cultural and educational backgrounds. Thus when two or more adults with similar backgrounds are asked to say any word at all in response to a specific stimulus word, such as "dog" or "sour," they will often come up with similar word associations (Deese, 1962; Palermo & Jenkins, 1964; Riegel, 1965).

If competent speakers of a language are asked to say as many words as they can think of during a given time period, their responses have certain characteristics. The words are not produced in random sequence. Instead, they tend to be grouped in short or longer sequences in which the words are related by meaning or semantic class membership. For example, a free association response may start with the word "tell." This word may be followed by the sequence "ask-give-sell-buy," an associated word series. The next related sequence may be "buy-car-truck-bus-boat-plane-train" and so on. The strategy of grouping associated words has been found to facilitate and increase both the quantity and speed of word recall on word association tasks (Bousfield, Cohen, & Whitmarsh, 1958).

Free association tasks in which the child is required to say as many different words as possible within a given time period are not common among standardized language tests. This task is featured as a subtest in the Detroit Tests of Learning Aptitude (Baker & Leland, 1967). Quantitative and qualitative analyses of the youngster's responses permit the examiner to discern:

(1) Limitations in the availability and use of associative grouping strategies to facilitate word recall.
(2) Random search strategies in word recall.
(3) Perseverative repetitions of words and word sequences.
(4) Deficits in the speed of word retrieval even though the child uses associative grouping strategies.
(5) Bizarre, neologistic, or jargon responses.

Controlled association tasks in which the youngster is required to name as many members of a semantic category as possible within a given time period are featured in at least two current tests of language abilities in children (McCarthy, 1970; Semel & Wiig, 1980). Both tests require the child to recall and retrieve the members of more than one semantic category. The McCarthy Scales of Children's Abilities require controlled associative recall of members of four semantic categories. They are:

(1) Things to eat.
(2) Animals.
(3) Things to wear.
(4) Things to ride.

The Clinical Évaluation of Language Functions features two semantic categories, Foods and Animals. The rationale for including more than one semantic category is based on the assumption that the child learns the organization within categories differently. The child's experiences with foods begin early, and foods are experienced in sensori-motor activities. You can assume that the child is familiar with many food items, which can be grouped around either meals or within subcategories such as meats, breads, fruits, vegetables, and snacks.

In contrast, with the exception of pets for some, most children today have no experience handling animals. Animals and animal categories are the subject of organized teaching efforts in the early grades. Children can learn the animals on the basis of perceptual (visual) characteristics and/or functional and geographical associations (Wiig & Semel, 1975). Controlled association lends itself to clinical observations which may discern:

(1) Limitations in the internal organization and use of associative grouping strategies for word recall and retrieval.
(2) Random search strategies in semantically associated word recall.
(3) Perseverative repetitions of previously produced labels and word sequences.
(4) Deficits in the speed of retrieval even though the child uses associative grouping strategies for the recall and retrieval of semantically related words.
(5) Bizarre and neologistic responses.
(6) Semantically unrelated naming responses.

# SELECTED TESTS FOR WORD RETRIEVAL

### Clinical Evaluation of Language Functions (CELF): Producing Names on Confrontation

This subtest of the CELF (Semel & Wiig, 1980) is designed to evaluate the accuracy, fluency, and speed of word retrieval in a repetitive word retrieval task. The subtest requires the child to retrieve color names, geometric form names, and color and form name combinations. The subtest taps the child's (1) accuracy in retrieving common words, (2) fluency and agility in producing words rapidly, and (3) speed in identifying and retrieving words.

The subtest contains three subsections. The first section requires rapid naming of randomly sequenced colored squares (red, blue, black, or yellow). The second section requires rapid naming of randomly sequenced geometric forms presented in black outlines (circle, square, or triangle). The last section combines colors and forms in rapid naming of randomly sequenced colored geometric shapes.

The visual stimuli designed to elicit the naming responses are presented on three separate cards. Card I, designed to elicit color naming, presents 36 randomly sequenced colored squares. Card II, designed to elicit form naming, presents 36 randomly sequenced geometric forms. Card III, designed to elicit naming of color-form combinations, presents 36 colored geometric forms which combine the features of the stimuli on Cards I and II. The responses are scored to reflect accuracy in naming and the speed or time required for naming each card.

The test-retest reliability of the subtest was evaluated with 30 randomly selected children in the age range from 8 years, 3 months to 8 years, 6 months. The test was readministered with a test-retest interval of 6 weeks. The correlation coefficient for the measure of accuracy was .97 and for speed .84, indicating good stability over time. The concurrent validity of the subtest was established by comparison with performances on the Spache Reading Passage. The correlation coefficients for the comparison were .43 for the measure of accuracy and .44 for the measure of speed. The comparison was made on the basis of the similarities between confrontation naming and word retrieval in oral reading. The Clinical Evaluation of Language Functions is a criterion-referenced language test. Criteria raw scores have been established for each subtest for Grades K through 10.

### Clinical Evaluation of Language Functions (CELF): Producing Word Series

This subtest of the CELF (Semel & Wiig, 1980) is designed to evaluate the child's accuracy, fluency, and speed in recalling and producing automatic-sequential word series. The subtest taps (1) memory for automatic word series, (2) accuracy in recalling stored word series, and (3) speed of retrieval and production of selected word series. The subtest contains two items, naming the days of the week and naming the months of the year.

The test-retest reliability of the subtest was established with 30 randomly selected children in the age range from 8 years, 3 months to 8 years, 6 months. The subtest was administered twice with a 6-week time interval. The correlation coefficients obtained were .56 for accuracy and .98 for speed, indicating that the measure of speed was highly stable over time. The concurrent validity was established by comparison with subtests of the ITPA. The correlation coefficients obtained in the comparison were .45 for the ITPA Auditory Association subtest and .42 for the ITPA Auditory Sequential Memory subtest. The Clinical Evaluation of Language Functions is a criterion-referenced test. Criteria raw scores have been established for each subtest for Grades K through 10.

## Detroit Tests of Learning Aptitude (DTLA): Free Association

The Free Association subtest of the DTLA (Baker & Leland, 1967) evaluates the fluency, flexibility, and speed of retrieval of words from long-term memory. The subtest requires the youngster to retrieve and produce a run-on series of words within a given time period. The directions given by the examiner include a word sequence designed to demonstrate the requirements of the task. The directions are as follows: "Say any words you think of like *tree, sky, train, boy*—any words at all" (p. 56).

The time allotted for responding depends upon the age of the child. It increases from 1 minute for children in the age range from 3 to 7 years to 5 minutes for children at ages 14 years and above. The responses are scored to reflect (1) the number of words produced during each 1-minute time interval, and (2) the total number of words produced. Words which appear in logical sequence, such as "one," "two," "three" (counting) or *a, b, c* (serial recitation) are not credited. The responses are recorded verbatim, and the total number of words produced is used as a measure to determine age level equivalence.

Language and learning disabled youngsters frequently run out of words after the first minute. Their subsequent responses may suggest a random and slow search for words with few apparent associative ties or groupings. An analysis of the quality of the responses may suggest whether the child is using associative organization and grouping strategies.

The Detroit Tests of Learning Aptitude were standardized on a sample of 150 children at each age level in the age range from 3 years, 0 months to 19 years, 0 months. All children attended the Detroit Public Schools. Test-retest reliability for the total test was determined for a sample of 48 children using an interval between tests of 5 months. The resulting correlation coefficient was .96, indicating high stability of performances. A second correlation coefficient of .68 was obtained for a sample of 792 children ranging in age from 7 to 10 years tested with a 3-year time interval. Normative data in the form of age level equivalents (Mental Age) are reported for each group in the age range from 3 years, 0 months to 19 years, 0 months.

This subtest is useful because measures of fluency and speed in word retrieval are not generally included in language tests. They allow the clinician-educator some insight into the child's verbal organization in memory and the availability of efficient strategies for retrieval from storage.

These clinical-educational assets are offset by limitations in the standardization of the DTLA, especially:

(1) The geographic and residential biases of the standardization sample.
(2) The lack of specification of socioeconomic and racial-ethnic characteristics of the children sampled.
(3) The age of the norms.

These limitations suggest that the norms should be applied with caution and that they should not be generalized to minorities and to rural children.

### McCarthy Scales of Children's Abilities: Verbal Fluency

The Verbal Fluency subtest of the McCarthy Scales of Children's Abilities (McCarthy, 1970) is designed to assess the fluency and speed of retrieval of words which belong to specific semantic categories. The responses provide a measure of the child's ability to classify words and to think categorically. The Verbal Fluency subtest is one of the five subtests which comprise the Verbal Scale.

The subtest requires the child to name as many items as possible within each of four semantic categories within 20 seconds. The semantic categories featured in the subtest are:

(1) Things to eat (bread, potatoes, etc.)
(2) Animals (cat, bear, etc.)
(3) Things to wear (shoes, socks, etc.)
(4) Things to ride (car, bus, etc.)

The child's responses in each category are recorded verbatim. The total number of items named, excluding repetitions, determines the raw score. An analysis of the quality of the responses may reveal characteristics of interest to the clinician-educator. Flexibility, originality, rigidity, and perseveration may all be observed.

The McCarthy Scales of Children's Abilities were standardized on a sample of 1032 children ranging in age from 2 years, 6 months to 8 years, 6 months. The sample was distributed evenly within 10 age groups at 6-month intervals. The standardization sample was selected to match the demographic characteristics of the general population, closely based on the 1970 Census of Population. Test-retest reliability coefficients for each of the 6 scales (Verbal, Perceptual-Performance, Quantitative, General Cognitive, Memory, Motor) were established with a sample of 125 children tested at a 1-month interval. The reliability coefficients for the Verbal Scale ranged from .89 at 3 to 3½ years to .82 at 7½ to 8½ years. Normative data in the form of Scale Index Equivalents of raw scores are available for each of the scales and for 25 age levels distributed at 3-month intervals in the age range from 2½ to 8½ years.

Among the assets of the test are:

(1) The standardization sample is representative, which allows the norms to be used with a wide range of children.

(2) The standardization and the norms are recent.
(3) Quantitative and qualitative analysis of the response patterns with regard to internal verbal organization, retrieval strategies, fluency and speed of retrieval, and characteristic response patterns gives valuable clinical information.

The test does, however, have several limitations.

(1) Normative data at each of the 25 age levels are not available for individual subtests.
(2) Test-retest reliability indices have not been reported for individual subtests.
(3) The subtest must be administered in conjunction with the remaining subtests of the Verbal Scale to provide a valid measure of verbal skills.
(4) The age range for which the subtest is appropriate is relatively limited.

## Clinical Evaluation of Language Functions (CELF): Producing Word Associations

This subtest of the CELF (Semel & Wiig, 1980) is designed to evaluate the fluency and speed of retrieval of associated words from long-term memory. The subtest requires the child to name as many members as possible from two semantic classes, (1) foods and (2) animals, within 60 seconds each. The subtest taps (1) fluency and speed in identifying and retrieving words that belong to the same class and (2) ability to use associative word grouping to facilitate word retrieval.

The semantic classes chosen are designed to elicit one word series, foods, formed on the basis of early and common experiences, and a second, animals, formed primarily on the basis of educational experiences. The responses are scored to reflect fluency, or the number of class members named. They may be analyzed for quality by determining the number of classes named, the presence of associative groupings, and the number of shifts from one class to the next. Table 12.2 analyzes the quality of the responses by one youngster.

The test-retest reliability of the subtest was evaluated with 30 randomly selected children in the age range from 8 years, 3 months to 8 years, 6 months. The subtest was administered twice with an interval of 6 weeks between tests. The correlation coefficient obtained was .56, suggesting that this subtest should be administered as part of the Language Production subsection of the CELF. The test-retest reliability coefficient for this subsection was established to be .89, indicating good stability over time for the subtests which comprise the Language Production section. Comparison of the performances on the Producing Word Associations subtest and subtests of the ITPA yielded correlation coefficients of .46 for the Verbal Expression subtest and .43 for the Auditory Sequential Memory subtest. The Clinical Evaluation of Language Functions is a criterion-referenced language test. Criteria raw scores have been established for each subtest for Grades K through 10.

Summaries of these tests of word retrieval are presented in Table 12.3.

**TABLE 12.2**

*Word association responses to the Producing Word Associations subtest of the CELF (Semel & Wiig, 1980)*

| | Meals | Meats | Breads | Fruits | Desserts | Snacks | Sandwich spreads | Sandwich meats | Vegetables | Dairy products | Staples | Soups | Main courses | Fast foods |
|---|---|---|---|---|---|---|---|---|---|---|---|---|---|---|
| 1. toast | √ | | √ | | | | | | | | | | | |
| 2. bacon | √ | √ | | | | | | | | | | | | |
| 3. cereal | √ | | | | | | | | | | √ | | | |
| 4. bread | √ | | √ | | | | | | | | | | | |
| 5. oatmeal | √ | | | | | | | | | | √ | | | |
| 6. crackers | | | | | | √ | | | | | | | | |
| 7. cookies | | | | | | √ | | | | | | | | |
| 8. sandwich | | | | | | √ | | | | | | | | |
| 9. ham | | √ | | | | | | √ | | | | | | |
| 10. turkey | | √ | | | | | | √ | | | | | | |
| 11. chicken | | √ | | | | | | √ | | | | | | |
| 12. pork chops | | √ | | | | | | | | | | | | |
| 13. stew | √ | | | | | | | | | | | | | |
| 14. liver | | √ | | | | | | | | | | | | |
| 15. cranberry | | | | | √ | | | | | | | | | |
| 16. jelly | | | | | √ | | √ | | | | | | | |
| 17. pudding | | | | | √ | | | | | | | | | |
| 18. tapioca | | | | | √ | | | | | | √ | | | |
| 19. gelatin | | | | | √ | | | | | | | | | |
| 20. peanut butter | | | | | | | √ | | | | | | | |
| 21. jelly | | | | | √ | | √ | | | | | | | |

**TABLE 12.3**

*Selected tests of retrieval of serially and associatively related words*

| Name | Purpose | Age Range | Stimuli | Responses | Scoring |
|---|---|---|---|---|---|
| CELF: Producing Names on Confrontation | Evaluates the accuracy and speed in retrieving and producing single and combined words on visual confrontation. | K to 10 | 3 parts. Each features an array of 36 visual stimuli on a card. Card I contains colored circles; Card II, geometric forms; Card III, colored geometric forms. | Each test card is presented for rapid sustained naming of colors, forms, and color-form combinations. | Responses to each stimulus card are timed in sec. and scored for accuracy. Criteria raw scores are presented for each grade level. |
| CELF: Producing Word Series | Evaluates the accuracy and speed of retrieval of automatic word series from long-term memory. | K to 10 | 2 tasks: rapid naming of the days of the week and rapid naming of the months of the year. | Upon verbal request, the child names first the days of the week and then the months of the year. | Responses to each task are scored for serial accuracy and timed in sec. Criteria raw scores are presented for each grade level. |

**TABLE 12.3** (*Continued*)

*Selected tests of retrieval of serially and associatively related words*

| Name | Purpose | Age Range | Stimuli | Responses | Scoring |
|------|---------|-----------|---------|-----------|---------|
| DTLA: Free Association | Evaluates the fluency, flexibility, and speed of retrieval of words from long-term memory. | 5–3 to 19–0 | The examiner tells the child to say any words he thinks of, "like tree, sky, train, boy—any words at all." | The child must say as many words as possible within a given time period. The time allowance ranges from 1 to 5 minutes, depending upon the child's age. | Responses are recorded and scored to reflect the number of different words produced during each 1-minute period and the total number produced. Raw scores are converted to age level equivalents (Mental Age). |
| McCarthy Scales: Verbal Fluency | Evaluates the fluency and speed of recall and retrieval of semantically related words. | 2–6 to 8–6 | 4 tasks. Part I requires rapid naming of things to eat; Part II of animals; Part III of things to wear; Part IV of things to ride. A time of 20 seconds is given for each category. | The child is required to name as many members of each semantic category as possible within the 20-sec. time allowance. | Raw scores are calculated to reflect the total number of different words produced. They are incorporated in the Verbal Scale total and converted to Scale Index Equivalents for each 3-months age interval. |
| CELF: Producing Word Associations | Evaluates fluency and speed in the recall and retrieval of semantically associated words. | K to 10 | 2 tasks. Part I requires rapid naming of foods and Part II of animals. A time allowance of 60 seconds is given for each semantic category. | The child is required to name as many members of each semantic category within a 60-sec. time period as possible. | Raw scores reflect the total number of different words produced. Criteria raw scores are presented for each grade level. |

# WORD FINDING, FLUENCY, AND FLEXIBILITY
## Intervention

# 13

## BACKGROUND

There are several important variables which are at work when you try to recall and retrieve words and concepts from long-term memory in order to speak. How the input is organized and stored in your memory and how efficient your retrieval mechanisms are affect your ability to come up with a particular idea or word, as do your attitudes, standards, values, and feelings at the moment. Your mental, physical, and emotional set also influence your recall and retrieval. The recall, retrieval, formulation, and production of spoken language occurs amazingly rapidly and automatically in efficient speakers. In order to produce an intelligent and appropriate message, you must do several things at the same time, including:

(1) Select concepts and relationships from storage to match the ideas, attitudes, and feelings you want to express.
(2) Select semantic-symbolic (vocabulary) equivalents for the concepts and relationships.
(3) Select and formulate appropriate syntactic structures and transformations (phrases, clauses, and sentences).
(4) Select and formulate the appropriate phonemic and morphemic characteristics and structures.
(5) Formulate and produce the auditory-verbal equivalents of the words, phrases, clauses, and sentences; that is, speak the words and structures you have chosen.

As we have seen, in spontaneous conversation, you usually have freedom in choosing your words and sentences to best match your immediate mood and appeal to your audience. The limitations and constraints placed on you for selecting specific words and sentence types are relatively minimal. Nonetheless, the characteristics of your message and your audience impose some constraints on your selection of words, phrases, clauses, and sentences. In formal language tasks, including those required in educational and academic settings, the

343

imposed constraints are often much stricter. Students are usually given a topic to discuss or to write about. Certain types of sentences are preferred and expected by the teacher. Some words are taboo and other words are expected and encouraged. All of these factors impose semantic, syntactic, and stylistic constraints on the students. Some language and learning disabled youngsters may not be able to perform successfully within these limitations and constraints. They may not be able to retrieve specific words speedily and accurately. Their word retrieval deficits may limit their success in the classroom as well as on the social scene, and an intervention program is indicated.

In order to recall and retrieve a specific word or structure speedily and accurately upon request, you must have adequate organization of storage. You must also be able to locate the stored words and structures and retrieve them. When you attempt to find a word which eludes you, you may direct your consciousness toward filling a shape of the word. You may vaguely perceive parts of the word in your mind. In the process, you may guide your word-finding attempts by an image of the word's structure. That image may be a visual-perceptual picture of the word in print, an auditory-verbal memory of how it sounds, or a motor-kinesthetic memory of how it feels to say the word. Some language and learning disabled youngsters may not have adequate organization in storage. Others may have difficulty in retrieving the words after having located them in storage. Still others may not have a clear perception of an image of the structure of the desired word. Others may just be unusually slow in all aspects of word recall and retrieval. And some will have some combination of these difficulties.

The word-finding efforts of some language and learning disabled youngsters result in idiosyncratic patterns of expression in spontaneous speech or writing. They produce word substitutions, circumlocutions, imprecise use and overuse of empty words, repetitions, perseverations, and dysfluencies. These errors may surface when the child has to answer a question, select a response from among multiple choices, fill in blanks on tests, read, write, or take notes. Their word substitution errors are common even on relatively easy naming and word-finding tasks, and the substituted words usually belong to the same semantic-grammatic class as the intended word. For instance, the intended word for a fruit such as an "orange" is generally replaced with the label for a strongly associated fruit, such as "lemon." These features make the errors somewhat predictable if you know the intended word, its semantic-grammatic class, and potential words which are strongly associated with the intended word. Functional definitions may also be used as substitutes for specific content words.

In intervention, the specific objectives will vary depending upon the bases for the youngster's word-finding problems. There are, however, overall objectives which hold in spite of the underlying bases. Among them are to facilitate accuracy and speed in identifying and retrieving target words from within a set of related words. A second objective may be to reduce the semantic problems, dysfluency, and redundancy of the child's spontaneous speech. A third objective may be to inhibit the retrieval of associated words. Each of these overall objectives may be met with a variety of strategies, procedures, or tasks which will be discussed in more detail in subsequent sections. But before we discuss intervention objectives, strategies, and tasks any further, let us look at the variables known to facilitate accuracy and speed in word retrieval.

## Facilitating Variables in Word Retrieval

The contents as well as the organization of storage and the available cues affect retrieval of verbal-symbolic information from storage (Dixon & Horton, 1968; Tulving, 1974). All other things being equal, the process of retrieving information depends upon the cues that are present. We can say that forgetting or the inability to recall and retrieve information is a cue-dependent phenomenon; because the cues for retrieval are no longer available, the person cannot retrieve perfectly intact information (Tulving, 1974, p. 74). According to this theory, the language and learning disabled youngster is unable to recall, reconstruct, or use cues to facilitate word retrieval. Thus it is important to use cues in intervention to help the child retrieve words accurately and quickly. The program should also teach the child to use cues on his own.

Several studies of verbal memory have provided information about the use of cues in intervention to facilitate or improve word recall and retrieval (Light, 1972; Tulving, 1974; Tulving & Pearlstone, 1966; Tulving & Psotka, 1971; Tulving & Thomson, 1973). The results are summarized below.

(1) Specific retrieval cues, presented after a noncued attempt to recall verbal materials or information, have a significant positive effect on the accuracy of recall and retrieval.
(2) Associative word cues ("sweet"–"sour"; "dog"–"cat") are generally more effective in improving the recall of target words than rhyming word cues ("hat"–"mat"–"sat").
(3) The accuracy of word recall may be improved by increasing the number of sounds or the size of the fragment (syllable or syllables) featured in a phonetic-phonemic word cue.
(4) Partial cue words (phonetic-phonemic cues) are more effective in improving word recall than homonyms or synonyms.
(5) The name of the semantic category to which the word belongs (*metal, insect, type of building,* etc.) may help restore word recall and retrieval to an optimum level.
(6) Retrieval of words is facilitated if the cues that were present when the child learned the word are introduced again.

The implications for intervention are evident. First, retrieval cues should be used when a youngster fails to recall or retrieve a word, substitutes a word, or produces other expressions characteristic of word-finding difficulties. Second, retrieval cues that name the conceptual category (semantic class) to which the intended word belongs may be the most efficient. This type of cue can be widely used if applied with ingenuity. It also generalizes readily from context to context. Third, while homonyms and synonyms may not be the most effective cues for word retrieval, they may help some youngsters better than others. When these cues are used, homonyms should be tried before synonyms. Fourth, parts of words (the initial sound, sounds, or syllable) may be used as retrieval cues. Larger word fragments such as syllables are more effective cues than small fragments such as the initial sounds. The word part cues (phonetic-phonemic) may not help the child with word recall and retrieval if he has auditory-perceptual deficits. Finally, cueing may be most effective if you can replicate the cues which were present during acquisition of the word. Thus you should probably select cues or cue combinations from the best exemplars or prototypical contexts for the target word. For example, the target word "balloon" may be cued by saying, "You blow it up. It goes up in the air."

The recall and retrieval of specific words may also be facilitated by nonverbal cues, including gestures, pretended actions, motor actions, and nonsymbolic sounds. Gestural cues may be used most appropriately with the names or labels for common objects such as toys, utensils, furniture, and the like that have a characteristic shape or outline. A pretended action cue may elicit the name of a common everyday utensil or object such as a comb, a knife, a cup, or a pencil. Motor actions may be used with specific action verbs or sequences. Nonsymbolic sound cues may be used with the names of objects such as trains, telephones, and doorbells that are associated with specific sounds. Nonverbal cues may be especially appropriate for the youngster with strong visual or motor-kinesthetic abilities.

## Associative Word Cues

Associative word cues are readily available for use in intervention. Several studies have explored the relationships among target word identifications and the stimulus situation, associative strength, and logical relationship of the verbal cues (Flavell, 1963; Wiig & Globus, 1971; Wyke, 1962; Zivian, 1966). The experimental evidence suggests that accurate verbal responses may be facilitated when the stimulus situation restricts the number of possible choices, as in a sentence completion task. More accurate target words are identified in response to verbal cues that are highly associated with them than to clues with low association strength. More correct target words are identified in response to so-called *logical cues* (semantic class cues) than to cues that are related by spatial or temporal contiguity. For instance, the cue word "bus" may be used to elicit the target word "car" by saying, "It is not a bus, it is a____." This cue may be more efficient than a spatial cue such as "It is in the garage. It is a ____." Evidence also shows that it takes longer to find and say a word if the cue restricts the choices from which the target word is to be selected. If a word is to be selected from only two possible choices, the recall and retrieval task seems to require more time and be more complex. Antonym recall and retrieval is an extreme case of limiting the set of words from which a target word can be selected, because only one word may be used in most instances.

There are several implications of these research findings for intervention. First, you can increase the probability that a child will retrieve an appropriate word in intervention by using word cues that are strongly associated with and belong to the same semantic class as the intended word. Second, restricting the size of the set from which the target word is to be selected may result in longer retrieval time. This result would not be desirable if the purpose of your intervention is to increase the child's speed of retrieval. In that case, you should keep the set of possible words as large as possible. Third, sentence completion and sentence and paragraph cloze tasks may be used effectively to increase accuracy of word retrieval. These tasks often introduce multiple syntactic and semantic cues for the retrieval of a word. The sentences and oral cloze paragraphs may be written to include exemplar or prototypical contexts to help even more.

## Cues to Facilitate Word Retrieval

After a child or adult has tried unsuccessfully to find a word without cues, presenting a specific retrieval cue may help. The following types of cues may be used to facilitate recall and retrieval from long-term memory.

*Phonetic Cues*

(1) Say the *beginning sound* of the intended word, as in saying *m-* to elicit the word "man."
(2) Say a word fragment containing one or more of the *beginning syllables* of an intended polysyllabic word, as in saying "hippo" to elicit the word "hippopotamus."
(3) Give a *rhyming word* cue, such as reciting "sing," "wing," to facilitate the recall of an intended word such as "ring."
(4) Use *phonetic placement*; that is, show the posture and position of the articulators for the beginning sound of the intended, as in pursing the lips for the *sh-* sound to elicit the word "shoe."

*Associative-Semantic Class Cues*

(5) Use *antonyms* to facilitate the recall and retrieval of their direct opposites, as in saying "The opposite of day is ___" to elicit "night."
(6) Use *synonyms* as cue words, as in saying "Another word for lady is ___" to elicit the word "woman."
(7) Use an *associated word* which belongs to the same semantic class as a cue, as in saying "Bread and ___" to elicit the word "butter."
(8) Use the name of a *semantic (conceptual) category* to elicit the name of a member of the group, as in saying "It's a building," "It's a fruit," "It's an insect," or "You can drink it," "You can eat it for dinner," and "You can use it to fix things."
(9) Use *serial cueing*, as in reciting part of a well-established series such as "Tuesday, Wednesday, ___" to elicit "Thursday."

*Sentence Completion*

(10) Use *sentence completion*, with a well-known and established sentence pattern such as "We decorated the _____" to elicit target words such as "cake," "tree," "package," "present," "table," or "room"; "We set the _____" to elicit the word "table"; or "We gave her a birthday _____" to elicit the word "present."

(11) Give a *nursery rhyme completion*, using well-established nursery rhymes such as "Jack and Jill went up the _____" to elicit the word "hill."

(12) Use cueing by *analogy*; present a metaphor or a simile such as "as white as _____" to elicit words such as "snow," "a cloud," "a sheet," or "a swan," or "It was like music to my _____" to elicit the intended word "ears."

(13) Use *proverb* cueing, as in saying "All that glitters is not _____" to elicit "gold."

*Melodic-Stress Cueing*

(14) Use *melodic cueing*; sing a well-known tune to elicit a specific word, number, or letter or hum a part of the alphabet song to elicit the letter *g*.

(15) Use cueing by *tapping* the syllabic stress pattern of a polysyllabic word, using a rhythmic pattern such as _ _ _____ _ _ to elicit the word "hippopotamus."

*Multiple-Choice Cueing*

(16) Provide *multiple choices* for cueing, as in saying "Is it a house, a tree, or a chair?" to elict the word "tree."

# INTERVENTION OBJECTIVES AND STRATEGIES

Any intervention program to improve accuracy, fluency, and speed in word retrieval should begin with several approaches or strategies used at the same time, in order to determine their relative efficacy for the youngster. While it is possible that one approach may turn out to be the most efficient for a specific child, it is unlikely. That seems to be the exception rather than the rule. In most cases, a variety of tasks are used to achieve several complementary objectives. Here are possible objectives for intervention.

*Objective 1*

To strengthen semantic classification and categorization in order to improve the semantic organization in long-term memory and storage.

*Objective 2*

To increase the child's use of associative grouping and other cueing strategies.

*Objective 3*

To increase the speed of word retrieval in the presence of accuracy.

*Objective 4*

To increase the use of imagery to facilitate retrieval and accuracy in naming.

*Objective 5*

To inhibit dysfluency, perseveration, redundancy, circumlocution, and word substitutions in spontaneous speech.

Let us look at each of these objectives in more detail.

### Strengthening Semantic Classification and Categorization

Strengthening a child's ability to classify words by semantic category should improve his long-term memory storage and thus help him recall and retrieve specific words. Picture, printed, and spoken word sorting and classification may be used to achieve this objective. The child should be required to name each semantic category and each member of the categories formed. The naming task may be followed by a discussion of essential similarities and differences in word and concept meaning or of differences and similarities among the semantic groups.

### Increasing the Use of Associative Grouping Strategies

When the intervention objective is to increase the child's use of associative grouping strategies, the emphasis is on the child's output and performance rather than on the organization and semantic categorization of the input. This objective may be achieved as a by-product of strengthening semantic categorization and input organization. It may also be achieved by direct intervention activities and tasks. Controlled word association drills may be used. In these drills, the task is to name as many members of a semantic class as possible within a given time period. Initially, the task may be to name a small section of a larger semantic group, such as naming breakfast foods. The smaller groups named may then be combined in drills to improve the fluency of retrieval for the larger semantic class. For example, you can combine the names of breakfast foods and of dinner foods to form the larger class of foods. Or the youngster may be asked to name some familiar animals (pets, farm animals, zoo animals) at first. When he can name the members of each group rapidly, accurately, fluently, and automatically, the small groups may be combined into the larger semantic group *animals*.

### Increasing the Speed of Word Retrieval

When the child is accurate but slow in retrieving words, rapid naming drills may be used. Initially, the criterion of accuracy may need to be sacrificed. As the child's speed increases, you can firm up your demands for accuracy. Rapid naming drills may require naming of grouped or ungrouped objects, pictures, or printed labels. They may also require random, free association responses. When pictures or printed words are used, you can gradually use shorter and shorter time intervals to make the task more difficult. A tachistoscope or slide projector may be used to display the stimuli. In each case, the time of exposure of the images may be controlled automatically. You can give tokens or other reinforcers for rapid responses within a predetermined

*For more detailed discussions of the use of behavior modification techniques in language intervention, consult Mowrer (1978).*

time limit, and present time out or other negative consequences if the child is too slow.

## Increasing the Use of Internal Imagery

Increasing the youngster's use of imagery and internal representations may have generalized benefits (Anderson & Bower, 1973; Bower, 1972; Kosslyn & Pomerantz, 1977; Paivio, 1971). It may lead to improvements in language processing, verbal association, and accuracy, speed, fluency, and flexibility in word recall and retrieval. This objective is appropriate when the youngster has strength in visual memory, re-visualization, and imagery. Use of imagery can allow the child to compensate for verbal-symbolic limitations. Here is one possible procedure and sequence of intervention for increasing the use of images.

First, ask the youngster to close his eyes, revisualize his own room, and name all the furniture in it. If the child's fluency and speed of retrieval increase, you have a "go-ahead" to extend the procedure. Ask the youngster to close his eyes and revisualize a supermarket aisle and name, for example, the fruits he sees in his mind's eye. He may be asked to name the food items he had for breakfast, lunch, or dinner. He may be asked to pretend he is at the zoo, a circus, the beach, a fair, and tell about all the things he sees there.

If these exercises consistently improve the child's word retrieval speed and fluency, you can continue to use the same procedure, to elicit hobbies, past events, television shows, whatever seems interesting. When the revisualization strategy becomes automatic and efficient, have the child try it without closing his eyes. You may ask the youngster to focus on and project the image on a piece of white, unlined paper placed in front of him. Later, you can instruct him to focus on a point behind the listener when he is talking to someone.

## Inhibiting Dysfluency, Redundancy, and Other Problems

Inhibiting dysfluency, redundancy, and other idiosyncratic problems associated with word finding may best be achieved by using operant conditioning or behavior modification procedures. Initially, you can tell the child that from now on his spontaneous speech will be monitored closely. Two lights—one red and one green—can be used to tell him whether he is being precise in what he says or not. The green light will be used as a GO light. It will be on as long as he uses precise content words to express his ideas. The red light will be used as a STOP light. When it comes on, the youngster must stop speaking. The red light will be activated if the youngster talks in a round-about fashion, uses placeholders while he searches for a word, repeats words or phrases, or loses the topic in his effort to find the right words. When the red light goes on, the youngster should describe what he was doing that was unacceptable. The purpose of his telling you what triggered the STOP light is to increase his awareness of his speech and language output.

As the youngster has increasing success in identifying his own unacceptable word-finding efforts and in monitoring, controlling, and revising his speech, you can gradually increase the criteria for accuracy and specificity. Be especially careful to tell the child the criteria for success and failure at all times. Other behavior modification techniques and procedures, as discussed by Mowrer (1978) may also be applied.

Let us now look at some of the task formats discussed above in more detail. We will emphasize specific word retrieval tasks and drills and possible contents.

## TASK FORMATS AND EXAMPLES FOR INTERVENTION

### Confrontation Naming

Accuracy in retrieving specific words and concepts may be taught with visual confrontation (picture) naming tasks. The contents of the pictures may progress from naming related objects to naming a series of unrelated objects, actions, or events. Initially, you may ask the youngster to name a group of related actual objects that are common in his everyday environment. You can also provide tactile-kinesthetic input or motor experiences with the objects to help. The naming tasks may feature one or more of these activities.

(1) Naming a series of toys such as a "ball," "boat," "car," "plane," or "train."
(2) Naming a series of fruits such as "apples," "pears," "bananas," "oranges," and "grapes."
(3) Naming a series of doll house furniture such as a "chair," "table," "couch," "bed," "refrigerator," and "sink."
(4) Naming a series of doll clothing items such as "pants," "shirt," "socks," "coat," "skirt," and "gloves."
(5) Naming a series of related pictured objects such as "toys," "foods," "furniture," "clothes," and "means of transportation."
(6) Naming a series of related pictured actions such as:
   (a) Actions related to getting up in the morning (brushing teeth, combing hair, putting on shirt, and eating breakfast).
   (b) Actions related to sports or gym sessions (running, walking, jogging, jumping, catching, throwing, swimming).
   (c) Actions related to hobbies (sewing, baking, knitting, weaving, model building, and mechanics).
   (d) Actions related to school activities (reading, writing, arts, music, gym, and sciences).
(7) Naming colors and colored objects beginning with the primary colors and progressing to other colors within the spectrum.
(8) Naming a series of unrelated pictured objects, actions, colors, and the like.

A programmed approach may also be used for eliciting and strengthening naming responses. Keenan (1966) describes a program designed for use with a Language Master and a set of Language Master Cards. The program consists of separate Noun, Verb, and Number programs. One set of Language Master cards (Set I) presents pictures of two referents for either nouns, action verbs, or numbers. The names of the pictured referents are recorded on the magnetic tape strip on the card. Each card has the name of one of the pictured referents printed above the two pictures. The reverse slide of each card repeats the printed word and the picture of its referent. An alternate set of cards (Set II) presents a printed word, the pictured referent for the word, and the recorded name of the referent. The child goes through the following steps.

STEP 1. Identifying each pictured referent, followed by imitating the recorded name and reading the printed word label (Set I).

STEP 2. Identifying each pictured referent after reading the printed name; then repeating the recorded name and reading the printed word label (Set I).

STEP 3. Identifying each pictured referent after hearing the recorded name; then imitating the recorded name and reading the printed word label (Set I).

STEP 4. Identifying each printed word label after listening to the recorded name and looking at the pictured referent (Set II).

STEP 5. Naming each pictured referent presented in association with its printed word label (Set II).

STEP 6. Identifying the printed word label after hearing the recorded name of a referent (Set II).

STEP 7. Naming or reading each printed word label (Set II).

STEP 8. Identifying the printed word label presented in association with the pictured referent (Set II).

STEP 9. Naming each pictured referent (Set II).

The program provides opportunities for the child to repeat the names for the pictured referents. It provides a confrontation naming task as well as reading practice, with built-in feedback. However, some language and learning disabled youngsters with poor reading skills may not be able to perform the steps that require them to recall the printed word labels. Steps 1, 3, 5, and 9 of the program may be especially appropriate for improving accuracy in confrontation naming.

## Sentence Completion

Sentence completion tasks may be incorporated into activities designed to work on accuracy and speed in word recall and retrieval. The incomplete sentences featured in the beginning of the program may be designed so that a wide range of words will satisfy the sentence frame, thus facilitating quick retrieval. Later, when the child has shown some improvement, the incomplete sentences may involve semantic and syntactic constraints that limit the number of words that will work. When the program is first changed this way, the speed with which the child answers will probably decrease. Your objective here would be to establish accuracy of word retrieval and increased use of semantic-referential and syntactic cues for retrieval. Here are examples of sentence completion tasks in a progression from relatively easy to relatively hard.

*Sentence completion with selection from a large word set*

Cars are _____.            (nice, fast, long, driven, fun, expensive, etc.)

Jets are _____.            (fast, big, flown, fun to ride, expensive, etc.)

Tigers are _____.     (dangerous, wild, fast, hungry, big, rare, etc.)
Elephants are _____.     (big, huge, fun, curious, grey, rare, slow, etc.)

Children like _____.     (toys, ice cream, cakes, pies, summer, fun, etc.)
Monkeys like _____.     (peanuts, climbing, swinging, jumping, each other)

You can eat _____.     (fruits, hamburgers, ice cream, hot dogs, etc.)
You can drink _____.     (coke, pepsi, ginger ale, water, orange juice)
You can wear _____.     (socks, shoes, gloves, glasses, pants, etc.)

*Sentence completion with selection from restricted word sets*

You can row _____.     (a rowboat, dinghy, raft, etc.)
You can drive _____.     (a car, bike, motorbike, tandem, tractor, jeep)
You can fly _____.     (a kite, glider, plane, helicopter, rocket)

You can live in _____.     (a house, tent, cottage, building, etc.)
You can swim in _____.     (a pool, the ocean, a lake, etc.)
You can cook in _____.     (a pan, casserole, saucepan, pot, etc.)

You can ride on _____.     (a bike, scooter, horse, etc.)
You can cook on _____.     (a stove, fire, burner, etc.)
You can sit on _____.     (a chair, sofa, couch, stool, etc.)

I comb my hair with _____.     (a comb)
I brush my teeth with _____.     (a toothbrush)
I cut meat with _____.     (a knife)
I play tennis with _____.     (a racket)

I like bread and _____.     (butter, jam, cream cheese, etc.)
I drink milk and _____.     (juice, coffee, tea, coke, etc.)
I fry bacon and _____.     (eggs, sausage, ham, etc.)
I fix my hair with a brush and _____.     (comb)
I draw with pencils and _____.     (crayons)

*Sentence completion with logically associated words*

(1) *Agent-action relationship*
Dogs bark and tigers _____.     (growl)
Birds fly and fish _____.     (swim)
Kangaroos hop and frogs _____.     (jump)
Planes fly and buses _____.  .     (drive)

(2) *Antonym relationship*
Some cars are big; some cars are _____.     (small, little)
Some fruits are sweet; some fruits are _____.     (sour, bitter)
Some elephants are wild; some elephants are _____.     (tame)
Some people are tall; some people are _____.     (short)

(3) *Spatial relationship*
I park my car in _____.     (a garage, carport, driveway)
I put my clothes in _____.     (a closet, drawer, etc.)
I type on _____.     (a typewriter)
I watch shows on _____.     (the television)

(4) *Temporal relationship*
In the winter we have _____.     (snow, cold weather, rain, etc.)
In the summer we can _____.     (swim, cook outside, etc.)
In the morning we have _____.     (breakfast)
At night it is _____.     (dark)

(5) *Semantic class relationships*
My favorite fruit is _____.     (apple, pear, orange, banana, etc.)
My favorite food is _____.     (ice cream, hotdogs, hamburger)

A tiger is one of many _____.        (animals)
A robin is one of many _____.        (birds)

*Relative orders of difficulty have been discussed earlier, on pages 162–63.*        Sentences that require the child to consider the comparative, spatial, temporal, familial, cause-effect, or other logical relationships expressed among words may also be used. You should consider the order of difficulty of various sentence types in sequencing them. Incomplete comparative sentences and sentences with spatial relationships may be completed by selecting from a relatively large set of words. They should therefore be relatively easy and fast to complete. Sentences that express temporal-sequential relationships require selection from a relatively smaller set of words, and may therefore require more time. Incomplete sentences that feature the linguistic concepts of inclusion or exclusion ("all," "some," "any," "none," "all . . . except," etc.) may be completed with a relatively large set of words. Cause-effect or conditional relationships, on the other hand, require completion from a much smaller set of choices. As a result, incomplete sentences involving inclusion and exclusion should be used before cause-effect or conditional relationships are introduced. The examples below show incomplete sentences with logical relationships among words.

*Comparative sentences*

Summer is warmer than _____.        (winter, spring, fall)
Elephants are bigger than _____.        (tigers, lions, etc.)
Children are smaller than _____.        (adults, older kids, etc.)
Sidewalks are narrower than _____.        (roads, streets, avenues)

*Spatial relationships*

Mother put the vase with flowers _____.        (on the table, counter, etc.)
The car drove in the middle of _____.        (the road, street, etc.)
The pilot landed the plane on _____.        (the runway, landing strip)
Planes take off from _____.        (runways, airports)

*Temporal-sequential relationships*

Breakfast comes before _____.        (lunch, dinner)
Summer comes after _____.        (spring, winter)
Saturday comes between _____.        (Friday and Sunday)
Halloween is in _____.        (October)

*Concepts of inclusion and exclusion*

I like all _____.        (people, children, dogs, etc.)
I like some kinds of _____.        (ice cream, cakes, breads, etc.)
I like all kinds of ice cream except _____.        (vanilla, chocolate, etc.)
I do not like any kind of _____.        (insect, snake, bully, etc.)
I like neither cats nor _____.        (dogs, rabbits, etc.)

*Fanny Doodles (ZOOM) with inclusion-exclusion*

Fanny Doodle loves sweets but hates _____.        (candies, chocolates, etc.)
Fanny Doodle loves apples but hates _____.        (fruits)
Fanny Doodle loves jogging but hates _____.        (sports)
Fanny Doodle loves babies but hates _____.        (children)

*Cause–effect and conditional relationships*

I wore a raincoat because it _____.        (rained)
I went skating because the lake was _____.        (frozen)

| | |
|---|---|
| I washed my clothes because they were _____. | (dirty) |
| When there is a fire there is _____. | (smoke) |
| When we see lightning we sometimes hear _____. | (thunder) |
| If it snows we can go _____. | (skiing, sledding, etc.) |

## Word Association

Many types of word association tasks may be used in intervention programs to increase accuracy, fluency, and speed of retrieval. Among them are free association tasks, in which the youngster can say any word or sequence of words he can think of, and controlled association tasks, in which the child can name all of or as many as possible of the members of a semantic class. In controlled association tasks, the set of words from which the selections can be made is limited by semantic class membership. Verbal analogies may also be used for associated word retrieval. In the completion of verbal analogies, the set of words from which the target is to be selected is restricted, usually to one specific word. This task is, therefore, relatively hard. Word association tasks may also require one-word or multiword responses. Depending upon the size of the set from which the word may be selected, they may be relatively easy or relatively hard. Word association tasks, other than free association tasks, should not be used until the child has learned the vocabulary items required. Here are examples of word association tasks.

*For procedures for teaching knowledge and internalization of semantic categorization and classification, see page 229.*

### Free association tasks (timed)

Name as many things as you can think of in the next minute. Start.

### Controlled association tasks (timed)

Name as many foods as you can think of in the next minute.
Name as many animals as you can think of in the next minute.
Name as many things to wear as you can think of in the next minute.
Name as many things to drink as you can think of in the next 30 seconds.

### Antonym recall and retrieval (untimed or timed)

*Listen to these words. Tell me the exact opposite word for each.*

| | |
|---|---|
| man | (woman) |
| girl | (boy) |
| walk | (run) |
| big | (little) |
| up | (down) |
| inside | (outside) |
| happy | (sad) |
| cold | (hot) |

### Synonym recall and retrieval (untimed or timed)

*Listen to these words. Tell me a word that means about the same thing.*

| | |
|---|---|
| rapid | (swift/fast) |
| blossom | (flower) |
| giggle | (laugh) |
| furious | (angry) |

*Semantic class name (untimed or timed)*

> *Listen to these words. Tell me what they are.*

|          |                |
|----------|----------------|
| dog      | (animal/pet)   |
| apple    | (fruit)        |
| ball     | (toy)          |
| robin    | (bird)         |
| sofa/couch | (furniture)  |
| shoes    | (footwear)     |

*Spatial relationship (location)*

> *Listen to these words. They tell the name of a place. Tell me something you can find there.*

|         |                      |
|---------|----------------------|
| garage  | (car/truck/bus)      |
| airport | (plane/helicopter)   |
| zoo     | (animals/tigers)     |
| circus  | (clowns/acrobats)    |

*Temporal relationships*

> *Listen to these words. They tell about time. Tell me what you think of when you hear each of the words.*

|           |                                |
|-----------|--------------------------------|
| winter    | (snow/ice/skiing/skating)      |
| summer    | (swimming/warm/sailing)        |
| morning   | (get up/breakfast/go to school)|
| Halloween | (goblin/trick or treat)        |

*Temporal-sequential relationships*

> *Listen to these words. They tell about time. Tell me what comes right after/before each of them.*

|           |                      |
|-----------|----------------------|
| Saturday  | (Sunday/Friday)      |
| noon      | (afternoon/morning)  |
| May       | (June/April)         |
| September | (October/August)     |

*Agent-action relationships*

> *Listen to these words. They tell names of animals or objects. Each of them does something special. Tell me what it does.*

|           |              |
|-----------|--------------|
| fish      | (swim)       |
| bird      | (fly)        |
| lion      | (roar/growl) |
| kite      | (fly)        |
| cat       | (meow)       |
| telephone | (ring)       |

*Action-object relationships*

> *Listen to these words. They tell the things you can do with objects. Each action is special for some object. Tell me what the object is.*

|       |                    |
|-------|--------------------|
| bake  | (cake/bread)       |
| fry   | (eggs/fish)        |
| ride  | (car/bike/horse)   |
| fly   | (plane/helicopter) |
| cook  | (potatoes/eggs)    |
| knit  | (socks/sweaters)   |

| | |
|---|---|
| A dog has hair. A bird has_____. | (feathers) |
| A roof belongs on a house. A feather belongs on a_____. | (bird) |
| A father is big. A baby is_____. | (small/little) |
| A car is parked in a garage. A plane is parked in a_____. | (hangar) |
| Summer comes before winter. Halloween comes before _____. | (Thanksgiving) |
| When I am happy I smile or laugh. When I am sad I_____. | (cry/weep) |
| A girl can be a sister. A boy can be a_____. | (brother) |
| A cat meows. A dog_____. | (barks) |
| You drive a car. You fly a_____. | (plane) |
| You play baseball with a bat. You play tennis with a_____. | (racket) |

At first, you may not wish to time these tasks, if your objective is to increase accuracy. When the tasks are timed, they require rapid recall and retrieval of words and can be used to increase the speed of retrieval.

## Rapid Naming Drills

Rapid naming drills may be used when the youngster is inordinately slow in responding. These drills should be timed, and should progress to shorter and shorter time intervals for responding to each stimulus word or shorter and shorter overall response times for a sequence of tasks. You should chart the child's times so he knows how well he is doing.

It may be necessary to sacrifice accuracy in responding for speed during the initial sessions, allowing the child to make as many errors as necessary. Later you can limit the errors acceptable to 15% (85% correct responses). As the child's speed in responding increases and stabilizes, the criterion for accuracy may be gradually increased from 85% to 100%. Behavior modification techniques may be used effectively to shape both the speed and fluency of responding (Mowrer, 1978).

The efficacy of word naming drills has been tested among adults with acquired aphasia and word retrieval and word finding deficits (Wiegel-Crump & Koenigsknecht, 1973). A group of four aphasic adults were provided with a total of 18 sessions of drill. The drill sessions were given two or three times weekly. The adults were drilled in naming 20 words (household items, clothes, foods, action verbs, and living things). All the words used were ones which the aphasics were not able to retrieve before intervention. The subjects were given with visual and auditory cues (gestures, associated words, synonyms, carrier phrases, or word fragments) to facilitate naming. A measure of word naming was taken after every six therapy sessions. Interestingly, the subjects improved both on recalling and naming the 20 drilled words and on 20 words within the same semantic classes which were not drilled. This observation suggests that there was a transfer of naming ability to other members of the semantic classes. While there is no specific research evidence with language and learning disabled youngsters, similar results should obtain.

## Cloze Tasks

*Cloze passages are narrative materials in which various words are deleted.*

Accuracy and speed in word retrieval may also be improved by using oral or written cloze paragraphs and passages. When the cloze passages are used to work on speed and accuracy in word recall and retrieval, the content words should be deleted. The deletions may include names for agents and objects, actions, and attributes or characteristics (nouns, verbs, adjectives). Of these deletions, noun deletions appear to result in better production of the intended words than any other types. Therefore noun deletions should be used first. You can delete other word categories as the child's speed and accuracy in retrieval and naming improve. Cloze paragraphs and passages encourage the child to use semantic-referential, syntactic, and topical cues for word recall and retrieval.

The cloze passage below illustrates a possible design. This passage was designed by deletion of phrase markers (Blackwell, 1975, pp. 115–116). Other passages may be designed by deletion from appropriate curriculum materials.

### The Lion and The Mouse

Long ago in the forest there lived a lion and some mice. One day the _____ wanted to play. They _____ up and down some hills and _____ jumped on piles of leaves. They ate some seeds and they _____ some sweet flowers. _____ was a happy day.

"_____ is fun," said the little gray _____.

But one _____ named Fuzzy did not _____.

"Look!" he said. "_____ is the lion. He is _____!"

The little _____ ran away. They hid _____ the forest. Only one mouse was _____.

"Don't be afraid," _____ said. "Come on! We can play _____ the soft fur."

"No, no!" _____ the other little _____. He will wake up and _____ us!"

"Well, I am _____ to play in the soft _____ even if you _____!" said Fuzzy. Then he ran up _____ lion's back. "Eek! Eek!" he said. "This is lots of _____!"

The big lion _____. "Roar!" said the _____.

"Eek! Eek!" said Fuzzy.

"I am _____ to eat you," said the lion. "You woke me up!"

"Oh, no!" _____ Fuzzy. "Do not eat _____! I will not _____ in your soft _____ again!"

"I _____ let you go this time," said the _____. "But do not bother me _____."

Quickly _____ poor little mouse ran away. _____ did not see the lion _____ a long time. _____ day he heard the lion roar. Fuzzy felt sorry _____ the lion. The _____ knew what he had to _____. He chewed and _____ the net. Soon the _____ was free! _____ lion had saved _____ mouse. The mouse had saved the lion.

# FLEXIBILITY AND ELABORATION IN LANGUAGE FORMULATION

Verbal fluency and flexibility may be developed by using general as well as specific training procedures. Five general training principles have been reported to result in significant gains in verbal elaboration, fluency, flexibility, and creativity or originality (Torrance, 1965). First of all, student questions should be encouraged and treated with respect. Second, creative and imaginative ideas—even the wildest ones—should be treated with attention and respect. Third, you should acknowledge and express the value of student-generated ideas and solutions. Fourth, students should have practice in developing and expressing creative and original ideas without being evaluated. Finally, your evaluations of student-generated creative and original ideas should be related to the causes and consequences of the ideas.

*See pages 330–32 for characteristics of verbal fluency problems in learning disabled children and adolescents.*

Specific training procedures to increase creativity have been found effective at both the first grade and college levels. A group of first graders were directed to think about how they could improve their toys in 25-minute daily sessions. They showed significant gains in verbal fluency, flexibility, and originality (Cartledge & Krauser, 1963). College students who were trained to produce remote and uncommon word associations showed similar gains (Maltzman, Bogartz, & Berger, 1958; Maltzman, Simon, Raskin, & Licht, 1960). These studies suggest that procedures designed to improve verbal fluency, flexibility, originality, and attention to details in descriptions may use several tasks formats. The tasks that can be used require extended verbal elaboration in responses to specific or general questions, word association, and formulation of a variety of solutions and descriptions. These formats and task requirements are illustrated in the examples below. Other examples are provided throughout the test in sections dealing with intervention in basic language areas (syntax, semantics, retention, recall, and retrieval).

### Extended Verbal Elaboration of Detail

Attention to details of objects and events and the ability to provide precision and flexibility in verbal descriptions of the details may be increased by intervention. You can begin by requiring the child to describe objects and pictures in response to direct questions. Later, you can require him to give verbal descriptions of past events and experiences either in response to direct questions or spontaneously. Specificity and flexibility in describing objects or events depends upon experiences, details, and the amount of information stored in long-term memory. It is therefore necessary to be sure that the objects, events, or experiences you ask the child to describe are highly familiar to him and that he knows the vocabulary he will need. To make sure the child has the tools he will need, you can demonstrate the use of the object or describe the event before you require any verbal descriptions from the youngster. Here is one sequence that can be used in an intervention program.

STEP 1. *Introduction of a familiar object or pictured object with associated demonstration or verbal description of attributes and functions*

For instance, you can present a toy car or a picture of a car to the youngster. You then tell the youngster about attributes of the specific car and of cars in general.

STEP 2. *Verbal elaboration of details in response to direct questions*

After the demonstration or verbal description of the specific car and of cars in general, ask specific questions or details. The question sequence could progress as follows.

(1) What is its name?
(2) What color is it?
(3) What make of car is it?
(4) What other makes of cars can you think of?
(5) What size is this car?
(6) How does it compare in size with other cars?
(7) Where can you find cars?
(8) What are some things cars can be used for?
(9) Who in your family has a car?
(10) Who else do you know who has a car?
(11) Where would you buy a car?
(12) What would you need to be able to buy a car?
(13) What are some ways you can get money to buy a car?

STEP 3. *Spontaneous verbal description of familiar pictured objects*

Present one or several familiar pictured objects. Among them may be objects such as a telephone, a refrigerator, a baseball mitt, and a hockey stick and puck. You can ask general questions to elicit verbal elaboration and description of details for each object. The questions may be phrased as follows.

(1) Tell me about this object.
(2) What else can you tell me about it?
(3) What more can you think of to tell me about it?
(4) Are there any other things about it that are important?

STEP 4. *Verbal elaboration of details of events in response to direct questions*

Present pictures of familiar events to the youngster for verbal elaboration and descriptions of details in response to specific questions. Appropriate events include washing a car, playing baseball, baking a cake, and making a Thanksgiving dinner. Specific questions may be asked to elicit description of spatial, temporal, cause-effect, and conditional relationships, specific details, and implications of events. For instance, use a picture of a family breakfast in association with the sequence of questions outlined below.

(1) What is happening here?
(2) What time of day is it?
(3) Where is the family?
(4) How many people are there in the family?
(5) What are they eating?
(6) Who are the people in the family?
(7) Tell me about breakfast in your family.

STEP 5. *Spontaneous verbal description of familiar pictured events*

Show the child a picture of a current event from a newspaper or magazine, perhaps a ball game or a tennis match. Ask general questions to elicit the verbal elaboration and description of details. Here are some possible questions.

(1) Can you tell me about the event in this picture?
(2) What else can you tell me?
(3) What else is happening?
(4) What else can you see?

STEP 6. *Verbal elaboration of details of an event sequence in response to direct questions* Present a slide or film show that features a sequence of interactions, happenings, or events. After the showing ask specific questions to elicit descriptions of details of the sequences. The questions may focus on people present, objects in view, attributes of people, objects, and events, consequences of actions, and the like. Sections of the slide show or film may be replayed to facilitate recall and to provide feedback. For example, a slide show of a shopping trip may be followed by specific questions such as:

(1) What did the people do?
(2) Where did they go?
(3) How did they get there?
(4) Who were the people?
(5) What did the store sell?
(6) What did they buy?
(7) What do you think happened before they went to the store?
(8) What do you think is going to happen when they get home from the store?

STEP 7. *Spontaneous verbal description of an event sequence* A sequence of events or happenings may be presented in a slide or film show. After viewing the show, ask the youngster general questions to elicit spontaneous verbal description of the event sequences, their causes, and their consequences. Among possible general questions are:

(1) What was this all about?
(2) What happened in this show?
(3) What else can you remember?
(4) What other things happened?

**Word Associations Tasks**
*See pages 355–57.*

Verbal fluency may also be encouraged by using the methods and task formats described earlier in this chapter for intervention with retrieval deficits.

**Flexibility and Elaboration**
*Specific procedures and task formats for intervention on syntax are described on pages 229–80.*

Flexibility, variety, and elaboration in language formulation may be improved in several task formats. One task may require the child to make up a range and variety of sentences that feature a specific key word. The emphasis in this task is on varying both the semantic-referential contexts, the word selections, and the syntactic structures used in the sentences. Before this task is introduced, the child must be

*Procedures for intervention on semantics are described on pages 229–80.*

able to use a variety of syntactic structures and sentence transformations. It is also essential that the child have adequate knowledge of word meanings. It only remains then to work on flexibility and variety in the semantic-referential contexts in which words are featured. This objective may be attained by requiring the child to formulate sentences, following specific directions. Here are possible tasks.

*Directed sentence formulation with incorporation of key words*

(1) Have the child formulate a variety of sentences which incorporate names of persons, animals, and objects (nouns) such as "boy," "cat," "car," and "telephone." The sentences may be combined to constitute a story about a boy, a cat, a car, or other topics.

(2) Have the child formulate a variety of sentences which incorporate names of actions and attitudes (verbs) such as "walk," "run," "drive," "have," "want," and "like." The various sentences generated with one or more of the verbs may be combined to make up a story.

(3) Have the child formulate a variety of sentences which incorporate names of attributes or characteristics (adjectives) such as "young," "old," "new," "big," and "fast." Again, the sentences may be used to create a story if appropriate.

The child's flexibility and variety in describing cause-effect relationships may be improved by using sentence and story completion tasks. The examples below illustrate some possible task requirements.

*Formulating plausible causes for actions*

John went to the store because . . .
a. _____
b. _____
c. _____

Jane went home because . . .
a. _____
b. _____
c. _____

George went to New York because . . .
a. _____
b. _____
c. _____

Yesterday school was closed because . . .
a. _____
b. _____
c. _____

*Formulating plausible effects of various causes*

Yesterday in the storm . . .
a. _____
b. _____
c. _____

When the car broke down, Mr. Jones . . .
a. _____
b. _____
c. _____

Paul was very hungry, so he . . .

a. _____

b. _____

c. _____

*Formulating a variety of plausible outcomes or stories*

Last summer Jorge went to the beach. He always brought his lunch and a snack. One day . . .

Last week Iris went to New York by bus. She sat right behind the driver. On the way . . .

Al bought a marvelous gadget last week. It looked like a wrench. He wanted to use it . . .

*Formulation of a serial story*

Ask a group of youngsters to make up a story. Give them a sentence to start the story, such as, "Last week, when I went for a walk, I . . . ." Each youngster should make one sentence. Each new sentence should be made on the basis of only the last sentence of the story. Each youngster may say or write down his or her sentence. After the youngsters have each made up a sentence, tell or read the resulting story to all of the youngsters.

### Establishing Awareness of Audience and of Social Register

Language and learning disabled children and youth frequently are unaware of audience characteristics, styles, or expectations. They may show a limited range of verbal and nonverbal communication registers and styles. Their interpersonal communications may be stereotypic and idiosyncratic; they may speak in a monotone. As a consequence, their responses may be inappropriate to the context or the social situation.

Academic tasks and educational interactions may require the child to use language skills in contexts where there are few cues to help out. The accurate interpretation and use of language depends upon the full and adequate use of all available syntactic and semantic cues. In interpersonal interactions, especially in the social domain, the situation changes. There contextual, environmental, and nonverbal communication cues add redundancy to the spoken language. For instance, posture and body language can add dimensions to a verbal message. They may serve to modify, negate, or enhance the verbal messages, to add an affective and intentional dimension. They also indicate the status and expectations of the listener or audience (Argyle, 1972; Birdwhistell, 1970).

Language and learning disabled youngsters have often been described as ineffective in dealing with nonverbal communication cues in interpersonal interactions. According to Johnson and Myklebust (1967), they show "social imperception." Their difficulties in handling nonverbal cues in social interactions may exist along with problems in dealing with the verbal messages (Bryan, 1978; Wiig & Harris, 1974; Wiig & Semel, 1976). These problems seem related in part to visual-spatial and visual-motor integration problems. The resulting confusion in the child's perceptions may in turn lead to inappropriate expressions of his own feelings, expectations, or social intentions.

One of the overall goals in any language intervention is competence in interpersonal communications. To achieve this competence, it may be necessary to work on more than knowledge and use of linguistic rules, words and sentences, and pragmatic meanings. It may be necessary to directly improve the child's perception and expression of nonverbal communication cues. Several strategies and methods facilitate and improve social perception and nonverbal communication (Wiig & Semel, 1976, pp. 297–318). As the child's awareness and recognition of the significance of nonverbal cues in communication improve, his awareness and sense of the social register and language style and expectations of his audience should improve. This awareness and sense of the subtle verbal and nonverbal cues in speaker-audience interactions and of differences in style and register among speakers and audiences may be further improved through guided observations of films and of role-playing interactions. Then role-playing activities can be used to give the child practice in using varied verbal and nonverbal registers and styles. Emphasis on interpersonal interactions may be especially appropriate in intervention during adolescence and young adulthood. The test and manual *Let's talk* (Sathre, Olson, & Whitney, 1973) appears particularly relevant for use with adolescents.

# SELECTED PROGRAMS AND SOURCE MATERIALS

1. *A student-centered language arts curriculum, Grade K-6, Grade K-13.*
   James Moffett. Houghton Mifflin Company, Boston, MA.

2. *Developing understanding of self and others: Play kit and manual.*
   D. Dinkmeyer. American Guidance Service, Circle Pines, MN.

3. *Ideas, images, I. The triple "I" series.*
   J. M. Franco, J. M. Kelley, and T. Whitman. American Book Company, Cincinnati, OH.

4. *Let's talk: Activities supplement.*
   C. I. Whitney, F. S. Sathre, and R. W. Olson. Scott Foresman Company, Glenview, IL.

5. *New dimensions in creativity.*
   J. S. Renzulli. Harper and Row, New York, NY.

6. *Semel auditory processing program.*
   Eleanor M. Semel. Follett Educational Publishing Company, Chicago, IL.

7. *Smiles, nods, and pauses: activities to enrich children's communication skills.*
   Dorothy Grant Hennings. Citation Press, 50 West 44th Street, New York, NY 10036.

8. *Sound-order-sense: a developmental program in auditory perception.*
   Eleanor M. Semel. Follett Educational Publishing Co., Chicago, IL.

9. *Teaching the universe of discourse.*
   James Moffett. Houghton Mifflin Company, Boston, MA.

10. *The structure of intellect: its interpretation and uses.*
    M. N. Meeker. Charles E. Merrill Publishing Company, 1300 Alum Creek Drive, Columbus, OH 43216.

11. *Experiences in language.*
    W. T. Petty, D. C. Petty, and M. F. Becking. Allyn and Bacon, Boston, MA.

*part* V

# Language Components of the Curriculum

# LANGUAGE DEMANDS OF THE CURRICULUM
## Reading

# 14

The language demands of the traditional curriculum change considerably during the youngster's educational career. The strategies emphasized in preschool programs focus mainly on sensorimotor and language development and on social and emotional growth. Auditory-perceptual, visual-perceptual, visual-spatial, and visual-motor experiences are used to help prepare the child for academic learning. The materials used tend to be manipulative, three-dimensional, and concrete.

During the early grades (K, 1, and 2), the curriculum shifts to provide opportunities for the child to develop perceptual-cognitive strategies. Here major emphasis is on developing basic academic skills, particularly reading and simple computations. The materials used in teaching tend to feature one-dimensional, more abstract, symbolic representations. The curriculum focuses on the preoperational development of the child (Piaget, 1969).

During the middle grades (3 and 4), an even greater demand is placed upon the child's linguistic and symbolic language skills. The emphasis in teaching shifts to include content areas such as social studies, science, mathematics, and health education. Basic skills may be reviewed, but they are no longer taught. The curriculum focuses on the concrete-operational development of the child (Piaget, 1969). Towards the end of this period, teaching strategies may emphasize the abstract-symbolic dimension of language more and more. Materials are abstract symbolic representations. The children are expected to show the ability to abstract, analyze, and synthesize. The contents and strategies provided in curricula focus on helping the child move from using concrete-externalized to abstract-internalized operations in learning and problem solving. Heavier demands are placed on the child's ability to express himself, his ideas, and abstract relationships in written language. The children are asked to give oral reports. Their reading selections and literature use higher level vocabulary, more complex sentence structures, and more abstract concepts. Comprehension and recall of meaning becomes critical to the reading process, while more elementary decoding skills are assumed.

In other content areas, reading is often treated differently for academically achieving and for learning disabled youngsters. Academic achievers may be encouraged to read assignments silently, while the learning disabled children may be asked to read orally. But reading out loud may impede the children's acquisition of information, as it emphasizes decoding individual words. Instead, learning disabled children should be encouraged to use contextual cues and synthesize phrase, clause, and sentence meaning. The language and learning disabled youngster with reading comprehension problems may benefit from short, silent reading periods no more than 7 to 9 minutes long.

The traditional curriculum in the upper elementary grades (5 and 6) provides even greater emphasis on content areas. The youngster is expected to have accuracy, fluency, and flexibility in using the basic academic skills and in recalling the information presented in the earlier grades. The curriculum focuses on the development of formal-operational strategies in problem solving (Piaget, 1969). The language demands require mature and efficient linguistic and cognitive-semantic processing and production of language. The gradual change in the curriculum from emphasizing basic skills to focusing exclusively on content areas is illustrated in Figure 14.1.

Learning the contents of the traditional curriculum depends upon acquiring a hierarchy of skills and knowledge. The child with language and learning disabilities may have problems and delays in acquiring and in demonstrating specific skills and the related contents. Unfortunately, the youngster's difficulties may be exacerbated inadvertently by common teaching styles.

Academic competence and skill acquisition are generally evaluated in the classroom through verbal or written questions from the teacher. Most classroom interactions are characterized by an overabundance of teacher questions paired with a dearth of student questions. Recitational or specific memory questions from the teacher tend to predominate. On the other hand, questions that reveal a grasp or understanding of cause-and-effect relationships, such as *why* questions, tend to occur rarely (Gall, 1970; Susskind, 1969; Zimmerman & Bergan, 1971).

*These concepts have been discussed throughout this book. See the index for specific references.*

Questioning for recall of specific information or for oral recitation may put language and learning disabled children at a disadvantage. Their ability to perform may be limited by problems in immediate and sequential auditory memory, internal rehearsal, input organization, word finding, and retrieval.

The youngster who brings a significant language problem to the classroom may come up against other barriers to learning. The youngster's language style may be different from the teacher's. Teachers tend to use formal language in the classroom. Language and learning disabled students may know and use only an informal language style and may be unable to switch codes to satisfy the teacher's language demands. The contrast in language styles may present a real barrier to comprehension, learning, and communication.

In the upper elementary grades and in high school, teachers frequently present information in long spoken monologues, and students are expected to take notes. The classroom presentations may make

**FIGURE 14.1**
*Illustration of the Primary Emphases on Basic Skills and Content Areas in the Traditional Curriculum*

**PRE-SCHOOL YEARS**

Language development & social-emotional growth. Visual- & auditory perceptual, visual-spatial & motor skills

**EARLY GRADES**
**(K, 1-2)**

Development of basic skills in reading and writing (letters, words, sentences), spelling (oral & written), and arithmetic

**MIDDLE GRADES**
**(3-4)**

Review of basic skills & introduction of content areas such as English, social studies, science, and mathematics

**UPPER GRADES**
**(5-6)**

Emphasis on acquisition of knowledge in content areas, including English, social studies, science, and mathematics

**JUNIOR & SENIOR HIGH**

Expansion of the content areas with emphasis on English (composition, literature, language arts, and study skills), social studies (American and world history, economics), foreign languages (French, Spanish, Latin), science (biology, chemistry, physics), mathematics (algebra, geometry), and vocational education

frequent reference to, but not highlight or specifically review, information that is assumed to have been acquired earlier.

The teachers assume that the children know and can use a variety of vocabulary items, concepts, and sentence structures. Unfortunately, the chronological or logical order of the events, actions, or relationships the teacher describes may not be apparent. The lecture may jump in space or time from one sentence to the next or from paragraph to paragraph. The students are expected to adjust to these abrupt jumps, and reorganize the material internally while they hear it. But this internal reorganization of spoken input may be impossible, inaccurate, or inefficient for the language and learning disabled youngster. The teacher may completely fail to provide the guidance, structure, and support the language disabled student needs to succeed.

An additional barrier to successful learning experiences may be the sheer volume of the information presented to be learned. Students are often given irrelevant information interspersed with relevant data. The two may not be easily differentiated by the language and learning disabled students. They need materials to be divided into manageable,

**FIGURE 14.2**
*Volume of Information*

logically sequenced, and relevant units of information. Irrelevant information must be reduced, and relevant facts and material identified and highlighted.

Vocabulary must be familiar and well below grade level (2 years or more) for these students. Only a limited number of unfamiliar words should be introduced in each content unit to facilitate vocabulary growth. Experience suggests that no more than five new and unfamiliar vocabulary items should be introduced within a single lesson or unit. Vocabulary words that denote abstract concepts such as "freedom," "liberty," and "democracy" should not be introduced until the students understand the concepts. The teacher should also control sentence length and structure to feature structurally simple and relatively short sentences of from approximately 8 to 10 words in length. These sentences may seem short and choppy to the teacher. They may not seem to flow easily or to allow stylistic variation and elegance. However, some students need these short structures if they are to be successful in learning the content information.

Abramowitz (1978) provides an illustration of the effects of reducing sentence length and vocabulary level on readability. He analyzed a reading sample of 105 words using the Dale-Chall readability quotient. The original sample contained 5 sentences with an average length of 21 words. The readability quotient indicated that it was at the 11th to 12th grade level. When the number of sentences was increased to 10 and average sentence length decreased to 10 words, the readability was at the 5th or 6th grade level. It remained at that level when adapted to include 15 sentences with an average length of 7 words. Adaptation of the vocabulary resulted in comparatively greater reductions in grade level equivalence.

The visual characteristics of materials may also influence learning success for the language and learning disabled. Materials and presentations may not have adequate and appropriate illustrations. Pictures may help these children interpret verbal materials and recode the message from the auditory-verbal code to an internal perceptual (visual) image. In some cases, textbook print may be too small or too dense. Long, typed materials may fail to attract the youngster's attention. Learning disabled children in the middle grades may respond to color coding of critical words, concepts, or relations. In the upper grades, underlining or italics may achieve the same goal of attracting and focusing the children's attention. A visually presented summary of important facts may provide an added focus for attention, storage, and recall.

Concomitant or isolated deficits in visual-motor, visual-spatial, and auditory-perceptual abilities may result in a spectrum of specific problems in learning to read, write, spell, and compute. The implications of these deficits on the curriculum have been discussed elsewhere by, among others, Frostig (1965) and Lerner (1971). The academic problems of children with learning disabilities may or may not include overt language deficits. In a similar vein, speech articulation problems may or may not be associated with language and learning disabilities.

The rest of this chapter discusses the potential impact of language disabilities on basic reading skills, and the various approaches that may be taken to teaching reading. Chapter 15 discusses the effect of language disabilities on specific curriculum content areas. The areas covered in chapter 15 are English, mathematics, social studies, science, and foreign languages. In this chapter and the next, we will focus on the curriculum demands and prerequisite language skills in the upper grades and at the high school level.

## READING TASK REQUIREMENTS

Reading comprehension is a secondary language skill that has phonetic, syntactic, semantic, and memory components. The beginning reader seems to be more dependent upon graphic information in decoding than the skilled reader. As the reader learns to process graphic-phonic cues more effectively, the syntactic and semantic information assumes greater importance. This shift in the reading process, from a primarily visual mode to auditory and intersensory modes, appears to occur around the fourth grade (Hallahan & Cruickshank, 1973).

Reading seems to depend upon knowledge of the structural (syntactic) and word selectional (semantic) rules of the native language. This relationship has been expressed in a variety of forms. For example, Kavanagh (1968) has stated that "reading is parasitic on language," while Venezky (1968) purports that "reading is translating from written symbols to a form of language to which the person can already attach meaning."

It is a basic goal of the educational process to develop proficiency in reading for accurate comprehension. We can differentiate poor and good readers on the basis of characteristics of the process they use (Clay, 1969). Good readers verify their predictions by reading at the sound-letter (phoneme-grapheme) level. Poor readers, in contrast, do not appear to verify their predictions. On this basis, Clay states that "motor, perceptual, and language differences would perhaps be of greater significance [in reading] than general intelligence" (p. 55). Clay suggests that children with language disabilities or reductions experience:

> difficulty in predicting constructions likely to occur and in noticing the redundant cues which signal that errors have occurred. There is good reason to believe that the very complexity that provides rich cue sources for the child who is able to discover the regularities of the code may present confusion to the child with limited language skill. (p. 55)

Mattingly (1972) suggests that the efficient reader must have two types of linguistic abilities: (1) primary linguistic activity and (2) linguistic awareness. Primary linguistic activity includes the ability to apply a set of internalized syntactic-semantic rules to the processing, comprehension, and production of language. Linguistic awareness refers to the ability to talk about or reflect on language, to segment spoken language into phoneme sequences, and to handle written text in alphabetic form.

Goodman (1967, 1969) has presented a model for reading for beginning and proficient readers based on analysis of miscue error. Within that model, reading is seen as a selective, tentative, anticipatory process. The proficient reader decodes directly from the graphic stimuli and encodes from the deep structure to reflect the underlying meaning. The verbal output in reading may therefore reflect transformations at the syntactic (surface-structure) and semantic (vocabulary) levels, even though the meaning (deep structure) is retained. The efficient reader also uses three types of information simultaneously: the graphic input, the syntactic structure, and the semantic interpretation. The reader formulates anticipatory hypotheses about the input on the basis of syntactic and semantic information. He then samples the graphic information to either confirm or reject his initial hypotheses.

Investigations of specific oral language components and their relationship to reading achievement suggest that the dependence on knowledge of morphology and syntax increases with advance in grade level. At the first grade level, when reading materials are syntactically simple, there is no significant relationship between oral syntax and reading (Bougere, 1969). At fourth grade level, when reading materials have increased in syntactic complexity, reading comprehension and oral syntax appear to related (Redell, 1965; Sauer, 1968). Similarly, knowledge of morphology relates to reading achievement at both the first and second grade levels when the reading materials contain expansions in the variety and use of morphological structures (Brittain, 1970). The link between the spoken and the read language is dramatically illustrated in this poem.

> I well remember my delight when first
> The meaning of a printed sentence burst
> Upon me; I had vaguely sensed a link
> Between the symbols reproduced in ink
> And what was read to me, but had not found,
> The kinship of the letters and the sound;
> Then suddenly the synthesis was clear,
> And all at once I understood that here

Incorporated in these symbols lay
The language I was speaking every day.

*WILLIAM S. CORWIN*

## APPROACHES TO READING

The proficient reader uses all of his knowledge of the spoken language and all of his language experiences when he reads (Goodman, 1969). He matches the printed phrases, clauses, and sentences with their previously learned and stored meaning counterparts. He anticipates what may come next, and he forms tentative hypotheses about possible structures and meanings. When he encounters a new sentence in the on-going process of reading, he either accepts or rejects the tentative hypothesis he formed about it and its meaning. The reader must rapidly link printed letter sequences, words, phrases, and clauses to their underlying meaning. He must accurately analyze and integrate the surface structure characteristics and their contributions to sentence meaning. He must be able to remember his tentative hypothesis to compare it to the printed sentence. At any one time, the reader must hold both the hypothesized meaning of the message and the actual structure and meaning of the printed message immediately available in his memory. At times, even a good and efficient reader may resort to skills and processes he depended upon years before if he encounters an unexpected or unfamiliar sentence.

For instance assume that you were to see the nonsense word "complyishment" in an otherwise meaningful printed sentence. You might approach the word in several ways. You might decide to discard the word since it is unfamiliar and not sound it out or read it at all. You might sound it out letter by letter. You might decide that the word is a noun, even though unfamiliar, since it has the familiar derivational ending -*ment*. You might decide that the noun has several meaningful components, *com-* (prefix), -*plyish-* (base), and -*ment* (derivational suffix). You might say about these components that they are also syllables. You might assign meaning to some of the components you have identified, either by familiarity and/or by analogy with words such as "comply" or "compartment." Chances are, however, that the word will remain an oral reading word without a base of meaning.

The beginning reader is struggling to learn the processes and strategies that will make him efficient and proficient. Any one of the processes involved in reading can cause problems. The child can have difficulty with:

(1) Visually decoding the printed, graphic input.
(2) Integrating the auditory-visual (sound-symbol) inputs.
(3) Associating printed words, phrases, concepts, and relations with their underlying meaning.
(4) Processing the surface structure of the printed sentences and relating it to the underlying meaning (deep structure).
(5) Generating tentative, anticipatory hypotheses about subsequent printed messages.

(6) Verifying, rejecting, or revising the anticipatory hypotheses with reference to the actual printed, graphic representations.

We can think of the process of learning to read as a process of superimposing a new, secondary symbol code upon an already known, spoken language code. We apply the same linguistic rules (phonology, morphology, syntax, semantics) to both the spoken and the read symbolic codes. When the normally developing child is confronted with the task to learn to read, he may bring to the task a listening vocabulary of from 8,000 to 10,000 words (McKee, 1966). He also brings knowledge of common morphological rules and syntactic structures and basic sentence transformations. He has the auditory and visual attention, the discrimination, and the memory abilities he will need for the task. He is entering into a stage of development in which his mode of behavior changes from being relatively impulsive to being relatively reflexive. His tendencies for impulsive, snap responses give way to more control (Kagan, Rosman, Kay, & Phillips, 1964; White, 1965). He has successfully completed the sensorimotor stage of cognitive development and is entering the concrete operational stage (Inhelder & Piaget, 1964; Piaget & Inhelder, 1969). The normally developing child has the potential to successfully transfer his skills from the auditory-oral or spoken language code to the graphic-symbolic or written language code.

Unfortunately, deficits, problems, or delays in acquiring basic prerequisite skills and competencies may lead to reading failure. Of course, failure to learn to read adequately may result from many other contributing factors, including cultural deprivation, bilingualism, emotional instability, sensory deficits, cognitive and intellectual limitations, restricted environmental opportunities, poor teaching, and lack of motivation. The way reading is taught may also enhance or detract from the child's potential for reading. The next sections discuss common approaches to reading and their relationship to basic language skills.

## Basal Reading and Language and Learning Disabilities

Basal reading emphasizes the "look-say," sight, or whole word approach to teaching reading. The vocabulary incorporated in basal readers is selected and sequenced for grade level based on word lists. In this approach, the child is exposed to multiple presentations of printed–spoken word combinations until he can identify and label the printed words. A sight vocabulary is then featured repeatedly in sentences, paragraphs, and stories.

In teaching a sight vocabulary, certain assumptions are made. It is assumed that the large majority of words, with the exception of homographs such as "wind"/"wind" (noun-verb) are unique in appearance. Similarities and differences in word configurations may be identified through one or more of the following features.

(1) Internal details such as:
  (a) Letters below, above, and below and above the lines, as in the words

"peg" [below]    "bet" [above]    "pet" [below and above]
"pig" [below]    "half" [above]    "girl" [below and above]

(b) Presence of double letters, as in the words:

kitten    mi<u>dd</u>le    su<u>pp</u>er    squi<u>rr</u>el

(c) Presence of "little" words embedded in "big" words, as in:

<u>sto</u>p – top    <u>sat</u> – at    <u>win</u> – in    difficult – if

(2) Unusual length, as in the words:

hippopotamus    Washington

(3) Configuration by outline, as in words such as:

pill ⌐⌐⌐    log ⌐⌐⌐    help ⌐⌐⌐

(4) Mnemonic devices, such as:

| | |
|---|---|
| fri<u>end</u> | (to the <u>end</u>) |
| prin<u>cipal</u> | (is your <u>pal</u>) |
| the<u>i</u>r | (only people have eyes—i) |
| the<u>r</u>e | (places do not have eyes; only people have eyes) |
| sepa<u>rat</u>e | (there is a rat in sepa<u>rat</u>e) |

(5) Associations, as in the case of the words:

l o͝o k    b͡e d

(6) Learned or known root words or bases, as in:

<u>cover</u>ed, dis<u>cover</u>ed, un<u>cover</u>ed    [cover]

(7) Context cues used to guess at a word, as in:

Grandmother baked a chocolate layer (<u>cake</u>).

The words incorporated in the initial sight vocabulary list are often selected from and taught in the child's immediate educational environment. They may be taught by placing printed word labels on objects in the room. They may be taught by associating printed words with pictures, in association with stories, charts, posters, ads, or activity notices. They may be featured in preprimers and other formal materials with controlled vocabulary or in word lists.

The sight or "look-say" approach to teaching reading has inherent limitations. Among them are that every word is introduced in isolation, without showing its semantic, linguistic, or phonetic relationships to already-established words or word categories. Second, at or after the second grade level, the needed inventory of sight words becomes so large that the visual differences among words may be obscured. Third, the approach may not be successful with children with visual-perceptual, visual memory, and visuo-spatial deficits. This approach may also be unsuccessful with children with language disabilities and word-finding problems. (Mattis, French, & Rapin, 1975). These limitations, whether inherent or in application, suggest that for some children this approach may be inefficient or uneconomical.

However, the approach does have advantages. Some words are difficult to decode from the printed to the spoken form by applying

*See the list at the end of the chapter for sources for word lists.*

phonetic-phonemic rules. The inventory of basic sight vocabulary items includes at least 200 words which make up at least 50% to 75% of all ordinary reading materials. These words are featured in Dolch's Basic Sight Vocabulary List in the *Manual for Remedial Reading*. These basic sight vocabulary items may be used along with any other approach to reading to assist children with reading difficulties. The sight approach to reading, adapted and expanded, may result in success in reading for children with auditory perception and processing and auditory-visual integration deficits. Adopting the "look-say" or sight approach to reading with these children should, however, not be taken to mean that intervention to strengthen auditory processing skills should be abandoned. The "look-say" method may be especially useful for establishing new reading vocabulary words. The youngster may be successful in using an auditory approach to eliciting and decoding highly familiar sight vocabulary. This added strategy may in many cases allow the language and learning disabled child to stay in the same reading program as his academically achieving age peers. The classroom teacher should be informed when and when not to use a sight approach with children with language and learning disabilities. With some of these children, the teacher may be advised to use a sight approach only with unfamiliar and new reading words, in combination with other approaches to facilitate reading.

The most widely used basal reading programs include those listed below. While these basal readers focus on a visual, whole word approach to reading, most also feature phonics programs as a vital part of the reading materials.

(1) *The New Basic Readers*. Scott, Foresman, and Company, 433 E. Erie Street, Chicago, ILL; and 1900 E. Lake Avenue, Glenview, ILL.

   This reading program features materials for the pre-primer level up to and including the sixth grade. The language at the lower levels may be considered stilted, bearing little resemblance to children's language.

(2) *Reading for Meaning*. Houghton Mifflin Company, Educational Division, 110 Tremont Street, Boston, MA 02107.

   The objective of this program is reading readiness. It features excellent readiness activities, manipulative materials with a multisensory emphasis, and specific and practical manuals.

(3) *Ginn Basic Readers*. Ginn and Company, 125 2nd Avenue, Waltham, MA 02154.

   This program ranges from readiness to the eighth grade level. The program is carefully conceived and executed, with exceptionally good teacher guides. Many good enrichment books are available as supplements to this program.

(4) *The Alice and Jerry Reading Program*. Harper and Row, 49 E. 33 Street, New York, NY 10016.

   The scope of this program spans from the readiness level to the fourth grade level. It is a typical basal reading series.

(5) *The Macmillan Readers*. Macmillan Company, 866 Third Avenue, New York, NY 10022.

The range of this program is from the preprimer to the eighth grade level.

## Auditory Approaches to Reading

In the auditory approaches to teaching reading, the emphasis is on establishing associations between speech sounds (phonemes) and their printed letter (grapheme) representations. Knowledge of speech sound and letter associations is thought to provide the key to unlocking new and unfamiliar words in reading. Within the range of auditory approaches to reading, it is possible to differentiate three major emphases. They are:

(1) Phonics,
(2) Linguistics,
(3) Phonetics.

### Phonics Systems

The phonics system focuses on developing the child's recognition that printed letters in printed words represent speech sounds. In the instructional phases, the children are taught which speech sounds are associated with which letters or combinations of letters. The stated instructional objectives suggest that reading programs using a phonics approach reconcile the dilemma of matching about 44 significant speech sounds to only 26 printed letters. Phonics programs tend to place heavy emphasis on the auditory discrimination of similarly spelled patterns in words. The vowel sounds are divided into three categories—long, short, and irregularly spelled. Printed words that contain identically spelled segments are grouped together and sounded out. The instructional pattern is to move from printed symbols to sound symbols, rather than from the familiar sounds to the unfamiliar printed symbols. The word groups featured below illustrate commonly used word group patterns. As can be seen, some regional pronunciation patterns may confuse the child, since the same sound may be used to pronounce the letter sequences *-ack* and *-uck* and *-in*, *-en*, and *-an*.

| Word group A | | Word group B | | |
| --- | --- | --- | --- | --- |
| *-ock* | *-uck* | *-in* | *-en* | *-an* |
| dock | duck | pin | pen | pan |
| lock | luck | tin | ten | tan |
| sock | tuck | win | when | can |
| rock | buck | bin | then | fan |

Traditionally, proponents of phonics introduce vowels before consonants for at least two reasons: (1) all syllables and all words contain at least one vowel; (2) vowels carry more of a clue to a word's pronunciation than do consonants. This last reason is interesting when we consider that at least one contemporary written language, Hebrew, uses no vowels. The vowels are "filled in" by the reader on the basis of his knowledge of the spoken language. If this task sounds difficult, consider the two sequences below. The first features consonants only.

The second features vowels only. Read each one without referring to the printed intended sentences at the bottom of the page.

(1)  CN  SH  RD  THS?

(2)  EE  A  I  OW.

We can offer several rationales for teaching consonants first in phonics analysis, especially with language and learning disabled youngsters. First, the majority of the early reading words begin with consonants. For instance, about 80% of the Dolch Basic Sight Words begin with consonants and about 87% of the words on the related *Dale List of 769 Easy Words* begin with consonants (Dale, 1931). Second, the child should be encouraged to attack printed words from left to right. Since most of the early words have initial consonants, the second rationale follows directly from the first. Third, consonants are featured strongly in English syllable configurations and hold more cues to their pronunciation than vowels do. Fourth, language and learning disabled youngsters with auditory processing deficits appear to have special problems in vowel discrimination.

Here is the basic sequence commonly followed in the phonics approach to reading.

STEP 1.  Auditory and visual discrimination of initial consonants or vowels, short and long.

STEP 2.  Auditory discrimination of rhyming words.

STEP 3.  Auditory and visual discrimination of consonant digraphs (*sh, ch, th, wh*).

STEP 4.  Syllabication.

STEP 5.  Auditory and visual discrimination of blends.

STEP 6.  Auditory and visual discrimination of "silent e" (tap-tap*e*).

STEP 7.  Auditory and visual discrimination of phonograms, word families, and vowel digraphs (b*oa*t, *ea*t, tr*ee*).

STEP 8.  Vowel exceptions, i.e., the effects of -*r* on preceding vowels (-*ir*, -*er*, -*ar*).

Among widely used phonics reading systems are the following:

(1)  *Reading with Phonics* ("Hay-Wingo"). J. Hay and C. Wingo. J. B. Lippincott, E. Washington Square, Philadelphia, PA 19105.

This system features a series of workbooks teaching phonics generalizations through deduction. Pictures are used to teach letter-sound associations.

(2)  *Phonics We Use.* M. Meighen, M. Pratt, and M. Halvorson. Lyons and Carnahan, 407 East 25th Street, Chicago, IL.

This program features auditory and visual discrimination practice and drill. Auditory and visual discrimination skills are then combined in practice to recognize various initial consonants.

---

(1)  Can she read this?

(2)  See a big cow.

(3) *Speech to Print Phonics.* D. D. Durrell and H. A. Murphy. Harcourt, Brace, Jovanovich, Inc., 757 Third Avenue, New York, NY.

The emphasis is on moving from speech which is already known to printed words or symbols for speech. The program features a kit containing 233 cards to use for practice on the phonics elements taught. A teacher's manual is provided. Connected reading materials, appropriate to the generalizations being taught, must accompany use of the kit.

(4) *Time for Phonics.* L. B. Scott. McGraw Hill Book Company, Manchester Road, Manchester, MO.

Development of listening skills is emphasized initially. Letter symbols are introduced as representations of speech sounds the youngster can discriminate and recognize. Key words are featured. These are subsequently used in the development of stories and poetry.

(5) *Functional Phonetics.* A. D. Cordts. Benefic Press, 10300 Roosevelt Road, Westchester, IL.

Readiness activities are provided to prepare for reading. The system features blending of parts of words into words, identifying beginning sounds in words, matching beginning elements in words, and matching final elements in words.

(6) *The Sound Way to Easy Reading.* A. J. Bremmer and J. Davis. Bremmer-Davis Phonics, Inc., 161 Green Bay Road, Wilmette, IL.

This approach features listening-looking-repeating sequences in phonics analysis. Letter sounds and key words are recorded on four phonographs. Charts that feature the letters and key words are provided.

(7) *Landon Phonics Program.* A. Landon. Chandler Publishing Company, 124 Spear Street, San Francisco, CA.

This system features a sequential program that combines auditory and visual discrimination and association training. The program includes 20 recordings of sounds and words and associated worksheets for the children. It emphasizes repeated practice, left-to-right progression in reading, and individualized learning.

*Linguistics Approaches*

The linguistic approaches to teaching reading have their origin in the descriptive linguistics or phonemic approach to classifying the significant speech sounds of the spoken language (Bloomfield & Barnhart, 1961; Fries, 1963; Lefevre, 1964). These approaches are based on the premise that children have already acquired the spoken linguistic forms (phonemes, morphemes, and basic syntactic structures) that are represented by the printed letter and word shapes. Therefore they already have an established meaning and structure base for the printed language forms. The process and objective in teaching reading is said to be to translate the unknown letters (graphemes) into their already known sound correlates (phonemes). The primary objective is best realized when the child associates the significant speech sounds with their corresponding letter representations.

The vocabulary used to teach phoneme-grapheme (sound-letter) associations initially is controlled to present monosyllabic, two- or three-letter familiar words. Picture cues to word meanings are eliminated to avoid distraction from the main learning objective. The process of forming phoneme-grapheme associations is based on inductive learning principles. The child is presented with phonemically and phonetically regular words (**graphones**) in which the spelling of a specific sound is consistent. This may result in word sequences such as:

> Dan ran to Fran and Stan.
> The fat cat played with a bat.
> Tim and Jim are slim and trim.
> Meg begs for a peg.

Linguistically based readers often include sound grids which the teacher can use to elicit rhyming words and word families. These word groups are at times indistinguishable from the word groups featured in the phonics system. The sound grids shown in Figure 14.3 are typical examples.

Here are some of the widely used linguistic reading programs.

(1) *Let's Read.* L. Bloomfield and C. Barnhart. Clarence L. Barnhart, Inc., Box 250, Bronxville, NY.

This program is structured and systematic. It features contrasting phoneme-grapheme patterns or minimal word pairs which are consistently different in meaning but similar in form ("Nat," "mat," "cat," "fat," "sat," etc.). Regular patterns are presented and repeated with contrasting sound-letter elements. The patterns are memorized by rote in isolation.

(2) *The Merrill Linguistic Reading Program.* C. C. Fries, R. Wilson, and M. K. Rudolph. Charles E. Merrill Publishing Company, 1300 Alum Creek Drive, Columbus, OH 43216.

This program features the "three major spelling patterns in English," a unique aspect. Words featured in the spelling patterns are first introduced in list format. They are then incorporated into a story. The emphasis is on learning to perceive and differentiate likenesses and differences in the printed words in a word family and among the various word families.

(3) *SRA Basic Reading Series.* D. E. Rasmussen and L. Goldberg. Science Research Associates, 259 East Erie Street, Chicago, IL.

This program features alphabet and letter names followed by phonetically regular word patterns as the basis for reading. Reading is done in unison in classroom activities.

(4) *The Linguistic Readers.* C. Stratemeyer and B. Weiss. Benziger, Inc., 8701 Wilshire Boulevard, Beverly Hills, CA.

This program features vocabulary items with more than three letters and one syllable. The vocabulary is introduced in a regularly evolving linguistic sequence. Sight words are introduced. Simple drawings are featured, and animals are the focus of events in the series.

(5) *The Miami Linguistic Readers.* P. M. Rojas, R. Robinett, P. W. Bell. D. C. Heath and Company, Lexington, MA.

These readers take a linguistics-oriented language arts approach to reading. The materials have been designed to be culture-free and to minimize

## WORD LIST FOR TEACHER REFERENCE

**FIGURE 14.3**
*Typical Sound Grids from Linguistically Based Reader*

| Pages | Words in Pattern | Sight Words |
|---|---|---|
| Unit 1 5-8 | cat fat Nat | is a |
| Unit 2 9-12 | pat mat sat | the on |
| Unit 3 13-16 | hat | not |
| Unit 4 17-20 | bat at | look he |
| Unit 5 21-26 | can man ran Dan Jan | |
| Unit 6 27-32 | fan pan van | to in |
| Unit 7 33-38 | cap lap nap Dan's Jan's | see her |
| Unit 8 39-44 | map tap | his |

| Pages | Words in Pattern | Sight Words |
|---|---|---|
| Unit 9 45-50 | Dad Dad's had bad Nat's | she |
| Unit 10 51-56 | mad sad | and |
| Unit 11 57-62 | ham jam Sam Sam's am | I |
| Unit 12 63-68 | bag rag tag wag | it |
| Unit 13 69-77 | bats pats taps maps bags rags  Rags wags | |

Source: Fries, C. C., Wilson, R., and Rudolph, M. K. *The Merrill Linguistic Reading Program* (Columbus: Charles E. Merrill, 1980).

phonemic irregularities. The focus is on the acquisition of phrase patterns. Imitation of the teacher's model with whole-word, sight reading is emphasized during the initial stages. Reading aloud is also emphasized.

(6) *Programmed Reading.* C. D. Buchanan and M. W. Sullivan. McGraw-Hill Book Company, Manchester Road, Manchester, MO.

This program features a sequence of programmed materials sequenced according to linguistic-phonemic principles. Vowels and consonants are featured in workbooks in 14 different settings in a series of teaching frames. A test is inserted after every 50 frames within the programmed materials. Storybooks which are to be used after each workbook has been completed are included. The emphasis is on individualized rates of learning, testing, and writing out of responses rather than upon response selection.

(7) *The Michigan Language Program.* D. E. P. Smith and P. Carrigan. L.R.I., 1501 Broadway, New York, NY.

This program features structured, step-by-step material frames. The frames were designed and programmed to provide auditory, spatial, sequential, and visual discrimination responses. The stimuli are controlled for complexity in developmental order. The program identifies skills in the order in which they are considered to emerge. It is self-instructional, with the teacher acting as a monitor.

(8) *Basic Reading.* G. McCracken and C. C. Walcutt. J. P. Lippincott Company, Educational Publications Division, East Washington Square, Philadelphia, PA.

This program is both linguistically and visually oriented. It features colorful illustrations in association with the texts. Readiness activities are provided for visual discrimination, likenesses and differences, left-to-right progression, and basic sounds. Sounds are introduced in isolation and then immediately incorporated in stories. A limited repertory of sight words introduced. The program provides readers, filmstrips, recordings, and enrichment materials.

(9) *The Palo Alto Program.* T. E. Glin. Harcourt, Brace, Jovanovich, Inc., 757 Third Avenue, New York, NY.

This program features step-by-step structured sequences with small incremental changes. Writing activities precede reading instruction. The program is individualized and self-correcting.

## Phonetic Approaches

The phonetic approaches to teaching reading may be called *one-to-one sound-symbol* approaches. In these approaches, a single symbol or a coded symbol represents one and only one speech sound. As a consequence, each of the 44 speech sounds is represented by a printed symbol. There are three major variations of the phonetic approach.

### Variation 1.

Additional symbols are invented to provide for one-to-one correspondences between the significant sounds (phonemes) and the corresponding printed letters.

### Variation 2.

A number code is attached to parts of words or to letters and letter combinations. The code indicates the most frequently occurring spelling (primary, secondary, tertiary) of the sound in the specific context.

Additional sensory cues in the form of color coding, texture, or shading are introduced. The letters/symbols are coded so that the phonetic-phonemic irregularities of the language are reconciled by consistent representation by the elements of the code.

The systems that feature a one-to-one sound-symbol approach to teaching reading include those summarized below. All variations of this approach provide some transition process from using the modified printed letters (graphemes) to using the regular printed alphabet and letters.

(1) *The Phonovisual Method.* L. D. Schoolfield, J. B. Timberlake, and M. Buckley. Phonovisual Products, Inc., 4708 Wisconsin Avenue, N. W., Washington, DC.

This program is organized in a sequential plan for teaching auditory and visual discrimination and integration. Phonovisual consonant and vowel charts are provided for teaching. After the initial acquisition of consonants and vowels, secondary spelling, structural analysis, compound words, polysyllabic words, roots, prefixes, and suffixes are introduced. No readiness activities are included. Phonemic and structural analysis is emphasized in the approach to unlocking unfamiliar and new words.

(2) *Initial Teaching Alphabet.* I. Pitman and J. Pitman. Initial Teaching Alphabet Publications, 20 East 46th Street, New York, NY.

The system features the ITA, a phonemically based alphabet which uses regular phonemic sound symbols in teaching. Letter names are not taught, and sight words are not used in rote learning activities. Only lower case letters are used. In the transition stage, the emphasis is on reconciling irregularities in spelling. Workbooks are used in association with storybooks.

(3) *Words in Color.* C. Gattegno. Schools for the Future, P. O. Box 349, Cooper Station, New York, NY.

This system provides a phonemic approach to teaching reading with the use of color cues to reconcile irregularities. Printed symbols with added color cues are translated into speech sounds. No letter names are used, and word families are not emphasized. The program provides colored letter charts for classroom use, descriptions or principles for the teacher, and workbooks and worksheets for the child.

(4) *The Writing Road to Reading.* R. B. Spalding. William Morrow and Company, 105 Madison Avenue, New York, NY.

This system relies on a so-called *unified phonics* approach to learning the phonemic bases of language. Notations are used in spelling to indicate the phonogram used in a particular word. The system features a highly structured and systematic approach to reading. It emphasizes repetition and stimulus-response association learning.

(5) *Psycholinguistic Color System.* A. Bannatyne. Learning Systems Press, P. O. Box 64, Urbana, IL.

This system features 17 vowel phonemes that are color coded. The program sequences the introduction of all phonemes, graphemes, auditory and visual discrimination activities, and words in meaningful contexts. Sensory input is provided through auditory, visual, and kinesthetic stimulation. This input elicits visual, articulatory, and motor outputs in the forms of speaking, reading, and writing. The writing activities emphasize the use of cursive writing.

(6) *Open Court Basic Readers.* A. Hughes, N. Thomas, and S. L. Bernier. Open Court Publishing Company, Box 399, LaSalle, IL.

This program provides for a sequential development of oral and reading skills, vocabulary and spelling, dictionary and research skills, composition techniques, sentence structure or grammar usage, style, capitalization, and punctuation. Traditional fables, folk tales, fairy tales, and poems are used as materials. Alphabet cards, songs, and puzzles are featured. The program uses alphabet paper with faintly outlined printed letters to develop tracing. Phonics analysis is provided.

(7) *UNIFON* (Uniformly Phonemic Representation of the Sounds of the English Language). J. R. Malone. Western Publishing, Educational Services, 1220 Mound Avenue, Racine, WI.

This program features consistent sound-symbol relationships through phonemic spellings. UNIFON symbols have been designed to account for diphthongs. Teacher-training films and videotapes are available. A UNIFON traditional spelling dictionary is provided.

(8) *Laubach Method.* F. C. Laubach. New Reader's Press, Box 131, Syracuse, NY.

This system features a revised English alphabet and a phonemic spelling system. Sequential steps are used to teach reading and writing skills. The program uses controlled cue reduction and association of pictures and letters.

(9) *Phonetic English Spelling.* T. Rohner. Fonetic English Spelling Association, 1418 Lake Street, Evanston, IL.

This system eliminates the inconsistencies and irregularities of English spelling by introducing a phonetically based alphabet. Five long vowel symbol representations are added. The program was designed to assist adult nonreaders. Although the program principles are described, no actual materials for use are currently available.

## Other Selected Approaches to Reading

(1) *Peabody Rebus Reading Program.* R. W. Woodstock and L. M. Dunn. American Guidance Service, Inc., Circle Pines, MN.

This program uses a rebus format to teach reading. Pictures of objects, persons, animals, or actions are substituted for printed words. The program has the same instructional objectives as the traditional basal readers. The rebus reading program has several positive features. It is carefully programmed, with built-in self-correction devices. Cue reduction is featured to facilitate the transfer from picture reading to printed word reading. The program uses a semantic approach to reading instruction.

(2) *Responsive-Environment Approach* (The Talking Typewriter). O. K. Moore and A. R. Anderson. Prentice-Hall Learning Systems, Prentice-Hall, Englewood Cliffs, NJ.

This approach is based on the premise that children should learn to read, spell, and write in a controlled, responsive environment. The environment should permit the learner to explore freely. It should inform the learner about the immediate consequences of his actions and permit him to make full use of his individual capacity to discover and abstract relationships. It should be structured and self-pacing to accommodate for individual differences among learners. Learning is viewed as an autotelic activity with its own intrinsic values and rewards. The approach was designed to be used in the environment of the Talking Typewriter.

(3) *Distar* (Direct Instruction System for Teaching Arithmetic and Reading). C. Bereiter and S. Englemann. Science Research Associates, 259 East Erie Street, Chicago, IL.

This approach features a highly structured, "teacher-centered" approach to teaching reading. The teacher of the system uses a presentation book. It contains directions for the teacher, acceptable answers from the learners, and instructions for feedback. The guidelines must be followed absolutely with this approach. Specific tasks are sequenced to promote step-by-step acquisition of skills. The program is intensive and demands rapid and immediate responses. A modified alphabet is used in the initial stages of teaching reading.

(4) *Organic Reading.* S. Ashton-Warner. Simon and Schuster, Inc., Rockefeller Center, 630 Fifth Avenue, New York, NY.

This approach to teaching reading resulted from the author's work with Maori children in New Zealand. She holds that words featured in reading should have the intensity of being associated with internalized emotions and reactions. They should be so-called *one-look* words. Reading in this approach is related to the self, to personal needs, to self-concepts, and to feelings. This approach results in language which is obviously less stilted than the language of most basal and linguistic readers. During the initial stages, the child's personalized vocabulary is uncovered. It may include anger and fear words as well as sex words. These words are introduced to establish a reading vocabulary. Subsequently, the child constructs a Make-It-Yourself book which features his own vocabulary. In learning the vocabulary, the child traces words and plays games that emphasize visual memory and perceptual discriminations. The approach has promise for children with poor motivation, emotional instability, attention deficits, and intellectual limitations. It also seems appropriate for nonreading adolescents and adults.

(5) *Mott Basic Language Skills Program.* B. E. Chapman and L. Schultz. Allied Education, Inc., Gallien, MI.

The primary objective of this program is to teach beginning reading to adults with minimal reading skills. The program is highly structured, with semiprogrammed materials. The beginning stages feature materials and activities to develop sound-symbol recognition and correspondences. Among the materials featured with the program are a teacher manual, workbooks, an "object box," and supplementary job applications, job training pamphlets, and personal loan application forms suitable for adults.

(6) *Language Experiences in Reading.* V. Allen and C. Allen. Encyclopedia Britannica Educational Corporation, 425 North Michigan Avenue, Chicago, IL.

The language-experience approach uses the spoken language, experiences, and reasoning of the child as the basis for skill development in reading. The approach is individualized and therefore unstructured. The child chooses the words he wants to read. These words are printed on paper for the child to read, copy, and reread. The system features two major programs, a continuing program for multiple exposures to hearing, seeing, reading, and writing experience stories, and a pupil activities program with suggestions for shared experiences (field trips, demonstrations, films, painting, listening to stories, etc.). Little emphasis is placed on skill-building activities.

(7) *Remedial Training for Children with Specific Disability in Reading, Spelling, and Penmanship (Orton-Gillingham Approach)*. A. Gillingham and B. Stilman. Educators Publishing Service, 301 Vassar Street, Cambridge, MA.

This remedial program uses tactile-kinesthetic input. It relies on auditory discrimination and begins training with the short vowels. Sounding and blending, letter names, sounds, and how to write letters are taught. The activities move from the letter level to the word and sentence levels in three stages. Within each stage, the teacher provides a spoken model to the child. The child repeats it, names the letter or letters, says a key word if the model is a letter, writes the model down, and rereads it. The complete remedial kit contains phonic drill cards, phonetic word cards, phonetic stories, and exercises on syllabification and use of dictionary.

### Supplementary Reading Programs and Materials

Several programs, methods, and materials may be used to supplement the reading programs discussed above. They should not be introduced before the child has mastered the basic phonetic-phonemic or phonic elements taught in the first and early second grades. Among available supplementary programs are:

(1) *Intersensory Reading Method*. Book Lab, Inc., 1449 37 Street, Brooklyn, NY 11218.

This method may be used to supplement materials and methods for readiness and early reading instruction. It may also be used for remediation. The method teaches letter sounds, but no letter names are taught. The program contains 48 illustrated, programmed lessons in which about 400 words are organized into linguistic spelling patterns. The program emphasizes the motor-kinesthetic modality in writing.

(2) *Primary Phonics*. B. Makar. Educators Publishing Service, 301 Vassar Street, Cambridge, MA.

The scope of this program is on reading instruction for kindergarten and first grade levels. It features several workbooks. The readers may serve as supplements to other programs which emphasize phonic generalizations and in which the contents are sequenced similarly.

(3) *The Structural Reading Program*. C. Stern. L. W. Singer Company, 249-259 W. Erie Boulevard, Syracuse, NY 13202.

This program features a series of workbook-reader combinations. It uses writing as a reinforcement for kinesthetic-motor input. The program introduces whole words to insure that there is a meaning base for the child.

(4) *Remedial Reading Drills*. T. Hegge, S. Kirk, and W. Kirk. George Wahr Publishing Company, 302½ S. State Street, Ann Arbor, MI.

This system presents an excellent handbook for teaching phonic elements. The drills were designed to be accompanied by appropriate reading materials. It has been expanded in a recent text (Kirk, Kiebhan, & Lerner, 1978).

## PHONOLOGICAL COMPONENTS OF READING ACQUISITION

Children who have problems in discriminating and differentiating speech sounds and/or in integrating sounds with letters (auditory-visual integration) may be delayed or disabled in learning to read. Their primary problems may be made worse by certain common techniques used in auditory approaches to teaching reading. For instance, such practice involves teaching the letter names for the alphabet. This practice has its origin in research that showed that children who were academic achievers and good readers all knew the alphabet and letter names. Children who were poor readers did not (Durell, 1956). We now have the evidence that this practice may be neither beneficial nor detrimental to normally developing children (Chall, 1967). It may, however, be confusing for language and learning disabled children (Myklebust, 1968). They may be confused because most of the letters do not carry their letter names when they are embedded in printed words. But some letters, on the other hand, *do* carry their letter names in some contexts. Take as examples the consonants in the initial position of the words "beep," "deed," "piece," "teeth," "veal," and "zeal." In other contexts the very same letters no longer carry their letter names. Examples are the words "big," "dog," "pat," "tap," "van," and "zip." All of these contexts or words are featured early in beginning reading programs. A different set of consonants, *f, l, m, n, s, h,* and *x,* never carry their letter names. The concrete and literal child, especially one who has heard repeatedly on children's TV programs that "the letters say their names," may listen attentively to hear a letter which actually does say its name.

A second problem which may arise from teaching letter names involves the letters *g, j, k, w,* and *y.* Children may not recognize or associate the pronunciation of these letters in words with their visual symbolic representations. They may expect to hear the letter names or at least variations of them when they encounter these letters in printed words. Other consonants may cause confusion because they have two distinctly different pronunciations. For instance, the letter *c* is pronounced as /k/ in words such as "cat," "cake," and "color." It is pronounced as /s/ in words such as "cent," "circus," and "celery." The letter *d* is pronounced as /d/ in words such as "dig," "dog," "doll." It is pronounced as /j/ in words such as "individual" and "gradual." The letter *g* is pronounced as /g/ in "go" and as /dj/ in "gem." The digraph *ch* is pronounced as /sh/ in "Chicago" and as /ch/ in "chips."

To add to the confusion one speech sound may be represented by several different letters. The sound /f/ is denoted by different letters in the words "fat," "cuff," "laugh," and "elephant." The sound /j/ is represented by different letters in the words "jump," "bridge," and "age." If these potential stumbling blocks appear contrived, you may be convinced if you read the poem below aloud.

> When the English tongue we speak
>    Why is break not rimed with freak?
> Will you tell me why it's true
>    We say sew but likewise few?
> And the maker of a verse
>    Cannot rime his horse with worse?
> Beard sounds not the same as heard,
>    Cord is different from word;

Cow is cow but low is low
   Shoe is never rimed with foe.
Think of hose and dose and lose;
   And think of goose and yet of choose.
Think of comb and tomb and bomb,
   Doll and roll and home and some.
And since pay is rimed with say,
   Why not paid with said, I pray?
Think of blood and food and good.
   Mould is not pronounced like could.
Wherefore done, but gone and lone—
   Is there any reason known?
To sum up all, it seems to me
   Sounds and letters don't agree.

*(Author unknown)*

## Vowels and Vowel Segments

Vowel sound and letter relationships are often taught by teaching the child to differentiate long and short vowels. This practice may lead to severe problems for the language and learning disabled youngster. These youngsters may not be able to understand that there are exceptions to rules they are taught formally. Some of these youngsters may not learn the rules for long and short vowels in the first place. To use that rule, you must be able to differentiate durational features accurately and consistently. Vowels and their pronunciation and spelling appear to represent a major problem for youngsters with auditory processing deficits. They represent the same problems as consonants: (1) there are multiple pronunciations for the same printed vowel and (2) there are multiple spellings or letters used for the same vowel sound. Table 14.1 summarizes these complexities.

Dialectical variations only add to the confusion. These variations are highlighted in Table 14.2.

To add another complication, some vowel sounds are represented by more than one letter in certain words. Because they are not included in the phonogram patterns taught in phonics analysis these vowel com-

**TABLE 14.1**

*Vowel sound/spelling*

**Uniformity of Spelling for Short Vowels**

| A | E | I | O | U |
|---|---|---|---|---|
| bat | bet | bit | box | blue |

**Multiple spellings of long vowels**

| A | E | I | O | U |
|---|---|---|---|---|
| bake | be | bike | boat | bug |
| pay | see | might | bone | boot |
| paid | Pete | mice | show | cute |
| great | ski | my | note | few |
| reign | key | height | hope | suit |
| they | deceive | buy | cold | you |
|  |  | guide |  |  |

**TABLE 14.1 (*Continued*)**

**Multiple pronunciations of the same letter**

| A | E | I | O | U |
|---|---|---|---|---|
| seat | each | mail | do | purse |
| boat | bake | boil | boat | thou |
| charın | few | paid | cow | taught |
| bread | blue | said | boy | thought |
| paid | bread˙ | guide | worm | through |
| sofa | bean | view | thou | suede |
| straw | water | reign | brother | tongue |
| taught | never | bike | room | rum |
| said | | | tongue | |
| any | | | | |
| bazaar | | | | |
| call | | | | |

**TABLE 14.2**

*Dialectical variations in vowel and diphthong articulation in common English words*

| Sample Word | General American | Eastern New England | New York city | Southern | Southwest | Northwest |
|---|---|---|---|---|---|---|
| | | | Dialectical Variation | | | |
| BOY | ɔɪ | | | ɔɪ | | |
| BASKET | æ | ɑ | | æja | | æ |
| EGG | ɛ | e | e | eja | | |
| PIE | aɪ | | | ɑɪja | | |
| CAKE | eɪ | | | eɪja | | |
| CAT | æ | | | æja | | |
| BOOK | ʊ | | | ʊː | | |
| FATHER | ɑr | ɑ | ɑ | ɑ | | |
| LOCK | ɒ | ɒ | ɑ | ɑ | | ɔ |
| TRUCK | ʌ | | | | | |
| HORSE | ɔr | ɔ | ɔː | ɔːwə | | ɔː |
| COW | ɑʊ | | | ɑwə | | |
| GOAT | oʊ | | | owə | | |
| SHEEP | iː | | | iːj | | |
| PIG | ɪ | | | ɪj | | |
| BIRD | ɝ | ɜː | | ɝɪ | | |
| FOOD | uː | | | uːwə | | |

binations can be confusing. Table 14.3 on p. 390 shows some of the more common words that contain combinations of two or more vowels.

Consonant **blends** are usually introduced in reading materials at the beginning of the second grade. These blends represent specific phonemes that are frequently misperceived or mispronounced by language and learning disabled children. The critical sound components in blends are /r/, /l/, /w/, and /s/. One or more of these sounds occur in all single and triple blends. The repertory of blends is summarized in Table 14.4.

## Consonant Clusters

*A* **blend** *is a combination of two or three consonants which feature either r, l, or w as the second consonant or s as the initial consonant. Examples include pr,- pl-, tw-, sp-, and str-.*

**TABLE 14.3**

*Vowel combinations*

| Vowel Sequence | Vowel Segment | | Word Examples |
|---|---|---|---|
| | **Diacritic** | **Phonetic** | |
| 1. -ea- | (ē) | /i:/ | beat |
| | (ĕ) | /e/ | head |
| | (ā) | /eĭ/ | great |
| 2. -ie- | (ē) | /i:/ | chief |
| | (ī) | /aĭ/ | pie |
| 3. -ei- | (ē) | /i:/ | ceiling |
| | (ā) | /eĭ/ | vein |
| 4. -eigh- | (ā) | /eĭ/ | neighbor |
| | (ī) | /aĭ/ | height |
| 5. -ou- | (ou) | /oŭ/ | out |
| | (o͞o) | /u:/ | soup |
| | (ō) | /ou/ | shoulder |
| 6. -ow- | (ō) | /ou/ | grow |
| | (ou) | /au/ | owl |
| 7. -ew- | (ū) | /u:/ | few |
| | (o͞o) | /u:/ | grew |
| 8. -ue- | (ū) | /u:/ | cue |
| | (o͞o) | /u:/ | true |
| 9. -oo- | (o͝o) | /u/ | look |
| | (o͞o) | /u:/ | pool |
| 10. -ey- | (ē) | /i:/ | monkey |
| | (a) | /eĭ/ | they |
| 11. -ough- | (ō) | /ou/ | though |
| | (ô) | /ɔ:/ | thought |
| | (ou) | /aŭ/ | bough |
| | (o͞o) | /u:/ | through |
| | (ŭf) | /ʌ/ | enough |
| 12. -augh- | (ò) | /ɔ:/ | caught |
| | (ăf) | /æ/ | laugh |

**TABLE 14.4**

*Blends with* r-, l-, *and* w- *and double and triple* s- *blends*

| Speech Sound | R- Blend | L- Blend | W- Blend | S₂- Blend | S₃- Blend |
|---|---|---|---|---|---|
| p | princess | plate | | spoon | spring |
| b | brother | black | | | |
| m | | | | smile | |
| w | | | | swim | |
| f | frog | flag | | | |
| t | tree | | twin | stove | string |
| d | drum | | dwarf | | |
| θ | three | | | | |
| n | | | | snowing | |
| l | | | | sled | |
| k | crown | clown | queen | skating | squirrel |
| g | green | glasses | | | |

If a youngster is unable to perceive or pronounce blends accurately and consistently, his ability to read and spell words with blends may be impaired. He may need individualized intervention in both auditory discrimination and articulation to help him learn to read words with blends. The intervention goals should be shared with the classroom teacher at regular intervals to encourage transfer of the new skills to classroom activities in reading, spelling, and writing.

Other multiple letter combinations, the **digraphs** may also cause confusion for language and learning disabled youngsters. They may find it hard to accept that a phoneme has to be broken up into two letters in spelling or writing a word. They may fail to grasp the correspondence between the one sound they hear and the two letters they see. Their problems may be compounded by the fact that some digraphs have only one pronunciation while others may have two or more pronunciations. Table 14.5 illustrates the sound-letter correspondences for digraphs.

*A consonant **digraph** is a combination of two or more printed consonants representing a single speech sound. Examples include sh, wh, ph, ch, and tch.*

**TABLE 14.5**
*Digraphs*

**Digraphs associated with one spoken sound**

| Digraph | Phoneme | Word Examples |
|---------|---------|---------------|
| sh | /ʃ/ | shop, dash |
| wh | /hw/ | whale, white |
| ph | /f/ | phone, elephant |
| ck | /k/ | deck, smack |
| tch | /tʃ/ | catch, pitcher |

**Digraphs associated with two or more spoken sounds**

| | | |
|---------|---------|---------------|
| ch | /tʃ/ | church, chime |
| | /ʃ/ | Chicago, chef |
| | /k/ | Christmas |
| th | /ð/ | this, them |
| | /θ/ | thin, think |

Silent consonants may present a different problem because they violate the principles for digraphs. In the case of silent consonants, two consonant letters are used in one printed sequence but only one of the letter sounds in the sequence is articulated. The principles associated with these consonant combinations differ from those associated with digraphs. In digraphs, the two letters are represented by one sound which combines elements of the two components. The rules for pronouncing consonant combinations with a silent consonant may have to be learned by rote. Table 14.6 on p. 392 shows examples of silent consonants in words.

**Homonyms**

The meanings of homonyms are generally discerned in spoken language from contextual, referential-semantic, and topical cues. In written language, the cues to word meaning are clear in the spelling of the

**TABLE 14.6**
*Silent consonants*

| Letter Combination | Phoneme | Word Examples |
|:---:|:---:|:---:|
| wr- | /r/ | write, wrist |
| kn- | /n/ | know, knife |
| pn- | /n/ | pneumonia, pneumatic |
| gn- | /n/ | gnaw, gnome |
| sc- | /s/ | scene, science |
| ps- | /s/ | psalm, psychology |
| rh- | /r/ | rhythm, rhyme |
| gh- | /g/ | ghost, ghastly |
| -bt | /t/ | doubt, debt |
| -lk | /k/ | walk, talk |
| -mb | /m/ | comb, lamb |
| -mn | /m/ | hymn, condemn |

words. Language and learning disabled youngsters may be confused by the identical pronunciation of two words which are obviously spelled differently. They may need extensive and repetitive experiences with reading, spelling, and writing the members of homonym pairs. The exercises should involve verbal or written definitions of each member of a homonym pair or best exemplar or prototypical sentences in which the homonyms are featured. The objective is to establish instant recognition that a word is a homonym and knowledge of the alternative meanings and spellings of homonyms. Table 14.7 gives an extensive list of common homonyms.

*See Semel (1970, 1976) for other specific intervention methods and activities.*

**Syllabification**

A good reader uses knowledge of syllabification to:

(1) Arrive at the accurate spelling of a variety of polysyllabic words.
(2) Pronounce words in reading which are not recognized immediately as sight words.
(3) Accommodate for word length in writing by breaking words at the end of the line.

A **syllable** can be defined as a group of letters that includes a vowel symbol and forms a pronounceable unit. For example, the word "apple" may be divided into only two syllables, "apple," even though it has three distinguishable sound units "a/pp/le." Syllables may carry identifiable meaning, and they then qualify as morphemes. The inflectional and derivational suffixes and prefixes qualify as both morphemes and syllables. Improving the child's knowledge of morphology and ability to identify the smallest meaningful units in words through segmentation may indirectly strengthen his syllabification skills. It is nonetheless necessary to teach some syllabification rules. These rules may need to be repeated if they are to become automatic for the child. Here are the commonly taught rules for syllabification.

(1) The number of vowel sounds heard in a word determines the number of syllables. For example, the word "precaution" contains

**TABLE 14.7**
*Common homonyms*

| | | | |
|---|---|---|---|
| air-heir | fowl-foul | meet-meat | scene-seen |
| aisle-isle | flea-flee | main-mane | shone-shown |
| ate-eight | frees-freeze | not-knot | sea-see |
| aye-eye-I | four-for | none-nun | seam-seem |
| bare-bear | fair-fare | oh-owe | seas-sees-seize |
| base-bass | grown-groan | or-oar-ore | sew-sow-so |
| be-bee | great-grate | our-hour | size-sighs |
| beat-beet | hole-whole | one-won | sole-soul |
| berth-birth | herd-heard | praise-prays-preys | stair-stare |
| blue-blew | hanger-hangar | peace-piece | sun-son |
| break-brake | hall-hull | peer-pier | steel-steal |
| by-buy | hair-hare | pain-pane | stake-steak |
| cent-sent-scent | horse-hoarse | pail-pale | tax-tacks |
| cellar-seller | holy-wholly | peel-peal | to-too-two |
| course-coarse | heel-heal | pear-pair | tail-tale |
| capital-capitol | him-hymn | peek-peak | there-their |
| cell-sell | hear-here | plane-plain | toe-tow |
| chews-choose | idle-idol-idyll | passed-past | threw-through |
| clause-claws | in-inn | peddle-pedal | vain-vein-vane |
| creak-creek | know-no | red-read | vice-vise |
| colonel-kernel | knows-nose | road-rode | veil-vale |
| days-daze | knew-new | rose-rows | week-weak |
| dear-deer | knead-need | rains-reigns-reins | way-weigh |
| do-dew-due | leak-leek | real-reel | waist-waste |
| die-dye | lone-loan | roll-role | wood-would |
| eight-ate | lane-lain | rap-wrap | wait-weight |
| earn-urn | lie-lye | rung-wrung | wade-weighed |
| flower-flour | light-lite | right-write-rite | war-wore |
| fur-fir | male-mail | ring-wring | warn-worn |
| feet-feat | minor-miner | sale-sail | waits-weights |
| fourth-forth | mail-male | sum-some | |

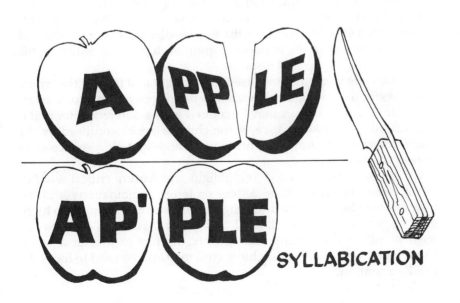

**FIGURE 14.4**
*Syllabication*

SYLLABICATION

five vowel symbols or letters, but only three vowel sounds are heard. Thus, the word contains three syllables (pre·cau·tion).

(2) Vowel combinations (diphthongs) serve as a syllable nucleus in the same way as single vowel symbols (main·tain).

(3) Letter sequences with a vowel followed by an -*r* serve as the nucleus of a syllable. These combinations are often spoken as one sound, a vowel phoneme. This combination is especially sensitive to dialectical variations and therefore deserves attention (firm; ra·*zor*; church; num·b*er*).

(4) When a double consonant symbol occurs in a written word, the syllable border occurs between the two consonants (sup·per; pic·nic).

(5) Prefixes and suffixes generally form a syllable (un·fair; great·er).

(6) The silent *e* cannot form the nucleus of a syllable (bak*e*; ex·cit*e*).

(7) When a word ends with a consonant followed by -*le*, the consonant and -*le* combination forms a syllable (a·ble; lit·tle; jun·gle; nee·dle; un·cle; an·kle).

## Adapting Reading Materials to Teach Sound-Letter Correspondence Level

Visual cues may help focus a child's attention on critical features in printed words. They may help him abstract and learn the principles and rules associated with the critical features highlighted by the visual cue. There are many easily constructed cues that may be used in adapting reading materials for children with language and learning disabilities.

A mask or a window may be used to guide the child's visual focus. This technique may also be used when the child can read the words in sentences or paragraphs but changes their sequences. It can be designed to expose a single critical element such as a letter or letter sequence, a syllable, a prefix or suffix, a word, phrase, clause, or sentence. The window area should initially expose the largest section within which the critical element occurs. This may mean exposing a sentence or a line. If the child does not respond correctly, you can reduce the window in small steps until he succeeds. After he responds correctly, you should strengthen the response by removing the mask or increasing the size of the window in gradual steps while requiring the child to repeat the desired response.

A color code is another tool used to highlight and feature the critical elements for the youngster. Vowels may be colored red and consonants blue. Or each new feature may be colored with a different color as it is introduced. As an alternative, if the child becomes confused by the many colors, all critical elements may be highlighted in one color as they occur.

Other codes may be used to highlight and feature critical word or letter elements. The critical letters or letter combinations and sequences may be underlined. Configuration cues may be used to highlight contrasts in word outlines. Modified configuration cues may be used in which the outline follows only the top or part of a word. Combinations of these highlighting cues may also be used to focus the child's attention.

**FIGURE 14.5**
*Mask Use for Sequence*

*Strengthening the Recall of Spelling Examples and Rules*

Visual memory and recall of printed words may be strengthened by using the game "Concentration." At first the game may feature word cards with printed words along with pictured objects. As the child's recall of the printed word forms increases, the pictured objects may be left on only one of the two matching cards. Finally, the cards may use only the printed words for matching. Along with the matching activity, the teacher and the child should read each word out loud at first. Later, the child may be asked to read each word aloud as he sees it. Finally, the child may be directed to read each word to himself silently as he sees it.

In a related activity, printed words may be categorized on the basis of similarities in spelling or syllabification. The activities may require the child to group words with multiple spellings of the same spoken sound. They may require him to group words with multiple pronunciations of the same spelling, words with the same number of syllables or identical syllables, etc. Tables 14.1 through 14.7 may be used as guidelines for emphasis and contents.

Printed word cards presented in rapid reading drills, can be used to make reading more automatic. These drills may also be used to teach spelling principles which can only be learned by rote. Rapid reading drills may also increase accuracy and speed in word retrieval among youngsters with word-finding problems and dysnomia. The words on the printed word cards may be highlighted with color cues or configuration cues. They may be modified to allow the child to use tactile-kinesthetic cues. For instance, sandpaper and pipecleaner letters are easy to construct. Or the words can be written on a card, outlined in glue, and then sprinked with sand or birdseeds. An alternative method of providing tactile-kinesthetic cues is to perforate the letters with a blunt point from the back of the card.

Match-to-sample activities with multiple word choices may be used to strengthen reading responses. The samples used in these activities may be single letters, letter combinations, syllables, prefixes and suffixes, words, phrases, clauses, or sentences. The choices in turn may be single words, phrases, clauses, or sentences. The frames or samples may be sequenced in small steps that feature small increments in level of difficulty. The samples and frames may be transferred from word cards to appropriate hardware such as teaching machines or computers. Existing programmed materials may be used for this activity.

*See the reviews of reading approaches and programs above.*

Meaning (semantic-referential) and topical cues may be used to strengthen the reading, spelling, and writing of words, phrases, and clauses. This objective may be achieved by using sentence completion, cloze, or rebus formats. If contextual cues do not help the child read, spell, or write accurately, phonetic-phonemic or syllabic cues may be added.

Mnemonic and adaptive devices may also be used to assist the child in the recall of specific spelling rules, principles, and/or exceptions to rules. Among possible adaptive devices are answer keys, charts and lists of words grouped according to rules and principles, dictionaries of commonly misspelled words, and symbol adaptations. Word associations may also be used as mnemonic devices—"mother is other with an *m*," "warm is arm with a *w*," and "there is here with a *t* in front."

Auditory discrimination activities may strengthen the associations among sounds and symbols and syllabification skills. Possible auditory discrimination activities require (1) tracing word configurations in association with listening; (2) judging spoken words same-different in association with their printed counterparts; (3) acting out spoken and printed word meanings; (4) responding to specific questions about spoken and read sentences or paragraphs; and (5) following directions in response to spoken and printed input.

*A variety of these activities are described in detail in SAPP (Semel, 1976).*

A new product in the field of electronics is a computerized spelling device which "speaks" letters and words. This piece of equipment, *Speak and Spell,* produced by Texas Instruments, holds promise for spelling drills and homework assignments for language and learning disabled children. As word modules which feature beginning reading words as well as advanced vocabulary or specific technical or scientific terminology become available its use may be expanded.

## CONCLUSION

This chapter has discussed the characteristics of several major approaches to teaching reading and given specific examples of reading materials that use each approach. In our discussions we focused on certain dimensions of these reading programs, such as whether the approach was modality specific, visual (whole word) or auditory (phonic, phonetic, or linguistic), synthetic (beginning with isolated, meaningless sounds) or analytic (beginning with whole ideas, phrases, or words), highly structured (programmed systems) or unstructured (some language experience approaches), and whether it used the traditional alphabet or a modified alphabet. We did not consider student variables such as learning styles, self-concept, affect, attentiveness, or counseling needs.

A variety of other dimensions could have been considered. As Frierson states,

> It would not be hard to identify other distinctive dimensions [of reading programs]. Some would argue for five modes (visual-auditory, tactile, kinesthetic, and combinations). Others would add environmental characteristics (stimuli-free, highly distracting, normal). Still others would demonstrate convincingly that the means of presentation makes a distinctive contribution (slides projected at far point vision, computerized typewriter feedback, animated films, etc.). In short, the list of characteristics would become infinite. (1976, p. 19)

In addition, we have not discussed process versus perception in reading. Nor have we focused on the impact of the wide variations in teacher training represented among teachers of reading or on the level of enthusiasm of teachers for the methods and materials they are required to use. The last issues have been researched and discussed eloquently by Chall (1967). Our discussions have also avoided the issues of whether or not remediation for reading problems should focus on teaching prerequisite skills, on selecting the best method for teaching reading, or on matching student deficits and individual differences to instructional methods. These issues have been discussed in depth by Guthrie (1978), Johnson (1978), and Zigmond (1978), among others.

Guthrie (1978) featured four principles of instruction applicable to teaching reading which have been supported by research. He states that the teacher should:

(1) Focus instruction on the deficient cognitive components of reading. They are decoding accuracy and speed, and semantic segmentation and construction.
(2) Instruct children in all the components of reading.
(3) Provide intensive interaction between the instructor and the student.
(4) Maximize instructional time.

It is generally acknowledged that we do not know all we need to know about factors that influence the process of acquisition of reading and about reading instruction. Future research must focus on the impact of deficits in specific components of oral language on the acquisition of the various components of reading.

# 15

# LANGUAGE DEMANDS
# OF THE CURRICULUM
## Content Areas

Chapter 14 focused on the language demands presented by reading and on approaches to teaching reading and reading programs. In this chapter we will take a look at the language demands presented by the content areas of the curriculum for the upper grades and at the high school level. The examples used to illustrate various aspects of the language demands of the curriculum were selected from representative curriculum materials. Chapter 16 will look at ways to adapt the curriculum and standard materials to accommodate the child with language and learning disabilities.

## ENGLISH AND LANGUAGE ARTS

### Implications of Language Deficits

When the youngster enters junior and senior high school, he is expected to bring certain skills to his reading comprehension. He must be accurate, efficient, mature, and rapid in processing the surface structures of a variety of sentences and retrieving their underlying meaning. He must process and interpret tense and time markers accurately. He must resolve and interpret complex sentences with conjunction, complementation, and relativization efficiently. He must perceive the equivalence of sentences which differ widely in structure but share the same underlying meaning immediately and consistently. He must perceive structural ambiguities in sentences instantaneously and resolve them accurately on the basis of available contextual, logical, or topical cues and relationships. He must interpret *wh-* questions accurately in both spoken and written questioning. And these are only a few of the necessary skill areas.

In the area of semantics, the high school student must understand abstract word meanings, antonymy, and synonymy or be able to learn them easily. He must interpret the linguistic concepts of spatial, temporal, and analogous relationships consistently and rapidly. He must be able to detect semantic ambiguities that arise from multiple meanings of one or more of the words in a sentence or multiple referents for persons, places, or events, resolve them, and recall them if he encounters them later. He must readily understand figurative language at the abstract level of interpretation. Implied but not stated causal and conditional relationships must be inferred and discerned. In recounting materials he has read, he must be able to use semantic elaboration, a wide variety of words, and the expected idiom.

In the area of memory skills, he must have accurate recall and retrieval of words and facts. He needs adequate auditory retention span, organization of input, and chunking of materials into perceptual-conceptual units in order to handle the language materials. Temporal-sequential relationships among events or actions are expected to be stored, retrieved, and recalled accurately and rapidly.

The language and learning disabled pre-adolescent and adolescent may not meet one or several of these expectations. He may have difficulties and delays in syntax, semantics, and/or memory and retrieval. These may negatively influence advanced reading comprehension and performances in grammar and language arts. Table 15.1 summarizes common language problems among the learning disabled that may influence the interpretation and use of spoken and read English.

**TABLE 15.1**

*Selected language problems that may limit the interpretation and formulation of spoken and written English*

| Syntax | Semantics | Memory |
|---|---|---|
| Tense and time markers. | Narrow word meanings with concrete rather than abstract interpretations. | Limited retention span. |
| *Wh-* questions. | | Lack of efficiency in organizing input and in chunking. |
| Complex sentences with: Conjunction, Complementation, Relativization. | Limitations in antonymy and synonymy. | Auditory sequential memory deficits. |
| | Concepts for relationships such as: spatial and temporal, comparisons, analogous. | Limited internal rehearsal. |
| Retrieval of the underlying meaning of sentences which differ in structure but share the same meaning. | | Limited recoding from the verbal code to an internal representation or image. |
| | | Deficits in delayed recall. |
| Ambiguities in sentences caused by surface or deep structure alternatives. | Ambiguities in sentences caused by multiple meanings of one or more of the words. | Limitations in the speed and accuracy of word retrieval. |
| Syntactic elaboration in recounting events, etc. | Figurative language. | |
| | Implied but not stated causal and conditional relationships. | |
| | Semantic elaboration and variety in word use in recounting events. | |

## Language Demands of the Curriculum

At the junior and senior high school levels, examples of the assignments and materials used in English literature and Language Arts readily reveal the level of the syntactic and semantic complexity of the language. We will use selected representative materials from current seventh, eighth, and tenth grade English texts to illustrate this point. Consider the assignment below, which is based on sentences featured in *Treasure Island*. This assignment requires accurate and efficient perception, syntactic processing, and semantic interpretation of figurative language.

*Example 1*

The following sentences contain imaginative comparisons. . . . Name these comparisons. . . . Decide what idea or impression the author wanted to give. . . .

(1) The stranger kept hanging about just inside the inn door, peering round the corner like a cat waiting for a mouse.

(7) My own accidental cut across the knuckles was a flea bite.

(8) I was dead tired, as you may fancy; and when I got to sleep, . . . I slept like a log of wood.

(11) The dirk, where it had pinned my shoulder to the mast, seemed to burn like a hot iron.

From: BUILDING BETTER ENGLISH, Harper and Row, 1961.

The next examples illustrate assignments from a text of English grammar for the high school level. The examples will give an idea of the syntactic complexity of the sentences which must be analyzed. Example 4 also illustrates the complexity of the visual-spatial components of materials used in advanced English grammar.

*Example 2*

"Still, with faith that the adult nature of my mission would give me unmolested passage, I approached the corner, which was guarded by a red fire alarm box, looked both ways for the cars that seldom came, and, swallowing, began to cross over."

With what attitude did he approach the corner?
What did he see on the corner?
What did he do after looking both ways?

*Example 3*

"The smallest snowshoes had been dragging in a stick of firewood from along-shore—the women."

What useful thing did the women do?

"When I stepped onto the porch again, I saw them playing on their corner—Valentine's Gang."

Who was playing on the corner?

From: PERSPECTIVES-GALAXY, Scott Foresman, 1963.

*Example 4*

*Apposition with Subject*
Our milkman, *Mr. Greer*, is a jolly man.

*Apposition with Direct Object*
Dan won the award, a *trip* to Cuba.

milkman (Mr. Greer) | is \ man

Dan | won | award (trip)

*Apposition with Predicate Nominative*
This dog is Prince, our family *pet*.

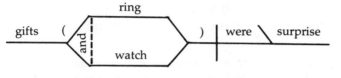

*Compound Appositives*
These gifts, a *ring* and a *watch*, were a real surprise.

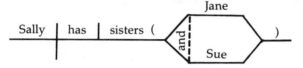

Sally has two sisters, *Jane* and *Sue*.

Diagram verbs, subjects, appositives, and any predicate nominatives or direct objects in these sentences.

(1) Sunday, my birthday, was a rainy day.

(4) Laura plays two games well, checkers and chess.

(6) Has your wife met our new leader, that tall man in the gray suit?

(10) Sitting on the fence were two birds, a robin and a sparrow.

From: BUILDING BETTER ENGLISH, Harper and Row, 1961, p. 200.

High school level assignments in Language Arts designed to develop dictionary skills and vocabulary meaning are shown in the next three examples. The first assignment requires word definition and demonstration of knowledge and use of multiple meanings of words. The second features examples of synonymy, and the last of antonymy in word meanings.

*Example 5*

In your dictionary, look up each underscored word in the sentences below. Indicate which dictionary definition most closely matches the sense in which the word is used. Then write a sentence that illustrates a different meaning of the same word.

(1) The cabin is *accessible*, even after the heavy winter snows.

(2) The motel can *accommodate* us.

(3) The organist will *accompany* him as he sings "The Star Spangled Banner."

(4) He *acknowledged* my first letter, but I have not heard from him since.

*Example 6*

A *valiant* foe.     (a) hostile   (b) weak   (c) cowardly   (d) brave

Entertainment *galore*.     (a) exciting   (b) free   (c) plentiful   (d) professional

The *original* owner.     (a) true   (b) first   (c) new   (d) legal

*Fragile* package.     (a) expensive   (b) genuine   (c) breakable   (d) intricate

*Example 7*

The lettering on the old monument is almost _____     (a) legible  (b) illegible

If the jury's verdict is _____, the defendant will be exonerated.
(a) guilty   (b) innocent

Should the new business prove lucrative, many investors will _____
it.     (a) enter   (b) avoid

From: VOCABULARY FOR THE HIGH SCHOOL STUDENT, Amsco School Publishers, 1964.

The next illustration lists common poetic devices. These must be perceived, interpreted, differentiated, discussed, and used by high school students in various assignments.

*Example 8. Common poetic devices and terms*

    (1) Theme.

    (2) Tone.

    (3) Repetition: (a) assonance, (b) consonance.

    (4) Alliteration.

    (5) Imagery.

    (6) Figures of speech: (a) simile, (b) metaphor, (c) onomatopoeia, (d) hyperbole.

    (7) Irony: (a) verbal, (b) situational.

    (8) Personification.

    (9) Symbolism.

   (10) Allusion.

Last, but not least, this example illustrates expected composition skills for first term high school students.

*Example 9*

"The ogre known as homework looms up before me in the form of a nineteenth-century school master in ill-fitting jacket and breeches, hair tied back with a scrap of black ribbon and a stout hickory stick in his hand. His face is thin and pinched as a dried acorn kernel. Perched on the end of his long, sharp nose, which closely resembles a wood-pecker's beak, is a pair of square-rimmed spectacles. Behind them his beady eyes rove incessantly for missing or mischievous pupils. He is a stern and relentless taskmaster, and his students cringe before him while he forces knowledge through their craniums."

From: FOR INSTANCE NUMBER 1, Technifax Corporation, 1958, p. 22.

# MATHEMATICS

## Task Requirements

The ability to solve verbal math problems depends in part upon language skills similar to those required in processing spoken and written language. Verbal math problems contain a syntactic (structure) and a semantic (meaning) component. Both the syntax and the semantics must be processed accurately and efficiently to figure out what operation is required to solve the problem. The task requirements involved in processing verbal math problems appear to tax general as well as specific syntactic, semantic, and memory capacities.

The specialized language of mathematics differs from that of social English (Aiken, 1972). It is very conceptually dense; that is, many complex concepts are carried in relatively few words, phrases, and sentences. The statements have limited redundancy and few contextual cues. Thus the student must understand the exact meaning of every word and concept and every expressed syntactic-semantic relationship must be understood. The interpretation is not aided by other cues such as topic, context, or body language, as it is in normal interpersonal interactions. In mathematical language, adjectives tend to carry more importance than in social language. Common words are used with a specific rather than a generalized meaning. Specific concepts that relate to size, number, space, time, and inclusion and exclusion (few, some, none, all . . . except) abound, and their meaning must be firmly established.

Two alternative processes appear to be involved in solving verbal problems in mathematics (Aiken, 1972). These problems may be thought of as (1) complex verbal stimuli with an extra arithmetical dimension or (2) English statements that must be translated into equivalent mathematical statements. Each approach seems to require sequential processing. The student must first read the verbal math problem to discern the overall situation or pattern. This initial reading may be followed by a second reading to identify difficult words or concepts. Finally, the problem may be read again to discern semantic and logical relationships among words, phrases, and clauses and to plan the mathematical solution.

Dahmus (1970) describes a similar sequential approach to verbal math problems called the DPPC (direct, pure, piecemeal, complete). This approach requires the student to translate the words and concepts used in social English statements into their equivalent mathematical statements. The translation is followed by recoding into a single equation or a system of equations. This approach to solving verbal math problems moves from the concrete level into varied levels of abstraction.

The relationships among syntactic complexity, vocabulary level, and verbal math problem-solving ability have been investigated. In one study, verbal math problems were presented to fourth graders (Linville, 1970). Four arithmetic word-problem tests were controlled and differed only in the levels and combinations of syntactic complexity and difficulty of vocabulary. One test featured easy syntax and vocabulary. A second test featured a combination of easy syntax and difficult vocabulary. The third contained difficult syntax and easy vocabulary, and the fourth difficult syntax and difficult vocabulary. The results indicated that problems with relatively simpler syntax and easier vocabulary were solved most easily. Vocabulary level appeared to be perhaps more significant than syntax in its effect on problem solving. A related study established that specific training in syntax improved verbal math problem-solving abilities among seventh graders (Sax & Ottina, 1958). In a similar vein, fifth graders who received training in interpreting quantitative terms made significantly greater gains in mathematical problem solving than their peers who did not receive training (Vander Linde, 1964).

Rosenthal and Resnick (1974) studied the effects of differences in three dimensions on math problem-solving ability. The dimensions were (1) order of mention (chronological or reverse), (2) identity of the unknown set (starting or ending), and (3) type of verb (associated with gain or loss). More errors were made when the order of mention was reverse than when it was chronological. The response time also proved to be significantly longer for these problems. The most significant variable was, however, the presence of an unknown starting set, as in the problem $? + y = z$, particularly when associated with gain verbs. The authors concluded that higher level linguistic and cognitive abilities were required to perform the necessary mental operations in these problems.

## Mathematics Examples

Verbal math problems at the high school level abound with spatial, temporal, causal, and conditional concepts. They feature concepts of exclusion and inclusion such as "some," "all . . . except," and "all . . . but." They may contain temporal-sequential events, comparative relationships, hidden questions, unnecessary details, or implied relationships. Sometimes the sentences are complex with conjunction, complementation, or relativization. At times the syntactic structures are idiosyncratic or unusual. At other times, verbal problems are associated with visual-spatial representations which are complex. Other problems may require recoding from the words to an internal perceptual (visual) representation. There are practically always *wh*-questions to elicit and focus the mathematical operations. The examples below, obtained from high school level texts, each illustrate one or more of these features.

### Example 1. Spatial and temporal-sequential terms

In multiplying decimals together, we first find the product, as in whole numbers. Then point off the decimal point according to the rule given in Section A above.

There are ___?___ decimal places in 3.93 and ___?___ decimal places in 41.3.

Therefore, we point off ___?___ decimal places in the product.

We must point off how many places in the product of 3.88 and .02?

Why did we put a zero to the left of 7 in the product?

### Example 2. Identification of hidden questions and unnecessary data

It is 1500 miles from Los Angeles to Chicago, and 2400 miles from Los Angeles to New York. A jet plane flew from Los Angeles to New York in four hours. What was the average speed?

Mr. Adams has 1600 apple trees in his 3-acre orchard. Last year the orchard produced 11,200 bushels. What was the yield per tree?

Mary receives 80¢ an hour for an 8-hour day 5 days a week clerking in a store. If she works overtime she gets 25% extra per hour. She worked 3 hours overtime each day on Monday, Tuesday, and Thursday. How much did she earn for the week?

*Example 3. Complex transformations and unusual structure*

The circle graph . . . shows the kinds of businesses 4,300,000 firms in this country were engaged in recently. In what business were the largest number engaged? How many firms were engaged in that business?

In what business were the smallest number engaged? How many firms were engaged in that business?

To the nearest tenth, the number of firms engaged in retail trade is how many times the number engaged in manufacturing?

From: GENERAL MATH, Holt, Rinehart, and Winston, 1960.

*Example 4. Complex spatial terms with required internal representation*

There are many examples in geometry of the union and intersection of sets. If A is the set of points on a line not in a plane $p$, and B the sets of points in the plane, the union set $A \cup B$ consists of points of the line together with points of the plane. The product set $A \cap B$ is the null set if the line is parallel to the plane and is the single point of intersection of the line and the plane when they intersect.

From: MODERN GEOMETRY, McGraw Hill, 1967.

### Implications of Language Disabilities

The relationships between receptive language deficits and difficulties in mathematics among learning disabled youth have been emphasized by, among others, Johnson and Myklebust (1967). They observe that "Some children with auditory receptive language disorders learn to calculate but do poorly in mathematical reasoning because they do not comprehend the words" (p. 84). They also suggested that there are inner, receptive, and expressive aspects of mathematical language which are similar to other forms of symbolic behavior. The hierarchical acquisition of mathematical language progresses from (1) assimilation and integration of nonverbal experiences and (2) associations between experiences and numerical symbols to (3) expression of quantity, space, and order using mathematical language (p. 245). This progression may be delayed or deficient in the presence of language disabilities.

Kaliski (1962) suggests that mathematical problem-solving difficulties relate to deficits in abstract thinking and reductions in organizational abilities. She relates difficulties experienced in mathematics to receptive and expressive language in the following statement:

> First of all, "casual" language must never be used because of the brain-injured child's deficient ability to focus visually and/or auditorily. Second, the child's receptive language capacity is often inadequate in regard to symbols. Third, the child's ability to express himself accurately and to the point with mathematically correct answers is limited. (p. 247)

At the high school levels, verbal math problems demand knowledge of specific terminology and efficiency in performing mathematical operations. The student must know the spatial terms for three-dimensional relations such as prism, pyramid, cylinder, cone, sphere, angle, central, radius, diameter, tangent, congruent figures, and polygon.

The operations which must be performed to solve verbal math problems at this level require complex syntactic-semantic processing and symbolic recoding abilities. Consider, for example, this verbal math problem below:

> A man working alone can paint a barn in four hours, while his son alone takes six hours. After they both work for an hour, the son leaves. How long does it take the father to finish the job alone?

In order to solve this problem, at least two steps must be completed. The student must:

STEP 1. Understand the concepts and expressions (phrases, clauses and sentences) to abstract the critical underlying meaning.

STEP 2. Translate the deep structure of the English sentences into number sentences or mathematical equations.

Studies of classroom mathematics activities suggest other factors which may contribute to the language disabled student's failures. In one math class at the sixth grade level, a verbal problem-solving test was given orally, and the teacher would not repeat the questions. One language and learning disabled student completely failed the test. This student could not recall the verbal math problems accurately and as a result was unable to either interpret them or solve them. Math classes

**TABLE 15.2**

*Selected areas of difficulty in interpreting and solving verbal mathematics problems*

| Syntax | Semantics | Memory |
|---|---|---|
| Complex sentences structures: conjunction complementation relativization. | Adjective meaning, specifically comparative and superlative forms. | Automatization of series and serial manipulations (multiplication tables, count by 5, etc.) |
| *Wh-* question designed to elicit problem solving. | Synonyms which describe the acts of computation (take away-minus- less than- subtract). | Sequential recall of numbers, actions, and operations. |
| Structural ambiguities, e.g. "Eating apples cost ten cents more a pound than cooking apples." | Linguistic concepts and relationships:    spatial and temporal    conditional    cause-effect    inclusion and exclusion    quantity    ordinal    analogous. | Internal auditory rehearsal for recall and storage. |
| | | Recoding from the verbal to an internal perceptual (visual) code or image and vice versa. |
| | | Delayed recall of numerical and computational detail. |
| | | Accuracy and speed in the retrieval of numbers, sums, and numerical products. |
| | | Limited capacity for concurrent processing and computation (Add 7 + 2; subtract 3; multiply by 7; etc.) |

at the seventh or eighth grade levels often begin with an orally presented series of verbal math problems. In the fifth or sixth grades, they may start off with an oral drill of the multiplication tables. For instance, the teacher may say "Jane, 9 x 4," "John, 6 x 9," and so on. The student with language disabilities may be confounded by the briefness of these presentations. He may need repetitions to recall the numbers accurately.

Table 15.2 summarizes areas of potential difficulty for language disabled students. Their problems may arise in dealing with the syntactic, semantic, or memory components of mathematics.

# SOCIAL STUDIES

The demands placed upon a child's language skills in subjects such as history and geography are clear. These subjects feature spatial and temporal terms, concepts, and relationships. At the high school level, lectures where note taking is required are frequent. Much of the terminology is abstract and advanced. The students must acquire new information by reading texts that use complex sentence transformations, high level vocabulary, and figurative language. Research projects and oral and written reports abound, and using texts, articles, and other references is emphasized in completing these assignments. These subjects tax the students' syntactic, semantic, and memory skills as well as their ability to produce oral and written language.

Illustrations of materials from high school texts reflect the complexity of the language used and the verbal responses required in social studies. The most obvious task the students are required to do to demonstrate knowledge in history courses is to be accurate in the retention, recall, and retrieval of the chronology of historical figures or events. The example below illustrates this task requirement.

*Example 1. Chronological order test*

Number the items in each of the following groups so that they are in chronological order.

A. ____ Pope Urban II.
____ Pope Innocent.
____ Richard the Lion-Hearted.

B. ____ University of Paris.
____ University of Cambridge.
____ University of Oxford.

C. ____ Knight.
____ Squire.
____ Page.

D. ____ Norse invasions of Europe.
____ Moorish invasions of Europe.
____ Germanic invasions of Europe.

E. ____ Journeyman.
____ Apprentice.
____ Master worker.

F. ____ Craft guilds.
____ Merchant guilds.
____ Trade unions.

Which one of the following occurred first? (a) The American Revolution, (b) The Glorious Revolution, (c) The execution of Charles II, (d) The Industrial Revolution.

The materials which the students must interpret and analyze may use structurally complex phrases, clauses, and sentences. Frequently cloze sentences or paragraphs are used to assess comprehension and recall. This procedure requires the student to be accurate in word retrieval and in the use of syntactic-semantic and contextual cues in the sentence or paragraph. The example below illustrates the syntactic complexity of the materials and test procedures used to assess comprehension and recall.

*Example 2*

The following information is about a Supreme Court case. Read the information carefully. Then write in each blank at the left the word or phrase that best completes the statement.

In June, 1971, *The New York Times* began publishing documents—the so-called Pentagon papers—about United States government policy in Vietnam. These secret documents had been stolen and given to the *Times* to publish. The Justice Department got an injunction, or a court order, to stop the *Times* from printing the documents. *The Washington Post*, which had begun to publish the papers shortly after the *Times*, was also stopped. The *Times* and the *Post* appealed their case to the Supreme Court of the United States.

    _____ 1. The *New York Times* first published the _____ papers.
    _____ 2. The papers were about American policy in _____.
    _____ 3. These secret government documents had been _____.
    _____ 4. A court order called an _____ stopped the publications.
    _____ 5. The case was appealed to the _____ of the United States.

Multiple-choice questions are often used to evaluate the knowledge of relationships among events, persons, dates, and places. The questions often involve structurally complex sentences with multiple embedded clauses. The example below illustrates a not-uncommon occurrence. The student must interpret spatial concepts embedded in a passive transformation with multiple embedded relative clauses.

*Example 3*

The theory that objects fall toward the earth according to the same laws that govern the motion of the planets around the sun was developed by (a) Roger Bacon, (b) Isaac Newton, (c) William Harvey, (d) Louis Pasteur.

The demands on the interpretation of multiple-meaning words and figurative language are often staggering in the materials presented in high school level history texts. This characteristic is illustrated in the excerpt below.

*Example 4*
*The italics indicate the difficult words.*

Title: "Peter the Great *opens the windows* to the West."

For 250 years the "Golden Horde" ruled Russia *with an iron fist*. But one prince, Ivan III, refused to pay tribute to the Tartar rules. With a strong army *at his back*, he conquered the important city of Novgorod, threw out the Tartars and set up an independent state.

Many social studies texts use comparative tables or charts to present relative comparisons and complex information. These charts often use long word strings rather than sentences. Without full sentence markers, the subject-action-object relationships may be obscure to language and learning disabled students. The visual-spatial features of the charts may add to the students' confusion. Example 5 shows the formats and tasks required in using some comparative charts.

To adequately demonstrate competence and skills in social studies, the student may need to produce complex syntactic-semantic

*Example 5. Skills: Using Comparative Charts*

*Study the chart below, and then in each blank at the left, write the letter of the best answer.*

### CULTURAL DIFFERENCES—THREE IMAGINARY INDIAN SOCIETIES

| | Society A | Society B | Society C |
|---|---|---|---|
| **Geography** | Land: Mountains; fertile valleys; dense forests; many rivers | Land: Arid with rugged, broken terrain | Land: heavy forests; fertile valleys; mountains; rivers and bays; coastal area |
| | Climate: Cold winters; hot summers; moderate rainfall | Climate: Desert climate, usually hot and dry | Climate: Mild winters; cool summers; heavy rainfall |
| **Food Supplies** | Vegetables, such as corn, beans, and squash; wild fruit; game, such as deer, beaver, fish and fowl | Seeds, nut, and roots; small animals and insects (rabbits, rats, lizards, caterpillars, and grasshoppers) | Fish (salmon), sea mammals, and game; wild fruit; wild greens; seaweed; products from domesticated animals |
| **Hunting and Fishing Methods** | Stalking game with arrows and spears; trapping and spearing fish; later, using guns obtained from the Dutch | Trapping insects and small game with snares, net, crooks, and clubs | Fishing with nets, weirs, harpoons, and hooks; hunting game with arrows, spears, traps, and snares |
| **Clothing** | Men: Leggings or trousers, moccasins, shirts—all made of animal skins; fur boots for winter | Men: Scanty clothing; some rabbit-skin robes | Men: Fur caps; deerskin robes, leggings; moccasins; rain capes |
| | Women: Skirts, blouses, moccasins—all made of animal skins; later, cloth dresses received from European traders | Women: Basket hats and sleeveless tunics of skins or woven grass | Women: Basket hats, goatskin skirts, rain capes |
| **Housing** | Longhouses for group living | Domed wickiups | Low plank houses with dome-shaped grass thatch roofs |

_____ (1) Which society existed in a geographical setting where conditions were probably least favorable for farming? (a) Society A, (b) Society B, (c) Society C

_____ (2) Which society developed special clothing designed for protection during rainfalls? (a) Society A, (b) Society B, (c) Society C

_____ (3) Which society apparently had the most direct contacts with Europeans? (a) Society A, (b) Society B, (c) Society C

_____ (4) Which society had the culture best adapted to severe winters? (a) Society A, (b) Society B, (c) Society C

_____ (5) Which of the three societies had the most primitive culture? (a) Society A, (b) Society B, (c) Society C

structures. Example 6 illustrates the complexity of the language tasks of one history assignment at the high school level. To complete the task, the student must (1) interpret a metaphor, (2) extend a metaphor to historical persons by analogy, (3) use logical sequencing, and (4) be fluent, accurate, and flexible in word selection and sentence transformation.

*Example 6.*

"The pen is mightier than the sword."

Tell the importance of the following writers on their times: (a) Adam Smith, (b) Charles Darwin, (c) George Bernard Shaw, (d) Victor Hugo, and (e) Leo Tolstoy.

The language difficulties the language disabled student encounters in social studies are similar to those he experiences in English. Table 15.3 emphasizes problems which are relatively content-specific to the emphasis on spatial and temporal information in social studies.

**TABLE 15.3**

*Selected areas of difficulty in interpreting and responding to materials and assignments in social studies*

| Syntax | Semantics | Memory |
|---|---|---|
| Tense and time markers. | Semantic ambiguities related to multiple referents for proper names. | Temporal-sequential memory. |
| Complex sentences: conjunction complementation passive constructions. | Linguistic concepts and relationships: spatial and temporal familial analogous. | Internal rehearsal of specific information (dates, names, places, etc.) |
| Structural ambiguities at the surface or deep-structure levels. | Figurative language: idioms metaphors. | Delayed recall of numerical details, proper names, and chronology. |
| *Wh-* questions. | Implied cause-effects, conditions, and relationships. | Accuracy and speed in retrieving specific names and dates, resulting in substitutions of names, dates, places, etc. |
| | Semantic elaboration in recounting events or issues. | |

# SCIENCE

There are several input-output modalities that can be used in learning the physical sciences. Experiments, lab assignments, and demonstrations allow the students to learn through visual and motor experiences. The need for language in learning may vary greatly from classroom to classroom, depending upon the teaching methods and materials. There are, however, specific language skills which the student must have if he is to process, retain, and recall the information presented for learning.

The language used in the sciences is space and time-related. As a result, the student must have a firm grasp of the meaning of linguistic concepts and relations that denote space-time relationships, including:

(1) Concepts that denote comparative spatial-temporal relationships such as *more than, less than, wider, widest,* and *later than.*
(2) Concepts that denote specific temporal-sequential relations such as *when . . . then, before, after,* and *until.*
(3) Concepts that denote cause-effect relationships such as *because, as, although,* and *even then.*
(4) Concepts that denote conditional relationships such as *if, not unless, only if,* and *instead.*
(5) Concepts of inclusion and exclusion such as *all, few, some, none,* and *all . . . except.*

The student will also need to learn and be able to use specific terminology such as:

(1) Terms that denote specific actions (verbs) such as "revolve," "focus," "replace," "increase," "decrease," "display," "deflect," and "oscillate."
(2) Terms that denote specific substances, objects, processes, relationships, or events such as "diaphragm," "molecule," "density," "photosynthesis," "brothymol blue," and "ammonium hydroxide."

We have selected illustrations of curriculum materials for high school science that highlight the semantic and structural characteristics of scientific language. The first examples show the syntactic complexity of the sentences in some science texts. They also indicate the number of expressed spatial, comparative, cause-effect, and conditional relationships.

*Example 1*

Now it happens that water molecules are lighter than the molecules of nitrogen or oxygen which they replace in the air. Hence, although both cubes have the same number of molecules, cube B has some lighter molecules than cube A, and so the dry air of cube A weighs more than the humid air of cube B. Air that contains water vapor is *less* dense than dry air, other things being equal.

*Example 2*

If pressure belts alone determined wind directions, then all winds would blow either due north or due south. However, because the earth is rotating, the winds in the northern hemisphere are deflected to their right, and those in the southern hemisphere are deflected to the left. This deflection is known as the CORIOLIS EFFECT. As an example of the Coriolis effect, notice how the winds we call "prevailing westerlies," that blow across the continental United States, are deflected toward the east.

The next example illustrates the topic-specific terminology featured in science texts.

*Example 3*

Prepare a dilute solution of bromthymol blue (¼ gram in 500 ml of water gives a .05% solution). To this solution add only enough ammonium hydroxide to cause the solution to turn light blue. Bromthymol blue is a carbon dioxide indicator. Place some of the solution in a test tube. Insert a straw and blow into the solution gently. If the solution is properly prepared, it should turn yellow. If it does not turn yellow you added too much ammonium hydroxide.

Science demands relatively high accuracy in the recall and retrieval of specific terminology. There are several methods that may be used to assess knowledge and skill acquisition. The students may be required to demonstrate their competence by selecting a term from among several choices or by naming an object, relationship or process they can visually observe. Each of these formats may cause problems for some language and learning disabled students and therefore fail to tap their actual knowledge of the subject. Cloze paragraphs are also frequently used in science texts. In this format the student must supply words deleted from a paragraph to demonstrate his knowledge. This format taxes syntactic, semantic, and memory and retrieval skills. Example 4 illustrates the use of a cloze paragraph in the sciences.

*Example 4*

1. If the diameter, density, and tension upon a string remain unchanged, shortening its length _____ its vibration rate and _____ its pitch.
2. If the length, density, and tension upon a string remain unchanged, a string of double a given diameter has a vibration rate just _____ that of the first string. A string of diameter three times that of the first has a vibration rate just a _____ that of the first.
3. If the length, density, and diameter of a string remain unchanged, the vibration rate is doubled when the tension is made _____ times as great. The vibration rate is trebled when the tension is _____ times as great.
4. If the length, diameter, and tension upon a string remain unchanged, the denser the string the more _____ it vibrates. A string of four times the density of another would vibrate just _____ as rapidly as the string of lighter density.
5. Among the stringed musical instruments are _____ and _____.
6. Musical instruments produce sounds pleasing to the ear by means of vibrating _____, and _____, reinforced in some cases by sounding boards.

The language and learning disabled high school student may have difficulties with the syntactic, semantic, and memory components of verbal and written science assignments. Table 15.4 outlines selected potential areas of difficulty in interpreting and using the language of science.

# FOREIGN LANGUAGES

Learning a foreign language requires the student to acquire a new symbol system with arbitrary rules. The differences between the linguistic rules of English and those of most other languages encompass the phonological (speech sound), morphological (word formation), syntactic (sentence formation), and morphophonemic (intonation and prosodic) levels, as well as semantic (meaning). The methods used to teach a foreign language will vary greatly from classroom to classroom.

**TABLE 15.4**
*Selected areas of difficulty in interpreting and expressing the language of science*

| Syntax | Semantics | Memory |
|---|---|---|
| Word derivations. | Topic-specific vocabulary. | Auditory-sequential memory for actions and events. |
| Prefixing. | Latin and Greek prefixes and base words. | Internal rehearsal of specific details for storage. |
| *Wh-* questions. | Linguistic concepts and relationships: | Delayed recall of details (numerical, formulas, etc.) |
| |     spatial and temporal | |
| |     cause-effect | Accuracy and speed in the retrieval of specific terms. |
| |     inclusion-exclusion | |
| |     conditional | Recoding from the verbal to an internal perceptual (visual) code or image and vice versa. |
| |     analogous | |
| |     computational. | |
| | Elaboration in verbal or written assignments. | |

In general, however, visual aids such as posters, photographs, maps, slides, and films are used to assist in teaching.

Foreign language learning may present one of the greatest barriers in the educational and academic career of the language and learning disabled child. The problems may come up from the very beginning, when basic vocabulary and phrase structure rules are emphasized. Or they may begin later, when more abstract vocabulary and complex sentence transformations are taught. Just the vast number of language rules that the student is expected to learn during the first year of studying a foreign language may in itself present a barrier.

In addition, the teacher may expect the students to learn more quickly than is possible for the language and learning disabled student. The teacher may not repeat specific rules or vocabulary items in the classroom often enough for the learning disabled. In general, however, the difficulties a child experiences in learning a foreign language tend to match those he has in his first language.

A curriculum outline of objectives for first year French and Spanish classes in one county is presented below (Table 15.5). It is evident from the outline that the process of learning a language is greatly telescoped when learning a foreign language compared to when learning the native tongue. Clearly, the language and learning disabled student may run into problems in learning even basic rules such as regular and irregular noun plurals, noun possessives, personal pronouns, and so on.

**TABLE 15.5**
*First-year French and Spanish language rules to be acquired*

**(1) Articles**
(a) Definite-indefinite.
(b) Contracted forms.
(c) Partitive constructions.
(d) Definite articles in general sense.

**TABLE 15.5** (*Continued*)

**(2) Nouns**
(a) Gender.
(b) Number.
(c) Regular-irregular forms of plural.
(d) Noun possessive.

**(3) Pronouns**
(a) Personal pronouns: Subjective and objective case.
(b) Possessive-possessive replacive (position).
(c) Interrogative.
(d) Demonstrative.
(e) Prepositional.
(f) Relative.
(g) Indefinite.

**(4) Adjectives**
(a) Gender.
(b) Regular-irregular.
(c) Agreement.
(d) Position.
(e) Comparison (regular-irregular).
(f) Possessive.
(g) Interrogative.
(h) Demonstrative.

**(5) Adverbs**
(a) Formation.
(b) Position.
(c) Comparison (regular-irregular).

**(6) Prepositions**
(a) Verb combinations.
(b) Idioms.

**(7) Verbs**
(a) Tenses (present; imperative; imperfect; past indefinite; future).
(b) Agreement of past participle.
(c) Irregular forms with orthographic changes.

**(8) Idioms**

**(9) Syntactic structures**
(a) Affirmative construction.
(b) Negative construction.
(d) Interrogative construction.

# ADAPTING AND ENHANCING LANGUAGE COMPONENTS OF THE CURRICULUM

# 16

## SYNTACTIC-SEMANTIC COMPONENTS IN READING

Youngsters with language and learning disabilities who are confronted with standard reading materials may be targeted for failure. The materials may be too complex syntactically, as we saw in chapters 14 and 15. The words, concepts, and relations featured in the materials may be too difficult. As a result, reading materials and assignments may be virtually illegible, incomprehensible, and incapable of evoking the student's interest in either the topic or the details. Learning is necessarily curtailed by the youngster's difficulties in dealing adequately with the syntactic and semantic aspects of the written language code.

Reading materials and assignments presented to the language and learning disabled student may be adapted or scaled down in complexity by analyzing them and applying readability formulas. Readability formulas may provide valuable information about the current level of difficulty of the materials and assignments and they give guidelines for reducing the complexity. In this context there are three components to readability: legibility, ease of understanding, and interest in relation to the subject matter and themes.

For any written material, readability may be determined by applying one or more of several formulas. Applicable formulas have been developed after extensive research by Dale and Chall (1948), Flesch (1948), and others. We have applied the Dale-Chall and Flesch formulas to two textbook samples (Figure 16.1). Table 16.1 on p. 417 shows a worksheet for applying the Dale-Chall readability formula.

Chall (1958) has reviewed the extensive results of investigations of readability. She summarizes several major generalizations about factors that contribute to readability which can be used with written materials presented to language and learning disabled students. They also can be used in determining whether spoken materials presented in the classroom to these youngsters are easy to listen to and interpret.

First, the syntactic structure of the sentences predicts the level of difficulty of the materials. In this respect, syntactic complexity of the language affects ease of processing and interpretation similarly in

**FIGURE 16.1**

*Application of the Flesch and Dale-Chall formulas*

*The slash shows where the passage ends for counting purposes.*

**Original Passage**

The first dictionary of the English language to become famous and widely used was written in London in 1755. Earlier attempts to list English words and their meanings had been scanty and unsystematic; simply by its thoroughness, this work was the first to deserve the title "dictionary," as we use the word today. Can you guess how many experts it took to compile this dictionary? How many people do you think were needed to read widely enough in the published writings in English—even in the 1750's—to find the words and meanings to include in a dictionary?

Surprisingly, the answer to this question is not hundreds, nor even many, but one, Dr. Samuel Johnson.*

*Readability:*    Dale-Chall 9th to 10th grades.
                  Flesch 10th to 12th grades.

**Revised Version**

The first English language dictionary to be known and used widely appeared in London. The year was 1755. People had tried before to list all English words and what they meant. These tries, though, had not been well-done. This work was thorough. It was the first to earn the name "dictionary" as we use the word now. Can you guess how many experts it took to write this book? How many people do you think it took to read enough English words to find all the words and meanings to put in such a book?

Oddly, the answer to this question is not hundreds, nor even many, but one, Dr. Samuel Johnson.

*Readability:*    Dale-Chall 7th grade.
                  Flesch 6th grade.

* From *Guide to Modern English* (Grade 9) published by Scott, Foresman, & Company, 1960, p. 172.

spoken and written deliveries. The syntactic complexity of written materials can be determined by various measures. The most frequently used measure is the average sentence length in number of syllables and/or words. In general, ease of comprehension and accuracy and speed with which materials are read are increased by shortening the sentences. The longer the sentences, the harder the reading task. Another measure of structural complexity is the relative proportion or percentage of simple to complex sentences. The more simple sentences, the easier the reading task. The relative number of prepositional phrases and the number of clauses are also used as indicators of sentence complexity. Measures of the relative number of prepositional phrases provide information about syntactic complexity as well as about idea density, a semantic component. The average sentence length and the relative number of prepositional phrases in sentences are related. Measures of the relative number of affixed morphemes (prefixes, suffixes, and derivational and inflectional suffixes) have been found to relate to the abstractness of the reading materials. These measures also tap syntactic complexity.

Second, the semantic content of the sentences presented predicts the relative level of difficulty or of readability. Some observations suggest

**TABLE 16.1**
*Application of the Dale-Chall readability formula to three reading samples*

Article: *Your Baby,* published by the National TB Association

| Steps in Applying the Dale-Chall Formula | Sample 1 "A happy . . . prevented." (p. 2) | Sample 2 "Diphtheria . . . often given." (p. 7) | Sample 3 "The germs . . . or boiled." (p. 12) |
|---|---|---|---|
| 1. Number of words in sample. | 132 | 131 | 111 |
| 2. Number of sentences in sample. | 7 | 9 | 6 |
| 3. Number of words not on Dale list of 3000 familiar words. | 6 | 20 | 17 |
| 4. Average sentence length (divide 1 by 2). | 19 | 15 | 19 |
| 5. Dale score (divide 3 by 1, multiply by 100). | 5 | 15 | 15 |
| 6. Multiply average sentence length (4) by .0496. | .9424 | .7440 | .9424 |
| 7. Multiply Dale score (5) by .1579. | .7895 | 2.3685 | 2.3685 |
| 8. Constant. | 3.6365 | 3.6365 | 3.6365 |
| 9. Formula raw score (add 6, 7, 8). | 5.3684 | 6.7490 | 6.9474 |

**Average raw score of three samples above:** 6.35

**Average corrected grade level:** 7–8

that the nature of the semantic content may take priority over the syntactic structure in predicting readability. The semantic content of reading materials may be measured by vocabulary diversity, vocabulary level and difficulty, degree of abstractness (concrete-abstract), degree of remoteness (nearness-remoteness), conceptual difficulty, supporting details, inferences, organization and logic, and directness of approach.

The vocabulary diversity or range is determined by the number of different words used. In general, the fewer different words used, the easier the reading task. Vocabulary difficulty refers to the reader's knowledge of the meanings of the individual words. Vocabulary difficulty may be determined by reference to developmental data, word lists, or word length. Word length is determined by the number of syllables per 100 words in the text, number of monosyllables, disyllables, or polysyllables. In general, the more familiar and the shorter the words, the easier the reading task. The more unfamiliar the words and the longer the word length, the harder the reading task.

*A bibliography of selected word lists and word frequency counts is presented at the end of this chapter.*

Conceptual difficulty may be measured along a continuum of word meanings from relatively concrete to relatively abstract. It may also be measured by the relative degree of nearness to or remoteness from the reader's life experiences. Conceptual difficulty is also reflected in the relative density of ideas in the reading materials. In general, the more concrete, closer to the reader's experiences, and the lower the idea density, the easier the reading task. The more abstract and remote the words and the greater the idea density, the harder the reading task. The relative degree of idea density is determined by the relative proportion of different content words (nouns and verbs) to the total number of words. As we mentioned above, the relative number of prepositional phrases also determines the degree of idea density. These phrases add to, qualify, or extend the range of the ideas stated in simple sentences and therefore add density of ideas.

The amount of human interest or directness of approach refers to stylistic characteristics of written materials. It is determined in part by the proportion of proper names, personal pronouns, gender nouns (father, mother, sister, etc.), colorful words, dialogue, and sentences directed to the reader. While this factor seems to affect the overall readability only slightly for normal, proficient readers, it may have greater effects for the language and learning disabled reader. These stylistic characteristics determine in part the perspective the reader must take vis-a-vis the content or information shared. Many language and learning disabled youngsters appear to have difficulties in assuming the perspective of other people. They should, therefore, have more trouble reading materials that are other than self-directed and require the reader to take another person's point of view.

Readability formulas may help classroom teachers and specialists to determine the degree of difficulty the child or youth is encountering in his reading assignments. They may be applied directly to make reading materials more readable. We can also apply our knowledge of the nature of language and communication deficits among learning disabled children to the formulas to come up with the following clinical-educational recommendations and suggestions for adapting reading materials.

## Adapting and Reducing Syntactic Complexity

The structural complexity of *all* written materials presented for the language and learning disabled student to read should be adapted or reduced. It should reflect the child's current knowledge of morphological, syntactic, and transformational rules. Both formal and informal assessments can be used to find the youngster's current level of linguistic competence.

*For appropriate formats for formal and informal assessment see pages 97–101.*

When structural aspects of written sentences are adapted or edited, the word, phrase, and clause order should be of primary importance. The order-of-mention of critical content words or phrases (noun phrase, verb phrase, etc.) should correspond to the order-of-action. The sentence "Before you go out to play, wash your hands" would be rewritten as "Wash your hands before you go out to play."

The order or sequence of the individual phrases in sentences should be controlled and adapted to conform as closely as possible to the order of kernel sentences. This principle is especially relevant during the early stages of reading. It applies also when the youngster is confronted with materials that are semantically complex and that use new terminology in specific subject areas such as social studies or the sciences. The phrase structure at the early levels should follow the basic order of agent-action-object. As the youngster's syntactic and semantic abilities improve, you can be less rigid in your adherence to this principle.

Sentence length should be strictly controlled at all levels and for all reading materials. Sentences introduced in reading materials at the early stages of reading, up to about the third grade level, should not exceed five to eight words. At the more advanced levels, they should be kept to within a range of eight to ten words. (In comparison, the average length of sentences in fourth grade reading materials is about 11 words per sentence. In seventh grade materials, it is 13.5 words per sentence [Stormzand & O'Shea, 1924].) As the youngster learns to read longer sentences, prepositional phrases of place or time and coordinated or subordinated clauses may be added towards the ends of sentences.

The length of the noun and verb phrases in sentences should also be controlled. Noun phrases (subject-object) with modification of the noun by more than two adjectives should be rewritten and shortened. No more than two adjectives, and at the beginning levels only one, should be featured in any one noun phrase. The length and complexity of the verb phrase should be reduced to the minimum possible while still retaining the meaning and intent. If the meaning or intent is changed by shortening the length and reducing the complexity, specific words may be added to indicate the intended mood or aspect. For example, the meaning of the verb phrase "might go" in the sentence "He might go to New York next week" could be highlighted by adding "perhaps" or "possibly," as in "Perhaps he might go to New York next week" or "He might possibly go to New York next week."

Sentences that feature conjunction deletion in either the noun (agent-object) or verb (action) phrase may need to be adapted during the early stages of reading. Each related idea stated in the phrase which involves the deletion may need to be presented by itself and in logical sequence in order for the child to grasp the intention of the sentence.

Sentences with embedded clauses (noun complements, adverbial phrases, relative clauses) or with nesting of embedded clauses should be rewritten. The related component sentences should be presented in a written out format, one by one, and in their logical sequence. This practice should be continued until the child can understand and produces these sentence transformations in his speech. If the content and the details presented in a reading selection are conceptually hard for the youngster to grasp, the complex sentences should be reduced— regardless of the child's knowledge of the linguistic rules involved.

In sentence sequences or paragraphs that feature a high proportion of pronouns, the references for the various pronouns should be reiterated at regular intervals. This practice may help the child interpret the stated personal references and relationships.

### Reducing the Semantic Complexity

The semantic content of all written sentences should be reduced or edited to reflect the child's current knowledge of word meanings, of linguistic concepts and relationships, and of figurative language.

*For appropriate formal and informal assessment methods of semantics, see pages 188– 228.*

Again, formal and informal tests of the youngster's receptive vocabulary, linguistic concepts and relationships, and figurative language can be used to assess the child's current abilities. The youngster's use of words and concepts in his spontaneous spoken language should also be considered.

When adapting the semantic contents of reading materials, the number of different content words featured in sentences and paragraphs is critical. Insofar as possible, the ratio of different words to the number of total words should be kept at a minimum. This may be achieved by substituting synonyms with one exemplar—the most familiar, most frequent, or earliest acquired word form. It may also be achieved by rewriting condensed and telescoped phrases and clauses in more elaborate forms that repeat a common vocabulary pool over and over.

The level of difficulty of vocabulary items and concepts used in reading selections may be adapted or reduced overall. In other cases, words from specific categories may need to be adapted or reduced. The specific word categories which you should consider for possible adaptation include multiple meaning words, prepositions, adjectives, and word combinations which result in a change of word meanings.

Among the repertory of prepositions, you may need to substitute for some spatial prepositions. High frequency and more commonly used prepositions should be substituted for low frequency and less commonly used spatial prepositions. In addition, multisyllabic prepositions or prepositions with two or more words should be replaced with prepositions with fewer syllables if the meaning and intent of the spatial relationship can be retained. For example, the preposition "beneath" may be replaced by a bisyllabic preposition, "under." The preposition "above" may be substituted by the preposition "over," and so on. Among the temporal prepositions, "during" may present specific difficulties in interpretation and reading comprehension. This preposition may be replaced by a word or phrase that specifies the beginning and one which specifies the end of the interval in question. For example, the phrase "During the second world war" may be rewritten to say "Between 1914 and 1918, during the second world war." When prepositions are used idiomatically, as in the sentence, "Jane ran into her aunt," they should be rewritten by substituting words with a literal interpretation. That sentence may be adapted to state that "Jane met her aunt" without any loss of intent.

We have already said that prepositional phrases contribute to the idea density of reading materials. In order to reduce the density of ideas and the conceptual level of difficulty, they should be controlled carefully. As a guideline, one prepositional phrase per sentence may be appropriate for most language and learning disabled youngsters. By limiting the number of prepositional phrases per sentence, a certain redundancy and repetitiveness is built into reading materials. This redundancy may help some youngsters understand what they are reading and make the material more readable, even though it may seem intolerable for proficient readers, even the youngster's age peers.

Multiple-meaning words may not always be readily controlled and edited in reading materials. In some cases there are no synonyms available that adequately convey the intent of a multiple meaning word. Take as an example the word "run." If it were featured in a written sentence such as "Lorna had a run in her stockings," it would be hard to find another word to convey the same information. Substitution of the word "rip" for "run" would resolve the problem to some degree, even though "rip" can act as a noun or a verb and therefore has multiple meanings of its own. To reduce the difficulties associated with multiple-meaning words in reading materials, you can define them in sentence contexts or with illustrations. The multiple word definitions and/or illustrations of meanings should be introduced to the youngster before he reads the materials, and they should be available to him during the reading.

In some cases, some words may be combined. In the process of the combination the meaning may, however, differ widely from the meanings of the component words. Take as examples the words "up," "blew," "traffic," and "jam." The two first words may be combined to form the phrase "blew up," as in "The balloon blew up." The last two may be combined into the phrase "traffic jam" as in "There was a traffic jam on the corner." When combinations of two or more words appear in reading materials, you should be careful to adapt or edit those in which the combined meaning is different from the sum of the meanings of the word elements. Usually you will need to elaborately write out the intended meaning and add descriptive terms. This process may result in redundancy, which benefits the language and learning disabled youngster's reading comprehension. Comprehension of these word combinations may also be facilitated by word definitions and illustrations of the meaning of the combination.

The level of difficulty of linguistic relationships such as comparative, spatial, temporal and temporal-sequential, and analogous relationships may need to be controlled in reading selections. This objective is best achieved by using the discussions of order of difficulty for each type of relationship, presented earlier as guidelines. These relationships may then be reworded.

Adjective strings should be reduced in all reading materials presented to language and learning disabled youngsters. The optimum number of adjectives used as noun modifiers may be rather small at the early reading levels. At most, two adjectives should be used in any one noun phrase. To describe other attributes or characteristics of persons, objects, or events sentences with predicate adjective constructions may be used. For instance, the sentence "The *tall, young* boy stood on the corner" may be reworded to read "The *young* boy stood on the corner. *He was tall*."

Verb tenses may cause problems in reading comprehension as well as in spoken language comprehension. To reduce the semantic complexity of verb phrases, the time denoted by the verb tense or by auxiliaries may be emphasized by prefacing sentences with time words such as "yesterday," "last week," and "in the future."

Figurative language in the form of idioms, metaphors, similes, proverbs, and maxims may need editing. The words that signal metaphors and similes may be underlined to signal their figurative status (*as* and *like* underlined). Other figurative expressions and language usages may need to be rewritten, defined, or illustrated. Riddles, jokes, and puns in reading materials may need extensive definitions of terms with double meanings or entendre. They may be elaborated upon to make their intentions clear, or they may be illustrated with pictures, drawings, or cartoons.

Restricted word meanings may be implied in the use of some terms and concepts. For example, the meanings of verbs used in math problems tend to be restricted and to need accurate interpretation. If words used in reading materials or assignments need to be interpreted with restricted meaning, they should be defined. The definitions may take the form of sentences that provide the referential-semantic context or exemplars. They may also take the form of illustrations of actions, objects, or relationships denoted by the restricted word meanings.

Other adaptations may increase readability of reading materials. Implied but not stated meanings and intents may be verbalized and spelled out. The main ideas in materials may be color-coded or underlined. Critical details and significant information may be highlighted or coded. Ideas may be polarized by adding an introductory paragraph that states the topic and main issues. The detailed statements in the body of the materials may be followed up by a restatement of significant topics, ideas, or details at the end. It may also be helpful to adapt reading materials by editing them to feature more and shorter paragraphs. These paragraphs should be sequenced to reflect underlying temporal order, required order of action, or other inherent logical-sequential features. An alternative strategy is to enumerate and number or label sentences and to present each sentence on a single line or two.

## ADAPTING AND ENHANCING LANGUAGE MATERIALS IN CLASSROOM INSTRUCTION

For the language and learning disabled youngster to function and learn optimally in the regular classroom, all the language used in classroom instruction may have to be adapted or enhanced. Classroom interactions center around the teacher, the student or learners, and/or the materials used for instruction. The classroom teacher controls two of these elements directly. She controls her own language and verbal interaction modes and styles, and she controls the materials used for instruction by selection. Both of these elements lend themselves to adaptation or enhancement. And the language and other behaviors of the students can be constantly modified. The teacher can control and adapt the response modes and response requirements, to allow the language and learning disabled youngster to demonstrate his skills and knowledge. We will now discuss some of the possible strategies for adapting and enhancing teacher instructions and directions, materials, and response modes and requirements.

### Adapting and Enhancing Spoken Language Input

Both the structural and semantic complexity and level of difficulty of the teacher's spoken language in the classroom can be adapted. The teacher may not immediately recognize the need to modify and adapt her own language in instructions and directions to the language and learning disabled student. It may therefore be necessary for the language clinician to share the diagnostic findings, observations, and conclusions regarding a specific child in some detail. This may best be accomplished using examples either tape-recorded or videotaped. Only when she thoroughly understands the child's problem areas in listening to and interpreting spoken language and in expressing himself, can the teacher adapt and modify her language appropriately. The teacher should also be informed of language changes and improvements with specific examples as they occur. This will allow her to adapt her modifications of her spoken language to the youngster's changing language status and abilities. In addition, there are other habits of the teacher you may need to change.

Modifying the spoken language in classroom instruction may be beneficial in several subject areas, including English, language arts, social studies, mathematics, and sciences. The spoken language in instruction, the materials used in the classroom, and the language used for questioning or testing may also be adapted.

To reduce the syntactic and transformational complexity of the language used in instruction, the teacher can use the guidelines we presented above for adapting reading materials. And there are other criteria to use as well when the language input is spoken. Sentences should be spoken at a rate which is slower than normal conversational speech if the contents or structures are unfamiliar or new to the child. It is essential that the teacher speak slowly without changing the normal conversational patterns of intonation, phrasing, and stress. Prosodic cues of stress, pauses, or phrasal cueing may be used to highlight certain phrases or clauses in the spoken sentences. Phrasal cueing may also be used to facilitate the immediate recall and rehearsal of the spoken instructions.

*See pages 418–19.*

The efficient and accurate interpretation of spoken instructions in the classroom depends upon short-term auditory memory factors. Therefore the teacher should keep in mind the variables which may facilitate the immediate recall and retention of spoken language, and control them when possible. The interpretation of spoken sentences, paragraphs, and oral directions in classroom instruction may also be facilitated by sequencing the order-of-mention of information, actions, computations, or directions in the order-of-action required in recall or execution.

*For a discussion of the facilitating variables, see pages 419–22.*

The semantic contents of classroom instruction may be controlled and adapted by applying the principles suggested for reading materials. The semantic contents may, however, be enhanced by several methods. The teacher can compile a list of significant details, facts, or information to be recalled later. The students can use the list for reference during the presentation and later questioning. A list of definitions or illustrations of the meaning of unusual or unfamiliar words, phrases, clauses, linguistic concepts and relationships, and idioms and other figurative language usages may be given to the youngster before the instruction begins. The student can then use the definitions for handy reference during instruction or later during recall and questioning sessions. An outline of the contents of materials and presentations may be provided for the youngster. The outline may emphasize focal and significant themes, events, facts to be recalled, or characterizations. It may be used as a reference during classroom instruction, for homework assignments, or for reviews and preparation.

The spoken classroom instructions and presentations may be adapted and organized into specific, self-contained, thematic, and logically or chronologically sequenced segments. This organization may facilitate later recall and use of the information in other tasks and activities such as writing and composition.

Tape recordings of written instructions or materials featured in the classroom may be provided for some youngsters. Tape recordings may be used when the youngster's ability to process and interpret spoken language surpasses his ability to deal with the written language code. The recordings may also provide opportunities for the student to replay and rehearse the materials for later recall. They provide opportunities for decreasing the rate of presentation, depending upon the equipment used for playback. Earphones may be used when the recordings are played back in order to reduce or eliminate extraneous noises. The use of earphones may help the youngster with auditory attention deficits and problems in differentiating spoken language from competing background noises.

Nonsymbolic visual materials may be used to enhance the verbal messages in classroom instruction. Among possible materials are flash cards, photographs, slides, and films. These visual materials may be used to enhance the teacher's verbal instructions in the classroom, the written language materials introduced in teaching, and classroom discussions.

Note taking may be replaced by tape recording classroom presentations and interactions. The tape recordings may later be transcribed, or notes taken from them. Lists and outlines may facilitate the process of abstracting for note taking in the classroom or from taped recordings. The teacher could also start a buddy system in which students with divergent but complementary abilities, in the face of limitations and deficits, help each other take notes and outline.

## Other Adaptations and Modifications

Even spelling assignments may be adapted for language and learning disabled students. They may be designed to permit the student to select a choice from among several possible or related choices. The words to be spelled may be tape recorded to allow the child to listen to the words several times before trying to spell them. The form of response required may also be modified. Written (graphic) rather than oral spelling responses may be allowed, and vice versa. Some youngsters may perform better on oral spelling than on written spelling tasks. Others may perform better on written spelling tasks. In either case, the response requirements may be tailored to the individual youngster's strength.

Vocabulary skill assignments may be adapted by making the word definitions more concrete and providing redundancy in the definitions given. Redundancy may be built in to definitions by using familiar antonyms, synonyms, and other associated words. It may also be built in by featuring the word in a prototypical or best exemplar sentence in which all the words other than the one to be defined are highly familiar.

Verbal math problems and science and lab assignments may be adapted by reducing the structural complexity of sentences to a minimum. The length of sentences may also be shortened to from five to eight words each. Unfamiliar terms for relationships and operations may be replaced by terms that are familiar to the youngster. Sentences and statements should be sequenced to match the computational or experimental steps required. Concrete, manipulative materials such as blocks, beads, rods, or geometric shapes may be used to explain terms by demonstration and action. The operations or computations required may also be demonstrated and illustrated with these concrete materials.

Verbal math and science problems may be further adapted by providing lists of definitions or illustrations of the meanings of concepts and relationships. A list of synonyms or phrase substitutions for terms that are commonly used in math and science problems may also be used to facilitate the interpretation of verbal assignments. The list may be used for handy reference in the classroom, for homework assignments, and during testing and evaluation. One example of a reference list for verbal math terms is featured below.

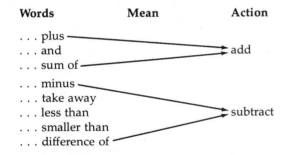

| Words | Mean | Action |
|-------|------|--------|

Science assignments may be adapted and/or enhanced by cutting reading to a minimum through the use of detailed work sheets. A detailed, sequenced outline may be provided for lab assignments and experiments. The steps to be executed may be numbered. The sheet may be arranged so that the student, a tutor, or the teacher can check off each step as it has been completed. The instructional steps should be associated with pictorial or graphic illustrations of the operations, actions, steps, and outcomes of each step. A list of definitions of topic-specific terminology should be provided for immediate reference.

Statements and questions presented in tests and evaluations should be adapted by reducing the syntactic and semantic complexity. *Wh-* questions used to elicit factual information may be rephrased to help the student interpret the question per se accurately. Statements and questions featured on written tests and evaluations may be tape recorded and word definitions provided to facilitate accurate interpretation. *Wh-* questions may be rephrased as follows:

| WHO | becomes | WHAT PERSON |
| WHERE | becomes | WHAT PLACE |
| WHEN | becomes | WHAT TIME |
| HOW | becomes | IN WHAT WAY |
| WHY | becomes | FOR WHAT REASON |

The response requirements of tests and evaluations may also need to be modified for the language and learning disabled student. These youngsters may not be able to demonstrate their actual knowledge and competence if the responses required limit their ability to respond accurately and speedily. There are several kinds of response requirements that can present barriers to the valid demonstration of skills and competencies. If complex written responses are required, the potential difficulty is evident. If specific words must be retrieved accurately and rapidly to complete sentences or label tables, graphs, or pictures, the learning disabled student may have trouble. The teacher should consider these response requirements in designing an evaluation. Multiple-choice tests may increase the accuracy and speed of response for some youngsters. However, they may have to be adapted with multiple cues. The teacher can add functional definitions and familiar synonyms in addition to the topic-specific terminology being tested. The cues will help the student choose the appropriate response. Multiple choices are often designed so that one of the choices is the exact opposite of the correct choice, and a second choice may be designed to be very closely parallel to the correct one. This design requires fine discriminations of word meanings. It may also make it nearly impossible for some language and learning disabled youngsters to display their knowledge. Youngsters with word-finding problems and dysnomia may select the exact opposite of the target or the word which is highly associated with the target. Their selections may appear to be random, and the teacher may assume that they have not learned the material. But with small changes in the design of the selections, their response accuracy may be improved drastically. The teacher should keep in mind that the foils for the target should not trigger associated word substitution errors for these youngsters.

Cloze sentences or paragraphs used for testing may present problems for some language and learning disabled youngsters. This format taxes both syntactic and semantic skills. Youngsters with inadequate syntactic knowledge may not be able to use the available syntactic cues in selecting the words to complete the frame. They are put at a disadvantage from the start, and their errors may reflect problems other than lack of knowledge of the topic. Youngsters with inadequate semantic knowledge may not be able to take advantage of the semantic cues presented for the word selections. They too are disadvantaged. Editing the sentence and paragraph cloze tests may reduce the disadvantage for these youngsters. The syntactic and transformational structure as well as the semantic contents of cloze test materials should be carefully adapted to reduce syntactic and semantic complexity.

Test responses often require labelling of objects, charts, or diagrams in visual confrontation with a picture or a drawing. Multiple choices, letter, syllable, or associative word cues may help the child recall and retrieve a response. A simple visual cue such as a series of lines to indicate the actual or approximate length of the target word may also aid recall and retrieval. Complex written responses are sometimes required on tests and evaluations. The language and learning disabled youngster may not be able to formulate the language for writing the response adequately. He may not be able to select accurate and specific content words. He may not be able to recall or formulate relationships among objects or events. He may not be able to formulate sentence structures that are adequate to the task. These problems may exist along with other writing-specific difficulties. Tape recoding of spoken responses to the test items may eliminate or at least reduce some of these barriers to performance. Using untimed rather than timed tests and evaluations for language and learning disabled youngsters may also help. The responses these youngsters make when they have adequate time and are no longer under pressure will probably be more valid and representative of their actual knowledge, competencies, or potential.

## SELECTED REFERENCES FOR WORD LISTS AND WORD FREQUENCY INDICES

(1) *The Most Common 100,000 Words Used in Conversation*. K. W. Berger. Herald Publishing House, Kent, OH. 1978.

(2) *Word Frequency Book*. J. B. Carroll, P. Davies and B. Richman. Houghton Mifflin. New York, NY.

(3) *Educational Research Bulletin*. E. A. Dale. "A Comparison of Two Word Lists." 1931, *10*, 484-489.

(4) *Elementary English*, E. W. Dolch. "The Use of Vocabulary Lists in Predicting Readability and in Developing Reading Materials." 1949, *26*, 142–149.

(5) *Problems in Reading*. E. W. Dolch. "The First Thousand Words for Children's Reading." Garrard Press. Champaign, IL 1948.

(6) *A Reading Vocabulary for Primary Grades*. A. I. Gates. Teacher's College, Columbia University, New York, NY. 1935.

(7) *A Semantic Count of English Words*. I. Lorge and E. L. Thorndike. Institute of Educational Research, Teachers College, Columbia University, New York, NY. 1938.

(8) *A Basic Vocabulary of Elementary School Children*. H. D. Rinsland. Macmillan Company, New York, NY. 1945.

(9) *A Teacher's Word Book of 10,000 Words*. E. L. Thorndike. Teachers College, Columbia University, New York, NY. 1921.

(10) *A Teacher's Word Book of 20,000 Words*. E. L. Thorndike. Teachers College, Columbia University, New York, NY. 1931.

(11) *The Teacher's Word Book of 30,000 Words*. E. L. Thorndike and I. Lorge. Teachers College, Columbia University, New York, NY. 1944.

# APPENDIX
# Morphology and Syntax

## 1. REGULAR WORD FORMATION RULES

| Rule | Morpheme–Allomorphs | Sample Word | Sample Sentence |
|---|---|---|---|
| 1. **Noun plural** | -s | | |
| | /s/ | cats | The cats are climbing. |
| | /z/ | boys | The boys are walking. |
| | /ez/ | glasses | The glasses are new. |
| 2. **Noun possessive** | | | |
| Singular | -'s | | |
| | /'s/ | cat's | The cat's food is gone. |
| | /'z/ | boy's | The boy's cat is missing. |
| | /'ez/ | glass's | The glass's stem is broken. |
| Plural | -s' | | |
| | /s'/ | cats' | The cats' food is gone. |
| | /z'/ | boys' | The boys' cats are missing. |
| | /ez'/ | glasses' | The glasses' stems are broken. |
| 3. **Present progressive** | | | |
| | -ing | walking | The boy is walking. |
| 4. **Third person singular-present tense** | | | |
| | -s | walks | The boy walks to school every day. |
| 5. **Past tense** | -t | | |
| | /t/ | walked | The boy walked home. |
| | /d/ | jogged | The boy jogged home. |
| | /ed/ | balanced | The boy balanced the scales. |
| 6. **Adjective form** | | | |
| Comparative | -er | bigger | The boy is bigger than me. |
| Superlative | -est | biggest | The boy is the biggest in his class. |

| Rule | Morpheme–Allomorphs | Sample Word | Sample Sentence |
|------|---------------------|-------------|-----------------|
| **7. Noun derivation** | | | |
| | -er | teach*er* | He is a teach*er*. |
| **8. Adverb derivation** | | | |
| | -ly | slow*ly* | The boy is walking slow*ly*. |
| **9. Diminutive of nouns** | | | |
| | -let | book*let* | The boy bought a book*let* on jogging. |

## 2. THE FINITE VERB PHRASE

| Verb Form | Noun Phrase 1 | Verb Phrase | Noun Phrase 2 |
|-----------|---------------|-------------|---------------|
| **Present tense: V + -s** | | | |
| θ | I | *eat* | apples |
| -s | She | *eats* | apples |
| **Present progressive: BE + V + -ing** | | | |
| θ | I | *am* eating | apples |
| -s | She | *is* eating | apples |
| **Past tense: V + -ed** | | | |
| -ed | I | *ate* | apples |
| -ed | She | *ate* | apples |
| **HAVE + V + en** | | | |
| θ | I | *have* eaten | apples |
| -s | She | *has* eaten | apples |
| **HAVE + -ed + V + -en** | | | |
| -ed | I | *had* eaten | apples |
| -ed | She | *had* eaten | apples |
| **HAVE + BE + -en + V + -ing** | | | |
| θ | I | *have* been eating | apples |
| -s | She | *has* been eating | apples |
| **HAVE + -ed + BE + -en + V + -ing** | | | |
| -ed | I | *had* been eating | apples |
| -ed | She | *had* been eating | apples |
| **HAVE + BE + -en + V + -en** | | | |
| θ | The apples *have* been eaten | | ——— |
| **HAVE + -ed + BE + -en + V + -en** | | | |
| -ed | The apples *had* been eaten | | ——— |
| **CAN + HAVE + BE + -en + V + -en** | | | |
| -ed | The apples *could* have been eaten | | ——— |
| **WILL + HAVE + BE + -en + V + -en** | | | |
| θ | The apples *will* have been eaten | | ——— |
| **SHALL + HAVE + BE + -en + V + -en** | | | |
| -ed | The apples *should* have been eaten | | ——— |

Italics indicate the inflected form. θ indicates no inflectional ending.

# 3. KERNEL SENTENCE AND SELECTED DERIVED SENTENCE TRANSFORMATIONS

| Transformation | Characteristics | Derived Sentence |
|---|---|---|
| Kernel sentence. | Active, affirmative, declarative. | The girl is flying the plane. |
| Negation. | Active, *negative*, declarative. | The girl is *not* flying the plane. |
| Passive. | *Passive*, affirmative, declarative. | The plane *is being* flown *by* the girl. |
| Interrogative. | Active, affirmative, *interrogative*. | *Is* the girl flying the plane? |
| Negative interrogative. | Active, *negative*, *interrogative*. | *Isn't* the girl flying the plane? |
| Negative passive. | *Passive*, *negative*, declarative. | The plane *is not being* flown *by* the girl. |
| Passive interrogative. | *Passive*, affirmative, *interrogative*. | *Is* the plane *being* flown *by* the girl? |
| Negative, passive interrogative. | *Passive*, *negative*, *interrogative*. | *Isn't* the plane *being* flown *by* the girl? |
| Emphatic. | Active, affirmative, declarative with *stress* on BE. | The girl *is* flying the plane. |
| Emphatic negative. | Active, *negative*, declarative with *stress* on BE + not. | The girl *is not* flying the plane. |
| Emphatic passive. | *Passive*, affirmative, declarative with *stress* on BE. | The plane *is* being flown by the girl. |
| Emphatic interrogative. | Active, affirmative, *interrogative* with *stress* on BE. | *Is* the girl flying the plane? |
| Emphatic negative interrogative. | Active, *negative*, *interrogative* with *stress* on BE + not. | *Isn't* the girl flying the plane? |
| Emphatic negative passive. | *Passive*, *negative*, declarative with *stress* on BE + not. | The plane *isn't* being flown by the girl. |
| Emphatic negative passive interrogative. | *Passive*, *negative*, *interrogative* with *stress* on BE + not. | *Isn't* the plane being flown by the girl? |
| Imperative. | Active, affirmative, *imperative*. | *Fly* the plane! |
| Negative imperative. | Active, *negative*, *imperative*. | *Don't fly* the plane! |

# 4. SELECTED SENTENCE TRANSFORMATIONS WITH CONJUNCTION OF CLAUSES

| Transformation | Clause 1 | Conjunction | Clause 2 | Derived Sentence |
|---|---|---|---|---|
| Coordination of clauses. | The dog barks. | *and, but,* etc. | The baby cries. | The dog barks *and* the baby cries. |
| Conjunction deletion | | | | |
| Subject. | The dog barks. | *and* | The dog howls. | The dog barks *and* howls. |

| Transformation | Clause 1 | Conjunction | Clause 2 | Derived Sentence |
|---|---|---|---|---|
| Predicate. | The dog howls. | *and* | The cat howls. | The dog *and* cat howl. |
| Object. | The dog eats the bone. | *and* | The cat eats the bone. | The dog *and* cat eat the bone. |
| Time conjunction. | The dog barks. | *when, after,* etc. | The mailman arrives. | The dog barks *when* the mailman arrives. |
| Conditional conjunction. | The dog barks. | *if,* etc. | The mailman arrives. | The dog barks *if* the mailman arrives. |
| Causal conjunction. | The dog barks. | *because, as,* etc. | The mailman arrives. | The dog barks *because* the mailman arrives. |
| Noun clause. | I believe/told/think it. | *that* | The mailman arrives. | I believe *that* the mailman arrives. |
| Adverbial clause | | | | |
| Time. | The dog barks. | *when* | It is late. | The dog barks *when* it is late. |
| Place. | The dog barks. | *where* | It is safe. | The dog barks *where* it is safe. |
| Relative clause | | | | |
| Subject-related. | The dog barks. | *that, who, which* | The dog lives next door. | The dog, *that* lives next door, barks. |
| Object-related. | She saw the dog. | *that, who, which* | The dog lives next door. | She saw the dog *that* lives next door. |
| Pronoun deletion. | She saw the dog. | —— | She likes the Dog. | She saw the dog she likes. |

# REFERENCES

Abramowitz, J. *Methods and materials for educationally deficient pupils.* Fort Lauderdale, Fl.: Instructional Advisory Services, 1978.

Ahmann, J.S., & Glock, M.D. *Evaluating pupil growth.* Boston: Allyn & Bacon, 1971.

Aiken, L.R., Jr. Language factors in learning mathematics. *Review of Educational Research,* 1972, *42,* 359–85.

Anderson, J.R., & Bower, G.H. *Human association memory.* New York: V.H. Winston & Sons, 1973.

Anglin, J. *Word, object, and conceptual development.* New York: W. W. Norton, 1977.

Argyle, M. *Non-verbal communication in human social interaction.* Cambridge: Cambridge University Press, 1972.

Aten, J., & Davis, J. Disturbances in the perception of auditory sequence in children with minimal cerebral dysfunction. *Journal of Speech and Hearing Disorders,* 1968, *11,* 236–45.

Baker, H., & Leland, B. *Detroit Tests of Learning Aptitude.* Indianapolis: Test Division of Bobbs-Merrill, 1967.

Bangs, T.E. *Language and learning disorders of the pre-academic child.* New York: Appleton-Century-Crofts, 1968.

Bangs, T.E. *Vocabulary comprehension scale.* Austin, Tex.: Learning Concepts, 1975.

Bannatyne, A. *Language, reading and learning disabilities.* Springfield, Ill.: Charles C. Thomas, 1971.

Barrie-Blackley, S. Six-year-old children's understanding of sentences adjoined with time adverbs. *Journal of Psycholinguistic Research,* 1973, *2,* 153–65.

Bartlett, F.C. *Remembering: a study in experimental and social psychology.* Cambridge: Cambridge University Press, 1932.

Beiswenger, H. Luria's model of the verbal control of behavior. *Merrill-Palmer Quarterly,* 1968, *14,* 267–83.

Bellugi-Klima, U. Some language comprehension tests. In C.S. Stendler (Ed.), *Language training in early childhood education.* Urbana: University of Illinois Press, 1971.

Berko, J. The child's learning of English morphology. *Word,* 1958, *14,* 150–77.

Birdwhistell, R.L. *Kinesics and context.* Philadelphia: University of Philadelphia Press, 1970.

Blackwell, J.M. An investigation into phrase-marked and nonphrase-marked cloze scores. Unpublished doctoral dissertation, Boston University, 1975.

Bloom, L. *Language development: Form and function in emerging grammars.* Cambridge: M.I.T. Press, 1970.

Bloomfield, L., & Barnhart, C. *Let's read, a linguistic approach.* Detroit: Wayne State University Press, 1961.

Boehm, A.E. *The Boehm Test of Basic Concepts. Manual.* New York: Psychological Corporation, 1969.

Boehm, A.E. *Boehm Test of Basic Concepts.* New York: Psychology Corporation, 1970.

Bolinger, D. *Aspects of language.* New York: Harcourt, 1968.

Bollinger, D., & Gerstman, L.J. Disjuncture as cue to construct. *Word,* 1957, *13,* 246–55.

Bougere, M. Selected factors in oral language related to first grade achievement. *Reading Research Quarterly,* 1969, *4,* 31–57.

Bousfield, W. Cohen, B., & Whitmarsh, G. Associative clustering of words of different taxonomic frequencies of occurrence. *Psychological Reports*, 1958, *4*, 39–44.

Bower, G.H. Mental imagery and associative learning. In L. Gregg (Ed.), *Cognition in learning and memory.* New York: Wiley, 1972.

Bowerman, M. The acquisition of word meaning: An investigation of some current conflicts. In N. Waterson & C. Snow (Eds.), *Development of communication: Social and pragmatic factors in language acquisition.* New York: Wiley (In press).

Brewer, W.F., & Stone, J.B. Acquisition of spatial antonym pairs. *Journal of Experimental Child Psychology*, 1975, *19*, 299–307.

Brittain, M.M. Inflection performance and early reading achievement. *Reading Research Quarterly*, 1970, *5*, 34–48.

Brown, R. The development of *wh-* questions in child speech. *Journal of Verbal Learning and Verbal Behavior*, 1968, *7*, 279–90.

Brown, R. *A first language: The early stages.* Cambridge: Harvard University Press, 1973.

Brown, R., Cazden, C., & Bellugi, U. The child's grammar from I to III. In J.P. Hill (Ed.), *The 1967 Minnesota Symposium on child psychology.* Minneapolis: University of Minnesota Press, 1968.

Brown, R., & McNeill, D. The "tip of the tongue" phenomenon. In R. Brown (Ed.), *Psycholinguistics.* New York: Free Press, 1970.

Brutten, M., Richardson, S.O., & Mangel, C. *Something is wrong with my child.* New York: Harcourt, Brace, Jovanovich, 1973.

Bryan, T.H. An observational analysis of classroom behaviors of children with learning disabilities. *Journal of Learning Disabilities*, 1974, *7*, 26–34.(a)

Bryan, T.H. Peer popularity of learning disabled children: A replication. *Journal of Learning Disabilities*, 1974, *7*, 621–25.(b)

Bryan, T.H. Social relationships and verbal interactions of learning disabled children. *Journal of Learning Disabilities*, 1978, *11*, 107–15.

Bryan, T.H., & Bryan, J.H. *Understanding learning disabilities.* Port Washington, N.Y.: Alfred Publishing, 1975.

Bryan, T.H., Wheeler, R., Felcan, J., & Henek, T. "Come on dummy": An observational study of children's communications. *Journal of Learning Disabilities*, 1976, *9*, 661–69.

Carey, P., Mehler, J., & Bever, T. Judging the veracity of ambiguous sentences. *Journal of Verbal Learning & Verbal Behavior*, 1970, *9*, 243–54.

Caroll, J.B., Davies, P., & Richman, B. *Word frequency book.* New York: Houghton Mifflin, 1971.

Carrow, E. *Test of Auditory Comprehension of Language.* Austin, Tex.: Urban Research Group, 1973.

Carrow, E. *Carrow Elicited Language Inventory.* Austin, Tex.: Learning Concepts, 1974.

Cartledge, C.J., & Krauser, E.L. Training first-grade children in creative thinking under quantitative and qualitative motivation. *Journal of Educational Psychology*, 1963, *54*, 295–99.

Cazden, C.B. Children's questions: their forms, functions, and roles in education. *Young Children*, 1970, *25*, 202–20.(a)

Cazden, C.B. The neglected situation in child language research and education. In F. Williams (Ed.), *Language and poverty.* Chicago: Markham, 1970. (b)

Cazden, C.B. *Child language and education.* New York: Holt, Rinehart, & Winston, 1972.

Chall, J.S. *Readability: An appraisal of research and application.* Columbus; Ohio State University, 1958.

Chall, J.S. *Learning to read: The great debate.* New York: McGraw Hill, 1967.

Chambers, J.M., & Tavuchis, N. Kids and kin: Children's understanding of American kin terms. *Journal of Child Language*, 1976, *3*, 63–80.

Chipman, H.H., & deDardel, C. Developmental study of the comprehension and production of the pronoun "it." *Journal of Psycholinguistic Research*, 1974, *3*, 91–99.

Chomsky, C. *The acquisition of syntax in children from 5 to 10.* Cambridge: M.I.T. Press, 1969.

Chomsky, N. *Syntactic structures.* The Hague: Mouton, 1957.

Chomsky, N. *Aspects of the theory of syntax.* Cambridge: M.I.T. Press, 1965.

Clark, E.V. On the acquisition of the meaning of "before" and "after." *Journal of Verbal Learning & Verbal Behavior,* 1971, *10*, 266–75.

Clark, E.V. On the child's acquisition of antonyms in two semantic fields. *Journal of Verbal Learning & Verbal Behavior,* 1973, *11*, 750–58.(a)

Clark, E.V. How children describe time and order. In C.A. Ferguson & D.I. Slobin (Eds.), *Studies of child language development.* New York: Holt, Rinehart, & Winston, 1973. (b)

Clark, E.V. Some aspects of the conceptual basis for first language acquisition. In R.L. Schiefelbusch & L.L. Lloyd (Eds.), *Language perspectives—Acquisition, retardation, and intervention.* Baltimore: University Park Press, 1974.

Clark, E.V. Knowledge, context, and strategy in the acquisition of meaning. In D. Dato (Ed.), *Developmental psycholinguistics: theory and applications.* Washington, D.C.: 26th Annual Georgetown University Round-table, Georgetown University Press, 1975.

Clark, H.H., Carpenter, P.A., & Just, M.A. On the meeting of semantics and perception. In W.G. Chase (Ed.), *Visual information processing.* New York: Academic Press, 1973.

Clay, M.M. Reading errors and self-correction behavior. *British Journal of Educational Psychology,* 1969, *39*, 47–56.

Cofer, C.N. Constructive processes in memory. *American Scientist,* 1973, *61*, 537–43.

Cohen, J. The factorial structure of the WISC at ages 7½, 10½, and 13½. *Journal of Consulting Psychology,* 1959, *23*, 285–99.

Coker, P.L. On the acquisition of temporal terms: Before and after. Stanford University Department of Linguistics, *Papers and Reports on Child Language Development,* 1975, *10*, 166–77.

Cronbach, L.J. *Essentials of psychological testing.* 3rd Edition. New York: Harper & Row, 1970.

Crystal, D., Fletcher, P., & Garman, M. *The grammatical analysis of language disability.* New York: Elsevier, 1975.

Dahmus, M.E. How to teach verbal problems. *School Science and Mathematics,* 1970, *70*, 121–38.

Dale, E. A comparison of two words lists. *Educational Research Bulletin,* 1931, *9*, 484–89.

Dale, E., & Chall, J.S. A formula for predicting readability and "instructions." *Educational Research Bulletin,* 1948, *27*, 11–20, 37–54.

Deese, J. *The structure of association in language and thought.* Baltimore: Johns Hopkins Press, 1962.

Denckla, M.B., & Rudel, R.G. Naming of object-drawings by dyslexic and other learning disabled children. *Brain and Language,* 1976, *3*, 1–15.

DeRenzi, E., & Vignolo, L.A. The token test: A sensitive test to detect receptive disturbances in aphasia. *Brain,* 1962, *85*, 665–78.

deVilliers, J.G., & deVilliers, P.A. A cross-sectional study of the acquisition of grammatical morphemes in child speech. *Journal of Psycholinguistic Research,* 1973, *2*, 267–78.

DiPietro, R.J. New vistas in a post-transformational era. In R. Shuy (Ed.), *Some new directions in linguistics.* Washington, D.C.: Georgetown University Press, 1973.

DiVesta, F., & Stauber, K. Identification of verbal concepts by preschool children. *Developmental Psychology,* 1971, *5*, 81–85.

Dixon, T., & Horton, D. (Eds.). *Verbal behavior and general behavior theory.* Englewood Cliffs, N.J.: Prentice-Hall, 1968.

Donaldson, M., & Wales, R.J. On the acquisition of some relational terms. In J.R. Hayes (Ed.), *Cognition and the development of language.* New York: Wiley, 1970.

Dunn, L.M. *Peabody Picture Vocabulary Test.* Minneapolis: American Guidance Service, 1959.

Durrell, D.D. *Durell Analysis of Reading Difficulty.* New York: Harcourt, Brace, & World, 1955.

Durrell, D.D. *Improving reading instruction.* New York: Harcourt, Brace, & World, 1956.

Eilers, R.E., Oller, D.K., & Ellington, J. The acquisition of word meaning for dimensional adjectives: The long and short of it. *Journal of Child Language,* 1974, *1*, 195–204.

Eisenson, J. *Examining for aphasia.* (Rev. ed.). New York: Psychological Corporation, 1954.

Ellis, J., & Ure, J.N. Language varieties: Register. In A.R. Meecham (Ed.), *Encyclopedia of linguistics.* Oxford: Pergamon Press, 1969.

Erven, S.M. Imitation and structural changes in children's language. In E.H. Lenneberg (Ed.), *New directions in the study of language.* Cambridge: M.I.T. Press, 1964.

Fillmore, C.J. Santa Cruz lectures on deixis 1971. Indiana University Linguistics Club, Bloomington, Indiana, 1975.

Fishbein, H.D., & Osborne, M. The effects of feedback variations on referential communication of children. *Merrill-Palmer Quarterly,* 1971, *17*, 243–50.

Fishman, J.A. *Sociolinguistics.* Rowley, Mass.: Newbury House, 1971.

Flavell, J.H. *The developmental psychology of Piaget.* Princeton: Van Nostrand, 1963.

Flavell, J.H. Botkin, P.T., Fry, C.L., Wright, J.C., & Jarvis, P.E. *The development of role-taking and communication skills in children.* New York: Wiley, 1968.

Flesch, R. A new readability yardstick. *Journal of Applied Psychology,* 1948, *32*, 221–33.

Fodor, J.A., & Bever, T.G. The psychological reality of linguistic segments. *Journal of Verbal Learning and Verbal Behavior,* 1965, *4*, 414–20.

Fodor, J.A., & Garrett, M.F. Some reflections on competence and performance. In J. Lyons & R.J. Wales (Eds.), *Psycholinguistics papers.* Edinburgh: Edinburgh University Press, 1966.

Ford, W., & Olson, D. The elaboration of the noun phrase in children's description of objects. *Journal of Experimental Child Psychology,* 1975, *19*, 371–82.

Foss, D.J., Bever, T., & Silver, M. The comprehension and verification of ambiguous sentences. *Perception and Psychophysics,* 1968, *4*, 304–6.

Foster, C.R., Giddan, J.J., & Stark, J. ACLC: *Assessment of Children's Language Comprehension.* Palo Alto: Consulting Psychologists Press, 1972.

Fraser, C., Bellugi, U., & Brown, R. Control of grammar in imitation, comprehension, and production. *Journal of Verbal Learning and Verbal Behavior,* 1963, *2*, 121–35.

French, J.W. The description of aptitude and achievement tests in terms of rotational factors. *Psychometric Monographs,* 1951, No. 5.

Freston, C.W., & Drew, C.J. Verbal performance of learning disabled children as a function of input organization. *Journal of Learning Disabilities,* 1974, *7*, 424–28.

Freud, S. *Psychopathology of everyday life.* New York: Norton, 1971.

Frierson, E. The educator's dilemma in dyslexia and learning disability. CEC DCLD *Newsletter*, 1976, *1*, 15–21.

Fries, C.C. *The structure of English.* New York: Harcourt, Brace & World, 1952.

Fries, C.C. *Linguistics and reading.* New York: Holt, Rinehart, & Winston, 1963.

Fromkin, V.A. Slips of the tongue. *Scientific American,* 1973, *229*, 110–17.

Frostig, M. Corrective reading in the classroom. *The Reading Teacher,* 1965, *18*, 573–80.

Frostig, M. *Move, grow, learn.* Chicago: Follett, 1975.

Gall, M.D. The use of questions in teaching. *Review of Educational Research,* 1970, *40*, 707–21.

Gardner, H., Kircher, M., Winner, E., & Perkins, D. Children's metaphoric productions and preferences. *Journal of Child Language,* 1975, *2*, 125–41.

Garmiza, C., & Anisfeld, M. Factors reducing the efficiency of referent-communication in children. *Merrill-Palmer Quarterly*, 1976, *22*, 125–36.

Gentner, D. Validation of a related-component model of verb meaning. Stanford University Department of Linguistics, *Papers and Reports on Child Language,* 1975, *10*, 69–79.

Geschwind, N. The varieties of naming errors. In M.T. Sarno (Ed.), *Aphasia: Selected readings.* New York: Appleton-Century Crofts, 1972.

Glasser, A.J., & Zimmerman, I.L. *Clinical interpretation of the Wechsler Intelligence Scale for Children.* New York: Grune & Stratton, 1967.

Glucksberg, S., & Kraus, R.M. What do people say after they have learned how to talk? Studies of the development of referential communication. *Merrill-Palmer Quarterly,* 1967, *13*, 309–16.

Glucksberg, S., Kraus, R.M., & Weisberg, R. Referential communication in nursery school children: method and some preliminary findings. *Journal of Experimental Child Psychology, 1966, 3*, 333–42.

Goldstein, K. *Language and language disorders.* New York: Grune & Stratton, 1948.

Golick, M. Language disorders in children: A linguistic investigation. Doctoral dissertation, McGill University, 1976.

Goodglass, H., & Kaplan, E. *The assessment of aphasia and related disorders.* Philadelphia: Lea & Ferbiger, 1972.

Goodman, K. Reading: A psycholinguistic guessing game. *Journal of Reading Specialist, 1967, 4*, 126–35.

Goodman, K. Analysis of oral reading miscues: Applied psycholinguistics. *Reading Research Quarterly, 1969, 4*, 9–30.

Greenfield, P.M., & Smith, J.H. *The structure of communication in early language development.* New York: Academic Press, 1976.

Guthrie, J.T. Principles of instruction: A critique of Johnson's "Remedial approaches to dyslexia." In A.L. Benton & D. Pearl (Eds.), *Dyslexia: An appraisal of current knowledge.* New York: Oxford University Press, 1978. Pp. 425–33.

Hallahan, D.P., & Cruickshank, W.M. *Psychoeducational foundations of learning disabilities.* Englewood Cliffs, N.J.: Prentice-Hall, 1973.

Harris, P. Children's comprehension of complex sentences. *Journal of Experimental Child Psychology, 1975, 19*, 420–33.

Hass, W.A., & Wepman, J.M. Dimensions of individual differences in the spoken syntax of school children. *Journal of Speech and Hearing Research, 1974, 17*, 455–69.

Hoar, N. Paraphrase capabilities of language impaired children. Paper presented at the Second Annual Boston University Conference on Language Development, 1977.

Hunt, K. *Grammatical structure written at three grade levels.* Champaign, Ill.: National Council of Teachers of English, 1965.

Ingram, D. Toward a theory of person deixis. *Papers in Linguistics, 1971, 4*, 37–53.

Inhelder, B., & Piaget, J. *The early growth of logic in the child.* New York: Norton, 1964, 1969.

Inhelder, B., Sinclair, H., & Bovet, M. *Learning and the development of cognition.* Cambridge: Harvard University Press, 1974.

Jeter, I.K. (ed.) *Social dialects: differences vs. disorders.* Rockville, Maryland: American Speech and Hearing Association, 1977.

Johnson, D.J. Remedial approaches to dyslexia. In A.L. Benton & D. Pearl (Eds.), *Dyslexia: An appraisal of current knowledge.* New York: Oxford University Press, 1978. Pp. 399–421.

Johnson, D.J., & Myklebust, H.R. *Learning disabilities: educational principles and practices.* New York: Grune & Stratton, 1967.

Johnson, H.L. The meaning of *before* and *after* for preschool children. *Journal of Experimental Child Psychology, 1975, 19*, 88–99.

Johnson, W., Darley, F.L., & Spriestersbach, D.C. *Diagnostic methods in speech pathology.* New York: Harper & Row, 1963.

Kagan, J., Rosman, B.L., Kay, D., Albert, J., & Phillips, W. Information processing in the child: Significance of analytic and reflective attitudes. *Psychological Monographs: General and Applied, 1964, 78*, 1–37.

Kaliski, L. Arithmetic and the brain-injured child. *The Arithmetic Teacher, 1962, 9*, 245–51.

Kavanagh, J.F. (Ed.). *Communicating by language: the reading process.* Bethesda, Md.: National Institute of Child Health and Human Development, 1968.

Keenan, J.S. A method of eliciting naming behavior from aphasic patients. *Journal of Speech and Hearing Disorders, 1966, 31*, 261–66.

Keogh, B.K., Tchir, C., & Windeguth-Behn, A. Teacher's perceptions of educationally high risk children. *Journal of Learning Disabilities, 1974, 7*, 367–74.

Kirk, S.A., Kliebhan, J.M., & Lerner, J.W. *Teaching reading to slow and disabled learners.* Boston: Houghton Mifflin, 1978.

Kirk, S.A., McCarthy, J.J., & Kirk, W.D. *Illinois Test of Psycholinguistic Ability: Revised Edition.* Urbana: University of Illinois Press, 1968.

Klees, M., & Lebrun, A. Analysis of the figurative and operative processes of thought of 40 dyslexic children. *Journal of Learning Disabilities*, 1972, *5*, 389–96.

Kolers, P.A. Experiments in reading. *Scientific American*, 1972, *227*, 1, 84–91.

Kosslyn, S.M., & Pomerantz, J.R. Imagery, propositions, and the form of internal representations. *Cognitive Psychology*, 1977, *9*, 52–76.

Koziol, S. The development of noun plural rules during the primary grades. *Research in the Teaching of English*, 1973, *7*, 30–50.

Kraus, R., & Rotter, G. Communication abilities of children as a function of status and age. *Merrill-Palmer Quarterly*, 1968, *14*, 161–73.

Lapointe, C.M. Token Test performances by learning disabled and academically achieving adolescents. *British Journal of Disorders of Communication*, 1976, *11*, 121–33.

Lavatelli, C. *Piaget's theory applied to an early childhood curriculum.* Boston: American Science & Engineering, 1970.

Lee, L.L. *Northwestern Syntax Screening Test.* Evanston, Ill.: Northwestern University Press, 1971.

Lee, L.L. *Developmental Sentence Analysis.* Evanston, Ill.: Northwestern University Press, 1974.

Lee, L.L., Koenigsknecht, R.A., & Mulhern, S.T. *Interactive language development teaching.* Evanston, Ill.: Northwestern University Press, 1975.

Lefevre, C.A. *Linguistics and the teaching of reading.* New York: McGraw-Hill, 1964.

Lenneberg, E. *Biological foundations of language.* New York: Wiley, 1967.

Leonard, L.B., Wilcox, M.J., Fulmer, K.C., & Davis, G.A. Understanding indirect requests: An investigation of children's comprehension of pragmatic meanings. *Journal of Speech and Hearing Research*, 1978, *21*, 528–37.

Lerner, J.W. *Children with learning disabilities.* Boston: Houghton Mifflin, 1971.

Levin, H., & Kaplan, E.L. Listening, reading, and grammatical structure. In D.L. Horton & J.J. Perkins (Eds.), *Perception of language.* Columbus, Ohio: Charles E. Merrill, 1971.

Light, L.L. Homonyms and synonyms as retrieval cues. *Journal of Experimental Psychology*, 1972, *96*, 255–62.

Linville, W.J. The effects of syntax and vocabulary upon the difficulty of verbal arithmetic problems with fourth-grade students. Doctoral dissertation, State University of Iowa, 1970.

Lodge, D., & Leach, E. Children's acquisitions of idioms in the English language. *Journal of Speech and Hearing Research*, 1975, *18*, 521–29.

Long, A., & Looft, W. Development of directionality in children ages 6 through 12. *Developmental Psychology*, 1972, *6*, 375–80.

Longhurst, T.M., & Reichle, J.E. The applied communication game: A comment on Muma's "communication game: dump and play." *Journal of Speech and Hearing Disorders*, 1975, *40*, 315–19.

Lumsden, E., & Poteat, B. The salience of the vertical dimension in the concept of "bigger" in 5 and 6 year olds. *Journal of Verbal Learning and Verbal Behavior*, 1968, *7*, 404–8.

Luria, A.R. *Higher cortical functions in man.* New York: Basic Books, 1966.

Luria, A.R. *The working brain.* New York: Basic Books, 1973.

Lyons, J. *Introduction to theoretical linguistics.* Cambridge: Cambridge University Press, 1971.

MacKay, D.G. To end ambiguous sentences. *Perception and Psychophysics*, 1966, *1*, 426–36.

Maltzman, I., Bogartz, W., & Berger, L. A procedure for increasing word association originality and its transfer-effects. *Journal of Experimental Psychology*, 1958, *56*, 392–98.

Maltzman, I., Simon, S., Raskin, D., & Licht, L. Experimental studies in the training of originality. *Psychological Monographs*, 1960, *74*, No. 6 (Whole No. 493).

Maratsos, M.P. The effects of stress on the understanding of pronominal co-reference in children. *Journal of Psycholinguistic Research*, 1973, *2*, 1–8.

Maratsos, M.P. Children who get worse at understanding the passive: A replication of Bever. *Journal of Psycholinguistic Research*, 1974, *3*, 65–74.(a)

Maratsos, M.P. When is a high thing a big one? *Developmental Psychology*, 1974, *10*, 367–75.(b)

Mattingly, I.G. Reading, the linguistic process, and linguistic awareness. In J.F. Kavanagh & I.G. Mattingly (Eds.), *Language by ear and by eye*. Cambridge: M.I.T. Press, 1972.

Mattis, S., French, J.H., & Rapin, I. Dyslexia in children and young adults: Three independent neuro-psychological syndromes. *Developmental Medicine and Child Neurology*, 1975, *17*, 150–63.

McCaffrey, A. Communicative competence: How it can be measured and how it can be fostered in young children. Paper presented at the Third International Child Language Symposium, London, 1975.

McCarthy, D. *The language development of the preschool child*. Minneapolis: University of Minnesota Press, 1930.

McCarthy, D. *McCarthy Scales of Children's Abilities*. New York: Psychological Corporation, 1970.

McCarthy, J.J., & McCarthy, J.F. *Learning disabilities*. Boston: Allyn & Bacon, 1969.

McKee, P. *Reading–A program of instruction for the elementary school*. Boston: Houghton Mifflin, 1966.

McNeill, D. *The acquisition of language: the study of developmental psycholinguistics*. New York: Harper & Row, 1970.

Mehler, J., Bever, T.G., & Carey, P. What we look at when we read. *Perception and Psychophysics*, 1967, *2*, 213–18.

Menyuk, P. A preliminary evaluation of grammatical capacity in children. *Journal of Verbal Learning and Verbal Behavior*, 1963, *2*, 429–39.(a)

Menyuk, P. Alternation of rules in children's grammar. *Journal of Verbal Learning and Verbal Behavior*, 1963, *3*, 480–88.(b)

Menyuk, P. Syntactic rules used by children from preschool through first grade. *Child Development*, 1964, *35*, 533–46.

Menyuk, P. *Sentences children use*. Cambridge: M.I.T. Press, 1969.

Menyuk, P., & Looney, P. A problem of language disorder: Length versus structure. *Journal of Speech and Hearing Research*, 1972, *15*, 264–79. (a)

Menyuk, P., & Looney, P. Relationships between components of the grammar in language disorders. *Journal of Speech and Hearing Research*, 1972, *15*, 395–406. (b)

Miller, G.A. The magical number seven, plus or minus two. *Psychological Review*, 1956, *63*, 81–97.

Miller, G.A., & Chomsky, N. Finitary models of language users. In R.D. Luce, R.R. Bush, & E. Galanter (Eds.), *Handbook of mathematical psychology*. Vol. 2. New York: Wiley, 1963.

Miller, W.R. The acquisition of grammatical rules by children. In C.A. Ferguson & D.A. Slobin (Eds.), *Studies of language development*. New York: Holt, Rinehart & Winston, 1973.

Moorehead, D.M., & Ingram, D. The development of base syntax in normal and linguistically deviant children. *Journal of Speech and Hearing Research*, 1973, *16*, 330–52.

Mower, D.E. *Methods of modifying speech behaviors*. Columbus, Ohio: Charles E. Merrill, 1978.

Myklebust, H.R. *Development and disorders of written language*. Vol. I. New York: Grune & Stratton, 1965.

Myklebust, H.R. *Development and disorders of written language*. Vol. II. New York: Grune & Stratton, 1973.

Newcombe, F., & Marshall, J.C. Immediate recall of sentences by subjects with unilateral cerebral lesions. *Neuropsychologia*, 1967, *5*, 329–34.

Newcomer, P.L., & Hammill, D.D. *The Test Of Language Development*. Austin, Tex.: Empiric Press, 1977.

Newcomer, P.L., Hare, B., Hammill, D.D., & McGettigan, J. Construct validity of the Illinois Test of Psycholinguistic Abilities. *Journal of Learning Disabilities*, 1975, *8*, 32–43.

Nice, M.M. Length of sentences as a criterion of a child's progress in speech. *Journal of Educational Psychology*, 1925, *16*, 370–79.

Noll, J.D. The use of the Token Test with children. Paper presented at the 46th Annual American Speech and Hearing Association Convention, New York, 1970.

Norman, D.A., Rumelhart, D.E. & the LNR Research Group *Explorations in cognition*. San Francisco: Freeman, 1975.

Paivio, A. *Imagery and verbal processes*. New York: Holt, Rinehart, & Winston, 1971.

Palermo, D.S., & Jenkins, J.J. *Word association norms: grade school through college*. Minneapolis: University of Minnesota Press, 1964.

Paris, S. Comprehension of language connectives and propositional logical relationships. *Journal of Experimental Child Psychology*, 1973, *16*, 278–91.

Parker, T.B., Freston, C.W., & Drew, C.J. Comparison of verbal performance of normal and learning disabled children as a function of input organization. *Journal of Learning Disabilities*, 1975, *8*, 386–92.

Piaget, J., & Inhelder, B. *The psychology of the child*. New York: Basic Books, 1969.

Piaget, J., & Inhelder, B. *Memory and intelligence*. New York: Basic Books, 1973.

Prutting, C.A., Gallagher, T.M., & Mulac, A. The expressive portion of the NSST compared to a spontaneous language sample. *Journal of Speech and Hearing Disorders*, 1975, *40*, 40–48.

Reddell, R.B. The effect of oral and written patterns of language structure on reading comprehension. *Reading Teacher*, 1965, *18*, 270–75.

Rees, N.S., Kruger, F., Bernstein, D., Kramer, L, & Bezas, M. The acquisition of a first language in a blind-deaf adult. *Journal of Rehabilitation of the Deaf*, 1974, *8*, 11–24.

Riegel, K.F. *The Michigan restricted association norms*. Ann Arbor: University of Michigan, Department of Psychology, Report No. 3, 1965.

Rinsland, H.D. *A basic vocabulary of elementary school children*. New York: Macmillan, 1945.

Rips, L.J., Shoben, E.J., & Smith, E.E. Semantic distance and the verification of semantic relations. *Journal of Verbal Learning and Verbal Behavior*, 1973, *12*, 1–20.

Robinson, H.M., Monroe, M., & Artley, A.S. *We read pictures*. Chicago: Scott Foresman, 1962.(a)

Robinson, H.M., Monroe, M., & Artley, A.S. *Before we read*. Chicago: Scott Foresman, 1962. (b)

Rosch, E.H. On the internal structure of perceptual and semantic categories. In T.E. Moore (Ed.), *Cognitive development and the acquisition of language*. New York: Academic Press, 1973.

Rosenthal, D.J., & Resnick, L.B. Children's solution processes in arithmetic word problems. *Journal of Educational Psychology*, 1974, *66*, 817–25.

Rosenthal, J.H. A preliminary psycholinguistic study of children with learning disabilities. *Journal of Learning Disabilities*, 1970, *3*, 11–15.

Rueda, R., & Perozzi, J. A comparison of two Spanish tests of receptive language. *Journal of Speech and Hearing Disorders*, 1977, *42*, 210–15.

Sachs, J.S. Recognition memory for syntactic and semantic aspects of connected discourse. *Perception and Psychophysics*, 1967, *2*, 391–95.

Sathre, F.S., Olson, R.W., & Whitney, C.I. *Let's talk: An introduction to interpersonal communication*. Glenview, Ill.: Scott Foresman, 1973.

Sauer, L.E. Fourth grade children's knowledge of grammatical structure and its relationship to reading comprehension. Doctoral dissertation, University of Wisconsin, 1968.

Savin, H.B., & Perchonock, E. Grammatical structure and the immediate recall of English sentences. *Journal of Verbal Learning and Verbal Behavior*, 1965, *4*, 348–53.

Saz, G., & Ottina, J.R. The arithmetic achievement of pupils differing in school experience. *California Journal of Educational Psychology*, 1958, *9*, 15–19.

Schuell, H. *Minnesota Test for Differential Diagnosis of Aphasia*. Minneapolis: University of Minnesota Press, 1965.

Schuell, H., & Jenkins, J.J. Reduction of vocabulary in aphasia. In M.T. Sarno (Ed.), *Aphasia: Selected readings*. New York: Appleton-Century-Crofts, 1972.

Schultz, T.R., & Pilon, R. Development of the ability to detect linguistic ambiguity. *Child Development*, 1973, *44*, 728–33.

Semel, E.M. *Sound-order-sense: A developmental program in auditory perception*. Chicago: Follett, 1970.

Semel, E.M. *Semel Auditory Processing Program*. Chicago: Follett, 1976.

Semel, E.M., & Wiig, E.H. Comprehension of syntactic structures and critical verbal elements by children with learning disabilities. *Journal of Learning Disabilities*, 1975, *8*, 53–58.

Semel, E.H., & Wiig, E.H. Auditory processing: Can it be improved? (Submitted for publication to *Journal of Learning Disabilities*.)

Semel, E.M., & Wiig, E.H. *Clinical Evaluation of Language Functions*. Columbus, Ohio: Charles E. Merrill.

Shriner, T.H. A review of mean length of response as a measure of expressive language development in children. *Journal of Speech and Hearing Disorders*, 1969, *14*, 61–67.

Shriner, T.H., & Sherman, D. An equation for assessing language development. *Journal of Speech and Hearing Research*, 1967, *10*, 41–48.

Simon, H.A., & Chase, W.G. Skill in chess. *American Scientist*, 1973, *61*, 394–403.

Skousen, R. *An explanatory theory of morphology*. Paper from the parasession on natural phonology, Linguistic Society, Chicago, 1974.

Slobin, D.I. Grammatical transformations in childhood and adulthood. Doctoral dissertation, Harvard University, 1963.

Slobin, D.I. Grammatical transformations in childhood and adulthood. *Journal of Verbal Learning and Verbal Behavior*, 1966, *5*, 219–27.

Slobin, D.I. *Psycholinguistics*. Glenview, Ill.: Scott Foresman, 1971.

Stormzand, M.J., & O'Shea, M.V. *How much English grammar*. Baltimore: Warwick & York, 1924.

Streng, A. *Syntax, speech and hearing: Applied linguistics for teachers of children with language and hearing disabilities*. New York: Grune & Stratton, 1972.

Sullivan, H.S. *The interpersonal theory of psychiatry*. New York: Norton, 1953.

Sullivan, H.S. *The psychiatric interview*. New York: Norton, 1954.

Sullivan, H.S. *The fusion of psychiatry and social science*. New York: Norton, 1964.

Susskind, E. The role of question-asking in the elementary classroom. In F. Kaplan & S. B. Sarason (Eds.), *The psychoeducational clinic: Papers and research studies*. Community Mental Health Monograph, Vol. 4, 1969.

Swope, S. Spectographic analyses of infant cries. Doctoral dissertation, Boston University, 1974.

Takahaski, G. Perception of space and the function of certain English prepositions. *Language Learning*, 1969, *19*, 217–33.

Templin, M. *Certain language skills in children*. Minneapolis: University of Minnesota Press, 1957.

Terman, L.M., & Merrill, M.A. *Stanford-Binet intelligence scale*. Boston: Houghton Mifflin, 1960.

Thorndike, E.L., & Lorge, F. *The teacher's word book of 30,000 words*. New York: Teacher's College, Columbia University, 1944.

Toronto, A.S. A developmental Spanish language analysis procedure for Spanish speaking children. Doctoral dissertation, Northwestern University, 1972.

Toronto, A.S. *Spanish Syntax Screening Test*. Evanston, Ill.: Northwestern University Press, 1973.

Toronto, A.S. *Toronto Tests of Receptive Vocabulary* (English/Spanish). Austin, Tex.: Academic Tests, 1977.

Torrance, E.P. Developing creative thinking through school experiences. In S.J. Parnes & H.F. Harding (Eds.), *A source book for creative thinking*. New York: Scribners, 1965. Pp. 31–47.

Townsend, D.J. Children's comprehension of comparative forms. *Journals of Experimental Child Psychology*, 1974, *18*, 293–303.

Tulving, E. Cue dependent forgetting. *American Scientist*, 1974, *62*, 74–82.

Tulving, E., & Pearlstone, Z. Availability versus accessibility of information in memory for words. *Journal of Verbal Learning and Verbal Behavior*, 1966, *5*, 381–91.

Tulving, E., & Psotka, J. Retroactive inhibition in free recall: Inaccessibility of information available in the memory store. *Journal of Experimental Psychology*, 1971, *87*, 1–8.

Tulving, E., & Thomson, D.M. Encoding specificity and retrieval processes in episodic memory. *Psychological Review*, 1973, *80*, 352–73.

Turner, E.A., & Rommetveit, R. Experimental manipulation of the production of active and passive voice in children. *Language and Speech*, 1967, *10*, 169–80.(a)

Turner, E.A., & Rommetveit, R. The acquisition of sentence voice and reversibility. *Child Development*, 1967, *38*, 649–60.(b)

Turner, E.A., & Rommetveit, R. Focus of attention in recall of active and passive sentences. *Journal of Verbal Learning and Verbal Behavior*, 1968, *7*, 543–48.

Turton, L. Status of prepositions in the verbal and nonverbal response patterns of children during third and fourth years of life. Doctoral dissertation, University of Kansas, 1966.

Tyack, D., & Gottsleben, R. *Language sampling: Analysis and training*. Palo Alto: Consulting Psychologists Press, 1974.

Utley, J. *What's its name*. Urbana: University of Illinois Press, 1950.

Vander Linde, L.F. Does the study of quantitative vocabulary improve problem solving? *Elementary School Journal*, 1964, *65*, 143–52.

Venezky, R.L. Discussion. In J.F. Kavanagh (Ed.), *Communicating by language: the reading process*. Bethesda, National Institute of Child Health and Human Development, 1968.

Vogel, S.A. Syntactic abilities in normal and dyslexic children. *Journal of Learning Disabilities*, 1974, *7*, 47–53.

Vygotsky, L.S. *Thought and language*. Cambridge: M.I.T. Press, 1962.

Warden, D.A. The influence of context on children's use of identifying expressions and references. *British Journal of Psychology*, 1976, *67*, 101–12.

Waryas, C.I. Psycholinguistic research in language intervention: The pronoun system. *Journal of Psycholinguistic Research*, 1973, *2*, 221–37.

Waryas, C.I., & Ruder, K. On the limitations of language comprehension procedures and an alternative. *Journal of Speech and Hearing Disorders*, 1974, *39*, 44–52.

Wechsler, D. *Wechsler Intelligence Scale for Children*. New York: Psychological Corporation, 1949.

Wechsler, D. *Wechsler Intelligence Scale for Children—Revised*. New York: Psychological Corporation, 1974.

Wender, P.H. *Minimal brain dysfunction*. New York: Wiley-Interscience, 1971.

Wertz, R.T., Keith, R.L., & Custer, D.D. Normal and aphasic behavior on a measure of auditory input and a measure of verbal output. Paper presented at the 47th Annual American Speech and Hearing Association Convention, Chicago, 1971.

Wertz, R.T., & Perkins, M.P. Measures of auditory input and verbal output in children. *Journal of the Colorado Speech and Hearing Association*, 1972, *5*, 11–18.

Whimby, A.E., & Fischhof, V. Memory span: A forgotten capacity. *Journal of Educational Psychology*, 1969, *60*, 56–58.

Whimby, A.E., & Ryan, S.F. Role of short-term memory and training in solving reasoning problems mentally. *Journal of Educational Psychology*, 1969, *60*, 361–64.

White, S. Evidence for a hierarchical arrangement of learning processes. In L.P. Lipsett & C.C. Spiker (Eds.), *Advances in child development and behavior*. Vol. II. New York: Academic Press, 1965.

Wiegel-Crump, C., & Koenigsknecht, R. Tapping the lexical store of the adult aphasic: Analysis of the improvement made in verbal retrieval skills. *Cortex*, 1973, 411–18.

Wiig, E.H., & Fleischmann, N. Knowledge of pronominalization, reflexivization, and relativization by learning disabled college students. Paper presented at the 54th Annual American Speech and Hearing Association Convention, San Francisco, 1978. *Journal of Learning Disabilities*, (in Press).

Wiig, E.H., Florence, D.P., Kutner, S.M., Sherman, B., & Semel, E.M. Perception and interpretation of explicit negations by learning disabled children and adolescents. *Perceptual and Motor Skills*, 1977, *44*, 1251–57.

Wiig, E.H., Gilbert, M.F., & Christian, S.H. Developmental sequences in the perception and interpretation of lexical and syntactic ambiguities. *Perceptual and Motor Skills*, 1978, *46*, 959–69.

Wiig, E.H., & Globus, D. Aphasic word identification as a function of logical relationship and association strength. *Journal of Speech and Hearing Research*, 1971, *14*, 195–204.

Wiig, E.H., & Harris, S.P. Perception and interpretation of nonverbally expressed emotions by adolescents with learning disabilities. *Perceptual and Motor Skills*, 1974, *38*, 239–45.

Wiig, E.H., & Roach, M.A. Immediate recall of semantically varied "sentences" by learning disabled adolescents. *Perceptual and Motor Skills, 1975, 40,* 119–25.

Wiig, E.H., & Semel, E.M. Comprehension of linguistic concepts requiring logical operations by learning disabled children. *Journal of Speech and Hearing Research, 1973, 16,* 627–36.

Wiig, E.H., & Semel, E.M. Logico-grammatical sentence comprehension by learning disabled adolescents. *Perceptual and Motor Skills, 1974, 38,* 1331–34.

Wiig, E.H., & Semel, E.M. Productive language abilities in learning disabled adolescents. *Journal of Learning Disabilities, 1975, 8,* 578–86.

Wiig, E.H., & Semel, E.M. Wiig-Semel test of linguistic concepts. In O.G. Johnson (Ed.), *Tests and measurements in child development. Handbook II, Vol. I.* San Francisco: Jossey-Bass, 1976.(a)

Wiig, E.H., & Semel, E.M. *Language disabilities in children and adolescents.* Columbus, Ohio: Charles E. Merrill, 1976.(b)

Wiig, E.H., Semel, E.M., & Abele, E. Perception and interpretation of ambiguous sentences by learning disabled twelve-year-olds. *Learning Disabilities Quarterly,* (in Press).

Wiig, E.H., Semel, E.M., & Crouse, M.A.B. The use of morphology by high-risk and learning disabled children. *Journal of Learning Disabilities, 1973, 6,* 457–65.

Wilson, M. *The Wilson Initial Syntax Program.* Cambridge: Educators Publishing Service, 1972.

Winitz, H. Problem solving and the delaying of speech as strategies for the teaching of language. *ASHA, 1973, 15,* 583–86.

Wyke, M.A. An experimental study of verbal association in aphasia. *Brain, 1962, 85,* 679–86.

Zigmond, N. Remediation of dyslexia: A discussion. In A.L. Benton & D. Pearl (Eds.), *Dyslexia: An appraisal of current knowledge.* New York: Oxford University Press, 1978. Pp. 437–48.

Zimmermann, B.J., & Bergan, J.R. Intellectual operations in teacher question-asking behavior. *Merrill-Palmer Quarterly, 1971, 17,* 19–26.

Zivian, M.T. *Word identification as a function of semantic clues and association strength.* Ann Arbor, Michigan: University of Michigan, Department of Psychology, Report No. 12, 1966.

# GLOSSARY

**Accusative case**  An inflected form of the personal pronouns which functions as the direct object of the verb, e.g., "She saw *him*."

**Addition**  The process of adding a word, phrase, or clause to an existing sentence or utterance.

**Amnestic aphasia**  An acquired disturbance of the ability to use words as labels for objects, actions, characteristics, or relationships accurately.

**Animate**  Referring to human beings or animals possessing life.

**Anomia**  An acquired disturbance of the ability to recall or find the intended names for persons, objects, actions, or characteristics.

**Antonym**  A word opposite in meaning to another as "fast" ("slow").

**Aphasic**  Having an acquired language disorder caused by brain damage with complete or partial impairment of language comprehension, formulation and use.

**Articulation**  The process of executing movements of the speech organs (tongue, lips, jaw, vocal folds) to produce speech sounds.

**Associative memory**  The assimilation, storage, and recall of connections between two or more words or concepts such as cat/dog, eat/drink, hot/cold, up/down, etc.

**Auditory discrimination**  The process of distinguishing among heard sounds.

**Auditory memory**  The process of assimilating, storing, and recalling what has been heard.

**Auditory-visual**  Referring to an established connection between what is heard and what is seen as in sound-letter associations.

**Auditory-vocal**  Referring to an established connection between what is heard and what is spoken as in repeating a spoken word.

**Blend**  A cluster of two or more consonants, e.g., br-, dr-, tr-, str-.

**Bound Morpheme**  A meaningful unit of the language which cannot occur alone but must be joined to a word base such as inflectional endings (cats), derivational endings (teach*er*), and prefixes (pro-, anti-).

**Circumlocution**  Refers to a "round-about" way of speaking when a person cannot find a specific word for an object, action, or event as in calling a *brush* "that thing that you fix your hair with."

**Concurrent validity**  Refers to an existing agreement in the performances on two tests which supports the quality of one of the tests as valid.

| | |
|---|---|
| **Coordinate** | (v.) (linguistic use) To combine two words, phrases, or clauses into one grammatical construction in which both components have equal rank or importance as in *"Jack* and *Jill* went up the hill," "Cars drive *on streets* and *on roads*," and *"The boys ate the cake* and *the girls ate the pie."* |
| **Copula** | Any form of "to be" used to link a subject noun with a predicate adjective or noun as in "The boy *is tall*" or "That woman *is my aunt.*" Also called a *linking verb*. |
| **Counterfactive** | A sentence or conditional statement in which the first clause expresses something which is false or contrary to fact. |
| **Dative** | An inflected word form which functions as the indirect object of the verb as in the personal pronoun form "him" in the sentence "She gave the book to *him."* |
| **Deep structure** | The structure of the ideas or meaning which underlies a sentence as in the interpretation of the question "Are lemons sour?" as "Lemons (are) sour—yes/no?" |
| **Deixis** | A relationship between word opposites in which the two words are interchanged to indicate changes in the perspectives of the speaker(s) and listener(s) in verbal interaction, space, or time, e.g., "I" (*we*), "you," "here-there," "this" (*these*)–"that" (*those*). |
| **Deletion** | The process of leaving out a redundant word, phrase, or clause when combining sentences in a transformation as in combining the sentences "Jack *went up the hill*" and "Jill *went up the hill*" into a conjunction deletion of the form "Jack and Jill went up the hill." |
| **Derivation** | The process of adding an ending to a base word form and thereby changing its grammatical class relationship to allow the derived word to function in different syntactic constructions as in adding *-er* to the base verb "teach" to form a noun, "teacher," which can function as the subject-object in sentences. |
| **Digraph** | A pair of letters which represent a single speech sound as in the case of *-oo* and *-th* in the printed word "tooth." |
| **Dysnomia** | A partial loss of the ability to recall and retrieve the names of persons, things, actions, or places for speech. |
| **Embedding** | The process of placing a word, phrase or clause in an existing sentence as in the case of placing a clause between the subject and the verb of a sentence to form a relative clause transformation such as "The boy, *who lives next door*, is my best friend." |
| **Etiology** | The cause or origin of a disorder or disability. |
| **Factive** | A sentence or conditional statement in which the first clause expresses something which agrees with fact or reality. |
| **Figurative language** | A language expression which involves a figure of speech and cannot be interpreted literally as in the case of idioms, metaphors, similes, or proverbs. |
| **Fine motor** | Referring to skillful, discrete, sequenced movements of small muscle sets such as for speaking, writing, drawing, and other learned motor activities. |
| **Fluency** | Referring to the ease and smoothness with which sounds, syllables, words, phrases, and clauses are retrieved for and joined together in speaking. |
| **Free morpheme** | A unit of meaning in the language which can stand alone in utterances and sentences, e.g., "dog," "big," "bark," "fur," "friend," etc. |
| **Gender** | The distinction of sex (male, female, neuter) by a word form as in the case of the third person singular personal pronoun forms, "he," "she," and "it." |
| **Graphone** | The smallest unit in a written language form used to represent the speech sounds of that language. In contrast to a grapheme (letter), a graphone can be related on a one-to-one basis to a speech sound (phoneme). |

| | |
|---|---|
| **Gross motor** | Referring to movements of large muscle groups for activities such as walking, running, or climbing. |
| **Homonym** | A word identical to another in sound and spelling but which has a different meaning as in the case of the word "drive" as an action, "drive a car" or a condition or state, "I put the car in drive." |
| **Ideation** | The process of forming ideas, thoughts, or images. |
| **Indefinite pronoun** | A pronoun without a fixed or specific reference as in the pronoun forms, "someone," "somewhere," "somehow," and "sometime." |
| **Indefinite references** | Words which do not refer to a fixed or specific person, action, object, or event such as indefinite pronouns (some-, any-, no-), or terms such as ". . . that thing." |
| **Infix** | A small, meaningful unit of the language (morpheme) placed between elements of a word. An example can be found in the word "anticoagulant" in which the prefix *co-* (together) is placed between the prefix *anti-* and the remaining elements of the word, therefore becoming an infix. |
| **Inflected** | A word form which has been changed by adding a word ending to indicate number, gender, or case. |
| **Internal reliability coefficient** | A statistical measure which indicates the degree to which agreement exists in the form or contents of and responses to items of a subtest, test, or questionnaire. |
| **Interrogative sentences** | Sentences derived by transformation of a simple, active, affirmative, declarative (kernel) sentence through a process of inverting the noun-verb sequence ("Are you home?"), preposing an auxiliary ("Did you walk home?"), or preposing a wh- form (*"where* is your home?") |
| **Intonation** | The pattern of pitch, stress, and juncture in spoken sentences which serves to express communicative effects or intents such as interrogation, exclamation, or assertion, and convey affect. |
| **Kernel** | A sentence with the characteristics that it is *simple* (has only one subject-verb-object/predicate adjective/predicate noun), *active* (the subject of the sentence is the agent of the action), *affirmative* (the sentence expresses an actual fact or true condition), and *declarative* (the sentence is a statement of a fact, idea, condition, or event). |
| **Kinesthetic** | Referring to the quality of sense resulting from movements or changes in the positions of muscles, structures, or body parts. |
| **Language processing** | The process of hearing, discriminating, assigning significance to, and interpreting spoken words, phrases, clauses, sentences, and discourse. |
| **Language production** | The process of forming ideas or thoughts, finding words to express them, formulating sentences to structure the words, and producing the combined product in a spoken language form. |
| **Lexical** | Pertaining to the words or vocabulary of a language. |
| **Marked** | Pertaining to a word opposite (antonym) with a negative, nonpreferred, unusual reference as in the case of the words "hate" (love), "empty" (full), or "enemy" (friend). |
| **Modality** | Referring to (1) the primary senses (hearing, vision, touch, etc.) and to (2) the quality or state of the sensory input (spoken language, written language, braille, etc.). |
| **Morpheme** | The smallest unit of meaning in a language. Morphemes can be classified as either **free** or **bound** morphemes, depending upon whether or not they can occur in isolation or as a word in a sentence. |

| | |
|---|---|
| **Nesting** | The process of embedding and telescoping several subordinated clauses and phrases in a sentence transformation as in the sentence, "The girl who is sitting next to the boy in the first row, wearing a red sweater, is my sister." |
| **Nominative case** | An inflected word form which functions as the subject of a sentence as in the case of the personal pronoun forms "I," "you," "he," "she," "it," "we," "you," "they" in sentences such as "*I* saw the boy." |
| **Nonfactive** | A sentence or conditional statement in which the first clause expresses something that is not in agreement with the facts, reality, or existing conditions. |
| **Oral language** | The spoken form of a language. |
| **Ordinal** | Pertaining to an order or a sequential arrangement of objects according to an increase in a dimension such as size, length, width, or the like. |
| **Permutation** | The process of changing the order of elements in or components of sentences as in changing word, phrase, or clause order. |
| **Perceptual adherence** | The process of clinging to observable visual-perceptual characteristics of objects or relationships in problem solving. |
| **Perfective aspect** | A verb form which expresses an unusual or one-time action or an action considered from the point of view of its relative time of completion in the past. |
| **Perseverative** | The quality of continuing or repeating an activity or response, motor, mental, or verbal, which has been started past the point in time when it is appropriate and becomes inappropriate. |
| **Phrase-structure rules** | The set of rules or grammar which accounts for the structural characteristics of simple, active, affirmative, delcarative (kernel) sentences. |
| **Place holders** | Words, utterances, or stereotypic expressions used to fill a pause or "hold the place" for the speaker while he is searching for a specific name for a person, object, action, place, or event he cannot readily find. |
| **Prefix** | A unit of meaning, word or syllable, placed before the root of another word to modify meaning or form a new meaning as in the words *un*cover, *anti*social, and *in*habited. |
| **Prepose** | To place a word, phrase or clause at the beginning of a sentence as in forming wh- questions such as "*Who* sent you?" or "*Where* did you go?" |
| **Pronominal** | Having the characteristics of a pronoun or relating to a pronoun. |
| **Pronominalization** | The process of substituting a pronoun for a noun or a word used as a noun. |
| **Proprioceptive** | The quality of sensory feedback arising from awareness of body movements and position and from the sense of touch or contact through touching. |
| **Prosody** | The superimposed stress and intonation patterns of spoken sentences, determined primarily by variations in pitch, loudness, and duration. |
| **Psycholinguistics** | The study of language and linguistics as they relate to human development and behavior. |
| **Reauditorization** | The process of reconstructing or rehearsing heard digits, words, phrases, or sentences internally to oneself in the "mind's ear." |
| **Recall** | The process of remembering something experienced in the past to recapture specific or essential features of the experience. |
| **Receptive** | Referring to the quality of receiving spoken messages and translating the acoustic patterns into words, phrases, clauses, and sentences. |
| **Recognition** | The process of identifying that something is familiar or has been heard, seen, or experienced previously. |
| **Referent** | The person, object, action, or event to which a word refers and for which it serves as a symbol. |

| | |
|---|---|
| **Register** | The range of word and sentence choices and language styles available to a speaker. |
| **Rehearsal** | The process of repeating, drilling, or practicing a response. |
| **Replacive** | The quality of a word form being able to assume the role and function of or substitute for another word as in the case of the possessive replacive pronouns "mine," "yours," etc. |
| **Retrieve** | To bring back or reconstruct a stimulus in the form of a familiar word, phrase, clause, or sentence. |
| **Revisualizing** | To reconstruct or rehearse something that has been seen in the past in an internal image form in the "mind's eye." |
| **Rewrite rules** | A set of rules which state how a basic sentence can be broken down into component phrases and phrases into component elements before reference is made to the possible word choices (lexicon). |
| **Semantics** | The study of the relationships between words and grammatical forms in a language and their underlying meaning. |
| **Span memory** | The number of units—words, digits, or the like—which can be recalled immediately after hearing or seeing them. |
| **Split-half reliability** | The degree to which agreement exists in the form or contents of and responses to each half of a subtest, test, or questionnaire. |
| **Stanine score** | (standard nine score) A standard score, obtained by converting raw scores to a standard scale and converting the scaled scores into a normal distribution, ranging from 1 to 9 with a mean of 5 and standard deviation of 2. |
| **Stereotyped** | Having the quality of a fixed or settled form. |
| **Substitution** | The process of replacing a word, phrase, or clause with another. |
| **Suffix** | A sound, syllable, or syllable sequence which when added to an existing word can change or modify its meaning. Examples are the plural -s, comparative -er, and superlative -est suffixes used for inflection. |
| **Surface structure** | The actual form of spoken sentences which includes the word and sentence formations in evidence. |
| **Synonym** | A word which has the same or nearly the same meaning as another word in the language as in "happy," "glad," "joyful," "delighted." |
| **Syntax** | A set of rules for relating words, phrases, and clauses to another in forming sentences. |
| **Syntactic compression** | The process of increasing the number of ideas expressed in a sentence by using a complex sentence transformation such as in the relative clause contained in "The boy whose leg was broken went to school last week." |
| **Tag question** | A question form in which a statement is followed by a clause which follows the rules for questions. The question "The weather is nice today, isn't it?" is an example. |
| **Test-retest reliability coefficient** | A statistical measure of the degree of agreement between a person's performances on a test or questionnaire at two independent times. |
| **Transformational grammar** | A set of rules for combining words, phrases, and clauses in a variety of ways to form all possible, grammatical sentences in the language. |
| **Transformations** | Sentence forms which have been derived from a simple, active, affirmative declarative (kernel) sentence by changing one or more of the features of the "kernel" as in changing (a) simple to complex, (b) active to passive, (c) affirmative to negative, and/or (d) declarative to interrogative. |

**Unmarked**          Pertaining to a word opposite (antonym) with a positive, preferred, and usual reference as in the case of the words "love" (hate), "full" (empty), or "friend" (enemy).

**Unvoiced**          (speech sounds) Pertaining to speech sounds that are produced without simultaneous vibration of the vocal folds.

**Utterance**         A self-sufficient unit of meaning in spoken language, preceded and followed by silence or pauses.

**Verbalism**         A verbal expression in the form of a word, phrase, or sentence, which may carry little meaning or information.

**Voiced**            (speech sound) Pertaining to a speech sound which is produced with simultaneous vibration of the vocal folds. Examples are all vowels and voiced consonants.

# INDEX

# CLINICAL EVALUATION OF LANGUAGE FUNCTIONS (CELF)

## Eleanor M. Semel and Elisabeth H. Wiig

The CELF test consists of three different sets of tests:

1. *Elementary Level Screening*—A screening test for children grades K–5, individually administered covering both receptive and expressive language (total administration time— about 15 minutes).

2. *Advanced Level Screening*—A screening test for children grades 5–12, similar in design and administration time to the screening test for grades K–5.

3. *Diagnostic Battery*—A comprehensive battery of six receptive language and two supplemental speech subtests, individually administered (time — one and one-half to three hours), designed for children grades K–12 who have been identified by either of the above screening tests or by other instruments.

For ease in ordering any part of the CELF test from the publisher, you may use the following order codes:

1. Screening

   | | | |
   |---|---|---|
   | Elementary Level Screening | #8123-8MM | $15.95 |
   | (Includes Examiner's Manual for Elementary and Advanced Level screening plus (25) Elementary Level Score Forms.) | | |
   | (25) Additional Score Forms | #8120-3MM | $6.95 |
   | Advanced Level Screening | #8124-6MM | $15.95 |
   | (Includes Examiner's Manual for Elementary and Advanced Level screening plus (25) Advanced Level Score Forms.) | | |
   | (25) Additional Score Forms | #8119-XMM | $6.95 |

2. Diagnostic Test

   | | | |
   |---|---|---|
   | Diagnostic Battery | #8122-XMM | $75.00 |
   | (Includes Examiner's Manual, Stimulus Manual, (12) Score Forms, Audiocassette, and vinyl carrying case.) | | |
   | (12) Additional Score Forms | #8114-9MM | $9.95 |

3. Optional Videotape     #8118-1MM     $195.00
   (Demonstrates how to administer the CELF test for examiners.)

You may order any of these components from the publisher:
**Charles E. Merrill Publishing Co.**
1300 Alum Creek Drive
Columbus, Ohio 43216
**ATTN: Marilyn Creager**
*Prices effective June 1, 1980. Subject to change without notice.